ENGAGING
the
NEW TESTAMENT

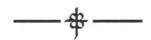

ENGAGING
the
NEW TESTAMENT

An Interdisciplinary Introduction

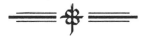

Russell Pregeant

Fortress Press   Minneapolis

ENGAGING THE NEW TESTAMENT
An Interdisciplinary Introduction

First Fortress Press paperback edition 1997

Illustration credits are found on p. xix.

Interior design; ediType
Cover design: Evans McCormick Creative

The Library of Congress has cataloged the hardcover edition as follows:

Library of Congress Cataloging-in-Publication Data

Pregeant, Russell.
    Engaging the New Testament : an interdisciplinary introduction /
    Russell Pregeant.
        p.   cm.
    Includes bibliographical references and indexes.
    ISBN 0-8006-2803-9 (alk. paper)
    1. Bible. N.T.—Introductions.   2. Bible. N.T.—Study and
teaching.   I. Title.
    BS2330.2.P69   1995
    225.6´1,dc20   95-5018
                                                    CIP

ISBN 0-8006-3115-3 (paperback)

The paper used in this publication meets the minimum requirements of American National
Standard for Information Sciences—Permanence of Paper for Printed Library Materials, ANSI
Z329.48-1984.

Manufactured in the U.S.A.   AF 1-3115

                                        5   6   7   8   9   10

To a special few among the many
from whom I have learned

William A. Beardslee   *John B. Cobb, Jr.*
Victor Paul Furnish   *Walter J. Harrelson*   *Leander E. Keck*
Schubert M. Ogden   *W. J. A. Power*

Education with inert ideas is not only useless: it is, above all things, harmful....

The solution...is to eradicate the fatal disconnection of subjects which kills the vitality of our modern curriculum. There is only one subject-matter for education, and that is Life in all its manifestations.
—Alfred North Whitehead,
The Aims of Education

What is written...? How do you read?
—Luke 10:26 (RSV)

Contents

Part Two
THE GOSPELS AND ACTS

Part Three

THE PAULINE CORPUS

List of Illustrations

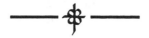

ACKNOWLEDGMENTS

The author and editors wish to express their gratitude to the following sources for granting permission to use these illustrations:

Photos

The photos on pp. 63, 82, 88, 92, 267, 271, 338, 340, 341, 357, 366, 369, and 373 (**Figs. 9, 13, 15, 16, 47, 48, 59–66**) are from Helmut Koester and Holland L. Hendrix, eds., *Archaeological Resources for New Testament Studies, Vol. 1* (Philadelphia: Fortress Press, 1987). The photos on pp. 60, 77, 83, and 463 (**Figs. 8, 12, 14, 72**) are by Marshall D. Johnson. The photos on pp. 178, 252, and 380 (**Figs. 28, 42, 67–68**) are by Thomas D. Hoffman, from Bruce J. Malina and Richard L. Rohrbaugh, *Social-Science Commentary on the Synoptic Gospels* (Minneapolis: Fortress Press, 1992). The photo on p. 124 (**Fig. 21**) is by Dennis Hamm from Malina and Rohrbaugh, *Social-Science Commentary on the Synoptic Gospels*. The text of Acts 5:12-21 on p. 9 (**Fig. 1, left**) is from the Nestle-Aland *Novum Testamentum Graece*, 26th ed. (Stuttgart: Deutsche Bibelstiftung, 1898, 1979). The photo on p. 9 (**Fig. 1, right**) is from the State Museum, Berlin (P11765) and used by permission. The photos on pp. 20 and 22 (**Figs. 2, 3**) are courtesy The Bettmann Archive and used by permission (Fig. 2 also courtesy UPI). The photo on p. 22 (**Fig. 4**) is from the BBC Hulton Picture Library. The photo on p. 46 (**Fig. 6**) is courtesy of Pontificia commissione di archeologia sacra. The photo on p. 317 (**Fig. 57**) is courtesy of the Institute for Antiquity and Christianity at the Claremont Graduate School, Claremont, California.

Maps, Charts, and Graphs

The maps on pp. 69, 128, 176, 218, and 265 (**Figs. 10, 22, 27, 35, 46**) are by Parrot Graphics. The map on p. 510 (**Fig. 76**) is by C. Kim Pickering.

The charts and graphs on pp. 37, 52–53, and 101 (**Figs. 5, 7, 17, 18**) are by Russell Pregeant. The graph on p. 74 (**Fig. 11**) is from Gerhard E. Lenski, *Power and Privilege: A Theory of Social Stratification*, copyright © 1966, 1984 The University of North Carolina Press, and reprinted by permission.

Appendix 2 and **Figs. 80–81** are by John A. Darr and are taken from Daniel Patte, *Paul's Faith and the Power of the Gospel: A Structural Introduction to the Pauline Letters* (Philadelphia: Fortress Press, 1983).

Artwork

The engravings on pp. 249, 293, 424, and 526 (**Figs. 41, 53, 71, and 78**) are by Paul Gustave Doré from *The Doré Bible Illustrations*. **Fig. 19, p. 107**: The etching "Christ Preaching to the Poor" by Rembrandt Van Rijn (Dutch, 17th cent.) is courtesy of The Minneapolis Museum of Arts. **Fig. 23, p. 140**: Allan Rohan Crite's "Rabboni," 1947 brush and ink drawing is used by permission of the artist. **Fig. 24, p. 146**: "Resurrection II," 1973, created by Paul T. Granlund and used by permission of the artist. Sculptures by Paul T. Granlund are available at Premier Gallery, 141 S. 7th St., Minneapolis, MN 55402. **Fig. 29, p. 184**: Petrus and Malchus. Arrest of Christ, The Entry into Jerusalem. West portal, capital zone. Cathedral, Chartres, France. Courtesy Foto Marburg/Art Resource, NY. **Fig. 30, p. 186**: "Headpiece to 'Apparition': Christ on the Cross" by Georges Rouault from André Saures, *Passion* (Paris: Ambrose Vollard, 1939), used by permission of Dover Publications, Inc. **Fig. 32, p. 201**: "The Adoration of the Magi," painting by Frank Wesley, 1987, used by permission of the artist. **Fig. 33, p. 205**: "Sermon on the Mount," 40 x 30", mixed media by Michael E. Coblyn used by permission of the artist. **Fig. 34, p. 213**: Theopan the Greek (14th–15th c). Transfiguration. Russian icon. Tretyakov Gallery, Moscow, Russia. Courtesy Art Resource, NY. **Fig. 36, p. 220**: "The Sacrament of the Last Supper," by Salvador Dali, National Gallery of Art in Washington, D.C. (Religious News

Service photo). **Fig. 37, p. 229:** Jusepe de Ribera, Spanish, 1591–1652, *Saint Matthew,* 1632. Oil on canvas, 50½ x 38½"(128.2 x 97.8 cm.). Courtesy Kimbell Art Museum, Fort Worth, Texas. **Fig. 38, p. 237:** Dante Gabriel Rossetti. Ecce Ancilla Domini (Annunciation), 1849–50. Tate Gallery, London, Great Britain. Courtesy Tate Gallery, London/Art Resource, NY. **Fig. 39, p. 240:** Baptism of Christ. Baptistry of the Orthodox, Ravenna, Italy. Courtesy Alinari/Art Resource, NY. **Fig. 40, p. 244:** "Jesus Feeding the Five Thousand," by Pablo Mayorga, 1982, is from *The Gospel in Art by the Peasants of Solentiname,* Phillip and Sally Scharper, eds. (Maryknoll, NY: Orbis Books, 1984) and courtesy Peter Hammer Verlag GmbH+, Wuppertal, Germany. **Fig. 41, p. 254:** "Días de Christo," lithograph and painting by Frank Diaz Escalet, 13 Fletcher St., Kennebunk, ME 04043, courtesy of the artist. **Fig. 50, p. 279:** "Christ of the Homeless" by Fritz Eichenberg (© 1982) by permission of Toni Eichenberg. **Fig. 51, p. 285:** Pieter Brueghel the Elder. Saint John the Baptist Preaching. Oil on Wood, Museum of Fine Arts, Budapest, Hungary. Courtesy Erich Lessing/Art Resource, NY. **Fig. 52, p. 288:** Max Beckmann, "Christ and the Woman Taken in Adultery," 1917. Oil on Canvas, 58¾ x 49⅞"(149.2 x 126.7 cm.). Courtesy The Saint Louis Art Museum Bequest of Curt Valentin. 185: 1955. **Fig. 55, p. 298:** *Pietà* by Bernard Buffet, 1946, Courtesy the National Museum of Modern Art, Paris. **Fig. 56, p. 302:** St. John the Evangelist, adapted from a Strassbourg/Johann Reinhard Gruninger Bible (German, 1485) in the rare books collection of the Burke Library at Union Theological Seminary in New York. **Fig. 69, p. 394:** "St. Paul" by Vicenzo Foppa (ca. 1427–1515) from The William Hood Dunwoody Fund. Tempura on panel. Courtesy of The Minneapolis Institute of Arts. **Fig. 70, p. 405:** "Christa," bronze sculpture by Edwina Sandys © 1975 used by permission of the artist. **Fig. 77, p. 519:** The Four Horsemen of the Apocalypse, etching by Frank Hawthorn, used by permission. **Fig. 79, p. 530:** Lucas Cranach, "New Jerusalem," engraving, 1522. Courtesy of Special Collections, Milton S. Eisenhower Library, The Johns Hopkins University, Baltimore, Maryland. **Figs. 20, 25, 26, 44, 45, 49, 54, 58, 73, 74, 75:** Courtesy Augsburg Fortress picture library.

Preface

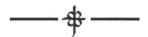

If necessity is indeed the mother of invention, then I can easily identify the driving force behind the production of this text. The necessity in this case arose early in my teaching career in the form of the conflicting expectations of two groups of students in my introductory course in New Testament at Curry College: those with explicitly religious interests and those with purely academic concerns. The dilemma posed by the legitimate demands of each led to a rather agonizing attempt on my part, now two decades in progress, to bridge the gap between them.

The first stage of this attempt involved the development of various classroom strategies, the success of which I must leave to those I taught during those years to judge. What I soon experienced, in any case, was the need for some help in implementing these strategies, some more explicit help, that is, from the reading material. So, on the theory that I was not alone in my agony, I eventually set out to write a text that could somehow provide the specific kind of assistance I wanted in such a task. Now it will fall to others to judge the success of this second stage.

The first persons I must thank for their help in bringing this text into existence are those students I encountered in my early years of teaching, whose honest conversation and bold suggestion led me to envision a project that otherwise would never have occurred to me. Close behind them are those later students who have helped me evaluate both the classroom strategies and the various forms of the manuscript as it has emerged, piece by piece, over the past several years and made its way into the course. More recently, a part-time teaching venture at Andover Newton Theological School has afforded me the opportunity to get the reactions of students at the seminary level.

Some other students, most of whom remain unknown to me, have participated in the process also. I am indebted both to them and to their professors,

Ron Farmer and John Darr. The former gave the text trial runs for several years at the University of Missouri–Columbia, and the latter has made use of it more recently at Boston College. It has, for obvious reasons, been of inestimable value to receive the comments of students who do not know me and who will not receive a grade from me! And both of these teachers have given me valuable advice on other levels as well. Ron Farmer made excellent suggestions regarding several areas in which the discussion needed strengthening, and John Darr has been an indispensable guide through the intricacies of reader-response criticism.

A number of other associates in the world of biblical studies have contributed much to the project also. William Beardslee read Parts One and Two, Paul Sampley critiqued an early draft of the first two chapters, and Victor Furnish read major portions of an intermediate draft of the whole. Gene Boring, with whom I have carried on an invigorating biblical/theological dialogue for some thirty years now, also reviewed the entire manuscript at an intermediate stage; and Mark Allan Powell provided an important evaluation of it following its submission to Fortress Press. More recently, Katheryn Pfisterer Darr saved me from a far too simplistic description of the development of Hebrew monotheism. And, beyond the bounds of biblical studies, Peter Hainer of Curry College helped me sharpen my understanding of structuralism, one of the several methodologies in which I have needed much instruction. I offer my gratitude to all of these for their assistance and hereby issue an unconditional declaration of their innocence with respect to whatever deficiencies remain in the final product—or have crept in since their perusal!

Others at Curry College have made important contributions of a different sort: Mary Ann Gallant, Director of Academic Computing, without whose patient guidance in the world of word processing I would have been swallowed up in some cosmic megabyte years ago; Paula Cabral, Administrative Assistant to the Humanities Division, who has given me innumerable forms of help, not the least of which has been getting the successive versions of this manuscript printed out for classroom use; and Gabe Rice, who did the copying, semester by semester, on top of the other mountains of material I burdened her with. All three will undoubtedly have their own reasons for rejoicing as the text goes into print.

I want also to thank the Division of Humanities, the Administration, and the Board of Trustees at Curry, who approved my sabbatical leave for the academic year 1986–87, when I began work on this project. By the same token, I must express my appreciation to the Release Time Committee for a course reduction that came at an important stage, to the Faculty Welfare Committee for helping to fund my yearly attendance at meetings of the Society of Biblical Literature, and to David Fedo, Dean of the College, for his many forms of support.

I am grateful also to the staff at Curry's Levin Library for their unfailing courtesy and eagerness to help. Thanks is due also to the personnel at the libraries of the Boston Theological Institute, particularly, those at the Episcopal Divinity School/Weston School of Theology and at Andover Newton Theological School. Without access to their resources my task would have been considerably more difficult.

Much of the help one receives on a project such as this is somewhat less tangible but no less important. And it is in that category that I place my continuing dialogue with my colleagues at Curry. One of the golden aspects of a small liberal arts college is the opportunity to transcend the boundaries of the academic disciplines. So I would like also to thank, collectively, the Curry faculty for their contributions to the atmosphere of open interchange that is the background of this interdisciplinary text. And, even at the risk of drawing an arbitrary limit, I feel the necessity of singling out a few with whom that interchange has been particularly extensive over the years or has had particular relevance for this project: Alan Anderson, in philosophy and religion; Bill Littlefield and Marvin Mandell, in English; Carol Hudson-Martin, Ann Levin, and Marlene Samuelson (whose primary fields are English, sociology, and biology, respectively) in women's studies; Dante Germanotta, in sociology; John Hill, in politics; George Wharton, in communication; and Joe Arsenault (in the Program in Assistance in Learning) and Debra-Lee Garren (in theater), our Catholic and Jewish chaplains respectively.

Among the more recent participants in the process have been Marshall Johnson and his amiable and highly professional staff members at Fortress Press. Their careful guidance and enthusiasm for the project have earned my sincere appreciation. It has also been a great pleasure to have worked, for a second time, with John Eagleson of ediType as my copy editor. And I would like to acknowledge the important contributions of those responsible for locating the illustrations that enhance the volume. David Lott of Fortress Press did a superb job in exercising the overall responsibility. And several others were of great help, either in locating specific materials or in discussing possibilities: Elizabeth Conde-Frazier and Robin Jensen, of Andover Newton; Charlotte Pridgen-Randolph, formerly of Andover Newton; Gertrude Webb, formerly of Curry; and Nelson Stevens of Spirit Wood Productions, Springfield, Massachusetts.

Although the manuscript was near completion when my association with Andover Newton began, it has been a great joy to bring it to completion in the company of others who share my passion for biblical studies. Conversations with Sze-kar Wan and John Yieh, my colleagues in New Testament, have been helpful in the final stages. And the contributions of my teaching assistants, Peggy Derick and Bill Jones, have ranged from freeing my schedule for last-minute labors to combing the manuscript for errors and points for reconsideration.

The seven persons to whom I have dedicated this book, some of whom I have already mentioned in other contexts, deserve words of appreciation in yet other ways. Victor Furnish and W. J. A. Power, my professors at Perkins School of Theology at Southern Methodist University, provided much of the inspiration and encouragement that led me to graduate school in the field of biblical studies. Schubert Ogden, also at Perkins, fueled my interest in theology, introduced me to life-changing perspectives, and held before me a model of rigorous thinking. At Vanderbilt University, Walter Harrelson not only gave me invaluable insight into the Jewish Scriptures, but also embodied an ideal of teaching that I still strive to emulate. And Leander Keck, my dissertation adviser, provided constant challenge, honest criticism, meaningful dialogue, and persistent encouragement. Years later, William Beardslee and John Cobb extended me a gracious welcome into an emerging circle of persons exploring the interaction between biblical interpretation and philosophical/theological reflection. To all of these—whom I honor as scholars, teachers, and human beings whose lives are shaped by the biblical visions of peace, justice, community, and love—I express my enduring gratitude.

Note to the Instructor

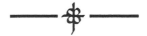

There are many ways to organize a study of the New Testament. The text as it stands takes a modified canonical approach. Beginning with chapters on methods of study, the historical context of early Christianity, the Jesus tradition, and the resurrection faith, it proceeds to treat the writings of the New Testament in roughly canonical order. For those who prefer other approaches, I have tried to write in such a way that some shuffling of materials is possible without a loss of continuity or coherence. It should be possible, for example, to move from Part One directly to the letters of Paul for a more chronological approach or to delay the treatment of the early Jesus tradition (chapter 3, section 2) until after the chapters on the Gospels.

Also, the sections of the chapters in Parts Two–Four that deal with specialized approaches such as redaction criticism, psychological or existentialist interpretation, etc., are relatively self-contained and therefore detachable. This should allow the instructor to be selective in the methods of study to be emphasized while at the same time providing opportunity for specialized detours based on individual student interest.

Introduction

Engaging the New Testament

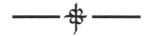

This is a book about the New Testament. But what *kind* of book is it? And just what is the "New Testament," anyway? These questions might seem simplistic, but they are of crucial importance to the reader. For before one approaches any piece of written material, it is helpful to have a clear idea of what kind of material it is.

The present book is an introductory text designed primarily as an aid to the study of the New Testament in an academic setting. As for the New Testament itself, it is a collection of ancient religious writings. Along with the Jewish Scriptures, which Christians have traditionally called the "Old Testament," these writings are sacred and authoritative for the Christian community. Together, the two collections constitute the Christian Bible.

1. The Aims of This Text

The study of sacred Scriptures in an academic environment presents certain problems, which can be overstated but should not be minimized. Although many of the students who come to a course in the New Testament will likely have some sense of identification with Christianity, some may be adherents of other faiths—such as Judaism, Islam, or Buddhism—and others may have no religious faith or background at all. Some will attach great importance to religion, but others will treat it more casually or even be quite certain they have no need of it. And some will not be quite sure where they stand.

Motives for taking the course, in any case, will probably be varied. If some students are seeking deeper knowledge of the Christian faith or confirmation

1

of their religious views, others may be searching for perspectives they can accept. Still others may have a purely secular interest in the historical development of Christianity or in the New Testament as literature. Quite obviously, neither instructor nor text should presuppose any particular religious commitment on the part of the students. Nor should an academic course in biblical studies become a means of indoctrinating students in one religious view.

As diverse as students' religious views may be, there is one thing virtually all who come to the course will share: they will all have some set of values, some sense of what life is about, or at least of whether life is in fact "about" anything at all. They will have views on human rights, politics, sexuality, ecology, and economics, or at least on whether the issues in these areas are of any real importance. Precisely as religious literature, the New Testament is addressed primarily to the intuitive side of the human psyche, which includes the capacity to make value decisions, to decide what is important in life and what is the best way for human beings to live. It thus has clear points of contact with the interests of both religious and nonreligious people.

Unfortunately, these points of contact can easily be overlooked. American education (along with Western education generally) has too often confused the legitimate demand for objectivity with a kind of value-neutrality that discourages personal involvement. But to study the New Testament writings only as relics from the past or as objects of curiosity is to miss their potential to engage the reader in reflection on life's deepest questions.

Ultimately, of course, it is up to students to make any connections between the course materials and their lives. But I have written this text out of the conviction that it is much more exciting, much sounder educationally, and much more human to have students, instructor, and text involved in an ongoing interchange about the possible importance of what is studied than to consign the text (and perhaps the instructor) to the external role of a provider of bare information—as if there were such a thing.

The matter is not fundamentally different in other fields of study. Should a history course approach the past as something dead or, instead, as a means of reflecting upon our present and our alternative futures? Is economics something (as is often claimed) that can be reduced to sheer quantification, or is every economic decision finally an expression of value judgments? It is arguable that, in actuality, the most subjective, doctrinaire books are those that claim to be value-free. For the illusion of neutrality may be the subtlest of all the tools of indoctrination.

Even though I hope that I have maintained an appropriate kind of objectivity, then, I disavow value-neutrality as an educational ideal. This text, far from addressing itself to students as disembodied intellects, is written to help them become actively engaged in the study of the New Testament. This means, in part, to provide them with information and with tools for discovering what the New Testament says. But it also means to invite them to ask some questions that call in varying degrees for personal involvement: the question of what the New Testament means by what it says; the question of how one can know what it means; and the question of the possible worth to them as human beings of what the New Testament both says and means. It is, in other words, my explicit intention to raise the question of whether the New Testament might interest students, challenge them, enlighten them, give them some actual help in the living of their lives. Chapter 1, which will be devoted to a discussion of various methods of biblical study, will explain more concretely how the text will proceed and how it will seek to encourage value judgments at some points without relinquishing objectivity.

2. The New Testament: Origin and Contents

Who wrote the New Testament? If the New Testament is a collection of writings, who were the authors of the various materials in this collection, and how did these specific works come to be included? Although these questions will require detailed discussions at later points, a brief overview of the early Christian movement can provide some preliminary answers.

a. The Origins of the Christian Faith

During the reign of the Roman Emperor Tiberius, the occupation government in the province of Judea executed an itinerant Jewish teacher from the town of Nazareth. In the decades that followed, small groups of his followers gathered regularly for worship, inspired in part by their belief that God had raised him from the dead. In the beginning, the movement was a small Jewish sect, composed of people who believed that through this crucified person, Jesus, God had fulfilled the ancient promises to the people of Israel. Soon, however, non-Jews—Gentiles—joined their ranks. Christians, as the followers of Jesus came to be called, eventually dropped some of their distinctively Jewish heritage, such as laws of ritual purity, although not without controversy. And before long, Jews were a small minority in a predominantly gentile faith.

In the Roman Empire, Christianity was at first but one among numerous religious cults. Sometimes viewed as oddities, sometimes seen as a threat and persecuted, Christians were nevertheless successful in winning converts to their faith. Slightly less than three hundred years after Jesus' death, the emperor Constantine gave Christianity a favored position in the empire and thus laid the foundation for its role in Western civilization. In time, a new system of reckoning history in the West made the presumed date of Jesus' birth the dividing point in the human drama.

b. The Origins of the New Testament

From the beginning, the figure of Jesus was central to the Christian faith. His followers passed along, by word of mouth, traditions about things he had said and done. In this earliest period, these oral accounts of the words of Jesus were received as authoritative in the Christian communities. But in time, various individuals and/or communities felt the need to bring such material together in written fashion. One form that the new, written tradition took was what came to be known as a Gospel, a narrative account of Jesus' life. The oral tradition did not vanish immediately when the various Gospels appeared, but its authority was eventually replaced by that of the written accounts.

The Gospels, however, were not the first writings that became authoritative in Christian communities. An important figure in one type of Christianity in the early decades was a man named Paul, a devout Jew who became a Christian and understood himself as commissioned by God to preach to Gentiles. Paul traveled widely in the Roman Empire, founding Christian churches as he went. And he frequently communicated with these communities by letter. His letters, written prior to the Gospels, were valued very highly by the recipients and later generations and were eventually brought together in collections and considered Scripture.

Other writings of various types appeared along the way also. In time there was an extensive body of Christian literature, and church leaders in different areas drew upon a variety of materials they considered in some sense authoritative. Not surprisingly, then, beginning around the middle of the second century, Christians began to define more precisely which books should be accepted. Scholars debate the extent to which this desire for a definite list was motivated by the need to combat teachings thought to be erroneous and to what it extent it was a response to other factors. In any case, Christians in various locales began to rank the writings in categories such as accepted, rejected, or disputed, and eventually church councils did the same. By the end of the fourth century, the present twenty-seven books of the New Testament had achieved wide acceptance. Controversies over specific writings continued, however, on into the fifth century and, in some areas, even later.

The Greek word for a list of authoritative books is *kanōn,* which means "rule" or "measure," and in the fourth century this term was applied to the writings of the New Testament. Through a long and complex process, then, Christianity developed its own canon, which became known as the "New Testament," to set alongside the Jewish canon, whose own boundaries were still somewhat in flux during the period of the early church.

c. The Contents of the New Testament

In shaping the New Testament canon, the churches chose those writings that they found meaningful and helpful in their community life, and they justified their choices (probably to some extent after the fact) by appealing to various criteria. One of these criteria was "apostolic" origin: they understood the writings included in the canon as in some (fairly loose) sense based upon the testimonies of the apostles, the first generation of leaders that was made up primarily, but not exclusively, of persons believed to have been called into their positions by Jesus himself.

The canon, as it eventually developed, begins with four Gospels. There follows a work called the Acts of the Apostles, which gives account of the early Christian movement in mission. Next come thirteen letters that bear the name of Paul. Appended to the body of Pauline letters is the book of Hebrews, which bears no author's name but was attributed to Paul by Christians in Egypt. The eight remaining works, seven of which are traditionally grouped together as the General (or Catholic) Letters, were attributed to various other apostolic figures.

Here, then, are the twenty-seven books of the New Testament canon:

The Gospels: Matthew, Mark, Luke, John

The Acts of the Apostles

The Pauline Letters: Romans, 1 Corinthians, 2 Corinthians, Galatians, Ephesians, Philippians, Colossians, 1 Thessalonians, 2 Thessalonians, 1 Timothy, 2 Timothy, Titus, Philemon, (Hebrews)

The General Letters: James, 1 Peter, 2 Peter, 1 John, 2 John, 3 John, Jude

Revelation

d. Questions about the Writings

Having given some idea of how the New Testament was formed, it is important now to make a distinction between what the ancient church believed about the canon and what may in fact have been the case. To begin with a minor point, tradition, largely because of the influence of Paul's writings, has understood most of the works other than the Gospels to be letters. As we will see, however, such a designation is questionable in some instances.

A much weightier matter is that in many cases the traditional views regarding authorship rest upon extremely shaky ground. Many scholars are convinced, for example, that Paul did not write all the letters that bear his name. And the actual identities of the authors of the Gospels is a matter of dispute. It is important, in this connection, to understand that the titles by which these writings are known appear as headings to the ancient manuscripts but do not occur in the bodies of the works themselves. These titles are probably the products of tradition and were not supplied by the authors.

In many cases, we do not know who the authors were or when they wrote. We do know that the authentic letters of Paul, some of which were written during the 50s of the first century, are the earliest of all the canonical writings. And we are fairly certain that the Gospels did not begin to appear until shortly before or shortly after the year 70, forty years or so after the death of Jesus.

The fact that those who drew the limits to the canon were not always correct in their historical judgments does not mean that they failed in their purpose. Apostolic origin was only one of the criteria that early church leaders used to define the canonical books. What they wanted most of all was to identify the materials that could mediate the authentic Christian faith and thereby meet their needs as a religious community. The precise relationship between the canonical materials on the one hand and the teachings of Jesus and the beliefs of his earliest followers on the other is a complex matter, as is the whole question of what constitutes "authentic" Christian teaching. There are, moreover, many factors to consider when evaluating the worth of specific materials, and the present text will encourage the student to reflect extensively on these questions. Nevertheless, there can be no doubt that the shaping of the canon was a major factor in maintaining coherence in the ongoing life of the church. At least to that extent, those who decided which materials to include in the New Testament accomplished precisely what they intended.

e. Unity and Diversity

The fact that the early church found it necessary to draw up a definitive list of authoritative books is a sign of the diversity of teaching and practice among the various communities. A significant number of writings in use were excluded from the list, often because their teachings were judged unacceptable.

There is reason to believe, also, that a certain amount of this diversity was present from a very early time.

Such diversity is in no way surprising. It is to some extent characteristic of religious movements in general. In addition, it was no simple matter for Christians to state just who they understood Jesus to be and precisely what his life, death, and resurrection meant. There were no preconceived categories into which they could easily fit him. Understanding themselves as heirs to God's promises to Israel, early Christians naturally looked to the Jewish Scriptures as their primary resource for understanding Jesus. These writings pointed to a hope for God's redemptive action in the future, and Christian interpreters connected that hope to Jesus. But the language of hope in these Scriptures took many forms and was subject to various interpretations. On the other hand, none of the many religious concepts available in the cultural world of the wider Roman Empire was fully adequate to the Christian experience of Jesus. Thus what eventually emerged as the "orthodox" view was without exact precedent. It was forged only through controversies and splits among groups with various interpretations.

By excluding some materials, the canon enforced some degree of unity and thus contributed to the "standardization" of Christian teaching. Yet considerable diversity remained even within the canon. The various writings, which tradition has designated as the "books" of the New Testament, were produced by many different authors, are of several different literary types, and express a wide range of interests and perspectives.

If interpreters have not always appreciated this fact, that is only because some of them have read the various texts from the point of view of an "official" teaching rather than approaching the works individually. The present text, following the generally accepted practice of modern scholarship, is designed to help the student engage each writing in its specificity and not impose the views of one upon another.

3. *Which* New Testament?
Translations, Manuscripts, and Textual Criticism

The vast majority of people who read the Bible today do not read it in the languages in which it was originally written; they read it in translation. It is therefore important to pay attention to which translation one uses. Most students of New Testament are aware of the existence of many versions of the Bible, particularly the newer ones that seek to capture the meaning of the original texts in clear, contemporary English. The movement in this direction is all to the good, but readability is not the only issue at stake. Translation is tricky business, and an important question to ask is whether the translators have made an attempt at objectivity or have presupposed some particular doctrinal point of view. Another question is whether a given version is in fact a genuine translation of the original or simply a paraphrase of an earlier translation that tries only to give the "general sense" of the text. Although all translation involves a measure of interpretation, a paraphrase offers far too much opportunity for the injection of some particular theological perspective.

But what precisely is it that translators translate? What do we mean, in other words, when we speak of "the original"? There is actually no such thing as the original New Testament as such, since each of the writings was produced separately. And neither do we have the original (or "autograph") copy of any of the individual books. What we do have is a great number of ancient manuscripts, some containing the entire New Testament and others containing portions of varying lengths.

Not surprisingly, there is considerable variation among the manuscripts as to what the original documents actually said. Copyists apparently made errors and sometimes even changed the text intentionally for various reasons. The variations are for the most part fairly minor, but they are not without significance. In any case, before setting out to translate a New Testament writing one must first try to establish how the original document read. And this is the task of a subdiscipline of biblical studies known as textual criticism.

A few scholars speculate that the Gospels were originally written in Aramaic, which was spoken by Jews in their homeland during the time of Jesus. The majority, however, are convinced that Greek was the language of composition of all the books of the Christian canon. What the textual critic must work from, in any case, is more than five thousand Greek manuscripts, along with many other manuscripts of early *versions,* that is, ancient translations into such languages as Latin, Syriac, and Coptic. In addition, the writings of early church leaders contain numerous quotations from New Testament writings. It is the task of textual criticism to compare all this material and produce the best approximation of the original Greek texts.

Our answer to the earlier question, then, is complex. What New Testament translators translate and what New Testament interpreters seek ultimately to interpret are the textual critics' reconstructions of the original Greek texts. And this observation leads to another reason why the choice of a translation is so important to the student of the Bible. Not only have textual critics refined their methods over time, but many formerly unknown manuscripts have been discovered in fairly recent history. The more recent translations that make use

333   ΠΡΑΞΕΙΣ ΑΠΟΣΤΟΛΩΝ   5,11-23

ψαν πρὸς τὸν ἄνδρα αὐτῆς, **11** καὶ ἐγένετο φόβος μέγας
ἐφ' ὅλην τὴν ἐκκλησίαν καὶ ἐπὶ πάντας τοὺς ἀκούοντας
ταῦτα.

12 Διὰ δὲ τῶν χειρῶν τῶν ἀποστόλων ἐγίνετο σημεῖα
καὶ τέρατα πολλὰ ἐν τῷ λαῷ. καὶ ἦσαν ὁμοθυμαδὸν Γἅ-
παντες ⸆ ἐν τῇ στοᾷ Σολομῶντος, **13** ⸆ τῶν δὲ λοιπῶν οὐδ-
εἰς ἐτόλμα κολλᾶσθαι αὐτοῖς, ἀλλ' ἐμεγάλυνεν αὐτοὺς ὁ
λαός. **14** μᾶλλον δὲ προσετίθεντο πιστεύοντες τῷ κυρίῳ,
πλήθη ἀνδρῶν τε καὶ γυναικῶν, **15** ὥστε καὶ εἰς τὰς πλα-
τείας ἐκφέρειν τοὺς ἀσθενεῖς ⸆ καὶ τιθέναι ἐπὶ κλιναρίων
καὶ κραβάττων, ἵνα ἐρχομένου Πέτρου κἂν ἡ σκιὰ Γἐπι-
σκιάσῃ τινὶ αὐτῶν⸆. **16** συνήρχετο δὲ καὶ τὸ πλῆθος τῶν
πέριξ πόλεων ⸆ Ἰερουσαλὴμ φέροντες ἀσθενεῖς καὶ ὀ-
χλουμένους ⸀ὑπὸ πνευμάτων ἀκαθάρτων, ⸀οἵτινες ἐθερα-
πεύοντο ἅπαντες⸃.

17 ⸋Ἀναστὰς δὲ⸌ ὁ ἀρχιερεὺς καὶ πάντες οἱ σὺν αὐτῷ,
ἡ οὖσα αἵρεσις τῶν Σαδδουκαίων, ἐπλήσθησαν Γζήλου
18 καὶ ἐπέβαλον τὰς χεῖρας ⸆ ἐπὶ τοὺς ἀποστόλους καὶ
ἔθεντο αὐτοὺς ἐν τηρήσει δημοσίᾳ⸆. **19** Ἄγγελος δὲ
κυρίου διὰ νυκτὸς⸀ ἀνοίξας τὰς θύρας τῆς φυλακῆς ἐξ-
αγαγών⸆ τε αὐτοὺς εἶπεν· **20** πορεύεσθε καὶ σταθέντες
λαλεῖτε ἐν ⸀τῷ ἱερῷ⸀ τῷ λαῷ πάντα τὰ ῥήματα τῆς ζωῆς
ταύτης. **21** ἀκούσαντες δὲ εἰσῆλθον ὑπὸ τὸν ὄρθρον εἰς
τὸ ἱερὸν καὶ ἐδίδασκον.   Παραγενόμενος δὲ ὁ ἀρχιερεὺς καὶ οἱ σὺν αὐτῷ⸀ συνεκάλεσαν τὸ συνέδριον καὶ
πᾶσαν τὴν γερουσίαν τῶν υἱῶν Ἰσραὴλ καὶ ἀπέστειλαν
εἰς τὸ δεσμωτήριον ἀχθῆναι αὐτούς. **22** οἱ δὲ ⸆παρα-
γενόμενοι ὑπηρέται ⸀οὐχ εὗρον αὐτοὺς ἐν τῇ φυλα-
κῇ⸃· ἀναστρέψαντες δὲ ἀπήγγειλαν **23** λέγοντες ὅτι τὸ

Cross-references:
2,43!
2,19.22.43; 4,30;
6,8; 7,36; 14,3; 15,
12; 7,7! 12,12!
1,14!; 3,11!
2,41! 11,24 - 18,8!
cf 19,12 Mc 5,56
8,7!
4,6
4,1 2.5.6ss • 13,45;
17,5
4,3! 16,23!; 12,4-10
16,37!
16,26s
J 6,68 cf Ph 2,16
Act 13,26
2,42; 4,2.18; 5,25.
28,42
Ex 12,21 1Mcc
12,6 2Mcc 1,10

12 ⸀τ παν- Α Β Ε 0189 pc ¦ txt 𝔓⁷⁴ⱽⁱᵈ א D Ψ 𝔐 ¦ Tεν τω
ναω συνηγμενοι Ε • **13** ¦και ουδ. τ. λ. D t (sy) • **15** Tαυτων D p ¦ Γ-σει Β 33. 614.
1241. 2495 al ¦ ⸀απηλλασσοντο γαρ απο πασης ασθενειας ως ειχεν εκαστος αυτων D
(mae) ¦ και ρυσθωσιν απο π. ασθ. ης ειχον. διο D Ε (it vgᵐˢ; Lcf) • **16** Tεις D Ε Ψ 𝔐
vgᵐˢˢ ¦ txt 𝔓⁷⁴ א Α Β 0189 pc lat sy ¦ Γαπο D ¦ ⸀και ιωντο παντες D it syᵖ; Lcf • **17** ⸋
Αννας δε p mae; [Blass cj]; και ταυτα βλεπων αναστας E ¦ Γ-ους B* • **18** Tαυτων E
𝔐 syʰ ¦ ⸀txt 𝔓⁷⁴ א Α Β D Ψ 0189. 36. 1175 pc lat syᵖ; Lcf ¦ Γκαι επορευθη εις εκαστος
εις τα ιδια D mae • **19** Γτοτε δια νυκ. αγγ. κυ. Dsyᵖ ¦ Γτ ηνοιξε B(D) Ε Ψ 0189
pc ¦ txt 𝔓⁷⁴ א Α 36. 453. 1175 pc ¦ Γδε Β Ψ 0189 • **20** Γ𝔓⁷⁴ • **21** Γεγερθεντες τοο
προσι και συνκαλεσαμενοι D mae • **22** ⸆D E Ψ 𝔐 ¦ txt 𝔓⁷⁴ א Α Β 36. 945. 1175.
1739 al ¦ Γκαι ανοιξαντες την φυλακην ουκ ευρ. ευρ. εσω D lat (syʰ**) mae

Fig. 1. *Left:* Acts 5:11–23 from the Nestle-Aland *Novum Testamentum Graece*, ed. 26. The small column on the right lists cross-references to other parts of the New Testament and both canonical and noncanonical Jewish writings; the notations on the bottom list important textual variations among the many ancient manuscripts. *Right:* Reverse side of uncial manuscript 0189, containing Acts 5:12–21; the oldest parchment manuscript of the New Testament, dating in the 2d/3d cent.

of the advances in textual criticism bring the reader considerably closer to what the New Testament authors actually wrote.

STUDY QUESTIONS

1. How would you describe the educational philosophy presented in section 1? State your agreements and/or disagreements with it. Should an academic text be "objective"? Should it be "value-neutral"? Do these two terms mean the same thing? Identify the specific interests you bring to the study of the New Testament.

2. Explain briefly the steps through which the New Testament came into being. Which writings are the earliest of all the canonical works? When, approximately, did the Gospels begin to appear?

3. How would you answer the question, "Who wrote the New Testament?"

4. Identify each of the following: apostle, canon, Gentile, manuscript.

5. Why is it important to approach each New Testament writing separately?

6. Why is it important to pay attention to which translation of the New Testament one uses?

7. What is the task of textual criticism?

8. In which language were the materials in the New Testament written?

FOR FURTHER READING

Bauer, Walter. *Orthodoxy and Heresy in Earliest Christianity.* Rev. by Georg Strecker; trans. Philadelphia Seminar on Christian Origins; trans. ed. Robert A. Kraft and Gerhard Krodel. Philadelphia: Fortress Press, 1971. An important work stressing the diversity of early Christianity.

Chadwick, Henry. *The Early Church.* Grand Rapids: Eerdmans, 1967. A clear, relatively brief presentation of Christian history through the sixth century.

Epp, Eldon Jay. "Textual Criticism, NT." *The Interpreter's Dictionary of the Bible, Supplementary Volume.* Nashville: Abingdon, 1962.

Gamble, Harry Y. "The Canon of the New Testament." *The New Testament and Its Modern Interpreters.* Ed. Eldon Jay Epp and George W. MacRae, S.J. Philadelphia: Fortress Press; Atlanta: Scholars Press, 1989. Discusses key issues in recent scholarship on the development of the canon.

Grant, Robert M. *The Formation of the New Testament.* New York: Harper & Row, 1965. A clear account of the development of the canon.

Lietzmann, Hans. *A History of the Early Church.* Vols. 1 and 2. Trans. Bertram Lee Wolf. Cleveland and New York: World Publishing Company, 1961. A detailed account, first published in 1937–38 and last revised in 1953.

Maslow, Abraham H. *Religions, Values, and Peak Experiences*. New York: Viking, 1973. Contains an important discussion of the question of value-free education.

Sundberg, A. C., Jr. "Canon of the NT." *The Interpreter's Dictionary of the Bible, Supplementary Volume*. Nashville: Abingdon, 1962. Argues for a distinction between Scripture and canon.

Taylor, Vincent. *The Text of the New Testament: A Short Introduction*. 2d ed. London: Macmillan; New York: St. Martin's, 1963. Brief and readable, but knowledge of New Testament Greek presupposed.

Weiss, Johannes. *Earliest Christianity: A History of the Period A.D. 30–150*. 2 vols. Trans. Frederick C. Grant. New York: Harper & Row, 1959. A detailed account, first published in 1937. Strong on the separate geographical areas.

Whitehead, Alfred North. *The Aims of Education*. New York: Macmillan, 1929. An early endorsement of the integration of education with life concerns.

Chapter 1

Some Ways of Reading the Bible

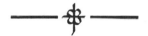

At a corner of Central Park, a man in a black suit waves a tattered Bible and pleads with a handful of bystanders: "Ye must be born again." In St. Patrick's Cathedral, worshipers at a weekday afternoon mass receive bread and wine that have been miraculously transformed into the body and blood of Christ; they would be as puzzled by the "born again" terminology as the man in the park would be with their understanding of the mass. At the same moment, in another part of the city, a college professor leads her class in a discussion of the psychological significance of the "Christ-*myth*," while a few blocks away a Unitarian minister, in a discussion with a parishioner, refers to Jesus as a moral hero worthy of imitation. Across the street, high above the city in an elegant apartment, a woman speaks with her guru over tea: they discuss the Buddha, meditation, and "Christ-consciousness."

The New Testament has been interpreted in innumerable ways. Not only are there sharp differences among Christians themselves, but the Jesus story has influenced many outside the Christian community also: Muslims recognize Jesus as a prophet; Jews, secular humanists, and devotees of various Eastern religions sometimes make room in their belief systems or value systems for either Jesus the historical person or a "Christ-principle" within every individual. Such persons obviously find in the New Testament something very different from what an Eastern Orthodox, a Baptist, or a Roman Catholic interpreter is likely to find.

Differing readings of the New Testament have also led to widely varying ways of applying it to contemporary life. In a mid-sized American city, a woman and a man sit before a television camera and speak of the "end of the world," which they believe, on the basis of the book of Revelation, to be very near. Their understanding of the Bible also leads them to specific positions on social and political issues: they oppose most government-funded social welfare programs but encourage voluntary giving to alleviate world hunger; they believe that capitalism is biblically based and that the United States is a Christian nation; they honor "womanhood" but oppose the ordination of women as Christian ministers. These media evangelists would identify themselves as Protestant.

In a study group in a small church across town, however, a minister representing a very different sort of Protestantism denies that any of the biblical prophecies apply literally to events in the modern world; but she does find biblical support for disarmament, the radical redistribution of wealth, and full equality for women. Her group learns about peasants in Latin America who, together with Catholic priests and nuns, discuss liberation theology, a school of thought that understands the Bible as announcing God's solidarity with oppressed people and calling for fundamental changes in the social and economic order. These peasants, priests, and nuns see in Jesus the one who frees them not only from sin and death but also from the economic domination they trace to North America, capitalism, and even certain segments of the Christian church. And their brand of Catholicism differs from that of some other Catholics as much as the minister's Protestantism differs from that of the media evangelists.

In light of the extreme diversity among biblical interpretations, what may at first have seemed a simple task—reading the New Testament and understanding it—may now appear insurmountable. If such radically different views can claim New Testament support, is there any hope at all of determining what the biblical texts "really" mean?

What would seem to be needed is some means of attaining objectivity, of moving beyond individual prejudices and cultural conditioning. But the search for objectivity raises serious questions. Not only is absolute objectivity unattainable, but one may even question its desirability. To be objective in dealing with a problem is to make that problem external to oneself. It is to become disinterested—not *un*interested, of course, but detached from the question in the sense of not allowing one's own interests to distort the evidence. But to the religious person, or even the person with religious questions, the interpretation of Scripture is not an external matter. The demand for detachment might thus seem to violate the religious person's point of view.

These are serious questions, and a book such as this cannot attempt final answers to them. My hope, however, is that the following discussion of various ways of studying the Bible will be of some help to students in formulating their own provisional answers and working perspectives from which they can begin their study of the New Testament. In the last two sections of this chapter, I will state how the present text will seek to provide an approach to biblical studies that violates neither the religious nor the nonreligious students' legitimate concerns.

1. The Historical-Critical Method

Modern scholars generally acknowledge the value of reading the biblical texts in light of the historical contexts in which they were written. Although biblical scholarship has sometimes come into conflict with religious groups over the practice and results of the historical-critical method, this approach to the Bible is now almost universally accepted as a valuable step toward objectivity. Interpreters employing this method do not begin with such questions as "What does this mean to me?" or "What does my religion teach about what this means?" They seek first to determine when and where the work in question was written, who wrote it, for whom it was written, and for what purpose it was written. The assumption is that answers to these questions will enable us better to understand what the author meant and what the original readers would have understood.

It is not always easy to read an ancient writing in this way. To view it in its historical context means learning about a time and place far removed from our own; it also means allowing that writing to say something that may strike us as unfamiliar, strange, and possibly untrue. Because people in ancient cultures held world-pictures (understandings of the nature of the universe) quite different from our own, we may even find that they were not only giving answers that appear strange in the modern context but were asking different questions from those that are important to us. It is natural to seek in the biblical materials some immediate point of contact with our own concerns, but the historian's point of view cautions us against forcing either "acceptability" or "relevance" upon the biblical text.

The historical approach to the Bible, in short, demands that we try to understand the biblical texts precisely in their "foreignness." Scholars employing this method must commit themselves to exercise their critical intellects, letting the evidence speak for itself and not allowing their own desires or religious perspectives to get in the way of an objective search for historical truth. This does not mean that one must give up one's prior beliefs as a prerequisite to historical inquiry, but it does mean that these must not be allowed to override the evidence and answer all questions before the investigation begins.

The present text presupposes the value of viewing the writings of the New Testament historically. But it is naive to think that the historical approach insures objectivity. There is no completely neutral perspective from which to view the past and no given set of questions a historian must ask; all questions reflect the perspectives of individual historians and their cultural settings. So it is important not only to try to allow the Bible to speak on its own terms but also to recognize that we cannot study the past objectively unless at the same time we identify our own biases and ask how they influence our interpretation.

2. Social-Scientific Criticism: Refinement of the Historical-Critical Method

Many of our biases are specifically social in nature, that is, they are rooted in the structure of our own societies and the values that permeate our own cultures. Scholars committed to the historical-critical method have long thought it important to learn as much as we can about the social and cultural contexts within which the New Testament writings were produced, precisely to avoid implanting our modern presuppositions upon these ancient texts. But it is only recently that they have made very explicit or sophisticated use of the tools of research developed in the social sciences such as sociology and anthropology. In doing so, they have helped to refine the historical-critical approach.

Biblical scholars employ several different socially oriented methods of study, each with its own set of interests and specific tools. One of these is "social description," an attempt to portray, in David Rhoads's words,

> every aspect of the social environment of the New Testament in its original setting: occupations, tools, houses, roads, means of travel, money, economic realities, architecture, villages and cities, laws, social classes, markets, clothes, foodstuffs, cooking practices, and so on.[1]

Another approach focuses on "social history," attempting to trace the social changes that took place over time. If, for example, we could determine that a particular New Testament author wrote for a specific community in a period of fundamental transition, we might learn a great deal about that author's intentions.

A number of recent interpreters have applied these and other socially oriented methods with interesting results. Some have read certain New Testament passages as reflections of class conflict within a community, and others

---

1. David Rhoads, "Social Criticism: Crossing Boundaries," in *Mark and Method,* ed. Janice Capel Anderson and Stephen D. Moore (Minneapolis: Fortress Press, 1992), 136.

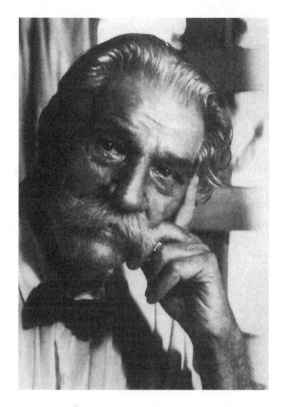

Fig. 2.
Albert Schweitzer
(1875–1965)*

have seen specific writings as reflecting the marginalized status of the recipients. Still others have focused upon the ways in which the communities to which Paul wrote were shaped by their specifically urban environments.

As an example of the way in which modern presuppositions can distort the ancient text, we may note that biblical scholars have often identified some groups mentioned in the New Testament as "middle class." Recent sociological study of ancient societies, however, suggests that there was no middle class in the modern sense of a group with an independent power base. People tended to be either rich or poor, although there were a number of different classes with different social functions and standing.

Biblical scholars are also making use of the methods of cultural anthropology. In the vocabulary of anthropologists, a culture is a complex of patterns

*A German scholar in the historical-critical school, he was also known as a musician and medical doctor. In later life, while administering a clinic in Africa, he became a world figure as a humanitarian and the proponent of a philosophy of "reverence for life." Among his most important and influential scholarly works were *The Quest of the Historical Jesus* and *The Mysticism of Paul the Apostle*. (*Photo courtesy UPI/Bettmann Archive*)

of thought and behavior that a society passes on through a set of symbols. On one level, a culture expresses itself through artifacts and institutions. But at its core it consists of the most fundamental ideas and values that hold a society together and give a sense of meaning to its members.

Drawing upon anthropologists' theories regarding the cultural context within which the New Testament was written, these scholars have identified some important differences between our way of thinking and that of the biblical authors. Those of us who live in the twentieth-century Western world, for example, tend to think of ourselves primarily as individuals. We speak of being responsible to ourselves, and we expect individuals to serve as their own moral guides. The people of ancient societies, however, saw themselves primarily as members of groups, and their actions were largely directed toward seeking the approval of the communities in which they lived. Unless we understand that the Bible reflects this ancient perspective, so radically different from our own, we are certain to miss or distort much of what it has to say.

Practitioners of the various socially oriented approaches have often worked in isolation from one another and have had considerable disagreements among themselves. But many scholars see the different methods as complementary, and John H. Elliott has tried to bring them together under the term "social-scientific criticism." This broad approach, he explains,

> studies the text as both a reflection of and response to the social and cultural settings in which the text was produced. Its aim is the determination of the meaning(s) explicit and implicit in the text, meanings made possible and shaped by the social and cultural systems inhabited by both authors and intended audiences.[2]

Some theologically minded interpreters have feared that the social-scientific approach might tend to "explain away" the religious content of the biblical writings as nothing more than the product of social and cultural forces. It is true that attention to such forces does place the theological content in a new light, but the social-scientific method does not in itself negate a theological or religiously based approach.

There are, of course, limitations to this way of reading the Bible. Because our sources for the social makeup of the New Testament world are sparse and fragmentary, much of the work in this field will remain somewhat speculative. But that is not to say it is useless. My sense is that the vast majority of con-

2. John H. Elliott, *What Is Social-Scientific Criticism?* Guides to Biblical Scholarship (Minneapolis: Fortress Press, 1993), 8.

temporary scholars believe that social-scientific criticism is making valuable contributions to our understanding.

The refinements that the social-scientific approaches have introduced into the historical-critical method show that the latter is capable of self-criticism. Some interpreters, however, want to go beyond the historical method in their attempt to understand the Bible. To the historian, the meaning of a writing is that which was intended by the author and/or that which the original audience would have found in it. But there are other ways of defining "meaning" that will become apparent as we examine other ways of studying the Bible.

3. Theological and Ideological Interpretation

As classically formulated, the historical-critical method requires that interpreters avoid making value judgments as they try to describe the meaning of a text in an objective way. Precisely for that reason, some religious interpreters have found limitations in this method and have proposed various types of "theological interpretation."

The term "theological interpretation" is sometimes used to refer to an objective description of the theological content of a writing. In that case, it is simply one aspect of historical interpretation. But what concerns us here is a second meaning of the term, that is, an interpretation designed specifically to serve the interests of a religious community. Theological interpretation in this sense tries to show the relevance of a writing for the contemporary readers' faith. The meaning it seeks to identify in the New Testament is the meaning a writing can have for Christian believers.

Interpreters who practice this second form of theological interpretation point out that the Bible is after all religious literature and to try to interpret it in a value-free way is to deny its fundamental nature. Many scholars object to this approach, however, because it seems to allow interpreters to distort the meaning of a text in order to satisfy the interests of official church doctrine or personal religious leanings.

Alongside theological interpretation, we have recently seen the emergence of various ways of reading the New Testament that draw upon specific ideologies that may or may not be complementary to Christianity but are in any case not explicitly Christian. Although the term "ideology" is sometimes used in a negative way, I use it here in a neutral sense. By ideology I mean simply a set of ideas and values to which someone is committed; and ideological interpretation is an approach to the biblical writings that openly identifies a specific set of interests and commitments on the part of the interpreter.

Fig. 3.
Elizabeth Cady Stanton
(1815–1902)*

Ideological interpretation is subject to the same criticisms as theological interpretation, but its proponents claim that all interpreters actually bring their own ideologies to the text, although they do not usually recognize them. One may note, for example, that until very recently, biblical interpretation was dominated by affluent white males in the industrialized West and tended to neglect questions of interest to women, persons of color, and people in the so-called Third World. When these latter groups began to offer their own readings of biblical materials, a new set of questions came to the fore.

One of the most prominent forms of ideological interpretation in recent years has been feminist criticism. Much of the work in this area is simply another refinement of the historical-critical method. By asking formerly neglected questions, feminist scholars have uncovered strong evidence that women played a much greater role in the leadership of early Christian com-

---

*A major figure in the women's suffrage movement in the nineteenth century. Although not a trained biblical scholar, she was the major contributor to *The Women's Bible*, a two-volume commentary (1895, 1898) that identified male bias in the Scriptures and challenged current understandings of divine inspiration. *(Photo courtesy Bettmann Archive)*

munities than was formerly believed. And they have found reason to speak of alternative strains of Christian tradition, which were eventually suppressed, that were passed on specifically by women.

Although feminist criticism overlaps with the historical-critical method, however, it is by no means value-neutral. Some feminist scholars have been particularly concerned to expose and critique the androcentric (male-centered) nature of many of the biblical materials. And some have spent much time doing the same with respect to male-centered biblical scholarship.

Feminist interpreters, moreover, often go explicitly beyond the historical method. Some, for example, make use of literary methods discussed later in this chapter. They add feminist twists by asking such questions as how the meaning of a writing might appear to a woman rather than a man and, more explicitly, to a woman who refuses to accept the male point of view that the writing might tend to impose upon her.

Persons of color and Third World peoples have also fostered various ideological approaches to biblical interpretation. And in some cases aspects of Marxian analysis of the class structure of society and economics play a role in their method. When these approaches are taken together with feminist interpretation, we may speak of a broad interest in "liberating" interpretations, intended to help free the reader from various forms of oppression. These forms of ideological interpretation overlap with theological interpretation, since some (but not all) of their proponents work from within the Christian community.

Another recent school of interpretation that stands on the borderline between theological and ideological interpretation makes uses of "process" philosophies and theologies. Process thought is a view of reality according to which all things in the universe are in continuous process and are related to one another as parts of one spiritual whole. It differs from traditional theology in various ways, particularly in its concept of God, and some theologians criticize it for that reason. Process interpreters, however, are convinced that the philosophical categories they bring to the text help them see aspects they would otherwise miss.[3]

Theological and ideological interpretations remain controversial in the eyes of many biblical scholars. Perhaps the key question to ask in evaluating any such approach is whether it actually illumines the writing being interpreted or simply imposes a meaning upon it. As we will see presently, however, this question itself raises further ones of an extremely difficult nature.

---

3. Process thought can be understood as one version of a "postmodern" worldview. See below, pp. 32–33, 49–51, 426–30, and 533–35.

Fig. 4.
Rudolf Bultmann
(1884–1976)*

4. Existentialist Interpretation

One school of interpretation that has been particularly influential on modern scholarship is grounded in the work of the mid-twentieth-century German biblical scholar and theologian Rudolf Bultmann. Although Bultmann was a lifelong defender of the historical-critical method against some proponents of a theological approach to the text, some interpreters have classified some of his work also as a specific type of theological interpretation.

According to Bultmann, the New Testament writers shared with ancient humanity generally a view of the universe as "a three-story structure, with earth in the middle, heaven above it, and hell below it."[4] They believed that

---

*A major figure in the historical-critical school, known also as a theologian and the proponent of demythologizing/existentialist interpretation. *(Photo from BBC Hulton Picture Library)*

their lives were subject to supernatural intervention, that God could send them heavenly visions, angels could come to their aid, demons could possess them, and Satan could take hold of their minds.

Bultmann terms this world-picture "mythological" and argues that modern people simply cannot accept it without involving themselves in serious contradiction. For the language of this world-picture naively speaks of what is understood as "other-worldly" in the same terms that we speak of this-worldly realities. The New Testament, for example, routinely understands God's transcendence ("apartness" from the world) as physical, spatial distance. And it views as supernatural interventions events that modern people would attribute to natural causation or human decision.

Bultmann thus proposes a method of interpretation that he names both "demythologizing" and "existentialist interpretation." The first term emphasizes the negative task of the interpreter, which is to "strip away" the mythology and look beneath the ancient world-picture that determined the authors' language and concepts. The positive term, "existentialist interpretation," indicates that the interpreter does so by identifying the "self-understanding"—the notion of what life is all about, or of what constitutes "authentic human existence"—that is expressed through the mythological language. In looking for the self-understanding conveyed in a text, one is searching for an "existential" meaning, one that speaks directly to life as all persons ordinarily experience it, without reference to supernatural occurrences.

For Bultmann, the real meaning of the New Testament has to do not with the claims it makes regarding supernatural interventions into the normal course of events but with the basic attitude toward life, or understanding of the meaning of human existence, to which it points. And to have faith on the New Testament's terms does not mean accepting an ancient world-picture or believing in miracles in any literal sense; it means embracing as one's own the self-understanding that the New Testament presents.

The New Testament, for example, speaks of a final judgment at which a heavenly court will pronounce the eternal fates of human beings. Many Christians throughout the ages have believed that such an event will actually occur at the end of history. Bultmann, however, looks beneath the notion of a supernatural end to history to find an existential meaning and interprets the final judgment as a symbol of the conviction that human beings stand before God in every moment of their lives. The proclamation of a final judgment is thus a powerful representation of the crucial nature of the

---

4. Rudolf Bultmann, *New Testament and Mythology and Other Basic Writings,* ed. and trans. Schubert M. Ogden (Philadelphia: Fortress Press, 1984), 1.

decisions human beings make regarding the meaning and purpose of their lives. Interpreted in this way, it has to do not with a literal end of history or with heaven and hell but with the choice between authentic and inauthentic human existence, between life that fulfills its God-given purpose and life that does not.

Existentialist interpretation has been criticized from several perspectives. Some opponents accuse Bultmann of imposing a modern point of view upon the Bible, arbitrarily rejecting everything that is incompatible with his own world-picture. They find his method to be ideological in a negative sense, criticizing him for his self-conscious use of the categories of the philosopher Martin Heidegger. Bultmann's reply is that the New Testament itself actually begins the process of existentialist interpretation, that at numerous points the authors unwittingly depart from their mythological world-picture and reveal the existential "intention" of their mythological language. We will examine some of these passage later in this text.

Some critics attack the theological nature of existentialist interpretation, claiming that it is less an explanation of what the text says than a form of contemporary theological reflection upon it. They ask whether scholar-theologians such as Bultmann see what they see in the New Testament only because they are trying, as Christians, to make it acceptable to the modern mind. For Bultmann, however, one need not be a Christian to perceive the existential meaning in the mythological language. One need only ask the "existential question," the question of what life is all about.

The very terms "myth" and "mythological" have also sparked controversy. Some critics charge that Bultmann assumes that there is something negative about myth, whereas most scholars in religion value it positively as a means of conveying religious understanding. A myth in this positive sense is simply a story that expresses a religious community's sense of the ultimate nature of the universe and their place in it. The dispute is in my estimation somewhat misdirected, since Bultmann clearly states that his intention is not to dispense with myth but to interpret it.

Another point of contention is Bultmann's emphasis upon the "self-understanding" conveyed in the New Testament. Some critics feel that to read the New Testament primarily as calling individuals to authentic existence obscures the collective outlook that the Bible shares with the ancient world in general. And interpreters concerned with sociological issues have complained that such an emphasis tends to ignore the concrete sociopolitical situations in which specific texts arose.

Each of these criticisms raises complex issues that could be discussed at length. But my purpose in discussing existentialist interpretation is neither to try to settle such issues nor to endorse or reject this approach. It is rather to stimulate reflection upon the difficult question of what interpreters are looking for when they seek to find "meaning" in a religious text.

5. Psychological Approaches to the Bible

Although existentialist interpretation can in principle be practiced by anyone who asks the "existential question," it was devised by Christian theologians and has been of interest primarily to Christians. There are other ways of seeking meaning in the Bible that, although used by Christians and Jews, have much less explicit ties to the interests of organized religion. Some recent interpreters, for example, have made use of the psychological theories of Sigmund Freud and C. G. Jung.

Whereas historical interpretation usually identifies the meaning of a work with the author's intentions, psychological interpretation views a writing as in part the product of the unconscious mind. Jung claims that the symbols used in religious lore are closely parallel to the imagery appearing in dreams. Religious writings thus have a special connection to the unconscious. They can express thoughts of which the author was unaware, and they can also affect the reader on the unconscious level. Psychological interpretation assumes that some psychological patterns are universal, cutting across history and cultures. It can thus to a large extent bypass historical questions. On the other hand, since each reader has an individual psychological history, meaning has a very personal dimension.

By way of example, it is interesting to view the New Testament stories of Jesus' resurrection from a Jungian perspective. Jung contends that all human beings share, in the depths of their unconscious minds, a set of "archetypes," or fixed patterns of thought. These archetypes are the products not of our individual experiences but of our biological inheritance through evolution; we have them simply by virtue of belonging to the human species.

According to Jung, the theme of death and resurrection is one of these archetypal patterns. This means not that all human beings subconsciously believe in a literal life after death, but that they have the innate capacity to understand the theme of death and resurrection as a symbol of a human experience in this world. We all have, in other words, unconscious knowledge of "a pattern of being, in which what appears to be irreparable loss is supplanted by unimaginable gain: being hopelessly lost and then found, being hopelessly ill and healed, being hopelessly locked into a destructive pattern of living and then forgiven and released."[5]

A psychological interpretation of the resurrection stories will have no interest in their literal truth but will focus upon ways in which they can release the power of the death/resurrection archetype in a reader's experience. Such a reading might enable some persons to acknowledge that destructive relationships in which they are involved constitute a kind of "death" from which they have been unconsciously seeking liberation. Others might come to realize that their dreams have been offering them a "resurrection" in the form of forgiveness for deeds that have burdened them with guilt for many years. Reading the New Testament in such a way can be an important tool for enhancing one's own psychological/spiritual healing.

Psychological interpretation can be criticized from the historian's perspective. Are psychological patterns really so universal? Might we not misread an ancient text if we try to correlate it with our own psychological patterns? Other critics will contend that the Bible not only expresses unconscious processes but also makes truth claims. Some will point out that the New Testament writers believed that God "really" raised Jesus from the dead, and others may note that it is not just any pattern of death and resurrection that is signified in the New Testament, but precisely that which moves from a life lived in estrangement from God and the neighbor to a life of love and unity with God and neighbor. And, finally, interpreters who stress the social context of the New Testament writings complain that psychological interpretation ignores the sociopolitical thrust of these materials. It is clear, however, that psychological approaches have an immediate point of contact in almost every reader's experience and therefore great potential for awakening interest in biblical studies.

6. Steps toward a Literary Approach: Form Criticism and Redaction Criticism

Because of the Bible's status as Scripture, Christian interpreters since early times have tended to treat it as a statement of Christian doctrine. As a result, they have focused largely on its rational content, that is, on the theological ideas it presents. Modern historical criticism reshaped this theological concern by insisting that we get at the meaning of a writing by placing it in its historical context. It also added a new interest: because a given work might

---

5. Wayne G. Rollins, *Jung and the Bible* (Atlanta: John Knox, 1983), 83.

have gone through one or more revisions and an author might have made use of various earlier materials, scholars sought to reconstruct the history of the work itself. In doing this they made use of source criticism, the attempt to identify preexisting written materials that the final author incorporated into the finished writing.[6]

The biblical writings, however, are more than sources for the reconstruction of history; and although they express theological ideas, very few if any of them can be designated theological treatises. Some of the books are narratives, or stories; and most of the others are letters or at least have some of the characteristics of a letter. The Bible is, in some sense at least, literature; and recent scholarship has given increased attention to the specifically literary aspects of its writings as completed works.

The new emphasis came in stages. Two methods of biblical study that have been extremely influential in twentieth-century scholarship can be understood as bridges between the historical and the literary approaches.

a. Form Criticism

The first of these is form criticism, which is based upon a recognition that the authors of some of the New Testament writings made use not only of written sources but of small units of oral tradition. The first task of form criticism is the recognition and classification of these small units of material according to their literary forms or types. The authors of some of the letters in the New Testament have apparently quoted early Christian hymns, and some seem to have reproduced standard lists of virtues and vices that scholars have named "household codes." The writers of the Gospels also seem to have made use of various kinds of earlier material. Each critic has a different scheme of classification, but typical categories are parables, various types of sayings, miracle stories, and pronouncement stories (short accounts ending in a dramatic saying of Jesus).

Insofar as scholars identify specific literary forms, they are involved in a kind of literary criticism. But form critics are also interested in the stages of development the material might have gone through before it found its way into the present writings. For that reason, it is also called form *history*.

This interest in development is particularly evident in the study of the Gospels. When we compare the different Gospels we sometimes find the same

---

6. Source criticism has traditionally been considered one aspect of literary criticism, but it has little to do with the newer emphases associated with that term. I reserve "literary criticism" to refer to approaches that focus on writings as finished products.

story or saying in several different versions. So the form critic tries to reconstruct the process of development that produced the variations and ultimately to identify the original version. The presupposition, almost self-evident to anyone who studies ancient cultures, is that the stories about what Jesus said and did circulated orally before anyone wrote them down. Presumably, they went through transformations as they moved from one environment to another. Form critics therefore try to determine what specific setting, or life situation, would produce a particular transformation. They are thus concerned not only with literary forms but with history and sociology as well.

Form criticism was highly controversial when first introduced into biblical studies, and it still has detractors. Some scholars are skeptical about the possibility of tracing the prehistory of specific materials, and others charge that form critics actually classify materials as much according to their content as according to their literary form.

b. Redaction Criticism

Application of form criticism to the Gospels eventually led to the development of redaction criticism. The term "redaction" is the English version of a German word that means "editing." Redaction critics presuppose the work of both source and form critics, but turn their attention away from the preexisting units of tradition back to the larger completed works themselves. Part of what *form* critics do is to separate tradition from redaction, that is, to strip away the final author's editorial changes, in order to find the earlier versions. But identification of the final author's editing can also be used in the opposite way: to identify the final author's own interests. For to show that in several cases a writer makes the same kind of change is to identify a consistent emphasis. What the *redaction* critic seeks to do then, is to identify the author's particular interests precisely by noting how that author has edited preexisting material.

Redaction critics, in contrast to form critics, are interested in a finished writing as a whole, not simply its component parts. Any student who has written a term paper, however, knows that it is possible to incorporate a quotation with which one does not fully agree or which one does not fully understand. To approach a writing as the product of editorial changes of existing material is to leave open the possibility that some incorporated material might not reflect the final author's point of view. So redaction critics will sometimes treat a given passage as an "undigested morsel," something that does not really serve the author's intentions.

Some interpreters have pointed out that redaction critics are actually interpreting something other than the writing itself, namely, the author's theology. While this is a valid goal, it is possible to approach a writing differently: one can simply ask what the text itself, as it stands, seems to signify. One could, in other words, ignore the possible sources that lie behind the text and interpret it as one would any other type of literature. One would then be unable to write off any passages as undigested material and would become responsible for the entire text as an integrated, coherent, literary whole.

By giving some attention to the final form of a text, redaction criticism constituted a step toward a truly literary approach to the Bible. But many biblical scholars are going beyond it and turning to the methods of interpretation used in the broader field of literature.

7. Literary Approaches to the Bible

While biblical scholars have traditionally focused on the theological content of the writings, literary approaches introduce another emphasis. To view the biblical writings as literature is to recognize that they are designed to appeal to the readers' imaginative powers, not simply their rational capacities.

To tell a story, for example, is to set up an imaginative world into which the reader is expected to enter. Understanding the story may involve grasping certain ideas, but more fundamentally it means entering the world the story creates and participating in what happens. As William Beardslee comments, "Literary criticism is not as eager as many modern theological interpreters to move out of the world of myth; its primary quest is for what the imaginative world of the work in question is."[7]

To say that the world of a story is imaginative has nothing to do with the question of historical truth—whether the events related "really happened" or not. The point here is simply that a good story, whether factual or not, reflects the imaginative powers of the author and appeals to those of the reader.

Literary approaches to the New Testament involve such traditional procedures, familiar to students of other literature, as identifying literary forms, tracing the development of plot and characters, recognizing themes, and appreciating rhetorical devices. Students who have encountered such methods in studying other types of literature may wonder why biblical studies has made so little use of them until recently. The reason is that the Bible's status as Scripture conditioned interpreters not only to look primarily for its doctri-

---

7. William A. Beardslee, *Literary Criticism of the New Testament* (Philadelphia: Fortress Press, 1970), 13.

nal content but also to focus upon the question of historical accuracy. It is because biblical scholars were so long preoccupied with doctrine on the one hand and the question of "what really happened" on the other that they gave scant attention to the Bible as literature.

a. Rhetorical Criticism

Some literary approaches are closely allied with historical study. Rhetorical criticism, for example, approaches ancient writings in light of the rhetorical patterns (the standardized forms of expression) that were current in the environments in which they were written. Seeking to understand how a given work would affect its intended audience, the rhetorical critic of the New Testament studies ancient Greek rhetoric and also tries to learn as much as possible about the historical situation of the original readers.

The Greek rhetoricians identified numerous specific patterns that speaking and writing followed. But in the most general terms they recognized three broad species of rhetoric: *judicial,* which is designed "to persuade the audience to make judgments about events occurring in the past"; *deliberative,* which encourages the audience "to take some action in the future"; and *epideictic,* which "celebrates or denounces some person or some quality."[8] As we will see, some biblical scholars have tried to classify the letters in the New Testament in terms of this delineation.

b. Structuralism

Other literary methods put much less emphasis upon the role of historical investigation. One of these, which is sometimes carried on in severe isolation from historical concerns, is structuralism. Structuralists base their work upon a distinction between two "levels" they find in certain kinds of texts. The first is familiar to readers and literary scholars generally—the "surface" level of plots, characters, themes, rational content, and the like. What interests structuralists, however, is the second level, on which they identify a type of pattern they call a "deep structure."

Different schools of structuralism identify different kinds of deep structures. The anthropologist Claude Lévi-Strauss studied myths from many societies and concluded that the function of these stories is to help people reconcile contradictory aspects of their experience. A given myth might exist

---

8. George A. Kennedy, *New Testament Interpretation through Rhetorical Criticism* (Chapel Hill: Univ. of North Carolina Press, 1984).

in several versions, with different plots and different meanings on the surface level; but what all versions will have in common is a series of pairs of opposites, such as raw/cooked, female/male, and nature/culture. These pairs constitute the deep structure of the myth and reveal its social function. So the structural interpreter's task is to identify the pairs of opposites and the contradictory aspects of experience the story tries to reconcile.

Despite Lévi-Strauss's own reservations, a number of scholars have applied his method to biblical materials. Because the results bear little resemblance to more familiar modes of biblical interpretation, however, structuralist analyses often puzzle students familiar with other modes of interpretation. The important point to understand is that the focus of structuralist interpretation is not the meaning that other interpreters might look for. The structuralists' interest is in the structure that is expressed not only in the stories but also in other aspects of the life of the group that passes the stories on, such as language and social organization. And what structuralists seek ultimately to describe is that which gives rise to this structure, namely, the human mind itself. In arguing that the myths of ancient societies seek to reconcile contradictions, Lévi-Strauss claims to have discovered a genetically based characteristic of the human mentality: we tend to think in patterns of "binary opposites."

New Testament scholar Daniel Patte seeks a type of deep structure quite different from that which interests Lévi-Strauss. Patte looks beneath the surface level of an author's rational argumentation, which can often vary and fall into contradiction, to the level of that author's faith or system of convictions. Because that system of convictions is what the author does not want to give up, he or she will often resort to odd argumentation—i.e., apparent contradiction, repetitions, and metaphorical language—to defend it. The presence of odd argumentation is thus the key to locating the deep structure, which is more fundamental than the rational content.

Structuralism has provided a new way of viewing texts for scholars impressed with the limitations of historical interpretation. It finds something embedded (or "encoded") in the writing that is the product neither of a historical situation nor of an author's explicit intentions. To opponents of structuralism, however, it seems as if one can find almost any deep structure one looks for in a text. Even some of the intellectual heirs of structuralism have questioned its objectivity. We may therefore speak of a "poststructuralist" school of thought that has contributed to the view that the meaning of a text depends in large part upon the perspective the reader brings to it. Many recent interpreters argue that a given text can produce a variety of meanings and that the reader has a share in the actual creation of meaning.

c. Reader-Response Criticism

Another approach that has contributed to the trend toward recognition of multiple meanings is reader-response criticism. Critics employing this method identify the ways in which a given text is designed to elicit responses from the readers: how it seeks to awaken specific emotions or judgments, how it prepares readers for turns in the plot by giving or withholding information, how it sometimes leaves it to the readers to fill in gaps in the plot and draw their own conclusions. To the extent that it acknowledges that the reader has real decisions to make, it leaves open the possibility of understanding the text in significantly different ways.

According to some interpreters, then, there is a sense in which each reader of a given writing reads a different text, since each brings her or his own interests and makes different decisions in reading; and even a single reader reads a different story every time he or she reads it. Quite obviously, we are at this point a long way from the purely historical approach and from the notion that the meaning of a work is to be identified with the author's intention. We are a long way also from the ideal of pure objectivity in interpretation, and one objection to the view that the reader creates meaning is that it allows interpreters to inject their own ideas into the text. Opponents of this view therefore charge that it leads to a pure subjectivism in which interpreters make the writing say whatever they want it to say, so that there is no way to distinguish valid readings from invalid ones.

Moderate reader-oriented critics avoid the charge by making clear that the reader has a limited range of options in creating meaning and that the role of historical criticism is to help define the limits. More radical proponents claim that the range of meanings is unlimited. However, they contend, their point is not that there is no valid or correct interpretation at all, "but rather that 'correct interpretation' is always relative to particular contexts and interests."[9] But, given the vastness of human contexts and interests, one may still ask whether this defense adequately speaks to the charge of subjectivism.

d. Deconstruction

A final literary approach, which is extremely difficult to grasp, is known as deconstruction. Developing out of structuralism as in part a reaction against it, deconstruction denies that texts are capable of presenting straightforward, consistent, and coherent points of view. Deconstructionist criticism thus consists in showing how texts tend to "deconstruct" themselves, how, for

---

9. A. K. M. Adam, "The Sign of Jonah: A Fish-Eye View," *Semeia* 51 (1990): 177.

example, one set of themes or values in a writing ends up actually making use of its opposite. It shares with the radical reader-response approaches the view that because meaning is open-ended, no interpretation can be final or definitive. But it is distinctive in its denial that a text constitutes a coherent literary whole, its denial that a text offers its reader a "climactic, completed understanding."[10]

Part of the reason that deconstruction is so difficult to grasp is that its goal is so radically different from other modes of interpretation. Rather than looking for an overall meaning in a writing, a deconstructionist seeks to identify strains of meaning that compete with and subvert what is generally accepted as the dominant strain. Although fiercely independent of any specific ideology such as Marxism or feminism, deconstruction self-consciously gives voice to points of view that are either neglected or suppressed.

e. The Problem of Multiple Interpretations[11]

Proponents of some of the newer literary methods tend to accept the validity of a variety of approaches to interpretation, including those based upon specific ideological commitments. Reader-oriented critics and deconstructionists will often grant that all such readings are valid within their own frames of reference but will deny universal validity to any one approach.

Not surprisingly, many biblical scholars are wary of such open-endedness in interpretation. They fear that deconstruction, the more radical forms of reader-response criticism, and the various theological and ideological interpretations are undermining the gains made by historical criticism. But proponents of the newer methods are convinced that they are coaxing biblical studies into exciting, if in some ways fearsome, new territory. So the debate goes on. And the man in the black suit still preaches at the corner of Central Park, as the Latin American peasants continue to read their Bibles as texts of liberation.

8. The Approach of the Present Text

What is the most important objective for beginning students in biblical studies? Should they gain a basic grasp of the content of the biblical "message"?

---

10. Stephen D. Moore, *Literary Criticism and the Gospels: The Theoretical Challenge* (New Haven: Yale Univ. Press, 1989), 160.

11. Acceptance of multiple interpretations is characteristic of "postmodern" worldviews. See above, p. 21, and below, pp. 49–51, 426–30.

Should they master a method of interpretation? Should they learn how the Bible came into being? These are all worthy goals, but they are all problematic. Which interpretation of the biblical message should they learn? Which method should they be taught? Does knowledge of the way the Bible was produced necessarily lead to an understanding of what it means? Without negating such goals as these, the present text has a prior, more basic objective: to help students become genuinely engaged in the study of the New Testament, to foster the process of questioning and "wrestling" with the biblical texts and with the life-and-death issues those texts raise.

It is precisely with the hope of genuine engagement in mind that I have chosen to write an interdisciplinary text, one that approaches the New Testament writings from several different perspectives influenced by various fields of study. To show that there are many ways in which people have found meaning and value in the New Testament is to invite students into an ongoing conversation; it is to encourage them to develop their own views as to the meaning and value of the materials they will be reading, even as they explore the opinions of others.

Paradoxically, this approach also contributes to objectivity. Whatever position one takes on the question of whether there can be more than one valid interpretation of a single text, the fact is that interpreters do come up with different readings. To give the student several different perspectives makes more difficult the uncritical acceptance of any perspective, whether this is the student's prior understanding, the teaching of a religious body, or the views of the instructor or the author of this text.

My hope is to encourage both objectivity and subjectivity in appropriate forms. In asking for objectivity, I affirm the academic environment and reject any attempt at indoctrination; but in asking for subjectivity, I acknowledge the nature of the New Testament materials as religious literature, the purpose of which is in fact to encourage readers to embrace certain options regarding faith, belief, thought, and action.

Although I will make some use of all the broad approaches to the Bible discussed above, I will emphasize two methods of study—historical criticism and a "moderate" version of reader-response analysis—by applying them to each of the New Testament writings. For I am convinced that the former, for all its limitations, still provides an important perspective on the text. And I have found the latter particularly useful in fostering an initial engagement with the text that can become the basis for further reflection.

Reflection, however, cannot take place in a vacuum but must be informed by the reader's own life experiences, concerns, and prior understanding. I have therefore not hesitated to allow current interests to influence my agenda.

Such matters as economic justice, race relations, and the status and role of women are pressing concerns in our contemporary world. Interest in psychology and the nature of the unconscious is mushrooming, while the debate over the compatibility of religion with a scientifically informed world-picture continues unabated. And the Christian community, in particular, is still faced with the age-old question of its relationship to Judaism, a question made all the more pressing by the Holocaust and the resurgence of anti-Semitism in recent years. These and similar concerns define the context within which biblical study in our day actually takes place. My goal has been to let such matters inform my approach to the New Testament without illicitly "modernizing" the ancient texts or ignoring their own frames of reference.

9. Exegesis, Hermeneutics, and Engagement

Another way of describing the intention of the present text is to say that it seeks to involve the student in reflection on what biblical interpreters call the "hermeneutical problem." The term "hermeneutics," which comes from a family of Greek words having to do with explanation or interpretation, has been employed in a variety of ways in modern biblical studies, theology, and philosophy. According to one influential school of thought, the heart of hermeneutics is the theoretical question of what is actually happening when an interpreter understands a text and/or communicates its meaning. Since theory affects practice, however, one may also speak of particular hermeneutical perspectives that inform given attempts to explain the meaning of a text.

One way of getting hold of the concept of hermeneutics is to contrast it with "exegesis," a term that comes from another group of Greek words with the root meaning of "leading out," which also refers to the process of interpretation. In current usage, exegesis refers in a rather simplistic way to a systematic explanation of what a biblical text means. The hermeneutical question, by contrast, comes into play whenever the process of finding the meaning of a text becomes problematic. It is at work, for example, when interpreters discover differences between their own world-pictures and those represented in the texts, competing strains of meaning within such texts, or different angles of vision from which to approach the task of interpretation. Scholars and theologians routinely refer to existentialist interpretation as a hermeneutical method, because it acknowledges the problem of differing worldviews. But the hermeneutical question is always "there," whether recognized or not. Sooner or later, every interpreter who does not cut the process short will have to face up to it, since every attempt at exegesis really presupposes a hermeneutical stance.

A central purpose of the present text is to demonstrate the unavoidability of the hermeneutical question, precisely as a way of inviting the student to engage the New Testament. That is why I have stressed the problems involved in interpretation. For it is my conviction that it is when a writing in some way presents itself as problematic that it has the greatest potential truly to engage us, to challenge our presuppositions and lure us into a deep and genuine struggle that affects our fundamental values and commitments.

The hermeneutical question is easiest to identify at the point at which the interpreter seeks to render an ancient text meaningful to readers centuries removed from it, to comment on its "contemporary relevance." It might at first seem that in relation to the New Testament the question arises only for Christian believers, those for whom this collection of writings is in some way authoritative. But many hermeneutical theorists insist that although there is a difference between understanding a text and appreciating it, that is, valuing it positively or negatively, the two cannot be separated in an absolute way. In other words, any understanding of a writing involves some kind of interest in it; and this means that we cannot really understand it without allowing it in some degree to engage us in a personal struggle for meaning and truth, whatever actual judgment we make about it.

To raise the questions of hermeneutical perspective and contemporary relevance is to risk the charge of introducing a personal agenda into an academic text. Certainly, the choice of which concerns to address has a certain subjectivity about it. But a decision to treat the New Testament from a purely historical perspective would in its own way constitute a hermeneutical move and, as we have seen, would carry no guarantee of objectivity.

It is impossible to write a totally unbiased text, and I certainly do not claim to have done so. I had no intention of writing one that is value-free. I do hope, however, that I have been fair enough on controversial issues to give students some tools for reaching their own conclusions. I hope also that this text will communicate some of the possibilities for excitement and self-examination that I believe the New Testament can open up. I hope, in other words, that it will serve as an invitation to its readers to approach the New Testament as students in the fullest sense, as whole human beings, exercising the critical intellect with enough detachment to see things clearly, yet deeply engaged in their own quest for meaning and value as they attend to voices that claim to speak the truth.

Fig. 5.

FORM CRITICISM, REDACTION CRITICISM, AND LITERARY APPROACHES
as applied to the study of the Gospels

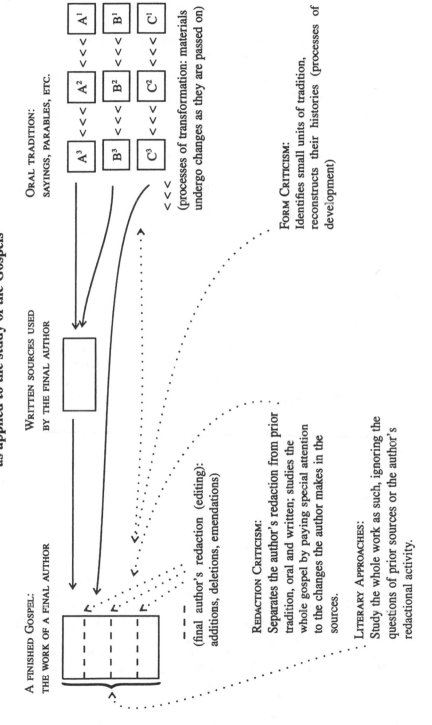

A FINISHED GOSPEL:
THE WORK OF A FINAL AUTHOR

WRITTEN SOURCES USED
BY THE FINAL AUTHOR

ORAL TRADITION:
SAYINGS, PARABLES, ETC.

A^3 <<< A^2 <<< A^1

B^3 <<< B^2 <<< B^1

C^3 <<< C^2 <<< C^1

<<<

(processes of transformation: materials
undergo changes as they are passed on)

FORM CRITICISM:
Identifies small units of tradition,
reconstructs their histories (processes of
development)

(final author's redaction (editing):
additions, deletions, emendations)

REDACTION CRITICISM:
Separates the author's redaction from prior
tradition, oral and written; studies the
whole gospel by paying special attention
to the changes the author makes in the
sources.

LITERARY APPROACHES:
Study the whole work as such, ignoring the
questions of prior sources or the author's
redactional activity.

STUDY QUESTIONS

1. What advantages and/or disadvantages do you see in the way the author of this text intends to approach the New Testament?

2. Explain what is meant by the historical-critical method and assess its advantages and disadvantages.

3. What specific questions does social-scientific criticism ask? Do you agree that it "refines" the historical-critical method?

4. Explain the terms "theological interpretation" and "ideological interpretation." What problems do you see in such approaches? What advantages? Do you think that feminist criticism "refines" the historical-critical method? Defend your answer.

5. Explain "existentialist interpretation," and give your initial reaction to it.

6. What advantages and/or disadvantages do you see in interpreting the Bible psychologically?

7. How do literary approaches to the Bible differ from the historical approach?

8. Explain what is meant by each of these terms: source criticism, form criticism, redaction criticism, structuralism, reader-response criticism, deconstruction, exegesis, hermeneutics.

9. Evaluate the statement, "You can make the Bible say anything you want it to say." How would a proponent of the historical-critical method respond to it? How would radical reader-response critics? Moderate reader-response critics? Deconstructionists?

10. Try to identify, in as specific terms as you can, the presuppositions, biases, and commitments that you bring to a study of the New Testament. How might each of these help you to become genuinely engaged with the New Testament? In what ways might each make such an engagement difficult? Do you think that you can maintain an appropriate balance of objectivity and subjectivity as you approach this study?

FOR FURTHER READING

Adam, A. K. M. "The Sign of Jonah: A Fish-Eye View," *Semeia* 51 (1990): 177.

Anderson, Janet Capel, and Stephen D. Moore, eds. *Mark and Method: New Approaches to Biblical Studies*. Minneapolis: Fortress Press, 1992. A readable introduction to literary, social-scientific, and feminist methods, as applied to Mark. A good complement to this book.

Bartsch, Hans Werner. *Kerygma and Myth: A Theological Debate*. New York: Harper & Row, 1961. Contains Bultmann's "New Testament and Mythology," essays by five critics of Bultmann, and Bultmann's reply.

Beardslee, William A. *Literary Criticism of the New Testament.* Guides to Biblical Scholarship. Philadelphia: Fortress Press, 1970. An early plea for a literary approach, with a chapter on the relationship between literary criticism and theological issues.

Bultmann, Rudolf. *New Testament and Mythology and Other Basic Writings.* Ed. and trans. Schubert M. Ogden. Philadelphia: Fortress Press, 1984. New translations of Bultmann's most important writings on existentialist interpretation.

Cannon, Katie Geneva, and Elisabeth Schüssler Fiorenza, eds. *Interpretation for Liberation. Semeia* 47 (1989). A journal issue by biblical scholars writing from black, feminist, and non-Western perspectives.

Conzelmann, Hans, and Andreas Lindemann. *Interpreting the New Testament: An Introduction to the Principles and Methods of N.T. Exegesis.* Trans. Siegfried S. Schatzmann. Peabody, Mass.: Hendrickson, 1988. A handbook for New Testament study based on historical-critical methods. Comprehensive and useful.

Croatto, J. Severino. *Biblical Hermeneutics: Toward a Theory of Reading as the Production of Meaning.* Maryknoll, N.Y.: Orbis Books, 1987. A brief review of hermeneutical theories and outline of a method that facilitates interpretation in light of contemporary experience with emphasis upon liberation of the oppressed.

Elliott, John H. *What Is Social-Scientific Criticism?* Guides to Biblical Scholarship. Minneapolis: Fortress Press, 1993. A readable, helpful introduction including a history of this approach and a comprehensive bibliography.

Felder, Cain Hope. *Troubling Biblical Waters: Race, Class, Family.* Maryknoll, N.Y.: Orbis Books, 1989. Interpretation of biblical texts from a perspective informed by the black experience.

Felder, Cain Hope, ed. *Stony the Road We Trod: African American Biblical Interpretation.* Minneapolis: Fortress Press, 1991. Essays reflecting the interests of the black church, stressing issues of race, class, and gender; an important contribution.

Kennedy, George A. *New Testament Interpretation through Rhetorical Criticism.* Chapel Hill: Univ. of North Carolina Press, 1984. A basic introduction to rhetorical categories and application to portions of the New Testament.

Krentz, Edgar. *The Historical Critical Method.* Guides to Biblical Scholarship. Philadelphia: Fortress Press, 1975. A basic introduction.

Mack, Burton L. *Rhetoric and the New Testament.* Guides to Biblical Scholarship. Minneapolis: Fortress Press, 1990. A useful guide; includes a history of the discipline, a discussion of classical theory, and applications to the New Testament.

McKenzie, Steven L., and Stephen R. Haynes. *To Each Its Own Meaning: An Introduction to Biblical Criticisms and Their Application.* Louisville: Westminster/John Knox, 1993. Helpful explanations and illustrations of both traditional and recent methods; an excellent complement to the present text.

McKnight, Edgar V. *What Is Form Criticism?* Guides to Biblical Scholarship. Philadelphia: Fortress Press, 1969. A basic introduction, with a chapter on the quest for the historical Jesus.

————. *Post-Modern Use of the Bible: The Emergence of Reader-Oriented Criticism.* Nashville: Abingdon, 1988. Discusses doctrinal approaches, the historical-critical method, existentialist interpretation, structuralism, and postmodern interpretation. Excellent but difficult.

Moore, Stephen D. *Literary Criticism and the Gospels: The Theoretical Challenge.* New Haven: Yale Univ. Press, 1989. A discussion of newer literary approaches to the Gospels, in particular reader-response and deconstruction. Complex but readable.

————. *Poststructuralism and the New Testament: Derrida and Foucault at the Foot of the Cross.* Minneapolis: Fortress Press, 1994. A brief and engaging account, focusing on deconstruction, with attention to the broader phenomenon of postmodernism.

Palmer, Richard E. *Hermeneutics: Interpretation Theory in Schleiermacher, Dilthey, Heidegger, and Gadamer.* Evanston, Ill.: Northwestern Univ. Press, 1969. An introduction to major theories informing the contemporary debate. Technical.

Patte, Daniel. *What Is Structural Exegesis?* Guides to Biblical Scholarship. Philadelphia: Fortress Press, 1983. Difficult, but good explanation and illustration of structuralism.

Perrin, Norman. *What Is Redaction Criticism?* Guides to Biblical Scholarship. Philadelphia: Fortress Press, 1969. A basic introduction, reviewing seminal works and giving examples.

Phillips, Gary A., ed. *Poststructural Criticism and the Bible: Text/History/Discourse.* *Semeia* 51 (1990), A journal issue containing important theoretical essays.

Powell, Mark Allan. *What Is Narrative Criticism?* Guides to Biblical Scholarship. Minneapolis: Fortress Press, 1990. A readable introduction to the major current literary approaches. A helpful complement to this book.

Rollins, Wayne G. *Jung and the Bible.* Atlanta: John Knox, 1983. Gives a brief introduction to Jung's theories and guidelines for Jungian interpretation.

Russell, Letty M., ed. *Feminist Interpretation of the Bible.* Philadelphia: Westminster, 1985. Essays by theologians, historians, and biblical scholars; a good introduction.

Sanders, E. P., and Margaret Davies. *Studying the Synoptic Gospels.* Philadelphia: Trinity Press International, 1989. An excellent introduction to several areas of research: the literary relationships among the first three Gospels, form criticism, literary approaches, and life-of-Jesus research.

Schüssler Fiorenza, Elisabeth. *Bread Not Stone: The Challenge of Feminist Biblical Interpretation.* Boston: Beacon, 1984. A leading scholar and theologian details her hermeneutical theory.

Schüssler Fiorenza, Elisabeth, ed. *Searching the Scriptures.* Vol. 1: *A Feminist Introduction;* vol. 2: *A Feminist Commentary.* New York: Crossroad, 1993, 1994. An important work by feminist scholars from around the world, including critical evaluations of various methods of biblical study.

Sugirtharajah, R. S., ed. *Voices from the Margins: Interpreting the Bible in the Third World.* Maryknoll, N.Y.: Orbis Books, 1991. A wide range of essays from the perspectives of the oppressed; an excellent collection.

Thistleton, Anthony C. *New Testament Hermeneutics and Philosophical Description with Special Reference to Heidegger, Bultmann, Gadamer, and Wittgenstein.* Grand Rapids: Eerdmans, 1980. A detailed examination of hermeneutical issues with a critical evaluation of Bultmann.

Tompkins, Jane P. *Reader-Response Criticism: From Formalism to Post-Structuralism.* Baltimore: Johns Hopkins Univ. Press, 1980. Key essays on the method; introduction provides an overview.

Part One

Before the New Testament

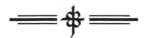

Prologue to Part One

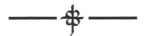

The primary subject matter of this text is the New Testament itself. Part Two, Part Three, and Part Four are devoted to treatments of the various writings that make up the canon. These writings as they presently stand, however, do not represent the earliest stages of the Christian tradition. Long before the appearance of the Gospels, and even before Paul wrote his letters, Christians passed on stories and sayings and composed materials for use in their worship. One way of gaining perspective on the New Testament writings, then, is to give attention to the historical process that lies behind them. In chapters 3 and 4 of Part One we will therefore turn our attention to two relatively distinct stages of the living traditions that constituted that process.

First, however, it is important to learn something about the broad historical context within which Jesus lived, the early tradition was transmitted, and the writings finally emerged. For as the early Christians shaped their understanding of Jesus and of what it meant to follow him, they had no tools to work with other than those drawn from their own cultural settings. Of necessity, they made use of the concepts, modes of expression, and styles of writing available in both the Jewish context and the wider Greek-speaking world. The new faith, although indeed new, was not created "out of nothing."

In chapter 2, then, I will try to describe the features of the New Testament "world" that are most relevant for understanding the early Christian tradition. In doing so, it will be important to give some attention to the history of both the Jewish people and the larger Greek-speaking environment. It will be important, also, to place both of these in the context of the human religious consciousness and of Western history as a preliminary way of studying ourselves—our preconceptions and our biases—as we approach the world of the past.

I will throughout the text make use of the designations "B.C.E." (Before the Common Era) and "C.E." (Common Era), rather than "B.C." and "A.D." In doing so, I follow a practice increasingly employed by biblical scholars "out of deference to those for whom the birth of Jesus marks the beginning of a new era only in a secular sense."[1]

---

1. Robert W. Funk with Mahlon H. Smith, *The Gospel of Mark: Red Letter Edition* (Sonoma, Calif.: Polebridge Press, 1991), 244.

Chapter 2

Christian Beginnings in Context

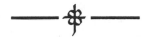

1. Nature Demystified: A Prologue to Western History

The ancient world-picture was a religious world-picture. The earliest human beings believed that all components of reality are bound together in a kind of cosmic empathy, or spiritual relatedness. In this view, the universe is pervaded by feeling; what affects one part affects all others. Human beings, animals, trees, mountains, moon, and stars—all alike participate in the same life-giving power. The many goddesses and gods that eventually developed were personifications of natural phenomena.

The world-picture prevalent in the modern West, by contrast, has made religious belief optional. It may not exclude a religious interpretation, but it no longer *expresses* such an interpretation. Modern people, even many who are religious, tend to see the forces of nature as subject to mechanistic laws of cause and effect. The modern mind-set, in short, has "demystified" nature, has taken the mystery out of it.

Although this demystification was not complete until the rise of modern science, its seeds were sown in ancient times. Two departures from belief in cosmic empathy were of great importance for the shaping of Western culture and the modern consciousness: Hebrew monotheism and Greek philosophy.

a. Hebrew Monotheism

In the mid-thirteenth century B.C.E., a revolution began in the central hill country of Canaan, the land known in later times under the alternative names "Israel" and "Palestine": a group of dispossessed people, the Hebrews, be-

45

Fig. 6. Moses and Israel crossing the Red Sea toward "Sinai."
Via Latina Catacomb, cubiculum C, 4th cent.

gan displacing a technologically more advanced society. These Hebrews, who organized themselves as a federation of tribes called Israel, possessed a rich heritage of ancestral lore. There were stories of Abraham and Sarah, who heard God's call and migrated from Mesopotamia; of Isaac and Rebekah, who lived in Canaan as semi-nomads; of Jacob and of his wives Leah and Rachel, and of their twelve sons and one daughter.

Most important of all was the tradition of the exodus, the story of how Moses led a band of Hebrew slaves out of Egypt to freedom. In conjunction with that tradition, the early Israelites began to break with the polytheism of the surrounding cultures by focusing their worship upon Moses' god Yahweh. They thus began a process that eventually developed into a true monotheism, the belief that only one god actually exists. That process took many centuries, but even its earlier stages brought a change in religious consciousness that had several important consequences.

First, there was a shift in emphasis from nature to history. The gods and goddesses of neighboring peoples functioned primarily to perpetuate the cyclical aspects of life, such as seedtime and harvest, birth and death. By focusing upon the one-time event of the exodus, the Hebrews came to think of their god not only as governing the cycles of nature but as causing new things to happen. As a result, they acquired a new historical consciousness that brought with it a sense of expectation, anticipation, and hope: they believed that God acted in history to bring about change.

Second, the worship of a god who acts in history laid the groundwork for a heightened moral conscience. As transcendent over against both nature and society, this god occupied a vantage point from which to exercise moral judgment. The Hebrews envisioned Yahweh not simply as sanctioning their society but as sometimes calling it into question.

They also understood Yahweh, who had identified with slaves and had given a land to the dispossessed, as having a particular concern for the downtrodden, a concern manifested in a remarkable set of social institutions. Farmers were expected to leave a portion of their crops for the poor and to leave their land uncultivated every seven years so that the landless could "harvest crops produced spontaneously by it."[1] And the Jubilee year provided that families who had lost their ancestral land through economic hardship would eventually receive it back in a general redistribution. Leviticus 25 refers to the Jubilee as the "fiftieth year," but there is some debate as to whether it was a one-time occurrence or took place on a regular basis. And some scholars doubt that the people ever practiced such a radical redistribution. The theological basis of the ideal, however, is clear: in Leviticus 25:23, Yahweh declares that "the land is not sold in perpetuity, for the land is mine."

This emphasis upon justice for the poor became even more pronounced with time. An eventual shift from the agricultural society of the tribal confederacy to a monarchy that encouraged international trade brought extreme discrepancies in wealth among the people. In the face of this situation, the prophets of the eighth through the sixth centuries B.C.E., who understood themselves as bringing God's message to the people, played a dramatic role. Confronting kings, priests, and people, they announced God's condemnation of the worship of other deities and the exploitation of the poor.

A third consequence of the movement toward monotheism was a tendency to identify the divine with the male gender. Whereas the pantheons of the surrounding peoples contained female as well as male deities, the imagery for Yahweh in the Jewish Scriptures is primarily (but not exclusively) male. How much the shift to a single god increased male domination is debatable, since

---

1. Sharon H. Ringe, *Jesus, Liberation, and the Biblical Jubilee: Images for Ethics and Christology* (Philadelphia: Fortress Press, 1985), 19; see also pp. 25–32 on the Jubilee.

the surrounding civilizations were also male-centered. But there is no doubt that in the long haul of Western history the tendency to think of God as male has often been used as a justification for the subordination of women.

A fourth consequence was a step toward the demystification of nature. Yahweh's apartness from the world meant that nature itself was no longer understood as divine. The full implications of this shift were not immediately apparent, however. It was many centuries later, long after the Hebrew heritage had merged with the Greek, that the Western view of nature as an object to be manipulated developed. As far as the ancient Hebrews were concerned, it was God, not human beings, who was sovereign over the world.

b. Greek Philosophy

The Greeks originally worshiped nature deities but eventually turned their attention to the gods and goddesses of Mount Olympus, who personified such ideals of civilization as law, justice, and intellect. As the political order came to manifest the divine more than did nature, the latter became subject to investigation. Inquiring minds began to ask such questions as "What is the fundamental substance out of which all things are made?" and "What is the relationship between the changing and the unchanging?" Questions like these led to scientific inquiry on the one hand and to philosophy on the other.

The philosopher Plato (427–347 B.C.E.) took a significant step toward the demystification of nature. He argued that physical objects (such as desks, trees, and dogs) are less real than the ideas, or eternal "forms," by which we identify these objects (desk*ness,* tree*ness,* dog*ness*). In his view, the universe is more basically mental than physical, since physical reality proceeds from a mental or spiritual ground, which he identified as the Idea of the Good. Plato also provided a basis for objective moral judgments, since he understood such values as truth, beauty, and goodness as eternal forms with objective reality.

From one perspective, Plato's philosophy is a form of idealism, the view that all reality is finally mental in nature, that only mind is in fact real. But Plato's thought also has characteristics of dualism, the view that there are two utterly different and irreducible kinds of reality, mind and matter. Dualism sometimes carries the implication that matter is a secondary and deficient form of reality, and later interpreters of Plato tended to view it in that way. So, when Platonic thought was eventually combined with Christianity, it led to the view of the universe as a "great chain of being," with the more spiritual kinds of being at the top and the more material (less spiritual) at the bottom. Such thinking lent support to the "divine right of kings," the subjugation of women, and hierarchical social structures in general. It has been used to justify theories of racial superiority and has governed the way we think about the division of labor, the governing of societies and organizations, and education. It would of course be simplistic to make Plato responsible for all later use of his ideas. But he did open the way for a dualism that in many ways shaped subsequent thought.

c. World-Pictures in Conflict:
The Context of the Contemporary Interpreter

Hebrew monotheism and Greek philosophy combined to provide Western civilization with a comprehensive world-picture that served for many centuries as a firm basis for human values. A transcendent god reigned over a universe arranged in hierarchical fashion. Moral standards, governmental structure, social organization—all were understood in terms of the will of God and Plato's eternal forms.

The legacy of these two modes of thought, however, was paradoxical: they also laid the groundwork for the destruction of the very world-picture they created. By breaking with the notion of cosmic empathy, they opened the way for the total demystification of nature that came with the rise of modern science. And this demystification ultimately undercut the spiritual basis of values as modern thinkers came to understand nature as composed of mere lifeless matter, without inherent value or purpose. In its most extreme form, the modern consciousness has involved the dissolution of the dualism that dominated the medieval world into sheer materialism, the view that only matter is real, that there is no spiritual or divine dimension to reality at all. The consistent materialist may affirm a heroic humanism and assert moral values but denies any transcendent basis for those values. Although many modern people have retained a belief in God or a spiritual reality, the modern worldview has made such a belief problematic for many and impossible for some. Nearly all forms of religious belief in the modern West involve a strategy for meeting the challenge posed by the modern consciousness.

One of the hallmarks of the modern consciousness is its confidence in the powers of human reason and the ability of the human mind to understand the universe and manipulate the environment for human benefit. This confidence, however, has broken down in recent decades, so much so that many thinkers are beginning to speak of the present as the *post*modern age.

For one thing, recent science itself has undermined our faith in our ability to grasp reality in a comprehensive way. Physicists, for example, have encountered extreme oddities in their studies of light. Observed in one way, light appears to be composed of particles; observed in another way, it consists of waves. The two views appear incompatible, but each seems to be true from within its own frame of reference. Also, it is increasingly clear that our values and understandings of truth are heavily dependent upon such factors as cultural background, social class, and family experience.

There are several recent styles of thought that are termed "postmodernism." All share a rejection of the confidence of the modern consciousness in the human ability to achieve absolute knowledge. One widespread variety of postmodernism is extremely skeptical regarding all claims to truth. The most radical reader-oriented methods of literary criticism are expressions of this view; for in arguing that the reader's perspective determines meaning they deny that there is any definitive interpretation of a text. Deconstruction also belongs in this camp. For its denial that texts contain coherent points of view is rooted in its insistence that all attempts to characterize reality as a whole—whether dualist, materialist, or idealist—are doomed to failure.

This does not necessarily mean that deconstruction envisions an absolute end to metaphysics (speculation on the nature of reality), however. For it is impossible to give a philosophical critique of metaphysics without making some metaphysical assumptions.[2]

In any case, not all types of postmodernism are quite so negative regarding human knowledge. A case in point is a school of thought sometimes called "constructive postmodernism," which agrees that human knowledge is limited by perspective but insists that it is possible to work out a provisional understanding of reality that takes this limitation into account.[3] This version involves a respiritualizing of nature that recovers a sense of the relatedness of all things without returning to the ancient world-picture or premodern ways of thinking. Based in process thought, it draws also upon Eastern religions, ecological consciousness, feminism, and liberation theology. Constructive postmodernists find it necessary and possible to speak of a god, but of one quite different from the absolute and all-powerful deity of traditional theology.

Both of these versions of postmodernism reject the hierarchical understanding of reality that emerged from the combination of Hebrew monotheism and Greek philosophy. Both also seek to hear the thoughts of groups long ex-

---

2. See Steven D. Moore, *Poststructuralism and the New Testament: Derrida and Foucault at the Foot of the Cross* (Minneapolis: Fortress Press, 1994), 20. Moore also notes another, considerably different, use of the term "postmodernism": "For many outside our field, postmodernism is first and foremost a global cultural phenomenon, one whose signal features include mass media, mass culture, information technology and multinational capitalism."

3. See David Ray Griffin, William A. Beardslee, and Joe Holland, *Varieties of Postmodern Theology* (Albany: SUNY Press, 1989), and David Ray Griffin, *God and Religion in the Postmodern World: Essays in Postmodern Theology* (Albany: SUNY Press, 1989).

cluded from the power centers of Western civilization. And both are inclined to say that literary texts are capable of generating more than one legitimate interpretation.

It is not my purpose to endorse or reject any version of the modern or postmodern consciousness; nor is it to make value judgments regarding monotheism, dualism, hierarchical thinking, or the alternative modes of thought. But it is important to identify our present ways of thinking and show that they are not simply "given" in human experience generally. They came about historically, in specific circumstances and under specific influences. To be a self-aware interpreter of the Bible is to have some sense of the particular consciousness one brings to the task, whether it be that of traditional Western theology or some version of a modern or postmodern world-picture. Put another way, it is to be aware of the hermeneutical problem.

The primary reason for discussing Hebrew monotheism and Greek dualism is to set the stage for the emerging Christian movement. But there are many steps we must take before we get to that point. The story that needs to be told now is the story of ancient Israel down to the beginning of the Common Era, as well as the story of that alien culture into whose sphere of influence that people was eventually drawn: Hellenism, the "Greek-like" culture that captured the Mediterranean world after the death of Alexander the Great.

2. Holiness, Memory, and Hope: The Jews and History

a. Holiness and Pollution

Despite their partial demystification of nature, the Hebrews continued to share many aspects of the ancient sense of cosmic empathy. And it is against this background that we must understand the emphasis in the Jewish Scriptures upon sacred rites, taboos, and dietary regulations. Otherwise we are likely to impose modern understandings upon texts that exhibit fundamentally different concerns.

Central to the value system of the Hebrews was the notion of holiness, a concept that had to do largely with separateness or apartness. They considered God, as the truly holy one, to be utterly beyond human beings and the things of the world—and therefore mysterious and incomprehensible, majestic and exalted. And because the Hebrews understood themselves as God's people, they participated in the divine holiness and were obligated to keep themselves in a state of holiness, or apartness from the world at large.

Holiness embraced a moral dimension, but it had other aspects as well. Par-

Fig. 7. CHRONOLOGICAL CHART

Hebrew/Jewish Civilization		Greek/Hellenistic/Roman Civilizations
	B.C.E.	
Exodus from Egypt	ca. 1290	
Conquest of Canaan begins	ca. 1250	
Period of tribal confederacy		
David king of all Israel	1000	
Divisions of monarchies	950	
	700–750	Homer's *Iliad* and *Odyssey*

Judah (south) **Israel** (north)

Assyrian conquest of Israel; end of northern monarchy	721	
Destruction of 1st temple; Babylonian Exile	587	

Beginning of Diaspora Judaism

Babylonia falls to Persia; band of exiles returns to Judah/Judea	538	
Persian rule of Judah/Judea		
Building of 2nd temple		
	347	Death of Plato
	338	Philip II, king of Macedon, defeats Greek states and forms Hellenic League
	336	Murder of Philip and accession of his son, Alexander
	333	Alexander defeats Persians at Issus
ALEXANDER	(332)	ENTERS JUDEA
	331	Founding of Alexandria in Egypt
	323	Death of Alexander

THE HELLENISTIC AGE BEGINS

		Hellenistic Dynasties: Antigonids, Seleucids, Ptolemies
	306	Epicurus founds school in Athens
	300	Zeno, founder of Stoicism, arrives in Athens
Seleucids take control of Judea	168	

CHRONOLOGICAL CHART (continued)

Hebrew/Jewish Civilization		Greek/Hellenistic/Roman Civilizations
Maccabean war begins	167	
Rededication of temple	165	
Hasmonean dynasty founded		
Formation of Pharisees, Sadducees, Essenes		
	POMPEY (63) enters Jerusalem	
Roman rule of Judea		
	60	First triumvirate rules Rome: Pompey, Crassus, Julius Caesar
	48–44	Julius Caesar dictator in Rome
	43	Second triumvirate rules Rome: Lepidus, Marc Antony, Octavian
Herod becomes king of Jews	37	
	31	Octavian defeats Marc Antony in the Battle of Actium and secures control of Rome
	27	Octavian proclaimed "Caesar Augustus"
Death of Herod	4	
Birth of Jesus (?)	C.E.	
	14	Tiberius becomes Roman emperor
Death of Jesus	ca. 30	
	37	Caligula becomes Roman emperor
	41	Claudius becomes Roman emperor
	54	Nero becomes Roman emperor
Jewish war of independence begins	66	
	68	Galba becomes Roman emperor
	69	After brief reigns of Otho and Vitellius Vespasian becomes Roman emperor
Romans destroy 2nd temple	70	
Jewish academy of Yabneh: beginnings of Rabbinic Judaism		
	79	Titus becomes Roman emperor
	81	Domitian becomes Roman emperor
	96	Nerva becomes Roman emperor
	98	Trajan becomes Roman emperor
	117–35	Hadrian Roman emperor
Bar Kochba War	132–35	

ticularly difficult for modern people to grasp is the distinction between clean and unclean, which was rooted in a notion of cultic pollution. Insights from cultural anthropology have been particularly helpful to recent biblical scholars in grasping this concept.[4] Pollution in this sense must not be confused with a modern interest in sanitation. Fundamental to the ancient mind was an overriding concern with order in a deeply cosmic sense. Since people believed that all components of reality were pervaded with power, they saw anything out of its proper place as unclean and therefore dangerous. And this, as David Rhoads notes, explains

> why blood, spit, or semen are unclean. They belong inside the body. When they come out of their place, such as in a menstrual flow, they are unclean and will defile people. Lepers are unclean because they have boils or breaks in the skin where pus or fluid comes out.[5]

This also explains why a person can become defiled, that is cultically polluted, by touching a holy object if that person is not qualified to do so or does so under the wrong circumstances.

Given this concern with pollution, it should be clear that everything—space, time, human activity—had to be ordered so as to meet the requirements of holiness. And it was the role of sacred rites—ceremonies and rituals—to carry out this ordering.

The rites were many. Like other ancient peoples, the Hebrews had a hereditary priesthood that presided over a system of animal and vegetable sacrifices. Modern people tend to view sacrificial cults as "primitive" attempts to manipulate the deity. But to the ancients themselves the sacrifice established relationship with the divine; it brought before the source of their being all the hope and fear and guilt that life entails. It kept order; it kept pollution in check; it insured holiness. The Hebrews also observed numerous festivals throughout the year, as well as the weekly Sabbath, a day of rest. By observing such sacred times, they gave meaning to the progression of time itself: life was not just "one day after another" but an existence in relation to the life-giving power.

Another aspect of holiness was "wholeness." "That which is pure and holy," Rhoads says, "is that which conforms wholly to its classification." And the notion of wholeness explains why

---

4. For a primary anthropological treatment, see Mary Douglas, *Purity and Danger: Analysis of Concepts of Pollution and Taboo* (New York: Frederick A. Praeger, 1966), 148–53.

5. David Rhoads, "Social Criticism: Crossing Boundaries," in *Mark and Method: New Approaches to Biblical Studies,* ed. Janet Capel Anderson and Stephen D. Moore (Minneapolis: Fortress Press, 1992), 151.

human beings with "deformities" were considered marginal and unclean and why animals with blemishes were considered unclean and not to be offered at the Temple.... Also, we can see why fish and cattle and doves are clean animals and do not defile people who eat them. These animals fit the Israelite classification of "normal" animals. Conversely, eels and pigs and ostriches do not fit the Hebrew classification of normal or whole animals.[6]

On the human and mundane level, holiness was measured in degrees. Space, time, and even persons could be ranked in specific order. The Sabbath was holier than other days. Priests were holier than ordinary Israelites. The land of Israel was itself holy, but within it Jerusalem and the temple were even holier; and finally within the temple there was the room that only the high priest could enter, and even he only once a year: the holy of holies.

b. Covenant, Memory, and Sacred History

The worshipers of Yahweh shared much of the ancient consciousness, but their god's transcendence over nature put their cultic activity in a distinctive light. At the heart of their faith was the notion of covenant—a compact between Yahweh and the people of Israel. Yahweh, who had led them out of Egypt, would continue to be their god and grant them abundant life in their land. They in turn would obey God's commands. Festivals originally connected with harvests or the birth of sheep came to signify the events through which God had acted on Israel's behalf, events such as the exodus from Egypt and the giving of the law on Mount Sinai. Their sacredness therefore came to consist largely in their capacity to evoke memory of what God had done in the past and hope for what God would do in the future. The history of the people was thus understood as sacred history. And woven together with such ancient notions as cultic pollution and cosmic order was that of God as a dynamic force for change, whose holiness was manifested in mighty acts in the course of human events.

c. Monarchy and Theology

If the establishment of a monarchy in Israel brought changes in the social sphere, it also altered the way people thought about God and the covenant relationship. The second king, David, turned the tiny nation into an empire. He

---

6. Ibid.

extended the borders and captured Jerusalem, which had remained in Canaanite hands. His son and successor, Solomon, built a magnificent temple there
to house the cult.

This new situation gave rise to several interrelated ideas, some of which
probably had Canaanite roots. First, both Jerusalem and the temple became
sacred places. People came to think of Zion, the mount on which the city was
built, as inviolable: it could never fall to an enemy. And they began to consider the kingly line of David as perpetual: God had promised that it would
last throughout the ages. Not everyone accepted this Davidic theology, but
the promise to David's line was to play an important role in later Jewish hope
for the future.

Another notion that probably entered Hebrew thought at this time was that
of God's sovereign Rule in the manner of a monarch, or, as the term is traditionally translated, the kingdom of God. According to a myth common in
the ancient Middle East, the god acted as monarch in creating 'the world and
in renewing the fertility of the earth each year. The Hebrews left aside various aspects of this myth, but the image of God as exercising sovereign Rule
became a primary vehicle for the expression of hope for the future. In earliest times people thought of God as exercising this Rule "eternally," i.e., "all
the time"; but they eventually began to look for a definitive act in the future
whereby God would establish this Rule fully. The reason, as we will see, is
that the present was too often filled with disappointment.

One expression of this hope for the Rule of God was the notion of God's
promise to David's line: people began to expect an ideal king through whom
God would truly reign. Because the Hebrew monarchs were consecrated
through the ritual of anointing with oil, they were sometimes called God's
"anointed." Through the centuries, the notion of an ideal king developed into
the formalized expectation of an "Anointed One," or "Messiah," i.e., a king
in David's line who would be God's agent in establishing a whole new order
on earth.

Since this concept has played such a large role in Christianity, it is important to note several points. First, the Messiah was understood as a human
being, a person through whom God would establish peace and justice on this
earth. Second, the figure of the Messiah was less important than the messianic age, the age of peace and justice. A messianic king was only one
of several means of conceiving the reign of peace and justice itself: some
people thought God would rule directly; others expected not an ideal king
but an ideal priest; still others spoke of a "prophet like Moses" who would
be God's agent. Third, the hope for a Messiah was not a clear-cut concept
passed on from early times. It developed only gradually, and it took many dif-

ferent forms. There was in fact no self-consistent "doctrine" of the Messiah when Jesus was born, and it was only later that Judaism itself set out formal definitions of that notion.

d. The Divided Monarchies and the Babylonian Exile

After the death of Solomon, the northern regions, unhappy with Jerusalem's oppressive policies, broke off to form a separate state. The northern monarchy kept the designation "Israel," while the southern came to be known by the tribal name "Judah." The stories of these two nations are in many ways tragic, involving constant struggle to maintain independence as mighty empires threatened their borders.

The prophets of this period interpreted the political crises in terms of God's judgment and mercy. When Assyria threatened Israel, they warned that Yahweh was bringing destruction because of the worship of foreign deities and the oppression of the poor. In 721 B.C.E., Assyria in fact conquered Israel, deporting much of the populace and bringing in foreigners to settle.

The fate of the northern monarchy then became a standard theme of prophetic preaching in the south, where Judah was threatened by Assyria and later by Babylonia. In 587 B.C.E., the Babylonians ravaged the land, destroyed the temple, and deported the community leaders to Babylon. The people of Judah were able, however, to retain their traditions and their sense of destiny and hope. How they did so is an interesting story.

Exiled in Babylon, the worshipers of Yahweh found more need than ever before to hold on to their traditions. They had already committed some material to writing, but there was as yet no Scripture in the formal sense. Thus the priests, deprived of the temple and the sacrificial cult, began to gather traditional materials into a foundational document. Whether completed during or after the exile, the result was what came to be called "Torah"—the first five books of the Bible, later attributed to Moses himself. "Torah" is often translated "law," but "teaching" is a better rendering; while containing much law, these books also tell a story beginning with creation, continuing through the Hebrew ancestors and the exodus from Egypt, and ending as the people prepare to enter the land of Canaan. It was largely by preserving this story that the people retained their distinctive heritage.

A more visible means of self-preservation was found in customs that set the worshipers of Yahweh apart from the surrounding culture. Whatever their role in earlier times, such observances as circumcision, dietary regulations, and Sabbath rest took on central importance in the period of the exile.

e. The Reestablishment of Judah/Judea

Empires rise and fall. Babylonia fell to Persia, which allowed its subject peoples a measure of home rule. In 538 B.C.E., the Persian king Cyrus issued an edict allowing the descendants of the exiles to return to Judah, which became known as Judea in the postexilic period. Two generations had passed since the deportations, and many people elected to remain in Babylonia. Some did make the long journey home, however, with high hopes of rebuilding Jerusalem and the temple.

Their task was difficult. Construction on the temple was completed by 515 B.C.E., but Jerusalem remained sparsely populated and without fortifications for some time. A part of the old northern monarchy now known as Samaria was under separate provincial rule by the Persians, and the Samaritans actively opposed the rebuilding of Jerusalem.

There were also conflicts within Judah/Judea itself. It was the wealthy and powerful who were taken into exile, and it was their descendants who returned. Those who had remained in the land were largely the poor, many of whom probably took over abandoned homes and farms after the deportations. We can thus imagine bitter conflicts over property rights after the return; and, in any case, we have clear evidence of the exploitation of the poor by the rich.

The rebuilding of the temple also contributed to class conflict. A dispute over who had legitimate rights to priestly service resulted in the exclusion of some groups. And those who assumed leadership gained enormous economic power, since the temple was responsible for collecting tithes and taxes.

Nearly a century after the edict of Cyrus, the Persian king took steps to stabilize the situation in Judah, sending two Jewish emissaries from Babylonia: Ezra and Nehemiah. The chronology of this period is unclear, but we do know the results of the work of these two men. For one thing, the Jewish community devised a system of defining membership. It involved enrolling citizens on the basis of genealogy and forbidding marriage to foreigners, a practice probably most common in the upper class. The motive had nothing to do with racial bigotry; the point was to strengthen the family and preserve tradition.

Nehemiah instituted reforms designed to alleviate the exploitative practices of the rich. His efforts were presumably successful in part but did not change the basic structure of society. He was, after all, an instrument of Persian colonial rule; and the empire's interest was not in dispersion of wealth and power but in stability. A strong temple aristocracy, tied to the ruling empire, remained securely in place.

Ezra was instrumental in making law central in Jewish life. Whether he introduced the completed Torah or simply an antecedent of it, he established obedience to the written law as the definitive mode of Jewish religious observance. This emphasis should not be understood as the reduction of religion to external details. In committing themselves to absolute obedience to God's commands, the people sought to insure that they would never again bring God's judgment upon them. For many had come to understand the Babylonian exile as punishment for sin. Commitment to Torah was an attempt to be faithful to the covenant and maintain holiness; it was a way of nurturing memory in order to call forth hope.

3. The Hellenistic Age: The Exportation of a Culture

The Persian Empire lasted two centuries, then crumbled before the invading army of Alexander the Great. After defeating the Persian king at Issus in Asia Minor in 333 B.C.E., Alexander took Egypt and then marched eastward to the edge of India. He conquered but hardly ruled at all: in 323 he died in Babylon, and the new empire disintegrated. He had, however, laid the foundations for a new world; in it he was remembered by many as a hero and often worshiped as a god.

a. The Impact of Hellenism

Alexander was a native of Macedonia, to the north of Greece, where a form of Greek was spoken. Historians debate whether he saw himself as a kind of cultural missionary bringing the glories of Greek civilization to the world. Whatever Alexander's intentions, his conquests resulted in the exportation of Greek culture, in however superficial a form. Throughout the new empire, he founded Greek-style cities and reorganized many older cities on the Greek model. The most notable of the new cities was Alexandria in Egypt, which became the intellectual center of this new world.

For nearly a century after Alexander's death, his generals and their successors fought over the remnants of the empire. When the dust had settled, three relatively stable dynasties remained: the Antigonids in Macedonia, the Seleucids in Syria, and the Ptolemies in Egypt. Although politically divided, the world Alexander left became a network in which the *koinē*, or "common," Greek was the primary language of government and business. Centuries later, the New Testament authors would compose their works in this popularized Greek.

The Greeks' own name for their homeland was "Hellas." The adjective "Hellenic" refers to ancient Greek culture, and "Hellenistic" pertains to the

Fig. 8. The Parthenon
(c. 432 B.C.E.)*

period following Alexander in which Greek culture spread throughout the Mediterranean world. The close of this period is usually dated in 31 B.C.E., which marks the ascendancy of Octavian, who became Roman emperor and was given the title Caesar Augustus in 27. Hellenistic culture, however, continued to dominate the Roman Empire, so that the period within which Christianity was born may aptly be termed that of Roman Hellenism.

It is unclear to what extent Hellenization reached the masses of people outside the new Greek-style cities; but within these cities, Greek ways prevailed, particularly among the affluent and educated. To gain acceptance among the elite who dominated government, education, business, and the social scene, it became necessary to speak Greek, wear Greek clothing, attend Greek baths and theaters, and participate in Greek athletic contests.

The combination of a common language and new trade routes brought a heightened awareness of the wider world. Local and national consciousness gave way to a cosmopolitan atmosphere. People began to think of themselves as citizens of the world and also as individuals, no longer bound by ancient traditions but free to choose from among various patterns of life and thought.

---

*Situated on the Acropolis, the "high city" in the middle of Athens, the Parthenon was built not as a functioning temple but as a national monument offered to Athena. goddess of Athens. Construction was completed in 432 B.C.E., five years before the birth of Plato. *(Photo by Marshall Johnson)*

The new world was one of intellectual vitality. The library at Alexandria amassed the largest collection of writings the world had ever known. Science and mathematics flourished; one astronomer even proposed the theory that the earth revolved around the sun. Significant advances were made in medicine, and seafaring expeditions extended the knowledge of geography.

There was also a great deal of literary activity. Biographies became popular, and a new literary genre was particularly reflective of the spirit of the times: the romance, or novel, which often combined the motifs of travel, adventure, and eroticism. In a typical romance, a hero would leave home and, after numerous battles against impediments, make a happy return. The appeal of such a story is obvious. Separated, cut loose from ancient traditions and set adrift in an unfamiliar world, is precisely how many people must have felt in the Hellenistic world. The cosmopolitan atmosphere was liberating for some, but to others it brought fear in the face of the unknown, a sense of having utterly lost one's moorings.

b. Hellenistic Religion

The provision of moorings, a sense of "at-homeness," had been to some extent the role religion. But the Hellenistic age was characterized by the break-up of traditional faiths. The old local deities seemed powerless in the face of Alexander's conquests. The Macedonians brought the Olympian gods and goddesses with them to the new cities, and the masses of people were drawn into the festivals and games associated with them. Faith in these deities had been dwindling for centuries among the educated, however. And in any case the Olympian cult was largely a political affair that offered little in terms of intense individual piety. The same must be said of the various ruler cults in which a dead or sometimes a living king was accorded divine honors.

How could people who had lost their traditional faith cope with life's difficulties? Many came to see life as ruled by either Fate (cosmic necessity, often imaged as a goddess) or Chance (sheer accident). Both options had positive and negative dimensions. They could encourage a kind of resignation that served as an antidote to complaint and worry, but they could also lead to a sense of hopelessness. Thus many turned to astrology, which spread from Babylonia throughout the Hellenistic world, as a way of discerning the future and perhaps modifying it in some way. Magic, which also gained popularity, offered a more immediate way of manipulating threatening forces.

Not everyone was satisfied with such answers as these. Many people sought enlightenment or salvation through various cults that offered initiation into secret "mysteries." Our knowledge of such cults is limited, but the sacred rites typically offered the renewal of the individual's life in this world and the promise of immortality. Generally speaking, they were originally associated with agricultural themes, particularly the renewal of nature, but then took on the new meaning of personal rebirth and immortality. Particularly popular was the cult of Demeter, "the Mother of Grain," housed at Eleusis near Athens; thousands flocked there yearly to become initiates. Worship of Dionysus, the god of wine, was also widespread. In the cult of Cybele, the Great Mother, priests cut themselves and sprinkled blood on a statue of the goddess; and at least some initiates castrated themselves while in a state of ecstasy. From Egypt came the cult of Isis and Serapis, a Hellenized version of the older religion of Isis and Osiris.

"Syncretism," the combination of motifs of various origins, was characteristic of Hellenistic religion in general. Greek ideas penetrated Eastern religions, and vice-versa. Eastern deities became identified with Greek gods and goddesses, and various deities combined into one. So it is not surprising to find some tendency toward belief in one universal divine being. The most notable example is Isis, who gradually shed her association with Serapis. A number of cultic hymns to her manifest a clear step toward genuine monotheism.

The mystery cults were very popular, but not everyone found their solutions to life's problems acceptable. For some, philosophy provided an alternative, although the distinction between religion and philosophy became somewhat blurred during this period.

c. Hellenistic Philosophy

For the Greeks, human beings were social beings; to be human in the fullest sense was to participate in society. Plato and Aristotle pursued their philosophy against the background of this assumption. Plato sought to know the nature of the universe in order to provide a foundation for just government and social norms. In the Hellenistic Age, however, people felt lost and powerless in a vast civilization. Thus philosophy underwent a shift of emphases: from concern with social structure to concern with the individual good, and from speculation on the nature of the universe to the development of a personal ethical code. The schools Plato and Aristotle had founded in Athens continued to exist, but it was the alternative philosophies that carried the day. Three of these are particularly important for our purposes—Epicureanism, Stoicism, and Cynicism.

Fig. 9. Hermes, divine messenger
of the gods, with Dionysus, god of
vegetation and wine.*

(1) **Epicureanism.** Epicurus, who established a school in Athens in 306 B.C.E., returned to a view of the universe that predated Plato. This was a pure materialism in which everything is made of atoms. Even deities and the human soul, in this view, are material in nature. There is thus no spiritual dimension undergirding the physical and no overarching purpose in the universe.

To the Epicureans it was self-evident that the pleasure of the individual is the ultimate good; the only question was how to attain it. It would be useless to seek aid from the gods and goddesses, since Epicureans believed these were unconcerned with human life. The quest for immortality was likewise futile, since Epicureans believed that the soul disintegrated at death; the atoms in both soul and body simply dispersed and eventually found their way into other entities. This view brought them great comfort, since they believed that nothing could hurt them after death.

The Epicureans also rejected overindulgence as a route to pleasure, noting that it becomes addictive. Their ideal, by contrast, was the pursuit of the simplest pleasures—to enjoy a bowl of porridge and the association of a few

---

*The Greek terms *hermēneia* and *hermēneuō*, which have to do with interpretation (and from which the English term "hermeneutics" is derived) are related to the name "Hermes." *(Photo: Koester/Hendrix)*

friends. One should live prudently, honorably, and cheerfully, and be just in one's treatment of others, simply because to do otherwise would ultimately bring pain upon oneself.

The emphasis upon friendship eventually worked itself out in the establishment of organizations that took on a religious character: members honored Epicurus and other leaders in sacred meals. They looked to one another for support and believed that in true friendship one comes to love one's friends as oneself. This ideal might seem contradictory to the egoistic premises of the philosophy, but the Epicureans recognized that friendship fulfilled a basic need; and they also encouraged a certain detachment, a freedom from desire, as a safeguard against pain.

(2) Stoicism. Founded by Zeno of Cyprus, who came to Athens in 300 B.C.E., Stoicism gained a much wider following than did Epicureanism. The name derives from the word *stoa,* which refers to the long, porch-like structures in the Greek cities, where people could gather for conversation or for activities such as exhibits or public debates: it was in such stoas that Zeno did much of his teaching.

The Stoics were materialists, but of a very different sort from the Epicureans. For them, fire was the basic element of which everything consists. The Stoics identified this fire with God, which they also called the universal Logos, or Reason. This Logos is the principle holding all reality together. The Stoic view of the universe is thus a form of pantheism, the view that the universe itself is divine, or that God *is* the universe. As pantheists, the Stoics believed that the world came forth from God, as God's body in which the Logos dwells as soul. Each human being, moreover, possesses an individual logos, a spark of the divine fire, capable of ordering itself in accordance with universal Reason.

Like the Epicureans, the Stoics were concerned with the problem of pain. But they made no attempt to avoid it, since they believed that everything is ruled by Fate or Providence, which they also identified with God. The Stoic's answer to life's difficulties was therefore simply to accept one's fate. Individuals have no control over external circumstances, but they can control their own inner attitudes. Thus the Stoic ideal was *apatheia,* the state of passionlessness: one should simply refuse to suffer internally no matter how great the external suffering.

There is some similarity to Epicureanism here, since *apatheia* demands a kind of detachment: one should neither depend too much on others nor expect to change society. But in contrast to the Epicureans the Stoics believed in duty: the individual is obligated to the whole, or God, in which a universal purpose resides. This has nothing to do with an eventual reward in a future life, however; since the Stoics believed that the universe is periodically consumed in fire, there was no place for individual immortality.

Stoic pantheism, which reflected the Hellenistic cosmopolitan atmosphere, also entailed the ideal of universal human relatedness. Even though belief in Fate tended to discourage attempts to change society, Stoics were frequent advocates of social reforms. On at least two occasions individual Stoics supported revolutionary movements: a Spartan king's attempt to abolish debts and nationalize the land, and a revolution against Rome in Asia Minor. Stoicism, moreover, produced some striking examples of utopian writings that envisioned thoroughly equalitarian societies.

The pantheistic deity of Stoicism sounds impersonal and was often spoken of as a principle. Some Stoics nevertheless found room for intense personal devotion to their god, as is evident from these lines from a famous hymn to Zeus by a Stoic:

> Thou, O Zeus, art praised above all gods:
> many are thy names and thine is all power for ever.
> The beginning of the world was from thee:
> and with law thou rulest over all things.
> Unto thee may all flesh speak: for we are
> thy offspring.[7]

Stoic pantheism led in one direction that seems strange to the modern mind. Plato, in his movement away from the Olympian religion with its human-like deities, regarded the sun, moon, stars, planets, and even the earth as divine. The Stoics accepted the divinity of these bodies, arguing that the Logos was manifest in them. With similar logic they justified traditional prayer to the gods and goddesses, and they even accepted astrology by reference to their belief in Fate.

(3) Cynicism. The third philosophical outlook, Cynicism, was distinguished less by specific doctrines than by the manner of instruction and life-style of the teachers, who rejected not only personal wealth and possessions but the conventions of society as well. The founder, Diogenes, who was born around 400, lived in a tub and was so flagrant in his violation of cultural norms that Aristotle called him *kyōn,* the Greek term for "dog." Out of this designation, apparently, grew the nickname *kynikos* ("dog-like"), Cynic, for those who embraced this philosophy and manner of living.

---

7. C. K. Barrett, *The New Testament Background: Selected Documents,* rev. ed. (London: SPCK, 1987), 67.

Cynicism actually gave rise to Stoicism and shared with it an emphasis upon detachment from the world. The Stoics, however, moderated what was in Cynicism an extreme denunciation of civilization itself. In stressing self-sufficiency and harmony with nature, the Cynics took animal behavior as their model. The typical Cynic sage lived an itinerant life, carrying only a bag, a staff, and a cloak, and slept on the ground or in public buildings. Water and vegetables were the typical diet, and begging often the means of support. By both manner and appearance, the Cynics exalted the natural state over the civilized and symbolically challenged standard values through intentionally offensive behavior. The Cynic sages generally taught in the market places, and they were known for their use of striking example stories, often about Diogenes, that illustrated their version of ethical behavior.

Cynicism and Stoicism influenced one another extensively during the Hellenistic age. In the New Testament period we find many popular philosophers wandering from place to place, living a Cynic life-style, and teaching in the marketplaces; their ideas generally reflected a Cynic-Stoic outlook.

d. The Spirit of the Age

Stoicism was more typical of one aspect of the Hellenistic Age than was Epicureanism: its pantheism constituted a partial "remystification" of nature. Epicureanism was virtually alone in moving in the opposite direction. For all the learning and sophistication of the age, there was an overwhelming resurgence of a sense of "the beyond" and of "mystery." Some historians have disparaged the change in consciousness as escapism. To what extent, however, is such a judgment the simplistic imposition of modern values on the ancient world? Was this change a "failure of nerve,"[8] as it has been called, or was it a creative attempt to see into the depths of human existence in this world?

4. Crosscurrents: Judaism in the Hellenistic Age

During the Hellenistic Age, the descendants of the ancient Hebrews were living in several distinct sets of circumstances. Many were outside Jewish Palestine.[9] There were probably scattered communities of such people even

---

8. Gilbert Murray, *Five Stages of Greek Religion*, 3d ed. (Boston: Beacon, 1951), chap. 4.

9. The preferred scholarly designation for the land as a whole in ancient times, i.e., as inclusive of both northern and southern regions. "Israel" is ambiguous, since it was once used to designate the northern monarchy alone.

before the Babylonian exile, but that event marked a new chapter in the history of what became known as the Diaspora ("Dispersion"), the great body of Jews living in the gentile world. By the dawn of Hellenism, there were particularly large groups in Babylon and Egypt. And at the time of Jesus, Jewish communities flourished in cities throughout the Mediterranean world.

Jewish Palestine was divided into three distinct regions: Judea; Samaria, to the immediate north; and, farther to the north, Galilee. The northern areas were suspect in the eyes of Judeans because of the gentile population that was imported after the destruction of the northern monarchy in 721. But worship of Yahweh was alive in both Galilee and Samaria, although in different forms. The Samaritans were a separate religious community, with their own Torah and temple. The history of their split with Judea is unclear, but by the time of Jesus it took the form of mutual hatred. Galilee, by contrast, was part of the Jewish community. But Galilean customs differed somewhat from Judean, and the religious leaders of Judea considered Galileans inferior and somewhat impure because of the gentile influence.

Both Judeans and Galileans related to the Jerusalem temple, but a new institution had by this time arisen as the site of worship in local communities: the synagogue. The term can apply to a physical structure, but its original and primary meaning was "congregation," or "assembly." The synagogue was in essence a formalized gathering of the people, with a broad range of functions related to community welfare. Among those functions were study of the Torah and services of worship that included prayer and the reading and exposition of the Scriptures, but not cultic sacrifice.

a. The Challenge of Hellenism

On his way to Egypt, Alexander brought Palestine under his control; at his death, it was caught up in the struggles among his successors. After more than a century of rule by the Ptolemies of Egypt, it passed into Seleucid (Syrian) hands in 198 B.C.E. Throughout the Hellenistic Age, Jews in both Palestine and the Diaspora struggled to retain their religious heritage in the face of a powerful and appealing culture.

In some ways, the Diaspora Jews had the more difficult time maintaining their identity. Frequent contact with Gentiles was unavoidable, and the Greek language was a necessity. Nevertheless, the Jews were able to live in closely knit communities and carry on their traditions. Dietary regulations and communal worship were of course crucial. And scholars eventually produced a Greek version of the Jewish Scriptures. It became known as the Septuagint, from a Greek root meaning "seventy": legend had it that seventy scholars made separate translations and came up with the exact same wording!

Diaspora Jews thus had resources for survival. Although sometimes ridiculed because of their dietary customs and refusal to participate in local religious practices, they generally gained acceptance and often made important contributions to public life. There were undoubtedly many Diaspora Jews who forsook their traditions, but Judaism survived as an important minority subculture and religion in the Hellenistic world.

Since Persian times, most of the people in Palestine had spoken Aramaic, although Hebrew was used in religious study and writing. Hellenism brought some Greek to the area, primarily the cities. As in other parts of the Hellenistic world, the upper classes embraced it along with other Greek ways as the passport to social and economic success. But Jewish Palestine was more resistant to Hellenization than was the Diaspora. When young men began to wear Greek clothes and participate in Greek games (and even to have operations to disguise circumcision, since the games required nudity), many pious Jews were scandalized. Even in the homeland, some Jews undoubtedly abandoned their traditions altogether. Others probably adopted some Greek ways but retained a basic Jewish identity. Some, however, believed that the only way to remain Jewish was through complete rejection of Hellenism.

b. The Maccabean War

The conflict between Judaism and Hellenism in Palestine came to a head during the reign of the Seleucid king Antiochus Epiphanes. Antiochus angered Jews by pursuing a policy of active Hellenization, but it was his selling of the office of high priest to the highest bidder that gave rise to an overt protest movement. An important component in that movement was a group known as the Hasidim—the "pious ones" or "faithful ones."

The actual revolution known as the Maccabean War came only after Antiochus raided the temple treasury following his failed military campaign in Egypt. Enraged by this action, a group of Jews seized control of Jerusalem. When the Seleucids had recaptured the city, they attempted to abolish the Jewish religion altogether in Jerusalem and Judea. In 168 (or 167) they forbade circumcision and Sabbath observance and destroyed copies of the Torah; they set up a Syrian-Hellenistic cult in the temple and ordered Jews throughout the land to offer sacrifices to foreign deities. Some Jews complied with the order, and some resisted passively and paid with their lives. But others, under the leadership of the family of one Judas, nicknamed Maccabeus ("the Hammer"), fled to the hills and organized armed resistance.

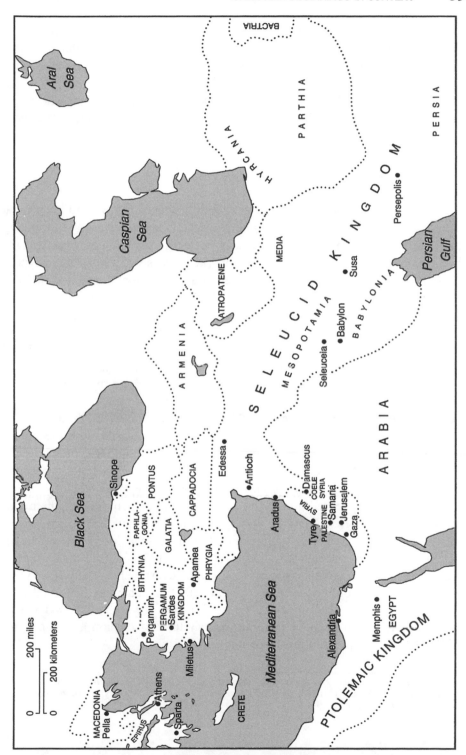

Fig. 10. The Hellenistic World. *(Map by Parrot Graphics)*

Judas's followers, the Maccabees, fought ferociously; by 165, they had forced a treaty restoring religious rights. Jews commemorate the rededication of the temple, following Judas's triumphant entry into Jerusalem, in the festival of Hanukkah. Not content with the treaty, Judas fought on for full freedom. After his death, leadership passed to his brother Simon, who negotiated independence and founded the Hasmonean dynasty, which lasted about a century.

c. Apocalyptic Literature

During the Maccabean War, a literary work appeared that was to have great influence on later Jewish and Christian thought. It expressed a way of thinking that had been developing since the early postexilic period. The work was the book of Daniel. In terms of literary form it is classified as an "apocalypse" (from the Greek work *apokalypsis*, meaning "revelation"), and the mode of thinking it expresses is called "apocalyptic."

According to one definition, an apocalypse is a narrative writing in which an other-worldly being mediates a revelation to a human recipient.[10] The revelation entails information on such subjects as (1) a supernatural world and (2) salvation, involving a personal afterlife, at the end of history. Apocalyptic teachings about matters such as the final judgment and the fate of human beings beyond the grave constitute a particular form of eschatology (from the Greek word *eschaton*, meaning "end"), or doctrine of the "last things."

In some apocalypses, the revelation has to do primarily with the nature of the heavenly world. Daniel, however, belongs to another type of apocalypse that is primarily concerned with human history. This latter type must be understood in light of the continuing hope for the Rule of God. Such a hope must have appeared dim to the Jewish people at many points; their enemies seemed always to have the upper hand. The prophets had wrestled with this issue and had frequently interpreted the misfortunes of Israel and Judah as God's punishment. But they had also promised God's Rule in the future. Now, after centuries of subjugation by foreign governments, many Jews were asking how they could deserve so much retribution. Thus the historical type of apocalypse gave the prophetic view of history a new twist: God would establish the divine Rule by bringing history to a conclusion and punishing those who had oppressed the righteous Jews.

---

10. See John J. Collins, *The Apocalyptic Imagination: An Introduction to the Jewish Matrix of Christianity* (New York: Crossroad, 1987), 4; also John J. Collins, "Apocalypse: Morphology of a Genre," *Semeia* 14 (1979): 9.

Historical apocalypses were written to encourage hope for the future in the face of difficult circumstances. They were, as many interpreters have noted, the "literature of the oppressed." Not surprisingly, then, apocalyptic writers often employed language that is highly charged emotionally. And the use of symbolism, which quite often takes the form of bizarre imagery, is also frequent in apocalyptic works.

Sometimes the imagery is terrifying. In Daniel, the recipient of the revelation (the character Daniel himself) describes a dream-vision in which he saw four monstrous beasts rising from the sea. There was one like a lion with an eagle's wings; another like a bear with the ribs of a victim in its mouth; another like a leopard with four heads and four wings. And then there was a fourth, which was "terrible and dreadful and exceedingly strong; and it had great iron teeth; it devoured and broke in pieces, and stamped the residue with its feet." This fourth beast had ten horns, but then grew a little one that had human eyes and a mouth that was "speaking arrogantly" (Dan. 7:7-8).

Later in the chapter, Daniel receives an explanation of the images from one of the angels at God's throne: the beasts represent successive empires, and the horns are kings. Although the angel names neither the empires nor the kings explicitly, the description leaves little doubt as to the meaning of the symbols: the fourth beast is Alexander's empire, the horns are the Hellenistic kings that succeeded him, and the arrogant little horn is Antiochus Epiphanes, the Seleucid ruler who tried to destroy the Jewish faith.

The book of Daniel also gives symbolic accounts of God's eventual defeat and destruction of Antiochus, the vindication of the Jewish people, and the final judgment and resurrection of the righteous. If the negative imagery helped the readers during the Maccabean Revolt identify their fears and face up to the extreme circumstances in which they lived, the positive imagery constituted a powerful encouragement to hope. Imagine the thoughts and feelings a passage like the following would have inspired among a group of faithful Jews wondering if God would ever bring in the Rule of peace and justice.

> As I watched,
> thrones were set in place,
>   and an Ancient One took his throne;
> his clothing was white as snow,
>   and the hair of his head like pure wool;
> his throne was fiery flames,
>   and its wheels were burning fire.

> A stream of fire issued
> and flowed out from his presence;
> A thousand thousands served him,
> and ten thousand times ten thousand stood attending him.
> The court sat in judgment, and the books were opened.
>
> (Dan. 7:9-10)

The ecstatic, imaginative language is all-important. It is the language not of reasoned argument but of religious inspiration. The arresting imagery conveys the awesomeness of God; it removes the readers from the world of daily troubles and historical despair and places them before the throne of God. The passage invites the readers to imagine that God is at last bringing history to its fulfillment.

Although written during the Maccabean War, the "story" told in Daniel is set during the Babylonian exile: Daniel's vision thus purports to look *ahead* in history. Readers living through the revolt therefore receive a word from a hero of the past who can assure them that God is in control of history and will eventually set things right.

The theme of the resurrection of the dead, which appears in Daniel 12, was unknown in earlier Hebrew thought. It is no accident that it showed up at this particular time in history, for as originally conceived it was intimately related to the problem of the suffering of the righteous. The point is not that human beings are by nature immortal. The raising of the dead is God's way of vindicating those righteous ones who have suffered unjustly in this life.

Apocalyptic literature is in part an outgrowth of Hebrew prophecy, but it owes much to other influences. The emphasis upon individual immortality is in keeping with the Hellenistic consciousness. Later apocalypses introduced the figure of Satan, or the devil, with a host of demonic assistants. These notions, along with that of a place of torment for the unrighteous, are characteristic of Zoroastrianism, a Persian religion that may have influenced Jewish thinking during Hellenistic times. The more important point is that it was a combination of disappointment with the present and a continuing hope for the Rule of God that brought all these influences together.

The book of Daniel found its way into the Hebrew canon, but there were many Jewish apocalypses that did not. Although Judaism eventually turned away from this type of writing, the apocalyptic imagination lived on in early Christianity.

d. The Sociological Makeup of Jewish Society

Recent sociological studies have cast important light on the social structure of the broad world within which Christianity was born.[11] Ancient agrarian societies were in general structured rather differently from modern societies. They were divided into two groups of classes, the upper and the lower, with no middle class in the modern sense.

It has been estimated that the upper classes in these societies constituted 5–7 percent of the population. The real power rested with a governing class that made up no more than 1–2 percent, but other groups were attached to the governing class and were able to enjoy some of its benefits. Among the latter was a "retainer" class, made up of such persons as bureaucrats, educators, officials, soldiers, priests, and to some extent merchants, whose function was to serve the needs of the governing class. Unlike the modern middle class, the retainers were directly dependent upon the governing class.

The lower classes were made up mostly of peasants, or farmers, the largest part of the population. Left to themselves, most peasants would produce only enough food for their families. But they were not left to themselves: the governing classes demanded not only excess produce to feed the rest of the population but high taxes to fund the government, including building projects and military endeavors. Although there was a wide range of economic status among peasants, from those who owned large plots of land to tenant farmers and hired workers, they were in general considerably poorer than those in the upper classes and lacked even the indirect access to power that the retainers had.

A small fraction of the population were artisans, who also belonged to the lower classes, and below them were persons without land or marketable skills who either performed society's most menial tasks or were left with no means of support at all. In difficult times, when peasants often lost their land, more and more persons fell into the very lowest categories—the unclean and degraded classes and, finally, the expendables. It is not surprising that many who lost status eventually turned to banditry or other means of support outside the law.

The governing class in Judea during the Hasmonean dynasty was comprised of the royal court and the temple aristocracy. The high priest and the upper echelons of the priesthood belonged to that class, but the majority of priests were among the retainers.

---

11. The following discussion draws particularly upon Anthony J. Saldarini, *Pharisees, Scribes, and Sadducees* (Wilmington, Del.: Michael Glazier, 1987), and Richard A. Horsley, *Jesus and the Spiral of Violence: Popular Jewish Resistance in Roman Palestine* (Minneapolis: Fortress Press, 1993).

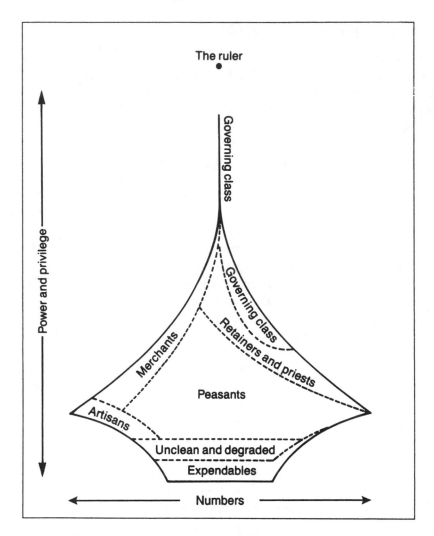

Fig. 11. A graphic representation of the relationship among classes in agrarian societies.
(From Gerhard E. Lenski, *Power and Privilege: A Theory of Social Stratification*
[New York: McGraw-Hill, 1966], 284)

The New Testament frequently mentions persons known as scribes. These also seem to fit primarily into the retainer class. Scholars have often treated the scribes as if they constituted a unified group, but the evidence is that there were many different kinds of scribes with a wide range of functions. In the most general terms, they were persons whose work demanded the ability to read and write. Some were undoubtedly teachers and high officials, but the majority seem to have performed middle-level bureaucratic functions such as record keeping, collection of taxes imposed by Jewish leaders, and copying documents. Many scribes were attached to the temple, and it was well-educated scribes who preserved much of ancient Jewish tradition in writing.

e. Pharisees, Sadducees, Essenes, and the Qumran Sect

The first-century c.e. Jewish historian Josephus describes three Jewish subgroups that were apparently formed during the Hasmonean period: the Pharisees, the Sadducees, and the Essenes. All are mentioned in other ancient sources as well, and the two most influential of them, the Pharisees and the Sadducees, appear in the New Testament. Modern archaeological finds are enhancing our understanding of the period in which these groups flourished, but the results of these finds are still in dispute. So before taking account of data gained in recent discoveries I will try to summarize the essentials of what we know of these groups apart from such new information.

Oddly enough, one point on which scholars have disagreed markedly is the question as to what kinds of groups these were. This is an issue particularly with regard to the Pharisees and the Sadducees. Seen from one perspective, they appear as political interest groups that competed for power. But each was defined also by specific religious teachings.

(1) The Pharisees. The origin of the Pharisees is uncertain, but many scholars think they were very likely heirs of the Hasidim, the vigorous opponents of Hellenism at the time of the Maccabean War. The Pharisees advocated meticulous obedience to the Torah and possessed an extensive oral tradition that supplemented the written law. They were known for observance of elaborate religious customs regarding such matters as tithing and Sabbath observance. Ritual purity was a primary concern, particularly with respect to regulations regarding meals. They believed in the resurrection of the dead and eternal reward and punishment.

Sociologically, the Pharisees seem to have belonged to the retainer class. As is often characteristic of groups in this class, they fell in and out of favor with the governing class over the years. It has been argued that by the New Testament period they had given up the struggle for political power, but the matter is disputed. In any case, their influence on the government was limited during the time of Jesus. Their relationship to the lower classes is somewhat unclear, although they did foster interpretations of the law designed to make it easier for common people to conform to its regulations.

(2) The Sadducees. We know considerably less about the Sadducees than about the Pharisees. They apparently belonged to the governing class and were probably a much smaller group than the Pharisees. Their membership seems to have come from the Jewish aristocracy, especially the upper levels of the priesthood. Concerned primarily with the temple cult, they had little interest in the application of Torah to daily life after the manner of the Pharisees. They also rejected the resurrection of the dead and eternal reward and punishment—notions that do not appear in the Torah. In this respect they reflected a conservatism that is typical of the governing class. Although power shifted back and forth between the Pharisees and Sadducees, the Sadducees generally had the greater influence in official affairs, which is hardly surprising, given their governing class makeup.

(3) The Essenes. According to Josephus, the Essenes resided in several different locales and practiced a type of communitarian life that involved elaborate rules of purity, far more extensive than those of the Pharisees. Membership entailed an extensive probationary period and the taking of strict vows, and life in the community was bounded by severe disciplinary rules. Another ancient source portrays them as a celibate order that perpetuated itself through adoptions, but Josephus's account indicates that not all groups of Essenes avoided marriage. The Roman writer Pliny the Elder refers to a group of Essenes living along the shore of the Dead Sea, although historians are uncertain as to the accuracy of his account.

The Essenes were apparently a fairly small group and considerably less influential on affairs of state during the time of Jesus than were the Pharisees and Sadducees. It would appear, in fact, that they had in large measure retreated from the wider Jewish community in protest against current practices.

(4) The Dead Sea Scrolls and the Qumran Sect. In 1897, an ancient writing that scholars named the Damascus Document was found in a synagogue in Cairo, Egypt. Then, in 1947, came the momentous discovery of an enormous deposit of manuscripts, largely in fragments, in caves near the ruins of an ancient settlement at Qumran, along the coast of the Dead Sea. Among these Dead Sea Scrolls, as the materials came to be called, were copies of the books of the Jewish Scriptures. There were also other writings, presumably reflecting the point of view of the residents of Qumran, that seem clearly sectarian in nature and that bear striking similarities to the Damascus Document.

The majority of scholars came to believe that both the Damascus Document and the sectarian materials among the Dead Sea Scrolls reflect the views of the Essenes and that the settlement at Qumran was in fact an Essene com-

Fig. 12. Caves in which the Dead Sea Scrolls were found. Near the ruins at Qumran, which scholars generally identify as the religious community that produced the scrolls. *(Photo by Marshall Johnson)*

munity. There are other theories, however, and a recent hypothesis is that the group at Qumran was a dissident faction of Sadducees. The evidence for this latter view is the fact that on several points the legal interpretations found in the sectarian scrolls parallel those of the Sadducees.[12]

Following the discovery of the scrolls, archaeologists excavated the site of the Qumran settlement. And the initial theory regarding the nature of the settlement dovetailed with the Essene hypothesis: it appeared to be a monastic community. More recent investigators have cast some doubt on this thesis, however. And it would appear that the debate over the precise nature of the Dead Sea community will continue for some time, especially in light of the fact that many of the scrolls are yet to be translated. Nevertheless, the most widely held interpretation of the excavated site is still that it was something akin to a monastery. And a majority of scholars still believe that the residents—and authors of the sectarian scrolls—were a group of Essenes.

Whoever the residents at Qumran were, they appear to have been highly

12. See the contrasting views of Lawrence H. Schiffmann, "The Sadducean Origins of the Dead Sea Scroll Sect," and James C. VanderKam, "The People of the Dead Sea Scrolls: Essenes or Sadducees?" in Hershel Shanks, ed., *Understanding the Dead Sea Scrolls: A Reader from the Biblical Archaeology Review* (New York: Random House, 1992).

sectarian in nature. The Hasmonean rulers strengthened the Jewish nation and extended the borders to include not only Samaria but Idumea, a region to the south. As they began to embrace Hellenism, however, they disappointed many pious Jews, in particular the Hasidim. Many scholars who identify the Qumran sect with the Essenes think that this movement was formed by a group of Hasidim in protest against Hasmonean policies. Thus some have argued that the group at Qumran shared a common origin with the Pharisees, who might also be heirs of the Hasidim. On the other hand, like the Sadducees, they seem to have had a priestly background. In sociological terms, in any case, the group at Qumran, at least after their withdrawal, seems to have been a "sect" in the narrow sense of a group that is almost completely alienated from the larger society.

The group's theology was eschatologically oriented, and some of their writings are highly apocalyptic. They expected a final battle between the forces of good and the forces of evil, and they awaited two messianic leaders, one political and one priestly, to lead them into the new age. The emphasis upon the final battle led them to adopt an attitude that was quite unusual in Judaism: they forbade marriage, not because they believed sex is immoral but because according to the purity laws in the Jewish Scriptures it brings a temporary ritual uncleanness that makes warriors unfit for battle. In expectation of the coming age, the sectarians sought to maintain a constant state of ritual purity. Thus they enforced a rigid set of community rules, believing themselves to be the only true Jews. Prospective members had to go through a period of probation, and strict regulations governed all aspects of life, particularly Sabbath observance.

The sectarian writings among the Dead Sea Scrolls are of particular importance to students of early Christianity because of their method of biblical interpretation. The settlers at Qumran read the Scriptures in light of their own experience; they took passages in the various books to refer to specific events in the history of their own community. Particularly good examples of their method are found in their commentary on the book of Habakkuk.

Modern scholars generally agree that the prophet Habakkuk wrote during the period of Babylonian power, shortly before the exile. In 1:5 he portrays God as announcing a divine action "that you would not believe if you were told," and in v. 6 it becomes clear that this action is the raising up of the Chaldeans (another name for the Babylonians) as God's own instrument. The sectarians, however, interpreted the Chaldeans as "the Kittim," their name for the Romans, who dominated the world of their own day. And they understood the phrase "you would not believe" as a reference to two other groups in their own time: the Jewish leaders who rejected the leader of the Qumran sect, the Righteous Teacher; and unfaithful members of the Qumran community itself.[13]

With such interpretation we are far removed from an attempt to read a passage in light of its original historical setting. The point is rather to bring the text to bear directly upon the needs and aspirations of the community to which one belongs. Similar approaches to interpretation were employed by other Jewish interpreters of the time and by the New Testament writers.

f. Hellenistic Influence on Diaspora Writings

Since well before the Babylonian exile, some Hebrew thinkers had begun to imitate a type of writing prevalent in the surrounding cultures: "wisdom" literature, which involved comment upon life in general, life as it might appear to anyone in any time. There was little room in this mode of reflection for such notions as God's special covenant with Israel, but the Hebrew version of such literature was able to retain a degree of distinctiveness by identifying Torah as the ultimate wisdom.

Not surprisingly, some Hellenistic ideas eventually found their way into Jewish wisdom materials. Probably around 100 B.C.E., an Alexandrian Jew produced a work known as the Wisdom of Solomon, which is included among the Apocryphal/Deuterocanonical books of the Bible (see below p. 85). Written in Greek, the work reflects Platonic, Stoic, and other forms of Hellenistic thought. The writer advances a notion of personal immortality based not upon resurrection but upon a dualism of body and soul (2:23; 8:19-20; 9:15), a Greek, not a Jewish, concept. We can also see in this work a tendency toward the personification of the figure of Wisdom. Because both the Greek and the Hebrew words for "wisdom" are feminine in form, the personified Wisdom appears as female. She is depicted as the agent through whom God created the world (7:22; 8:5; 9:9; cf. Prov. 8:22) and, like the Stoic Logos, as pervading all creation:

> For Wisdom is more mobile than any motion;
> because of her pureness she pervades and penetrates all things.
> For she is a breath of the power of God,
> and a pure emanation of the glory of the Almighty.
>
> (7:24-25b)

Jewish thought was even more fully accommodated to Hellenistic ideas in a later Alexandrian writer, Philo (20 B.C.E.–40 C.E.), an older contempo-

---

13. G. Vermes, *The Dead Sea Scrolls in English*, 3d ed. (Harmondsworth, Eng.: Penguin, 1975), 283–84.

rary of Jesus. Philo was deeply committed to Judaism, but his education was thoroughly Greek. He used the Septuagint as his Bible and had little knowledge of Hebrew, whereas his writings show the influence of such Hellenistic philosophies as later Platonic thought and Stoicism. His goal was to demonstrate the superiority of Judaism to other religious views, but he did this largely by arguing that the Jewish Scriptures contain the same truths put forth by the Greek philosophers. Philo thus identified the Torah with the "natural law" of the Stoics, and he interpreted biblical characters as embodiments of Greek virtues. He was aided in this endeavor by a method Greek philosophers had long used in relation to the Greek myths, namely, allegorical interpretation, which means finding a symbolic meaning behind the literal details of the text. Philo interpreted the Garden of Eden, for example, as a symbol for God's Wisdom, which he also identified with the Logos and the source of all virtue. And he understood the four rivers in the garden as the four cardinal virtues identified by Plato and the Stoics: prudence, temperance, fortitude, and justice.

Logos/Wisdom was an important notion in Philo's thought. It was for him a kind of emanation from God's own being, which gave the world its form, functioned as natural law, and became manifest in virtuous lives. It has been suggested that the figure of Isis influenced the way Philo understood Wisdom.

5. The Context of Emerging Christianity: The Roman Imperial Period

The Hellenistic monarchies eventually fell apart, but an eager new master lay waiting in the West to impose its might. The Hasmonean rulers thus suffered the fate of the whole western end of the Hellenistic world: while rival leaders contended for power, Rome stepped in. The independence of the Jewish nation came to an end in 63 B.C.E., when the general Pompey marched into Jerusalem.

a. The Roman Occupation of Jewish Palestine

Although many Jews were initially relieved to have Rome intervene in what had become a chaotic situation, there was some early resistance against the occupation government, particularly in Galilee, where many Gentiles had become enthusiastic converts to Judaism. The early years were also marked with political intrigue, since Rome itself was experiencing a power struggle and those contending for control of Judea switched sides as the tide turned. By

31 B.C.E., however, Octavian, who became known as Caesar Augustus, had gained control in Rome.

In the midst of this turmoil, a man named Herod received from the Romans the title "King of the Jews." Herod was a native of Idumea, a region south of Judea that had been annexed to the Jewish state during Hasmonean times. But the Jewish people did not consider him one of them. They saw him as a puppet of Rome and despised him intensely. He maintained foreign mercenaries and a network of informers among the people, and he met any hint of disorder with harsh repression. Although he made some attempts to win the favor of the people and even transformed the temple into a magnificent new structure, he was an avid proponent of Hellenism and intensely loyal to Rome; many people were scandalized when he placed a Roman eagle above the temple gate. His maintenance of a lavish royal court and his fetish for building projects, moreover, led to increased taxes that placed the population under an extreme economic burden.

When Herod died in 4 B.C.E., his territory went to his three sons. Philip ruled an area to the northeast of Galilee. Herod Antipas had Galilee and Perea (a district east of the Jordan river) and governed until shortly after Jesus' death. We will meet him later as the one who executes John the Baptist and who (while temporarily in Jerusalem) questions Jesus prior to his trial. Archelaus, who ruled Judea, was a complete disaster. His brutality provoked such constant unrest that the emperor removed him and put his district under a Roman governor.

Scholars have often characterized the time of Roman occupation as seething with revolutionary fervor. A recent study, however, reveals a more complex picture.[14] For the most part, Jewish resistance was sporadic and nonviolent.

There was, of course, widespread resentment of the occupation government, which was increased by economic hardship. And although Herod had stifled most overt manifestations of unrest, there was a series of insurrections in Jerusalem and the outlying regions shortly following his death. In Judea, Galilee, and Perea the revolutionaries proclaimed their leaders kings and were able to set up brief rules in their respective territories. These uprisings were popular in nature, involving mainly peasants. The leader in Galilee was a bandit chief, and the insurgents in Perea stormed the estates of the rich and confiscated their goods.

After these uprisings were put down, things remained relatively quiet until 26 C.E., when Pontius Pilate became governor of Judea. His rule, which

---

14. Horsley, *Jesus and the Spiral of Violence,* 59–145.

Fig. 13. Model of Athens in the Roman period, ca. 200 C.E. In the lower center is the ancient agora (marketplace), and on the lower left are the Library of Hadrian and the Roman agora. Above the agora are the Areopagus Hill (see Acts 17:16-39) and, to the left, the Acropolis (the "high city") in the center of Athens. The structure in the extreme upper left is the temple of Zeus Olympus. *(Photo: Koester/Hendrix)*

lasted for ten years and included the period of Jesus' ministry, was a complete failure. Consistently managing to offend the people's religious sensibilities, Pilate met their nonviolent protests with brutal repression. The situation deteriorated so much that the Romans removed him from office in 36 C.E., a few years after the crucifixion of Jesus. Then, in 41, they placed the whole of Jewish Palestine under a grandson of Herod, who ruled as King Agrippa I and who gained a good reputation among the Jews. Following his death in 44, the entire area came under the direct rule of a Roman governor. The king's son, Agrippa II, however, eventually received a small territory in Galilee and Perea. Completely subservient to Rome, he appears in the New Testament in connection with the trial of the apostle Paul.

The eight governors who served in succession from 44 to 66 were of mixed quality, but some were so insensitive and incompetent that they made almost inevitable the war of independence that came in 66. The immediate cause of the revolution seems to have been the brutality with which the governor

Fig. 14. Masada*

Florus responded to popular protests against his intention to appropriate funds from the temple treasury. As so often happens, repression led to further, more violent, resistance. Even a segment of the aristocracy turned against the occupation government. A son of the high priest, serving as temple captain, succeeded in stopping all sacrifices on behalf of Rome and eventually led an insurrection that expelled Florus from Jerusalem. When other members of the aristocracy took refuge in the Herodian palace, they lost all vestiges of authority with the people.

The entire country eventually united in a full-scale war. Gradually, however, the Roman troops regained control. After defeating resistance forces in Galilee, they marched through Judea, devastating the land. As they did so, many peasants were forced to flee from their land and formed bandit brigades. Several such groups eventually sought refuge in Jerusalem, forming a coalition known as the Zealots. They set up a makeshift government there but were opposed by the priestly aristocracy and eventually replaced by another revolutionary group. Scholars have often assumed that the Zealots

---

*Mosaic commemorating the last combatants in the Jewish war of independence, 66–70 C.E., who fled to a mountain fortress that had been built by Herod. According to Josephus, they held out until 74 and then and took their own lives rather than surrender to the Romans. *(Photo by Marshall Johnson)*

were a longstanding revolutionary party, but the evidence indicates that they were formed only during the Roman siege of Jerusalem.[15]

The final stage of that siege came in 70 C.E. After prolonged battle, the Romans recaptured Jerusalem and burned the temple and much of the city. In 73, they took the final group of holdouts at the mountain fortress of Masada, along the Dead Sea. Much later, in 132 C.E., a man named Bar Kochba led another war of independence, lasting two and a half years, which the Romans repressed at the price of enormous losses on both sides. When the fighting was over, they renamed the province Syria Palestina, forbade Jews to enter Jerusalem, and built a temple to Jupiter where Yahweh's once stood. The ancient Jewish state was at an end: all Jews, even those in Palestine, were henceforth Diaspora Jews.

If we remember that there was as yet no formalized concept of *the Messiah,* it is meaningful to speak of the time of Roman occupation as characterized by "messianic" expectations in the broad sense of hopes for a definitive and climactic act of God in history. These expectations are evidenced not only by the apocalyptic works produced during the period but also by social movements. In particular, the popular kingships set up temporarily after Herod's death, the revolutionary governments that appeared during the siege of Jerusalem, and the Bar Kochba war had clear messianic overtones. In addition, various prophetic movements and even some aspects of the activities of bandits, who generally attacked the holdings of the rich and were often glorified by the poor, in their own ways grew out of a hope for justice that was associated with the expected Rule of God.

b. The Continuation of Jewish Tradition

In 68 C.E., when the fate of Jerusalem was already apparent to many, a respected teacher among the Pharisees, Yohanan ben Zakkai, escaped from the city and went to the camp of the Roman general. With Roman approval, he then set up an academy in the town of Yabneh, near the seacoast, with the intention of preserving Jewish tradition. Revered teachers among the Jews were called rabbi, a title that did not at first involve formal ordination. Because of the succession of such teachers during the period that began with the establishment of the academy, the Judaism of the time is called "Rabbinic Judaism."

---

15. See Richard A. Horsley with John S. Hanson, *Bandits, Prophets, and Messiahs: Popular Movements at the Time of Jesus* (San Francisco: Harper & Row, 1988), xiii–xvi; also Horsley, *Jesus and the Spiral of Violence,* 77–78.

It was during the period of Rabbinic Judaism that the Hebrew canon took final shape. But the closing of the canon by no means brought the process of tradition to an end. Drawing upon centuries of lore, rabbinic schools in both Palestine and the Diaspora produced an enormous amount of literature during the early centuries C.E.

One type of such literature is known as midrash, a running commentary on Scriptures; another type is oral law arranged topically. In time, the Jewish leaders codified the topically arranged material as the Mishnah. And then, much later, they added to it an enormous body of interpretation to form two works called the Talmud—one produced in Babylon and the other in Palestine—which are second only to the Scriptures themselves as authoritative for Jews.

Rabbinic literature is far removed from doctrinal formulation, the presentation of ideas for intellectual assent. Contradictory assertions are allowed to stand side by side in a free-floating, open-ended discussion. As Christians in the early centuries C.E. turned more and more to the formulation of doctrine in the categories of Greek philosophy, Jews continued to wrestle with the application of God's commands to daily life and, simply, to tell stories. In the New Testament we find Christianity still living in both worlds: on the one hand engaged in their own open-ended discussion and telling stories, on the other hand moving toward a body of doctrine.

c. Christians and the Hebrew Canon

Some of the books included in the Septuagint were not subsequently accepted into the Jewish canon. Because the early church quickly became Greek-speaking and naturally used the Septuagint as its Bible, Christians found themselves with a version of the Jewish Scriptures containing books not accepted as fully authoritative by Jews themselves. Christians did not generally hold the "extra" books in as high regard as those in the Hebrew canon, but the inclusion of these books in the later Latin translation (the Vulgate) increased their standing. The Roman Catholic Church classifies these works as Deuterocanonical (i.e., canonical but at secondary status). During the Protestant Reformation, however, Martin Luther placed them at the end of his translation and designated them as "Apocrypha," thus emphasizing their subordinate standing, and in time most editions of Protestant Bibles excluded them altogether. They have therefore played a much less important role in Protestant churches than in Catholicism or Eastern Orthodoxy.

The early Christians supplemented the Jewish Scriptures with a collection of their own writings. Because Christians believed that God, who had once made a covenant with Israel, had now (in words taken from the prophet Jeremiah) made a *new* covenant with all humankind through Jesus, they called their own canon the "New Covenant." And, logically, the Jewish Scriptures became known as the "Old Covenant." The Greek term for covenant was translated into Latin as *testamentum.* Unfortunately, however, current usage of the English equivalent, "testament," obscures the original force of the term as applied to Scripture.

d. Christianity in the Greco-Roman World

The broad context into which Christianity was born was the Roman Empire, which was heir to the Hellenism that had flourished for two full centuries. The Romans were in fact admirers and imitators of the Greeks, and we may speak of the territory they ruled as the Greco-Roman world. The transition from a small Jewish sect in Palestine to a major religion within this wider world involved an agonizing conflict in values for the early church. In what sense was the Christian message for all humankind without qualification, and in what sense did it remain tied to God's covenant with Israel? This question was not settled without bitter debate and the permanent alienation of some of the factions. Not only did the early Christians face the task of defining their identity in relation to Judaism, but they did so in the context of an environment that was both a help and a hindrance in this process. This environment provided social, religious, and philosophical precedents that enabled the new faith to speak meaningfully to the world in which it found itself; but it also posed enormous threats to Christianity's own distinctive claims as well as to its Jewish heritage.

(1) Jewish Christians and Judaism. The earliest Christians were Jews and continued to think of themselves as such, not as members of a new religion. They understood Jesus as the fulfillment of Jewish hopes and designated him "Messiah," which they translated into Greek as *christos* (Christ). But what were the implications of such a designation? If Jewish messianic hopes had a nationalistic dimension, they also had broader implications: many Jews looked for a Rule of God that would bring peace and justice to the world at large. If Jesus was Messiah, could Gentiles now be included in the community of his followers? If so, on what basis? Must the males be circumcised, and were gentile Christians subject to the ritual requirements of the law? What, in fact, was the status of the Jewish law itself in this new situation?

Although Christians proclaimed Jesus as Messiah, the vast majority of Jews found no reason to accept him as such. After all, the messianic hope was associated with God's Rule. But did it make sense to say that God's Rule had in fact come? Was there peace? Was there justice? Most importantly, what actually became of Jesus? His life ended in apparent failure—worse, in the most shameful death the world had to give. How were Christians to answer these questions, not just to their non-Christian Jewish critics, but to *themselves* as Jews?

Like all Jews, these Christians also had to deal with the problem of Rome. During the war, they probably had to ask whether they should join the Jewish resistance. Later they faced the question of how to view the destruction of Jerusalem and the temple. As the church became more and more gentile, it lost all connection with Jewish nationalistic hopes. But what, then, were Christians to think of God's promises to Israel? How were they to relate to Israel's past? And how were they to relate to the Judaism that continued to exist?

(2) Christianity and the Sociopolitical Order. Somewhat like the Greek city-states, Rome had nurtured democratic ideals in its past; and even the transition from republic to empire, a transition completed with the accession of Augustus to the office of emperor, did not destroy these ideals entirely. The senate retained some power, and there was a strong sense of the rule of law as opposed to the arbitrary power of a monarch. Also, there were means by which people in the provinces under Rome's rule could obtain citizenship.

Nevertheless, in sociological terms Rome was a highly stratified society. Senate membership was a matter of social rank, and owners of large estates held a large percentage of the land.

The Roman Empire stretched over a vast area composed of agrarian societies that fit the general social pattern discussed earlier in relation to Jewish society (see section 4d above). Within this structure, it was taken for granted that persons relatively low on the social scale would look to persons higher up to be their patrons and would help them get what they needed in social or financial matters. In turn, those on the receiving end of the relationship were obligated to the patrons and thus became their clients, who would repay the debt in whatever ways the patrons demanded.

Because society was multileveled, persons who were clients of patrons above them could also function as patrons of others even farther down. Those who played such a dual role functioned as brokers, in the sense that they effectively negotiated power relationships between persons widely separated on

Fig. 15. The reconstructed Attalos Stoa in Athens. The doors on the left open into shops and offices, and the arched doorway at the far end leads to the street from the ancient agora to the Roman market. *(Photo: Koester/Hendrix)*

the social scale.[16] And brokerage was in fact a constant necessity, since the patron-client relationship with its system of continual indebtedness pervaded every aspect of human affairs.

Slavery, as in the ancient world generally, was widespread. Greco-Roman slavery was generally less brutal than its modern American counterpart: slaves were often well-educated, and steps had been taken, largely under Stoic influence, to improve their lot. But slavery is slavery nonetheless, and conditions were extremely severe in some areas. There were several slave revolts, which were harshly repressed.

The empire was male-dominated, but the rights of women had been expanded through the years, again largely under Stoic influence. In contrast to Jewish society, for example, women in the Roman world had the right to divorce.

How would Christians relate to these social structures? Would they pick up on the Jewish sense of social justice? Would they expand it to include

---

16. John Dominic Crossan, *The Historical Jesus: The Life of a Mediterranean Jewish Peasant* (San Francisco: HarperSanFrancisco, 1991), 89–90.

women in a fuller way? Would they embrace the Stoic notion of universal relatedness? Would they advocate social reform? The acceptance of Jesus as Messiah committed Christians to hope for the realization of God's Rule, but they had to work out for themselves just what that meant. Apocalyptic eschatology was popular when Christianity was born. The New Testament thus exhibits a tendency to replace the Jewish nationalistic hope with the hope for a supernatural end to history and eternal life in God's heavenly Rule. But given that hope, what attitudes would Christians take toward injustices in this world? How *un*worldly would their other-worldly hopes make them?

One issue Christians could not avoid was the emperor cult. Veneration of the emperor did not always mean what many Christians through the ages have thought it meant: that the emperor was literally worshiped as divine. Different emperors interpreted the matter differently (some actually discouraged the practice), but for the most part the implication was that divine power was present *in* the emperor. The point in any case was loyalty to the empire itself, an issue that was to the Romans strictly political. Even so, the practice of sacrificing to the emperor was unacceptable to both Jews and Christians, whose monotheism demanded ultimate loyalty to God alone. Given that attitude, however, the question remained: how were Christians to relate to human governments when such sacrifice was not demanded?

(3) Christianity and Mediterranean Culture. Both Hellenism and the Roman Empire superimposed themselves upon the preexisting world that surrounded the Mediterranean Sea. Although this broad region was composed of numerous distinct societies, modern anthropologists have been able to describe some specific characteristics of a general Mediterranean culture. And in recent years New Testament scholars have made use of their work.

Of particular importance is the identification of honor and shame as the pivotal values within this culture. "Honor," Bruce Malina explains, "is the value of a person in his or her own eyes (that is, one's claim to worth) *plus* that person's value in the eyes of his or her social group."[17] An enormous amount of human activity was directed toward the maintenance of the honor of one's family or other group to which one belonged. To preserve honor was to avoid shame, so that along with a sense of honor one also needed a sense of shame, that is, a "sensitivity for one's own reputation,"[18] a conscience informed by the fear of incurring dishonor.

---

17. Bruce J. Malina, *The New Testament World: Insights from Cultural Anthropology* (Atlanta: John Knox, 1981), 27.

18. Ibid., 44.

To grasp the meaning of honor and shame in New Testament times, the contemporary student must put aside the distinctively modern and Western notion of a human self that is highly individuated and psychologically introspective. The ancient mind, as represented in Mediterranean culture, thought largely in collective terms and was to a large extent dominated by the opinions of the group. To focus on honor and shame was to focus upon a person or group's standing, or "honor rating," within some larger group; it had little to do with the individual's attempt to look into her or his own "heart," or psychological depths.

Virtually all human activity had implications for the honor and shame scale, so that almost any instance of human interaction between members of different groups held the potential for gain or loss in honor rating. Each group member had specific responsibilities with respect to the maintenance of honor, and these were distributed according to a hierarchical order with clear differentiations according to sex. The father, as head of the family, was the person primarily responsible for honor, although the actions of other family members could bring shame upon him. The man's role in general was the active pursuit of honor in activities outside the home. The woman's domain, by contrast, was the home itself, and her role had to do largely with the maintenance of a sense of shame through which she protected this family honor.

The system of honor and shame revolved around the male. There was an institutionalized double standard that encompassed sexual activity. The woman's virginity prior to marriage was central to the family's honor. For a woman to engage in illicit sexual relations would bring shame, whereas for a male to do so would not. And both honor and shame fell ultimately upon the male. The men maintained their own honor by protecting the sexual purity of their women, and a woman's deviant behavior reflected ultimately upon the man. It was assumed that all women needed the protection and supervision of males. Thus those who were widowed or divorced or otherwise outside a male-headed household were "viewed as stripped of female honor, hence more like males than females, therefore sexually predatory, aggressive . . . hence dangerous."[19]

The value system of honor and shame was deeply ingrained in the first-century Mediterranean mind, and Christians could not simply abandon it altogether. From earliest times, however, their allegiance to Jesus brought them into tension with various aspects of that system. Thus even on the level of some of society's most tightly held norms they faced important questions.

---

19. Ibid.

To whom were they responsible in matters of honor and shame, and what in fact constituted honorable and shameful behavior in this new group?

(4) Christianity among the Religions in the Greco-Roman World. The Greco-Roman world was a fertile field for missionary activity, and Christianity was from an early point a missionary religion. Christians believed they were called to proclaim their message to the world at large. But Christianity was not alone in its missionary zeal, nor was it the only movement to meet with success.

Judaism itself was well-respected in many quarters. The extent to which Jews pursued an active missionary policy is debated, but we know that many people were profoundly attracted to Jewish monotheism and high ethical standards. The number of actual converts was limited because of circumcision and dietary regulations, but many Gentiles participated in synagogue worship without becoming Jews. In the New Testament such people are called "God-fearers."

The mystery cults were extremely popular, even in Rome itself, where religious secrecy was suspect and linked with superstition. Of particular importance was Mithraism, which was connected with sun-worship: initiates became "soldiers" of the god Mithras and eventually achieved unity with Sol, the sun. This cult spread rapidly among the military and at one point became the official religion of the empire.

In many ways, Christianity's most serious rival was not a religion but a philosophy: Stoicism. Like Judaism, it possessed a highly developed moral sense, and its notion of universal human relatedness suited an age of world-consciousness. As with all philosophical movements, however, its appeal was limited mostly to the educated. It did not offer initiation rites, the close communion of a religious fellowship, or the promise of immortality.

A different kind of competition came from a number of groups, treated by modern scholars under the general designation of Gnosticism, that propounded complex religious teachings. Not only did gnostic groups compete against Christianity, but the two movements overlapped to some extent. There were at one time numerous groups of Christian Gnostics; they were, however, eventually forced by the development of official doctrine and organizational structure to leave the church. The conflict with Gnosticism, which came to a head in the mid-second century C.E., was a crucial point in the development of Christian self-definition. For it brought the question of Christianity's relationship to its Jewish heritage together with the broader question of how Christians should balance this-worldly and other-worldly concerns.

According to the general gnostic mythology, the present world came into

Fig. 16. Emperor Claudius as Zeus*

being not as a creation of the supreme deity, but through some sort of cosmic accident. From the true god, who is pure Light, there somehow emanated several lesser orders of being. Sometimes the Jewish god is seen as belonging to one of these lesser orders. According to the Gnostics it was this god who—being ignorant of the true god—arrogantly decided to create this world. The present world, therefore, is seen as inherently flawed; it is less than fully real and actually an evil place that never should have come into existence.

Human beings within this world have a dual nature. Their material bodies, as parts of this "lower" world, are corrupt. But trapped within these bodies are spirits, "sparks" from the realm of Light. To remedy this situation, the true god sends a redeemer, or revealer, from the realm of Light to enter this world. This redeemer comes in the *appearance* of a human being, but is not truly human (since to be material is to be corrupt) and teaches a secret knowledge (Greek: *gnōsis*) that enables people to escape from this world at death and return to the realm of Light.

---

*From the mid-first century c.e; found at Olympia in Greece. Claudius ruled Rome from 41 to 54 c.e. He introduced several reforms in both governmental policy and religion and added Britain to the empire. When he was poisoned by his second wife, Agrippina, Nero, her son by a former marriage, took the throne. *(Photo: Koester/Hendrix)*

There are several theories of the origin of Gnosticism. The general opinion for a long time was that it was an extreme Hellenization of an already existing Christianity. Later scholars, however, argued that some forms of Gnosticism preceded Christianity and that Christians patterned their understanding of Jesus' redemptive role on that of the gnostic redeemer. Neither view is generally accepted today. There is still dispute over how much one movement owes to the other, but most scholars now see them as developing concurrently and interacting in a complex way.

Some scholars think that the negative use of the Jewish god in Gnosticism points to sectarian Judaism as a major factor in gnostic origins. The settlers at Qumran, for example, might have turned in such a direction after the disillusioning experiences of 70 c.e.; their literature is pervaded by dualistic imagery (light vs. darkness, etc.), which is clearly suggestive of the radical dualism characteristic of Gnosticism.

There are some real similarities between Christianity and Gnosticism. But the latter involved a total rejection of the Jewish god and the material world. Where were Christians, who accepted Jesus as the Jewish Messiah, to stand in relation to such a view? In what sense should they reject the world, and in what sense should they accept it?

6. The Life and Mission of the Christian Communities

The early Christians faced many questions, and the New Testament reflects their attempts to answer them. There were several factors that helped shape their responses. Jewish heritage, Hellenistic religious and philosophical ideas, and social realities all contributed to the various forms of Christian consciousness that emerged. But the reality of the early Christian movement was more than the sum of all these factors. The Christian communities constituted distinct entities within their various environments, held together by what is known in social-scientific terminology as a symbolic universe, a shared way of perceiving reality. They had a distinctive set of beliefs and practices that set them apart from the larger societies in which they lived and from other religious groups. Christians embraced the Jewish belief in one god, adding to it the conviction that through Jesus of Nazareth God had acted decisively not only to fulfill the ancient promises to Israel but to make salvation available to all people. They also believed that this Jesus, whom God had raised from the dead, would eventually return at the end of the age to bring to completion God's plan for the world. And along with such basic beliefs, they also passed on moral teachings and tried to maintain cohesive relationships within the communities.

Like other religious communities, Christians practiced certain rites. These served in sociological terms to define their boundaries and create internal cohesion and in theological terms to link them to the power of the divine. Their ritual of initiation was baptism, immersion in water, which Jews had long practiced as a way of incorporating gentile converts into their ranks. They also met together for worship, which was modeled after Jewish worship in the synagogues, involving such practices as prayer, reading of the Jewish Scriptures, and preaching. Originally meeting on the seventh day of the week, the Jewish Sabbath, they eventually adopted the first day as their holy day, associating it with the resurrection of Jesus.

At the heart of their worship life was a sacred meal, the Lord's Supper, which later became known as Holy Communion, or the Eucharist. It was a reenactment of Jesus' final meal with his disciples before his death. In earliest times, the Lord's Supper seems to have been identical to what was known as the love feast, an actual fellowship meal. But eventually the ceremonial reenactment was separated from the full meal and consisted only of the giving and receiving of bread and wine.

As important as their internal life was, Christians also understood themselves as in mission to the world. It was part of their self-definition that they should proclaim their message about Jesus to the world at large. So before we come to the New Testament writings as they now stand within the canon, it will be important to look in on the earliest stages of the Christian proclamation. What exactly did the earliest Christians say about Jesus? What was the precise nature and meaning of their claims?

STUDY QUESTIONS

1. How did Hebrew monotheism and Plato's thought alter the ancient consciousness? How does the modern consciousness differ from the ancient, and how does the postmodern differ from both of these?

2. Describe the main aspects of ancient Hebrew religion. Which beliefs were distinctive? Which were shared with other cultures? Explain the "logic" of clean/unclean.

3. How did the development of a monarchy change the social structure and religious outlook of ancient Israel? What changes came about as the result of the Babylonian exile?

4. Give a brief description of the Hellenistic "world," with particular emphasis upon the religious and philosophical options it offered.

5. Explain each of the following terms: cosmic empathy, demystification, materialism, idealism, dualism, exodus, prophet, Yahweh, covenant, Rule of God, Messiah, messianic age, Torah, Judah, Judea, Samaria, *koinē,* syncretism, Logos, Septuagint, eschatology.

6. How was Judaism affected by Hellenism?

7. What is apocalyptic literature, and why are historical apocalypses written? Discuss the benefits and dangers of apocalyptic literature from the point of view of a religious community.

8. Briefly describe the sociological makeup of Jewish society during the Hellenistic Age.

9. Describe the main characteristics of the Essenes, Pharisees, Sadducees, and the Dead Sea sect. What are the main theories regarding the identity of the last named?

10. What specific Hellenistic ideas can be found in writings of the Jewish Diaspora during the Hellenistic Age?

11. What would it have been like to have been a Palestinian Jew during the Roman occupation? How might your social standing have affected your evaluation of the occupation government?

12. Explain the origin of the terms "New Testament" and "Old Testament." Many recent scholars and theologians have abandoned the use of the latter in favor of such terms as "Jewish Scriptures," "Hebrew Bible," and "First Testament" (replacing "New Testament" with "Second Testament"). Can you state why this might be appropriate in our time?

13. Identify the following: Apocrypha, Zealots, midrash, Mishnah, Talmud, Philo, Herod, Antipas, Pontius Pilate.

14. Give a brief description of the patron-client relationship in the world of the Roman Empire. How does the concept of debt figure into this relationship?

15. Give a brief description of how the concepts of honor and shame functioned in the ancient Mediterranean culture. Compare that culture's understanding of the human self to our own view.

16. Discuss the status and role of women in the world into which Christianity was born.

17. What are the specific characteristics of Gnosticism, and what are the various theories of its origins?

18. In what ways did Gnosticism reflect the "spirit" of the Hellenistic Age? Compare Gnosticism to Christianity as you understand the latter.

19. Give a brief description of the "internal life" of the Christian community.

FOR FURTHER READING

Barrett, C. K. *The New Testament Background: Selected Documents.* Rev. ed. London: SPCK, 1987.

Bright, John. *The Kingdom of God: The Biblical Concept and Its Meaning for the Church.* New York and Nashville: Abingdon-Cokesbury, 1943. Traces the historical development of the notion of the kingdom (Rule) of God in ancient Israel.

Collins, John J. *The Apocalyptic Imagination: An Introduction to the Jewish Matrix of Christianity.* New York: Crossroad, 1989. Reflects a new phase in the study of apocalyptic literature. Technical.

Grant, Frederick C. *Roman Hellenism and the New Testament.* New York: Charles Scribner's Sons, 1962. A brief, readable overview.

Hanson, Paul D. *The Dawn of Apocalyptic: The Historical and Sociological Roots of Jewish Apocalyptic Eschatology.* Rev. ed. Philadelphia: Fortress Press, 1979. A detailed reconstruction of the development of apocalyptic thought that challenges many earlier assumptions.

————. *Old Testament Apocalyptic.* Nashville: Abingdon, 1987. A brief, readable introduction to the topic.

Horsley, Richard A., with John S. Hanson. *Bandits, Prophets, and Messiahs: Popular Movements at the Time of Jesus.* San Francisco: Harper & Row, 1988; first published in 1985. A readable account, drawing largely upon the writings of Josephus, that sheds new light on social movements among the common people in first-century Palestine.

Hengel, Martin. *Judaism and Hellenism: Studies in Their Encounter in Palestine during the Early Hellenistic Period.* 2 vols. Trans. John Bowden. Philadelphia: Fortress Press, 1974, 1 vol. ed., 1991. A detailed study, demonstrating the extensive Hellenization of Jewish society. Excellent bibliography.

Jonas, Hans. *The Gnostic Religion: The Message of the Alien God and the Beginnings of Christianity.* 2d ed., enlarged. Boston: Beacon Press, 1963. A classic description of the gnostic worldview.

Kee, Howard Clark. *The Origins of Christianity: Sources and Documents.* Englewood Cliffs, N.J.: Prentice-Hall, 1973.

Koester, Helmut. *Introduction to the New Testament.* Vol. 1: *History, Culture, and Religion of the Hellenistic Age.* Philadelphia: Fortress Press, 1982. A detailed but readable account.

Malina, Bruce J. *The New Testament World: Insights from Cultural Anthropology.* Atlanta: John Knox, 1981. A ground-breaking application of anthropological categories to the New Testament environment.

Neusner, Jacob. *From Politics to Piety: The Emergence of Pharisaic Judaism.* Englewood Cliffs, N.J.: Prentice-Hall, 1973. Argues that Pharisees withdrew from the political sphere.

Nock, Arthur Darby. *Early Gentile Christianity and Its Hellenistic Background.* New York: Harper & Row, 1964. A brief, readable overview.

Pagels, Elaine. *The Gnostic Gospels.* New York: Random House, 1979. A highly readable and interesting account for the general reader.

Peters, F. E. *The Harvest of Hellenism: A History of the Near East from Alexander the Great to the Triumph of Christianity.* New York: Simon and Schuster, 1970. A thorough study of the period; a valuable resource.

Pfeiffer, Robert H. *History of New Testament Times with an Introduction to the Apocrypha.* New York: Harper & Brothers, 1949. Good overview.

Rivkin, Ellis. *A Hidden Revolution: The Pharisees' Search for the Kingdom Within.* Nashville: Abingdon, 1978. Interprets the Pharisees as a reform movement.

Robinson, James M., gen. ed. *The Nag Hammadi Library in English.* 3d ed. San Francisco: Harper & Row, 1988. Translations of gnostic documents discovered in a major archaeological find.

Roetzel, Calvin J. *The World That Shaped the New Testament.* Atlanta: John Knox, 1985. A brief, readable overview.

Saldarini, Anthony J. *Pharisees, Scribes, and Sadducees.* Wilmington, Del.: Michael Glazier, 1987. A sociological study challenging standard assumptions; takes issue with both Neusner and Rivkin.

Tarn, William Woodthrope, and G. T. Griffith. *Hellenistic Civilization.* 3d ed. London: E. Arnold, 1952. A classic study; detailed and thorough.

Tcherikover, Victor. *Hellenistic Civilization and the Jews.* Trans. S. Applebaum. Philadelphia: Jewish Publication Society of America, 1959. A detailed study with a sociological interest.

Vermes, G. *The Dead Sea Scrolls in English.* 3d ed. Harmondsworth, Eng.: Penguin, 1987.

Chapter 3

The Gospels, Jesus,
and the Earliest Tradition

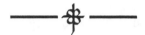

Alongside the early Christians' proclamation that God had raised Jesus from the dead, they transmitted another body of tradition: stories and sayings attributed to Jesus and accounts of incidents in his life. This tradition must have begun during Jesus' lifetime, as those who heard his words and saw his deeds told others what they had seen and heard. A period of oral tradition thus preceded the written accounts of Jesus' life we have in the four Gospels. The primary subject matter of this chapter is the earliest stage of this Jesus tradition. In chapter 4 I will consider its later stages, in connection with a discussion of the resurrection faith.

One cannot, however, consider the Jesus tradition apart from the Gospels themselves, for these writings constitute our primary sources for knowledge of the oral period. So it is important to begin by noting what contemporary scholarship has to say about the nature of the Gospels and how they came to be. And a good starting point is the question of the relationship between the Gospels and the actual, historical person Jesus, who lived and carried out his ministry in first-century Jewish Palestine.

1. Jesus and the Gospels

a. The Intentions of the Gospel Writers

Where does one go to find information about Jesus? Almost anyone who has any familiarity with Christianity will reply that such information is to be found in the Gospels. This answer is correct as far as it goes, but the task of gaining an accurate picture of the life and teachings of Jesus is far more complex than persons unfamiliar with modern biblical scholarship might imagine.

The Gospel writers were apparently less concerned with historical accuracy than with making clear to their readers the *meaning* of Jesus' life, death, and resurrection. The author of John, in fact, implies as much in a statement of purpose in 20:30-31: "Now Jesus did many other signs in the presence of his disciples, which are not written in this book. But these are written *so that you may come to believe that Jesus is the Messiah, the Son of God, and that through believing you may have life in his name.*"

If we may take these words as in some sense indicative of the intentions of all four authors, it is clear that what they set out to do was not to report factual material in disinterested fashion, but to tell the story of Jesus in such a way as to persuade readers to follow him. They intended their works, in other words, to be much more like sermons than newspaper accounts. This does not mean that the Gospels are pure invention, containing no historical facts at all. But it does mean that if we want to learn something about the actual person Jesus, we will have to read them critically, distinguishing between expressions of faith and the historical realities that lie behind those expressions.

b. "Apostolic Origin" and "Eyewitness Accounts"

Who wrote the Gospels? We saw in the Introduction that the early Christians accepted into the canon those writings that they believed were of apostolic origin. But in what precise sense did they understand the Gospels to be apostolic? To whom do the titles "Matthew," "Mark," "Luke," and "John" refer?

The first point that needs to be made is that in no case does the actual text of a Gospel make a direct claim regarding its authorship. The Gospels get their traditional names from the headings of the Greek manuscripts, the oldest of which (with the exception of a fragment of the Gospel of John) date from around 200 C.E. These manuscripts employ the stereotyped titles, "According to Matthew," "According to Mark," etc.

But where did these titles come from? Because it seems unlikely that four authors would have arrived independently at the exact same mode of designation, scholars conclude that they were added after these books had been widely accepted as authoritative. There must therefore have been oral traditions ascribing the books to particular authors.

We cannot be certain to whom the names originally referred. At some stage, however, early Christians took "Matthew" and "John" to be two of "the Twelve," the group that according to tradition formed the inner circle of Jesus' disciples during his lifetime. The general assumption is that "Mark" referred to John Mark, mentioned in Acts as a companion of Paul. A second-century bishop named Papias claimed that "Mark" made use of information given him by Peter, who was one of the Twelve. Second-century tradition also identified "Luke" with a co-worker Paul mentions in his letter to Philemon (v. 24), and the assumption has been that he is identical with the Luke of 2 Timothy 4:11 and "Luke, the beloved physician" of Colossians 4:14. The early church thus thought the author was a companion of Paul's, but not someone who actually knew Jesus. Clearly, then, apostolic origin had a fairly loose meaning; only Matthew and John were supposed to have been eyewitness accounts.

But are Matthew and John really eyewitness accounts? It is difficult to believe that *both* are, since they tell different stories; very few incidents occur in both, while a crucial event—Jesus' assault on the temple—comes at different points in the two accounts. They also contain entirely different types of material: Matthew (like Mark and Luke) is composed of short literary units—accounts of Jesus' conversations with various people, miracle-stories, sayings, etc.—while John is filled with long speeches by Jesus. An early Christian writer described John as a "spiritual" Gospel, recognizing it as a highly meditative work with little interest in reporting actual historical details. So if we had to compare the type of material found in Matthew and that found in John with respect to historical accuracy, the choice would have to be with material of the Matthean type. However much historical information John might contain, it is clearly not an eyewitness account.

c. The "Synoptic" Problem

But what of Matthew? The question is complicated by the fact that Matthew seems to bear a literary relationship to Mark and Luke. Not only do Matthew, Mark, and Luke tell roughly the same story, but their wording is so close at so many points that it is difficult to avoid the conclusion that some actual copying was involved. Because of their close interrelationships, scholars have designated these three works the "Synoptics" (from Greek words meaning "seeing together"), or Synoptic Gospels. They have also tried to solve the "Synoptic problem," the question of how to account for the literary relationships, through the discipline of source criticism.

Two basic solutions to the Synoptic problem have commended themselves to most modern scholars. The view that has dominated critical scholarship since the late nineteenth century is known as the "two-document hypothesis." According to this theory, a comparison of materials common to all three Synoptic Gospels leads to the conclusion that Mark appeared first, then the authors of Matthew and Luke used Mark independently in creating their own works. This leaves unexplained, however, the large body of material common to Matthew and Luke but not present in Mark. Thus proponents of this view posit a second written source, besides Mark, which both Matthew and Luke used. The designation for this hypothetical document is "Q," after the German word *Quelle,* meaning "source." Some scholars expand this solution to a four-source theory, positing two further documents to account for material that is peculiar to Matthew (M) and Luke (L).

Fig. 17. TWO (FOUR)-DOCUMENT HYPOTHESIS

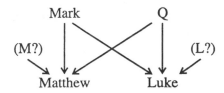

Fig. 18. TWO-GOSPEL HYPOTHESIS

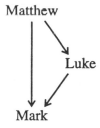

According to the other solution, Matthew was written first; then the author of Luke revised Matthew while combining it with other available traditions, and the author of Mark eventually wove Matthew and Luke together in summary fashion, deleting a great deal of material. This theory, which is termed the "two-Gospel hypothesis," has the advantage of simplicity: it has no need for hypothetical sources. It also accounts for some minor agreements between Matthew and Luke that are problematic for the view that both authors made independent use of Mark. Although out of favor for many years, the two-Gospel hypothesis has made a recent comeback and has quite a few articulate proponents.

The majority of scholars, however, continue to hold to the two-document hypothesis. Although its opponents have recently challenged some of the standard arguments in its favor, many scholars simply find it easier to explain why the author of Matthew (and Luke) would in individual instances have changed Mark rather than vice-versa. Sometimes it appears that the author of Matthew or Luke is cleaning up the Greek in Mark or avoiding a possible misunderstanding; in other instances it is easier to attribute a theological motive to either of these than to the author of Mark. Although the minor agreements between Matthew and Luke constitute a problem for the two-document hypothesis, most scholars are content with such explanations as the tendency of manuscript copyists to accommodate the Gospels to one another.

But how does all this affect the question of eyewitness accounts? However one solves the Synoptic problem, not all three Synoptics can be the reports of eyewitnesses, since a person who actually knew Jesus would not have had to copy someone else's story. At best, either Matthew or Mark is an eyewitness account. But the early church never claimed that the author of Mark knew Jesus, and the tradition that this writer got his material from Peter sounds too much like an attempt to lend authority to a document whose origin had been forgotten. So the one slim hope rests with Matthew, but most scholars think it was dependent upon Mark. And even if one accepts the view that Matthew appeared first, there are compelling reasons for denying that the author of this Gospel was an eyewitness to Jesus' ministry. The reasons have to do with the nature of the materials found in the Synoptic Gospels.

d. The Nature of the Synoptic Materials

When scholars settled on the view that Mark was the earliest Gospel, they at first thought this meant that Mark accurately reported the sequence of events in Jesus' life. Later studies, however, called this judgment into question. William Wrede noted the theological motives at work in the Gospel authors' presentations, and Karl Ludwig Schmidt showed that the Synoptic Gospels are composed of short pericopes, that is, self-contained units of tradition. Schmidt argued convincingly that the passages in Mark that tie the pericopes together in a continuous narrative show a common style and vocabulary not present in the pericopes. He concluded that the author of Mark had created the "framework" of the story of Jesus' life by linking together preexisting units of tradition.

This judgment might seem surprising to many modern readers, but in some ways it might have been less so to early Christians. It is worthy of note that Papias, the same second-century bishop who thought Mark drew upon Peter's testimony, also said that Mark did not recount the events of Jesus' life in accurate historical order.

Schmidt's insight, in any case, became the basis of form criticism, which laid to rest the notion of the Gospels as eyewitness accounts. It has become almost impossible to deny that behind the Synoptic Gospels stands a long process of oral tradition.

e. Christian Faith and the Problem
of the "Historical Jesus"

Two important questions arise at this point. The first is a historical one: whether, given the nature of the materials at our disposal, we can gain any reliable information at all about the historical person Jesus. The fact that the Gospel writers' materials were shaped by oral tradition does not, however, mean that they contain no historical reminiscences whatsoever. While some scholars are extremely skeptical about knowledge regarding the historical Jesus, most think we can reconstruct the main outlines of his teaching and the main thrust of his ministry. But there is wide agreement that the Jesus of history is to be found not through an uncritical reading of the Gospel narratives as they stand but through a complex process of evaluating the individual units of tradition found within them.

The second question is theological: What does the view of the origin of the Gospels taken in this book imply regarding Christian faith? Because of a particular understanding of the divine inspiration of the Scriptures that some Christians hold, people are sometimes disturbed to learn that our knowledge of Jesus depends upon oral tradition and that the Gospels are less than fully accurate in a historical sense.

Although the theological question lies to some extent beyond the scope of this book, it is legitimate to ask whether the religious value of these writings necessarily depends upon their accuracy in historical details. Not all Christians link the doctrine of divine inspiration to such a standard. Many theologians in fact believe that because the Gospel writers themselves focused on the meaning of Jesus' life rather than historical accuracy, believers should do the same—precisely as a way of honoring those writers' own intentions. In any case, as I have said, most scholars think we can in fact gain some knowledge about the historical Jesus.

f. "Historical Jesus" and "Jesus Tradition"

The remainder of this chapter will be devoted to an attempt to sift through the Gospel materials to identify the earliest components of the Jesus tradition and get as close as we can to an accurate portrayal of the historical Jesus. At a few points this will mean identifying specific events in his life that seem indisputable. More often it will mean identifying teachings and characteristic actions.

I would like, however, to add a note regarding my personal understanding of this attempt. If the Gospel writers understood their task as more analogous to preaching than to reporting, the same was undoubtedly true of those anonymous Christians who passed on the oral tradition before them. They told the stories of Jesus as a way of proclaiming his decisive importance in their lives and in the life of the world, not out of a neutral interest in bare facts. This means that the material we have is highly selective; the tradition passes on only what serves its purposes.

Thus my own view of life-of-Jesus research, one with which not all New Testament scholars or theologians agree, is that although it is legitimate to try to identify teachings and incidents that do in fact reflect the historical Jesus, there is a sense in which we never get "behind" tradition to the realm of neutral fact. The only Jesus we can know through historical research is the Jesus who is already part of his followers' proclamation.

But whether or not one distinguishes between the earliest tradition and the historical person Jesus, the fact remains that an oral tradition about his words and deeds preceded the written Gospels. And the task at hand is in any case to identify the oldest accounts of what he said and did. For all intents and purposes, the reader of the present text may treat the "historical Jesus" and the earliest level of the Jesus tradition as identical.

2. Jesus as Remembered: Words and Deeds

a. Identifying "Authentic" Teachings of Jesus

Recognizing that much of the teaching material attributed to Jesus in the Gospels belongs to later stages of the tradition, scholars have sought to develop criteria for identifying what is "authentic," that is, what actually comes from the historical Jesus himself. I will note five such criteria that many scholars accept.[1]

---

1. See the following for more extended discussions of criteria: Norman Perrin, *Rediscovering the Teachings of Jesus* (New York: Harper & Row, 1967), 39–49; John P. Meier, *A Marginal Jew: Re-*

(1) Environmental Appropriateness. Some passages can be ruled out immediately because they reflect an environment different from that of first-century Jewish Palestine, where Jesus lived. Mark 10:12, for example, presupposes the right of a woman to divorce her husband. Since Jewish law granted no such right to women, we must regard this verse as a later Hellenistic expansion of Mark 10:11, in which Jesus speaks on the question of whether a *man* may divorce his *wife*. We may thus speak of a criterion of environmental appropriateness. For most scholars, however, it functions only negatively, since not all material that could have come from first-century Palestine necessarily goes back to Jesus himself.

(2) Dissimilarity (or Distinctiveness). On the positive side, many scholars look to the "criterion of dissimilarity" as a way of establishing a core of relatively indisputable material. In their view, we can be certain a teaching comes from Jesus only if it is distinctive over against both first-century Judaism and early Christianity. Material that parallels early Christian theology could easily be the product of the early church. And material that is typical of Judaism could have come from some other Jewish teacher and only later have been attributed to Jesus.

This search for what is dissimilar is probably the only way to achieve relative certainty, but it entails a subtle prejudice. Jesus was, after all, a Jew; to rule out all passages paralleled in Judaism is to stack the cards in favor of a Jesus at odds with his own tradition. So the search for distinctive material should be bracketed by a recognition that Jesus must have shared much with his fellow Jews, however much he might have disagreed with some particular school on a given issue.

The matter is somewhat different when we come to parallels with early Christian theology. It is easy to imagine the postresurrection community reading its own faith back into Jesus' teachings. And it does in fact seem possible to distinguish between materials that reflect a distinctly postresurrection perspective and materials that do not. Even so, some scholars caution against assuming that Jesus' views were entirely different from those of the early Christian communities.

(3) Embarrassment. Closely related to the criterion of dissimilarity is that of embarrassment. Some scholars argue that there are some Gospel passages

---

or motifs that would have been so embarrassing to the early church that it is inconceivable that they are the product of invention.

(4) Coherence. Scholars who accept the criterion of dissimilarity sometimes supplement it with that of "coherence." Thus Norman Perrin argues that once one has established the characteristics of Jesus' teaching, "these character-istics can be used to validate sayings which themselves would not meet... the criterion of dissimilarity."[2] One can, in other words, include as authentic other material that is in some significant way similar to that which meets the stiffer requirements.

(5) Multiple Attestation. A final criterion is that of "multiple attestation." Scholars who use this test accept material as authentic if it appears in a cross-section of the sources and types of material that lie behind the Synoptic Gospels. It is more applicable to general themes than to specific segments of material. "We may say," Perrin comments, "that a motif which can be detected in a multiplicity of strands of tradition and in various forms (pronouncement stories, parables, sayings, etc.) will have a high claim to authenticity."[3]

b. The Parables of Jesus

Although the parable was common in Jewish teaching, the earliest layer of parable tradition in the New Testament exhibits a highly distinctive use of this form. The parables, in other words, tend to meet the criterion of dissimilarity; and many scholars believe that it is in the parables that we come closest to the original tradition regarding what Jesus taught.

Parables are on the surface simple stories; understanding them, however, is not a simplistic matter. So I begin with two uncomplicated examples as a way of getting an initial sense of what a parable is and what, according to the earliest tradition, Jesus taught.

(1) "The Treasure" (Matt. 13:44) and "the Pearl" (Matt. 13:45). Both of these parables make explicit reference to the "kingdom [Rule] of heaven," a circumlocution for "kingdom [Rule] of God." While not all of Jesus' parables and sayings are so explicit, there is something of a scholarly consensus that the announcement of God's Rule was central to Jesus' mission and that the

---

2. Perrin, *Rediscovering the Teachings of Jesus,* 43.
3. Ibid., 47.

Fig. 19. "Christ Preaching to the Poor" (Rembrandt Van Rijn; Dutch, 17th cent.)

saying in Mark 1:15 expresses a major component in his teaching: "The time is fulfilled, and the kingdom of God has come near."

In each of these two parables, God's Rule is the subject of a comparison; something that is known, because it is ordinary, reveals the character of the Rule, which is unknown in that it cannot simply be observed. We should be careful, however, about identifying what constitutes the point of comparison. Since Matthew 13:44 says that God's Rule is "like a treasure," it seems natural to think of the treasure itself as corresponding directly to that Rule. But 13:45 says the Rule is "like a merchant," when we would logically expect the *pearl* to be the point of comparison. Likewise the parable of the Sower in Matthew 13:24-30 presents God's Rule as like a person "who sowed good seed," whereas it is clearly not the sower but the whole situation described that corresponds to the Rule. In both the Pearl and the Treasure, then, it is the *action in the story,* not some individual element, that discloses something about the Rule of God.

A person, presumably by accident, finds a treasure in a field that belongs to someone else; and then, after hiding the treasure, goes and sells everything to buy the field. What does this story mean? To understand it *as parable,* we must get beyond questions based upon the story's literal meaning, such as whether it was moral to buy the field without telling the owner about the treasure. To grasp what is being said about God's Rule we must make an imaginative leap from the literal meaning to a metaphorical level. A parable is not an *example* story, and this story is not a lesson in business practice. Before we ask what the parable implies one should do, it is important to ask what happens to the character in the story.

The finder's normal way of planning and carrying out activities is, in the words of John Dominic Crossan, "rudely but happily shattered."[4] Something utterly unexpected and overwhelmingly good happens to this person, who goes joyfully to sell everything and buy the field. So what, then, does the parable invite us to say about the Rule of God? Perhaps that it interrupts, shatters everyday existence; that it is of such inestimable value and is the source of such unimaginable joy that those who encounter it will find themselves challenged to give their total selves to live within it.

A similar leap is required by the story of the Pearl. We should not be misled by the fact that the merchant was looking for pearls. Such a person would hardly have expected to find one so valuable as to demand selling everything to obtain it. Here again the Rule of God occurs as surprise. Like the Treasure, the Pearl is a parable of grace, in which God's Rule appears precisely as gift. Yet the gift demands a response, and a radical one at that. In the end, both parables call not only for imaginative interpretation but for imaginative action.

(2) Defining "Parable." There are several things we should note about these stories. First, they deal with common activities; they depict scenes ordinary people would recognize. Second, they command attention, partly through a note of extravagance: selling everything is extreme behavior! Later, we will see how some longer parables gain attention through vivid description. Third, these stories leave the reader somewhat puzzled about their exact meaning; that is why they demand an imaginative leap.

The indefiniteness of a parable is the clue to its mode of presenting meaning. Why does anyone tell such a story rather than simply stating what she or he means? In part because a vivid story captures the attention, but this is not the only reason. The fact is that we cannot reduce the meaning of a

---

4. John Dominic Crossan, *In Parables: The Challenge of the Historical Jesus* (New York: Harper & Row, 1973), 34.

parable to propositional statements, since that meaning depends to some extent upon who the hearers or readers are and the circumstances in which they live. Another interpreter might have derived somewhat different characteristics of God's Rule from the Pearl and the Treasure than I have. And the hearer/reader's concrete life situation will play a major role in determining what specific action God's Rule requires. It would seem, then, that one tells a parable precisely in order to *engage* those who hear it, to encourage people to make personal decisions and take action.

For this reason, it may be less meaningful to ask "what" a parable means than "how" it means—how it might affect a person's feelings and reasoning processes.[5] To state how a parable works would help define the parameters of its meaning without suggesting that the interpreter has found "the" meaning.

So what, then, is a parable, as exemplified in the earliest level of the Jesus tradition? In the classic definition of C. H. Dodd,

> At its simplest the parable is a metaphor or simile drawn from nature or the common life, arresting the hearer by its vividness or strangeness, and leaving the mind in sufficient doubt about its precise application as to tease it into active thought.[6]

Not all the stories called parables in the Gospels conform to this definition. Many of them are really allegories, and it is important to understand how they differ from parables. The individual elements in an allegory (characters, events, places) point outside the story to realities with which the hearers are already familiar. Thus the way to understand an allegory is to decode it piece-by-piece, i.e., figure out what person, event, etc. in the actual world each element in the story signifies.

A good example is Matthew 21:33-41: although introduced as a parable, it is clearly an allegory, as the following interpretation will show. A householder (God) plants a vineyard (a frequent symbol for Israel in the Jewish Scriptures) and then departs for another country. At harvest time, the householder sends a first set of servants (the early Hebrew prophets) to get his fruit, but the people reject and kill them; when a second set of servants (the later prophets) arrive, the people reject them also. Finally, the householder's own son (Jesus) appears; but he is killed (crucifixion) outside the vineyard (Golgotha, outside Jerusalem). Then the vineyard owner resolves to put the murderers to

---

5. James Breech, *The Silence of Jesus: The Authentic Voice of the Historical Man* (Philadelphia: Fortress Press, 1983), 134.

6. C. H. Dodd, *The Parables of the Kingdom*, rev. ed. (New York: Charles Scribner's Sons, 1961), 5.

death (the destruction of Jerusalem, 70 c.e.) and give their vineyard (Israel's relationship to God's Rule) to other tenants (the followers of Jesus).

When we come to the Gospel of Matthew, we will see evidence to confirm this allegorical reading. What is important at this point is to note that scholars do not generally accept allegories as authentic teachings of Jesus. They belong, in their present forms, to some later stage of tradition.

Despite a surface similarity, then, a parable is quite different from an allegory. Because a genuine parable demands acts of the imagination, it cannot be decoded. Its individual elements do not point to anything outside the story; these have no meaning except their contribution to the story itself. Thus a parable makes its point as a unified whole: one understands it not by mechanically translating it into other terms but by letting the story make an impact as an integrated totality. Neither the merchant nor the man in the field signifies anything or anyone in the "outside world"; each character is simply "everyone." The field, similarly, is a piece of furniture in the story—nothing more and nothing less. That is why one should beware of the simplistic equation, treasure = kingdom.

Study of the parables is complicated by the fact that many of them have been altered through transmission. Some have been turned into allegories or have been placed in contexts that invite allegorical interpretation. In other cases, the Gospel writers or those who transmitted the stories earlier have added interpretive comments. Thus sometimes we have to try to reconstruct the original form of a parable before we can interpret it as parable.

This procedure does not necessarily involve a value judgment; we can understand the instances of "tampering" with parables as ways of applying them to new situations. Nor is it absolutely impossible that some allegories belong to the earliest Jesus tradition. But materials such as Matthew 21:33-41 clearly presuppose the postresurrection situation. The safer course is to consider clearly allegorical elements secondary.

(3) "The Prodigal Son" (Luke 15:11-32). The disruption brought by the Rule of God in the preceding parables is occasion for undiluted joy. In some other parables, however, the matter is more complex; for God's Rule brings with it a disarming reversal of conventional expectations and values. Such a reversal is evident in the Prodigal Son.

To get the full impact of this story, we must imagine the response of someone who does not know the outcome. The character of the younger son, whom tradition has named the "prodigal," is a study in self-destruction: he demands what is not yet rightfully his, then wastes it in foolish ways; he reduces himself to a level where, tending ritually unclean beasts, he violates his religious heritage and his family's honor. He does nothing to deserve his father's approval, but in the end he receives not only acceptance but an extravagant welcome home. Ignoring social standards of dignity, the father actually runs to meet him and then lavishes gifts upon him. The older brother's reaction is understandable.

The author of Luke has placed the parable in a context that encourages allegorization of the father into a God-figure. Certainly the story itself asks the reader to imagine that God acts toward human beings as the father does toward the son, that is, in an accepting and forgiving way; but the allusion to God in verses 18 and 21[7] shows that the father does not signify God directly. To get the full shock of the story we need the reality of this human father's extreme behavior. Hearers need to feel the legitimacy of the older brother's reaction in order to have their own expectations shattered. But what specific expectations would be at work in a first-century Jewish audience? What metaphorical leaps would the hearers of this parable make?

Against the background of a proclamation of God's Rule, the story has the potential to convey unexpected acceptance by God. There were people in Jewish society who—sometimes because of the nature of their profession—led lives far beyond the boundaries of the demands of the Torah. Such persons, rejected by the community at large, would naturally identify with the younger son; to them the reversal of expectations and values would come as a word of overwhelming grace.

But some hearers, we can imagine, would hear the story differently. In fact, the parable has actually set the audience up for a negative response by its depiction of the extreme behavior of both the erring son and the father. Some among the religiously observant would naturally feel that, to the extent that the father's acceptance mirrors God's attitude toward the disobedient, the story makes a mockery of both divine justice and the demands of the Torah.

It is the genius of the parable, however, that it undermines this latter response by building it into the plot and subjecting it to criticism. Rather than rejoice in the return of his brother, the older son withdraws in resentment; he will not in fact name the younger as his brother, but refers to him as "this son of yours."

But resentment is not the only attitude the story holds open to the religiously observant. As Dan Via comments, "The father not only goes out to the prodigal son; he also goes out to the elder brother."[8] Reminded that he has always had access to his father's wealth and that the younger son is in fact

---

7. "Heaven" is a Jewish circumlocution for God.
8. Dan Otto Via, Jr., *The Parables: Their Literary and Existential Dimension* (Philadelphia: Fortress Press, 1967), 171.

his brother, the older son stands at a crossroads as the story closes: he can continue in resentment, or he can embrace his brother and come to know his father in a new way. Those who react negatively to the first part of the story face a similar choice. In the end, the parable offers grace to them no less than to those who thought themselves unacceptable.

Christian interpreters sometimes identify the attitude of the older brother as a specifically "Jewish" or "Pharisaic" form of "legalism," the view that human beings can merit divine acceptance by their own actions, apart from God's grace. But such interpretation is based upon an uncritical acceptance of the New Testament's negative presentation of the Pharisees, not upon anything we can learn from Jewish sources about the Pharisees or first-century Jews in general. Jewish teaching included an emphasis upon God's grace and forgiveness: there were clear provisions for the reacceptance of sinful persons into the community through repentance. And no Jew would have ever claimed that human beings earn God's favor.

The parable does, however, criticize a tendency common to any society and any religious community. And, as a story told in a Jewish context, it does so in Jewish terms. The note of extravagance circumvents the procedures associated with repentance in Judaism, such as making restitution for wrongs: the father accepts the erring son before he has a chance to do anything beyond the mere act of returning home in desperation. But the parable does not attack Jewish teaching; it proclaims the Rule of God as a gracious gift and, secondarily, undermines the attitude of resentment that prevents some people from understanding it as such.

(4) "The Workers in the Vineyard" (Matt. 20:1-16). It is generally agreed that the present ending of the Workers in the Vineyard was not part of the original story. This is true at least of v. 16, which is not an apt conclusion, since the order of payment ("last first") is not the point of the parable but a device to enable the early workers to observe the payment of the latecomers. It is a free-floating saying, found also in Mark 10:31, Luke 13:30, and Matthew 19:30; the author of Matthew must have added it as a way of fitting the parable into its present context. Some commentators exclude verses 14 and 15 from the original also, although most include the first half of 14. In any case, the story ends with a confrontation between the all-day workers and the landowner.

Just as it was necessary to feel the weight of the older brother's view in the Prodigal Son, so in the Workers in the Vineyard we need to experience the reasonableness of the full-day workers' complaints when the late-comers receive the same wage. Although the landowner fulfilled the contracts made with all the workers, "the parable's skillful strategy still maneuvers him into the appearance of injustice."[9] There is a profound sense in which the method of payment was unfair, and fair-minded persons in the audience can scarcely help but object. But the story undermines conventional expectations precisely by challenging a particular application of fairness as an adequate approach to the Rule of God, which appears, once again, as a gracious gift.

"The parable," Luise Schottroff writes, "has two focuses: the goodness of God and—as a consequence of this goodness—the solidarity of human beings."[10] The all-day workers miss the goodness of God precisely because they allow their sense of fairness to become a weapon to use against other human beings. Their comment, in fact, bristles with resentment: "you have made them equal to us who have borne the burden of the day and the scorching heat." The grumblers are, of course, ironically correct: all have, indeed, been made equal. And in that irony lies the parable's radical proclamation of the grace of God.

(5) "The Great Supper" (Luke 14:16-24). Another version of the Great Supper appears in Matthew 22:1-14. This parable is a convenient illustration of the process of allegorization, since Matthew's story contains some elements (vv. 7, 11-14) not found in Luke that make little sense as part of the plot. When the Matthean version is placed beside Matthew 21:33-41, which we examined above (pp. 109–10), one can easily see that it is a partial replay of that allegory. Even the Lukan version probably contains some editorial additions. The notation in 14:21 that the new guests are drawn from "the poor, the crippled, the blind, and the lame" (which is absent from Matthew) reflects a specific interest of the author of Luke in social outcasts. Nevertheless, the rich/poor contrast is implicit in the original; for it is only the affluent who are invited to banquets, and people rounded up at the last minute in the streets would almost certainly be poor.

When the story is stripped of its allegorical additions, we have once again a tale of the reversal of expectations: invited guests remain outside a banquet hall, while uninvited strangers sit at table! How might a first-century audience hear such a story? The socially acceptable and affluent would naturally identify with those originally invited but would be surprised that these characters

---

9. Bernard Brandon Scott, *Hear Then the Parable: A Commentary on the Parables of Jesus* (Minneapolis: Fortress Press, 1989), 297.

10. Luise Schottroff, "Human Solidarity and the Goodness of God," *God of the Lowly: Socio-Historical Interpretations of the Bible,* ed. Willy Schottroff and Wolfgang Stegemann, trans. Matthew J. O'Connell (Maryknoll, N.Y.: Orbis Books, 1984), 138.

make refusals. And, recognizing the banquet as a metaphor for the Rule of God, they would be deeply offended.

"There are those, on the other hand," Robert Funk comments,

> whose mouths water at the thought of so sumptuous a repast. They secretly aspire to be of sufficient social standing and affluence to be the recipients of invitations. But they know they will not be invited. . . . Only in fairy tales do beggars sit at the tables of aristocrats.[11]

Here again the Rule of God appears as a surprising and gracious gift, and here again we have the criticism of an attitude that prevents the recognition of that gift. In this parable, however, there is a particularly sharp social bite: it is the social standing of those originally invited that is their downfall. Preoccupied with other matters, they ultimately miss the feast that the rabble from the streets enjoy.

(6) "The Talents" (Matt. 25:14-30). The Gospel of Matthew presents the Talents as an allegory of the final judgment. This is evident not only from the context, but from v. 30, with its images of the agony of final punishment: "weeping and gnashing of teeth." That this phrase occurs at several other points in Matthew (Matt. 8:12, 22:13) but is absent from Luke's parallel parable (Luke 19:12-27) suggests that v. 30 is an addition by the Gospel author. Verse 29, also a free-floating saying,[12] must have been added before the author of Matthew received it, since it is found in Luke's story as well (Luke 19:26).

Originally, then, the parable ended with the master upbraiding the one-talent slave and taking away this hapless person's responsibilities. The story has nothing to do with the final judgment but is the account of someone who loses out on an opportunity. To make an appropriate leap to the metaphorical level, we must identify the cause of this loss.

Via finds this cause in the slave's self-defensive attitude, the refusal to take a risk.[13] Those who understand themselves as victims actually become victims of their own inability to act. The final scene shows simply that action and inaction have consequences. Those who refuse to make decisions find that time catches up with them. Metaphorically, in the context of Jesus' proclamation of God's Rule, the parable calls for decision and action even in the face of the risk that the advent of that Rule demands.

---

11. Robert W. Funk, *Language, Hermeneutic, and Word of God: The Problem of Language in the New Testament* (New York: Harper & Row, 1966), 191.

12. See Mark 4:25, Matthew 13:12, Luke 8:18.

13. Via, *The Parables,* 118ff.

(7) "The Unjust Manager" (Luke 16:1-9). If the Talents makes its impact through an image of tragic failure, the Unjust Manager does so through an image of success; and its impact is heightened through the shocking nature of its conclusion. Here again, tradition has added to the original parable. Verse 9 seems to be the attempt of the author of Luke to fit the story into its context, and the second half of v. 8 appears to be an earlier addition that comments on the first half of the verse. Scholars disagree as to whether the first part of v. 8 is original.

Either way, the story ends with a manager, who has been fired for either dishonesty or incompetence (it is not clear which), striking a bargain with the employer's creditors in order to have them as allies when things get tough—and at least getting away with it, if not actually receiving the employer's praise. How does a story like this proclaim the Rule of God? Clearly, not by offering a good example!

What the story does is to invite the hearer/reader to reflect upon the critical nature of the advent of God's Rule. The manager took action, which is precisely what the one-talent slave failed to do. But why so "shady" an image of resolute action? Why not rather a "good" steward, like the first two slaves in the Talents? The effect of the shadiness is to play up the radical character of the manager's action. As we will see more clearly in some of Jesus' *sayings*, the Rule of God demands action that goes beyond conventional piety, a kind of obedience that sometimes flies in the face of conventional practice.

(8) "The Good Samaritan" (Luke 10:29-37) and "the Yeast" (Matt. 13:33; Luke 13:20-21). Interpreters who accept the Good Samaritan as it stands in Luke generally understand it as an example story enjoining the hearer to imitate the action of the Samaritan. There is evidence, however, that both the introduction ("Jesus replied...") and the conclusion (v. 37) are attempts to fit the story into its Lukan context. The introductory question asks *whom one should consider neighbor*—i.e., who should *receive* neighborly acts—whereas the conclusion holds up the Samaritan as one who *acts* in a neighborly way. Neither introduction nor conclusion, moreover, picks up on the key point, which is the identity of the one who acts charitably: the Samaritan, archenemy of the Jew.

How would this parable affect first-century Jews? The first character to appear on the scene is the man who is beaten and robbed. The hearers, who know the treacherousness of the road from Jerusalem to Jericho, will have sympathy for him. They will view the priest and the Levite as potential heroes of the story and will feel shock and disappointment when these characters fail to show mercy to this unfortunate person. Bernard Scott notes that the hearers

Fig. 20.
The Good Samaritan
(Luke 10:29-37) (Asian)

will also be familiar with a standard triad of priest, Levite, and Israelite (i.e., a layperson or ordinary Jew), which signified the Jewish people as a whole. So perhaps they will now expect "an Israelite" to appear on the scene. But they will undoubtedly have thought of the victim as an Israelite, so that this role is no longer available. What happens instead is something they would never expect: a hated Samaritan enters the story, precisely as the hero.

Where does this leave the hearers? With whom can they identify in the story? Their only course at this point, Scott comments, "is to identify with the half-dead [the victim] and be saved by a mortal enemy or else to dismiss the narrative as not like real life."[14] To accept the Samaritan as hero, however, is to experience the disruption of one's routine ways of thinking. And it is precisely that point, according to Crossan, that the hearer is supposed to grasp with respect to the Rule of God: just as acceptance of the Samaritan turns one's world upside and shatters one's presuppositions, so does God's Rule "break abruptly into human consciousness and demand the overthrow of prior values, closed options, set judgments, and established conclusions."[15]

Crossan argues that the parable does not really teach mercy as a value but simply assumes it: the real point of the story is that God's Rule shat-

---

14. Scott, *Hear Then the Parable*, 201.
15. Crossan, *In Parables*, 65

ters conventional wisdom. The parable, however, does not stop with upsetting prior values but points forward to some specific qualities of life within God's Rule. As Robert Funk comments, the Samaritan acts in freedom from the constraints society imposes.[16] But this freedom is not utterly formless; it is freedom to risk an act of human love, unrestrained by society's prejudices. To accept the Samaritan as good is to acknowledge that God's Rule, in Scott's words, "does not separate insiders and outsiders on the basis or religious categories."[17] The hearer who has identified with the traveler in the ditch is in a position, if she or he can accept the Samaritan as "good," to enter that world of risk and freedom precisely through commitment to human solidarity.

There is a "scandalous" quality about the Good Samaritan that Scott finds also in the Yeast. In the ancient Mediterranean world, yeast or leaven was a metaphor for a corrupting influence (parallel to the proverbial "rotten apple" in our own culture). The parable thus creates the scandal of God's Rule appearing in the most unexpected context and subverts the audience's "dependency on the rules of the sacred, the predictability of what is good."[18]

One of the "rules" or boundaries that is shattered, in this reading of the Yeast, is the traditional attitude toward women. In symbolic terms, woman stood for impurity. So in comparing God's Rule to a woman's act of leavening dough, the parable attacks the patriarchal structure that was so integral a part of ancient civilization.

(9) A Psychological Reading. Some recent scholars have approached the parables through psychological criticism. Mary Ann Tolbert, for example, has proposed a Freudian reading of the Prodigal Son in which the characters in the story represent different facets of a human personality, much as they would in a dream. From this perspective, the father represents the ego, which must moderate between unrestrained desires (the id) and the constraints of society (the superego). The younger son images the id, while his older brother speaks for the superego. The father's acceptance of the younger son signifies an acceptance of sexuality, not, of course, in an utterly unrestrained form but "under the control, judgment, and mediation of the adult, the father in the parable."[19]

The father's final speech to the older brother indicates the role of the superego in the process of integration. This son, as far as we know, remains angry;

---

16. Funk, *Language, Hermeneutic, and Word of God,* 219.

17. Scott, *Hear Then the Parable,* 202.

18. Ibid., 328.

19. Mary Ann Tolbert, *Perspectives on the Parables: An Approach to Multiple Interpretations* (Philadelphia: Fortress Press, 1979), 104.

and we do not really hear of a change in the younger brother. Thus Tolbert concludes that the psychological integration remains partial, as it does in human experience. The parable "depicts the continuing conflict and attempt at resolution that form the basic fabric of everyday life" and expresses "the wish for harmony within, for unity no matter how partial nor how precarious."

The implication of Tolbert's reading is not that this is the sole meaning of the story or that first-century hearers would have consciously understood it in these terms. The point is that the story is capable of working in this fashion on peoples' subconscious minds. One could also argue that the self-integration Tolbert finds in the parable is at least partially correlative with reconciliation with that which lies outside the self. In fostering internal harmony, then, the psychological level of the story would in its own way contribute to that freedom to risk and love that parables seek on another level to bring about.

c. The Sayings of Jesus

Many sayings attributed to Jesus are paralleled in other Jewish literature of the time or reflect the interests of the early church. So we cannot be sure they belong to the earliest tradition. There are, however, enough sayings of distinctive character to give us a broad idea of the content of that earliest level. But because we find them in settings created by the Gospel writers or earlier collectors of tradition, we must take them completely out of context in order to interpret them.

(1) Paradox and Hyperbole: Sayings That "Jolt." Some of the most distinctive sayings are closely akin to the parables that jolt the hearer out of ordinary patterns of thought and action. Consider Mark 10:25: "It is easier for a camel to go through the eye of a needle than for someone who is rich to enter the [Rule] of God." This saying constituted a direct challenge to a standard theme in Jewish thought: that material well-being is a reward for righteousness and a sign of God's favor. Equally radical are the words of Luke 6:20-21, which may be close to the original version of the sayings known as the Beatitudes:

> Blessed are you who are poor, for yours is the [Rule] of God.
> Blessed are you who are hungry now, for you will be filled.
> Blessed are you who weep now, for you will laugh.

As F. W. Beare comments, "The Beatitudes put forward a conception of human blessedness which completely reverses all the values of any social order that ever existed."[20] We have seen such reversal in the parables, but its economic and social dimensions are even more prominent in the sayings we have just examined. For here we find a clear social radicalism that is neatly summarized in Mark 10:31: "many who are first will be last, and the last will be first." Those in a socially favored position in society tend to think of themselves as religiously and morally superior, as the parable of the Great Supper implies. According to these sayings, however, their attitude is among the expectations that are overturned in the Rule of God, which belongs most especially to the poor!

Reversal sayings such as these take the form of *antitheses*. As William Beardslee notes, however, an antithesis can become so sharp that it constitutes a *paradox*, such as Luke 17:33: "those who lose their life will keep it." This saying, Beardslee comments, jolts hearers out of their projects of making a continuity out of their lives, out of the normal human attempt to make rational sense of existence and plan for the future.[21] The greater part of human activity goes into survival, but according to this saying one finds survival only paradoxically: by losing one's life! How could anyone who tried to take such advice carry on the normal round of human activities?

The saying about the needle's eye makes its point through hyperbole— intentional exaggeration. The force of hyperbole becomes particularly clear in the sayings in Matthew 5:39-41:

> But if anyone strikes you on the right cheek, turn the other also; and if anyone wants to sue you and take your coat, give your cloak as well; and if anyone forces you to go one mile, go also the second mile.

The actions recommended here are so extreme as to be almost ridiculous. In the Mediterranean world, with its emphasis upon honor, a blow on the right cheek was the height of insult. And since the words for "coat" and "cloak" refer to the standard inner and outer garments, the second saying actually asks the hearers to give away their last possessions to people unkind enough to bring them to court.

The extreme nature of the commands prevents one from literalizing them. Life is full of complexities, but these sayings ignore such matters and give absolute, simplistic advice. Their effect is thus to force the hearers to exercise

---

20. F. W. Beare, *The Earliest Records of Jesus: A Companion to the Synopsis of the First Three Gospels by Albert Huck* (New York: Abingdon, 1962), 55.

21. William A. Beardslee, "Saving One's Life by Losing It," *Journal of the American Academy of Religion* 47 (1979): 67, and "Uses of the Proverb in the Synoptic Gospels," *Interpretation* 24 (1970): 61–73.

their moral imaginations, to question the patterns of revenge and self-concern that often motivate human behavior.[22]

(2) Ethical Content: The Parameters of "Open-Endedness." The parables and sayings we have seen challenge existing social and religious patterns; they remain open-ended, inviting people to use their own imaginations in making decisions. This is not to say that they give no direction at all. They in fact contain a decided moral content. The Good Samaritan calls the hearer to a freedom specifically to love, and the Workers in the Vineyard challenges the denial of human solidarity.

The saying on turning one's cheek is also a radical statement of human solidarity. The ethical content of the claim imposed by God's Rule, however, becomes clearest in the explicit injunction to love one's enemies:

> But I say to you, Love your enemies and pray for those who persecute you, so that you may be children of your Father in heaven; for he makes his sun rise on the evil and on the good, and sends rain on the righteous and on the unrighteous. For if you love those who love you, what reward do you have? Do not even the tax collectors do the same? And if you greet only your brothers and sisters, what more are you doing than others? Do not even the Gentiles do the same? (Matt. 5:44-47)

In its own way, this material too is disruptive of traditional values, which is evidence that it belongs to the earliest Jesus tradition. But it is not couched in antithetical form and does not resort to hyperbole. It is a straightforward command regarding one's dealings with other human beings.

It is less certain that the specific joining of the first commandment (love for God) with the injunction to love one's neighbor as it occurs in the Gospels (Mark 12:28-34; Matt. 22:34-40; Luke 10:25-27) belongs to the earliest tradition. There are "several near-contemporary Jewish summaries of the law which...juxtapose commands to love God and one's fellows." Nevertheless, it is only in the Synoptic stories that we find the specific link between Deuteronomy 6:5 and Leviticus 19:18.[23] And the command to love one's enemies is unparalleled in the entire ancient world.

There is thus no doubt that some form of a demand for love of one's human fellows, which permeates the New Testament, was a central component in the earliest Jesus tradition. But if we ask about moral regulations in a broader sense, we run into the problem of distinguishing earlier and later tradition,

---

22. Robert C. Tannehill, *The Sword of His Mouth* (Philadelphia: Fortress Press; Missoula, Mont.: Scholars Press, 1975), 69–70.

23. Victor Paul Furnish, *The Love Command in the New Testament* (Nashville: Abingdon, 1972), 62.

since the early church would have been inclined to produce such material to settle debates.

d. The Deeds of Jesus: General Activities

Those who originally followed Jesus told stories about what he did, as well as about what he said; for they understood his deeds as part of his mission. One must proceed somewhat differently in treating Jesus' deeds than in relation to his teachings, for only in a very few cases can we give solid evidence that a specific incident goes back to the earliest tradition. But there are some general activities that are deeply imbedded in the whole Jesus tradition: his healings and exorcisms, his association with "marginalized" people, and his maintenance of a group of disciples who shared his mission.

(1) Healings and Exorcisms. However one might choose to explain them, it is specifically the healings and exorcisms among the various miracles attributed to Jesus that scholars most often assign to the earliest tradition. The stories involving more elaborate wonders, such as walking on the water and stilling the storm, are generally viewed as belonging to a later phase. Some recent analysts have argued that the stories of healing and exorcisms are also late, but the majority hold that Jesus' earliest followers knew him as one who healed illnesses and cast out demons.

But what specific meaning would such actions have had in first-century Jewish Palestine? It is important, in beginning, to note what meaning it did not have. Modern people often think of a miracle as the suspension of the laws of nature. But ancient people did not have the concept of a rigid natural order that developed in the course of Western history—and that is now disintegrating under the weight of modern physics. Stories of miracle workers abounded in the ancient world in general and in Jewish culture as well. Jews were impressed with miraculous deeds but did not interpret them within the framework of a dualism of "the natural" and "the supernatural." It would therefore be erroneous to think that those who observed Jesus' amazing deeds would have somehow made the leap to later christological formulations and concluded that Jesus was a "divine" being.

People did consider miraculous works as manifestations of God's power, however. It is true that they were subject to more than one interpretation, as is clear from the apparent fact that some observers attributed Jesus' exorcisms to an evil power (Mark 3:21-27). Nevertheless, such deeds constituted evidence that those who performed them were emissaries of God. So, whatever other meaning Jesus' followers would have found in his powerful deeds, they must have understood them as attestations that he was in fact commissioned by God.[24]

It is also likely that they understood the exorcisms as signs that the Rule of God was breaking in; for in apocalyptic thought demons were agents of Satan, who held sway over the present age. And the view that through the exorcisms Jesus was breaking Satan's hold on the world is explicit in Luke 11:20: "But if it is by the finger of God that I cast out demons, then the [Rule] of God has come to you."

We should not, however, assume that those who told the stories of the exorcisms understood them in an exclusively other-worldly way. Jews who believed that Satanic power ruled the present world order would have viewed the Roman presence in their land as a manifestation of that power. Thus when the demon in Mark 5:1-13 identifies itself as "legion," a designation for Roman troops, the natural inference is that in breaking the power of demons Jesus is breaking that of Rome as well.

(2) Association with "Marginalized" People. The Gospels abound with stories of Jesus' associations with "marginalized" people, those denied full participation in society. His opponents ridicule his friendship with "sinners and prostitutes" and "sinners and tax collectors." The Beatitudes (Luke 6:20-22) and other sayings link Jesus with the hungry, the poor, and the miserable, as his healings do with the physically infirm. Some recent scholars doubt various aspects of this traditional picture,[25] but there is wide agreement that Jesus did attract people who were for one reason or another considered outcasts.

Marginalization was in part the result of economic factors: people were often forced into dishonorable professions by adverse circumstances. The story of Zacchaeus (Luke 19) has taught us to view tax collectors as rich, but most of those "who did the actual work were impoverished, or were slaves employed by a 'tax agency,' and quickly dismissed if problems arose."[26] The reality of economic distress is reflected in the fact that when speaking of "the poor" the Synoptic tradition regularly uses the Greek term for the destitute rather than that for the relatively poor. We have no reason to view this terminology as exaggeration. There is strong evidence of abject poverty and homelessness throughout the Roman Empire and in Jewish Palestine

---

24. E. P. Sanders, *Jesus and Judaism* (Philadelphia: Fortress Press, 1985), 157–73.

25. Richard A. Horsley, *Jesus and the Spiral of Violence: Popular Jewish Resistance in Roman Palestine* (Minneapolis: Fortress Press, 1993), 212–17.

26. Elisabeth Schüssler Fiorenza, *In Memory of Her: A Feminist Theological Reconstruction of Christian Origins* (New York: Crossroad, 1983), 127.

specifically, brought on by a combination of crop failures and insensitive government policy.[27]

In the ancient Middle East, to be a woman was in and of itself to experience marginalization. It is thus a remarkable feature of the Jesus tradition that it continually depicts Jesus in the company of women, without any hint that he shared the traditional restrictions regarding male-female contact and the role of women. We have already seen that in subtle ways the teachings of Jesus reflect this attitude of openness.

(3) Maintenance of Disciples. Not only does the Jesus tradition make constant reference to a group of disciples surrounding Jesus, but the very existence of that tradition is incomprehensible apart from the activities of such a body. The Gospels also speak of an inner circle of twelve. Although there are slight discrepancies in the lists of names, Paul's citation (1 Cor. 15:5) of an early testimony mentioning this group suggests that the tradition about such an inner circle goes back to the earliest level, whether or not the membership was stable.

The Synoptic accounts of the week before Jesus' death include a story of a final meal with the Twelve, during which Jesus institutes the later Christian cultic meal: the Lord's Supper, or Eucharist. Scholars disagree on several points: the extent to which later worship practices have been read back into this event; whether it really was a Passover meal as the Synoptic texts claim; and whether such an event actually took place at all. Most scholars acknowledge, however, that the story does at least reflect the memory that Jesus and his disciples shared fellowship meals during his ministry, a memory also reflected in the stories of the miraculous feedings (Mark 6:30-44, 8:1-10).

In the context of a proclamation of God's Rule, such meals carried a specific meaning. Jewish tradition frequently imaged the Age to Come as a great banquet. Sometimes it is God who presides at the banquet, but in other traditions, notably the Qumran literature, the Messiah assumes this function. Either way, the banquet has "messianic" implications. It symbolizes life free from want, injustice, and suffering, life that is in some sense a restoration of Paradise, the Garden of Eden. Like the cultic meals at Qumran, the meals shared by Jesus and his followers must in some way have symbolized the joy of the Rule of God.

The tradition regarding these meals also said something very specific about life in that Rule. For if we take the parable of the Great Supper as mirroring

---

27. Luise Schottroff and Wolfgang Stegemann, *Jesus and the Hope of the Poor,* trans. Matthew J. O'Connell (Maryknoll, N.Y.: Orbis Books, 1986), 16–17.

Fig. 21. Dining Table for Passover meal. The diners reclined on mats or couches while eating (the Greek word used here can also refer to lying in bed). The couches were arranged around three sides of the table. The servants had access from the fourth side.
(Photo by Dennis Hamm)

Jesus' own practice, then it is apparent that the gatherings involved a mixture of social classes. And, according to Crossan, it is precisely this mixture, rather than the presence of the poor in and of itself, that was so distinctive—and so offensive. For it was an outright violation the Mediterranean system of honor and shame, with its distinctions based on class, rank, and sex. What would respectable people say about someone who hosted such inclusive affairs? "He makes . . . no appropriate distinctions and discriminations. He has no honor. He has no shame."[28]

e. Jesus and the Jewish Law: Deeds and Teachings

One finds in the New Testament several accounts of Jesus' conflicts with the Pharisees over observance of the Jewish law, most notably because of his

---

28. John Dominic Crossan, *The Historical Jesus: The Life of a Mediterranean Jewish Peasant* (San Francisco: HarperSanFrancisco, 1991), 262.

practice of healing on the Sabbath. In Mark 7:15, moreover, we have a saying that seems to undercut the entire system of dietary regulations: "There is nothing outside a person that by going in can defile, but the things that come out are what defile." Not surprisingly, scholars frequently argue that Jesus disagreed pointedly with the Pharisees' interpretation of the law and/or actually spoke against the law itself.

Not all interpreters are convinced of the authenticity of Mark 7:15, however, and some recent analysts have argued that Jesus' healings did not constitute work and therefore were not violations of the Sabbath law.[29] In any case, scholars have long held that most of the stories of Jesus' conflicts with opponents are products of the later tradition, constructed to give concrete illustration to specific points. The early Christian communities probably came into more serious conflict with the Pharisees than did Jesus himself, and to some extent they projected these conflicts back into the time of Jesus.

There is, however, one account of Jesus' teaching that does suggest a willingness to forego the demands of the law in some instances. The statement in Matthew 8:22/Luke 9:60—"let the dead bury their own dead"—is simply astonishing. For, as Norman Perrin comments, "In Judaism the responsibility for burying the dead was one that took precedence over all other duties enjoined in the law."[30] We see here once again a radicalism found in some parables and other sayings. Jesus presents the demands of God's Rule not only as all-encompassing but as requiring a response that flies in the face of certain standard expectations.

It would be absurd to conclude from this one passage that the earliest tradition remembered Jesus as opposing the Torah itself. Perhaps the saying on burying the dead is an indication that in God's Rule the law would in some way be transformed.[31] It is also possible that Jesus and his earliest followers appealed to a "popular tradition," as opposed to the "official tradition" of the established leadership groups.[32] But there is no real basis for concluding that he rejected the law as such.

The question of Jesus' conflict with the Pharisees is related to the tradition regarding his association with marginalized persons. Scholars have generally assumed that his contact with members of the lower classes offended the Pharisees' standards of ritual purity, basing their view on materials such as

---

29. Geza Vermes, *Jesus the Jew: A Historian's Reading of the Gospels* (Philadelphia: Fortress Press, 1981), 25, and Sanders, *Jesus and Judaism*, 266.

30. Perrin, *Rediscovering the Teachings of Jesus* (New York: Harper & Row, 1967), 144.

31. Sanders, *Jesus and Judaism*, 267, suggests that Jesus did not think of the Mosaic law as final.

32. See Richard A. Horsley, *Sociology and the Jesus Movement* (New York: Crossroad, 1989), 136, who makes this suggestion in relation to the Jesus movement, or early Palestinian Christianity.

Mark 7:1-8. This passage combines an argument between Jesus and the Pharisees, over the fact that his disciples do not observe certain rites surrounding meals, with a description of the Pharisees' purity rules. Sanders argues, however, that Jews who adhered to extreme purity regulations were consciously taking upon themselves obligations that normally belonged only to priests. They were going far beyond the Torah itself and did not expect other Jews to follow suit.[33] It is therefore uncertain whether the earliest tradition remembered the Pharisees as attacking Jesus for associating with persons considered ritually impure.

Wholly apart from the question of the Pharisees, however, the diversity of the Jesus tradition shows that the earliest Christians were sharply divided among themselves on the question of where Jesus stood regarding the ritual aspects of the Jewish law. It is thus important to ask about the source of these differing opinions. According to Crossan, the only reasonable explanation is that he simply ignored them because "he did not care enough about such ritual laws to attack or to acknowledge them."[34] But that is still not to say that Jesus simply rejected the Torah.

f. Specific Incidents: Baptism, Action in the Temple, Death

There are a few accounts of specific incidents in the Gospels that scholars regard as indisputably historical, since the early church would have had no conceivable motive for inventing them. Although the accounts that we have of these incidents in the New Testament are the products not of neutral observation but of theological interpretation, it is reasonably certain that actual events stand behind them.

One of these events is Jesus' baptism by John the Baptist. Such elements in the Gospel accounts as the voice from heaven and the descent of the dove are probably added by tradition, but there can be little doubt that Jesus was actually baptized by John. For, as Matthew 3:14-15 reveals, the church was somewhat embarrassed by the memory of the event and sought to explain it. Many scholars take the baptism story as evidence that Jesus began as a disciple of John and then moved out on his own. This may in fact be the historical truth, but Christian tradition makes John a self-conscious forerunner of Jesus and understands the baptism as a kind of divine commissioning for Jesus' mission.

---

33. Sanders, *Jesus and Judaism*, 264–67. Sanders also contends that it is not absolutely certain that the Pharisees were actually *ḥaberim*, that is, persons who took upon themselves extraordinary regulations regarding purity.

34. Crossan, *The Historical Jesus*, 263.

Another indisputable event is Jesus' death on a cross. No group who understood the stigma of crucifixion in the Roman world would have invented such a story about their hero. The reason for Jesus' execution, however, is a matter of dispute. It is clear that it was the Romans who actually put him to death: it was they and not the Jews who used crucifixion as a means of capital punishment. The Gospels also implicate the Jewish leaders, but it is evident that the New Testament writers went to some lengths to shift the blame from the Romans to the Jews. Considerable disagreement remains as to precisely how and why Jesus came to die.

Some scholars have argued that the Pharisees instigated a plot against Jesus because of his views on the law. Whether or not Jesus came into significant conflict with the Pharisees over his teaching, it is improbable that the latter had the power to manipulate the legal system for their ends. Nor is it likely that conflict over fine points in the law or tradition would have constituted grounds for handing him over to the Romans for execution. It is significant, finally, that the Pharisees are almost entirely absent from the Gospel accounts of the events leading to Jesus' death.

Why, then, did Jesus die? According to Sanders, if we ask what among the things we know about Jesus could have led to his arrest, the obvious answer lies in another event with a strong claim to historicity: Jesus' disruption of the activity in the temple court (Mark 11:15-19).[35] To strike at the temple was to strike at the very heart of the established sociopolitical and religious power structure.

If we ask who would have had both the motive and the means to move against Jesus after this event, the answer has to be the priestly aristocracy. Why was Jesus a threat to them? For the same reason that he was a threat to the Roman occupation government. Not because he taught a particular doctrine about the law and not because he had an army that could have threatened the Roman legions. He was a threat in general terms because his proclamation of the Rule of God had the potential to create a public disturbance by raising "messianic" expectations. And his assault on the temple made the threat concrete. The Romans had no desire to deal with yet another popular uprising. And any unrest among the populace could only damage the positions of those among the Jews whose measure of authority depended upon the Romans' good graces.

The Gospel accounts of both these events, the action in the temple and the crucifixion, are heavily overlaid with theological interpretation. But behind the accounts lie genuinely historical incidents that can provide some insight

---

35. Sanders, *Jesus and Judaism*, 301–2.

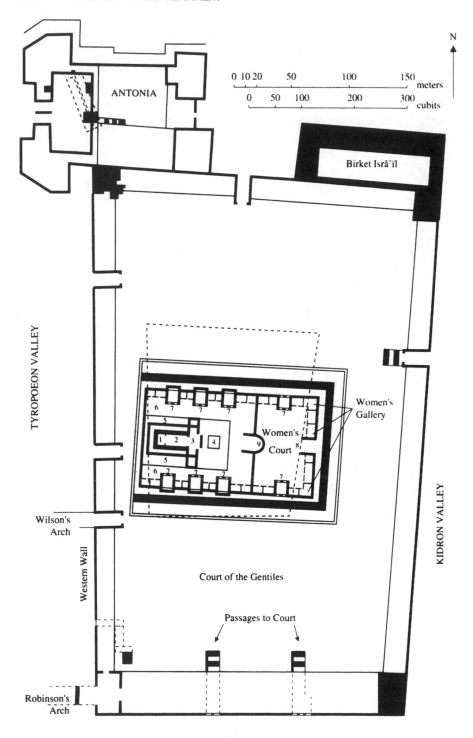

Fig. 22. Map of Temple. *(Map by Parrot Graphics)*

into how those who followed Jesus during his lifetime must have understood what he meant by the Rule of God.

g. Jesus, the Rule of God, and the Future

The proclamation of God's Rule was central to Jesus' mission. But what did the Rule of God mean? Was it still in the future or already present? Was it to come into the public, communal world of social and political structures, or into the experience of the individual? Would it bring the "end of the world"? And what was the relationship between the message about God's Rule and the person who brought that message? How, in other words, did the earliest tradition understand Jesus himself? I have delayed these difficult questions to give readers a chance to form their own impressions from the primary data, but it is important now to attempt some partial answers.

(1) Present or Future? Critical scholars are unanimous on one point: the earliest tradition does not speak of the Rule of God as something in the *distant* future. Here the agreement ends, however. Some scholars maintain that in this tradition God's Rule is expected in the immediate future, while others think it is understood as already present. A mediating position is that it is in the process of realization—as beginning to break in, but not yet fully realized.

The question is complicated by a point Crossan has emphasized. The notion of God's Rule was present not only in apocalyptic but also in wisdom literature, in which it signified not a future hope but God's ongoing Rule of the world, into which the individual can enter at any time "by wisdom or goodness, by virtue, justice, or freedom."[36] Crossan therefore argues that although (under the influence of John the Baptist) Jesus began as an apocalyptic preacher, he eventually turned away from this perspective in favor of the *always*-present Rule of God as envisioned in the wisdom tradition.[37]

A further complication is that a few scholars have denied that Jesus taught about the Rule of God at all. Burton L. Mack interprets Jesus along the lines of a Cynic sage, considering almost all elements in the Jesus tradition that are specifically Jewish to be secondary.[38] The vast majority of scholars, however, consider the Rule of God to have been central to Jesus' teaching.

---

36. Crossan, *The Historical Jesus*, 292.

37. Ibid., 235–38.

38. Burton L. Mack, *A Myth of Innocence: Mark and Christian Origins* (Minneapolis: Fortress Press, 1988), 67–74; also Burton L. Mack, *The Lost Gospel: The Book of Q and Christian Origins* (San Francisco: HarperSanFrancisco, 1993).

An answer to the question of present and future depends to some extent upon which materials one assigns to the earliest tradition, but also upon how one interprets the language employed in those materials. The present book sides with those scholars who think the heavily apocalyptic passages attributed to Jesus in the Gospels are products of later tradition. It is also influenced by the view that we should not force the language about God's Rule into a rigidly literal mold. Thus, particularly with respect to the parables, I am inclined to view this Rule as in some sense already present for those who are open to it.

Nevertheless, there are elements with strong claim to authenticity that seem to involve a future expectation. Consider, for example, the third Beatitude, Luke 6:21: "Blessed are you that weep now, for you will laugh." Certainly the blessing is available in the present, but the future tense indicates that something is yet to come. Similarly, the petition "Your kingdom come" in the Lord's Prayer (Matt. 6:10) seems to contain an irreducibly futuristic element. While Crossan and some other scholars believe the prayer is an early Christian summary rather than the actual words of Jesus, they do think it is based closely upon Jesus' teachings. And although Crossan interprets this petition in a nonapocalyptic way, it is not clear that he is correct in doing so.

The earliest level of the Jesus tradition did embrace a wisdom element, and it does seem to have contained the notion of a Rule of God that was already present in human experience. I find it difficult to deny, however, that it also contained a futuristic component. So perhaps the mediating position mentioned earlier is about as close as we can come to a resolution of the problem: for the first followers of Jesus, God's Rule was in the process of realization.

(2) Individual or Communal? To the extent that one understands the Rule of God as present for Jesus' first followers, one will also tend to see it as a matter of the individual's experience. Conversely, futuristic interpretations tend toward an understanding of that Rule as communal, or publicly observable. These issues converge in the consideration of a key saying that clearly denies the practice, typical of the apocalyptic outlook, of calculating the coming of God's Rule by observing historical events: "The kingdom of God is not coming with things that can be observed; nor will they say, 'Look, here it is!' or 'There it is!' For, in fact, the kingdom of God is among you" (Luke 17:20-21). Granted a critical attitude toward apocalyptic *speculation,* the question is whether this saying envisions God's Rule as already present in the individual's experience or as a future reality that will one day be "visible" to all. Some interpreters have understood the passage in a highly individualistic way on the basis of a translation of the closing phrase as *"within* you." Most recent scholars, however, understand that phrase to mean "among you," or "in your midst," i.e., in the social-communal setting in which you live.

But does this saying mean that God's Rule is understood as now present among the people, and therefore experienced by individuals, or does the present tense refer to a future time when it will be present? It is difficult to tell. It is reasonable, however, in light of the preceding discussion, to interpret it in this way: individuals are able to experience in the present the power of God's Rule, which will soon be publicly visible.

(3) The "End of the World"? What would the coming order be like? Would it be in heaven or on earth? Would the disruption it brought be historical, or of cosmic proportions? Would it involve the resurrection of the dead, a final judgment, and eternal life for the righteous? Answers to these questions hinge to some extent upon whether one believes that the earliest tradition contained an apocalyptic element, and upon how one chooses to interpret that element. Given the rapidity with which the early Christians adopted a fully apocalyptic outlook, it is difficult to deny that some of the apocalyptic material belongs to the earliest level. To say this, however, does not answer the crucial question of precisely how the apocalyptic language was intended. Richard Horsley has recently made a strong case for understanding it in a highly metaphorical way.[39]

One indication that the Rule of God in the earliest tradition did not refer to a heavenly reality disconnected from the present earthly sphere is to be found in a saying (Matt. 19:28) that assigns to the disciples the task of "judging" the twelve tribes of Israel, which should be understood in the sense of "doing justice for," or even "liberating" them.[40] Sanders makes much of this point in arguing that Jesus' mission was a Jewish renewal movement that expected the "restoration" of Israel in the eschatological age.[41] That is to say, the earliest level of tradition apparently understood God's Rule as involving, in some sense, the reestablishment of the nation of Israel. We should therefore not imagine that Jesus gathered disciples to assign them work that would be swept away when the new age had come. If his mission had to do with the renewal of Israel, then we must assume that the renewed society was supposed to continue in the new order, that it *was* in fact *to be* the new order.

That Jesus did not understand the Rule of God as a purely heavenly reality is also indicated by the circumstances surrounding his death. Not only does

---

39. Horsley, *Jesus and the Spiral of Violence,* 167–77.
40. Ibid., 203–5.
41. Sanders, *Jesus and Judaism,* 90–119.

his execution show that the existing power structure saw political implications in his movement, but his action in the temple suggests that he did also. This does not mean that he intended to lead a rebellion against Rome; there is no evidence that he gathered an army. His assault on the temple was clearly a symbolic act, foreshadowing the expected activity of God. But it does suggest that the Rule that God was bringing necessarily meant an end to the present political order and the establishment of a new one on this earth.

I do not mean to deny that in the earliest tradition Jesus and his followers envisioned the eventual resurrection of the dead and a final judgment or that a "heavenly" reality would somehow be superimposed upon the earthly. But it appears that they did not think of God's Rule in abstraction from the ancient hopes of Israel, the human longing for peace and justice, and the specific desire of the poor for vindication. Whatever else their hope entailed, what they worked and prayed for most immediately was an environment in which the traditional barriers between rich and poor, between the acceptable and the outcast, between men and women, were obliterated, and in which one's love for God was expressed through solidarity with one's neighbor.

(4) Jesus in the Tradition. What role did Jesus himself play in his disciples' understanding? They apparently did not apply explicitly "messianic" titles to him during his lifetime, but they almost certainly understood him as fulfilling "messianic" functions in the broader sense. It is clear that Jesus appears in the earliest tradition as one with special authority, as the final messenger before the full establishment of God's Rule. And it is likely that his first followers believed that he would play a special role within the new order.

It is also clear that these followers believed that Jesus enjoyed a special relationship to God. This is evident in the memory, preserved at a few points in the New Testament (Mark 14:36, Rom. 8:15, Gal. 4:6), that Jesus called God *abba,* an Aramaic term by which children addressed their fathers and which carried the connotation of "*dear* Father," or even "Daddy." Joachim Jeremias claims that such usage was unique to Jesus, but Geza Vermes argues that it was typical of Galilean charismatics.[42] Either way, it suggests a sense of special closeness between Jesus and God without implying the notion of a "divine nature" that was characteristic of later christology.

It should be emphasized that if Jesus' first followers thought of him as having a special relationship to God, their interest was not in that relationship as a matter of speculation but in what it meant for them. They felt themselves

---

42. Joachim Jeremias, *The Prayers of Jesus,* trans. John Bowden and Christoph Burchard (Philadelphia: Fortress Press, 1978) 11–65; Vermes, *Jesus the Jew,* 210–13.

drawn into that relationship; they, too, could address God as *abba*. Questions regarding Jesus' metaphysical nature would not have been to the point. What mattered was that they believed they were actually experiencing, in this person's words and deeds, the beginnings of the Rule of God.

h. Summary and Conclusion: "Radical Grace/Radical Demand"

"The time is fulfilled, and the [Rule] of God has come near." Many scholars regard this proclamation, attributed to Jesus in Mark 1:14, as an accurate summary of what he actually taught. In any case, for those who first followed Jesus the Rule of God was indeed breaking in: it was experienced in his fellowship meals and manifest in his association with outcasts.

The Rule of God was coming, on the one hand, as surprise and gift, reversing human expectations and traditional standards of acceptability. But it also brought with it a call to risky and courageous action, action offensive to the social and religious sensibilities of many sincere people, action that challenged accepted forms of authority. Herbert Braun therefore summarizes the teachings of Jesus in the succinct formula, radical grace/radical demand.[43] The announcement of God's rule was a proclamation of grace because it offered acceptance by God precisely as a gift; yet it was, paradoxically, a message of radical demand, since what it asked of those who responded was nothing less than total commitment.

For the Jews who first followed Jesus, to accept the announcement of God's Rule meant experiencing the disruption of their former lives, but it did not mean denying their Jewish religion, their Jewish god, or their Jewish law. They heard Jesus' words as they would have heard a Hebrew prophet who spoke on behalf of God's covenant with Israel. They found in his presence an energizing, renewing power. And they received the hope that Jesus brought precisely as a renewal of *the hope of Israel,* the hope that God's ancient promises to their ancestors, Abraham and Sarah, were now to be fulfilled.

But was this hope in fact fulfilled? Those who followed Jesus presumably experienced a renewal in their personal lives and in their fellowship groups that they understood as the power of God's Rule. But what they had hoped for on the public and observable level simply did not take place. Jesus suffered a painful and humiliating death. The world did not change in any visible way: Rome continued its brutal rule, and the suffering of the oppressed remained unrelieved.

---

43. Herbert Braun, "The Meaning of New Testament Christology," *Journal of Theology and Church* 5 (1968): 89–127.

What Jesus' followers had hoped for did not take place. But, as we will see, the movement he initiated was nevertheless able to survive. It is important to ask how.

STUDY QUESTIONS

1. In what sense did the early church understand the four Gospels as of "apostolic" origin?

2. Explain the terms "Synoptic Gospels" and "Synoptic problem."

3. Explain the "two-document" and the "two-Gospel" hypotheses.

4. What criteria do scholars use in determining the authentic teachings of Jesus (or the earliest level of the Jesus tradition)? Are there any problems entailed in the use of these criteria?

5. What is a parable, and how does a parable differ from an allegory?

6. What do the parables of the Treasure and the Pearl teach about the Rule of God?

7. Illustrate each of the following themes by references to specific parables: reversal, demand, freedom, grace. In what sense are the parables "scandalous"?

8. What specific types of deeds seem to belong to the earliest level of the Jesus tradition? How do these deeds complement the teachings attributed to Jesus in the earliest tradition?

9. Did Jesus come into conflict with the Pharisees? What are the problems entailed in answering this question?

10. What are the three specific events presented in the Gospels that most scholars view as most certainly historical? How would you respond to someone who says, "The Jews crucified Jesus"?

11. Does the earliest tradition present the Rule of God as present or as future? As individual or as communal? Does it present that Rule as the "end of the world"?

12. Show how the formula "radical grace/radical demand" does or does not adequately summarize the content of Jesus' ministry.

FOR FURTHER READING

Aulen, Gustaf. *Jesus in Contemporary Historical Research*. Trans. Ingallil H. Hjelm. Philadelphia: Fortress Press, 1976. A good, readable summary of early twentieth-century research.

Borg, Marcus. *Jesus: A New Vision: Spirit, Culture, and the Life of Discipleship.* New York: HarperCollins, 1987. An accessible characterization of Jesus against the background of Jewish spirituality.

———. *Meeting Jesus Again for the First Time.* San Francisco: HarperSanFrancisco, 1994. Presents Jesus as a charismatic wisdom teacher and social prophet and reflects on the significance of this portrait for Christian faith.

Bornkamm, Günther. *Jesus of Nazareth.* Trans. Irene and Fraser McLuskey with James M. Robinson. New York: Harper & Row, 1960; enlarged edition, Minneapolis: Fortress Press, 1995. For many years considered the "standard" treatment of Jesus by a critical scholar.

Breech, James. *The Silence of Jesus: The Authentic Voice of the Historical Man.* Philadelphia: Fortress Press, 1983. Interesting reading, but in my estimation forces Jesus into the mold of a modern existentialist.

Crossan, John Dominic. *In Parables: The Challenge of the Historical Jesus.* New York: Harper & Row, 1973. Subtle, but readable; an excellent work.

———. *The Historical Jesus: The Life of a Mediterranean Peasant.* San Francisco: HarperSanFrancisco, 1991. An exhaustive study, drawing upon recent insights from a variety of perspectives. Detailed but engaging; characterizes Jesus' view of God's Rule as informed by the wisdom tradition as known among the peasant class. An important contribution.

Dodd, C. H. *The Parables of the Kingdom.* Rev. ed. New York: Charles Scribner's Sons, 1961. An essential work; basic to later studies of the parables. A classic.

Farmer, William R. *The Synoptic Problem: A Critical Analysis.* New York: Macmillan, 1964. A history of the Synoptic problem with a critique of the two-document hypothesis in favor of the two-Gospel hypothesis.

———. *Jesus and the Gospel: Tradition, Scripture, and Canon.* Philadelphia: Fortress Press, 1982. Traces the history of the Gospel tradition from Jesus to the closing of the canon; challenges the two-source hypothesis.

Horsley, Richard A. *Jesus and the Spiral of Violence: Popular Jewish Resistance in Roman Palestine.* San Francisco: Harper & Row, 1987; paperback edition, Minneapolis: Fortress Press, 1993. Employs sociological methods and interprets Jesus against the background of Jewish resistance movements. An important study that challenges many standard assumptions.

Jeremias, Joachim. *The Parables of Jesus.* Rev. ed. Trans. S. H. Hooke. New York: Charles Scribner's Sons, 1963. An essential work, basic to later studies. Important for reconstruction of parables and recognizing allegorical elements. A classic.

Mack, Burton L. *A Myth of Innocence: Mark and Christian Origins.* Minneapolis: Fortress Press, 1988. Interprets Jesus along the lines of a Cynic sage, with only a thin relationship to Judaism and the Christianity that developed after his death.

———. *The Lost Gospel: The Book of Q and Christian Origins.* San Francisco: HarperSanFrancisco, 1993. A reconstruction and translation of the hypothetical document Q, followed by a discussion of Christian origins. See preceding entry.

Meier, John P. *A Marginal Jew: Rethinking the Historical Jesus.* Vol. 1: *The Roots of the Problem and the Person;* vol. 2: *Rethinking the Historical Jesus.* New York: Doubleday, 1991, 1994. Thorough, competent, and highly readable; an important work. Includes the best contemporary treatment of questions of particular interest to Roman Catholic readers.

Perrin, Norman. *Rediscovering the Teachings of Jesus.* New York: Harper & Row, 1967. A key work, in terms of both content and method.

Perkins, Pheme. *Hearing the Parables of Jesus.* New York: Paulist, 1981. A nontechnical but solid treatment, including interesting attempts at contemporary application.

Sanders, E. P. *Jesus and Judaism.* Philadelphia: Fortress Press, 1985. A major contribution to life-of-Jesus research. Interprets Jesus in terms of Jewish restoration eschatology. Important for correcting the view of Jesus as at odds with his Jewish heritage.

————. *The Historical Figure of Jesus.* London and New York: Penguin, 1993. A more broadly focused and less technical treatment by the author of *Jesus and Judaism.*

Schweitzer, Albert. *The Quest of the Historical Jesus: A Critical Study of its Progress from Reimarus to Wrede.* 3d ed., with a new introduction by the author. Trans. W. Montgomery. London: A. & C. Black, 1954. The classic treatment of an early period of life-of-Jesus research and speculation.

Scott, Bernard Brandon. *Hear Then the Parable: A Commentary on the Parables of Jesus.* Minneapolis: Fortress Press, 1989. A major work; thorough and comprehensive. Contains a wealth of helpful background material on each parable. Interpretations sometimes overly subtle in my estimation. Excellent bibliography.

Streeter, B. H. *The Four Gospels: A Study of Origins.* Rev. ed. London: Macmillan, 1930. Chapter 8 contains the classic statement of an early version of the two-source hypothesis.

Tolbert, Mary Ann. *Perspectives on the Parables: An Approach to Multiple Interpretations.* Philadelphia: Fortress Press, 1979. Theoretical investigation of the problem of multiple interpretations.

Vermes, Geza. *Jesus the Jew: A Historian's Reading of the Gospels.* New York: Macmillan, 1973. A treatment by a Jewish scholar interpreting Jesus against the background of Galilean charismatics. An important contribution.

————. *The Religion of Jesus the Jew.* Minneapolis: Fortress Press, 1993. Explains the author's previous work with close attention to Jesus' preaching.

Via, Dan Otto. *The Parables: Their Literary and Existential Dimension.* Philadelphia: Fortress Press, 1967. A good, solid treatment. The methodological section is complex, but the interpretations are highly readable.

Wilson, William Riley. *The Execution of Jesus: A Judicial, Literary and Historical Investigation.* New York: Charles Scribner's Sons, 1970. A sound treatment, arguing that Jesus did not intend to lead a rebellion against Rome and that attempts to blame the Pharisees or the Jewish people as a whole for Jesus' death are not supported by the evidence.

Chapter 4

The Resurrection Faith
and the Expanded Tradition

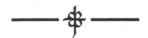

1. Christianity in Transition

The Christianity that eventually became a major force in the Roman Empire
was the result of several stages of development in various geographical loca-
tions and cultural settings. For the early Christians naturally drew upon the
specific environments in which they found themselves as they expanded and
elaborated upon the traditions they passed on.

Palestinian Judaism was the first environment, since it was in this particular milieu that Jesus and his very first followers lived and worked. The
Jesus movement (as scholars have termed this earliest stage of Christianity)
took root in various towns and villages of Jewish Palestine and continued
there after his death. Following the crucifixion, moreover, a church formed in
Jerusalem that was to be of great significance in the early postresurrection
period.

Christianity thus began in a Jewish setting. But influences from the broader
Hellenistic world were at work from the very beginning. Greek culture
had penetrated various parts of Palestine, and Acts 6 mentions a group
within the Jerusalem church called "the Hellenists," who were presumably
Greek-speaking Jews who had become Christians. The Hellenistic influence
increased greatly as Christianity began to spread into the world of Diaspora
Judaism and an important, mission-oriented Jewish-Christian congregation
developed in Antioch of Syria. Then, when the movement began to push beyond the bounds of the Jewish population to embrace Gentiles, the way was

137

open for a new level of cultural interaction and the eventual development of distinctively gentile forms of the Christian faith.

Early Christianity thus found itself in a variety of settings, each of which left distinctive marks upon the tradition. And it is important to understand that the original result was not amalgamation but diversity. In time, the church would define the limits of acceptable belief, in part through the designation of canonical materials. But in its earliest stages the Christian movement was able to tolerate a fairly wide variety of perspectives.

In the final section of this chapter we will take a brief look at the expansion the Jesus tradition underwent as it moved through time and varying environments. First, however, it is important to take note of the other stream of tradition that played into the form of Christianity that eventually became the dominant one. This other stream is the resurrection faith, the conviction that God raised Jesus from the dead.

2. The Origin of the Resurrection Faith

Despite the fact that Jesus' ministry ended with his arrest and crucifixion, within a few decades after his death the Mediterranean world was dotted with Christian congregations filled with hope and enthusiasm, aggressively proclaiming their message to the world. If we ask how this turn of events came about, traditional Christian faith has a ready answer: God raised Jesus from the dead, just as the early proclamation indicated. It should be obvious, however, that this claim is a matter of faith, not something that can be proved or disproved through historical research. Even if it were somehow possible to show that Jesus did in fact survive death, there would be no way to demonstrate that it was by the power of God that he did so.

It would thus be inappropriate, in a book such as this, to take a position for or against the traditional Christian claim regarding the resurrection. What is appropriate, however, is to examine some of the theories as to how Jesus' followers came to believe that he was raised from the dead. These theories fall into three broad categories. Some of them are obviously more compatible with traditional Christian faith than others, so that any evaluation of them will of course have some implications regarding belief. But the purpose of this section is only to gain insight into Christian origins, not to make a pronouncement for or against the validity of the early Christians' claim.

a. Theories of Intentional Deception

One approach sees the resurrection faith as the result of an intentional deception on the part of Jesus' followers. Over the years a number of writers, exhibiting varying degrees of familiarity with biblical scholarship, have argued along these lines. Typical theories are that the disciples stole Jesus' body or revived him after he merely fainted on the cross, and then set out to convince people he had been raised.

Not only are such hypotheses purely conjectural, but they show little understanding of first-century Judaism. Belief in the resurrection of the dead was indeed current, but people expected it at the end of the age. And it was something that was supposed to happen generally—either to all the dead, who would then face the judgment, or only to "the righteous," who would inherit eternal life. Theories of intentional deception could claim some credibility if there had been a widespread expectation among Jews of a Messiah who would undergo death and resurrection as part of his mission. But that was apparently not the case. When the early Christians proclaimed Jesus as the risen Christ, they were making an assertion that to some extent demanded a leap beyond existing categories of thought.

b. The Theory of Gradual Construction

A number of recent scholars have assumed that the movement that Jesus founded was strong enough to survive without him, strong enough to withstand the dramatic loss of a leader. And some of these scholars have gone on to argue that the New Testament stories regarding Jesus' resurrection are not the product of any dramatic event. There are carefully crafted expressions, constructed over a long period of time, of the early Christians' deeply felt conviction that he was somehow still present, spiritually, in their midst.[1]

This approach is certainly more plausible than the first, and it can be argued that the Q document (the hypothetical source used by Matthew and Luke), if its existence is accepted, lends some support to it. Since scholars have generally believed that Q contained no stories of Jesus' death and resurrection, it may have come from a community in which these themes played no part, which would tend to indicate that the Jesus movement continued after Jesus' death wholly apart from belief in the resurrection.

---

1. See John Dominic Crossan, *The Historical Jesus: The Life of a Mediterranean Jewish Peasant* (San Francisco: HarperSanFrancisco, 1991), 395–417; Burton L. Mack, *A Myth of Innocence: Mark and Christian Origins* (Minneapolis: Fortress Press, 1988), chaps. 3–4, and Burton L. Mack, *The Lost Gospel: The Book of Q and Christian Origins* (San Francisco: HarperSanFrancisco, 1993), part 4.

Fig. 23.
"Rabboni"
(Allan Rohan Crite; 1947 Brush
and India Ink Drawing)

c. The Resurrection Tradition and the Theory of Dramatic Events

Whether or not the Jesus movement continued under its own impetus, however, the vast majority of scholars have assumed that only some dramatic event or events could have given rise to the resurrection faith. Proceeding from this basic assumption, they have made some very interesting observations about the resurrection claims made in the New Testament.

These scholars have identified three distinct types of material in which the resurrection is proclaimed in a direct way: (1) the Gospel stories about the women (or woman) finding the empty tomb; (2) the Gospel stories about the appearance of the risen Jesus to various disciples; and (3) creed-like "proclamations" of Jesus' resurrection, such as Luke 24:34 and 1 Corinthians 15:3-7 (or 3-5),[2] which also contain references to the appearances.

(1) The Empty Tomb Tradition. If we come to these three types of materials asking which ones give us the best clues as to how Jesus' followers came

---

2. It is unclear where the traditional material ends and Paul's own comments begin; v. 6 breaks the grammatical pattern of "that . . . that. . . ."

to believe that he had been raised from the dead, we may begin by noting that the first of the three is of minimal help. The stories of the empty tomb are, taken by themselves, simply unconvincing. A story in Matthew (27:62-66; 28:11-14) shows that, not surprisingly, some people in the first century drew the same conclusion as others have done in more modern times, that is, that someone came and took the body away. It is simply inconceivable that Jesus' dispirited followers would have come to believe in the resurrection on the basis of the mere report that his tomb was empty.

(2) The Developed Appearance Accounts. We must therefore look to the appearance tradition to find what it was that convinced the disciples. But the appearance accounts in the Gospels are shot through with ambiguities and inconsistencies. At some points it seems clear that a physical body is involved (Luke 24:37-43; John 20:27). But at others the nature of the resurrection body is ambiguous: the disciples do not recognize Jesus (Luke 24:15-16), and he appears and disappears in ghostly fashion (Luke 24:31, 36; John 20:26). So it seems likely that these accounts reflect a good deal of embellishment; they stand far removed from the earliest level of the resurrection tradition. We can learn from them that the early Christians believed that Jesus appeared to his followers after his death, but we cannot use them to reconstruct, with any confidence, any actual, historical events.

(3) The Creed-Like Proclamations and Briefer Appearance Accounts. Our remaining category of materials is that of the creed-like proclamations, which contain briefer references to the resurrection appearances. Notice below three important features of 1 Corinthians 15:3-7: (1) Paul explicitly acknowledges that he is passing on a traditional formulation; (2) the entire formulation constitutes a proclamation that Jesus has been raised, a proclamation that also interprets the meaning of the resurrection; and (3) the formulation includes references to the appearances of the resurrected Jesus to various figures in the early community.

> For I handed on to you as of first importance what I in turn had received: that Christ died for our sins in accordance with the scriptures, and that he was buried, and that he was raised on the third day in accordance with the scriptures, and that he appeared to Cephas [= Peter], then to the Twelve. Then he appeared to more than five hundred brothers and sisters at one time, most of whom are still alive, though some have died. Then he appeared to James, then to all the apostles.

In another passage, Luke 24:34, we find a single sentence that has all the marks of a perhaps even earlier version of such a creed-like proclamation: "The Lord has risen indeed, and he has appeared to Simon" (= Peter).

It is in material such as this that many scholars find the root of the resurrection faith.[3] Here, at last, they contend, is the "something" that happened to the disciples: a series of experiences that Jesus' followers interpreted as his appearances to them.

It is important to say "interpreted as," because we cannot be certain about the nature of these experiences. After quoting the traditional formulation in 1 Corinthians 15:3-7, Paul then makes a statement (v. 8) that clearly interprets his own vision of Jesus, a considerable period after the crucifixion, as belonging to the same category as these earlier experiences: "Last of all, as to one untimely born, he appeared also to me." It seems unlikely, then, that the appearances were such that a neutral observer would have understood them as appearances of the risen Jesus: they may well have been of a "visionary" nature. It is in any case clear that, as Reginald Fuller remarks, the early tradition understood the resurrection "not as the resuscitation of a corpse, but as the transformation of the body" into a "heavenly" or "eschatological" form.[4]

d. Women in the Empty Tomb Tradition

Although the appearance tradition may have the greater claim to originality, it is important now to note a remarkable feature of the empty tomb stories. In all three Synoptics, it is women who discover that the body is missing and receive the message (Matt. 28:1-10; Luke 24:1-11; Mark 16:1-8) that Jesus has been raised. And in John (20:1-18) Mary Magdalene not only comes first to the tomb but also has a postresurrection encounter with Jesus.

This consistent linking of women with the resurrection faith may well reflect a historical memory. Elisabeth Schüssler Fiorenza argues that the women were in fact the first to proclaim the resurrection,[5] and her thesis is strengthened by the fact that the tradition is consistent also in claiming that the women did not abandon Jesus before his death, as the male disciples did. We can say, in any case, that there is good reason to believe that the women were among those who had experiences of Jesus after his death and that they were

---

3. See Willi Marxsen, *The Resurrection of Jesus of Nazareth,* trans. Margaret Kohl (Philadelphia: Fortress Press, 1970).

4. Reginald Fuller, *The Formation of the Resurrection Narratives* (New York: Macmillan, 1971), 57.

5. Elisabeth Schüssler Fiorenza, *In Memory of Her: A Feminist Theological Reconstruction of Christian Origins* (New York: Crossroad, 1983), 138–40.

indeed active in the earliest stages of proclaiming that God had raised him from the dead.

One may object to this thesis on the grounds that the creed-like proclamations do not mention the women. But it does not take much imagination to offer an explanation of that fact. Although women seem to have exercised some leadership in the early Christian communities, the culture at large was male-dominated. As we will see later, the church itself seems to have moved, in time, from a relatively equalitarian structure to a patriarchal one. It is entirely possible that, already at a very early stage, the tradition simply suppressed the role of the women in the resurrection proclamation.

e. Resurrection and Exaltation

A key point to note regarding the resurrection tradition is that it never says that anyone witnessed the resurrection itself. The claim is that the already risen Jesus appeared to believers. This means that the resurrection was not something the disciples experienced directly but something they *inferred* from the appearances.[6] But resurrection was not the only inference one could draw from such experiences. Alongside resurrection-language, the New Testament writers also employed *exaltation*-language—language that spoke of God's elevation of Jesus to a lofty status. Thus in Philippians 2:6-11 Paul quotes an early Christian hymn that moves from Jesus' death to an affirmation not of resurrection but of exaltation: "Therefore God has highly exalted him and bestowed on him the name which is above every name." A similar motif appears in Hebrews 1:3: "When he had made purification for sins, he sat down at the right hand of the Majesty on high."

The author of Luke and Acts, alone among New Testament writers, accommodates the two modes of Jesus' vindication by making his ascension to heaven (exaltation) a separate event that takes place *after* the resurrection. But the ascension/exaltation motif makes the same point as the resurrection: that Jesus' mission did not end on a cross, that the post-Easter Christians experienced Jesus as alive and working in their midst.

f. Summary

There are various ways of accounting for the resurrection faith. All credible theories refer to a sense of Jesus' continuing presence among his followers.

---

6. Philip E. Devenish, "The So-Called Resurrection of Jesus and Explicit Christian Faith: Wittgenstein's Philosophy, Marxsen's Exegesis as Linguistic Therapy," *Journal of the American Academy of Religion* 51 (June 1983): 171–90.

Some scholars think this was a generalized experience and that the resurrection stories are intentional symbolizations of it. The majority, however, believe that the appearance tradition is based upon one or more specific experiences of a dramatic nature. From these experiences the disciples inferred that Jesus had been raised from the dead and/or that he had been exalted and granted a lofty status in heaven.

3. The Meaning of the Resurrection Faith

Why did the disciples' experience of Jesus' presence with them suggest the notion of "resurrection"? Most Jews in the first century expected the collective resurrection of the dead at the end of the age. While Jesus lived, the disciples hoped for the Rule of God; when he appeared to them after his death, they concluded that the age of resurrection had actually begun. That is why they spoke of Jesus as "the firstborn from the dead" (Col. 1:18): they understood his resurrection as the inauguration of the eschatological events that played such an important role in apocalyptic thought.

The resurrection thus gave early Christianity a strong apocalyptic content. But it also necessitated a revision of the typical apocalyptic scheme. Obviously, the fullness of God's Rule had still not come. So the early believers came to think of the new age as arriving in two stages. The risen Jesus had been taken to heaven (exalted), but would eventually return "in his glory" (Matt. 25:31): *then* would come the general resurrection, the final judgment, and entrance into eternal life.

At first, Christians expected Jesus' return very soon, within their own generation (1 Thess. 4:15). So when decades passed and he had still not come, they had to wrestle yet again with the disappointment they had experienced. But by this time they had developed ways of thinking to aid them in that process.

If the resurrection signified for the first Christians the inauguration of the eschatological events, it also implied that God had approved Jesus, had confirmed the validity of his mission and the truth of his words. It meant, in other words, that Jesus was after all the one through whom God would bring in the new age. Thus it was natural that as they awaited Jesus' return these Christians expressed their renewed faith and hope in ways that gave Jesus himself a central role.

4. The Expression of the Resurrection Faith

a. The Titles of Jesus

Those early Christians naturally drew upon Jewish tradition for their terminology regarding Jesus. They addressed him in prayer as *Mar,* an Aramaic term of respect meaning "Lord." In specific relation to his expected return, they spoke of him as the "Son of man"—the awesome heavenly figure in Daniel 7. And, convinced that God had initiated the divine Rule through Jesus, they drew upon the still rather fluid complex of "messsianic" notions and titles and called him "Messiah," "Son of David," and "Son of God."

This last title had a rather complex background and is easily subject to misunderstanding. It had an ancient usage, rooted in Judaism's polytheistic past, as a reference to divine beings such as angels. In more recent times, however, it had been applied to human beings who stood particularly close to God: the king, the *messianic* king, a particularly just person, or a miracle-working charismatic. And it could also refer to the nation of Israel itself.

It is difficult to know precisely which nuances were included in the earliest application of this term to Jesus. But the important point is that the early Christians did not simply take over a prior Jewish usage; for Judaism knew nothing of a "Son of God" in the precise sense of later Christology.

The first Christians probably did not think of Jesus as having functioned as Messiah during his lifetime. They believed either that God had appointed him to assume that role at the time of eschatological fulfillment (Acts 3:20) or had already installed him as Messiah following his crucifixion (Acts 2:36). In time, however, they read Jesus' messiahship back into his earthly ministry.

As Christianity spread from Palestine into the world of Diaspora Judaism and finally into the gentile world itself, the meanings of the terms Christians used about Jesus underwent change. When "Messiah" was translated into Greek as *christos,* it tended to lose its specific meaning and become almost a proper name. "Son of David" and "Son of man," with little appeal to Gentiles, began to drop out of use as titles. In the post–New Testament period "Son of man" became a designation for Jesus' humanity as opposed to his divinity.

The titles "Lord" and "Son of God" blossomed in the Hellenistic world. Since the Septuagint translates "Yahweh" as "Lord" (Greek: *kyrios*), Hellenistic Jewish Christians probably began to transfer *"functions* from God to the exalted Jesus."[7] Then, among gentile Christians, both "Lord" and "Son of God" came finally to embrace the notion of Jesus' divine nature. It is unlikely,

---

7. Reginald Fuller, *The Foundations of New Testament Christology* (New York: Charles Scribner's Sons, 1965), 186.

Fig. 24. "Resurrection II" (Paul T. Granlund, 1973)

however, that either of these titles was in and of itself responsible for the development of the notion that Jesus was Son of God in the "metaphysical" sense of being a divine *incarnation*.

b. Christ as God Incarnate

How did the idea of Christ as God incarnate arise? Some scholars believe that prior to Christianity the Gnostics embraced a redeemer myth, that is, the story of a divine being sent from the world of light to release spiritual beings held captive in the flesh. Christianity, these scholars argue, simply borrowed this notion from Gnosticism. Not all scholars, however, are convinced that such a myth was already current when Christianity was in its early stages. An alternative theory is that Christians came to think of Jesus as divine under the influence of personified Wisdom, which appeared in the literature of pre-Christian Hellenistic Judaism. Some scholars think this happened very early, but others believe that the notion of the incarnation developed only gradually and came to flower in the Gospel of John, where the parallel term "Logos" displaced Wisdom: "In the beginning was the Word [Logos], and the Word was with God, and the Word was God" (John 1:1).[8] According to any of these theories, Wisdom played some role, since those who believe that there was an early gnostic redeemer myth think Wisdom also played a part in its development.

The gnostic thesis is largely discredited, but an early date for the notion of incarnation seems the more likely, in light of Paul's apparent belief in Christ's preexistence (see below, p. 346). And Larry W. Hurtado has argued that not only personified Wisdom, but related Jewish ideas regarding secondary divine agents of God (such as principal angels and exalted patriarchs) played into the development of that conception. But the early Christians' belief in Jesus' divinity, he argues, was the result not of speculative thinking but of the religious experience of corporate worship.[9]

However it happened, Christians came to think of Jesus in terms of the related notions of incarnation and preexistence. This move gave rise, of course, to the difficult questions with which the later church councils dealt. The early Christians had no desire to deny the unity of God or to identify Jesus Christ with God in simplistic fashion. But they did believe that God was present in Jesus in a unique way.

c. Worship, Witness, and the "Point" of Christology

As Hurtado has stressed, the honorific language early Christians applied to Jesus was the product of their worship and witness, not philosophical speculation. Those who believed in Jesus reflected upon his status because it was through him that they had experienced God in a new way. But their experience of Jesus as the incarnation of God was inseparable from the belief that he had performed a particular function on God's behalf. Even the christological hymns in the New Testament tend to connect Christ's exalted status to that function. And the point is crystal clear in Colossians 1:15-20. Beginning

---

8. See James D. G. Dunn, *Christology in the Making: A New Testament Inquiry into the Origins of the Doctrine of the Incarnation* (Philadelphia: Westminster, 1980).

9. Larry W. Hurtado, *One God, One Lord: Early Christian Devotion and Ancient Jewish Monotheism* (Philadelphia: Fortress Press, 1988).

with lofty statements on Christ's "nature"—"He is the image of the invisible God, the firstborn of all creation"—this hymn ends in a declaration of what he *accomplished:* "and through him God was pleased to reconcile to himself all things... by making peace through the blood of his cross."

It would thus appear that the interest of those who first came to think in terms of incarnation was not in Christ-in-himself but in Christ-for-them. But what, specifically, was the function they believed he had performed? And how did they come to embrace the notion that God had accomplished something through Jesus?

5. The Death of Jesus as a Redemptive Event

Deeply embedded in the ancient Hebrew faith was the hope that God would "save" or "redeem" Israel, i.e., establish the nation in security. Apocalyptic thought modified this collective hope by introducing the notion of an individual salvation consisting of eternal life in God's eschatological Rule. In neither case, however, was sheer survival the main idea. Jews hoped for survival *as the people of God,* which meant as an obedient society in which justice prevailed. And the eternal life envisioned in apocalypticism was explicitly for "the righteous" among human beings and was characterized by abundance, joy, and the absence of suffering.

Those who responded to Jesus' preaching presumably experienced both hope for the future and the power of God's Rule in the present. Then, when the early Christians announced Jesus' resurrection, they also proclaimed a future salvation that could in some measure be experienced in the present. But an important shift had taken place. They now understood Jesus not simply as the one who had announced God's Rule or brought it near, but as the one through whom God had actually *brought about* the salvation associated with that Rule. They began to think of Jesus' life and, most particularly, his death and resurrection as a redemptive event, an event that somehow wiped away or atoned for human sin and thereby made salvation available.

Christians must have come to interpret Jesus' death in this way very early, since Paul seems to be drawing upon an existing formulation when he writes, at Romans 3:25, of Christ as the one "whom God put forward as a sacrifice of atonement by his blood." But there is no consensus as to how far back such views can be traced. Some scholars believe that Jesus himself interpreted his anticipated death as an atonement for human sin. Their views depend upon the acceptance of certain New Testament passages as containing cores of authentic material. Among these are Jesus' words over the bread and wine at the last supper (1 Cor. 11:24-25; Mark 14:22-25) and Mark 10:45, where Jesus speaks of giving his life as "a ransom for many."[10] Many scholars dispute the authenticity of such passages, however, and trace the notion of Jesus' death as a saving event to one or another phase of the postresurrection community.

It is as difficult to determine how Christians came to think of Jesus' death as redemptive as it is to establish when they began to do so. By some accounts, they simply took over the concept of atonement associated with ritual sacrifices in the Jewish Scriptures and applied it to Jesus. Certainly, the New Testament makes use of some of the terminology relating to the sacrificial cult. "Ransom" belongs in this category, as do the Greek term *hilasterion* in Romans 3:25 (translated as "atonement" in the New Revised Standard Version) and the epithet "lamb of God" as applied to Jesus. Recent scholars, however, have rejected the notion of a simplistic transfer of this terminology to Jesus and have looked for some intervening factor.

A number of scholars find such a factor in the figure of the "suffering servant" depicted in Isaiah 52:13—53:12. This "servant," whose identity is not explicitly stated, is presented as "despised and rejected by others" (53:3); and it is said of him that

> ... he was wounded for our transgressions, crushed for our iniquities; upon him was the punishment that made us whole; and by his bruises we are healed. (53:5)

Christians through the centuries have understood these words as a prophecy of Jesus' death on the cross as a vicarious sacrifice for human sin, and at two points the New Testament seems in fact to make such a connection: Hebrews 9:28 and 1 Peter 2:22-25. As we will see, however, both Hebrews and 1 Peter were probably composed at relatively late dates. And although actual quotations from the "servant song" in Isaiah 52–53 can be identified at other points in the New Testament,[11] in none of these cases is the passage from the Jewish Scriptures used in order to make a point regarding vicarious atonement. It is significant also that in none of the Jewish literature of this period was this passage interpreted in that way. So although Christians came eventually to understand Jesus as the suffering servant, it is not at all clear that this passage is the source of the understanding of Jesus' death as a saving event.

Many scholars look to Hellenistic culture as the catalytic agent in the development of the Christian view of atonement; Greek literature was filled

---

10. See, for example, Martin Hengel, *The Atonement: The Origins of the Doctrine in the New Testament,* trans. John Bowden (Philadelphia: Fortress Press, 1981), and Joachim Jeremias, *The Eucharistic Words of Jesus,* trans. Norman Perrin (New York: Charles Scribner's Sons, 1966).

11. Romans 15:21; 10:16; John 12:38; Matthew 8:17; Luke 22:37; Acts 8:32-33.

with such notions as the worthiness of dying for one's friends or one's lands and the beneficial effects of a sacrificial death. A recent theory is that early Christians drew explicitly upon a noncanonical Jewish writing, known as 4 Maccabees, that shows heavy Hellenistic influence and contains an explicit notion of vicarious sacrifice.[12] Reflecting upon a family of pious Jews who were killed by the Seleucids because they would not renounce their faith, the author speaks of these martyrs as "a ransom for the sin of our nation" and says that "through the blood of these devout ones and their atoning sacrifice, divine Providence preserved Israel" (17:21-11).

Whatever the specific origin of the notion of Jesus' death as a saving event, the language the New Testament writers employ in this regard is highly metaphorical and cannot be translated simplistically into hard and fast concepts. Theologians in later centuries tended to take the biblical metaphors literally, however, in their efforts to explain the "mechanics" of Christ's vicarious sacrifice by developing formal doctrines of the atonement. Confronted with the term "ransom," for example, they asked the logical question: if God gave Jesus as a ransom for human sin, to whom was the ransom paid? Some answered "to God's own self," while others said "to Satan." Both answers raise enormous questions on the logical, moral, and theological levels. But most New Testament scholars would see the whole argument as based upon a failure to grasp the metaphorical nature of the term in question. And they would argue that the biblical writers were not at all interested in explaining the "how" of the atonement, but were concerned only to proclaim it.

Whenever and however the concept of Jesus' atoning death appeared, it eventually became an integral part of Christian thought. But it was apparently not universal among Christians in the beginning. As we will presently see, there was at least one other way in which believers understood Jesus' "saving" power.

6. The Expansion of the Jesus Tradition

a. The Process of Expansion

The proclamation of the resurrection could not stand alone. Every religious community needs to nurture its constituents in the faith, and every religious community needs rules of moral conduct and organizational structure.

---

12. Sam K. Williams, *Jesus' Death as a Saving Event: The Background and Origin of a Concept* (Missoula, Mont.: Scholars Press, 1975). Although never canonized and not formally counted among the Apocryphal/Deuterocanonical books, 4 Maccabees was read by early Christians and appears in an appendix to the Greek Bible. It is included in the Apocrypha section of the NRSV.

To what sources could the early Christians look as they faced the task of *teaching?*

They could of course look to the Jewish Scriptures. They could engage in their own *midrash*, that is, the "updating" of Scripture through commentary, and this is to some extent what they did. But it was the words and deeds of Jesus himself that had called them into a new consciousness, and it was the proclamation of Jesus' resurrection that had renewed their hopes. The real center of their life was thus Jesus, and it was primarily to his own teachings that they turned.

The problem, though, was that Jesus had not taught a comprehensive ethic and had probably said nothing directly related to community organization. His open-ended parables and sayings provided little help in meeting the needs of the community in relation to concrete situations. As was inevitable, Jesus' postresurrection followers expanded the tradition of his words and deeds.

This expansion took place in several ways. As Jews, the earliest Christians would have been familiar with the stories and sayings of many Jewish teachers without knowing the exact sources. Faced with a situation that called for a decision, they would naturally draw upon this wider body of teaching if an explicit memory of Jesus were not available. Because their lives were so centered on Jesus, they might naturally attribute to him whatever teaching seemed appropriate. Or even if the first person to introduce a teaching did not claim it was from Jesus, those to whom it was quoted later might naturally assume that it was. On the other hand, if a particular teaching of Jesus did not quite fit a particular situation it would be natural to add an interpretive comment to it and for later hearers to regard the comment as part of the original. And then there were probably situations in which the community could find no appropriate guidelines in any traditional source and had to make a decision on their own. Once again it would have been natural for later Christians to attribute the new teaching to Jesus himself.

Such indirect and unconscious expansion was not the only way in which the Jesus tradition underwent transformation. Prophecy was a major aspect of the Jewish heritage, and the New Testament reveals at numerous points that Christian prophets played an important role in the early Palestinian communities. Classically, a Jewish prophet was someone inspired by God's Spirit to speak a word to the people in some moment of crisis. But Christian prophets, speaking to communities that believed Jesus was spiritually present among them, spoke specifically on behalf of the risen Christ. And the communities apparently made no distinction between the words they received in this way and their memories of Jesus: they passed on the sayings of Christian prophets *as sayings of Jesus.* This should not be surprising. It is a sign that most Christians felt strongly that the risen Christ and the Jesus of history were one and the same.

b. Outside the "Mainstream"

In what eventually emerged as the mainstream of Christianity, the Jesus tradition and the proclamation of the resurrection complemented one another. But not all Christians found these two streams of tradition so compatible, and the "mainstream" was not the only line of development the Jesus tradition followed. A very different mode of expansion is attested by the Gospel of Thomas, a work discovered in an archaeological find at Nag Hammadi in Egypt in 1945.

The Gospel of Thomas does not tell a story of Jesus' life or death. It takes the form of secret teachings delivered by the risen Jesus to the author. Among the teachings, which are generally very esoteric in nature, we find a few parables that are obvious variants of materials found in the Synoptic Gospels. Some scholars think Thomas is directly dependent upon the Synoptics, that the author reshaped canonical materials to fit an esoteric theological perspective. The evidence is strong, however, that Thomas is independent of the Synoptics and therefore simply represents another direction in which the Jesus tradition developed. In a few cases it preserves materials that appear, under form-critical analysis, to be closer to the original in minor details than the Synoptic counterparts.

But what is the "other direction" that Thomas represents? The discovery at Nag Hammadi was the library of an ancient Christian monastery containing numerous works that are clearly gnostic in orientation. In the eyes of the Gnostics who read such materials, the postresurrection teaching in Thomas constituted the secret knowledge, or *gnōsis,* that set the gnostic (= knowing) Christian above the ordinary believer. And from their point of view it was the teaching itself, not Jesus' death and resurrection, that was redemptive. This is necessarily so for Gnostics, since they believed that the redeemer could not have been human in the sense of having a physical body and therefore could not really have died. The death was thus an illusion, and the "resurrection" could not mean what it did for "mainstream" Christians.

Some scholars who accept the existence of Q believe it also exhibits this tendency to understand Jesus' teachings as having saving power in themselves. But the authors of the New Testament writings curbed this tendency as they brought Jesus' teaching into the canonical writings. The Christianity that prevailed was that which proclaimed the life, death, and resurrection of Jesus of Nazareth as a saving event. It is nevertheless important to remember

Fig. 25. "Thus saith he unto Thomas, Reach hither thy finger, and behold my hands; and reach hither thy hand, and thrust it into my side: and be not faithless, but believing" (John 20:27 KJV) (Stone carving, late eleventh century)

that it is only in retrospect that we can speak of that form of Christianity as the "mainstream." Each of the widely variant Christian groups was undoubtedly convinced that it possessed the authentic interpretation of the meaning of Jesus' life.

c. The "Shape" of the Expansion[13]

We saw in chapter 3 one way in which the earliest level of the Jesus tradition was expanded, that is, through the allegorization of the parables. Since we have referred to the expansion only in an abstract way in the present chapter, however, it should be helpful now to give some concrete examples of materials belonging to the later tradition.

(1) Legal Materials. Matthew 5:18—in which Jesus says "until heaven and earth pass away, not one letter, not one stroke of a letter, will pass from the

---

13. This section is based largely upon categories delineated by Rudolf Bultmann in his *History of the Synoptic Tradition,* trans. John Marsh (New York: Harper & Row, 1963).

law"—makes the details of the Jewish law binding upon Christians, probably reflecting the position of conservatives in the Palestinian communities who opposed those who were dispensing with ritual requirements. In Matthew 18:15-17 we find a rule for church discipline, outlining procedures to be followed regarding one member's grievance against another.

(2) Prophetic Statements. Luke 10:16 is probably the utterance of a Christian prophet, designed to give encouragement to missionaries by portraying Jesus as pronouncing judgment on those who reject their message: "Whoever listens to you listens to me, and whoever rejects you rejects me, and whoever rejects me rejects the one who sent me." Mark 3:29 is best understood in a similar light: "Whoever blasphemes against the Holy Spirit can never have forgiveness, but is guilty of an eternal sin." Interpreted as a prophetic statement, this probably means that those who reject the words of Christian prophets will not be forgiven, not because they have committed too great a sin but because the impending eschatological crisis leaves no further opportunity for repentance.[14]

(3) Apocalyptic Materials. The expanded tradition also contains a wealth of apocalyptic sayings, produced by the community or borrowed from Jewish sources. Mark 13:24-27 is a striking example:

> But in those days, after that suffering,
> the sun will be darkened,
>   and the moon will not give its light,
> and the stars will be falling from heaven,
>   and the powers in the heavens will be shaken.

Then they will see "the Son of man coming in clouds" with great power and glory. Then he will send out the angels, and gather his elect from the four winds, from the ends of the earth to the ends of heaven.

(4) "Glorification" of the Earthly Jesus. One of the more interesting developments in the expansion of the Jesus tradition was that it attributed characteristics of the risen Christ to the earthly Jesus. In Mark 9:2-8 Jesus' disciples get a preview of the "glorified" Jesus: "And he was transfigured before them, and his clothes became dazzling white, as no one on earth could

---

14. M. Eugene Boring, *The Continuing Voice of Jesus: Christian Prophecy and the Gospel Tradition* (Louisville: Westminster/John Knox, 1991), 219-20.

bleach them." Also, beside the stories of healings and exorcisms there now appeared nature miracles in which Jesus walks on water (Mark 6:45-52), stills a storm (Mark 4:37-41), or feeds multitudes with a few loaves and fishes (Mark 6:34-44). The healing theme, finally, was heightened to include raising the dead (Mark 5:21-43).

Even the earlier miracle stories are largely the product of the expanded tradition. Whether pre- or post-Easter in origin, they are less reflective of memories of specific incidents than of the general recollection of Jesus as healer and exorcist. Undoubtedly, miracle stories of all types provided a powerful vehicle through which the community could communicate its faith. As Eugene Boring comments, each story constitutes a kind of "gospel in miniature."[15] As such, it focuses on the Jesus of the past only to convey the power of the risen Jesus as potentially working in the lives of those who hear it.

Thus, according to Boring, the story of the healing of a demoniac in Mark 5:1-20 was told "not to memorialize an incident at Gerasa...but to declare the meaning of the whole Christ-event: God is victor over the demonic."[16] Such a story would motivate those who heard it not merely to ask historical questions about a Jesus of the past but to consider whether the Jesus now presented in Christian preaching might be able to deliver them from oppressive forces in their own lives.

This particular story, moreover, would be a fertile field for both existentialist and psychological interpretation. The latter is clearly invited by the striking comment, "And they came to Jesus, and saw the demoniac sitting there, clothed *and in his right mind*." Certainly Gerd Theissen's understanding of the existential meaning of miracle stories in general is applicable here: in the face of deep suffering such stories articulate not simply the wish to move beyond what is normally understood as human limitations but the hope that through contact with the sacred such suffering and negativity can actually be overcome.[17]

(5) Controversies and Dialogues.

Several other types of stories grew up to illustrate general memories of Jesus' activities or to provide settings for remembered sayings. There are numerous accounts in which Jesus comes into conflict with religious representatives regarding such matters as his healings

---

15. M. Eugene Boring, *Truly Human/Truly Divine: Christological Language and the Gospel Form* (St. Louis: CBP Press, 1984), 21.

16. Ibid., 31.

17. Gerd Theissen, *The Miracle Stories of the Early Christian Tradition*, trans. Francis McDonagh, ed. John Riches (Philadelphia: Fortress Press, 1983), 300–301.

or exorcisms (Mark 3:1-6, 22-30) and his association with outcasts (Mark 2:15-17). And there are instances in which questions by either disciples or opponents lead to a response by Jesus (Mark 10:17-22). To assign such material to the expanded tradition does not mean that in no case whatsoever is the memory of an actual event preserved; the point is that the stories themselves were shaped through the process of tradition and that one cannot simply *assume* a historical incident.

(6) Historical Stories and Legends. Bultmann identifies a broad spectrum of stories, ranging from those with a strong historical element to those that are totally legendary, which do not fit into any of the previous categories. It is hard to know which elements in any given story are historical and which are legendary, but we can identify materials clearly on either end of the spectrum. Critical scholars generally take the accounts of Jesus' birth in Matthew 1:18—2:23 and Luke 1–2, for example, to be very late stories showing much Hellenistic influence. We have already seen that the stories of Jesus' baptism (Mark 1:9-10) and action in the temple (Mark 11:15-19), however, are undoubtedly based upon actual incidents. None of the stories, of course, are the product of neutral observation; they all come to us through the tradition—which means *theologically interpreted.* This is true in one sense even of the pre-Easter Jesus tradition, as we saw in chapter 2. The difference now is that these materials are influenced specifically by the *resurrection* faith.

This latter point is particularly significant in relation to the stories that make up the "passion narratives," that is, the accounts of the crucifixion and the events immediately leading up to it. Those who in the postresurrection communities reflected upon this tragic and puzzling event quite naturally interpreted it in light of the Jewish Scriptures. Thus passion narratives are replete with scriptural quotations and allusions. Far from the reports of neutral observers, they are theologically weighted accounts in which Jesus' death is interpreted as the fulfillment of prophecy, part of God's redemptive plan.

On the other hand, the fact that the early Christians went to such lengths to make sense of the crucifixion shows that for them the exalted Christ of the resurrection faith was identical with the Jesus of history. The one spiritually present to them in their worship and witness was that same Galilean Jew who taught, healed, cast out demons, drew to himself the poor and despised, and died a truly human death on a Roman cross outside Jerusalem.

7. The Formation of Orthodox Christology: Through the New Testament and Beyond

The expansion of the Jesus tradition and the proclamation of the resurrection faith were forms of reflection on who Jesus was and on his role in human salvation. Such reflection continued as the written materials that now constitute the New Testament supplemented the oral tradition. But in neither the oral nor the written materials do we find a systematic "Christology," a formal doctrinal statement of "the person and work Jesus Christ," to use the vocabulary of later theology. The New Testament ascribes titles of honor to Jesus—"Christ" (= Messiah), "Son of God," "Lord," etc.—but it neither explains them nor elaborates on their meaning. As the New Testament period drew to a close, however, Christians began to articulate their understandings of Jesus in more self-consciously ordered ways.

Early Christians came to think of Jesus as in some sense a divine being, but they also maintained that he was really human. In the second century, however, a tendency began to flourish that many prominent leaders found disturbing. Some Christians, partly under gnostic influence, denied that Jesus was human at all. Their doctrine of Christ is termed "docetic"—from a Greek word meaning "to seem"—because for them Jesus only seemed to have a human body.

To combat such notions, the church instituted such tests of "right teaching" as the Apostles' Creed, which emphasizes Jesus' humanity with the phrase "[Jesus] suffered under Pontius Pilate, was crucified, dead, and buried." The creed also affirms Jesus' divine status, however, by the phrase "[I believe] in Jesus Christ, [God's] only Son, our Lord." In later centuries the church formalized its Christology by employing the Greek philosophical notion of "substance." Jesus Christ, according to what became the "orthodox" formulation, is, as Son of God, of one "substance" with God the Father; and Father, Son, and Holy Spirit together constitute the Triune God, or Trinity. The Son, moreover, has two "natures," one human and one divine, which are neither separate (as if he were two persons) nor confused (so that one would negate the other). Those Christians who, in distinction from various groups of dissenters, accepted this view spoke of their faith as both "catholic" (= universal) and "apostolic." This christological formula, adopted at the Council of Chalcedon in 451 C.E., has remained definitive for most Christians through the centuries.

STUDY QUESTIONS

1. Through what specific stages of development, defined by geography and culture, did the early Christian tradition pass?

2. What are the different kinds of resurrection traditions found in the New Testament? What seems to be the origin of the resurrection faith?

3. What evidence is there that women were among the first, or even perhaps the very first, to proclaim the resurrection?

4. What was the "meaning" of the proclamation that God had raised Jesus from the dead?

5. How did the early Christians come to think of Jesus as "God incarnate"?

6. What are the various theories of when and how Christians began to think of Jesus' death having atoning, redeeming, or saving power?

7. What is the "other direction" of the development of the Jesus tradition that is represented in the Gospel of Thomas?

8. In what specific ways was the Jesus tradition expanded in the postresurrection community?

FOR FURTHER READING

Bultmann, Rudolf. *The History of the Synoptic Tradition.* Trans. John Marsh. New York: Harper & Row, 1963. A classic work in form criticism.

Cullmann, Oscar. *The Christology of the New Testament.* Trans. Shirley C. Guthrie and Charles A. M. Hall. Rev. ed. Philadelphia: Westminster, 1963. An influential treatment of the development of Christology.

Duling, Dennis C. *Jesus Christ through History.* New York: Harcourt, Brace, Jovanovich, 1979. A good, clear exposition of differing views of Jesus from earliest times to the present.

Dunn, James D. G. *Christology in the Making: A New Testament Inquiry into the Origins of the Doctrine of the Incarnation.* Philadelphia, Westminster, 1980. An important study, arguing for the late date and gradual development of the doctrine.

Fredriksen, Paula. *From Jesus to Christ: The Origins of the New Testament Images of Jesus.* New Haven: Yale University Press, 1988. A competent and highly readable interpretation of the development of Christology; an important contribution.

Fuller, Reginald H. *The Foundations of New Testament Christology.* New York: Charles Scribner's Sons, 1965. An influential treatment of the development of Christology.

————. *The Formation of the Resurrection Narratives.* New York: Macmillan, 1971. Traces the development of the resurrection tradition. Places the empty tomb tradition early, rather than late, in contrast to Marxsen.

Hengel, Martin. *The Atonement: The Origins of the Doctrine in the New Testament.* Trans. John Bowden. Philadelphia: Fortress Press, 1981. Brief but technical. Argues that Jesus himself understood his death as redemptive. An excellent review of related themes in Greek literature.

Hurtado, Larry W. *One God, One Lord: Early Christian Devotion and Ancient Jewish Monotheism.* Philadelphia: Fortress Press, 1988. An innovative and important study, tracing the belief in Jesus' divinity to Jewish notions of divine agency.

Jeremias, Joachim. *The Eucharistic Words of Jesus.* Trans. Norman Perrin. New York: Charles Scribner's Sons, 1966. Technical defense of the authenticity of Jesus' words at the last supper.

Marxsen, Willi. *The Resurrection of Jesus of Nazareth.* Trans. Margaret Kohl (Philadelphia: Fortress Press, 1970). Treats the resurrection from both historical and theological perspectives. Interprets the empty tomb tradition as a late development.

Pelikan, Jaroslav. *Jesus through the Centuries: His Place in the History of Culture.* New Haven: Yale Univ. Press, 1985. An engaging treatment, illustrated with classical art works; stresses the place of Jesus in the wider culture, beyond the religious establishment.

Perkins, Pheme. *Resurrection: New Testament Witness and Contemporary Reflection.* Garden City, N.Y.: Doubleday, 1984. A comprehensive study; makes an important contribution.

Perrin, Norman. *The Resurrection according to Matthew, Mark, and Luke.* (Philadelphia: Fortress Press, 1977). Discusses each of the Synoptic resurrection narratives as an expression of the theology of the author.

Epilogue to Part One

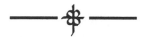

1. The Sociology of the Jesus Movement

Recent scholarship has produced much debate on the sociological nature of early Christianity. Some analysts view it as a movement of the lower classes, while others think it cut across all social groups. It is important, in dealing with this question, to distinguish between early Jewish Christianity in Palestine, often called the "Jesus movement," and the forms of Christianity that developed in the wider reaches of the empire. It is with the Jesus movement that we are concerned at this point.

We know from Paul's letters that the Jerusalem church was impoverished, and we have seen that the earliest Jesus tradition, which was preserved in the Palestinian communities, reveals a deep sense of identification with the poor. Theissen has argued, however, that most of the adherents of the Jesus movement were not among the very poor, but many were in danger of falling into that category.[1] From his perspective, the Jesus movement was liberal in orientation, comprised of persons from various strata of society who opposed the policies of the aristocracy and stood in solidarity with the poor. But it depended upon the generosity of affluent persons to subsidize those who formed its core and were its true leaders, namely, wandering charismatic prophets who voluntarily abandoned home and possessions and accepted poverty. According to Theissen, it was to these vagabond charismatics that sayings such as Luke 14:26 were directed: "Whoever comes to me and does not hate father and mother, wife and children, brothers and sisters, yes, and even life itself, cannot be my disciple."

---

1. Gerd Theissen, *Sociology of Early Palestinian Christianity,* trans. John Bowden (Philadelphia: Fortress Press, 1978).

Drawing upon a sociological method known as functionalism, which analyzes the ways in which various groups contribute to a total societal system, Theissen identifies the social function of the Jesus movement as containing and overcoming aggression. This movement, he argues, served to counteract the negative emotions generated by social tensions. On the one hand, it transformed aggression into a radical version of its opposite, that is, love of enemies, but also turned it inward through a demand for radical repentance and an insistence that all are sinners. On the other hand, the Jesus movement transferred the aggression of its adherents onto other objects, such as demons and persons who refused the Christian message.

According to Theissen, the Jesus movement in Jewish Palestine died out because it was ultimately unsuccessful in its social role. But the Christianity that developed in the wider Hellenistic world met with success precisely because it underwent a sociological transformation in which authority rested no longer with the vagabond charismatics but with the local communities themselves.

Theissen's view has been influential, but critics have challenged him on numerous points. It is not at all clear, for example, that the poverty indicated in the early Jesus tradition is voluntary. Wolfgang Stegemann notes that texts such as Matthew 6:25 ("do not be anxious about your life, what you shall eat or what you shall drink, nor about your body, what you shall put on") are best understood as words spoken to people who are worried about the basic necessities of life.[2] And Richard Horsley argues that it was not the wandering charismatics but the people in the local communities who were the core of the movement.[3]

Horsley has also charged that Theissen's sociological method—functionalism—is itself flawed.[4] By stressing the ways in which groups fit into a societal system, it tends to overlook the more disruptive aspects of some groups. Rather than a liberal group in solidarity with the poor, then, the Jesus movement was, in the eyes of some analysts, a more radical movement comprised of the very poor themselves. And its "function" was by no means to contain aggression.

Another aspect of the sociology of the Jesus movement that has attracted attention is the question of the status and role of women in its ranks. It is striking, to begin with, that Jesus appears in the early Palestinian tradition

2. Wolfgang Stegemann, "Vagabond Radicalism in Early Christianity," in Willy Schottroff and Wolfgang Stegemann, eds., *God of the Lowly: Socio-Historical Interpretations of the Bible* (Maryknoll, N.Y.: Orbis Books, 1984), 161–62.

3. Richard A. Horsley, *Sociology and the Jesus Movement* (New York: Crossroad, 1989), 112–16.

4. Ibid., 147–55.

in close association with the female Wisdom. Luke 7:35, for example, defends both John the Baptist and Jesus with a saying that casts them in the role of Wisdom's envoys: "wisdom is vindicated by all her children." But is this openness to female imagery matched by a social equalitarianism? There is some indication that it is.

Matthew 23:9 ("And call no one on earth your father, for you have one Father—the one in heaven") is of course a recognition of God's sovereignty. But as Elisabeth Schüssler Fiorenza has shown, it is also an implicit critique of male-dominated society. This is clear, at least, if one reads it in relation to Mark 10:29-30: "there is no one who has left house or brothers or sisters or mother or father or children or fields who will not receive a hundredfold now in this age—houses, brothers and sisters, mothers and children, and fields. . . . " Whereas fathers are among the items left behind, they do not appear among the items one *regains* in the new community: "Insofar as the new 'family' of Jesus has no room for 'fathers,' it implicitly rejects their power and status and thus claims that in the messianic community all patriarchal structures are abolished."[5]

We have in fact a striking example of the new community's abolition of an important patriarchal privilege. Since divorce was an exclusively male prerogative in Jewish society of the time, the early Christian prohibition of it functions in and of itself as an endorsement of women's rights. And Mark 10:8, which follows a quotation from Genesis on marriage, further emphasizes the point by proclaiming male-female solidarity: "So they are no longer two but one."

In a similar vein, Schüssler Fiorenza sees an expression of broad social radicalism in Mark 10:15: "whoever does not receive the kingdom of God like a child shall not enter it." This statement, she says, "is not an invitation to childlike innocence and naivete but a challenge to relinquish all claims of power and domination over others."[6]

It should now be evident that to some extent the early followers of Jesus challenged certain social norms and stood in opposition to the ruling aristocracy. And it might seem natural at this point to ask whether they were content to manifest an "alternative" life-style among themselves or made active attempts to change society as a whole. To pose the question this way, however, may rest upon a misunderstanding. If we take seriously the view that Jesus led a Jewish renewal movement, then we must be careful not to view the early Palestinian "Christians" as severely cut off from the communities in which

---

5. Elisabeth Schüssler Fiorenza, *In Memory of Her: A Feminist Theological Reconstruction of Christian Origins* (New York: Crossroad, 1983), 147–50.

6. Ibid., 148.

they lived. They had no sense of constituting a new "religion," nor did they retire from society as did the Qumran sect. They probably thought of themselves as the nucleus of the new order, the vanguard of God's coming Rule. They would thus have expected that the kind of community life they tried to manifest among themselves was precisely what would characterize Israel as a whole when the Rule of God became present in its fullness.

2. A Continuing Question: Christianity and the Social Order

The preceding questions should be of interest to anyone considering the relationship between religious faith and the social order. They are particularly important for Christian theology insofar as it wrestles with that issue. Some liberation theology attempts to move directly from those words and deeds of Jesus that challenge the power structures of his time to a contemporary rejection of analogous systems. From this perspective it becomes important to document the specifics of Jesus' social views. Another approach is to begin not with Jesus' solidarity with the poor specifically but with his general love ethic and then apply it to a wide range of situations.

Both these approaches take the Jesus tradition as normative for Christianity. While they do not deny the importance of the resurrection faith, they understand it as deriving its meaning from the stories of a Jesus who associated with the outcast and was opposed by the powerful. Because of this emphasis upon the human Jesus (or the earliest Jesus tradition), these views might be of significant personal interest to persons beyond the bounds of the Christian faith.

A fundamentally different option, which in fact became the "orthodox" view, is to understand the resurrection faith and incarnational theology as normative for interpreting the life and teachings of Jesus, rather than vice-versa. This approach would tend to support a somewhat more doctrinally oriented and other-worldly version of Christianity.

One should not, of course, assume a one-to-one correlation between a given approach and a specific position on religion and society. The "orthodox" view has often been enlisted in liberation causes, and the "historical Jesus" approach has sometimes produced an individualistic piety that de-emphasizes the social dimension of faith. Nevertheless, it makes some difference where one comes down on this issue when considering the question, "What is Christianity?" Theologians who start with the historical Jesus or the Jesus tradition are highly critical of theology that begins with the incarnation rather than their more "concrete" Jesus, while those who take the incarnational theology of the early church creeds as normative are highly suspicious of attempts to find a Jesus behind the canonical materials.

I will not attempt to settle this issue in this text; it belongs more to Christian theology than to biblical studies. In the ensuing chapters, however, I will explore some of the ways the New Testament writers themselves appropriated both the Jesus tradition and the resurrection faith. The issue of Christianity and society is only one of many issues it will be important to discuss as we turn from the tradition that lies behind the New Testament to the canonical texts themselves.

STUDY QUESTIONS

1. In what specific ways did the Jesus movement depart from existing social norms?

2. What specific issues are at stake between Theissen and his critics?

3. How might a Christian's choice between the historical Jesus (or earliest Jesus tradition) and the resurrection faith as a starting point for theological reflection affect her or his views on the relationship between Christianity and the social order?

FOR FURTHER READING

Horsley, Richard A. *Sociology and the Jesus Movement.* New York: Crossroad, 1989. Complex and technical, with extended attention to method; critical of Theissen.

Schottroff, Luise, and Wolfgang Stegemann. *Jesus and the Hope of the Poor.* Maryknoll, N.Y.: Orbis Books, 1986. A sociohistorical investigation of the Jesus movement. Critical of Theissen.

Schottroff, Willy, and Wolfgang Stegemann, eds. *God of the Lowly: Socio-Historical Interpretations of the Bible.* Trans. Matthew J. O'Connell. Maryknoll, N.Y.: Orbis Books, 1984. Application of the method to texts in Jewish Scriptures and New Testament, emphasizing themes of human oppression and divine justice.

Schüssler Fiorenza, Elisabeth. *In Memory of Her: A Feminist Theological Reconstruction of Christian Origins.* New York: Crossroad, 1983. A highly acclaimed, ground-breaking application of a feminist historical method. Challenges many standard assumptions. Demanding but rewarding reading; already a classic.

————. *Jesus: Miriam's Child, Sophia's Prophet: Critical Issues in Feminist Christology.* New York: Continuum, 1994. Combines historical reconstruction of the Jesus movement with feminist theology. A landmark contribution.

Theissen, Gerd. *Sociology of Early Palestinian Christianity.* Trans. John Bowden. Philadelphia: Fortress Press, 1978. An important attempt to employ sociology in New Testament studies.

Part Two

The Gospels and Acts

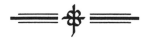

Prologue to Part Two

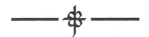

1. Getting Started

The New Testament begins with four stories of Jesus' life: the Gospels. In the canonical arrangement, the Acts of the Apostles is placed after the fourth Gospel, John. It is apparent, however, that the author of Luke also wrote Acts and that the two volumes constitute a genuine narrative unity. For that reason, I will depart slightly from the canonical order to study Luke-Acts as a single two-volume work. I will also begin with Mark rather than Matthew, not because of any theory regarding the order of composition but simply because I find a study of Mark helpful in dispelling preconceptions.

As indicated in chapter 1, I will approach each writing from several perspectives. For the Gospels and Acts, the specific procedure will be as follows. An early section in each chapter ("The Story of Jesus in . . .") will employ a reader-response methodology in guiding the student through the work under consideration. Subsequent sections will raise questions arising from historical criticism and other methods of study.

2. Entering the Story-Worlds

The fact that our primary method of study is to be a type of literary criticism has some important implications, of which the student should be aware. In dealing with the precanonical levels of tradition, we intentionally took passages out of their present contexts in order to understand what they meant to the earliest followers of Jesus. Now we are going to read the canonical books as they stand, that is, as whole, integrated literary works. Passages that meant

167

one thing when read in light of the pre-Easter or the early church situation may mean something quite different within the context of a Gospel narrative.

To read the Gospels and Acts in this way, we must let each of the books establish its own story-world for us to enter. We will have no interest in whether the events described in any of these stories "really happened." Our only concern will be for the story each narrative tells, how it attempts to engage the reader in reflection upon the meaning of Jesus' life.

It may at some points be difficult, particularly for those very familiar with the New Testament, to maintain this perspective. Perhaps the hardest task is to remember to treat the characters in the story *as characters*, and not make an unconscious leap to actual human beings who once lived. If Jesus does something puzzling in the story (as he will often do in Mark), we must not ask why the historical person Jesus would have done that. The appropriate question is why, in the context of the Markan (or Lukan, etc.) story-world, the *character* Jesus did that.

The other half of the matter is that the Gospel writers present their stories as interpretations of a person who actually lived and died. In this regard, what they did in constructing their story-worlds is not fundamentally different from what Jesus' earliest followers did in passing on the original stories of what he said and did. For the pre-Gospel Jesus tradition was itself *interpretation* of Jesus.

It is also important to grant each Gospel its unique perspective and not read into it the perspective of another. We have no right, for example, to import into Luke the particular form of incarnational theology, based largely upon the Gospel of John, that made its way into the orthodox creeds. Only when we allow each writing its own way of depicting Jesus will we be able to understand what each has to say individually about the meaning of his life. And what is true of Jesus is true of other characters as well. The disciples, for example, play differing roles in each of the four stories; and each story has its own distinctive cast of characters. The same point holds with respect to plot. We have no right to read into John the very different order of events found in Mark.

3. "The Narrator," "the Reader," and the Reading Process

The various schools of literary criticism necessarily employ particular technical vocabularies. I have sought to reduce such terminology to a bare minimum by limiting myself to two technical terms: "the narrator" and "the reader." In explaining my use of these two terms, I will also define more precisely the reader-response approach I will employ.[1]

a. The Narrator

By "the narrator," literary critics do not mean the author, the actual person who wrote the story. They mean the "voice" that tells the story. In some literary works, the narrator is one of the characters in the story. More frequently, the narrator is anonymous. All four Gospels employ an anonymous narrator, although in a few passages in Acts—written in the first-person plural—the narrator appears to be an unidentified character in the story.

Narrators, as Mark Allan Powell puts the matter, "vary as to how much they know and how much they choose to tell." When narrators are characters, their knowledge will probably be limited to what such characters would reasonably know. The narrators in the Gospels, however, fall near the other end of the spectrum. Powell describes them as "highly knowledgeable," noting that they know "the inner thoughts and motivations of the characters they describe." But, at least in the case of the Synoptics, they do show some limitations. They neither offer "descriptions of heaven and hell" nor "presume to speak directly for God" as Jesus does.[2]

b. The Reader

"The reader" might seem to be a self-explanatory term, but it is easily misunderstood. When reader-oriented critics refer to the reader, they are not speaking of some actual person, whether past or present. They are referring to a construct of their own devising, designed as an aid to interpretation. The critic, in other words, tries to imagine how a reader who follows the narrator's leads would read the story. By intentionally taking up the stance of this hypothetical reader, the critic sharpens her or his perceptions and approaches the narrative in a focused and systematic way.

The various schools of literary interpretation vary somewhat in their definitions of the reader. Narrative criticism, which is closely akin to the reader-response approach, tends to think of the reader as someone who knows the entire story very well, who has read it before and is therefore able to per-

---

1. See John A. Darr, *On Character Building: The Reader and the Rhetoric of Characterization in Luke-Acts* (Louisville: Westminster/John Knox, 1992), chap. 1, for a fuller statement of the approach that has most influenced my own. Darr's views are presented in more detail in his doctoral dissertation: "'Glorified in the Presence of Kings': A Literary-Critical Study of Herod the Tetrarch in Luke-Acts" (Vanderbilt, 1987).

2. Mark Allan Powell, *What Is Narrative Criticism?* Guides to Biblical Scholarship (Minneapolis: Fortress Press, 1990), 25–26.

ceive all sorts of relationships between the various parts of the story.[3] The advantage of defining the reader this way is that it allows the critic great freedom in noting such relationships.

Reader-response criticism, by contrast, tends to posit a first-time reader, who does not know the ultimate outcome of the story. Such a reader may make guesses about what is to happen next, but may in fact be surprised as the story unfolds. The advantage of this approach is that it helps to preserve the sequential nature of the narrative. In taking up the perspective of the reader who is naive regarding what is to come, the critic is able to imagine that reader's questions, remembrances, and feelings, such as disappointment, confusion, or amazement.

Neither of these schools of criticism is primarily interested in who the actual first readers of the work were. But many representatives of both camps recognize that the critic's historical knowledge is often essential, precisely because the text itself sometimes implies a reader who has such knowledge. The Gospels, for example, presuppose readers who are familiar with the Jewish Scriptures. To the extent that critics stress the importance of identifying presupposed knowledge, they are attempting to endow their hypothetical readers with some of the qualities of actual readers.

c. The Reading Process

It is as important to specify what the reader does as it is to say who the reader is. In other words, a reader-response approach requires some definition of what happens in the reading process. When actual readers read a story, they remember a good bit of what has happened before, and they anticipate what is to come. They form opinions about the characters, becoming attached to some and repelled by others; and they hope for certain turns of events and build up dreads about others. In doing all this, they are active participants in the story.

But their participation goes even farther. A story does not—indeed, cannot—tell everything. It always leaves something to its readers' imaginative powers. So they must make concrete what the narrator leaves in general terms, and they must even fill in gaps in the plot and in the development of characters. In the end, they try to understand the story as a coherent whole and often assign some specific meaning to what they have read. And they sometimes come away with insights regarding life in general or their own lives. Readers do not write their own stories, but they do participate in making narrators' stories complete and in bringing them to life.

---

3. Ibid., 19–21.

Fig. 26. Wycliffe Bible (Egerton Ms. 618, British Museum, 14th cent.)

Readers also move "in" and "out" of the story, sometimes utterly caught up in it but at other times disengaging themselves in order to reflect on ideas and even to assess their own reactions. Sometimes readers finish a story with a keen sense of satisfaction. But they must often revise their judgments and expectations along the way, and sometimes they must acknowledge that their hopes were dashed by the development of the story.

Because actual readers perform all these actions, reader-response critics try to bring to expression some of the key thoughts and feelings that a reader focused intently on the narrator's clues might reasonably have. There is, of course, a certain subjectivity in this method of criticism, since it involves the critic's own imagination. And the possibilities for a reader's actions are of course far broader than any critic could begin to "record"—or put into an essay of reasonable length! But the value of this approach is that, by focusing precisely on the reading process, it can help actual readers with their own task of truly engaging the text.

d. The Approach of the Present Text

In the initial approach to each of our four narratives, I will assume the role of the reader-response critic, which means trying to take up the perspective of "the reader." In doing so, I will posit a first-time reader who does not know the ultimate outcome of the story but who is able to remember in perfect detail everything that has gone before. In terms of more specific knowledge, my reader also knows the Jewish Scriptures in Greek (the Septuagint) and shares the broad outlines of the common knowledge of the Hellenistic culture.

I will, of necessity, be selective in actions I assign to this reader. But I will always seek to focus on lines of thinking and feeling that are in fact invited by the narrator's voice.

My attempt at "objectivity," however, cannot provide assurance to the reader of *this* text that the reader I posit is approaching these stories in a valid way. The point of the critic's observations is to assist others in doing their own reading and evaluation. I should also say that I do not assume that my reader's responses are the only possible, or only valid, ones. I present them as specific "performances" of the texts, which are not intended to rule out other, perhaps quite different, ways in which one might find meaning in them.

One final note on terminology: when I want to indicate the actual author of a New Testament writing I will say so explicitly; I will refer to "the author," "the author of Mark," etc. I have reserved the names "Matthew," "Mark," "Luke," and "John" to refer to the writings themselves.

4. What Is a "Gospel"?

The English word "gospel," derived from the Anglo-Saxon *godspel,* translates the Greek *euangelion:* the meaning, in each case, is "good news." The Gospel of Mark begins with an indication that the story of Jesus is to be understood as precisely that: "The beginning of the good news of Jesus Christ...." In designating the four stories of Jesus' life as "Gospels" and placing them together at the head of the canon, church tradition does more than recognize the literary similarities among these works. It indicates the centrality of the Jesus story in Christian faith, and it characterizes that story precisely as did the author of Mark: "good news" for humankind.

This fact in itself should tell us something about the nature of these writings. Scholars have long debated whether and in what sense they are to be understood as "biographies" of Jesus. Some have argued that the Gospels constitute a unique literary genre in the ancient world, while others have found significant ways in which they parallel ancient biographies. This debate need not concern us here. The important point for our purposes is that the Gospel writers, sometimes called "the evangelists" (those who announced the good news), obviously wrote with the explicit intention of engendering or nurturing Christian faith. Their purpose, we should remember, was not to report factual material in a neutral way but to convince those for whom they wrote of the truth of their witness.

STUDY QUESTIONS

1. Explain the terms "narrator" and "reader" as used in reader-response criticism.

2. Explain the difference between reader-response criticism and narrative criticism.

3. Are the Gospels written from an "objective" point of view? Should they be?

FOR FURTHER READING

Shuler, Philip. *A Genre for the Gospels: The Biographical Character of Matthew.* Philadelphia: Fortress Press, 1982. Argues that Matthew has some characteristics of an ancient encomium, a type of biography that heaps praise upon its subject.

Talbert, Charles. *What Is a Gospel? The Genre of the Canonical Gospels.* Philadelphia: Fortress Press, 1977. Argues that the Gospels conform to the genre of biography, as known in the ancient world.

Chapter 5

Mark

———— ✠ ————

1. The Story of Jesus in Mark

a. 1:1-13[1]

In the very first sentence of Mark, the narrator indicates that what is to follow is "good news" and concerns Jesus, Messiah (Christ) and Son of God. The reader is therefore prepared to hear a story about God's fulfillment of the ancient promises to Israel and will identify Jesus as the figure mentioned in the quotation from the Jewish Scriptures: the "voice of one crying in the wilderness," sent to "prepare the way of the Lord."[2]

In v. 4 a character named John appears, preaching baptism, forgiveness, and repentance. His message suggests both renewal and fulfillment, as does the place of his baptismal activity, that is, the river Jordan, scene of the Hebrews' entrance into the promised land. In the announcement that someone else is to come, who will baptize with the Holy Spirit, the reader will recognize another sign of fulfillment, since many Jews believed that the Spirit had departed Israel and would return only in the coming age. It will also be clear that the reference is to Jesus, who in fact comes on the scene and is baptized (1:9).

By treating the reader to Jesus' vision of the Holy Spirit and audition of the voice of God, the narrator establishes credibility regarding the earlier proclamation of who Jesus is and reinforces the term used earlier—Son of God. When the Spirit then drives Jesus into the wilderness the reader can begin to

---

1. Text divisions are based on Vernon K. Robbins, *Jesus the Teacher: A Socio-Rhetorical Interpretation of Mark* (Philadelphia: Fortress Press, 1984).

2. See Mary Ann Tolbert, *Sowing the Gospel: Mark's World in Literary Perspective* (Minneapolis: Fortress Press, 1989), 239–48. In both Matthew and Luke this passage is applied to John the Baptist. But in Mark the passage occurs before John's appearance, so the natural association is with Jesus.

sense a "cosmic" conflict. Satan tempts Jesus, seeking to subvert his mission, and the wild beasts suggest danger. But the ministering angels signify God's presence with Jesus and approval of his mission.

b. 1:14—3:6

There is a turn in the plot in 1:14-15, where the narrator notes John's arrest and the beginning of Jesus' proclamation, in Galilee, of the Rule of God. The immediate response of the Galilean fishermen to Jesus' invitation to discipleship creates a sense of rapid movement: the mission is underway.

When Jesus begins to teach in a synagogue (1:21), the narrator hints at a rift between Jesus and the religious authorities by observing that the people contrast his authoritative words to the teachings of the scribes (1:22). But the reader's attention will focus on the encounter with the unclean spirit, which increases the sense of cosmic warfare. The demon's recognition of Jesus provides a new and eerie confirmation of Jesus' status, and the exorcism impresses the reader with his uncanny power.

Jesus commands the spirit to silence before casting it out (1:25). The narrator eventually offers a partial explanation, but at the same time introduces a new theme that will puzzle the reader. Jesus continues his activities, and his fame spreads (1:28). But he attempts to maintain some sort of secrecy. The narrator explains his silencing of the demons with the phrase "because they knew him" (1:34), and in 1:44 Jesus tells a leper he has healed to "say nothing to anyone." The reader will want to know why Jesus is hiding his identity.

In the stories in 2:1—3:6, the theme of conflict with the religious authorities becomes explicit. Scribes and Pharisees criticize Jesus for pronouncing a man's sins forgiven, for eating with "tax collectors and sinners," and for Sabbath violation. In each of the stories Jesus in some way "bests" his opponents, quoting scriptural precedent or uttering a saying that presumably silences them. He also makes oblique references to his own status, speaking of the "Son of man" and of the "bridegroom" who will soon be "taken away." The reader will sense that these terms are Jesus' self-references, but the narrator gives no help in interpreting precisely what they mean.

Clearer in its import is the saying on new wine and old wineskins (2:22): Jesus is in some way a new beginning. But the reader is aware that the expected Rule is dawning in the midst of conflict, a point underscored by the conclusion to the series of stories: the Pharisees begin to hatch a plot "to destroy him" (3:6).

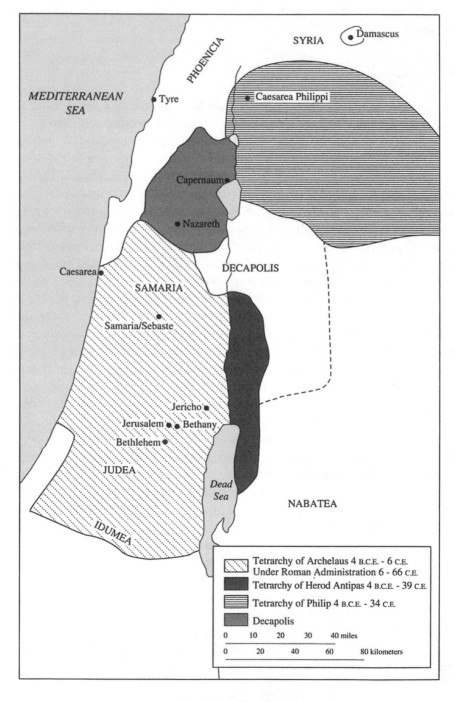

Fig. 27. Jewish Palestine and Surrounding Territory. *(Map by Parrot Graphics)*

c. 3:7—5:43

In 3:7-12 the narrator shifts the scene and again summarizes Jesus' activity. Demons continue to recognize Jesus, who explicitly forbids them to make his identity known. Then in 3:13 Jesus withdraws to a mountain, where he appoints twelve disciples as an inner circle, gives them authority to preach and cast out demons, and gives the nickname "Peter" to Simon. The reader will assume that these chosen ones will play a positive role in the drama, although the reference to Judas' betrayal adds a qualifying note.

An unexpected twist is added to the conflict in 3:21: the narrator introduces Jesus' own family members, who try to stop his activity, as the scribes contend that he is demonically possessed. The reader will be able to draw some conclusions from Jesus' logical victory over the scribes: Jesus is in mortal combat with Satan (the "strong man" of 3:27), and in casting out demons he is binding Satan in order to plunder his house, that is, to break the demonic hold upon the world. When Jesus later declares that only those who do God's will are his true family (3:33-35), the reader can push the point one step further. In the face of Jesus' conflict with evil, all who hear him must make a decision that may wrench them away from prior commitments, even those to their own families. The implication is that to reject Jesus' mission is to side with the demonic.

In chapter 4, where Jesus begins to teach beside the sea (of Galilee), the reader learns something of the specific content of his teaching. But here things get more complex and confusing. When the disciples ask for an explanation of the parable of the sower, Jesus comments that the parables are intended to keep those "outside" from getting the point, while the disciples have been given the "secret" of God's Rule. Then, disheartened at the disciples' dullness, he chastises them for not understanding but gives an allegorical explanation of the parable (4:13-20).

The reader will try to identify the various types of soil in the parable and explanation with varying responses to Jesus' own preaching (sowing), and it is already apparent that the Jewish authorities constitute the first type, in which the word takes no root at all. But Jesus' question and statement in 4:21-22, which transmute the metaphor from sowing seed to shedding light, speak directly to the reader's own life: those who desire to be disciples must preach the word themselves. After some additional parables and sayings, the narrator makes the summary statement that Jesus taught in parables "as they were able to hear it" (4:33).

Because the narrator also notes that Jesus explains things privately to his disciples (4:34), the reader, who still expects them to serve as model followers

Fig. 28. The Temple of Artemis (Goddess of the Moon). Located in ancient Gerasa, a city of the southern Decapolis, the heavily Hellenized district to the east of Jewish Palestine. Some manuscripts of Mark 5:1-13 relate a healing of a demoniac in Gerasa, but Matthew 8:28-34, along with other manuscripts of Mark, places the incident at Gadara in the northern Decapolis. *(Photo by Thomas Hoffman)*

of Jesus, will presume that they are beginning to understand. Immediately, however, the narrator foils this positive expectation. Caught in a storm in their little boat, the disciples are terror-stricken. When Jesus miraculously calms the storm but rebukes the disciples for their lack of faith, two themes are raised to a higher pitch. Jesus' awesome power extends now even to nature itself; but the disciples cannot grasp what is happening. *"Who is this,"* they ask? The reader will empathize with their fear, but will be disappointed at their lack of understanding. Although given the secret of God's Rule, those closest to Jesus seem to resemble the good soil less than the rocky soil—which starts well, but ends in failure!

The heightening of Jesus' powers continues. Across the lake—in gentile territory, which is unclean in Jewish eyes—he heals a demoniac possessed by a "legion" of demons and sends them away in a dramatic fashion (5:1-13). The reader will notice that, in sharp contrast to his practice in Galilee, Jesus commands the man to tell what has been done for him. The man in fact does so, exemplifying the good soil of the parable far better than do the disciples.

Back on Jewish territory, Jesus performs two even more astonishing feats. A woman is healed merely by touching his garment, and he actually raises a twelve-year-old girl from the dead. Then the note of secrecy reemerges: Jesus insists that no one should know of this latter deed (5:43). Thus a certain paradox cannot escape the reader. In his conflict with Satan, Jesus is exercising enormous power, which will strike the reader as evidence of his status as Son of God. Yet his identity and mission are cloaked in an air of secrecy and mystery. Why?

d. 6:1—8:26

Following these dramatic events, Jesus returns to his home area only to be met with rejection. His saying on a prophet's lack of honor among his own people (6:4) reminds the reader of the earlier conflict with his family, just as his surprise at the unbelief he now encounters is reminiscent of his reaction to the disciples' dullness. The reader will thus view Jesus as striving unsuccessfully to get his point across and distressed at the response; he will appear to the reader as powerful, but not omniscient or omnipotent. His ability to perform miracles depends upon the faith of those to whom he ministers.

When Jesus now sends his disciples on a mission, giving them "authority over the unclean spirits" (6:7), the reader will surmise that they are at last realizing their potential. For they are successful both in healings and in exorcisms, the very works Jesus himself has performed.

The speculation about Jesus in 6:14-16 encourages the reader to treat his identity as a crucial issue. And the flashback revealing Herod's execution of John the baptizer in 6:17-29 keeps the motif of conflict alive as a series of accounts dramatize Jesus' power. Highlighted by a miraculous feeding (6:30-44) and an eerie scene on the sea, the series ends with a description of how the masses flock to Jesus for healing (6:56). The reader is thus impressed with Jesus' success. Along the way, however, the narrator has undermined the positive view of the disciples by describing their obtuseness in the feeding story (6:37) and their display of fear on the sea (6:49), but most of all by the pronouncement in 6:52 that "their hearts were hardened."

The note of success in 6:56 will encourage the reader to contrast the people's reaction with that of the Pharisees in the ensuing material, as the narrator brings the conflict with them back into the foreground. A dispute over "the tradition of the elders" regarding ritual law (7:1-16) gives Jesus the opportunity to brand the Pharisees hypocrites who neglect human need and place human tradition above God's own commandments. Intruding in 7:19 to point out that Jesus' words effectively abolish the dietary regulations, the narrator invites the conclusion that Jesus is breaking sharply with established tradition, but precisely in order to honor God's command.

In 7:24, the narrator brings Jesus once again into gentile territory, where he is "bested" by a Syrophoenician woman in a verbal encounter regarding the "rights" of Gentiles to his ministry. The reader will be initially surprised but will, after Jesus pronounces the woman's daughter healed from afar, reflect on the place of Gentiles in Jesus' mission and contrast the gentile woman's faith to the attitude of the Pharisees. When, after another miraculous feeding, the Pharisees approach Jesus (8:11-13), the reader sees their full hypocrisy. They converse with him only to test him, asking for a sign on the heels of awesome deeds of power!

Jesus' warning to the disciples in 8:15 will reinforce the negative view of the Pharisees, but the reader's attention quickly shifts back to the failings of the disciples. They take Jesus' symbolic statement about yeast in a crudely literal fashion. And his displeasure is evident in the question he poses regarding the significance of the twelve and seven baskets of bread left over from the feedings: "Do you not yet understand?" The implication is that they do not, indeed, understand. But neither does the reader, who has received much information the disciples lack. The seven and the twelve seem to have significance, but it remains unexplained.

The note of mystery and secrecy thus reasserts itself with a vengeance, and it continues in 8:22-26. Jesus heals a blind man—half way! Has Jesus failed? He tries again, and the man sees clearly. What is the reader to make of this?

e. 8:27—10:45

In 8:27, Jesus, again in gentile territory, suddenly confronts the disciples, for the first time, with the question of his identity. The reader will remember not only the speculation in 6:14-16 but all the ways in which the evidence for Jesus' status has accumulated throughout the story. Peter's forthright answer will thus seem correct: "You are the Messiah." But Jesus' reply is puzzling. Employing the same Greek verb (*epitimaō*) with which he earlier silenced demons—but using it in a very odd way—he rebukes (NRSV: "sternly ordered") the disciples "not to tell anyone about him." Has he accepted Peter's confession that he is the Messiah? Has he rejected it? The reader cannot be sure.

The narrator does not answer the reader's questions directly. Jesus immediately begins to teach the disciples privately, telling them "quite openly" about the coming death and resurrection of the Son of man, whom the reader will identify with Jesus himself. But Peter now rebukes (*epitimaō*) Jesus, indicating his unwillingness for Jesus to die. In the harshest terms, Jesus again rebukes Peter, calling him "Satan"! Then he speaks to the crowd and the disciples, linking the role of discipleship to his own coming fate.

The reader will not miss the contrast between Jesus' present openness and his earlier secrecy and will sense that he has made an important disclosure. At least part of what has been hidden, and must remain hidden to outsiders, is that Jesus, to fulfill his mission, must die. And to follow Jesus means to bear one's own cross. Hiddenness and mystery thus give rise to paradox and irony. One must lose one's life to find it (8:35). Was this what Peter could not—would not—understand? The reader can sympathize with Peter's reaction. Impressed with the awesome power of the Son of God, the reader too will find Jesus' talk of death and denial abrasive—and must wrestle with the paradox.

When in 9:2 Jesus takes the disciples to a mountaintop and is transfigured before them, the reader receives additional, dramatic testimony to Jesus' status: the appearances of Moses and Elijah, and once again the voice from heaven proclaiming him Son of God. But the reassuring vision will clash with the narrator's presentation of the disciples. Peter does not know what to say, and all the disciples are afraid and cannot understand Jesus' reference to his coming resurrection. Then, at the foot of the mountain, Jesus finds that those left behind have failed in an attempt to cast out a demon. He performs the exorcism, but not before he has accused the disciples: "O faithless generation. . . . " The reader is clearer than ever about who Jesus is, but is increasingly aware of the disciples' inadequacies.

Noting in 9:30-32 that Jesus is traveling *secretly* through Galilee and speaking for a second time about his coming death, the narrator calls attention yet again to the disciples' fear and lack of comprehension. Then, in 9:34, it becomes clear that the disciples have been haggling over who among them is the greatest. Could any conversation be less appropriate to the situation? The pattern following the first prediction is repeated: again Jesus teaches about discipleship. But the reader knows that the disciples do not really understand him and are not prepared for the kind of discipleship he demands.

In 10:1, the scene shifts and Jesus is in a public setting, where he continues his teaching by addressing specific areas of ethical concern. When he reprimands the man who calls him "good" (10:17-18), noting that God alone deserves such praise, the reader will note that the narrator has consistently presented Jesus as Messiah/Son of God, but not *as God*. It is God's Rule that Jesus has proclaimed. And in now directing the inquirer to God's commandments (10:19), Jesus begins a characterization of that Rule that continues into the material that follows (10:23-31). The radical character of this teaching—evident, for example, in the demand he makes on the inquirer in 10:21—invites the reader to reflect upon the nature of life in the new age. And Jesus' promise of goods and families "now in this age" (10:30) suggests that the community he is gathering is called to manifest God's Rule in the here and now. Already informed in the abstract about the nature of discipleship, the reader now gets a glimpse of life, as it should be, in the Christian community. Like the call to discipleship, it is full of paradoxes: one leaves everything, but gains more—"with persecutions" (10:30)!

In 10:32-34, Jesus informs his followers that they are headed to Jerusalem, where he will die. In this account of Jesus' third prediction of his death and resurrection, the narrator takes pains to reemphasize the aura of terror and mystery and also repeats the familiar pattern linking Jesus' death with discipleship. The paradoxes of 10:43-44—great among you/your servant; first among you/slave of all—are powerful reminders of the earlier irony of losing one's life to find it. But the narrator now provides a new element, a statement on the meaning of Jesus' death: "For the Son of Man came not to be served but to serve, *and to give his life as a ransom for many*." Somehow, in a way that is not elaborated but only suggested through the metaphor of "ransom," Jesus' death and resurrection will *set human beings free*.

The reader has thus gained some insight into the secrecy that has shrouded the narrator's tale from the beginning. But this insight is couched in paradoxical form, and central characters in the drama do not grasp it. The air of mystery prevails. Nevertheless, the theme of prediction, linked to the narrator's use of the Jewish Scriptures, keeps alive the impression that in all that is happening God is somehow active. Jesus knows what is to come.

f. 10:46—12:44

When Jesus and his followers come to Jericho, which lies at the base of the mountain atop which Jerusalem is set, the reader will sense that this is the last leg of the fateful journey. And the incident that occurs here directs attention forward to Jerusalem. A blind man addresses Jesus as "Son of David"—that is to say, as Messiah-king—and Jesus heals him without a word of rebuke. Jewish monarchs reign from Jerusalem: will Jesus claim his crown when he arrives? No, the reader remembers that in 10:32-34 Jesus said that he will die in Jerusalem. But what, then, of the messianic title?

The incident at Jericho also points backward. The reader will remember an earlier story of a blind man, the odd two-stage healing that preceded the three instances in which Jesus predicted his death and linked it to discipleship. Together the two stories "frame" these predictions and invite the reader to reconsider them in light of the metaphors of blindness and sight and of the distinction between partial "seeing" and full "seeing." The reader has already come to understand that Jesus' mission involves his death, and that discipleship means bearing one's cross. What the metaphor of stages of sight adds is a confirmation that acceptance of Jesus' suffering, and of one's own as a disciple, represents a deeper level of understanding than is possessed by those who expect a more visible, less paradoxical victory of their Messiah. But precisely how does one reconcile the notion of a suffering Messiah and suffering disciples with the expectation of a messianic king who would establish peace and justice? The reader will want to read on—and "see" more clearly.

There is, however, no immediate answer to these questions. The reader may in fact be surprised that the narrator now relates a scene in which Jesus appears as a quite public and apparently triumphant Messiah. Not only do the crowd's accolades imply his status as Davidic king (11:9-10), but the colt on which he rides conjures up the image of the "messianic" procession in Zechariah 9:9.

The reader will thus understand that Jesus is wielding messianic authority when, on a second incursion into the city, he carries out a brief "occupation" of the temple and condemns both the commerce in the court and the exclusiveness of the temple worship. His citation of a scriptural passage that designates the temple "a house of prayer *for all the nations*" (11:17) will call to mind that Jesus had earlier extended his ministry of healing and exorcism into gentile territory and had abolished the system of clean and unclean foods. The reader will therefore conclude that Jesus is in some way opening God's Rule to the Gentiles.

The precise connection between the temple incident and the story that frames it, the strange account of the cursing of the fig tree, will be difficult to grasp at this point. But the reader will note the contrast between the unfruitful tree and the promise Jesus gives in verses 22-25. Faithlessness bears no fruit, while faith can move mountains!

Informed in 11:18 of the intent of the chief priests and scribes to kill Jesus, the reader will understand his interchanges with the Jewish leaders in 11:27—12:44 as a sign of the irreparable breach between the two opposing camps. The narrator makes certain in 12:12 that the reader interprets the preceding parable as a condemnation of Jesus' opponents, and the inquiring scribe's approval of Jesus' words in 12:32-34 draws an implicit contrast between this questioner's attitude and that of his fellows who have attacked Jesus. More explicit is the sharp contrast between the pretentious scribes and the rich on the one hand and the poor widow, who gave "everything she had," on the

Fig. 29. The Arrest of Christ/The Entry into Jerusalem
(Petrus and Malchus. West portal, capital zone. Cathedral, Chartres, France)

other (12:38-44). The reader will thus make a sharp distinction between those of sincere faith, who stand for love of God and neighbor (12:28-34), and those who pretend faith but "devour widows' houses" (12:40). The Jesus now on his way to his death is also the compassionate friend of the poor and the one who truly understands the nature of God's coming Rule.

Less clear to the reader will be the implications of Jesus' rejection of the scribes' identification of the Messiah as Son of David (12:35-37), arguing that the Messiah is in fact David's lord! Jesus has already passed up two opportunities to disclaim the title "Son of David" if that were his intention. The matter remains obscure.

The movement of the plot, however, is clear. The reader knows that Jesus is on his way to his death—and senses that this event is very near.

g. 13:1—15:47

(1) 13:1-37. Jesus' prediction of the destruction of the temple in 13:1-2 directs attention to the future. Then the disciples' question, put to him as he sits "on the Mount of olives, opposite the temple" (13:3), encourages the reader to listen for specific information about the expected end of the age. The first part of Jesus' answer—predictions of tumultuous events and the persecution of his followers, qualified by the disclaimer "but the end is still to come" (13:7)—disconnects the events surrounding the temple's destruction from the actual end of the age. And the narrator's "aside" in 13:14 ("let the reader understand") suggests that the reader should recognize the "desolating sacrilege" as an event predicted in Daniel 9:27 and fulfilled in the reader's own time. The point is that Jesus' followers after his death should not be led astray by false prophets and false Christs who interpret contemporary events as the actual end of the age.

The reader gets not only information about the future, but also encouragement. For Jesus promises that those who endure the terrible trials to come will "be saved" (13:13) and underscores the point with the reminder, "I have already told you everything" (13:23). Knowledge thus has the function of supporting courage and faithfulness in a time of crisis.

Having made clear to the reader that the destruction of the temple is only the prelude to the end of the age, the narrator can now (13:24-27) have Jesus speak of the actual end: the whole cosmos will finally be disrupted, but then the Son of man will return. The reader, recalling Jesus' predictions of his death and resurrection, will understand that Jesus will return in glory at the end of the age and will thus be encouraged to endure the sufferings ahead in confidence of the final deliverance of those who remain faithful.

The saying about the fig tree (13:28-31) continues the hopeful mood, making clear that the signs just elaborated will indicate the nearness of Jesus' return. The positive image of the tree nevertheless calls back the negative image of the tree Jesus cursed in 11:14, and the reader can now make the connection between that tree and the temple. Like the fig tree, the temple, which was not bearing fruit, had to die!

The reader has been asked to read the signs of the time and take heart. But immediately there comes a disclaimer. No one but the Father—not even the Son!—knows the time of the end (13:32). The narrator thus weds the note of hope to a solemn injunction to "watchfulness" (13:33-37).

The long discourse in chapter 13 combines with Jesus' earlier predictions to give the reader a certain clarity on one level. The paradox of a suffering Messiah is "explained" by his eventual return, at the close of the age, as the triumphant Son of Man. Yet the disciples' own inability to grasp the matter and Jesus' ominous words about the persecution of his followers keep the themes of mystery, paradox, and irony alive. The reader has only a promise, qualified by warnings of grave difficulties that lie ahead. In the present,

Fig. 30. "Headpiece to 'Apparition': Christ on the Cross"
(Georges Rouault; French, c. 1939)

one must still follow a suffering Messiah by taking up one's cross. No intellectual clarification can unravel the inherent irony of such a proclamation of "good news." But there is that promise—by Jesus, whom the narrator has encouraged the reader to accept as Son of God.

(2) **14:1—15:47.** Through reference to the plot of the chief priests and scribes (14:1-2) and the story of the woman who anoints Jesus, the narrator now brings the focus back to his death. As events unfold, the reader is encouraged not only to anticipate that event but to give a negative evaluation to the disciples' behavior as it draws near. It is Judas, one of the Twelve, who gives the chief priests the opportunity to carry out their intentions; and during the Passover meal Jesus predicts that they will "all become deserters." Quickly, events bear him out: the disciples sleep while he prays (14:32-42), and Peter denies him three times (14:66-72).

The crowds of people also fail Jesus in the end, in effect pronouncing his death sentence (15:1-15). But there are minor characters who appear momentarily to minister to Jesus and share his suffering: Simon the leper, who has him to dinner (14:3); the woman who anoints him; Simon of Cyrene, who is compelled to carry his cross (15:21); a group of women among his followers, some of whom had "provided for him" in Galilee, who watch his crucifixion "from a distance" (15:40-41); and Joseph of Arimathea, who provides a tomb (15:46). The reader will see their actions as examples of "faith, being least, being a servant"[3]—that is, as models of discipleship—and will contrast these people with the Twelve and the crowds, who neither took up their crosses nor followed Jesus. The actions of those around Jesus during his final days thus serve as positive and negative paradigms for action in the postresurrection situation.

If the reader must evaluate the disciples and the crowds negatively, the harshest judgment must fall upon the various "authorities." They are cowardly types who fear the reaction of the masses and must arrest Jesus secretly and convict him by false witnesses. Utterly unable to comprehend Jesus' message, they are outright opponents of all that he stands for. Pilate, it is true, makes an attempt to set Jesus free. But, in the end, he acquiesces to the crowds out of fear (15:14-15). The reader will see the authorities involved in the arrest, trial, and crucifixion as of a piece with the earlier Jewish leaders whose intention in questioning him was always to entrap him, never really to hear him.

The reader will focus attention largely on Jesus himself and will observe a figure that in some ways contrasts with the powerful wonderworker of the early chapters. He admits to intense agony and prays for deliverance from his fate (14:34-36); he utters a cry of despair from the cross and dies with a cry of pain (15:34, 37). Yet he is resolute and obedient to God's will throughout the drama. He has the strength of silence in the face of false accusations, and he at last makes the open claim to messiahship that leads directly to his condemnation (14:62). In everything, he carries out the intention of God. As he has predicted many things before, now he predicts his disciples' failure but also a reunion with them in Galilee after his resurrection (14:27-28). As he had spoken of his death as a "ransom," now at the Passover meal he interprets his death in terms of the renewal of the covenant and points ahead to the new community and the Rule of God (14:24-25). Even his cry of despair is a quotation from the Jewish Scriptures.

The reader thus confronts in a new way the irony that has pervaded the story. Jesus, the powerful wonderworker, suffers a humiliating death; yet he wins a moral victory in facing it courageously, fulfilling the mandate he has

---

3. David Rhoads and Donald Michie, *Mark as Story: An Introduction to the Narrative of a Gospel* (Philadelphia: Fortress Press, 1982), 29–30.

received from God. The Roman centurion's words at the cross, in fact, provide a confirmation of the victory: "Truly this man was God's Son!" (15:39). Recalling the narrator's own presentation of Jesus as Son of God in 1:1, the reader will be inclined to accept this statement as an accurate portrayal of Jesus' status.

The centurion's confession, however, leaves the reader in a paradoxical position. Just when Jesus' weakness and helplessness become most apparent, someone is finally able to understand fully who he is. He has suffered humiliation and death, and the reader quickly learns that he is buried (15:46); so the note of tragedy is real. Yet Jesus has predicted his resurrection and triumphant return, and the reader has learned to trust his predictions. At his death, moreover, there are signs of God's reading of this tragic event: the darkness covering the land and the rending of the temple veil (15:33, 38), which suggests the renewal of the covenant to include Gentiles. Despite the solemnity of the moment, then, the reader reads on in the hope that Jesus' victory is more than the *merely* moral victory of the one who dies nobly in an ultimately lost cause. The paradox must be unraveled, the ambiguity dispelled.

h. 16:1-8

The reader's hopes are immediately raised. The women come early Sunday morning to anoint the body that was buried Friday afternoon. But the tomb is empty! And a mysterious young man in white proclaims Jesus' resurrection, reminding the women of Jesus' promise that he will "go before" his followers to Galilee. So far so good—a fitting *beginning* for an ending. But then the women flee in utter astonishment and, ignoring the command of the mysterious figure, tell no one about what has happened, *"for they were afraid."* On this ambiguous note, the Gospel ends abruptly.[4] Where *now* does the reader stand?

The clear implication is that Jesus has in fact been raised. But no one actually encounters the risen Jesus. There are no appearances, and the reader thus has no experience of Jesus' presence. Nor does the reader learn anything about the establishment of the postresurrection Christian community. The Twelve have vanished from the story; the last the reader heard of them was that they deserted Jesus! Only the women among his followers stood by

---

4. Some ancient manuscripts contain additional verses that bring Mark's ending into closer conformity with Matthew and Luke by depicting Jesus' appearances to various followers. The scholarly consensus, however, is that none of the longer endings belong to the original versions; they represent the attempts of manuscript copyists to provide a more "suitable" conclusion.

him, and it is appropriate that they witness the empty tomb. But in the end the reader learns that they were too fearful to carry out their task.

Ultimately, the reader stands in ambiguity, caught between hope and fear— precisely where human beings often find themselves as they struggle in the midst of life's difficulties. This ambiguity, however, is not a void. Jesus has made promises, and the reader has "heard" them. He has performed wonders, and the reader has "seen" them.

True, the reader has seen hopes dashed and has experienced tragedy. But the narrator has also prepared the reader, through the story of how Jesus met his own fate, to choose hope rather than fear even in the face of difficult circumstances. In the ambiguity that prevails at the end, the reader can now think back to the theme of secrecy at the beginning of the story. In the context of his powerful deeds, Jesus commands secrecy about his Messiahship. Facing death, however, he openly asserts his identity; and at his death the centurion recognizes him as Son of God. The reader is thus invited to apprehend Jesus' identity in a paradoxical way: to see in his "weakness" the power of God; to see in his "failure" God's way of ransoming the world; and to see in the ambiguous witness of the empty tomb a sign of ultimate victory. The reader is thus encouraged to maintain a hope that is appropriate to a mode of discipleship in which one must lose one's life to save it.

A question remains, however. If even the women who witness the empty tomb do not in the story line pick up the task of witnessing, then is there anyone else equipped to do so? "Of course there is: the audience itself."[5] The narrator's abrupt ending thus contains an implicit demand upon the reader, a call to tell again the story that has just been read.

2. Historical Readings of Mark: The Question of "Corrective Christology"

In order to gain understanding of the author's theological intentions, some scholars have sought to identify that author's historical context. Theodore J. Weeden and Werner Kelber, along with many others, have dated Mark just after the destruction of the temple in 70 C.E. and have interpreted the Gospel in light of those tumultuous years in which Christians may have suffered hardship and persecution.

Weeden argues, on the basis of a redaction-critical study, that the author shaped existing materials in order to deal with a conflict within the Chris-

---

5. Tolbert, *Sowing the Gospel*, 297.

tian community. According to this reading, the references to "false Messiahs and false prophets" in 13:6, 21-23 refer to Christians who have come into the author's community from outside, promoting claims that appear attractive to people facing difficulties. These "false Christs" claim such a close spiritual union with the risen Jesus that it enables them actually to claim a kind of "identity" with Christ, saying "I am he" (13:6). Corresponding to their notion of spiritual union is a specific type of Christology: these "false Christs" emphasize Jesus' awesome power, understanding him in light of a particular type of Hellenistic wonderworker known as a "divine man," which some scholars think was a currently popular figure.

Many interpreters have termed this christological perspective "triumphalist." For it stresses Jesus' triumph over death to the exclusion of his suffering, and it understands the life of discipleship as so spirit-filled that it overcomes virtually all human problems.

Weeden believes that the author of Mark wrote in order to undermine these views. The first part of the Gospel presents a "divine man" Christology that depicts Jesus as a miracle-worker; from 8:27 on, however, this "triumphalist" understanding gives way to the image of a Jesus on his way to suffering and death, calling his followers to a similar life-style. Weeden makes much of the point that the Twelve do not in fact embrace this life-style. He denies that the Gospel implies their later restoration, arguing that in Mark they appear as surrogates for the "false Christs" of the author's situation! They stand as totally negative examples.

Kelber too believes that the Gospel of Mark portrays the disciples in a totally negative way. For him, however, they are surrogates for the Jerusalem church, with which tradition associated them. In his view, the author wrote in Galilee, shortly after the destruction of the temple, to explain how such an event could have happened. And the explanation is that the disciples themselves sowed the seeds of this disaster. The Gospel thus rejects both the Twelve and the Jerusalem church as failures and hints that the Galilean community is the authentic "heart" of the Christian movement.

Kelber emphasizes the theme of Jewish-gentile unity in Mark. Jesus' early ministry in Galilee, for example, which entailed periodic treks into gentile territory, appears as a way of establishing a base community that unites Jews and Gentiles. And much of the disciples' obtuseness is a result of their failure to accept this unity: they should have been able to grasp this point from Jesus' two feedings, one on Jewish soil and one on gentile, and from the presence of the "one loaf" in their boat (8:14).

Kelber, like Weeden, thinks the author of Mark tried to undermine a "divine man" Christology. Along similar lines, Norman Perrin has argued that

Fig. 31. St. Mark

the author intentionally balanced the title "Son of God" with "Son of man," which is particularly associated with Jesus' death.[6] Here again a Christology of suffering corrects a triumphalist, "divine man" Christology.

It is clear that Mark links both Christology and discipleship to the "way of the cross." Many scholars doubt, however, that the notion of "divine man" was as clearly developed a concept in the Hellenistic world as these theories suppose. And Jack D. Kingsbury has argued that while the christological view of Mark's early chapters is developed and deepened in the later chapters, it is by no means corrected.[7]

Mary Ann Tolbert, moreover, contends that attempts to interpret Mark in light of a specific historical setting do less than justice to the character of this work as narrative. While such a format would have been a poor choice as a vehicle for the correction of a theological view, it was an excellent means of arousing "the emotions of the reader on Jesus' behalf.".[8] And it was a power-

6. Norman Perrin, "Towards an Interpretation of the Gospel of Mark," in Hans Dieter Betz, ed., *A Modern Pilgrimage in Christology: A Discussion with Norman Perrin* (Missoula, Mont.: Society of Biblical Literature, 1974), 1–52.

7. Jack Dean Kingsbury, *The Christology of Mark's Gospel* (Philadelphia: Fortress Press, 1983).

8. Tolbert, *Sowing the Gospel,* 303–4.

ful way of offering encouragement to Christians facing persecution and of persuading others who had not yet made a Christian commitment

3. The Problem of the Disciples

For many scholars, the judgment that the disciples are seen in a totally negative light goes too far. Some therefore argue that the narrative invites the reader to look beyond the plotted events and imagine Jesus' eventual reunion with the disciples that is indicated in 16:7.[9] Many interpreters, however, think that 16:7 refers to Jesus' return at the end of the age, not a resurrection appearance. And Robert Fowler finds speculation about the ultimate fate of the disciples irrelevant to the reader, since Mark is designed less to make assertions about the characters in the story than to have an effect upon the reader.[10] So the question with which those who read Mark are left is not what becomes of the disciples but how they themselves will respond to the story the narrator has told.

It is nevertheless important to note that the narrative consistently presupposes the existence of a postresurrection Christian community. So it makes some sense to argue that one effect of the ending is to encourage the reader to imagine a postresurrection appearance that calls Jesus' followers back together. But Fowler and Tolbert are surely correct in identifying the primary effect of that ending as a call for the reader's self-examination. And the clarity of that call is partly dependent upon the fact that, insofar as the actually plotted events are concerned, not only the disciples but all other candidates for "good soil" end up as failures.

4. A Structuralist Reading

Elizabeth Struthers Malbon has carried out a structuralist study of all the spatial terminology in Mark: geopolitical, topographical, and architectural. The particular form of structuralism she employs is that of Claude Lévi-Strauss, who believes that myths arise in order to mediate between "irreconcilable opposites" in the experiences of given peoples. Although Mark is not a "myth"

---

9. See Norman R. Petersen, *Literary Criticism for New Testament Critics* (Philadelphia: Fortress Press, 1978), 49–80.

10. Robert M. Fowler, *Let the Reader Understand: Reader-Response Criticism and the Gospel of Mark* (Minneapolis: Fortress Press, 1991), 79.

in the strict sense applied to the creation-stories of archaic societies, Malbon argues that it has a mythic dimension that justifies her analysis.

In Malbon's view, the spatial terminology in Mark reveals an underlying opposition between order and chaos, which is progressively mediated by a series of "third terms." For example: the Jewish homeland stands for the familiar (order) and foreign lands for the strange (chaos); Jesus' travels across the Sea of Galilee, which stands between them, becomes a way of reconciling these opposites. Or again, heaven stands for promise (order) and earth—the scene of sickness, danger, etc.—for threat (chaos); mountain, which is the scene of divine-human encounters, particularly in relation to Jesus—mediates between them.

The comprehensive mediating term for the whole gospel is "way," the way on which Jesus travels and on which he calls his followers. This leads to an interesting observation about the Markan ending. The mysterious figure at the tomb commands the women to tell the disciples that Jesus is "going ahead of" them to Galilee, implying that Jesus himself is "on the way" to Galilee and that the disciples soon will be also. Thus Malbon concludes: "The tension of the Markan ending reflects the tension of the Good News according to Mark: conflict between the chaos and order of life is overcome not in arriving but in being on the way."[11]

5. Mark's Response to Social Context: Competing Evaluations

a. Mark as a Call to Nonviolent Revolution

Several scholars have found the Gospel of Mark particularly amenable to interpretation through sociopolitical categories. Ched Myers has argued that the story of Jesus in Mark presents a call to discipleship that explicitly embraces the social, economic, and political aspects of life.[12] According to Myers, the author of Mark wrote in Galilee, shortly before (rather than after) the destruction of the temple, at a time when Christians were subject to persecution from the oppressive Romans on the one hand and Jews pressuring them to join the rebellion on the other. Rejecting the standard alternatives of armed rebellion, collaboration, and withdrawal from society, this author wrote in order to offer another path: nonviolent resistance.

---

11. Elizabeth Struthers Malbon, *Narrative Space and Mythic Meaning in Mark* (San Francisco: Harper & Row, 1986), 168.

12. Ched Myers, *Binding the Strong Man: A Political Reading of Mark's Story of Jesus* (Maryknoll, N.Y.: Orbis Books, 1990).

Mark is, according to this reading, a profoundly "subversive" document in the sense that it presents an alternative to the existing societal structures. Myers finds a critique of Roman power already in the designation of the story as *euangelion,* that is, "gospel," or "good news." Because it was common to use the term *euangelion* in relation to military victories, the application of this term to the story of Jesus constitutes a challenge to the sovereignty of the empire. And the story of the exorcism in 5:1-13 symbolizes the downfall of Roman power. To call the demons "legion" is to associate them with the legions of Roman soldiers that imprisoned the land, and to have them drowned in the sea is to suggest their destruction in a new exodus. Even the Markan metaphor for discipleship, to take up one's cross, has, in light of the corpses of rebels that hung from Roman crosses along the Palestinian roadsides, a clearly political thrust.

According to Myers, however, Mark's subversiveness is pointed more directly at the Jewish establishment. Jesus' early activities in Galilee challenge the system of ritual purity and the authority of the established leadership, and the parable in 12:1-11 is a condemnation of the ruling class in the guise of the evil tenants of the landowner's vineyard. Economics, moreover, stands at the very heart of the power structure under attack. Jesus condemns the scribes in 12:40 because they "devour widows' houses," and in 11:17 he declares that the temple itself has become "a den of robbers." And, in contrast to the exploitative economics of the existing system, the Gospel of Mark presents the alternative of a new economic order based upon sharing. This, according to Myers, is the meaning of the promise of the reception of houses, lands, and families in 10:29-31. This new order, however, will not come through military endeavor; nor will it simply appear out of nowhere. It will grow slowly, like the seeds in 4:26-32, from a small beginning. It is a revolution from below—nonviolent, but thoroughly subversive of the present order. Those who wish to be disciples must take up the task of "sowing"—along with their crosses!

b. Mark as Anti-worldly and Vindictive

If we read Mark as Myers proposes, it will merit a highly positive evaluation from a perspective, such as that of liberation theology, that values an indictment of the oppressive forces in society. Burton Mack, however, gives a very different evaluation of this Gospel in terms of its impact upon social issues.[13] Seeking to place Mark in a particular social history, he concludes that it was

---

13. Burton L. Mack, *A Myth of Innocence: Mark and Christian Origins* (Philadelphia: Fortress Press, 1988).

a response of a writer within a group of Jesus' followers, probably in southern Syria shortly *after* the destruction of the temple, to the group's failure to convince the Jewish synagogues of the truth of their point of view.

Mack is highly critical of what he calls "pious" readings of Mark that see it as a call to humility, self-criticism, and service. While such themes are present in one sense, he argues, they must be viewed against the background of Mark's apocalyptic point of view. If Mark calls readers to service, it is only to others within the Christian community. Those outside stand utterly condemned, and the destruction of the temple comes precisely as God's judgment against the Jewish people for rejecting Jesus.

Mack therefore judges Mark to be an extremely violent and vindictive writing. Its plot of the conflict between the perfectly righteous and innocent Son of God against the forces of evil, he argues, "lies at the very foundation of the long, ugly history of Christian attitudes toward Jews and Judaism."[14] And on the political level it has even fed the notion of pure and innocent savior-nations whose moral duty it is to intervene in the affairs of others. Far from a text of liberation, then, this Gospel is for Mack an anti-worldly document with nothing positive to offer to contemporary attempts to live peacefully and well within the world.

Most New Testament scholars will view Mack's evaluation as one-sided, but one cannot easily dismiss his arguments. We will return to the question of anti-Judaism in connection with the Gospel of Matthew and to that of apocalyptic anti-worldliness in connection with the book of Revelation. For now, it is important to focus on a broader issue raised by the competing evaluations of Myers and Mack. One way of dealing with the discrepancy is to pronounce one (or perhaps both) of these readings simply wrong. But another way would be to point out that part of the difference between Myers and Mack is that they employ very different evaluative schemes. Perhaps, then, the discrepancy between the two is not simply one of exegesis but is, more profoundly, one of hermeneutics, involving the question of how one approaches a text in order to find meaning in it.

6. Philosophical/Theological Problems

The hermeneutical question surfaces again when we consider the tension between determinism and contingency in this Gospel. Mark presents Jesus' death as in accordance with God's will, and the notations that the events in

---

14. Ibid., 375.

the story are fulfillment of Scripture lend a predestinarian air to the whole drama. The secrecy theme reinforces this aspect of the story: the fact that Jesus teaches in parables to prevent outsiders from understanding suggests that the course of events is indeed foreordained. On the other hand, there are elements in the story that make no sense apart from the assumption of contingency. When Jesus is surprised by his disciples' misunderstanding, the implication is that he is genuinely trying to communicate with them and that their response is not predetermined. Similarly, the condemnation of Judas for his betrayal implies his freedom to have acted otherwise (14:21), although it is said in the same breath that Jesus' death is predicted in Scripture!

On a more comprehensive level, the story loses its dramatic punch if the actions of the characters have been totally programmed in the mind of God ahead of time. Jesus' struggles with the authorities, the faith of the people who ask for healing, the wavering attitude of the crowds: none of these crucial elements in the action carries any real weight apart from the assumption of contingency. Nor indeed does the pivotal scene in Gethsemane, which certainly implies that Jesus could have acted other than as he did and even suggests that *God* might have acted otherwise by coming up with an alternative plan.

From a strictly literary point of view, it may be satisfactory to say that Mark is finally paradoxical, combing contingency and predestination in a way that defies logic. But if one wants to render Mark intelligible and usable in one's own reflections on reality, it may be helpful to ask which is finally more important on the conceptual (as opposed to literary) level: the predestination or the contingency. Thus some scholars influenced by process theology (which stresses freedom) have suggested that one can read Mark as saying not that Jesus' death was predestined but that it became necessary under the circumstances of his rejection.[15]

The theme of predestination overlaps with the problem of God's power. Predestination assumes that God wields power unilaterally, while contingency implies that God's power is "relational," that it is not utterly coercive and does not utterly control other beings. Certainly Mark presents God as in some sense in control of the drama that is Jesus' life. Yet for the most part God acts only through Jesus and, at the crucial point, not through Jesus' power but through his weakness. In the end, of course, God raises Jesus from the dead; but this is not strictly speaking a unilateral act, since it was contingent upon

---

15. William A. Beardslee, John B. Cobb, Jr., David J. Lull, Russell Pregeant, Theodore J. Weeden, Sr., and Barry Woodbridge, *Biblical Preaching on the Death of Jesus* (Nashville: Abingdon, 1989), chaps. 4–5.

Jesus' obedience. Thus Mark can lead to critical reflection upon the question of God's power as presented in Scripture.

The paradox surrounding predestination and the power of God is not unique to Mark but is deeply embedded in the whole biblical mode of thought. In Mark, however, the often neglected pole of the paradox, that of contingency and relationality, is particularly visible. One cannot speak so glibly of either predestination or God's unilateral power in the Bible after a careful reading of this Gospel.

STUDY QUESTIONS

1. In what specific ways does the narrator try to convince the reader of Jesus' identity in Mark 1–5? Describe Jesus' ministry in these chapters. What is the "strange tension" that develops as he carries out this ministry?

2. What is the meaning of the "strong man" story?

3. Why, according to Mark, does Jesus tell parables?

4. How does Jesus relate to each of these groups in Mark 6–12: Gentiles, the Jewish leaders, the disciples?

5. Does Jesus accept Peter's confession of faith in Mark 8? Explain your answer.

6. What distinctive themes hold the section 8:27—10:45 together? What is the specific role and meaning of the two stories of healing the blind?

7. What questions does Mark 13 answer, and what effects might it have on the reader?

8. Where does the ending of Mark leave the reader? Explain why you do or do not think this ending is effective.

9. Evaluate the theories of Kelber and Weeden regarding the role of the disciples in Mark.

10. Compare and contrast the portrayal of Jesus in 1:1—8:26 to that in 8:27—16:8. Then give reasons for and against the view that Mark contains a "corrective" Christology.

11. Explain why you do or do not find Malbon's structuralist reading helpful in your own interpretation of Mark.

12. Compare and contrast the readings of Mark given by Ched Myers and Burton Mack and give your own evaluation of each.

13. Evaluate the suggestion of "process" interpreters "that Mark can be read as saying not that Jesus' death was predestined but that it became necessary under the circumstances of his rejection." In your answer, take into account the discussion in chapter 1, section 7, "Literary Approaches to the Bible."

FOR FURTHER READING

Beardslee, William A., John B. Cobb, Jr., David J. Lull, Russell Pregeant, Theodore J. Weeden, Sr., and Barry A. Woodbridge. *Biblical Preaching on the Death of Jesus.* Nashville: Abingdon, 1989. Approaches the Gospel of Mark and the letters of Paul from a "process" perspective.

Boring, M. Eugene. *Truly Human/Divine.* St. Louis: CBP Press, 1984. A study of the nature of christological language in Mark. Treats complex theoretical issues in an accessible way.

Fowler, Robert M. *Let the Reader Understand: Reader-Response Criticism and the Gospel of Mark.* Minneapolis: Fortress Press, 1991. A somewhat technical, but highly rewarding, explanation of one version of the method and an application to Mark.

Heil, John Paul, *The Gospel of Mark as a Model for Action: A Reader-Response Commentary.* Mahwah, N.J.: Paulist, 1992. An engaging treatment, from an explicitly faith-oriented perspective; stresses the action-learning model Mark presents.

Hooker, Morna D. *The Gospel according to Mark.* Peabody, Mass.: Hendrickson, 1991. A strong, competent commentary.

Kee, Howard Clark. *Community of the New Age: Studies in Mark's Gospel.* Philadelphia: Westminster, 1977. A detailed study of Mark and the author's community. Stresses the apocalyptic aspects of the Gospel and employs sociological methods.

Kelber, Werner H. *Mark's Story of Jesus.* Philadelphia: Fortress Press, 1979. A brief, readable account, combining historical, redaction-critical, and literary approaches.

Kingsbury, Jack Dean. *Conflict in Mark: Jesus, Authorities, Disciples.* Minneapolis: Fortress Press, 1989. A readable application of narrative criticism.

Lane, William. *The Gospel according to Mark.* Grand Rapids: Eerdmans, 1974. A thorough and competent commentary.

Mack, Burton L. *A Myth of Innocence: Mark and Christian Origins.* Philadelphia: Fortress Press, 1988. An attempt to place Mark in a particular social history, starting with Jesus' career in Galilee. Lengthy and complex, but raises important questions. A severe critique of Mark and the Christianity that developed in its wake.

Malbon, Elizabeth Struthers. *Narrative Space and Mythic Meaning in Mark.* San Francisco: Harper & Row, 1986. An application of a type of structuralism to Mark; extremely intricate, but remarkably readable for this kind of work.

Myers, Ched. *Binding the Strong Man: A Political Reading of Mark's Story of Jesus.* Maryknoll, N.Y.: Orbis Books, 1990. A detailed commentary, interpreting Mark as a call to nonviolent resistance to oppression. Fascinating reading.

Michie, Donald, and David Rhoads. *Mark as Story: An Introduction to the Narrative of a Gospel.* Philadelphia: Fortress Press, 1982. A readable application of narrative criticism.

Perrin, Norman. "Towards an Interpretation of the Gospel of Mark." In *A Modern Pilgrimage in Christology: A Discussion with Norman Perrin.* Ed. Hans Dieter Betz. Missoula, Mont.: Society of Biblical Literature, 1974, 1–52. A brief but influential study, focusing on literary structure and Christology.

Robbins, Vernon K. *Jesus the Teacher: A Socio-Rhetorical Interpretation of Mark.* Philadelphia: Fortress Press, 1984. A detailed study of Mark in light of ancient rhetoric, drawing upon Jewish and Greco-Roman parallels. Interesting treatment of Mark's formal structure.

Schweizer, Eduard. *The Good News according to Mark.* Trans. D. H. Madvig. Atlanta: John Knox, 1976. A solid, readable commentary.

Tolbert, Mary Ann. *Sowing the Gospel: Mark's World in Literary-Historical Perspective.* Minneapolis: Fortress Press, 1989. An approach to Mark in light of the literary conventions of the ancient world. A major contribution, stressing the coherence of the narrative and the function of parables as plot synopses.

Weeden, Theodore J. *Mark—Traditions in Conflict.* Philadelphia: Fortress Press, 1971. A redaction-critical study arguing that Mark corrects a "divine man" Christology.

Chapter 6

Matthew

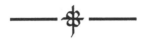

1. The Story of Jesus in Matthew

a. 1:1—4:16

In the opening sentence of Matthew the narrator indicates that what is to follow concerns Jesus, the Jewish Messiah (Christ). The reader will thus approach the ensuing genealogy as attestation of Jesus' Abrahamic and Davidic lineage. The genealogy fulfills this expectation, and its schematic nature conveys a sense that God is at work in the story that is unfolding; but it holds some surprises. Although tracing the lineage through males, at four points it mentions women, each of whom is in some way suspect. Tamar's intercourse with her father-in-law was incestuous; Rahab was a harlot; David's liaison with "the wife of Uriah" was adulterous and led to murder; and Ruth, though admirable, was, like Rahab, a Gentile. The reader thus learns that God works in unexpected ways, beyond the bounds of propriety.

Divine activity becomes more explicit in the story of Jesus' miraculous conception by a virgin, and Joseph's dream-revelation reinforces the point. The angel's comments also add to the reader's understanding of Jesus' role. As his name indicates ("Jesus" means "savior"), he will "save his people from their sins." He is also associated with Emmanuel ("God [is] with us") in Isaiah's prophecy, so the reader learns that in some way Jesus will make God present.

The sense of God's activity is enhanced by a series of scriptural quotations in the ensuing stories, several of which are introduced by the same Greek construction, "(might be/was) fulfilled [e.g., 1:22], what was spoken by the prophet(s)...." And divine guidance is evident in dreams and in the star the

200

Fig. 32.
"The Adoration of the Magi"
(Matt. 2:1-12)*

Magi follow. But there is a subtle subversion of the reader's expectations. Although Jesus is the Jewish Messiah, it is the gentile Magi who first acknowledge him. The Jewish leaders, even though the Magi have told them who Jesus is, seek to kill him, apparently fearing a threat to their own power. Already the reader confronts divergent evaluations of Jesus.

The narrator links the appearance of John the Baptist in 3:1 to the preceding material by a Greek conjunction (which does not usually appear in English translations) meaning "and" or "but," thus signaling the reader that the subject at hand is still the origins of Jesus. John introduces the theme of repentance in the face of God's Rule and the judgment ("wrath to come") associated with it; but he also directs attention back to Jesus by mentioning the one who is coming after him.

John's harsh words in 3:7-10 encourage the reader to view the Pharisees

*The Gospel of Matthew employs the term "magi" presumably to designate court priests from the Gentile world who were practitioners of astrology. Their homage to the Christ child is symbolic in this Gospel of his universal significance and is a precursor to the mission to the Gentiles commissioned by the resurrected Jesus in Matthew 28:16-20. (Painting by Frank Wesley)

and Sadducees in a negative light, and his declaration that God can make the stones on the ground into "children for Abraham" recalls the earlier positive treatment of Gentiles. The reader will understand that God's promise to Abraham is still in effect, but also that God is free to look outside the Jewish ethnic identity for recipients of that promise.

The narrator's identification of John as the "voice" of whom Isaiah prophesied (3:1-3) encourages the reader to trust what he says. In the story of Jesus' baptism (3:13-17), however, John shows incomplete understanding by at first refusing to perform the rite. Jesus corrects him with the statement that they must "fulfill all righteousness," i.e., do precisely what God requires. The story reaches a climax when God's voice enters the story to proclaim who Jesus is. The reader thus learns something more about how Jesus will make God present: he is God's own son. And the phrase "in whom I am well pleased" encourages the reader to understand that Jesus' sonship, even though he is in some sense born into this role, consists in his obedience to God's commands.

This impression is strengthened in the story that follows. Led into the desert by the Spirit, Jesus undergoes temptation by the devil, who dares him to test God and offers him power and glory. The reader will assume that the temptations are real, that Jesus *could* make the wrong choice, and will therefore understand that in withstanding Satan Jesus proves himself obedient.

After the temptation story, the narrator notes that John has been arrested and Jesus moves to Capernaum by the sea. Jesus' dwelling thus provides the setting for another scriptural quotation introduced by the "fulfillment" formula. And the point of the quotation itself is fulfillment, which the reader will associate with Jesus. But the unexpected prevails: the Messiah is in Galilee, not David's Judah. It is from Galilee that the light shines—"Galilee *of the Gentiles!*"

b. 4:17—9:34

The phrase "from that time" in 4:17 alerts the reader to a turn in the plot: Jesus now begins his ministry, which initially parallels John's, since he preaches repentance in the face of God's coming rule. The account in 4:23-25 combines with the call of the disciples (4:18-22) to create the impression of initial success, and it also gives the narrator opportunity to add teaching and healing to the list of Jesus' activities.

By having Jesus ascend a mountain in 5:1 in order to teach, the narrator encourages the reader to pay attention to what Jesus says and to receive it as authoritative. But the initial content will come as something of a surprise after the earlier emphasis upon the coming judgment. The "beatitudes" (5:3-

11) speak rather of the blessings associated with God's Rule. The last in the series, though, introduces another note: those who follow Jesus can expect persecution such as the prophets faced. The reader will understand that Jesus is issuing the promises and demands that pertain to those who follow him.

The metaphors of salt and light in 5:13-16 indicate that Jesus is calling his hearers into a mission: to glorify God by bringing light to others through their own good works. And the sayings in 5:17-19 clarify a point regarding what his followers should teach and practice regarding the Jewish law: it remains fully in effect for them, because Jesus came not to abolish but to fulfill it. Not only that, but in 5:20 the reader learns that those who follow Jesus must pursue an even higher standard of righteousness in their obedience to the law than do the scribes and Pharisees.

Quickly, however, it becomes clear that this "higher righteousness" is not defined in merely quantitative terms. For Jesus illustrates it in a series of antitheses (5:21-48) that pit his own teaching, i.e., interpretation of Scripture, against what his audience has "heard." Jesus' "fulfillment" of Scripture thus entails an intensification or radicalization of the commandments: it is not enough to love the neighbor, for example; one must love the enemy also. The reader will therefore understand that it is the law as interpreted by Jesus that remains authoritative and that Jesus' interpretation exposes the deepest intention of the law, not just its surface meaning.

In 6:1-18 Jesus defines the "higher righteousness" through contrast with the ways the "hypocrites" (whom the reader will identify with the scribes and Pharisees) practice almsgiving and fasting, and with the way Gentiles pray. Understanding the prayer in 6:9-13 as an alternative model, the reader will notice the focus on God's will and the correlation between the petition for God's forgiveness and the disciple's own commitment to the practice of forgiveness.

The theme of "higher righteousness" comes to its focal point in 6:19-24, where the metaphors of the treasure and the sound eye lead to the saying on serving two masters. The righteousness Jesus demands is thus wholeheartedness, complete dedication to God's will alone. Then verses 24-34 draw out the implications for the reader: God's wholehearted servants will be free from anxiety over mundane needs, depending totally upon God's provision.

Jesus begins a new series of commands by prohibiting the condemnation of others and presents the "golden rule" in 7:12 as the essence of the ethical demands of Scripture: "this is the Law and the Prophets." But demand is not the only emphasis; verses 7-11 stress that God's help is available to those who seek it. The references to "entering" (v. 13) and to the Rule of God (v. 21) remind the reader of what the discourse is all about: Jesus' authoritative teaching outlines the life-style or ethic that is appropriate to God's Rule and hence demanded of disciples. And neither knowing what is right nor even performing miracles in Jesus' name (vv. 21-27) is adequate apart from *doing* God's will.

With the phrase "and when Jesus had finished these sayings" in 7:28, the narrator signals the reader that the discourse is finished. Despite the earlier implication (5:1) that Jesus was speaking to disciples only, the narrator now says that the *crowds* were astonished at his teaching (7:29). Presumably, they have heard his words and may be considered potential disciples. And the reason for their astonishment is important to the narrator: it is Jesus' authority—precisely what the scribes lack—that has impressed them. The reader will understand the discourse as something Jesus said during his lifetime but intended for the postresurrection community as well. The sermon thus addresses the reader, along with the crowds, as at least a potential disciple.

Impressed by the authority with which Jesus teaches, the reader begins in 8:1 to see him exercising a similar authority in a series of mighty deeds. The narrator's use of the now-familiar formula (8:17) to interpret these works as fulfillment of Scripture combines with Jesus' action of sending the leper to the priest and emphasizes Jesus' link to the Jewish tradition. But Jesus praises the centurion's faith as unparalleled in Israel and announces that Gentiles will sit at table with Abraham. The reader will remember John's words about God's making stones into children for Abraham.

The sayings in 8:18-23 reintroduce the theme of discipleship, stressing its stringent demands that challenge conventional piety, and the story of the storm-stilling encourages the reader to concur in Jesus' evaluation of the performance of the disciples. Beset by fear in the beginning and unclear about Jesus' identity at the end, they merit only a mediocre rating: persons of "little faith." This story and the subsequent healing of the paralytic increase the reader's sense of Jesus' power and authority, and his words in 9:2-8 imply that this authority extends to his followers: "God ... had given such authority to human beings."

The scribes' reaction to Jesus' exercise of authority adds to the reader's negative impression of the Jewish leadership. And the point is reinforced as the narrator relates the call of Matthew the tax collector (9:9) and the stories of Jesus' conflict with the Pharisees over his association with "sinners and tax collectors" and his disciples' failure to fast. The reader will conclude that Pharisees cannot accept Jesus' association with outcasts for the same reason they do not understand the sayings (9:15-17) on the bridegroom, the garment, and the wineskins: something new is happening, which is why Jesus is free to break convention; but the Pharisees will not accept that fact.

Fig. 33. "Sermon on the Mount" (Matt. 5:1—7:29).
(40" x 30"; mixed media by Michael E. Coblyn)

The narrator now relates three more miracles (9:18-34), the last of which encourages the reader to recall all Jesus' remarkable deeds since 8:1. When Jesus casts the demon from the mute man, the Pharisees reject his miracles altogether, attributing his power to "the prince of demons." The crowds, however, stand amazed because "never has anything like this been seen in Israel." This complements the saying on wineskins: Jesus' ministry announces the new, and those who will not break with the past will be left behind.

The reader may now look back and discern two contrasting ways of responding to Jesus. Matthew, like the Galilean fishermen, followed Jesus without a word; the Pharisees, who remain locked into traditional piety, cannot see Jesus' deeds for what they obviously are. The narrator also pits Jesus against the Pharisees on the interpretation of tradition. To justify his eating with sinners, Jesus quotes Hosea 6:6: "I desire mercy, not sacrifice" (9:13). Just as the golden rule summarizes the law, so now mercy takes precedence over ritual requirements. The implication is that the Pharisees lack mercy, caring more for their traditional piety than the salvation of sinners.

Not all the responses to Jesus, however, are so clear-cut. There are degrees of faith. The crowds are impressed by Jesus, but the reader is not told that they become disciples; and while the centurion shows an overwhelming faith, Jesus must say "take heart" to the paralytic and the woman who touches his garment. The blind men show enough faith to be healed, but they disobey Jesus' command to silence. Finally, Jesus castigates the disciples precisely because of their "little faith." Clearly, the narrator is encouraging the reader to have greater faith: because Jesus can calm the sea, heal the sick, and raise the dead, one should be able to follow him without faltering.

c. 9:35—11:1

Through the summary in 9:35-38 and the story of the appointment of the Twelve as apostles, the narrator encourages the reader to reflect further on Jesus' mission. The reader will associate the term "apostle" (one who is sent) with missionary activity;[1] it will thus be clear that Jesus, who is himself the needed shepherd of the helpless sheep (crowds), designates the Twelve as co-workers (laborers) in a ministry that is carried out in the face of God's coming Rule (harvest). The reader will also notice that Jesus gives authority to the apostles to perform works similar to his own. The naming of each of the Twelve underscores their importance and encourages the reader to view them

---

1. "Disciple," the term used up to this point, means simply "learner," and does not in itself carry connotations of mission activity or authority.

positively; but mention of Judas's betrayal, pointing ahead to Jesus' death, suggests that their obedience is not insured.

In the instructions that follow, Jesus sends the apostles exclusively to "the lost sheep of the house of Israel." The reader will therefore understand their mission as something that took place in Jesus' lifetime. Yet the notation that this mission to Israel will not be completed "before the Son of man comes" invites the postresurrection reader into the apostles' task. The fact that the narrator gives no account of either the apostles' actual going out or their return subtly indicates that the mission, at least in some form, continues into the reader's time. And many of the instructions Jesus issues to the apostles in 10:5-42 have particular relevance for readers in the postresurrection situation. The prediction of persecution from both Jews and Gentiles shows the reader that the gentile mission is in view here also.

The reader will note the close parallel between Jesus' own activity and what is expected of his representatives. These too will suffer rejection and must bear their own crosses. And just as his own role embraces both that of eventual judge (10:32-33) and compassionate shepherd, so their mission will bring judgment upon those who reject them (10:14-15), but peace and reward to those who receive them (10:13, 40-42).

In 11:1 the narrator signals the reader that the discourse is finished by using the same grammatical construction that closed Jesus' teaching in chapters 5–7: "And when Jesus had finished. . . ." The reader is thus prepared to recognize another formulary expression parallel to that which introduces Scripture quotations.

d. 11:2—12:50

The narrator's phrase "what the Messiah was doing" (more literally translated, "the deeds of the Messiah") in 11:2 reminds the reader that Jesus' miraculous works reflect his divine authority and are a central aspect of his mission. And Jesus' answer to the question John the Baptist sends from prison underscores the point. Mention of John also affords the narrator opportunity, through Jesus' comments, to identify John with Elijah. The fact that "Elijah" is now in prison, however, suggests something ominous about the present situation; and the narrator capitalizes on the point by having Jesus compare those who have rejected both John and himself to petulant children.

The reader will recognize in the statement, "wisdom is vindicated by her deeds" (11:19), not only an echo of 11:2 but an allusion to personified Wisdom, through whom in Jewish tradition (see, e.g., Prov. 8:22, 27) God created the world. The deeds of Jesus and John are thus associated with Wisdom's own deeds, which the reader will probably interpret as a metaphorical reference to God's own self-expression at creation. The implication is that the works Jesus has performed testify to his messianic office, so that those who have rejected him and John show that they are not among those "with ears" (11:15).

When Jesus then proceeds (11:20-24) to pronounce condemnation on the Galilean towns that (it is now revealed) have failed to respond to him, the reader becomes aware of a turn in the plot: not only is the opposition to Jesus growing more serious, but Jesus for the first time begins to speak explicitly of judgment, as did John. The tone is more positive in 11:25-30, but the note of judgment is retained. The same Jesus who is gentle and lowly in heart is also the Son who has unique knowledge of God: those who reject him are rejecting God also. Other points, however, will puzzle the reader. Jesus' "yoke"—which the reader will recognize as an allusion to the rabbinic metaphor of the "yoke of the law" and will therefore associate with Jesus' interpretation of the Torah—is "easy" and "light." But is the "higher righteousness" of 5:17-48 *easy?* And even as the passage speaks of revelation, it maintains a note of secrecy. God has "hidden" something, presumably the significance of Jesus' earlier deeds, from the "wise." But why?

The ensuing stories (12:1-14) enable the reader to answer the first of these questions. Jesus' defense against the charges of Sabbath violation combines scriptural interpretation with appeal to human need and again entails quotation of the mercy-not-sacrifice passage from Hosea. The reader will thus contrast Jesus' presentation of mercy as the core of the law with the Pharisees' inhumane approach and can now identify the "easiness" of Jesus' yoke. His "higher righteousness" is centered upon a concern for human welfare, and it ultimately provides "rest" (11:28) for the human soul. And the narrator confirms the Pharisees' malicious attitude by reporting their plot to destroy Jesus.

The narrator's quotation of Isaiah in 12:18-21, interpreting Jesus' command to silence in v. 16, recalls the theme of "hiddenness" in 11:25. And the positive references to Gentiles in the quotation contrast with the negative responses of the Galilean cities, while the line "until he brings justice to victory" hints at a future vindication. The reader thus learns that despite sharp opposition, Jesus' mission will eventually be accomplished. But the reason for "hiddenness" remains unexplained.

The sayings on "lord of the Sabbath" and "greater than the temple" in the grainfield incident showed that it is not just Jesus' teaching but his authority that is at stake in the growing conflict. This becomes clear in the Beelzebul controversy in 12:22-32, which also softens the exclusivism of 11:27: the issue is not the rejection of Jesus in and of itself but the rejection of God's spirit working through him. Appropriately, the reader hears of the two contrasting ways of receiving Jesus and their consequences: good trees bring forth good fruit, and evil trees evil fruit (12:33-35).

When the Pharisees demand a sign from Jesus in 12:38, the reader will remember that he has already performed many miraculous works and will conclude that his opponents betray an understanding of authority exactly the opposite of his own. Because they look for crude, outward manifestations of power, they cannot discern the authority of the "gentle" and "lowly" one. Even when confronted with power as in the exorcisms, they attribute it to Satan rather than God. And it is against this background that Jesus speaks the words in 12:43-50. Although he has plundered Satan's house and "cleansed" this generation, the Pharisees' rejection of him results in a more serious form of demonic possession. By contrast, those who receive him, who do God's will, become his "family." But it is clear to the reader at this point (12:50) that the Pharisees, engaged in vicious opposition to Jesus' mission, do not belong to that family but have brought condemnation upon themselves.

e. 13:1—16:20

At the beginning of chapter 13, Jesus begins to address the crowds "in parables" and, in response to the disciples' question, explains that he does so precisely because the crowds of people do not understand (13:13). The reader, remembering the theme of "hiddenness" in 11:25, can now understand that God hides understanding precisely from those who have by their own choice made understanding impossible.

Chapter 13 thus explains why Jesus used parables and helps make the rejection of his ministry understandable; it also speaks to the reader as disciple or potential disciple. The allegorical explanations of the parables of the sower and the weeds (vv. 18-23, 36-43) address those who have heard the word but now face the problems of living faithful lives. The teaching in Matthew 13 alerts them to impediments to faith and, especially in the concluding parable and interpretation in 13:47-50, warns of the coming judgment.

The conversation in 13:51-52 encourages the reader to make an evaluation of the disciples that modifies the earlier judgment of "little faith" (8:26). They profess to understand all that Jesus has said, and his reply indicates acceptance of their declaration. They are scribes "trained for the [Rule] of heaven," who can draw upon both Jewish tradition and Jesus' authoritative teaching; as such, they stand in some sense as models for the reader.

Immediately, however, the reader will have occasion to contrast the disciples' understanding with the incomprehension of others. The familiar conclusion formula in 13:53, marking the parable-chapter off as a third major discourse, leads into an account in which Jesus' authority is disputed: the people in his home area question the source of his wisdom and mighty works. The theme of opposition is continued in the story of the death of John the Baptist, which explains the fact that Herod, also grasping for an explanation of Jesus' power, takes Jesus to be John raised from the dead.

The material that follows encourages the reader to reflect further on the disciples. Obedient to Jesus' commands, they are able to feed a huge crowd with five loaves and two fish (14:13-21); and Peter is able actually to walk on water (vv. 22-33). Jesus does reprimand Peter for his "little faith," but the reader will contrast the disciples' response to their less adequate attitude in an earlier situation (8:27). This time, instead of questioning Jesus' identity, they worship him and declare, "Truly you are the Son of God." The reader will accept this confession as appropriate but will see in those who are healed by merely touching Jesus' garment (14:34-36) an even more unqualified faith. The disciples thus appear not as models of perfection, but as examples of followers "on the way" to a deeper faith.

The reader must continue to identify contrasting responses to Jesus in chapter 15. The Pharisees challenge Jesus on his disciples' transgressions of the traditions of the elders, but Jesus turns the tables: the Pharisees use human traditions to transgress *God's* commands. They treat religion as something external, not a matter of the heart that affects one's relations with other human beings (vv. 18-20). In contrast, a Canaanite woman shows "great faith" by cajoling Jesus into healing her daughter. And, again in contrast to the Jewish leadership, the crowds show faith in 15:29-31 by bringing those who suffer to Jesus for healing.

At this point the reader discerns in the disciples a lack of faith. They are concerned about the fact that the Pharisees are offended by Jesus' comments (v. 12), and Peter must ask for an explanation and thus merits Jesus' rebuke (vv. 15-16). Nor have the disciples achieved full understanding after a second feeding miracle (15:32-38) and Jesus' additional condemnation of the Pharisees (16:1-4). They take his reference to the Pharisees' "leaven" literally, showing that they are not yet willing to trust God to provide. Finally, however, when Jesus explains that "leaven" means the teaching of the Pharisees and Sadducees, they do understand. In all this, the reader is learning that faith is a matter of degrees, that it is a process of learning and growth.

The reader will sense a climactic moment when, in the scene at Caesarea Philippi, Jesus confronts the disciples directly, for the first time, with the crucial question: "But who do you say that I am?" (16:15). Peter's response contrasts with the views of Herod and the Pharisees, echoing the disciples' preliminary confession on the lake but adding to it the term "Messiah." Jesus' response is overwhelmingly positive: Peter's confession could only be the product of revelation. Jesus thus gives him the symbolic name of Peter, "the rock," and speaks for the first time of the *church*. He also gives Peter the authority to "bind and loose," technical terms in the rabbinic vocabulary indicating pronouncement on what is and what is not required by law.

The reader will understand that Jesus has thus founded the church that exists in the postresurrection situation. It will also be clear that this church rests upon a confession of Jesus as Messiah/Son of God and that Jesus has conferred authority upon it and has acknowledged a special role of some sort for Peter.

Despite the positive response to Peter, the scene concludes with Jesus' injunction to the disciples "to tell no one that he was the Messiah," a command that reminds the reader of subtler notes of secrecy earlier in the Gospel (8:4; 9:30; 11:25; 12:16). This is the first time, however, that it is the disciples who are commanded to silence specifically on Jesus' identity. The reader will wonder what is going on here; but it is clear that Jesus wishes his identity to remain unknown to the public at this point.

f. 16:21—20:34

With the phrase "from that time" in 16:21, the narrator indicates a shift in Jesus' emphasis: he begins to concentrate upon the disciples, teaching them about his coming death and resurrection. But the reader's positive image of the disciples is shaken by what follows. Because Peter cannot accept Jesus' suffering, Jesus links him with Satan, who had earlier tried to tempt him away from his mission. When Jesus then defines discipleship in relation to his own suffering, the reader will conclude that the disciples' unwillingness to suffer is at the root of their inability to accept his mission. And the motive behind Jesus' secrecy regarding his identity begins to emerge. Unwilling to grasp the necessity of Jesus' death, they are not yet ready to proclaim his messiahship.

The negative impression of the Twelve continues in the ensuing stories. Peter makes an inept statement when Jesus is transfigured on the mountain, all three of the disciples who are present manifest fear, and those left behind are unable to cast out a demon (17:14-20). But there is subtle indication of growth in the disciples' understanding. Lifting up their eyes after Jesus' touch, Peter, James, and John see "no one but Jesus" (17:8). And the narrator notes that they do understand Jesus' reference to John the Baptist (17:13). Later, the conclusion to Jesus' second prediction of his death cuts with a double edge: the disciples become "greatly distressed" (17:23), which suggests some understanding, if not full acceptance, of what must take place!

The divine voice in the transfiguration scene encourages the reader to accept the narrator's understanding of Jesus. And the command to the disciples to listen to Jesus in 17:5 also coaches the reader to pay close attention to what Jesus will say as the story continues to unfold. An opportunity to do so arises in 17:24-27, the conversation on the half-shekel tax collected on behalf of the temple. Although Jesus tells Peter to pay in order to avoid offense, he makes a declaration with clear implications for the postresurrection church: "the children are free." The community Jesus is building is in some sense free from traditional obligations.

The reader will recognize further material relevant to the postresurrection community as Jesus responds to a question of the disciples with extended teaching in chapter 18. A statement on childlike humility leads into a series of statements on community life that ends with a parable containing a stern warning (18:35). Along the way, Jesus outlines procedures for dealing with community members who injure others in the group and extends the authority to "bind and loose" to the community as a whole. Apparently the power to interpret legal regulations includes the power of exclusion from the community. Clearly, however, exclusion is a last resort; the overwhelming emphasis is upon forgiveness.

It will be clear by the end of the chapter that Jesus, on his way to die, has been preparing the disciples for life in the postresurrection time, and the reader will be encouraged by the promise that the resurrected Jesus will be present (18:20) with the community. Aware that the divine presence was in a similar way promised to those who study Torah, the reader will also understand that Jesus assumes the role of that presence, empowering his followers and guiding their decisions. The name "Emmanuel" in 1:23 thus takes on more explicit meaning.

The conclusion formula in 19:1 signals the reader to understand the preceding material on church life as a fourth distinct discourse. From the second half of the verse, the reader, learning that Jesus moves from Galilee to Judea, will sense that the story is moving toward its climax.

When, in a dispute with the Pharisees regarding divorce, Jesus overturns Moses' concession by reference to God's primordial will (19:8: "from the beginning it was not so"), the reader will remember Jesus' earlier intensifications of the law (5:21-48). It will also be clear that the term "hard-hearted" describes the Pharisees' basic disposition, which is what necessitated the concession.

Following the material on "eunuchs" (19:10-12) and children (19:13-15),

Fig. 34. "The Transfiguration of Christ" (Icon c. 1403 by Theopan the Greek)

Jesus' response to the man seeking eternal life concludes with a reference to the commandment to love one's neighbor and an junction to sell his possessions and give the proceeds to the poor. The reader will not only notice that Jesus once again affirms the validity of the law but will also be able to put the preceding material in context. The comments of the narrator in v. 22 and Jesus in 23-26, emphasizing that wealth was the barrier for this man, suggest a contrast with the children in the preceding story. The children, absolutely dependent and possessing nothing, receive God's Rule, while the man with everything is excluded, precisely because he cannot let go of what he has. Unlike the voluntary "eunuchs" who receive God's gift of celibacy (presumably not actual castration), he is more like the Pharisees, with his own brand of "hardness of heart"; for he turns away from the poor.

Even the disciples appear rather like the Pharisees, since they turn the children away. But Jesus points to God's gift, which makes possible what is humanly impossible! So despite the disciples' imperfections, Jesus acknowledges that they have left everything to follow him and promises them both the fellowship of the new community and eternal life (19:27-30). Here again, the reader will understand the disciples as models of persons in the process of becoming faithful followers, not of those who have reached it.

The "first/last" saying in 19:30 may at first strike the reader as puzzling. But the parable beginning in 20:1 picks up on this saying and draws together all the material beginning at 19:1. The grumbling workers again illustrate "hardheartedness" and will stand for the Pharisees in the reader's mind. When the parable closes with another "first/last" saying, the reader will contrast the grumblers with the disciples who have "left everything." In the judgment, those who are "first"—and cling to what they have, whether wealth or religious pride—will be excluded from God's rule; but the "last"—who, like children, are able to receive a gift—will enter.

Jesus' third prediction of his death (20:17-19) is coupled with the narrator's notation that he is at this point "going up to Jerusalem," which signals the reader that the final events are not far off. That Jesus now speaks in the plural is a subtle indication that he expects the disciples to participate in the coming events. Immediately, however, his followers manifest incomplete understanding: the mother of two disciples asks for special privileges for her sons, and Jesus counters with a presentation of discipleship as humility and acceptance of suffering. In the process, he presents his own ministry as service to others and his death as a "ransom for many" (20:28) The meaning of "ransom," however, remains unexplained: the emphasis is upon the way in which Jesus' activity becomes a model for those who follow him. The reader will thus associate discipleship with Jesus' gentleness and humility (11:29).

The reader will also notice a related characteristic of Jesus' ministry in 20:29-33. As the disciples had tried to keep the children from Jesus, so now the crowds try to silence two blind men who ask Jesus for mercy. But Jesus, "moved with compassion," gives them their sight.

g. 21:1—25:46

When the blind men in 20:29-33 twice address Jesus as "Son of David," the reader will sense a degree of tension. Although the term is approved by the narrator (1:1), it conjures up images of worldly-political power at odds with the words about humility in 20:25-28. The story of Jesus' entry into Jerusalem mediates this tension. Citing the Jewish Scriptures (Zech. 9:9), the narrator claims that Jesus' action fulfills the prediction that a king would come, "humble, and mounted on a donkey, and on a colt, the foal of a donkey."[2] The reader will thus know that when the crowds correctly hail Jesus as "Son of David" the worldly-political meaning of this term has already been undercut. And the crowds' partial misunderstanding is evident in that they speak of him simply as a prophet. By contrast, when the powerless children call him "Son of David," Jesus gives approval by quoting Scripture.

The reader continues to be aware of the dialectic of power and humility as the story proceeds. Jesus exercises overt power and authority in his assault upon the temple (21:12-13) and his cursing the fig tree (21:18-22), an act interpreted as a demonstration of the power of faith. But the theme of Jesus' gentleness and compassion reappears in the notation about his healing the blind and crippled (21:14) in the temple, from which they are normally excluded.

Jesus' authority becomes a matter of explicit dispute when the chief priests and elders object to the children's acclamations (21:14-17). Attributing Jesus' opponents' refusal to answer his counterquestion to their fear of the crowd, the narrator discloses their true attitude: they have no interest in who really speaks with God's authority but are concerned only to preserve their own; nor are they interested in the sufferings of those he has healed. Against this background the reader can easily decipher the parables Jesus now tells. The son who says he will go into the vineyard but does not (21:28-32) represents the Jewish leaders themselves. And the story of the wicked tenants (21:33-41) is an allegory of Israel's relationship to God's Rule. When Jesus states in 21:42-

---

2. The passage from the Jewish Scriptures is taken so literally that the narrator puts Jesus in the odd position of riding two animals at once! The phrase "and on a colt" is actually an instance of a device, common in Hebrew poetry, known as "synonymous parallelism." That is, *in the Hebrew text* the "donkey" and the "colt, the foal of a donkey," are one and the same.

44 that Israel's rejection of him results in the transfer of that relationship to "a people that produces the fruits" of God's Rule, the reader will think of the postresurrection Christian community.[3]

The reader will interpret the story of the wedding banquet as another allegory of Israel's history, this time with a symbolization of the destruction of Jerusalem (22:7). But the ending (22:11-14) will come as a surprise: one of the new guests, whom the reader will identify as members of the Christian community, is thrown out for lack of proper attire. The eschatological overtones in v. 13 make the point unmistakable. Although the church has inherited the established (or majority) Israel's relationship to God, it too is responsible for bearing fruit and is subject to judgment.

The Jewish leaders' actions at this point will further confirm the reader's negative evaluation of them. Although they rightly interpret the story of the two sons (21:31) and they know that the parables are directed against them (21:45), they do not repent but set out to entrap Jesus (22:15). But Jesus' answers to their questions only further discredit them. The saying on God and the emperor (22:21) shows that the Pharisees and Herodians do not know what belongs to God; and in undermining the Sadducees' attempt to render the notion of resurrection absurd (22:29-33) Jesus shows that they read Scripture incorrectly.

The narrator indicates that even the Pharisaic lawyer's question about the greatest commandment (22:35) is a test, by placing it in the context of the continuing conflict. While Jesus does not explicitly criticize the question, his answer exposes its inadequacy: the questioner asks for *one* commandment, but Jesus gives *two* that are inseparable. The reader will understand that the lawyer was looking for an externalized command that could be abstracted from one's relationship to one's fellow human beings. It will also be plain that the issue at hand expresses a crucial difference between Jesus and his opponents: for Jesus, but not for them, the dual command to love constitutes the core principle of the law, the starting and ending point for all interpretation.

Jesus himself initiates the controversy over the relationship between David and the Messiah. Without denying the Messiah's Davidic descent, he quotes Scripture to place the Messiah above David. His concluding remark brings the issue of his authority back to the foreground, and the narrator's comment in 22:46 signals the reader that the controversy on that matter has reached a climax: "nor from that day did anyone dare to ask him any more questions."

Remembering the earlier charges that the Jewish leaders misread Scripture,

---

3. There is disagreement among scholars, however, as to whether "a people" refers more specifically to the church or to Gentiles.

the reader may be surprised when in 23:1 Jesus begins a speech by acknowledging the validity of the teachings of the scribes and Pharisees. Although the
tension is never resolved, the reader will understand that the point is to expose these teachers as hypocrites who do not practice what they preach. And
whatever authority they do have, it is merely formal, since in practice even
their teaching is perverse. They "bind heavy burdens" on human beings, using their law not to help people but to preserve their own authority—thus in
effect usurping *God's* authority (23:4-7); and they emphasize details of the
law to the neglect of what is central (23:23).

By painting the Jewish leaders in a totally negative light, the speech encourages the reader to render a negative judgment regarding the faithfulness
of the established Israel to God. But because it is directed (23:1) not to these
leaders but to the crowds and disciples, the reader will also see in it a message for the postresurrection church and view the scribes and Pharisees as
models of a religious hypocrisy that exists in the church. Verse 39, moreover,
contains a subtle qualification of the judgment theme. Here, immediately preceding a prediction of the destruction of the temple, Jesus suggests that the
day will come when Jerusalem actually acknowledges him. Although the narrator never elaborates the point, this verse encourages the reader to imagine
some possibility for the Jewish people beyond the punishment.

Throughout the speech, the reader has a complex task of integrating Jesus'
words in the past to the present situation of the church. The justification of
God's punishment of Israel, which the reader will associate with the destruction of the temple in 70 c.e., is a consistent pattern of the Jewish leaders' own
rejection of God, which reaches into the postresurrection situation. As they
rejected the prophets in the distant past (23:30-31) and now in the "present"
of the narrative they reject "justice and mercy and faith" (23:23) as well as
Jesus himself, so will they reject the postresurrection Christian witnesses by
persecuting them in the synagogues (23:34). It is this consistent pattern more
than any single event that merits Jesus' ironic condemnation: "Fill up, then,
the measure of your ancestors" (23:33).

This integration of past, present, and future also keeps the issue of Jesus'
authority in view for the reader. At two points Jesus speaks directly for God,
from a transhistorical perspective. In 23:34 he says, "*I* send you prophets,
sages, and scribes," and in 23:37: "How often have *I* desired to gather your
children together. . . . " His words and role are thus reminiscent of personified
Wisdom, who, in a widespread strain of tradition, had sought unsuccessfully
for centuries to woo Israelites back to God. The reader will understand the
"prophets, sages, and scribes" as referring both to the earlier Jewish emissaries of God and to their counterparts in the later Christian community.

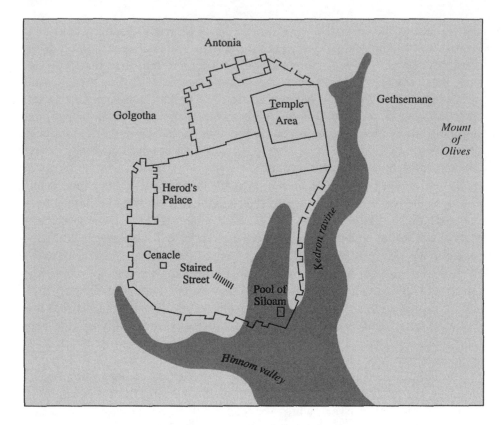

Fig. 35. Jerusalem at the time of Jesus' passion and death. *(Map by Parrot Graphics)*

The more general point is that Jesus himself now speaks with God's own authority; rejection of him is the focal point in the long history of Israel's rejection of God. But the later persecution of Christian prophets is a piece of the same cloth.

When the scene shifts in 24:1-2 and Jesus leaves the temple as he predicts its destruction, the reader will understand that the preceding material provides a programmatic justification for that destruction. The very act of departure from the temple, moreover, will carry symbolic weight.

The disciples' question in 24:3 encourages the reader to think more specifically about future events. Coming immediately after his comment about the temple, it presupposes that the destruction of the temple will happen *at the end.* But Jesus corrects this view by declaring that "the end is not yet" (24:6). Thus the events described in 24:4-28 belong not to the actual end-time but to a period preceding it. In this interim period, the Christian message "will be proclaimed throughout the world" (24:14). The sign of the actual end, moreover, will be straightforward (24:29-32). The reader will understand that no one should engage in apocalyptic speculation about the time of the end, since not even the Son knows this (24:36)!

Nor should anyone make the mistake of following "false prophets" who will cause many of Jesus' followers to "fall away" and will undermine the most central of Jesus' ethical teachings by causing love to "grow cold." Thus the narrator encourages the reader to "be ready" for the coming of the Son of man by "watching" and remaining faithful. This comes through clearly in the warnings in 24:37-44 and the allegories of 24:45—25:30, which depict Jesus' return as Son of man and judge. The reader should understand that although the end might seem a long time coming, it will indeed come.

The description of the final judgment in 25:31-46 portrays, in dramatic fashion, the specific content of faithfulness. It is love—mercy and compassion for the poor, the needy, and the imprisoned—that is the heart and soul of righteous action. This is what the reader might have expected in light of the Gospel's consistent emphasis. But the point is made with an unexpected twist: both the righteous and the unrighteous are surprised at the end to learn that the Son of man has identified himself with the needy. The scene thus encourages the reader not only to perform deeds of love and mercy but also to reject the self-centered, calculating attitude that makes such deeds a means toward achieving one's own reward. Spontaneous, merciful, unselfish love thus stands as the criterion for entering eternal life.

h. 26:1—28:20

After the conclusion formula in 26:1, marking off the fifth major discourse, the narrator alerts the reader that the climax of the story is near. Jesus refers explicitly to the imminence of his crucifixion, and the chief priests and elders make plans for his arrest. Then Jesus' words regarding the woman who anoints him not only connect this act to his death but point beyond it to the mission of the church: "wherever this good news is proclaimed in the whole world . . ." (26:13). With the report of Judas's deal with the high priest, the stage is fully set. Jesus' comment in 26:18 only underlines what the reader already knows: the Passover meal is a prelude to his death.

Jesus' prediction of Judas's betrayal (26:20-25) suggests that what is happening is under God's direction, and his designation of the bread and wine as his body and blood points to the later cultic meal of the church as a mode of his presence with his followers after his death. The phrase "forgiveness of sins" reminds the reader that Jesus has spoken of his death as a ransom

Fig. 36. "The Sacrament of the Last Supper" (Salvador Dali; Spanish, c. 1964)

(20:28), and the reference to the eschatological banquet in 26:29 provides assurance that the ultimate outcome of the tragic events to come will be victory.

The reader will thus feel a sense of preparation for what is to come but will be disappointed in the disciples, who should also be prepared. Jesus predicts their defection, and his words are borne out in the scene in Gethsemane (26:36-56) and in Peter's denials (26:69-75). But when Jesus interprets their actions as fulfillment of Scripture and refers to a reunion with them in Galilee after the resurrection (26:32), the reader will conclude that seeming defeat will lead to a fortunate outcome.

Although accepting the emphasis upon God's control of events, the reader will notice elements of contingency in the story also. As Jesus faced the temptation to deny his role at the beginning of his ministry, so now in the Garden of Gethsemane he faces the temptation to abandon it. And, as in the earlier case, he accepts God's will. Similarly, at his arrest he indicates that he *could* appeal to God for intervention; but he will not, because this would apparently interfere with the fulfillment of Scripture (26:54). Necessity and contingency stand side by side in an unresolved tension; the reader will have to balance the view that God is sovereign over events in the world with the conviction that human beings, like Jesus himself, have real choices to make.

In the account of Jesus' condemnation, the narrator brings the conflict that has pervaded the story to its conclusion, making certain that the reader is aware of the malevolence of the Jewish authorities. When Jesus is brought before the high priest, those who hear his case seek false testimony against him. And the fact that it is his own disclosure of his identity (26:64) that leads to the charge of blasphemy and the conclusion that he must be executed serves further to place his accusers in a bad light: the reader will understand that they are rejecting the Son of God. The reader will also note an additional significance in Jesus' disclosure. It is only now, in the face of imminent death, that he "goes public" with who he truly is.

The portrayal of the Gentiles involved in the matter reinforces the negative view of the Jewish participants. The narrator notes Pilate's knowledge of the "jealousy" (27:18) that motivated those who brought Jesus to trial and reports his attempts to avoid condemning Jesus to death (27:15-26). Even Pilate's wife counsels him to avoid the affair (27:19). In the end, the narrator has the Jewish leaders prevail by convincing the masses to ask for Jesus' death, and the effect is a broadening of responsibility. Noting the crowd's glib and ironical acceptance of responsibility for Jesus' death (27:25), the reader will understand the destruction of Jerusalem as punishment of those who rejected Jesus, leading to the forfeiting of their relationship to God's Rule to the followers of Jesus (21:43).

The reader will find a double significance in the portrayal of those who put Jesus to death, however. Beyond the explanation of God's punishment of Israel, the characters in the story serve also to illustrate typical human attitudes that enable or prevent participation in God's Rule. The Jewish leaders represent a kind of self-seeking, a preoccupation with one's own power, authority, and position that excludes compassion for the neighbor and prevents a recognition of the humble Jesus as the Messiah. The crowds, at an earlier stage portrayed as potential disciples, illustrate a shallow fickleness that is attracted by the promise of God's Rule but in the end prefers a criminal to the seemingly powerless Jesus. Judas, finally, shows that betrayal is a possibility even for those within the most intimate circle. The story of his suicide (27:3-10) not only plays up Jesus' innocence (27:4) but also shows that there is a point beyond which repentance is too late.

Most importantly, Jesus himself manifests humility, steadfast obedience to God's commands, and the refusal to "test" God (4:7) or to use power for personal ends in defiance of God's will (26:52-54). His example is important for his followers: although he was subject to temptation and even experienced despair at the moment of his death (27:46), he remained faithful to his role.

The reader, however, will identify more easily with the disciples. Like most who strive to follow a religious teaching, they are ambiguous characters throughout the story—showing understanding at one point, misunderstanding at another; faithfulness at one point, unfaithfulness at another. They are particularly important because it is with them, despite their fallibility and doubt, that Jesus has entrusted his teaching and promised ultimate reunion. They stand for the unexpected possibilities of ordinary people who come to faith.

The reader will sense a tragic irony in the scenes in which Jesus is mocked and crucified. For by now the reader knows many things: that Jesus indeed is "king," but in a sense his tormentors do not understand; that although humble and apparently powerless, he has access to God's power; and that while he does not "save himself" he does in fact "save others"! The narrator confirms all this for the reader immediately after Jesus' death by reporting dramatic signs that signify *God's* evaluation of what has taken place: the rending of the temple curtain, the "preliminary" resurrection of the saints, and the earthquake (27:51-54). Then the words of the Roman soldiers underscore the point: "Truly this was God's Son."

New characters enter the scene unexpectedly. The narrator now reveals that there were after all some who did not totally desert Jesus: a group of women (27:55-56). And the reader will remember that it was a woman who, against the disciples' protest, anointed Jesus for burial in the home of another marginalized person, Simon the leper. Here, then, is another model for discipleship: humble people have attended the humble Jesus in his moment of greatest vulnerability. The other new character, Joseph of Arimathea, is by contrast rich; but the notation about his wealth explains how he could own a tomb.

The narrator presupposes that the reader will know that some opponents of Christianity have sought to discredit the resurrection story by claiming that the disciples stole Jesus' body. Thus, woven into the stories of the empty tomb and resurrection appearances there are accounts that answer this accusation: the guarding of the tomb and the bribing of the soldiers (27:62-66; 28:11-15). The latter story also further discredits the Jewish authorities, who, even in the face of the empty tomb and reports of the dramatic event involving the angel, never consider belief but immediately resort again to treachery.

The narrator's straightforward presentation of the resurrection will encourage the reader to believe the reports. The guards themselves witness both the earthquake and the angel, and the women run not only with "fear" but also with "great joy," indicating their full belief, to tell the disciples what has happened. But it is of course the report of Jesus' actual appearance to the women that provides the major incentive to belief, and their response to this appearance serves as a model to the reader: they worship him (28:9).

Both the angel and Jesus reiterate Jesus' promise, in 26:32, of a reunion with the disciples in Galilee. The repetition of this motif, together with the suspense created by the shift back to the story of the guards, coaches the reader to anticipate a dramatic event. And the narrator's presentation fulfills the reader's expectations. On a mountain, which will recall earlier scenes in the story, the disciples meet Jesus and worship him, just as the women did earlier.

The reader will understand that the narrator is proclaiming worship of the resurrected Jesus as appropriate, will conclude that the disciples are now ready for a new stage of discipleship, and will attach particular significance to Jesus' final words. It will be clear that as Jesus draws together central themes from the entire gospel he is giving a direct command to the postresurrection community. Once again claiming authority from God, Jesus implicitly passes it on to the disciples in a threefold command: to "make disciples of all nations," to baptize, and to teach. The reader will know that the first two commands mean to preach the good news to the entire world, including the Gentiles, and to draw those whom they encounter into their own fold. And the baptismal formula—"Father, Son, and Holy Spirit"—will remind the reader of John the Baptist's promise that Jesus would baptize with the Holy Spirit and that the Spirit descended upon Jesus at his baptism.

The third command, to teach the converts what he himself has taught, will remind the reader of all that Jesus has said throughout the Gospel on such subjects as the ethics of God's Rule, life in the new community, and things to come. But when Jesus specifies that the disciples are to teach the converts *to obey* his commands, the narrator calls attention to the difference between hearing and doing: the reader will remember that the dual command to love is the principle by which Jesus interprets the law and also that love must be manifested in concrete deeds of mercy.

It will be clear that these final commands define the mission of the church as to carry on Jesus' own ministry. But this task will not appear as a burden. For the commands are followed by a promise, which brings the Gospel to a close: "I am with you always, to the end of the age." The reader will remember Jesus' words about the end of all things, knowing that the time of final fulfillment is incalculable. Reflecting upon the difficulties that will precede that fulfillment, the reader will also remember the earlier promises of Jesus' abiding presence with the community and will be encouraged to live courageously in the present.

2. Historical Questions Concerning Matthew

Considerable scholarly effort has gone into attempts to answer historical questions regarding the author of Matthew and the community for which this person wrote. The majority of scholars have viewed Matthew as the "most Jewish" of the four Gospels. Its positive view of the Jewish law (5:17-20) and, at points, even of Pharisaic tradition (23:2), as well as the frequent use of rabbinic modes of argument, are among the factors that create this impression.

A number of scholars claim that the Matthean community was not fully separated from Judaism, that the bitter dispute between Christians and Jews reflected in the Gospel is a family affair. A more frequent view is that this community, although totally separated from the synagogue, was comprised largely of Jewish Christians who were somewhat unsure of the implications of their Christian identity for their relationship to Judaism. Thus some scholars have seen Matthew as an attempt to forge a Christian alternative to the assertion of authority by the Jewish teachers at Yabneh. The frequent phrase "*their* synagogues" is often cited as evidence for the separateness of church and synagogue.

Other scholars find this Gospel quite "un-Jewish." Matthew 28:16-20 is a ringing affirmation of the gentile mission. And we have seen ample evidence of a positive attitude toward Gentiles. Kenneth Clark speaks of a "Gentile bias" in Matthew,[4] and John Meier claims that the author betrays an ignorance of Jewish traditions: it is, for example, apparently a failure to grasp the Hebrew poetic device of parallelism used in Zechariah 9:9 that has Jesus seated upon two animals at the same time in Matthew 21:4-7![5]

That such contrasting historical judgments can be derived from Matthew is a sign of its complexity. Clearly, there are tensions within the text. From a strictly literary point of view, it is meaningful to look for the "function" of such tensions, to ask how competing emphases create particular meanings. But historical critics ask whether the competing points of view are products of layers of tradition embedded in the text. Did the author, in other words, make use of earlier material not entirely compatible with that author's own view? Redaction critics have often assigned the heavily Jewish material to an earlier stage. They assume that the author, living in a mixed community of Jews and Gentiles, made use of material preserved by the Jewish contingent but accommodated it to the dominant gentile outlook.

---

4. Kenneth Clark, "The Gentile Bias in Matthew," *Journal of Biblical Literature* 66 (1947): 165–72.
5. John P. Meier, *The Vision of Matthew: Christ, Church and Morality in the First Gospel* (New York: Paulist, 1978).

Although most scholars think that the author of Matthew used sources with competing viewpoints, it is difficult to claim that the Jewish-Christian material has no real function on the level of the text as it stands. And while many scholars endorse the "Gentile bias" thesis, the majority continue to think of the author of Matthew as Jewish and the community as predominantly Jewish. As Donald Senior comments, "The gospel's occasional bitter critique of the Jewish leaders can be explained by the rupture between the church and synagogue. And [the author's] alleged 'errors' are extremely subtle" and are the more understandable if Matthew was written in the Diaspora.[6]

The debate on these issues is far from settled, and some recent studies have challenged some of the premises of earlier arguments. Anthony J. Saldarini thinks that the sharp distinction between a community "in" or "out" of Judaism is too simplistic. Drawing upon the sociological notion of deviance, he understands Matthew's group as a marginalized sect within the larger community that has its own identity but does not think of itself as beyond the bounds of Judaism, whatever others might have thought of it. In this view, the author still has hopes that other Jews will join the messianic movement. "However," Saldarini goes on, "the orientation of the Matthean community is changing from reformist to isolationist (vis-à-vis Jewish society), and it is beginning to create a new community withdrawn from Judaism and the empire as well."[7]

The most frequently suggested place of composition is Antioch in Syria, a large city with a mixed Jewish and gentile population, but others have suggested the Syrian hinterland or even Galilee. Any conclusion on this point remains highly speculative. As to the date of writing, scholars who accept Markan priority generally place Matthew around 85–90 C.E.

3. Theological Questions

Many scholars have sought to determine the author's position on various theological issues. Three of these issues are the Jewish law, the church, and Christology.

---

6. Donald Senior, *What Are They Saying about Matthew?* (New York: Paulist, 1978), 12.

7. Anthony J. Saldarini, "The Gospel of Matthew and Jewish-Christian Conflict," in David L. Balch, ed., *Social History of the Matthean Community: Cross-Disciplinary Approaches* (Minneapolis: Fortress Press, 1991), 60. See also Saldarini's more extensive arguments in *Matthew's Christian-Jewish Community* (Chicago: Univ. of Chicago Press, 1994).

a. The Jewish Law

B. W. Bacon, who first noticed the five formulary passages that conclude the long discourses, argued that Matthew was comprised of five "books," each including a narrative section followed by a discourse, plus an introduction and a conclusion to the Gospel as a whole.[8] In this view, the Gospel constitutes a "new law" presented by Jesus, the "new Moses." More recent scholars note that the narrative sections actually contain short discourses, and the major discourses are as closely connected to the material that follows them as to that which precedes them; so the book scheme appears forced. Also, while Jesus' legal interpretation is important in Matthew, it is hardly Jesus' only role. And scholars are divided on the Moses-Jesus correlation.

Jesus probably does not appear as the giver of a *new* law in Matthew, but neither does he simply endorse the law as it stands, as 5:21-48 shows. So the precise relationship between Jesus and the law remains unclear. A key passage in the debate is 5:17-20, Jesus' statement that he has come to "fulfill" the Law and the Prophets. One view is that "fulfill" means to "establish" or "actualize" the Scriptures by teaching and acting in such a way that what God promised through the prophets and demanded through the law is now realized. In Jesus the time of fulfillment becomes present, enabling true obedience and making salvation available. Jesus' interpretation, anchored in the love commands, involves some modification of the actual content of the law, but in some sense it remains valid as a totality.

Some scholars who adopt this view take the phrase "until all is accomplished" in 5:18 to mean that the law remains in effect throughout the life of the church. Meier argues, however, that what is "accomplished" is the fulfillment of prophetic prediction through Jesus' ministry, so that the law is no longer valid after the resurrection.[9] This reading of the passage illustrates the difference between redaction-critical and literary approaches to interpretation. For Meier regards 5:19, an affirmation of the law's continuing validity, as an "undigested morsel" of earlier tradition, but literary critics insist on interpreting the text as it stands.

b. The Church

Matthew is the only Gospel to use the term *ekklēsia* (church), and there is general agreement that "ecclesiology" (doctrine regarding the nature of the

---

8. Benjamin W. Bacon, *Studies in Matthew* (New York: Henry Holt, 1930).
9. Meier, *The Vision of Matthew*, 224–34.

church) plays some role in the Matthean theology. There is a clear interest in community problems and in defining discipleship, but scholars debate
the relative weight to be given to ecclesiology, as contrasted to Christology,
and whether and/or in what sense the church constitutes a "displacement" of
historical Israel. There is no need to elaborate these issues in detail. Both
Christology and ecclesiology are important, and the emphasis upon the shift
from Israel to the church is balanced by an emphasis upon the eschatological
judgment the church too must undergo.

There is also general agreement that Peter plays a special role in Matthew, but not on how this role affects the Gospel's ecclesiology. Traditionally,
Catholic interpretation has understood 16:16-19 as representing the founding of the papacy, a reading that Protestants, not surprisingly, have resisted.
But few contemporary Catholic scholars would defend this traditional position, and few Protestants still "survey the biblical evidence on Peter with the
object of discrediting the papacy."[10] At issue in the more current debate is
whether Peter symbolizes church leadership or, more generally, discipleship
per se. Certainly in 16:16-19 Peter receives certain powers and responsibilities. But are these prerogatives of certain offices within the church or are they
the responsibility of the church as a whole?

There is a strong equalitarian strain in Matthew: the power to "bind and
loose" given Peter in 16:19 is given to the whole community in 18:18;
and 23:9-12 warns against exalting some members above others. Thus Jack
Kingsbury claims that Peter's "primacy" in Matthew is purely temporal—i.e.,
he is the first to confess Jesus and thus becomes the spokesperson for the disciples.[11] Other scholars point out, however, that only Peter is given the "keys"
to God's Rule, called "blessed," and named as the "rock" on which Jesus
founds the church. Thus, they argue, the Matthean emphasis upon Peter is of
a piece with other portions of the New Testament (John 21, Luke 5:1-11 and
22:31-32, 1 and 2 Peter, etc.) that understand Peter as a symbol of "pastoral
leadership."[12]

c. Christology

Scholars have given a great deal of attention to Matthew's Christology, and
much of it has centered around the relative importance of the various titles
given to Jesus: Son of God, Son of man, Christ, and Lord. Kingsbury has

---

10. Senior, *What Are They Saying about Matthew?*, 74.

11. Jack Dean Kingsbury, "The Figure of Peter in Matthew's Gospel as a Theological Problem,"
Journal of Biblical Literature 98 (1979): 67–83.

12. Senior, *What Are They Saying about Matthew?* 76.

been a strong defender of the view that the title "Son of God" is preeminent,[13] but others have disputed this claim. Meier, for example, thinks that Matthew balances this title with "Son of man."

There is general agreement that Matthew's Christology is relatively "high,"—that in Matthew Jesus more clearly embodies "divine" character-istics (miraculous power, knowledge of others' thoughts, etc.) than he does in Mark or Luke. Some interpreters, however, also detect a "functionalist" element in Matthean Christology, a tendency to understand Jesus' identity less in terms of his "being" in a metaphysical sense than in terms of the role he plays in God's plan. One indication of this element is the empha-sis upon Jesus' obedience to God's will. And given Matthew's emphasis upon the law, some scholars have found a strain in Matthew in which it is Jesus' interpretation of the law, rather than his death and resurrection, that actually brings about salvation. I have argued elsewhere, for example, that there are points at which the notion of a salvation actually effected by Jesus' death seems to break down.[14] In one reading of 25:31-46, the criterion of eschatological salvation has nothing directly to do with explicit confession of Jesus but is based solely upon concrete deeds of love. How one evaluates the significance of such a possible "undercurrent" in Matthew is, of course, a hermeneutical question.

Another issue in Matthean Christology concerns the role of wisdom termi-nology in this Gospel. Jack Suggs has argued that a comparison of Matthew and Luke shows that the author has revised certain Q-passages to have Jesus assume the role that personified Wisdom originally played in those passages.[15] And Fred Burnett has interpreted 24:3-31 as Jesus/Wisdom's final statement to the disciples, following his/her final rejection by the Jewish people.[16] Suggs further claims that in Matthew Jesus is actually the incarnation of Wisdom and, since Wisdom and Torah were already identified in some Jewish thought, of Torah as well. In this view, Matthew constitutes a major step toward the ex-plicitly incarnational Christology in John. Some interpreters, however think that the author has Jesus assume Wisdom's role precisely as a way of avoid-ing reference to Wisdom herself. And there is reason to doubt that a purely

---

13. Jack Dean Kingsbury, *Matthew: Structure, Christology, Kingdom* (Philadelphia: Fortress Press, 1975).

14. Russell Pregeant, *Christology beyond Dogma: Matthew's Christ in Process Hermeneutic* (Missoula, Mont.: Scholars Press; Philadelphia: Fortress Press, 1978).

15. M. Jack Suggs, *Wisdom, Christology, and Law in Matthew's Gospel* (Cambridge: Harvard Univ. Press, 1970).

16. Fred W. Burnett, *The Testament of Jesus-Sophia: A Redaction-Critical Study of the Eschatologi-cal Discourse in Matthew* (Washington, D.C.: University Press of America, 1981).

Fig. 37.
St. Matthew
(Jusepe de Ribera;
Spanish, 1632)

literary reading of the Gospel, without regard to the author's revision of Q, can attest the incarnation motif.[17]

However one views the question of Wisdom Christology in Matthew, in this Gospel Jesus appears as definitive interpreter of the law in a way that occurs in no other New Testament materials. Salvation has an ethical aspect throughout the New Testament, but only here is it tied in such a specific way to the Jewish law.

---

17. See Russell Pregeant, "The Wisdom Passages in Matthew's Story," in David J. Lull, ed., "Society of Biblical Literature: 1990 Seminar Papers" (Atlanta: Scholars Press, 1990): 469–93.

4. Matthew's Theology and Jewish-Christian Relations

Anyone sensitive to the problem of Christian anti-Semitism will read certain aspects of the Gospel of Matthew with some degree of horror: the sweeping denunciation of the Pharisees, the notion of the destruction of the temple as God's punishment, and especially the verse in which the narrator has the Jewish crowds assume responsibility for Jesus' death: "His blood be on us and on our children" (27:25). Such material has undoubtedly fed the Christian hatred of Jews that contributed so much to the tragedy of the Holocaust. What is found in lesser degrees in other New Testament materials reaches its height in Matthew and John. Thus Lloyd Gaston argues that Matthew "can no longer be part of the personal canon of many" and that much Christian theology "needs to be rethought after Auschwitz, and one good place to begin is Matthew."[18]

Both Jewish and Christian scholars have given a great deal of attention to this problem in recent years, and a helpful distinction has emerged from the discussion. It is important to note the difference between a racially based anti-Semitism, which is a clear form of bigotry, and an anti-Judaism that is a religious polemic grounded in theological disagreement. Although a few interpreters find actual anti-Semitism in the New Testament, the majority do not. It is clear, nevertheless, that Matthew and other New Testament writings contain severe statements that appear to be anti-Judaic, that is, condemnatory of the Jewish religion.

There is no doubt that New Testament passages have in fact fed both anti-Judaism and anti-Semitism through the centuries. But this does not mean that those who have used the New Testament in this way have rightly understood the writings they quote. It is particularly important to place the harsh statements of the New Testament in the context of their ancient environment and its rhetorical conventions. As Scot McKnight notes,

> Rhetorically potent language is used throughout the ancient world to erect, fortify, and maintain the boundaries that distinguish one religious community from another or to separate, within the same religious community, the obedient from the disobedient. This form of religious rhetoric is especially prevalent in the Hebrew prophetic tradition that, through this kind of communication, seeks repentance on the part of the sinful.[19]

---

18. Lloyd Gaston, "The Messiah of Israel as Teacher of the Gentiles," *Interpretation* 29 (1975): 34.
19. Scot McKnight, "A Loyal Critic: Matthew's Polemic with Judaism in Theological Perspective," in *Anti-Semitism in Early Christianity,* ed. Craig A. Evans and Donald A. Hagner (Minneapolis: Fortress Press, 1993), 55.

The last sentence is crucial. The strong language of the New Testament stands clearly in the tradition of the Hebrew prophets, who themselves hurled bitter condemnations against their own kings, religious leaders, and people.

This defense, of course, works best on the assumption that Matthew's community is still closely related to Judaism. The greater the degree of separation one imagines, the more the harsh language appears as invective against *another* group. But even if the Matthean community is essentially separate from Judaism, the recentness of the split would lend an air of "family fight" to the conflict.

Bruce Malina and Jerome Neyrey address the issue in a slightly different way by explicitly focusing upon the pre-Matthean level of tradition, which they trace to a period in which the followers of Jesus were a deviant group within the Jewish community. As a sub-group with strong internal solidarity but weak influence on the larger society, they did what was typical in such situations: they attacked their fellow Jews with charges that fit the anthropological model of "witchcraft" accusations. In other words, they "demonized" their opponents. And, as is evident from Matthew 12:24, their rivals the Pharisees, who were apparently unable to counter completely the Jesus-group's influence, did the same.[20]]

The tragedy is that Christians have often read these polemical statements in Matthew, as well as the Jewish prophets' criticisms of Israel, as objective descriptions of the Jewish people as a whole. To do so, of course, is no more valid than to take the Pharisees' charges against Jesus in Matthew 12:24 as a just description of his intentions.

The insights of Malina and Neyrey are important, but they do not speak to the question of how we are to interpret the invectives in Matthew on the level of the Gospel as it stands. Precisely at this point, however, insights from literary criticism can add a point worth considering. If we focus upon the possible functions of the polemical language for readers within the Matthean community, it appears that *to some extent* the Pharisees, as characters in the story, represent a type of distorted religious consciousness that can exist within any religious community. This point is supported by the emphasis in Matthew upon the judgment against the church.

Matthew's treatment of the Pharisees nevertheless remains problematic, and some of the statements on the broader Jewish community are even more troublesome. To hold the Jewish people as such responsible for Jesus' death and to speak of God's rejection of Israel can scarcely appear to Jews them-

---

20. Bruce J. Malina, and Jerome H. Neyrey, *Calling Jesus Names: The Social Value of Labels in Matthew* (Sonoma, Calif.: Polebridge, 1988), chap. 1.

selves as anything other than anti-Judaism, and perhaps even anti-Semitism. There is some reason to believe, however, that traditional interpretations of Matthew may be in error on both these points. What does it mean that the crowds accept responsibility for Jesus' death on behalf of themselves and their children in 27:25? This verse is traditionally understood as signifying the guilt of the Jewish people as such. Some recent commentators, however, argue that the narrator means quite specifically that two generations are held responsible, namely, the generation contemporary with Jesus and the next one, which suffered the destruction of the temple in 70 C.E.[21] Even this notion is problematic for many modern readers, but it is a far cry from condemning all future generations of Jews.

It is important to observe, in any case, that Matthew's way of dealing with the relationship between Judaism and Christianity is not the only option the New Testament offers. Paul, for example, presents a very different view; and this alone should encourage one to ask whether a literal acceptance of Matthew's view, however we might interpret it, is a necessary part of a Christian's affirmation. In a rather dramatic way, then, an attempt to evaluate the Gospel of Matthew raises one aspect of the hermeneutical question discussed in the Introduction.

STUDY QUESTIONS

1. What specific contributions does each of the following make to the reader's understanding of Jesus, prior to the beginning of his ministry: the genealogy (1:2-17); the birth (1:18-25); the baptism (3:13-17)?

2. Identify as many elements as you can in 1:1—4:16 that stress the Jewish nature of the story being told. Now identify the passages that stress Gentiles. How, at this point in the story, would you explain the meaning of this dual emphasis?

3. How would you summarize Jesus' teaching in chapters 5-7 (the Sermon on the Mount)? Why do you think scholars refer to Jesus' demands as constituting a "higher righteousness"?

4. What does the discourse in chapter 10 tell the reader about the role of the disciples? Which aspects of the discourse apply most directly to the postresurrection church?

5. What contrasting views of Jesus are found in 13:52—16:20? What is the significance of 16:13-20?

6. What is the purpose of Jesus' teaching of the disciples in 16:1—18:35?

---

21. Daniel J. Harrington, *The Gospel of Matthew* (Collegeville, Minn.: Liturgical Press, 1991), 390.

7. How does the "parable" (allegory) beginning in 20:1 draw together all the material from 19:1 to 19:30?

8. Give allegorical interpretations of the "parables" in chapters 21–22. How are they related to the conflicts in which Jesus has been involved?

9. Describe the dual role played by chapter 23. What is the function of chapters 24–25?

10. What is the significance, for the reader, of the behavior of the disciples as Jesus is arrested, tried, and executed?

11. What is the importance of Jesus' reunion with the disciples in Galilee?

12. In what ways does 28:16-20 draw together themes from the Gospel as a whole?

13. Compare the treatment of the resurrection in Matthew to that in Mark.

14. Looking back over the entire Gospel, compare Matthew's overall treatment of the disciples to Mark's.

15. In what specific ways does Jesus' relationship to the law in Matthew "remain unclear"?

16. Do you think that in Matthew Peter represents church leadership specifically or discipleship per se? Give evidence for your view.

17. In what ways does Matthew exhibit a "high" Christology? What aspects of Matthew might be viewed as in tension with this high Christology?

18. Imagine that two of your friends, one of whom is Christian and one of whom is Jewish, are discussing the question of whether the New Testament is anti-Judaic or possibly anti-Semitic? What would you contribute to the discussion?

FOR FURTHER READING

Balch, David L., ed. *Social History of the Matthean Community: Cross-Disciplinary Approaches*. Minneapolis: Fortress Press, 1991. Essays on such topics as Hellenistic and Jewish aspects of Matthew, social location of the community, and gender roles.

Baur, David R. *The Structure of Matthew's Gospel: A Study in Literary Design*. Sheffield, Eng.: Almond Press, 1988, 1989. A helpful analysis of the literary structure of Matthew, with implications for Christology, making use of Greek rhetorical categories.

Bornkamm, Günther, Gerhard Barth, and Heinz Joachim Held. *Tradition and Interpretation in Matthew*. Philadelphia: Westminster, 1963. Essays on eschatology and ecclesiology, law, and miracle stories.

Edwards, Richard A. *Matthew's Story of Jesus*. Philadelphia: Fortress Press, 1985. A brief, nontechnical treatment employing reader-response criticism.

Ellis, Peter. *Matthew: His Mind and His Message.* Collegeville, Minn.: Liturgical Press, 1974. Employs a variant of redaction criticism, which focuses on the completed text; emphasizes Matthew's Christology and understanding of the church.

Gundry, Robert H. *Matthew: A Commentary on His Literary and Theological Art.* Grand Rapids: Eerdmans, 1982. Detailed and technical, making extensive use of Greek. Employs redaction criticism based on the two-document hypothesis, but identifies the author with Matthew, one of the Twelve. Highly competent

Harrington, Daniel J. *The Gospel of Matthew.* Collegeville, Minn.: Liturgical Press, 1991. Detailed and thorough, stressing the work's Jewish character; a major contribution.

Howell, David B. *Matthew's Inclusive Story: A Study in the Narrative Rhetoric of the First Gospel.* Sheffield, Eng.: Almond Press, 1990. A reader-response analysis stressing Jesus' role as model; critiques the category of salvation history.

Kingsbury, Jack Dean. *Matthew: Structure, Christology, Kingdom.* Philadelphia: Fortress Press, 1975. An important redaction-critical study.

———. *Matthew.* Proclamation Commentaries. 2d ed. Philadelphia: Fortress Press, 1986. A brief, readable commentary employing a form of redaction criticism.

———. *Matthew as Story.* Philadelphia: Fortress Press, 1986. A highly readable treatment employing narrative criticism.

Luz, Ulrich. *Matthew 1–7.* A Continental Commentary. Minneapolis: Fortress Press, 1989. Trans. Wilhelm C. Linss. First volume in an exhaustive work, distinguished by attention to history of interpretation. Comprehensive bibliography.

Meier, John P. *The Vision of Matthew: Christ, Church and Morality in the First Gospel.* New York: Paulist, 1978. A detailed work, employing redaction criticism. Includes a treatment of the formation of Matthew and a commentary on the entire work.

Overman, J. Andrew. *Matthew's Gospel and Formative Judaism: The Social World of the Matthean Community.* Minneapolis: Fortress Press, 1990. An important argument that the Matthean community is still within the bounds of Judaism.

Patte, Daniel. *The Gospel of Matthew: A Structural Commentary on Matthew's Faith.* Philadelphia: Fortress Press, 1983. A detailed commentary employing a simplified form of structuralism. Good bibliography.

Pregeant, Russell. *Christology beyond Dogma: Matthew's Christ in Process Hermeneutic.* Philadelphia: Fortress; Missoula, Mont: Scholars Press, 1978. Somewhat technical; outlines a process hermeneutic and applies it to the question of exclusivism and universalism in Matthean Christology.

Saldarini, Anthony J. *Matthew's Christian-Jewish Community.* Chicago: Univ. of Chicago Press, 1994. Makes a strong case that the Matthean community remains a marginalized group within Judaism.

Schweizer, Eduard. *The Good News according to Matthew.* Trans. D. Green. Atlanta: John Knox, 1975. A solid, readable commentary.

Senior, Donald. *Invitation to Matthew.* Garden City, N.Y.: Doubleday, 1977. A brief, nontechnical commentary.

———. *What Are They Saying about Matthew?* New York: Paulist, 1983. A brief, highly readable summary of current issues. A good introduction to the study of Matthew.

Stanton, Graham, ed. *The Interpretation of Matthew.* Philadelphia: Fortress Press; London: SPCK, 1983. Essays, some of them classics, on key issues. Contains a helpful introduction.

———. *A Gospel for a New People: Studies in Matthew.* Louisville: Westminster/John Knox Press, 1994. A major contribution that covers a wide range of topics and shows the separation between Matthew's community and the synagogue.

Weaver, Dorothy Jean. *Matthew's Missionary Discourse: A Literary Critical Analysis.* Sheffield, Eng.: Almond Press, 1990. A competent, helpful study of the role of the discourse in the narrative as a whole.

Chapter 7

Luke-Acts

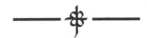

1. Preliminary Comments

It is best to discuss two issues regarding Luke-Acts prior to a literary analysis. First, it is important to state why scholars believe the same person wrote Luke and Acts. Both are addressed to someone named "Theophilus," and Acts 1:1 refers back to a "first" writing, which tells the story of Jesus. The two books, moreover, share a distinctive literary style that entails sophisticated use of the Greek language, and they also show unmistakable signs of narrative and theological unity. This point will become clearer as we work our way through the story of Jesus in Luke and the story of the early days of the Christian "way" in Acts.

The second matter is the identity of Theophilus, which has been the subject of much speculation. Some scholars think he was a Roman official. Others point out that the name means "God-lover" and suggest that the author used it symbolically, as a way of addressing readers who are new or potential Christians. The dedication of historical works to particular individuals, however, was common in the Greco-Roman world. Whether Christian or not, Theophilus was most likely an actual person.

2. The Story of Jesus in Luke

a. 1:1—2:52

The preface, directed to Theophilus, gives the narrator opportunity for a statement of purpose: to provide an "orderly" account of "the events that

Fig. 38.
The Annunciation
(Luke 1:26-38)
(*Ecce Ancilla Domini!*
Dante Gabriel Rossetti;
Italian, 1849–50)

have been fulfilled among us." The reader will presume that Theophilus has either heard reports about the Christian movement or actually received some instruction in the faith. Either way, the account is given so that he, along with other potential readers, might come to know "the truth" about the events in question, the truth the narrator claims is in some sense related by eyewitnesses.

From the beginning, the reader knows that the story is a Jewish one. The account of Zechariah and Elizabeth and the birth of their son, John, takes place in the reign of "Herod, king of Judea"; and the reader first encounters Zechariah, a priest, while he is on duty in the temple. Not only is the style of writing in the first two chapters reminiscent of Septuagint Greek, but the theme of the gift of pregnancy to an elderly, infertile woman echoes a familiar biblical theme.

Divine activity is also evident from the beginning. The angel Gabriel announces the pregnancy to Zechariah and indicates that the child will "be filled with the Holy Spirit," lead many Israelites back to God, and "make ready a people prepared for the Lord" (1:14-17). Gabriel then appears to a virgin named Mary and tells her she will conceive a son, to be named Jesus, by the power of the Holy Spirit. The angel's reference to Jesus as "Son of God" coaches the reader to understand Jesus' role as more prominent than John's—a point underscored by John's startling prenatal recognition of Jesus in 1:41.

The overriding mood of the opening scenes is joy. John's birth is cause for rejoicing (1:14), and the poetic responses of Mary and Zechariah celebrate the fulfillment of God's promise to Abraham (1:55, 73). The narrator interprets this fulfillment, this "salvation" of Israel (1:69), partly in terms of God's worldly-political reestablishment of Israel, the chosen people. Jesus comes to occupy the Davidic office (1:32-33) and to depose "the powerful from their thrones" (1:52). It is specifically Israel (1:16, 54) that receives God's help and is saved from its enemies (1:68-71).

The reader will see a socioeconomic element in the fulfillment of God's promise. Mary's poem is rich with the theme of reversal of fortunes: God has "sent the rich away empty" and exalted the lowly. And the theme continues as Mary, already identified as of "low estate" (1:48), is forced by circumstance to give birth in a manger, and Jesus' first visitors are lowly shepherds (2:8-20).

In 2:21-40 the narrator again stresses the Jewish nature of the story. Jesus' parents do everything in relation to his birth according to the Torah, and the two characters who give oracles regarding the child Jesus are identified in specifically Jewish terms. Simeon is a devout person who is "looking for the consolation of Israel," and Anna is a prophet. Jesus' own Jewish devotion is central to the story from his childhood, and the temple itself is the focus of activity in this chapter. The reader will think of Jesus as emerging from a pious Jewish family.

Simeon's oracle also discloses that God's salvation is for Gentiles as well as Jews (2:32). And, in the midst of stories full of joy and fulfillment, Simeon injects an ambiguous note regarding Israel: "This child," he says, is set for the *falling* and the rising of many in Israel," and through him "the inner thoughts of many will be revealed" (2:34-35). Precisely as the one who comes to save Israel, Jesus will cause *division*. It is now possible to detect a similar motif in the earlier statement that John's role is to call Israelites *back* to God (1:16-17) and to offer "forgiveness of sins" (1:77). The narrator has thus prepared the reader for the notion that it is a "purified" Israel within which God's promises will be fulfilled.

The incident regarding Anna contributes something else to the reader's consciousness. Women have already played strong roles in the story, with Mary completely overshadowing Joseph in the account of Jesus' birth. Now, finding the male prophet Simeon paralleled by a female prophet, the reader is learning to meet women in roles equal in importance to those of men.

The reader finishes the first phase of the story of Jesus with a strong sense of Jesus' special role in a course of events through which the Holy Spirit is fulfilling the ancient promises to Israel. An angelic messenger and two inspired Israelites have announced that the time of salvation has come: the child Jesus has been born into the world as Davidic Messiah, Son of God, who will establish God's Rule. The reader will hear in all this a continuation of the story told in the Jewish Scriptures and also recognize a pattern, typical of Hellenistic biographies of famous persons,[1] in which childhood incidents foreshadow greatness. They will be prepared to understand Jesus as a benefactor who confers wonderful gifts on humankind in the manner of great emperors and heroes.[2]

When the narrator comments in 2:52 on Jesus' growth "in wisdom and in years, and in divine and human favor," the reader will anticipate further indication of Jesus' understanding, acceptance, and actual performance of his special role. The narrator makes clear, however, that Jesus is no ordinary hero. The comment in 2:52 combines with the preceding incident in the temple to emphasize that he is totally committed to the purpose of God.

b. 3:1—9:50

The narrator signals a new phase of the story in 3:1 by providing a historical context for the ensuing events. The reference to the emperor Tiberius encourages the reader to think not only of Jewish history, but of world history, a point that recalls the earlier indication of the inclusion of Gentiles.

The new beginning is marked by the immediate fulfillment of one of the predictions in the birth stories: John calls Israel to repentance. The preface to his ministry parallels the introductions to prophetic books in the Jewish Scriptures, and John quotes a passage from Isaiah. The reader will thus remember that Zechariah had termed John a prophet who would prepare the way before the Lord (1:76). The theme of an inclusive salvation also reappears at the end of the quotation: "all flesh shall see the salvation of God." And the reader will note again, in John's definition of repentance (3:10-14), the socioeconomic dimension of God's Rule. The high point of the account of John's ministry,

---

1. See Charles H. Talbert, "Prophecies of Future Greatness: The Contribution of Greco-Roman Biographies to an Understanding of Luke 1:5–4:15," in *The Divine Helmsman: Studies on God's Control of Human Events, Presented to Lou H. Silberman*, ed. James L. Crenshaw and Samuel Sandmel (New York: Ktav, 1980).

2. See Frederick W. Danker, *Benefactor: Epigraphic Study of a Greco-Roman and New Testament Semantic Field* (St. Louis: Clayton, 1982).

Fig. 39. The Baptism of Jesus (Luke 3:21-22). (Ravenna mosaic)

however, is his witness to the one who comes after him, who will baptize "with the Holy Spirit and fire" (3:16). The reader will therefore anticipate Jesus' appearance, which in fact comes immediately after the narrator's preview of John's imprisonment. Jesus' reception of the Spirit in baptism will not only connect with John's prediction but will remind the reader that the Holy Spirit has been active from the start.

The genealogy in 3:23-38 encourages the reader to accept Jesus' messianic status through the linkage with David and Abraham, but it also reiterates the universality of the salvation he brings by tracing his lineage ultimately to "Adam, the son of God." Then, on the basis of the encounter with the devil in the wilderness, the reader will evaluate Jesus' actual behavior in a positive way: making a decision about how to understand his sonship, he chooses to worship God rather than the one who tempts him to use his power for selfish ends. But the conclusion of this story in 4:13 suggests that Jesus' victory is incomplete: Satan departs, but only to await "an opportune time."

The reader can surmise from 4:1 that it is through the power of the Holy Spirit that Jesus conquers temptation, and 4:14 places his entire mission in the context of the Spirit's empowerment. The latter point is reemphasized by the scene in the synagogue at Nazareth (4:16-30), where Jesus reads the passage from Isaiah beginning, "The Spirit of the Lord is upon me...." The implication is that Jesus' baptism was his anointment, in messianic fashion, by the Spirit. And the reader will see in the remainder of the quotation a description of Jesus' role in terms that yet again define God's Rule in a "material" way: his messianic practice brings deliverance to the poor, the blind, the captive, and the oppressed.

The scene at Nazareth also picks up on other notes from the earlier chapters. John was successful in attracting crowds, and in the present story the congregation's initial reaction to Jesus is positive. John's castigation of his audience, however, implied that not all who came to him were sincere. Similarly, Jesus now predicts his own rejection and tells two scriptural stories implying God's graciousness toward Gentiles. When the people then run Jesus out of town, the reader will remember the prediction in 2:34-35 that he would reveal peoples' inner thoughts and cause the "falling and the rising of many."

The reader has already been coached to understand John as a prophet. In predicting his own rejection at Nazareth (4:23-24), Jesus now identifies himself in the same way. The two stories he tells, moreover, concern the prophets Elijah and Elisha. As Jesus moves out of Nazareth to continue his ministry, the reader will be inclined to interpret his messianic activities with the prophetic model in mind. The accounts of Elijah and Elisha also give scriptural sanction for the Gentiles' inclusion in the fulfillment of God's promise, since they illustrate acceptance of non-Israelites.

"Messiah," "Son of God," "prophet," "benefactor"—the reader is now prepared to understand Jesus in light of all these categories. In the stories that follow the scene at Nazareth, the narrator injects specific content into Jesus' fulfillment of these roles by relating the words and deeds through which he carries out the commission given in the quotation from Isaiah in 4:18-19. Jesus brings release to those possessed by demons (4:31-37) and afflicted by disease and infirmity (4:38-41; 5:12-16, 17-26; 6:6-11). He accepts outcasts: a leper (5:12-16), tax collectors (5:27-32), and (in an account that again parallels a story involving a man) also a woman (4:38-39; 4:31-37). In line with

John's earlier proclamation (3:3), Jesus defends his association with tax collectors with the statement that he has "come to call not the righteous, but sinners to repentance" (5:32). And in his actual pronouncement of the forgiveness of sins (5:20) he further dramatizes that the longed-for salvation is now available. The theme of forgiveness appears also in the call of the fishers, since Peter pronounces himself a sinner (5:8). And this story combines with the designation of twelve apostles in 6:12-16 to give the reader a strong sense of his messianic mission.

The reader learned in 4:18 that Jesus' commission is not only for messianic deeds but also for preaching, and in 4:43 he explicitly acknowledges proclamation of the Rule of God as his task. The narrator can alternately speak of Jesus "preaching" (4:44) or "teaching" (4:15) in the synagogues, and in 6:17-49 he delivers a lengthy discourse. The opening sentence places this teaching in the context of God's Rule, and related themes already familiar to the reader reappear. In a series of beatitudes/woes (6:20-26) permeated with the theme of eschatological reversal, Jesus pronounces the poor and the unfortunate blessed and gives a severe warning to the rich. Along with the prohibition of revenge, the golden rule, and other injunctions, the narrator reports his command to "give to everyone who begs from you."

The reader will understand the stories of the healing of the centurion's slave (7:1-10) and the raising of the widow's son (7:11-17) as further demonstration of Jesus' role as Messiah and benefactor. The former story also encourages further reflection on the Jewish-gentile theme. The narrator has the Jewish leaders justify Jesus' dealing with the centurion on the basis of this man's contribution to a synagogue. But Jesus, in a statement that recalls his earlier stories of Elijah and Elisha, praises this Roman's faith as greater than any he has found in Israel.

In response to the raising of the dead man, the onlookers not only repeat Jesus' self-designation in 4:24 by calling him a prophet, but in words that echo Zechariah's in 1:68 they proclaim that "God has looked favorably on his people!" (7:16). The narrator thus encourages the reader to connect Jesus' words and deeds to God's promised redemption in specific ways. The point becomes even clearer in 7:22-23, where Jesus alludes to his scriptural commission in 4:18-19: "The blind receive their sight . . . the dead are raised up, the poor have good news brought to them. And blessed is anyone who takes no offense in me."

The reader will find a double edge in this last sentence. Jesus has been conferring benefits upon those who have accepted him and, despite his rejection at Nazareth, has achieved recognition (4:14; 5:1, 15). But some have in fact taken offense at him. The scribes and Pharisees have objected to his forgiveness of sins and acceptance of tax collectors and attacked him for Sabbath violations (6:1-10). Considering him a blasphemer and lawbreaker, they begin to wonder what to do about him (6:11).

The reader, by contrast, has come to think of Jesus as a pious Jew, who justifies his actions on the basis of Scripture (6:3-5) and seeks to know God's will and clarify his own mission through prayer (3:21; 5:16; 6:12). But the fulfillment he brings represents something new: in the saying on wineskins (5:33-39), he attacks his opponents because they cling to tradition in a way that blocks out the significance of the present moment. He is in fact causing division, and in 7:24-35 the reader finds help in understanding the reason for it. Intruding into Jesus' reply to the criticisms against himself and John, the narrator portrays one's response to John's message as a decision for or against God. In refusing John's baptism, the narrator says, the Pharisees and lawyers had *"rejected the purpose of God for themselves."*

When, at dinner in a Pharisee's home (7:36-50), Jesus defends his acceptance of the ministrations of a "sinful" woman and pronounces her forgiven, the reader will remember the saying on the physician and the ill in 5:31. And the contrast Jesus draws between the woman's gratefulness and the Pharisee's self-righteous rigidity makes the issue between Jesus and the Pharisees more concrete. By having this unlikely person ask Jesus to dinner, however, the narrator suggests that there is still hope that Jesus will get through to the Jewish leaders—a point reinforced by the fact that he continues in dialogue with them. That all Jewish leaders are not opponents of Jesus, moreover, is apparent from the faith of Jairus, a "leader of the synagogue" (8:41-42). The reader will nevertheless see the Pharisees demonstrating the wrong response to Jesus.

The notation in 8:1-2 that as Jesus continued his ministry the Twelve and some women he had healed were with him reminds the reader of the emphasis upon eyewitnesses in 1:2. And the point is elaborated as the story proceeds. Jesus' statement in 8:9-10 that the disciples are given the secrets of God's Rule emphasizes their special status. They are with Jesus when he calms a storm on the lake (8:22-25), when he casts a "legion" of demons from a man in the country of the Gerasenes (8:26-39), and when his power heals a woman who simply touches him (8:43-48). Peter, John, and James are then privileged to be present when he raises Jairus's daughter from the dead (8:40-42, 49-56). Remembering that the Twelve have been designated apostles (6:13), the reader will not be surprised that Jesus sends them out briefly on their own, empowered to preach and to heal (9:1-6). It will be clear that they are witnesses of what Jesus has done as well as the ones who share in and extend his mission.

Fig. 40. "Jesus Feeds the Five Thousand" (Luke 9:10-17).
(Pablo Mayorga; Nicaraguan, 1982)

The notation about Herod in 9:7-9 serves both to inform the reader that John the Baptist has been executed and to raise the question of Jesus' identity. Following a miraculous feeding of the crowds, Jesus himself raises this question with the disciples. When Peter confesses him as "the Messiah of God," Jesus apparently accepts the designation. But he also enjoins secrecy about this matter and solemnly predicts his death and resurrection. In the ensuing teaching (9:23-27), Jesus indicates that those who follow him must take up their own crosses; and the term "daily" coaches the reader to understand this demand metaphorically, as the practice of self-denial.

The reason for Jesus' injunction to silence, however, remains a matter of speculation for the reader. Is it simply not the time for disclosure of his identity? Is the disciples' understanding not clear enough? The disciples in fact show very limited faith and understanding in the stories that follow. When Jesus' glory is made manifest in the transfiguration scene (9:28-36), the narrator emphasizes Peter's incomprehension (9:33). And as Jesus returns from the mountain he upbraids the disciples who have failed in an attempt at exorcism. They show incomprehension also in 9:45, when Jesus again refers to his coming death; and in vying with one another for greatness (9:46) they utterly negate the call to discipleship as self-denial. Finally, in 9:49-50, ignoring the counsel to childlike humility, they persist in their self-centered, controlling attitude by forbidding an exorcist outside their band to use the name of Jesus.

The reader who finished the stories of the births of John and Jesus expecting the fulfillment of God's promises now faces a complex situation. Both John and Jesus have met with some success, and Jesus is dispensing blessings, both the forgiveness of sins and the material well-being associated with God's Rule. Yet he has encountered opposition from the Jewish leadership, and his own disciples, although recipients of his power, appear strangely inept. Jesus has said, moreover, that he must die. What now of the promised restoration of Israel? The reader, of course, has a clue as to the resolution of the problem: Jesus has twice said that the Messiah must suffer, die, and be raised from the dead.

c. 9:51—13:30

In 9:51 the narrator indicates that Jesus sets out for Jerusalem, noting that the time "for him to be taken up" has drawn near. Understanding this phrase as a reference to Jesus' coming death, the reader will accept the interchanges in 9:57-62 as pointing to the metaphorical meaning of Jesus' journey. They are reminders of the cost of discipleship, of "following" Jesus on his way. The disciples' arrogant response to the Samaritans' rejection of Jesus in 9:52-56, however, shows that they still have much to learn.

The account of the sending of the seventy (10:1-22) raises the reader's hopes, even as it embraces the theme of Jesus' rejection. The emissaries' joyous return and Jesus' positive response, including a saying on Satan's fall from heaven (vv. 17-23), indicate a successful journey that points toward an ultimate victory. It will be clear that the journey prefigures the later worldwide Christian mission.

The reader will find further definition of following Jesus in the material that ensues. In an encounter with a lawyer (10:25-37), Jesus endorses the dual love commandment as the central requirement for "eternal life." Then, in the parable of the Good Samaritan, he plays upon the term "neighbor" to reiterate the theme of the inclusion of outcasts at the same time as he commends deeds of mercy. The story of Mary and Martha redefines the role of women through Jesus' approval of the sister who neglects the traditional "women's work" to hear his teaching. When the disciples ask Jesus to teach them to pray (11:1), he not only teaches them the Lord's Prayer but delivers a brief discourse on God's willingness to give to those who ask. While those who follow Jesus are asked to leave everything behind them, they are nevertheless promised the bounty of God's goodness.

It is becoming apparent to the reader by now that Jesus' death is not as imminent as 9:51 might have suggested and that the narrator is using the journey format to expand upon Jesus' teachings. From 11:14 to 13:30 Jesus is speaking almost constantly, although he changes locales several times. In the Beelzebul controversy, he indicates that in deciding how to interpret his exorcisms people are deciding for or against God's Rule (11:20, 23). The statement that the Rule of God "has come upon you" echoes Jesus' counsel to the seventy in 10:9 and so interprets the later Christian mission as an extension of Jesus' own.

The reader will recognize the theme of decision about Jesus as it continues in the encounter with the woman in 11:27-28, the condemnation of "this generation" in 11:29-32, and the sayings on light/darkness in 11:33-36. And then in vv. 37-52 there is a reminder of the decision the Jewish leadership has been making throughout the story. At a dinner at a Pharisee's house, Jesus attacks the Pharisees and lawyers on the specific details that set them apart from his own version of God's Rule. Although he points to the coming judgment against "this generation" (11:51), however, he also leaves the door open for his opponents' repentance. Attacking them for "greed and wickedness," he then exhorts them: "So give alms for those things that are within" (11:41). Yet in 11:53 the narrator makes their decision clear: they lie "in wait for him, to catch him at something he might say." The reader will thus remember the ominous destination of Jesus' *literal* journey.

In the following scene (12:1-12), Jesus warns his followers against the Pharisees and then places the issue in the context of the final judgment: one's response to Jesus has eschatological consequences. Even here, however, the narrator provides a qualification (12:10): denial of Jesus is a forgivable offense, but blasphemy against the Holy Spirit is not. In light of the clear reference to the persecution of the future church in vv. 11-12, the reader will conclude that those who rejected Jesus during his life will have a second (but final) chance when confronted with Christian preaching.

The parable of the rich fool (12:13-21) reiterates the need for decision and also introduces the theme of the danger of riches. The latter becomes the subject of Jesus' statement in 12:22-34, where he enjoins the disciples to trust in God rather than worldly goods and to sell their possessions and give alms. The discourse then turns to eschatological preparedness in 12:35-40, a theme illustrated in the following story of the master and the servant (vv. 41-48) and woven together with a call to decision in vv. 49-59. Jesus' denial that he has come to bring peace is jolting, especially in light of Zechariah's prophecy of peace in 1:79 and the angels' song in 2:14: "and on earth peace...." In 13:1 some listeners' remarks about Pilate's massacre of Galileans provide the occasion for Jesus to continue his eschatological warnings, which he illustrates with the story of the vineyard owner and the gardener (13:6-9). In all of this the reader is garnering teaching pertinent to life in the postresurrection situation, but also observing Jesus in conflict and on his way to his death.

After the Pharisees show their true nature yet again by criticizing Jesus' healing of a woman on the Sabbath, the narrator notes that Jesus' opponents are "put to shame," while the crowd rejoices "at all the wonderful things" Jesus is doing (13:17). Jesus then tells two parables (13:18-21) emphasizing the paradox of God's Rule: insignificant to the eye, it bursts forth with marvelous results! The reader will thus reflect upon the paradox of Jesus' own ministry. He is indeed conferring benefits that bespeak the presence of God's Rule; and yet he is opposed by the Jewish leadership. One may wonder what will come of all this confusion; and yet the narrator is clearly pointing to a final victory.

In 13:22 the narrator, reminding the reader that Jesus is on a journey to Jerusalem, again has Jesus teach about the eschatological judgment, decision, and division based upon one's attitude toward himself. Verses 28-29 reintroduce the theme of the inclusion of Gentiles, now placed over against the exclusion of "evildoers" (13:27). And the saying on "first and last" reminds the reader of all that has been said about eschatological reversal, while the qualification "some" subtly indicates that the fate of those who hear Jesus (as well as that of the readers of the gospel) remains a matter of decision.

d. 13:31—19:27

When the Pharisees warn Jesus in 13:31 of Herod's intentions, the reader will hold out hope for at least some of the Jewish leadership. This verse leads into a statement by Jesus that weaves together the familiar themes of his prophetic status, his coming death in Jerusalem, and an ultimate victory. The reader will also note a new emphasis: Jesus' sorrow for those among his people who reject him.

Dining again at a Pharisee's table on a Sabbath (14:1-24), Jesus uses the healing of a man with dropsy to enter once again into argument. After pitting concern for human suffering against rigid adherence to legal technicalities, he launches a discourse—combining the themes of humility, reversal of status, and inclusion of the outcast—that culminates in the parable of the banquet. Again Jesus tries to teach his opponents, whom he castigates for their love of status. But the reader will also hear both defense of and instruction to the postresurrection community.

In Jesus' speech to the multitudes in 14:25-35, the reader will recognize a resumption of the theme of the cost of discipleship and the wrenching division it brings. Then his three parables (15:1-32), in response to the Pharisees and scribes who murmur about his dealings with tax collectors and sinners, stress inclusion of the outcast and forgiveness of sins. The story of the Prodigal Son also constitutes a powerful challenge to Jesus' opponents.

The reader may at first be puzzled by the story with which Jesus introduces teaching to the disciples in 16:1-9, but his words in the following verses express the narrator's interpretation. By "giving away property in his control,"[3] the steward shows that faithfulness in "dishonest wealth" means nonattachment to it, since human beings can serve only one master. And the reader will find the point illustrated when in 16:14 the narrator characterizes the Pharisees as persons attached to money. Jesus replies to their scoffing first with sayings that place God's Rule in opposition to their values (16:15-18) and then with the story of the rich man and Lazarus (16:19-31), a searing indictment of attachment to money and lack of mercy for the poor. The story not only categorizes the Pharisees as opponents of Jesus during his lifetime but also points to the postresurrection situation. Verse 31 is a clear allusion to Jesus' own resurrection and the failure of some to repent even in the face of God's confirmation of Jesus' ministry. In context, it also links the resurrection faith closely to justice for the poor and inclusion of the outcast.

In 17:1-10 the narrator directs the reader's attention more directly to the postresurrection situation by having Jesus address the disciples on matters that concern the later community: forgiveness of one's fellows, maintenance of faith, and humility in service. Then, in the story of the ten lepers, the reader is surprised to find that, as in 10:29-37, it is the outcast Samaritan who receives Jesus' praise.

When in 17:20 the Pharisees ask Jesus when God's Rule is coming, he launches a discourse, most of which is directed to the disciples, that constitutes an implicit exhortation to preparedness. The eschatological material, however, is bracketed by sayings that refocus the issue in terms of the "now." Despite the reference to future events in 17:22-37, verses 20-21 speak of God's Rule as already present. And 18:8, following upon an exhortation to the disciples to pray and have confidence in God, subordinates the question of the "when" of God's Rule to the question of faith in the present. The reader

---

3. Robert C. Tannehill, *The Narrative Unity of Luke-Acts: A Literary Interpretation*, vol. 1: *The Gospel according to Luke* (Philadelphia: Fortress Press, 1986), 247.

Fig. 41. "The Return of the Prodigal Son" (Luke 15:20).
(Engraving by Gustave Doré, 1865)

should understand God's Rule as in some sense already present, yet awaiting future fulfillment.

The parable of the Pharisee and the tax collector (18:9-14) reminds the reader of the familiar themes of reversal, inclusion of the outcast, and forgiveness of sins. The story of Jesus and the children not only illustrates inclusiveness but exposes the disciples' inadequate understanding. Despite the connection Jesus made in 9:46-48 between acceptance of children and the humility necessary for discipleship, they try to turn the children away and once again display a self-centered, controlling attitude.

When a "ruler" asks how to obtain eternal life (18:18), Jesus refers to the commandments, thus reminding the reader that he remains a pious Jew. But his radical view of God's Rule reappears in his interpretive addition: "Sell all that you own and distribute the money to the poor." Following with a statement on the seductive character of riches, Jesus then answers Peter's question by indicating a "way out" of the rich person's dilemma: God can make salvation possible for anyone. But this statement is followed by more interpretive material: the reader is expected to view the disciples, who have left their homes and followed Jesus, as models of those who will in fact receive eternal life.

In 18:31 Jesus abruptly announces to the Twelve that they are now ready to enter Jerusalem, reminding them (and the reader) of what must happen there. The narrator notes, however, in an extremely emphatic statement, that they do not understand his words.

Outside Jericho, Jesus heals a blind man who calls him Son of David; and the people respond by praising God. The reader will now recall all the benefits Jesus has dispensed throughout the story and will remember that early in the story Jesus was heralded as the messianic king. So here is the king, ready to enter Jerusalem; yet the reader knows what the disciples do not grasp, that this king and prophet has come to Jerusalem to die.

In Jericho itself, Jesus encounters Zacchaeus, a tax collector (19:1-10). The story draws together several familiar themes for the reader: Jesus proclaims salvation present in the "now," stresses Zacchaeus's Jewishness, and defines his own mission precisely as "to seek out and to save the lost." It also serves to comment yet again on wealth and poverty, since Zacchaeus does what the rich ruler would not do: he not only restores fourfold to those he has defrauded, but gives (the remaining?) half of his wealth to the poor.

In 19:11 the narrator notes Jesus' proximity to Jerusalem and has him tell a parable to dispel the impression that God's Rule is "to appear immediately." It will be clear that the reader must interpret the story allegorically: the image of the nobleman who had gone away to receive sovereignty over the people stands for Jesus himself. Thus just before taking the reader into Jerusalem, the narrator points beyond Jesus' death to his glorious return and indicates that the real fulfillment of God's promise will come not during Jesus' visit to Jerusalem but at the end of history.

But there is more to the allegory than this. Not only does it encourage the reader to reflect upon the actions of the servants as models of good and bad discipleship, but it reaches its climax in a note of judgment. The nobleman's punishment of the citizens who tried to sabotage his reign is the narrator's pronouncement of judgment against those who rejected Jesus.

e. 19:28—24:53

The narrator's description of Jesus' entry into Jerusalem in 19:28-44 will remind the reader that from the beginning he has been presented as the messianic king destined to bring fulfillment of God's promises to Israel. But the Pharisees' confrontation of Jesus in 19:39 will contrast with the recitation of the kingship psalm by "the whole multitude of the disciples" in v. 38. The "triumphal entry" will thus appear as ambiguous, fraught with conflict. In a similar way, Jesus' lament over Jerusalem clashes with the proclamation of peace in v. 38, which echoes the words of the shepherds in 2:14. The tragedy will thus be clear: Jerusalem does not in fact recognize "the things that make for peace." But the reader will also look for a resolution of the peace/conflict tension.

Against this background, Jesus addresses the city, predicting its destruction because it fails to recognize its time of "visitation from God." In 1:68 Zechariah's oracle proclaimed that in Jesus God had "visited" (NRSV: looked favorably on) the people for the purpose of redemption. Now, however, the visitation of Jerusalem brings judgment, because the rejection of Jesus is the rejection of the peace that God's redemption brings. The reader must conclude that Jesus brought the real possibility of the restoration of Israel under God's Rule, but that in failing to recognize him as the messianic king the people turned down that possibility. That is why the one whose mission is peace brings not peace but division (12:51-53). But the reader will also hope that the peace of God's Rule will eventually prevail.

In what follows, the reader is aware of escalating conflict. When Jesus enters the temple, ejecting "those who were selling things," and proceeds to teach, the "chief priests, the scribes and the leaders of the people" seek a way to get rid of him (19:45-48). This same group then engages him in controversy as he teaches in the temple for several days. He outwits them on the questions of his own authority and of tribute to Caesar, however. And his al-

Fig. 42. Temple area of a model of the city of Jerusalem, about 50 C.E. This model is located behind the Holy Land Hotel in the new city of Jerusalem. It gives a good idea of the Temple precincts, although the Temple building itself occupied a relatively small part of the Temple area. Public worship took place outside the Temple building. Sacrifices were offered on the altar immediately outside the building and the liturgical worship took place in the Court of Women (see Fig. 22). *(Photo by Thomas Hoffman)*

legory of the tenants foreshadows Israel's rejection of him and subsequent punishment (20:9-18).

When the Sadducees try their own trick question regarding the resurrection of the dead (which they reject), Jesus' answer not only shows the coherence of the doctrine but grounds it in Scripture. And this prompts some of the scribes, who presumably accept the doctrine, to acknowledge his point. The reader will thus entertain the possibility that even among the Jewish leaders the rejection of Jesus is not absolute. Nevertheless, after demonstrating from Scripture that the Messiah is not subordinate to David, Jesus tells his disciples to beware of the scribes, whose love of status and injustice toward the poor will merit condemnation, and then contrasts the scribes to the poor widow who gives proportionately more than they do to the treasury (21:1-4). The reader will understand all this on two levels: Jesus' words both illustrate true discipleship and point to the nature of the conflict that sends him to his death.

In 21:5 Jesus begins a discourse on things to come. Predicting the destruction of the temple, he separates that event from the actual end of history (21:9), which will come only when the gentile mission is completed (21:24). The reader, looking back on the destruction of Jerusalem as an event in the past, will hear the prediction (21:25-28) of the coming of the Son of man as an encouragement to hope. Through Jesus' concluding words in verses 29-38, the narrator then enjoins the reader to take heart—but also to "be alert" and pray.

Suddenly, the reader is aware that Jesus' death is imminent (22:1-3). As the chief priests and scribes seek a way to put Jesus to death, Satan, having found the "opportune time" mentioned in 4:13, reenters the story to prompt Judas to betray his leader.

In the account of the Passover meal (22:14-38), the narrator directs the reader's attention to the future, both immediate and distant, with a focus on the present deficiencies but future role of the Twelve. Jesus speaks of his coming betrayal and death and must deal with the disciples' dispute about greatness by emphasizing his own role as servant. He also predicts Peter's triple denial. By designating the Twelve as "apostles," however, the narrator points to their role in the postresurrection church. And Jesus not only speaks of eating and drinking with them in God's coming Rule but acknowledges that they have so far accompanied him in his trials and will in fact "sit on thrones judging the twelve tribes of Israel." Even his rebuke of their self-centeredness, when taken together with his prediction of Peter's renewal (22:32), contains a positive implication: they will someday learn what it means to follow a crucified leader!

The final interchange at the meal may leave the reader puzzled: Jesus commands his followers to buy swords. Is this a metaphorical statement, indicating that perilous times are ahead? Or does the reference to fulfillment of Scripture mean that Jesus is recognizing the disciples' misunderstanding of the situation, that they, in other words, have already become "transgressors" in the sense of outlaws? What will be clearer to the reader in the stories that follow (22:39-62) is the contrast between Jesus' steadfast obedience to God and the disciples' failure.

In the trial sequence, the narrator moves from the disciples' failure to Jesus' rejection by the people. The "assembly of the elders of the people, both chief priests and scribes," deliver Jesus to Pilate and bring charges that the reader knows are false. After an unsuccessful attempt to pawn Jesus off on Herod, Pilate suggests letting him off with a flogging. The narrator presents

Fig. 43.
"Días de Christo."
Painting and
lithograph by
Frank Diaz Escalet,
13 Fletcher St.,
Kennebunk, ME
04043.

the scene dramatically: three times Pilate tries to release Jesus, and three times the people, ever more emphatically, demand crucifixion. The final irony is that as they demand Jesus' death they also insist upon the release of Barabbas, a man who, the narrator twice notes, was an insurrectionist and a murderer!

The reader will conclude that the people as a whole wanted Jesus' death, but will then have to qualify the judgment. The abandonment of Jesus is real, but not absolute. The soldiers treat him brutally, but Simon of Cyrene is made to carry his cross (23:26), while a great multitude follows him and women weep for him. Then, after Jesus dies, the narrator discloses that "his acquaintances, including the women who had followed him from Galilee," had stood at a distance and watched. The reader also learns that Joseph of Arimathea, who procures Jesus' body, had not assented to Jesus' death even though he was a member of the council.

Throughout the account, the narrator hammers home the theme of Jesus' innocence. Pilate himself had reached that verdict, and at the death scene it is reiterated first by one of the criminals with whom Jesus is executed and then by a centurion: "Certainly this man was innocent" (23:47).

The reader will notice that Jesus remains God's faithful servant to the end. He prays at the Mount of Olives before his arrest, and at the moment of his death he commends his spirit to God. He retains, moreover, his beneficent character, offers forgiveness to the repentant criminal at his side, and even asks forgiveness for those who put him to death (23:34). This attribution of Jesus' rejection to ignorance complements the narrator's subtle indications that the rejection was not really unanimous.

The reader may now draw some conclusions. Jesus gained acceptance by some, although in the end the faith of those followers entrusted with the greatest responsibility was imperfect. In some sense the people as a whole turned away from him, yet all—both those of imperfect faith and those who rejected him outright—could from the point of Jesus' death look forward to the possibility of forgiveness and renewal.

The renewal of Jesus' followers begins immediately, although it does not happen all at once. Three women come to the tomb on the first day of the week and receive the resurrection proclamation from the two men in dazzling apparel (24:1-12). When the apostles are informed of this incident, however, they consider the report "an idle tale."

The narrator moves from this inconclusive account of the empty tomb to the road to Emmaus, where two of Jesus' followers unknowingly encounter the risen Jesus and ironically try to fill him in on the recent events in Jerusalem. After he has documented from Scripture that it was necessary for the Messiah to suffer and then enter into glory and has then broken bread with them, they suddenly recognize him. And then he vanishes. Hurrying back to Jerusalem, they find that the risen Jesus also appeared to Simon Peter. Then comes the climatic moment: he appears in the midst of the disciples and gives proof that he is not a "spirit." They are joyous but only half-believe. So Jesus proceeds once again to document the scriptural necessity of his death in terms that more clearly recall his earlier predictions.

The reader may now surmise the root of the disciples' inadequate faith throughout the story. It was precisely their inability to grasp that the Messiah could suffer, rather than bring the restoration of Israel directly, that stood in the way. Failing to understand that, they also failed to understand that their own roles must involve humility and suffering. Then, in the face of his death, they were driven to despair. Thus the two on the road to Emmaus could only say—ironically, in light of the resurrection—that they "had hoped that he was the one to redeem Israel."

With the resurrection accomplished, Jesus can project from his own completed mission to that of his followers: they are to preach the familiar message of "repentance and forgiveness of sins," but now specifically in his name, "to all nations, beginning in Jerusalem." The disciples are qualified for this mission because they are, as the narrator has indicated throughout the story, witnesses of "these things," that is, his deeds, his death, and his miraculous presence with them after his death. And they will be further qualified in the future, because Jesus promises that they will be "clothed with power from on high."

When Jesus is taken into heaven, the disciples return to Jerusalem, where the narrator leaves them, joyously blessing God in the temple. The story thus remains a Jewish story: pious Jews, disciples of Israel's Messiah, await the fulfillment of his promise. Their mission, which will be a mission to all the world, must begin right here in the heart of Judaism.

The reader will have some sense of closure. The story of Jesus has reached its conclusion. The Messiah has taken the path Scripture had said he must take; thus his strange rejection somehow fulfills God's redemptive purpose after all. But issues remain unresolved. What, specifically, of Israel itself, which put its own Messiah to death? How is one to interpret God's promise that Israel itself should be redeemed? And what of the gentile mission predicted in Scripture? How does it fit into the promise to Israel? The reader finishes also with a sense of anticipation.

3. The Story of the Christian "Way" in Acts

a. 1:1-26

Referring to the "first book," Acts 1:1-4 points the reader back to Luke 24, to Jesus' resurrection appearances, his ascension, and his command to wait in Jerusalem. The passage also expands upon the account in Luke, for Acts 1:4-8 makes clear that the awaited "power from on high" (Luke 24:49) is precisely the baptism of the Holy Spirit of which John the Baptist spoke (Luke 3:16), and v. 3 discloses (in contradiction to Luke 24, however) that Jesus remained on earth for forty days after the resurrection, teaching the apostles.

The narrator also uses the term "apostles" here, although other disciples figured in the stories in Luke 24. The reason becomes clear in 1:6-11, the expanded ascension scene: the emphasis is upon the apostolic mission. Since Jesus has now been raised from the dead, the apostles expect him to proceed immediately with the restoration of Israel as they originally understood it. Jesus answers their question by referring to the "times and periods" that God alone knows and commissioning them to be his witnesses "in Jerusalem, in all Judea and Samaria, and to the ends of the earth." Those who earlier did not understand that Jesus' own mission involved death and that discipleship entails suffering appear here unable to understand that God's purpose includes a mission to the whole world in which they themselves will be key figures.

The scene closes with the words of two heavenly figures, words that point to Jesus' eventual return and the completion of God's redemptive activity.

On that note of hope, the narrator proceeds to the story of the reconstitution of the Twelve, symbolic of the twelve tribes of Israel, through the replacement of Judas. The reader understands that the worldwide mission is about to begin.

b. 2:1—9:43

Then it happens! On the Jewish feast of Pentecost, Jesus' followers receive the Holy Spirit and begin to speak in other languages (2:1-13). There are in Jerusalem, the narrator notes, "devout Jews from every nation under heaven," who are bewildered: the speakers are Galileans, but they are communicating with people from all over the world. The reader, remembering that the apostolic mission is destined for "the ends of the earth," will see here a dramatic demonstration of the power of this mission to unite all humankind.

Peter seizes the moment, addressing the crowd with an interpretation of what is happening. The passage from Joel reflects the widespread notion that the Spirit had long since departed from Israel but would return just prior to the end of the age. The people, Peter declares, have just experienced the Spirit's return. Then he makes his case by recounting the story of Jesus—his great deeds and his resurrection, to which Peter and the others are witnesses (2:32). The latter claim will remind the reader of the emphasis in the first volume on the role of disciples as witnesses, whose testimony has made possible the "orderly account" promised in Luke 1:1.

When Peter speaks of God's "definite plan and foreknowledge" (2:23) and finds prophecies of Jesus' resurrection and lordship in the Psalms (2:25-35), the reader will be inclined to accept the view that God is in control of history and that Jesus' death was part of God's overarching plan. But the narrator is also presenting the resurrection as God's answer to a human decision: Peter tells his Jewish audience that they killed Jesus through "those outside the law," the gentile Romans, but God intervened by raising Jesus from the dead. When Peter also declares that God "made" Jesus both Lord and Messiah (2:36), the reader, who has thought of Jesus as Messiah since birth, will conclude that the resurrection confirmed Jesus' status and brought his lordship into another phase.

Peter's call for repentance and baptism for the forgiveness of sins and his promise of the Spirit recall the emphasis in Luke on all these items, as well as the definition of the content of the Christian message in Luke 24:45-47. The reader will understand that Peter is offering the "second chance" to the Jewish people implied in the Gospel. When the narrator recounts the mass baptism

Fig. 44. "Descent of the Holy Ghost" (Acts 2:1-13).
(Jerome Wierix; Netherlands, 16th cent.)

and the wonders worked by the apostles (2:41-43), the reader will feel that the mission is now underway with great success.

The references to the temple and the "goodwill of all the people" (2:46-47) coach the reader to think of the new community in terms of God's promises to Israel. But the mission is rooted specifically in Jesus. The apostles' miracles (2:43) will appear as a continuation of the benefits Jesus himself conferred, and the communitarian economic structure of the new group will appear as a practical application of the emphasis upon justice for the poor in the Gospel. The idyllic description of the movement in 2:43-48 creates the impression of a "purified" Israel-within-Israel as the locus of the Spirit's activities.

Peter has two more occasions to speak, first in response to the crowd that gathers after the healing of the lame man (3:12-26) and then in answer to the authorities after he and John are arrested (4:8-12). In both instances he again places Jesus in the context of God's plan of salvation, proclaims the resurrection, refers to the apostles' role as witnesses, and offers forgiveness to those who crucified Jesus. Added notes, which supplement the reader's grasp of the details of God's "plan," are his explicit acknowledgment that in rejecting Jesus the people acted *in ignorance* (3:17), his reference to Jesus' eventual return at "the time of universal restoration," and his declaration that salvation is made available in Jesus' name alone (4:12).

The reference to ignorance will remind the reader of Jesus' statement from the cross (Luke 23:34) and will help illumine the notion of the "second chance." And this latter notion becomes clearer in 4:1-4, where the narrator distinguishes between the Jewish leaders, who arrest Peter and John, and the people at large, some of whom respond to the preaching and join the movement. Although historical Israel as a formal whole has rejected Jesus, individuals may respond to the mission now underway.

When confronted by the authorities, Peter and John boldly declare, "we cannot keep from speaking of what we have seen and heard" (4:20). Hardly recognizable as the faint-hearted followers depicted in the Gospel, these two now appear to the reader as sterling models of persons who in fact fulfill the role of witnesses. Their release from custody also gives the narrator opportunity to present a model of another type, through further descriptions of the Spirit-filled community's piety and economic communitarianism. The latter theme receives dramatic emphasis in the story of Ananias and Sapphira (5:1-11), whose attempt to defraud the community ends disastrously. The point is not to inspire fear but to play up the atmosphere of miracle, wonder, and expectation that pervades the movement. This story leads directly into an account of other "signs and wonders" that took place among the believers, an account that stresses the benefits conferred by the apostles. The reader reads on with an image in mind of an idyllic community fearlessly preaching its message in the power of the Spirit.

The sense of wonder prevails. Although arrested (5:17-18), the apostles resume preaching after their miraculous release. When Peter is again before the council and makes another courageous witness, an honored teacher named Gamaliel, a Pharisee, convinces the body to delay action, warning that the movement might after all be "of God"! The narrator thus suggests that even the Jewish leadership is not entirely against the new movement, and the reader will remember that it was the temple hierarchy, not the Pharisees, who were the prime movers both in Jesus' death and in the opposition to the apostles' preaching. The reader will also note further evidence of the change in the apostles. After suffering a beating, they rejoice in being able to suffer for Jesus' name (5:41). Their deeds now attest their understanding of what it means to follow a crucified Messiah.

The narrator has so far presented the fledgling community's internal life as idyllic, but in 6:1-6 the reader gets a glimpse of an internal conflict between "Hellenists" and "Hebrews" (i.e., presumably, between Greek-speaking Jewish Christians and Aramaic-speaking Jewish Christians). In response to charges of discrimination against the Hellenists among the widows in the distribution of supplies, the Twelve appoint seven Hellenistic deacons to oversee this matter. The story thus shows the happy resolution of a community problem. It also introduces Stephen to the reader.

The narrator presents Stephen as a powerful figure, full of the Spirit, whose deeds parallel those of the apostles. Arrested and charged with speaking against the temple and the law, he defends himself by recounting the whole history of Israel as the history of God's graciousness and the people's mixed response, again adding specific content to the reader's understanding of God's dealings with Israel. In contrast to faithful servants such as Abraham, Moses, and Joseph, Stephen sets Joseph's treacherous brothers (7:9) and the opponents of Moses (7:27, 35, 38-42). Coming finally to the matter of the temple, he declares that God "does not dwell in houses made with human hands" (7:48). The reader, remembering earlier positive references to the temple, will interpret this statement to mean only that true worship does not depend upon the temple, and—given Israel's rejection of its Messiah—that this true worship is to be found within the community of those who have accepted that Messiah. In 7:51 Stephen brings the matter home: the people, he says, "are forever opposing the Holy Spirit." The same recalcitrance that opposed Joseph and Moses and killed the prophets has now resulted in the murder of Jesus.

Stephen dies courageously, full of the Spirit and beholding a vision of the

Fig. 45. "Saul, Saul, why do you persecute me?" (Acts 9:4).
(French manuscript, 15th cent.)

Son of man at God's right hand. Like Jesus, he is put to death outside the city; like Jesus, he delivers his spirit to God; and, like Jesus, he asks forgiveness for those who kill him. The reader understands that discipleship can involve not only persecution but actual martyrdom. That is the pattern set by the prophets, Jesus himself, and now Stephen. But the reader can discern another pattern also: although many individual Jews respond to the missionary preaching, the leadership stands in stark opposition. And the theme of opposition continues as the narrator makes passing reference to a young man named Saul, who observes and approves the stoning of Stephen. Then in 8:1-3 the reader learns of a general persecution of the Jerusalem church, in which Saul is a vigorous participant.

The reader will be curious about this Saul, but must put this interest aside as the narrator relates the consequences of the persecution. Except for the apostles, the Jerusalem Christians are scattered throughout Judea and Samaria, where they preach the word (8:1-8). The reader will remember Jesus' command in 1:8 and will sense that the mission is still in progress, even if through tragic means. The apostles also witness in Samaria: after Philip's successful mission, Peter and John come and lay their hands upon the people so that they receive the Holy Spirit (8:14-24). But the faith of the Samaritans stands in implicit contrast to the attitude of one Simon, who, mistaking the laying on of hands for magic, proposes to buy Peter's power from him (8:9-13).

The narrator next (8:26) follows Philip, who is divinely directed to Gaza for an encounter with an Ethiopian eunuch. The eunuch is presumably a Gentile,[4] but his reading of the Jewish Scriptures suggests that he is a believer in Israel's god. Although he is identified as a high official in his nation, he also appears as a marginalized person, since his mutilated body would exclude him from potential membership in the covenant community of Israel. Thus, in recounting this person's reception of baptism and the Spirit, the narrator signifies that the Christian mission has been extended to someone no less outcast than the Samaritans themselves. The reader may also associate Ethiopia with "the end of the earth" and view the incident as a partial, symbolic fulfillment of the final destiny of the mission. In any case, explicitly identifying Ethiopians as black, the reader will once again be led to reflect on the universal and inclusive character of the Christian way.[5]

In 9:1 the reader's attention is directed back to Saul, who is journeying to Damascus to continue his harassment of the movement, which the narrator now terms "the Way." Dramatically, the narrator recounts Saul's encounter with the risen Jesus, who identifies himself with his followers: to persecute them is to persecute Jesus himself. More divine interventions follow. God speaks both to Saul and a disciple named Ananias, arranging their meeting, despite the latter's hesitancy. But God insists that Saul is a chosen instrument for a mission to Gentiles and Jews and even kings. The reader can thus look forward to the further extension of the mission as outlined in Acts 1:8. There is also a reminder of the cost of bearing witness, for God proposes to show Paul "how much he must suffer" (9:16).

Struck blind on the road, Saul eventually recovers his sight in the presence of Jesus' followers; he is then baptized and proclaims Jesus the "Son of God." At first mistrusted by some Christians, Saul becomes a powerful witness and, under the sponsorship of Barnabas, tells his story to the apostles in Jerusalem. Following this story, the narrator comments (9:31) on the well-being of the church in Judea, Galilee, and Samaria and then relates a story in which Peter raises a woman from the dead. The reader retains a strong sense of the progress of the mission under the guidance of the Spirit.

---

4. The narrator, however, does not at this point draw attention to the issue of the inclusion of Gentiles, a matter that is given dramatic treatment in chapter 10.

5. See below, section 7, "A Matter of Race in Acts."

c. 10:1—15:35

In chapter 10 the narrator relates the encounter between Peter and the centurion Cornelius, guiding the reader through four scenes that gradually focus upon the issue of Jewish-gentile relations in the church. By the time the two actually meet, the reader not only knows that Cornelius is devoted to God and the Jewish people but has also heard a heavenly voice interpret Peter's vision of the "unclean" food: "What God has made clean, you must not call profane." If the precise meaning of the vision remains unclear, its triple occurrence signifies its importance and creates anticipation as the reader comes to the actual encounter.

Peter's words to Cornelius provide the final interpretation. The issue for the narrator is whether any *person*— i.e., specifically a Gentile—can be called "common or unclean." Peter, citing God's direct command, answers negatively (10:28). With the door thus open to the inclusion of Gentiles, he delivers an account of God's actions through Jesus, beginning with a declaration that "God shows no partiality" and ending with a reference to Jesus' eventual return as judge and an offer of forgiveness of sins in his name.

The speech itself reminds the reader of many familiar themes, such as God's historical dealings with Israel, the role of disciples as witnesses, forgiveness of sins, and Jesus' return at the end of the age. The subsequent events—the descent of the Spirit, the speaking in tongues, the baptism, and finally the controversy with the "circumcised believers"—lead up to the statement in 11:18, in which the reader will find the meaning of the entire sequence: "God has given even to the Gentiles the repentance that leads to life." Then, against the background of this explicit statement of the equality of Jews and Gentiles in the church, the narrator notes that some of the believers scattered in the Diaspora have begun to preach not only to Jews, but to Gentiles as well (11:19-20). The reader will now expect to hear more about the gentile mission, which has been foreshadowed in numerous ways since the beginning of the Gospel.

Further justification for this mission comes as Barnabas, whom the narrator introduces as someone sent from Jerusalem to Antioch to evaluate the matter (11:22), gives his approval. Saul also receives additional sanction, as Barnabas invites him there. These two are entrusted with a collection, in response to the prediction of a famine, for the church in Jerusalem. Following another miraculous arrest-escape sequence involving Peter, which ends with Herod's ghastly death, the Holy Spirit commissions Saul and Barnabas for special work. Immediately (13:4), they set sail and land on Cyprus, where Paul confounds a magician and converts a proconsul. The narrator, having brought the story deep into the gentile world, notes that Saul is also called (the Greek equivalent) Paul and proceeds now to employ the latter version of his name.

The reader will have sensed in the commissioning of Paul and Barnabas a turn in the plot, and its direction becomes clear as their journey begins. In Antioch of Pisidia (in Asia Minor), the missionaries worship in a synagogue, where Paul delivers a speech that ends with an invitation to repentance and a stern warning. Many hearers are interested, but when a multitude gathers to hear the message on the next Sabbath there is general outrage among the Jews that is increased by Paul's statement of intention to go the Gentiles. The result is that many Gentiles are converted, but the Jews drive the missionaries away (13:50). Events follow a similar pattern as Paul and his company travel in Asia Minor and preach in the synagogues. Returning to Antioch, Syria, they joyously report their success among the Gentiles (14:27-28). The reader will understand that Paul and Barnabas are now systematically preaching in the world at large, to both Jews and Gentiles.

"Unless you are circumcised according to the custom of Moses, you cannot be saved" (15:1): in reporting these words of the Judean critics of the gentile mission, the narrator poses the issue debated at the conference Paul and Barnabas attend in Jerusalem. The question is not whether Gentiles can become Christians, but whether they must be circumcised and accept the regulations of the Jewish law. Peter speaks against the necessity of gentile circumcision, stating that salvation is through grace (15:11). Then, after Paul and Barnabas report on the "signs and wonders that God had done through them among the Gentiles," James (whom the reader is expected to recognize as James "the lord's brother," since the other James is dead) affirms Peter's judgment and proposes that Gentiles simply be required to follow the regulations that, according to Jewish teaching, apply to all humankind.

Paul and Barnabas then return to Antioch, accompanied by emissaries who carry an official letter attributing this momentous decision to the Holy Spirit. The narrator wants the reader to know that a major problem faced by the early church has now been solved. Israel's salvation is now, as God had always intended, on its way to the Gentiles—to the "ends of the earth."

d. 15:36—19:20

The reader will sense a new phase of the story as Paul and Barnabas, back in Antioch, decide to visit the churches they have founded but part company over a dispute regarding John Mark (to whom later tradition attributed the Gospel of Mark). This incident injects a note of human frailty into the drama,

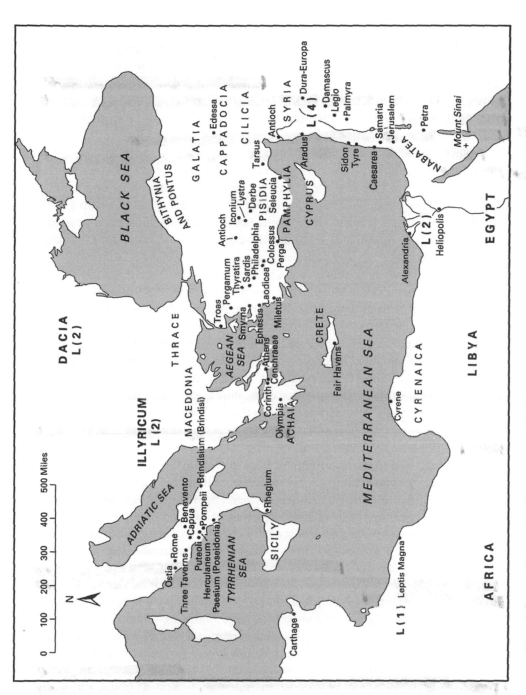

Fig. 46. Roman Eastern Mediterranean world, first century C.E. The location of the legions is indicated by **L** followed by their number (23 C.E.). The four legions of Syria were: in the north, X *Fretensis*; in the center, III *Galicia* and IV *Ferrata*; in the south, XII *Fulminata*. (*Map by Parrot Graphics*)

but the narrator quickly reinforces the aura of divine guidance. Paul chooses Silas as his new companion and adds to the entourage a man named Timothy, son of a Jewish mother and a gentile father, whom he circumcises out of deference to the Jews. Making clear that the mission to strengthen the churches is underway and successful (15:41; 16:5), the narrator employs three references to divine intervention (16:6-10) to assure the reader that God is directing the course of events. When Paul departs from his itinerary to sail for Macedonia, both he and the reader are clear that it is at God's command.

The miraculous events that attend the missionary party underscore this impression. Paul casts out a demon from a female slave in 16:16-18; then, when this event leads to imprisonment, an earthquake provides the party a possible escape. These events also suggest parallels between Paul and both Jesus and Peter. And the exorcism ties Paul to Jesus' emphasis upon good news to the economically oppressed, since the slave's owners had used her affliction to their profit.

In 16:10 the narrator subtly enters the story by shifting from the third-person to the first-person plural, thus giving the reader the sense of reading a report of events from within the circle of travelers. This device is dropped, however, after the story of the exorcism.

In Thessalonica (17:1-9), Paul preaches in a synagogue where he has some success among the Jews but receives a greater response from the Gentiles (persons who worshiped in the synagogue but did not become full members of the Jewish community). The narrator notes, however, that other Jews become "jealous" and bring Paul and Silas before the city authorities. The reader will grasp the irony of the charge that "they have been turning the world upside down." A developing pattern will also be apparent to the reader as the believers escape to Beroea, where many Jews and some Gentiles respond to the word but angry opponents from Thessalonica still pursue Paul.

Paul's friends send him on to Athens, where, provoked by the "idols" in the city, he argues with both Greek philosophers and Jews and finally addresses a large crowd in the Areopagus. His speech (17:22-31) is designed to meet "pagans" on their own ground by making known the "unknown god" to whom a local altar is dedicated. Affirming God's omnipresence, Paul nevertheless implies the inadequacy of "pagan" religion by calling for repentance in light of Jesus' resurrection. Although it avoids Jewish history per se, the speech elaborates upon God's plan for history by mentioning the creation (v. 24) and the final judgment (v. 31) and by characterizing past history as the "times of human ignorance," a phrase that echoes both Jesus' statement from the cross (Luke 23:34) and Peter's second speech (Acts 3:17). It should thus be clear to the reader that before the resurrection, human beings were not fully re-

Fig. 47. Votive relief in the Serapeion (Temple of Serapis) in Thessalonica*

sponsible for their deeds, since God's truth was not completely known. Now, however, it is. And the reader may piece together from all the speeches a comprehensive outline of God's plan, from the creation to the judgment, with the resurrection of Jesus as a kind of hinge-point.

Most of Paul's listeners are put off by the strange notion of resurrection. The reader, however, will be impressed that Paul does gain a few believers and some of the listeners remain open to further argument (17:32).

In Corinth, Paul lives with a couple, Priscilla and Aquila, and the narrator uses this arrangement to inform the reader of Paul's tentmaking trade. Here Paul again gains converts among both Jews and Greeks; but opposition from other Jews provokes his declaration, "From now on I will go to the Gentiles" (18:6), which the reader will understand as signaling another turning point in the story. This opposition also leads to Jewish accusations before a proconsul, which gives the narrator opportunity to have a Roman official declare the matter an internal Jewish affair with no relevance to the empire as such (18:12-18). Having returned to Antioch, Syria, Paul then strikes out for Galatia in Asia Minor.

---

*Late 2nd cent. B.C.E. Given by someone named Demetrios in honor of his parents. The figure in the center is Osiris, and the two beside the altar may be Demetrios's mother and father. (Photo: Koester/Hendrix)

In 18:24, the narrator introduces Apollos, a powerful missionary from Alexandria who knew only the baptism of John but taught about Jesus. Priscilla and Aquila complete his instruction in Ephesus, where they had journeyed with Paul, and provide him with a letter of introduction to another congregation. This story leads into an account of Paul's dealings with converts in Ephesus who had received only John's baptism and knew nothing of the Holy Spirit. Paul's laying on of hands leads to a mini-Pentecost, replete with speaking in tongues, that not only reminds the reader of the Spirit's role in the mission but once again shows Paul's work as parallel to Peter's. When Paul and the other disciples withdraw from the synagogue in Ephesus after encountering stiff Jewish opposition, the reader senses a widening breach between those who accept Jesus and those who do not (19:8-10).

The dramatic account of Paul's deeds in 19:11-17 not only shows the parallel between Paul and Jesus but also distinguishes Christian exorcism from a magical approach in which Jesus' name carries power in and of itself. The book-burning in vv. 18-19 suggests the victory of the Way over magic, and the summary statement in 19:20 informs to the reader that, despite serious obstacles, the mission is successful and the church is growing.

e. 19:21—28:21

The reader will discern in 19:21 a major turn in the plot, as the Spirit convinces Paul that after some further journeying he must go back to Jerusalem and then to Rome, the heart of the gentile world. Before his departure from Ephesus, however, a controversy arises: the "Way" has turned so many residents away from "idolatry" that the local artisans who make images of the deities are losing business! The account thus links idolatry with greed and pits Christianity against both. Defended by a local official, Paul avoids arrest; and in 20:1 he takes leave for Macedonia.

In a brief account, given partly in the first-person plural, the narrator follows Paul's movements back to Troas in Asia Minor, where he raises a young boy from the dead, and then down the coast to Miletus. Having summoned the elders of the Christian congregation in nearby Ephesus, he delivers a touching farewell speech (20:18-35), telling his friends he must go to Jerusalem, never to see them again. He also stresses that because he has declared God's whole plan (NRSV: purpose), he is innocent of the blood of all who heard him, indicating that it is not his fault if anyone has rejected the call to repentance. The reference to God's plan will remind the reader of the whole history of God's action as outlined in the other speeches in Acts, while the emphasis upon repentance offered to both Jews and Greeks (20:21) will recall the themes of a "second chance" for Jews and of God's longstanding intention to bring salvation to the Gentiles. The reader will also understand from the farewell theme that danger awaits Paul in Jerusalem.

After a tearful farewell (20:36-38), Paul and his party set sail again. In a long "we"-passage—which heightens the drama through another farewell, a prophecy of imprisonment, and efforts to dissuade Paul from continuing—the narrator finally brings the group to Jerusalem, where their fellow Christians greet them warmly. In a meeting with James and the elders of the community (21:17-25), Paul learns that many Jews in Jerusalem have become believers; but these leaders are concerned about reports that Paul is turning Diaspora Jews away from the law, so they convince him to undergo a rite of purification in the temple to demonstrate his Jewish "orthodoxy." The reader will note Paul's attempt to avoid a total break with Judaism. Nevertheless, aware of the opposition Paul has encountered throughout the story, the reader will also sense that such a break is unavoidable.

The reader's intuition is confirmed as some Asian Jews accuse Paul of teaching against the law and bringing a Gentile into the temple. They cause a commotion that results in Paul's arrest by a Roman tribune who, however, allows him to speak to the crowd. Stressing his Jewish credentials, Paul states that although born in the Diaspora (at Tarsus in Cilicia), he was educated in the law and studied in Jerusalem under the teacher Gamaliel. Then, having noted his own persecution of the "Way," he recounts his vision on the Damascus road (22:6-21). The people listen until he mentions his commission to go to the Gentiles; at this, they begin to cry out against him. The reader will remember that talk of Gentiles has caused such problems as far back in the story as Jesus' rejection at Nazareth (Luke 4:16-30).

The tribune takes Paul away, but, learning of his Roman citizenship, foregoes a flogging and brings him before the Jewish council. Paul, however, pits the Pharisees against the Sadducees by casting the issue in terms of the resurrection of the dead. The session thus ends in confusion, and, following a Jewish plot on Paul's life, the tribune sends Paul to Caesarea to stand before the Roman governor Felix. The reader will accept the Pharisees' reluctance to condemn Paul, as well as Paul's deference for the office of the high priest (23:1-5), as further indication that the Christian movement stands in full continuity with God's promises to Israel and that it is those who reject the Way who fail to recognize God's plan. Despite the Pharisees' ambiguity, however, the reader knows that Paul will not be freed. And the narrator adds in 23:11 a reminder why, according to divine purpose, this must be so: having testified in Jerusalem, Paul will now bear witness at Rome.

In the meantime, Paul gives his testimony in Caesarea (24:1-27). Confronted by some Jews, he stresses his "orthodoxy" and claims again that the issue is the resurrection of the dead. But Felix refuses to decide the case immediately and keeps Paul imprisoned for two years, frequently conversing with him on the matter. Standing eventually before Felix's successor, Festus, Paul finally appeals directly to the Roman emperor. The reader is thus prepared for the final leg of Paul's journey with Festus's declaration, "to the emperor you shall go" (25:12). But the narrator also seizes the opportunity to sound a familiar theme: in his comments to King Agrippa (25:18, 25), before whom Paul will now appear, Festus pronounces Paul innocent.

In Agrippa's presence (26:1-29), Paul stresses his Jewish heritage, claims he is on trial because of God's promise to Israel, and mentions the resurrection of the dead. Recounting again his vision on the Damascus road, he adds important elements: Jesus has appointed him to witness, has delivered him from both Jews and Gentiles, and sends him specifically to open the eyes of the blind and offer forgiveness of sins. Through this account of Paul's mission and Paul's subsequent summary of his message, the narrator not only recalls familiar themes from the entire story but reaches back to the very beginning: through Paul, God continues Jesus' own work—"to give light to those who sit in darkness" (Luke 1:79).

Through the final interchange (26:24-29), the narrator presents Paul as a model of faithful Christian witness; and the scene involving Agrippa, his wife, and Festus (26:30-32) underscores the reader's sense that Paul is innocent of any crime against the empire. Seen from the perspective of these characters, it is ironical that Paul must nevertheless, because of his appeal to Caesar, stand trial in Rome. And yet the reader will remember that it is really God's hand that guides Paul in that direction.

In 27:1 the narrator, again using the first-person plural, begins an account of Paul's voyage to Rome. The interaction of the Roman soldiers, the crew, and Paul through storm and shipwreck lends an air of dramatic realism to the report. Other elements remind the reader that God's hand is at work in all that happens. Paul shows prior knowledge of the dangers that lie ahead (27:9-10), and an angel gives him assurance in the midst of danger that he will in fact stand before Caesar. The narrator, moreover, blends in two more examples of the miraculous power working through Paul. Impervious to an adder's bite, he also performs healings (28:1-9). These healings, together with the scene in which Paul breaks bread and prays (27:35), again suggest parallels between Paul and Jesus.

Greeted by fellow Christians in Rome, Paul eventually speaks before the local Jewish community and tries "to convince them about Jesus" from Scripture (28:23). Some are convinced, but others disbelieve. So he quotes a

Fig. 48.
Statue of Augustus Caesar (Octavian)
from the Serapeion (Temple of Serapis)
in Thessalonica*

passage from Isaiah about hearing and not understanding and announces that "this salvation of God has been sent to the Gentiles; they will listen" (28:28). The reader will sense a momentous turn in the progress of the mission.

The notation that Paul lived "for two whole years" in Rome shows that he was no threat to the empire and thus reminds the reader yet again of the theme of innocence. Against the background of the tearful farewell at Miletus, it also gives a subtle hint that he is eventually put to death by the Romans. Implicitly, then, Paul appears as parallel to Jesus not only as a wonderworking, Spirit-filled benefactor, but as one unjustly arrested, convicted, and martyred.

The narrator embraces this faintly tragic note, however, within an over-whelmingly positive concluding sentence. Under house arrest, Paul continues his teaching and preaching "with all boldness and without hindrance." The reader thus finishes the story with a strong sense that God will powerfully bring the mission to its conclusion. The salvation promised to Abraham and proclaimed at the beginning of the story of Jesus has now reached from Jerusalem, the heart of Judaism, to Rome, center of the gentile world.

---

*The end of the Hellenistic Age is generally placed at 31 C.E., the year in which Octavian defeated his rival Marc Antony at Actium in Greece. In 27 C.E., Octavian was given the title Caesar Augustus. *(Photo: Koester/Hendrix)*

The church, to be sure, faces opposition. But God, who raised Jesus from the dead, also stands by those who preach forgiveness of sins in his name. Although many Jews have rejected this message, thousands of other Jews have accepted it, as have many Gentiles. And the church, personified in Paul, continues to make that word known, confident of ultimate victory. The mission is well on its way "to the ends of the earth." And the reader experiences a strong appeal to become, or remain, a faithful participant in it—a witness.

4. Questions about the Author: Identity, Purpose, Historical Accuracy

In the Letter to Philemon, Paul mentions someone named Luke as a fellow-worker. This name also appears in two other letters attributed to Paul—2 Timothy (4:9-11) and Colossians. Tradition accepted this Luke as the author of both Luke and Acts, believing him to be a physician (Col. 4:14) and a Gentile who had firsthand knowledge of Paul's journeys. Many modern scholars have defended this ancient view, often citing the "we"-passages in Acts as a sign of eyewitness reporting and sometimes arguing that the author shows unusual knowledge of medical terminology.

Recent scholarship has tended to dispute these claims. Perhaps the most damaging argument is that the Paul we meet in his own letters is very different from the character depicted in Acts, whose speeches show only the slightest trace of Paul's distinctive interests and theological ideas. Also, the description in Galatians 2:1-10 of the conference in Jerusalem regarding the "gentile issue" is so much at odds with the account given in Acts 15 that it is scarcely credible that Paul would have accepted the settlement reported there. And while Paul understood himself as commissioned to preach to the Gentiles as Peter was commissioned to preach to Jews (Gal. 1:16; 2:2, 7-8), the character Paul in Acts spends much of his time offering a "second chance" to Jews. As to the "we"-passages, recent study of the literature of the period suggests that the author is using an accepted literary device to draw the reader into the story.[6] And many scholars are unconvinced by the argument regarding medical knowledge.

If, as critical scholars now tend to conclude, the author of Luke-Acts was not an actual companion of Paul, one may still ask whether this author presents an accurate picture of the early church. This issue is more complex than

---

6. Vernon K. Robbins, "By Land and by Sea: The 'We' Passages and Ancient Sea Voyages," in Charles H. Talbert, ed., *Perspectives on Luke-Acts* (Danville, Va.: Association of Baptist Professors, 1978).

that of authorship, and it overlaps the question of whether the author was attempting to function as a historian. Scholars generally agree that literary sources lie behind Acts, just as (according to the two-document hypothesis) Mark, Q, and perhaps other written sources stand behind Luke. It is equally clear, however, that the author has revised those sources to make theological points. So if we speak of Luke-Acts as a "history," we must do so in a highly qualified way. It is in no sense a neutral history, but is very much a "theological" one. The author wrote not in order to communicate factual data but to present the stories of Jesus and the early church as the avenues through which God has acted and is acting in the world. Although there is much to learn about the early church from Acts, one may not simply assume the historical factuality of any particular account but must view all material critically.

If the author has reworked source materials, it is important to ask what purposes might have been at work in such revisions. Many interpreters have noted the emphasis upon the innocence of both Jesus and Paul regarding the charges against them and have understood Luke-Acts as a piece of political apologetic. According to this interpretation, the author wrote to show Roman officials that the empire had nothing to fear from Christianity. Not only is it difficult to accommodate the clearly theological interests of Acts to this narrowly political reading, however, but some interpreters have questioned whether the author's view of Rome is as conciliatory as this view supposes. Pilate, Felix, and Festus are hardly heroic characters, even if they do pronounce their prisoners innocent.

Other readings of Luke-Acts see the way the author has presented Peter and Paul as reflective of the central purpose. Paul appears in Acts as completely at one with the Jerusalem leadership, and it is Peter who makes the initial breakthrough in converting Gentiles and who, along with James, is most vocal in defending the gentile mission. Judging from Paul's own writing, however, not only did Paul understand himself as commissioned to preach to the Gentiles, but he came into conflict with Peter and the Jerusalem leadership on certain aspects of this matter. Some scholars thus argue that Luke-Acts was an attempt to reconcile the Pauline and Petrine wings of the church or to defend Paul against the attacks of Jewish Christians. A variant of the latter view is that the author was not in fact a Gentile, as has generally been thought, but a Hellenistic Jew who wrote in order to show the validity of the gentile mission precisely from the perspective of the Jewish Scriptures.

Yet another theory is that the author wrote specifically in order to combat some form of Gnosticism that was gaining ground in Christian communities. There is a good bit of material one can use in order to make this case. Luke 24 emphasizes the physical nature of Jesus' resurrected body, and there are fre-

Fig. 49.
St. Luke

quent references to Jesus as a "man" in Acts. One can understand all this as refutation of docetic Christology, typical of Gnosticism, just as one can see the emphasis upon the apostolic witness as a way of setting the "mainline" tradition over against "heretical" teachings.

All these readings of Luke-Acts assume that the author was trying to deal with some specific problem, whether in the church or between the church and the empire. Another way of understanding Luke-Acts is to see it as an evangelistic document, e.g., as written to convert people in the Greco-Roman world to Christianity or as instruction for new converts.

I will not go further in assessing these views, other than to suggest that some of them err in attributing too narrow a purpose to a rich and complex document. Whether Jew or Gentile, the author seems to have been writing in order to declare an understanding of the Christian message to Christians and/or potential Christians and thus to engender and enhance faith. Along the way, of course, this author undoubtedly sought to clear up numerous "misconceptions" held by people and groups within the churches.

There is one more understanding of the purpose of Luke-Acts that has been particularly influential in recent decades. It is best discussed, however, in the following section, which is dedicated to more specifically theological concerns.

5. Theological Questions

a. History and Eschatology

Hans Conzelmann's *The Theology of St. Luke*, originally published in German in 1953, was a major force in developing the methodology of redaction criticism. It also put forth an understanding of the purpose and theological perspective of Luke-Acts that has provided a point of reference for much subsequent scholarship.

According to Conzelmann, Luke-Acts was a response to a crisis of faith within the church. Near the end of the first century, Christians were becoming disillusioned and disheartened because Christ's expected return in glory had not taken place. The author's solution to this problem was to offer a revised eschatology. According to this scheme, the end of history should not be expected in the near future. For the present age was but part of a three-period scheme of salvation history, a history of God's actions in behalf of human salvation.

The first period was the time of the "law and the prophets," which lasted through the ministry of John the Baptist. The second was the "middle of time"—the time of Jesus, in which Satan was absent and salvation was fully present. The third was the time of the church and its mission to the world. This was the period in which the original readers of Luke-Acts lived; the author's message to these people was that rather than expecting deliverance in the near future they should order their daily lives in accordance with Christian teaching. That is why Jesus tells his disciples to take up his cross "daily" (Luke 9:23): the author presents a call to discipleship for the "long haul," a message for a church that must learn to settle down and live in the world.

Despite the enormous influence of Conzelmann's views, there have been numerous challenges to several of his claims. William C. Robinson, for example, has argued that much of what Conzelmann attributes to the author's redactional activity was already present in the author's sources and that at many points the reasons Conzelmann gives for the revision of the sources are disputable.[7] And many recent interpreters have doubted that the writer of

---

7. William C. Robinson, *Der Weg des Herrn: Studien zur Geschichte und Eschatologie im Lukas-Evangelium; Ein Gespräch mit Hans Conzelmann* (Hamburg-Bergstedt: Herbert Reich, 1964).

Luke-Acts really intended the complex historical periodization—which even breaks Jesus' life down into three phases—that Conzelmann imagined. For them, it is more accurate simply to speak of the author's interest in the theme of promise and fulfillment.

Along with doubt about Conzelmann's periodization goes doubt that the delay of Jesus' return constitutes the author's main concern. Scholars disagree as to whether this question was as problematic for first-century Christians as others have thought. In any case, it seems clear that Luke-Acts contains both an element of "realized" eschatology and a strong emphasis upon a final consummation; what is less clear is whether the author specifically envisions that consummation as lying in the *distant* future.

b. Jews and Judaism

Many scholars, including Conzelmann, have found a harsh anti-Judaic strain in Luke-Acts. In seeking to make Jesus and his later followers look innocent before the Romans, it is argued, the author put all the blame for the deaths of these martyrs on the Jews. Along similar lines, a typical understanding of the gentile mission is that it arises specifically out of the Jews' refusal of the message. That is to say, the church preaches to the Gentiles *because* the Jews refuse to hear it.

Luke-Acts certainly attributes guilt to the Jews, but it also stresses that many Jews embraced the Christian proclamation. And although the refusal of the message by some Jews in Acts becomes the occasion for the gentile mission, it is clear from the beginning of Luke that this mission is part of God's plan.

A related question has to do with the relationship between Christianity and Judaism in Luke-Acts. Many scholars see the church as a kind of "new Israel," a replacement for "old" Israel. Jacob Jervell, however, has made a good case for a very different understanding.[8] Given the extreme emphasis upon the loyalty of Jesus and his followers to Jewish institutions and given the early emphasis upon the gentile mission, it makes sense to see the church more as a "purified" Israel, in which Gentiles are included, than a new institution. This view also explains the emphasis in Acts upon the success of the Christians among Jews. From this perspective, those Jews who refuse the Christian message actually cut themselves off from God's people.

---

8. Jacob Jervell, *Luke and the People of God: A New Look at Luke-Acts* (Minneapolis: Augsburg, 1972).

c. Christology

One of the more interesting features of the theology of Luke-Acts is the apparent absence of any notion of the saving significance of Jesus' death. There is, for example, no Lukan parallel to the description of the meaning of Jesus' death in terms of "ransom" in Mark (10:45) and Matthew (20:28). Jesus' death and resurrection are central to Christian preaching in Acts, as is an emphasis upon forgiveness of sins; yet there is no causal connection between the two. The missionaries preach repentance for the forgiveness of sins in Jesus' name, but they never state that it is won by his death. One must therefore ask what precise role Jesus' death and resurrection play in the theology of Luke-Acts.

One key to this problem may be the presentation of Jesus as a prophet. Robert Tannehill has argued that in Luke-Acts Jesus' death appears as necessary because persecution and death belong to the prophetic model on which Jesus' role is fashioned.[9] The author's use of the "suffering servant" motif would fit well with this view. Another key may be found at Acts 17:31: following upon a reference to the final judgment, Paul concludes that "of this [God] has given assurance...by raising [Jesus] from the dead." Jesus had offered God's benefits and had preached the coming of God's Rule, repentance, forgiveness of sins, and his own glorious return at the judgment. To say that the resurrection constitutes God's "assurance" regarding the judgment is therefore to present it as a confirmation of Jesus' words and deeds. Through the resurrection, God confirmed him as Son of God-Messiah and gave assurance that all he said, including his prediction of the judgment and God's final Rule, was indeed the truth.

d. "The Way"

However one understands the relationship between Jesus' death and human salvation, it is clear that the concept of "way" is central to the author's theology. This becomes evident when one notices the role of movement in Luke-Acts. The central section in the Gospel describes Jesus' journey to Jerusalem, while the latter part of Acts traces Paul's journey to Rome, via Jerusalem. In Acts, of course, the narrator speaks of Christianity itself as "the Way." And in a broad sense the whole story of God's dealings with Israel is the recitation of God's movement through history. But the definitive element in all this is Jesus' own "way," symbolized in his journey to his death in Jerusalem. Just as the lives of Peter and Paul parallel the life of Jesus, so

---

9. Tannehill, *Narrative Unity*, 286–89.

Luke-Acts calls the Christian to follow in the footsteps of all these who have followed God's way. This means participating in the mission of proclaiming forgiveness of sins in Jesus' name, and it means "following" Jesus precisely through the daily acceptance of one's own cross.

e. The Rule of God and the Hope of Israel

There are, finally, some remaining questions about the precise nature of God's Rule in Luke-Acts. We noted a strong sociopolitical element in the poems in Luke 1, not only an emphasis upon vindication of the poor but a specific recognition of the hope for the restoration of Israel. The "material" aspect of salvation appears prominently also in Jesus' teachings and deeds and in the life of the church in Acts. One may ask, however, what becomes of Israel's hope of restoration.

One way to answer this question is to interpret the specifically political component as a false understanding. In this view, the disciples' misunderstanding of Jesus flows from their "nationalistic" view of God's promise to Abraham. Luke 24:21 and Acts 1:6-7 thus appear as reflections of this false view, which Jesus corrects: salvation means life in God's *heavenly* Rule.

The problem with this interpretation, as Tannehill shows, is that not only do the poems in Luke 1 clearly endorse the political hope but Peter in Acts 3:21 "still holds out the hope of the 'restoration of all things which God spoke through the mouth of his holy prophets from of old' ... provided the people repent."[10] According to Tannehill's reading, when Jesus mourns that Jerusalem does not know "the things that make for peace" in Luke 19:42, he is mourning the loss of a real possibility. That is to say, Jesus' coming to Jerusalem gives to the Jewish nation the genuine option of accepting him, which would in fact lead to peace and justice in the political sense.

One may of course ask how the notion of a real possibility of Israel's repentance can be combined with the notion that Jesus predicted his death as part of God's plan. We have already seen, however, that this kind of paradox is part and parcel of biblical thought.

One may also ask how this earthly-political hope would fit in with the author's view of salvation as entailing resurrection and eternal life. We should beware, however, of imposing modern distinctions upon the biblical writers' framework. There is no reason the author could not have imagined a hypothetical role for a restored Israel within world history that reaches its end in a general resurrection of the dead followed by an eternity of peace and justice.

---

10. Ibid., 26, 34–35.

Fig. 50. "Christ of the Homeless" (Fritz Eichenberg, © 1982)

To ask whether God's Rule at that point is "in heaven" or "on earth" may not have been within the writer's purview. The truth is that the apocalyptic tradition in general becomes extremely vague precisely at this point. What is clear enough, in any case, is that for the author of Luke-Acts God's Rule was not some *merely* heavenly/spiritual reality that could be divorced from peace, justice, and material well-being in human society.

6. Deconstructing Luke-Acts on Poverty and Riches

William A. Beardslee has applied a deconstructionist approach to the theme of poverty and riches in Luke-Acts. When one reads this work as a whole, Beardslee notes, one finds a rather moderate stance on the question. Although the earliest Christian community is depicted as eliminating poverty altogether through the communal ownership of all goods, it is clear that the narrator does not expect the later churches to imitate this practice in a literal way. The ideal of this earliest community serves rather as an inspiration to a generalized concern for the poor that is to be expressed largely through almsgiving.

When a passage such as Luke 6:20 ("blessed are you who are poor") is read in light of the whole narrative of Luke-Acts, then, its radical implications are moderated. A deconstructionist approach, however, refuses to gloss over the tensions between individual strands of meaning and the overall thrust of the work. Thus Beardslee asks the pointed question: "Can the hearer's identification with the poor, which the beatitude calls for, be so readily expressed in the limited moves for the poor which Acts describes?" The saying, he notes, resists integration into the whole. And it is the negative function of a deconstructionist approach to note resistance and thereby upset the attempt to find in the narrative an integrated, consistent point of view.

The positive function, in the present instance, is to enable the reader to hear the radical challenge of the saying itself. And what happens when we do that, Beardslee explains,

> is exactly the opposite of finding a place for the poor in a structured society. The structure is broken; the line between the hearer and the poor is erased; we find ourselves open to, at times perhaps even identified with, the subjects of the saying. A vivid, shattering awareness of the possibility that there, among the poor, is the place of happiness or blessedness, does not produce a plan of action. . . . It does break the established lines of relatedness, by opening up a new and hitherto unrecognized relatedness to the poor. It challenges the structure of power which established a place for the poor.[11]

7. A Matter of Race in Acts

In a study of Acts 8:26-40, the conversion of the Ethiopian eunuch, Clarice J. Martin shows that Ethiopians were known in the Roman empire as black and goes on to argue that the eunuch's blackness has thematic value in the Acts narrative as illustrative of the universality of the Christian mission.[12] She also gives reason to believe that Ethiopia was viewed as "the end of the earth,"

---

11. William A. Beardslee, "Post-Structuralist Criticism," in *To Each Its Own Meaning: An Introduction to Biblical Criticisms and Their Application*, ed. Steven L. McKenzie and Stephen R. Haynes (Louisville: Westminster/John Knox, 1993), 229-30.

12. Clarice J. Martin, "A Chamberlain's Journey and the Challenge of Interpretation for Liberation," *Semeia* 47 (1989): 105-35.

thus supporting the view that the Ethiopian's conversion anticipates the projected extension of the Christian mission to the world at large (Acts 1:8). A striking aspect of Martin's argument is her documentation of the way in which commentators have routinely dismissed the question of ethnicity: while some have contended that the eunuch's race is indeterminate, others have denied its importance in the narrative. This careful study thus stands as a sterling illustration of the way in which the historical-critical method is limited by the perspectives of those who practice it.

Suppression of the racial motif began long before the historical-critical method was born, however. As Cain Hope Felder shows, this motif is largely overshadowed in Acts itself by a concentration on the Roman centurion Cornelius as representative of the mission to Gentiles—a role the Ethiopian could conceivably have played. The reason, Felder argues, is the author's acceptance of the notion of "a Roman-centered world."[13]

We may thus observe a tension between competing elements in the narrative itself. The author uses a story of a black person to signify inclusiveness but partially disempowers it by giving a related story programmatic status. Attention to the subtle racial motif in Acts therefore gives another important illustration of the need to read the biblical writings both carefully and critically.

STUDY QUESTIONS

1. In what specific ways does Luke 1-2 prepare the reader to understand the role of Jesus? In what ways does this material encourage the reader to connect Jesus to the history of Israel? In what ways does it point beyond historical Israel?

2. How does Jesus define his own mission in the story in 4:16-30? What links can you find between his definition and the themes in Luke 1-2?

3. In what ways does Jesus fulfill the role of "benefactor" in 3:1-9:50?

4. How does the narrator play up the theme of decision regarding Jesus in Luke 9:51-13:30?

5. Pick materials in 13:31-19:27 that seem particularly relevant for life in the postresurrection community. At what specific points does the narrator focus on economic concerns? At what earlier points were such concerns emphasized?

6. In what ways does Jesus, as his death grows imminent, point beyond the disciples' coming betrayal to their positive role in the postresurrection community?

---

13. Cain Hope Felder, *Troubling Biblical Waters: Race, Class, and Family* (Maryknoll, N.Y.: Orbis Books, 1989), 48.

7. How do Jesus' words on the cross pick up on themes already familiar to the reader?

8. How does the ending of Luke parallel its beginning? Describe the role of the disciples as Jesus defines it in Luke 24.

9. What specific links can you find between Acts 1 and Luke 24?

10. What is the significance of the dramatic event described in Acts 2?

11. What does the reader learn from the speeches of Peter and Stephen in the early chapters of Acts?

12. What is the significance of the prolonged account of Peter's encounter with Cornelius?

13. What is the issue at the "conference" described in Acts 15, and how is it resolved?

14. What does the reader learn from Paul's speech in Athens in Acts 17?

15. How do Jews respond to Paul's preaching? How do Gentiles respond? How does the narrator want the reader to evaluate the progress of the mission?

16. Give a brief description of how Paul eventually comes to Rome. What familiar themes does the narrator emphasize in describing the events that lead Paul to that destination?

17. What is the significance of Paul's final speech to the Jewish elders in Rome?

18. Identify the themes that you think are most prominent in Luke-Acts.

19. Do you think the author of Luke-Acts was an actual companion of Paul? State your reasons.

20. Was the author a historian? Explain your answer.

21. Assess the various attempts to describe the author's central purpose in writing.

22. What are the main points in Conzelmann's understanding of Luke-Acts? On what points do many scholars disagree with him?

23. Give your own views regarding the relationship between Christianity and Judaism in Luke-Acts.

24. What seems to be the significance of Jesus' death and resurrection in Luke-Acts? How does the treatment of this theme in Luke-Acts differ from that in Mark?

25. Explain and evaluate Beardslee's deconstructionist reading of the theme of the poor in Luke-Acts. Which strain of teaching do you personally prefer—the moderate stance of the author of Luke-Acts or the more radical undercurrent Beardslee identifies? Why?

FOR FURTHER READING

Cadbury, Henry J. *The Making of Luke-Acts*. New York: Macmillan, 1928. A detailed study of the author's use of source material, with attention to such matters as style, social and religious/theological interests, and general purpose. A classic.

Conzelmann, Hans. *The Theology of St. Luke*. Trans. Geoffrey Buswell. New York: Harper & Row, 1961. A groundbreaking and influential redaction-critical study. Conclusions remain controversial.

Danker, Frederick W. *Luke*. Proclamation Commentaries. 2d ed. Philadelphia: Fortress Press, 1987. A brief, nontechnical commentary, stressing the concept of benefactor.

Darr, John A. *On Character Building: The Reader and the Rhetoric of Characterization in Luke-Acts*. Louisville: Westminster/John Knox, 1992. A readable and helpful study of John the Baptist, Herod, and the Pharisees as characters in Luke-Acts; stresses the reader's role and contains a clear and concise chapter on reader-response criticism.

Edwards, O. C., Jr. *Luke's Story of Jesus*. Philadelphia: Fortress Press, 1981. A brief, nontechnical study, employing a literary approach and stressing the theme of fulfillment of prophecy.

Haenchen, Ernst. *The Acts of the Apostles: A Commentary*. Trans. Bernard Noble and Gerald Shinn. Philadelphia: Westminster, 1971. A massive work, stressing the theme of political apologetic to Rome and the gentile orientation.

Jervell, Jacob. *Luke and the People of God: A New Look at Luke-Acts*. Minneapolis: Augsburg, 1972. Important essays articulating a major alternative to Conzelmann's interpretation.

Juel, Donald. *Luke-Acts: The Promise of History*. Atlanta: John Knox, 1983. A brief and readable study, combining historical and literary interests; views the author as a Jew.

Keck, Leander, and Louis J. Martyn, eds. *Studies in Luke-Acts: Essays Presented in Honor of Paul Schubert*. Nashville: Abingdon, 1966. A collection of important and influential essays, some of them classics.

Kingsbury, Jack Dean. *Conflict in Luke: Jesus, Authorities, Disciples*. Minneapolis: Fortress Press, 1991. A readable treatment, employing narrative criticism.

Krodel, Gerhard. *Acts*. Proclamation Commentaries. Philadelphia: Fortress Press, 1981. A brief and readable commentary, with a final chapter on historical problems.

Marshall, I. Howard. *Luke: Historian and Theologian*. Enlarged edition. Grand Rapids: Zondervan, 1989. A redaction-critical treatment, critical of recent trends in Luke-Acts studies. Combines an interest in the author's theology with a defense of that author's reliability as a historian.

Powell, Mark Allan. *What Are They Saying about Acts?* New York: Paulist, 1990; *What Are They Saying about Luke?* New York: Paulist, 1989. Solid, readable surveys of recent scholarship.

Tannehill, Robert. *The Narrative Unity of Luke-Acts: A Literary Interpretation*. 2 vols. Philadelphia/Minneapolis: Fortress Press, 1986, 1990. A comprehensive treatment from the perspective of narrative criticism, exhibiting a wealth of knowledge. Excellent bibliographies.

Chapter 8

John

———— ✠ ————

1. The Story of Jesus in John

a. 1:1-18

"In the beginning was the Word," the Logos. Thus begins the Gospel of John, inviting the reader into a "world" beyond the world of human events and a "time" before historical time. More poetry than narrative, the opening verses evoke a deeply reflective and meditative mood.

There is an implicit narrative element here, since the initial phrase echoes the beginning of the creation story in Genesis 1 and gently encourages the reader to expect something to happen. The narrator's focus, however, is on the term "Logos," which reminds the reader that in the creation story it is through the divine word that God creates the world. The role of the Logos in creation also evokes overtones of the figure of personified Wisdom, who assumes this role in wisdom literature,[1] as well as fainter echoes of related motifs in Philo. Told alternately that the Logos "was with God" and "was God," and is "light" and "life," the reader will associate this Logos with God in a paradox of identity/not-quite-identity. The contrast of light with darkness also introduces a stark dualism of opposing forces locked in mortal combat.

Verse 6 intrudes abruptly, injecting a narrative element from the world of human events. Someone named John, whom the reader will recognize as John the Baptist, appears. But the interlude is long enough only to establish John as witness to the light, in distinction from the light itself.

---

1. See, e.g., Proverbs 3:19, 8:22-31, and Wisdom of Solomon 9:1-2 (which also uses the term "logos"); personified Wisdom speaks of herself as having gone out from God's mouth in Sirach (Ecclesiasticus) 24:3.

Fig. 51. "Saint John the Baptist Preaching"
(Pieter Brueghel the Elder; Netherlands, 1566)

The poetic treatment of the Logos/light reappears with stronger narrative elements in 1:10-11. The light was in the world but was rejected by his own people. The reader might think already of Jesus, but perhaps of God's word spoken through the prophets, or even of a divine communication to the world at large. Then the declaration in vv. 12-13, that those who believe in the light become children of God, encourages a dualistic distinction between "natural" and "divine" birth and a negative view of the world as it is. The narrator, however, does not utterly negate the world. Pointedly—even abrasively, according to both Jewish and Hellenistic presuppositions—v. 14 asserts that the Logos became *flesh!* God's eternal Word thus enters human history in the most radical way. Here, in the flesh, the narrator declares, "we have seen his glory." And in the narrator's "we" the reader hears the voice of the Christian community, witnessing to its faith.

Reminded once again of the witness of John the Baptist and of his subordinate status (1:15), the reader then comes to the end of the poetic introduction. The Son, now named explicitly as Jesus Christ, is the source of fullness, grace, and truth. Contrasted with Moses, who brought only the law, he is the one "close to the Father's heart, who has made [God] known."

The reader, who has already learned to understand things from the "heavenly" world beyond that of human events, thus reads on with the expectation of encountering Jesus as the one who, as Logos-made-flesh and light of the world, is the true and full revealer of God. And the contrasts the reader knows to make will enhance this focus on Jesus. John the Baptist and Moses are positive figures but are clearly subordinate to Jesus. More sharply, Jesus as the light of the world stands in direct opposition to the forces of darkness.

b. 1:19-51

With v. 19 the reader enters historical time unambiguously, finding John the Baptist under questioning by religious authorities. Four brief scenes reinforce the reader's contrast between Jesus and John, who denies that he is the Messiah or even Elijah or "the prophet"[2] and performs his stated task of witnessing to Jesus. John's grounding of his witness outside his own perceptions teaches the reader to look beyond human testimony to that of God, who has prepared John to recognize the "sign" of the Spirit/dove. The reader must fill in a gap here with prior knowledge of Jesus' baptism, but the significant point is that John identifies Jesus as "Son of God" and "the Lamb of God who takes away the sin of the world" (1:29).

In the third scene (1:35-42), the reader must carry the contrast between John and Jesus one step further. When two of John's own disciples follow Jesus to the place where he is staying, the reader learns both of the demand upon those who identify Jesus as Son of God, lamb of God, etc., and what "following" him in the symbolic sense means. Andrew, one of these two disciples of John, repeats the pattern of witnessing to Jesus: he enlists his own brother, Simon Peter, and this pattern of following/witnessing occurs yet again in the fourth scene as Jesus calls Philip, who in turn brings Nathanael to him.

Nathanael's response also confronts the reader with a new set of judgments to make. His question, "Can anything good come out of Nazareth?" corresponds to the difficulty in believing that the Logos has become flesh and thus places the problem of Jesus' identity squarely before the reader. Then Jesus' response to his eventual confession raises the question of what constitutes an adequate basis for belief. As Jesus promises a vision of heaven, with "the angels of God ascending and descending upon the Son of man," the reader will want to read further in quest of "evidence" of Jesus' identity.

---

2. Presumably the eschatological "prophet like Moses" expected in some Jewish circles on the basis of Deuteronomy 18:15-18; see Raymond E. Brown, *The Gospel according to John (i–xii)* (Garden City, N.Y.: Doubleday, 1966), 49.

c. 2:1—4:54

The narrator immediately addresses the issue of identity by presenting the reader with "signs," notably the changing of water into wine in 2:1-11 and the healing of the official's son in 4:46-54. The status of the signs as "evidence," however, is ambiguous. For although the narrator notes that the sign manifests Jesus' "glory" and evokes faith from the disciples (2:11), the reader also learns that Jesus does not entrust himself to those in Jerusalem who believe in him because of his signs (2:23-25). And then in 4:48 Jesus explicitly criticizes the desire for a sign. The reader will thus reflect upon the relationship between such signs and mature belief.

In a subtler fashion, the narrator also encourages the reader to understand the signs in a particular way. On the literal level, the changing of water into wine seems a rather picayune miracle. But Jesus' words in 2:10-11 suggest a deeper meaning: the "good wine," through which Jesus reveals his "glory," symbolizes the qualitative difference he brings to the world. What human beings have formerly settled for is no longer good enough. Such a reading is underscored in two ways by the ensuing story of Jesus' assault on the temple. First, the narrator's intrusion (2:21), which explains Jesus' comment on destroying the temple as a reference to his body, sanctions symbolic interpretation. Second, Jesus' assault upon the temple is an act of renewal, parallel to the changing of water into wine.

The reader is also learning to identify *mis*-understanding. Not only do the Jews miss the symbolic nature of Jesus' words about the "temple," but Nicodemus, a Jewish official, takes his statement on the new birth, the spiritual birth "from above,"[3]—in a crassly literal way (3:4). In 4:11 the Samaritan woman similarly misunderstands Jesus' reference to "living water," giving him an opportunity to speak about "eternal life," and in 4:33 the disciples miss the spiritual meaning of "food."

The narrator teaches the reader also to look for double meanings in Jesus' words. Jesus' explanation of the new birth to Nicodemus employs an analogy between "wind" and "spirit," both signified by the single Greek word *pneuma*. Likewise the Samaritan woman's misunderstanding results from the fact that the Greek term for "living water" would normally indicate *spring* water.

Jesus' identity is never in doubt from the narrator's perspective. Not only does the prologue identify him as the Logos incarnate, but characters in the story immediately invest him with explicit christological titles, and he openly declares his messianic role in 4:26. This concentration on the identity issue

---

3. NRSV: the literal meaning of the Greek term that is often rendered "again" because of the implication of new birth derived from the context.

Fig. 52.
"Christ and the Woman
Taken in Adultery"
(John 8:3-11)
(Max Beckmann;
German, 1917)

encourages the reader to reflect on the specific nature and meaning of Jesus'
status as Son of God, etc. And this emphasis is reinforced by the way the narrator treats the theme of Jesus' death at this early stage in the Gospel. John the
Baptist's designation of Jesus as "lamb of God" alludes to his coming death/
resurrection, as do the reference to his "hour" in 2:4 and the term "lifted up"
in 3:14. In 2:21-22 the narrator mentions this theme explicitly and even gives
the reader a glimpse of the postresurrection community. The result is that the
reader will experience little tension regarding Jesus' historical fate and will
be free to give full attention to the task of meditating on Jesus' identity and
the content of his words.

In the encounter with Nicodemus, the question of Jesus' identity merges
with that of what he accomplishes: Jesus not only refers to himself as the
Son but also explains that God's gift of the Son brings eternal life. But the
narrator wants more from the reader than understanding of this point. Jesus
goes on to speak in dualistic terms of the consequences of one's response to
the Son: those who choose the Son, or the light, receive eternal life; but those
who refuse him side with darkness and bring judgment upon themselves. The
narrator thus encourages the reader to make a definite decision about Jesus.

The characters in the stories represent varying ways of responding to

Jesus. John the Baptist and the disciples are the initial believers, even if their faith needs development. Nicodemus shows great interest, and the Samaritan woman raises the question of his messiahship and even tells others about his miraculous powers. Yet neither makes an explicit confession of faith. Others believe simply because of the signs, and Jesus remains untrusting of their faith. The Samaritans to whom the woman witnesses, however, go a step further. They believe first because of the woman's testimony but then because of what they hear him say; and then they proclaim him "Savior of the world" (4:42). Implicitly, then, the narrator encourages the reader to look through the signs and come to complete faith in Jesus through hearing his own words.

Jesus' condemnation of those who reject him (3:18) underscores the urgency of decision and locates the judgment upon unbelief in the present, not only of the characters in the story, but of the reader. Similarly in 4:23 Jesus speaks of the eschatological age in which the Jewish-Samaritan distinction is abolished as "now here." The reader will thus understand that if Jesus is the light of the world/Logos incarnate, in him the eschatological realities of judgment/eternal life are already present.

The healing of the official's son (4:46-54) underscores the view that life is present in Jesus. And the faith of the official and his household further encourages the reader's own belief and adds to the impression of Jesus' success in revealing his identity.

d. 5:1—10:42[4]

The picture becomes more complicated in chapter 5. After attributing the persecution of Jesus by "the Jews" to a Sabbath healing, the narrator discloses that they now seek to kill him because he "called God his Father, making himself equal to God" (5:16-18). Thus as Jesus travels back and forth between Galilee and Jerusalem, where he attends Jewish festivals, the reader finds him increasingly facing opposition over the issue of his identity.

Typically, the questions put to Jesus afford him the opportunity to launch lengthy discourses elaborating his identity and exposing the misunderstanding of his questioners. And typically their misunderstandings flow from the attempt to understand heavenly things from an earthly perspective. The interchanges are thus packed with glaring ironies that the reader, trained to understand from the heavenly perspective, will detect. "The Jews" search the Scriptures to find eternal life, but fail to understand that these Scriptures point

---

4. This treatment omits 7:53—8:11, the story of the woman caught in the act of adultery, because it does not appear in some of the best ancient manuscripts and was probably not found in the original text of John.

to Jesus as the bearer of life—and are ironically accused by Moses himself (5:39-47)! They reject Jesus as Messiah because they know his earthly origin, thereby missing his heavenly origin (7:27-29). And when Jesus tells the Pharisees he will return to the one who sent him, the reader decodes a reference to the resurrection; but the Pharisees ask whether he intends to go into the Dispersion to teach the Greeks. The irony is that Jesus' mission will indeed lead into that larger world—through his death and resurrection!

In all this interchange, the reader is refining the ability to read on more than one level and also to reflect in a more complex way on the identity issue. When "the Jews" accuse Jesus of claiming "equality with God," the implied charge is attempted displacement of God, or idolatry. Jesus' reply, however, unmasks a misunderstanding: the Son "does nothing on his own" (5:19). Thus in claiming God as his Father, Jesus does not displace but simply *reveals* God. His work is God's work, which is to give life (5:21); and God's work, conversely, is to bring about belief in Jesus as revealer (6:29).

The reply does not satisfy Jesus' opponents. And the narrator, although carefully answering the objections of "the Jews" in one sense, is in another sense deliberately provocative. When the disciples encounter Jesus walking on the sea, he identifies himself by employing the Greek phrase *egō eimi*—"It is I," or "I am," which the reader will recognize as a formulary statement of God's self-revelation in the Septuagint and of Hellenistic deities as well. The allusion becomes even clearer in 8:58, where Jesus says, "before Abraham was, I am."

This provocation contains a central component in what the narrator wants to teach about Jesus' identity. The "I am" in 8:58 occurs in a conversation with "the Jews who had believed in him" (8:31), and it is against these believers that Jesus makes the blistering charge, "You are from your father the devil" (8:44). The narrator clearly expects the reader to conclude that belief in Jesus is not enough if it does not involve acceptance of his status as incarnation of the preexistent Logos, the one who "was God" and "was with God" from eternity! From one angle and then another, Jesus proclaims his identity as the one from above. "I am [*egō eimi*] the bread of life" (6:35), he says, and "I am the light of the world" (9:5); finally, in a term rich in scriptural associations with God, he says, "I am the good shepherd" (10:11; see, e.g., Ezek. 34:11, 15).

All these terms say in essence the same thing: that Jesus is the true giver of life. The reader learned early on to think of the life he gives as a present reality, and that theme is reiterated in 5:24. The narrator, however, now has Jesus add a futuristic element: there will be a final resurrection and judgment (5:28-29; 6:39-40). And both aspects of true life, the present and the future, come into play as Jesus uses language the reader will associate with the eucharistic meal of the church: "those who eat my flesh and drink my blood have eternal life, and I will raise them up on the last day" (6:54).

This language, together with the contrast between Jesus as the bread of life and Moses' manna, turns out to be offensive even to many of Jesus' disciples (6:61). Thus when some disciples turn away from Jesus in 6:66, the reader will perhaps associate them (and "the Jews who had believed in him" in 8:31) with later Christians who do not share the "high" Christology of the Gospel of John. That would seem to be the implication of 6:70-71: if one of the Twelve could turn out to be a "devil," then others among the believers could also have a false understanding. The reader will thus link a particular interpretation of the Eucharist with a true grasp of Jesus' identity.

The reader will also recognize the postresurrection situation in 9:22. The parents of the blind man "were afraid of the Jews; for the Jews had already agreed that anyone who confessed Jesus to be the Messiah would be put out of the synagogue." The narrator thus tells the reader that Christian exclusion from the synagogue, which is in the reader's time an accomplished fact, was rooted precisely in the failure of the Jews to grasp who Jesus was.

There is another complex point the reader must consider. The false understanding of Jesus is not a matter of simple misperception. Those who fail to grasp who Jesus is do so because they think in earthly terms; and they think in earthly terms because they are "from below" (8:23). But those who accept Jesus are precisely those whom God "draws" (6:44). One might thus conclude that salvation is purely deterministic: some have the power of perception, and some do not. In 9:40-41, however, the narrator has Jesus clear this matter up. When the Pharisees ask if they are blind, Jesus replies, "If you were blind, you would not have sin. But now that you say, 'We see,' your sin remains." So although one's decision about Jesus flows from one's origins, from above or below, Jesus' coming as the light now enables people to *choose their origins.* In the presence of the light, one becomes free to decide whether to see or to step back into the darkness. The reader will thus solve the problem and pronounce guilty those who reject Jesus.

In chapter 10, Jesus' conflict with his opponents comes to a head. In 9:38 the blind man's confession exemplifies the proper response to Jesus: he worships him. Against that background, Jesus launches his discourse on the good shepherd, which leads to an attempt to stone him (10:31) and a renewal of the charge that he claims to be God. Following an argument from Scripture, Jesus points back to his "works" as evidence, evidence that should not be necessary, of who he is; but this leads to an attempted arrest.

Following Jesus' escape, the narrator adds that many came to believe in him. The reader thus finds Jesus in a paradoxical situation: many believe, but "the Jews" are now clearly against him. And the reason is clear: he claims equality with God!

e. 11:1—12:50

The narrator now introduces a family in Bethany, the sisters Mary and Martha and their brother Lazarus, who has fallen ill. The reader will sense the importance of what is to come when Jesus indicates that both God and the Son will be glorified by this illness (11:4), but will be puzzled that Jesus tarries before proceeding to Bethany. The explanation, however, comes quickly: correcting the disciples' misunderstanding of his words about awakening Lazarus from his "sleep," Jesus says that Lazarus is dead (11:14). So the reader will understand that it will be through Lazarus's "awakening" that the glorification will come.

Anticipation blends with foreboding, however; the disciples are reluctant to go to Judea because "the Jews" are seeking Jesus' life. Yet in the end Thomas articulates their decision: "Let us also go, that we may die with him" (11:16). The reader thus thinks of Jesus' coming death and will reflect upon the cost of following him—but may also question the completeness of Thomas's faith: he is willing to die, but is there a note of despair in his statement?

In Jesus' encounter with Martha (11:20-27), the reader gets an explicit lesson in faith development. Following her initial expressions of faith in Jesus' power and confidence in the final resurrection, Jesus insists that *he is* the resurrection and the life. Then, when she makes a strong confession of faith, the reader will understand that Jesus is correcting a purely futuristic eschatology by presenting "resurrection" / "life" as a present possibility.

The characters in the story, however, do not grasp the point so quickly. Mary and "the Jews" who are with her can only weep. The reader, who has learned to identify misunderstandings, will know that it is precisely this weeping, not Lazarus's death, that distresses Jesus. Grief over death is inappropriate, since death means nothing in the presence of the one who *is* resurrection and life! Yet "the Jews" show misunderstanding once again in their interpretation of Jesus' tears. And even Martha cannot apply her new understanding to the immediate situation but can only voice concern about the odor of the body.

Against the background of such limited understanding, the reader hears Jesus' comment and prayer (11:40-42) that combine to emphasize that the miracle takes place through God's power and that Jesus is sent by God. Then Jesus calls Lazarus, who emerges from the tomb, symbolizing to

Fig. 53. "The Resurrection of Lazarus" (John 11:44).
(Engraving by Gustave Doré, 1865)

the reader that Jesus indeed brings life, here and now, to those who have faith.

In a Gospel abounding in irony, the next bit of irony stands out. The raising of Lazarus, Jesus' most dramatic sign of his God-given power, leads directly to the decision of the Jewish leaders to put him to death (11:45-53). These leaders are afraid that Jesus' popularity will lead to a Roman reaction and the destruction of the temple, but the reader knows that disposing of Jesus did not save the temple. The high priest argues that it would be expedient for one person to "die for the people," but the narrator intrudes with the ironical truth: the high priest unwittingly prophesies that Jesus' death "saves" the nation in a paradoxical sense that also involves the gathering in of the non-Jewish world. This point reappears in 12:19 in the Pharisees' declaration, again true in an ironical sense they do not understand, that "the world has gone after him."

As the reader reads on, Jesus' death looms large. So thick is the air with the plot against him that the people in Jerusalem wonder whether he will show up for Passover. Judas, the betrayer, stands out in the story (12:1-8) of Jesus' anointing by Mary, the sister of Martha and Lazarus, which Jesus interprets in relation to his death. In 12:16, however, the narrator takes the reader beyond the resurrection to a time in which the disciples look back and reinterpret everything that has happened in light of Scripture.

Thinking for the moment in postresurrection terms, the reader will penetrate the subtleties of 12:20-26. The "Greeks" who seek Jesus never actually encounter him, but the reader hears Jesus speak first of his glorification and then of losing one's life to find it. Beyond the resurrection, then, the "Greeks," like the reader, will be able to know Jesus precisely by "serving" him!

In 12:27-50 the words of Jesus, the narrator, and a heavenly voice combine to encourage several conclusions regarding Jesus' ministry and coming death. Jesus' death is, paradoxically, a victory through which he will draw all humanity to himself; it is simultaneously the judgment of the world, which defeats Satan. Not only will God's name be glorified through this death, but it has already been glorified, presumably through Jesus' total ministry (12:28). The miraculous signs will naturally come to mind, but Jesus emphasizes the saving power of his *sayings* (12:47-48). The reader will thus understand Jesus' words, deeds, and death as bringing salvation precisely by revealing God and confronting the world with the choice between light and darkness, judgment and eternal life. The decision one makes regarding Jesus is thus not about this person in himself, but about God.

Fig. 54.
The Last Supper (John 13)

f. 13:1—17:26

In 13:1 the narrator reinforces the reader's sense that Jesus' earthly ministry has drawn to a close and summarizes that ministry in a new way: Jesus has *loved* his followers to the end. The reader will not only remember 3:16, which speaks of God's love in sending the Son, but will feel drawn into the ensuing supper scene through the phrase "his own." Precisely as a member or potential member of the community, the reader will experience the "cleansing" power of Jesus' act of radical humility and also hear the commands to wash one another's feet (13:14) and love one another (13:34; 15:10-12) as defining the life of the community in Jesus' absence.

As one living in the time of Jesus' absence, the reader will also identify with the disciples' anxiety at his departure. Thus the questions and answers regarding "where" Jesus goes have great importance. That he goes to God (14:2, 28), that he will come again and take the believers with him (14:3), and that in the meantime he will send the Spirit of truth (14:16-17, 26; 15:26; 16:13) are promises of enormous comfort. The predictions of Judas's betrayal and Peter's denial, together with Jesus' own warnings about the hostile world

(15:18-20; 16:2), point up the difficulties of discipleship. But the reader learns of the ultimate resource: the Spirit will serve as the Advocate (14:26), who will teach whatever is needed in the later situation; and the one who has loved his followers while he was with them now leaves his "peace" with them. It will be consoling to the reader that even as Jesus predicts the disciples' defection he declares his own victory over the world (16:33). Cleansed by Jesus' word (15:3) and understanding themselves as branches of the "vine" (15:1-10) that Jesus is, believers in all times receive empowerment.

The hostility of the world most explicitly defines the need for such empowerment, but in 17:20-24 the narrator subtly suggests the missional nature of the community. As believers in the reader's time have come to faith through the witness of the original disciples (17:20), so the eventual unity of that community will constitute a witness to the entire world (17:24). And the subject of that witness is a point with which the narrator has confronted the reader from the beginning: that Jesus is the one sent from God. This point is hammered home in 14:8-11 in Jesus' exchange with Philip, and at the conclusion of Jesus' prayer it blends with the love theme: just as to know Jesus is to know God, to know that Jesus is sent by God is to know God's love for the Son and to share love within the community (17:25-26).

The movement toward Jesus' death includes the naming of his betrayer, and this latter theme gives the narrator opportunity to introduce the disciple "whom Jesus loved" (13:23) This unnamed figure remains mysterious at this point; but the fact that Peter asks him to interpret Jesus' words leads the reader to suspect that he has great importance.

The theme of Jesus' death is entwined with that of the world's hostility. Disciples can expect rejection by the world precisely because Jesus himself was rejected. The reader will thus understand discipleship as costly. Jesus, however, promises "peace" to the followers who must remain in the world: like him, they "do not belong to the world" (17:16). And the "unworldliness" of the community explains the sense in which Jesus' love commandment is "new," even though it is contained in the Jewish Scriptures. The love envisioned for the Christian community is a possibility that comes not from this world but from beyond. To live in its power is to have "eternal life," which the narrator draws into the present by having Jesus define it as a *quality* of life: "And this is eternal life, that they may know you, the only true God, and Jesus Christ whom you have sent" (17:3). The reader thus reaches the end of the supper scene understanding that the present community, insofar as it is obedient to Jesus' love commandment, is empowered to withstand a hostile world.

g. 18:1—21:25

The reader comes to the arrest, trial, and crucifixion scenes with a clear image of Jesus as totally in command of the unfolding events, fully knowledgeable of the future, and concerned with the future welfare of the community of believers. The image holds: the narrator stresses Jesus' knowledge of "all that was to happen to him" (18:4), and Jesus' only concern is for his followers (18:8). Before Caiaphas he declares that he has always spoken openly (18:20), and he informs Pilate not only of his own divine origin and purpose (18:33) but of the power "from above" upon which Pilate himself depends. The narrator's references to fulfillment of Scripture (18:9; 19:24, 36-37), moreover, increase the reader's impression of divine activity in all these events.

Trained by the narrator to appreciate irony, the reader now encounters it everywhere. While the high priest questions the innocent Jesus, Peter, undergoing a less formal interrogation inside the high priest's court, saves his own neck by denying his leader. Confronted with their true king, the Jews demand his death and the release of a robber. As concerned as they are with their law (19:7, 31), they condemn an innocent person and charge the Son of God with blasphemy. And then there are Pilate's words and deeds. His claim to power (19:10) is itself ironic, in light of Jesus' reply, as is his mocking designation of Jesus as king, through which he hopes to shame the Jews into relenting (19:14-16). Even more glaring are his cynical attitude toward truth, even as he stands in the presence of it (18:38), and his inscription on the cross (19:19-22): Jesus will indeed be recognized as king by speakers of Hebrew, Latin, and Greek, which is to say, throughout the world.

The reader encounters some negative models in these scenes. If the Jews embody a false religious attitude and Pilate illustrates the misuse of secular power, Peter's denial stands for a failure in discipleship. Joseph of Arimathea and Nicodemus, however, appear as ambiguous figures, mixtures of devotion and fear (19:38-42), while the four women who stand near the cross serve as models of faithfulness. The reader will also find a positive model in the other figure at the cross—the "disciple whom [Jesus] loved"—and will ponder the identity of this mysterious person.

Although presenting Jesus as fully in command and knowledgeable of the future, the narrator wants the reader to understand that Jesus really dies. This point is underscored by the notation that it was unnecessary to break his legs and by the reference to an unnamed eyewitness (19:35), which also reminds the reader that the purpose of the narrative is to bring about belief.

The process of coming to mature faith is precisely what the reader witnesses in the stories of the resurrection appearances. Mary Magdalene, first

Fig. 55. *Pietà.* (Bernard Buffet; French, 1946)

to see the empty tomb, thinks the body has been stolen. Later recognizing the risen Jesus, she at first seeks to "hold onto" him (20:17), unable to grasp that in the postresurrection situation one has a different relationship to him. In the end, however, she becomes a witness. The larger group of disciples are hiding in fear when Jesus encounters them; but then Jesus grants them peace and breathes the Holy Spirit upon them (20:22), thus fulfilling his earlier promise. Thomas, for his part, proceeds from doubt to the fullest confession of faith in Jesus in the entire Gospel (20:28), a confession that recognizes his unity with God as stated in the prologue.

These transformations define the faith of the later community for the reader. Jesus' response to Thomas's confession, in fact, shows that the faith of the postresurrection believers is in no way inferior to that of the eyewitnesses. And it is to such faith that the narrator now explicitly invites the reader in 20:30-31.

Despite the climactic sound of 20:30-31, the narrator is not yet finished. The scene at the empty tomb (20:1-10) left the state of Peter's faith unresolved. That story, moreover, forced the reader into a comparison of Peter with the disciple whom Jesus loved. This still mysterious figure not only beats Peter to the tomb but comes to faith immediately upon seeing that the body is gone. In 20:29, then, the reader can look back and understand him as the truest model of faith for the later community: he alone believes without seeing! But even at this point the reader must still wonder who the unnamed disciple is and still have questions about Peter. The narrator addresses these concerns in chapter 21. Finding the disciples once again fishing in Galilee, the reader will surmise that despite the dramatic encounters of chapter 20 they still lack full understanding. Thus Peter's interchange with the risen Jesus serves as another example of the maturation of faith: both Peter and the reader learn that love of Jesus means service to the Christian community itself. The narrator also makes sure the reader understands that Jesus predicts Peter's martyrdom (21:19).

Peter also serves as a foil to inform the reader further about the disciple whom Jesus loved. Peter dives into the sea to meet Jesus, but it is the unnamed disciple who first recognizes him following the miraculous catch of fish. And Peter's question regarding this disciple sets up the solution of a problem in the community. The narrator assumes the reader's knowledge of a tradition that Jesus had said that the disciple whom he loved would not die. The narrator, however, not only has Jesus phrase the matter differently but also intrudes with an explanatory comment: Jesus said only that this disciple would "remain until I come" (21:22). The reader will conclude that Jesus' reference was to his resurrection appearance, not an eschatological return.

But who is this mysterious disciple? He is, the narrator finally discloses, precisely the one who "is testifying to these things" (21:24), i.e., the one who has written the story the reader has just read. The reader must thus recognize a second narrator, who provides a second conclusion to the story. That narrator, looking back over the whole story of Jesus' words and deeds, then adds the final note in the second conclusion: Jesus in fact did so many things the entire world could not contain a record of them!

2. Historical and Theological Questions concerning John

a. Authorship and Sources

Critical problems regarding the Gospel of John appear in abundance and are notoriously complex. Historical questions such as authorship, historical background, and sources are bewilderingly entangled with one another on the one hand and with problems of interpretation on the other. And the perplexing question of John's relationship to the Synoptic Gospels is matched by that of its relationship to the three Johannine letters.

Early church tradition assigned the fourth Gospel to John the son of Zebedee, one of "the Twelve," whom it also identified with the mysterious disciple "whom Jesus loved." We have already noted the difficulties in attributing any of the Gospels to an eyewitness, and even the ancient tradition was not unanimous in this case. An alternative suggestion for the author was a "presbyter John" from Ephesus, although there is no solid evidence that there ever was such a person.

This question is complicated by speculation that we might not have John in its original form. Not only does chapter 21 appear to be a later addition, but there are at least seeming discrepancies in theological outlook within the main body of the work. A radical emphasis upon "realized," or present, eschatology sometimes gives way to statements of the more traditional, futuristic view. And some scholars have found it strange that a Gospel that gives no account of Jesus' words over the bread and wine at his final meal with the disciples should nevertheless contain clear allusions to the Christian sacraments of Eucharist and Baptism. There is, moreover, some reason to believe that the sequence of materials found in the present text is not that of the original. As one of many possible examples, in 14:31 Jesus seems to be concluding his discourse at the final meal with the words, "Rise, let us be on our way," yet he speaks on for three more chapters, and it is only in 18:1 that he and his disciples in fact leave the scene of the supper and go to the garden.

Scholars have accounted for the displacements in several different ways. Some have suggested that the pages somehow got mixed up. Others have argued that the original author left only fragments, never having finished the work, and someone else put the parts together rather incompetently.

One way of accounting for the discrepancies, and to some extent the displacements, is to posit an editor, or perhaps a series of editors, who altered an original text. Some scholars taking this view have maintained that John the son of Zebedee was in fact responsible for the original document, but this view does little to solve the problems entailed in attributing the kind of material John contains to an eyewitness. Bultmann's view, by contrast, is that the original author borrowed heavily from Gnosticism and put forth a view, critical of sacramentalism and futuristic eschatology, that a later editor brought into closer conformity with "mainstream" Christian thought.[5]

---

5. Rudolf Bultmann, *The Gospel of John: A Commentary*, trans. G. R. Beasley-Murray, et al. (Philadelphia: Westminster, 1971), 6–12.

According to Bultmann, the original author drew upon two sources. One was a "signs" source, which presented a series of mighty deeds of Jesus as a way of calling forth faith, and the other was a gnostic "revelation discourse." This author supposedly modified the "signs" source by taking a position critical of faith based upon miracles and departed sharply from the Gnosticism of the revelation discourse by maintaining that "the word became flesh." Then the final editor moved even farther from the gnostic view.

A major problem with Bultmann's view is that it is debatable whether the developed form of Gnosticism he envisions was already in existence in the early stages of Christianity. Not many scholars have been convinced by his evidence for the revelation discourse, but more have been inclined to grant the possibility of the "signs" source.

A seemingly more manageable question is whether the author used one or more of the Synoptic Gospels, but scholars have not reached much of a consensus on this question either. The story told in John is on the whole very different from those told in Matthew, Mark, and Luke; yet at some points it seems to presuppose elements in the others. The question is whether the author drew directly upon the written Gospels or simply upon a fund of oral tradition, and there seems to be no way really to tell.

b. Historical Reliability

To the extent that we imagine an independent strain of tradition, we also open up the question of relative historical reliability. The vast majority of scholars grant far greater historical credibility to the Synoptics on most counts. Few indeed would follow John in placing Jesus' assault on the temple at the beginning of his ministry, since such an act would almost necessarily have led to his arrest. And it is scarcely imaginable that the raising of Lazarus, recounted only in John, would not have found its way into the Synoptic tradition had it been a historical event.

Some scholars have asked, however, whether John might not be based upon more historically accurate tradition in a few instances. A case in point is the date and nature of Jesus' final meal with his disciples. In the Synoptics, it is a Passover meal, but in John it takes place on the day before Passover. The question is whether the author of John altered tradition to make Jesus' death coincide with the slaughter of the Passover lamb in the temple or the Synoptic tradition modified an earlier version to make the final meal into a Passover celebration.

Fig. 56.
St. John the Evangelist
(German, 1485)

c. The "Beloved Disciple" and the Johannine Community

A particularly intriguing question is the identity of the "beloved disciple," the one "whom Jesus loved." If we reject the traditional view of authorship, what are we to make of this figure? Bultmann followed earlier suggestions in understanding him as a purely "ideal" figure, that is to say, as a "type" of the perfect follower of Jesus. This is a real possibility. Raymond E. Brown, however, has made a plausible case that this "beloved disciple" was in fact a historical figure, although not the son of Zebedee and not the author of the Gospel.[6] An eyewitness to Jesus' ministry, he was a key figure in a specific community of Jesus' followers that passed on a variant form of early tradition.

There is widespread scholarly agreement on the existence of such a "Johannine" community, i.e., a form of Christianity whose theology is represented in the Gospel and letters of John. Brown has gone so far as to offer a reconstruction of the history of this group. According to his hypothesis, the man later called the "beloved disciple" was a member of a community of Jews in or

---

6. Raymond E. Brown, *The Community of the Beloved Disciple: The Life, Loves, and Hates of an Individual Church in New Testament Times* (New York: Paulist, 1979). This view is a departure from Brown's earlier work, *The Gospel according to John (i–xii)*, in which he argued that John the son of Zebedee was indeed the beloved disciple.

near Palestine who deviated from the mainstream of Jewish teaching only in accepting Jesus as the Davidic Messiah. They eventually included in their fellowship, however, other Jewish Christians who held anti-temple views and understood Jesus on a Mosaic rather than a Davidic model, believing that Jesus had been with and seen God and had made God's words known. The acceptance of this latter group brought the Johannine Christians into sharp conflict with other Jews who accused them of abandoning monotheism and finally expelled them from the synagogue.

The "beloved disciple," according to Brown, earned his epithet by exercising leadership as the community struggled toward a new self-definition. Alienated from the larger Jewish community, the Johannine Christians forged a tightly cohesive group supported by well-honed beliefs. They branded other Jews as children of the devil and came to believe that the eschatological promises were already fulfilled within their own community.

Assuming that it was at this stage that the author of the Gospel wrote, Brown identifies several groups regarding whom the author expresses varying attitudes. The term "the Jews" designates Jewish people who do not accept Jesus as Messiah; for them the Gospel of John apparently holds out no hope. Use of the broader term "the world" in an equally negative fashion indicates that the community was also experiencing some sense of alienation within the wider Hellenistic environment. And some surprisingly negative statements regarding John the Baptist suggest that a community of his followers might still have existed outside the church at this time. But the author, more inclined to correct their views than to condemn them, seems to leave open the possibility of their conversion.

There are indications also that the author takes a negative, but not absolutely condemnatory, attitude toward Jews who secretly believe in Jesus but will not say so publicly, perhaps because they blame the Johannine Christians and their high Christology for the tragic split that had occurred. More moderate still is the author's position on non-Johannine Christians, whom Brown sees represented in Peter and the other members of the Twelve. While the author clearly asserts the superiority of the "beloved disciple" over Peter—and hence Johannine over "apostolic" (or what eventually became "mainstream") Christianity—the inclusion of the Twelve at the last supper clearly places these disciples and their later followers among Jesus' "own," for whom he prays in his final prayers.

According to this reading, the story of Thomas's postresurrection doubts may point to an inadequacy Johannine Christians found in the teaching of the early "apostolic" church. "We may make an informed guess," Brown writes, "that the precise aspect missing in the faith of the Apostolic Christians is the perception of the pre-existence of Jesus and of his origins from above."[7] In time, of course, the "mainstream" church adopted the Johannine view of Jesus as the incarnation of the preexisting Logos. So, even though the sectarian Johannine community did not prevail over the majority church, its Christology did win out.

Brown consigns the three Johannine letters to a later phase of the community, which we will deal with in chapter 16. He thus sides with those scholars who do not think that the same author wrote both the Gospel and the letters. His view also supports the growing tendency to understand John, once thought of as a radically Hellenistic Gospel, in large part against the background of Jewish thought. And, as will become clearer when we examine the letters, he reverses Bultmann's understanding of the relationship between Johannine thought and Gnosticism. It is not that John represents the Christianization of a preexistent Gnosticism but that the perspective found in John moved progressively *toward* a developing gnostic point of view.

3. The Gospel of John and Bultmann's Existentialist Interpretation

According to Bultmann, a modern person simply cannot, without serious contradiction, believe the New Testament message in a literal way. All talk of the incarnation of a divine preexistent being, the end of the age, or of Christ's atoning sacrifice, resurrection, and eventual return is inherently mythological. For it rests upon presuppositions radically at variance with those that undergird the modern turn of mind. Not only that, but the New Testament's eschatological expectations run headlong into the brute fact that Christ's second coming did not take place as expected.

The discrepancy between ancient and modern presuppositions is not, however, Bultmann's only justification for his attempt to demythologize the New Testament or interpret it in existentialist terms. He claims that "there is nothing specifically Christian in the mythical world picture," that it "is simply the world picture of a time now past that was not yet formed by scientific thinking."[8] As evidence that the real message of the New Testament was not bound to this ancient worldview, Bultmann points to early forms of existentialist interpretation within the New Testament itself. He finds steps in this direction in the letters of Paul, but a more radical move in John.

---

7. Ibid., 79.
8. Rudolf Bultmann, *New Testament and Mythology and Other Basic Writings*, ed. and trans. Schubert M. Ogden (Philadelphia: Fortress Press, 1984), 3.

Most notably, Bultmann argues, the Gospel of John entails a demythologizing of the primitive Christian eschatology:

> For John the coming and departing of Jesus is the eschatological event. "And this is the judgment, that the light has come into the world, and men loved the darkness rather than light, because their deeds were evil" (John 3:19). "Now is the judgment of this world, now shall the ruler of this world be cast out" (12:31). For John the resurrection of Jesus, Pentecost and the [second coming] of Jesus are one and the same event, and those who believe have already eternal life.[9]

In Bultmann's view, then, the Gospel of John makes all talk of Christ's return at the end of history into a symbolic representation of what happens, through faith, in the experience of believers in the here and now. It is clear, for example, that John 14:23 "is not talking about a realistic [second coming] of Jesus":[10] "Those who love me will keep my word, and my Father will love them, and we will come to them and make our home with them."

Eschatology is not the only element of early tradition that Bultmann finds challenged in John. John 16:26-27 explicitly rejects the mythological view of Jesus as a heavenly intercessor between God and humanity: "and I do not say to you that I will ask the Father on your behalf; for the Father himself loves you, because you have loved me."[11] And in making Jesus' crucifixion itself already a "triumph over the world and its ruler,"[12] Bultmann argues, John in effect deprives the resurrection of its significance. While the author may have believed the Easter stories, they do not appear as indispensable—any more than do the miracles of Jesus!

Needless to say, Bultmann's treatment of John opens up a host of questions and necessitates consideration of one's own presuppositions and hermeneutical perspective. It should be noted that Bultmann's characterization of John is based in part upon his view that we do not have this Gospel in its original form. Thus he consigns the clear instances of futuristic eschatology in John to the editor who made the work more acceptable to the larger church community. Wholly apart from this issue, however, it should be clear that there is at least a strain of teaching in John that stands in marked contrast to that found in the Synoptics and in early Christianity generally. Every interpreter must in some way come to terms with this evidence when evaluating Bult-

---

9. Rudolf Bultmann, *Jesus Christ and Mythology* (New York: Charles Scribner's Sons, 1958), 33.

10. Rudolf Bultmann, *Theology of the New Testament*, vol. 2, trans. Kendrick Grobel (New York: Charles Scribner's Sons, 1955), 84.

11. Ibid., 87.

12. Ibid., 56.

mann's claim that the New Testament itself begins the process of existentialist interpretation.

4. The Gospel of John and Jungian Psychology

John is a particularly fertile field for psychological interpretation, and Jung's interpretation of the Christ-symbol owes much to this Gospel. Five basic concepts in Jungian psychology—"collective unconscious," "archetype," "individuation," "ego," and "self"—will be helpful for understanding the psychological significance he saw in this symbol.

In addition to Freud's notion of the unconscious dimension of the individual mind, Jung spoke of a collective unconscious, that is, a fund of psychological patterns shared by the entire human species by virtue of its evolutionary history. Within this collective unconscious are innumerable archetypes, or "tendencies to structure images of our experience in a particular fashion."[13] We cannot know the archetypes directly, but we can identify the specific images through which they express themselves.

Jung's positive view of religion was rooted in his perception that religious symbolism parallels material that comes to expression in dreams, that religious symbols reflect the archetypes of the collective unconscious. Far from the neurotic phenomenon that Freud proclaimed it, religion appeared to Jung as something constitutively human: its symbols tell us something of fundamental importance about who we are in our deepest psychological depths.

"Individuation" is Jung's term for healthy psychological development, or self-realization. This process takes place in two stages. During roughly the first half of life, a person is faced with the task of developing a strong ego, of distinguishing oneself from parents and environment. In the second half of life, however, a person will ideally develop a new center of the psyche, which Jung called the "Self." "In Jung's model, the Self is the regulating center of the entire psyche, while the ego is only the center of personal consciousness."[14] Persons who have developed the Self have transcended a narrow understanding of who they are and experience themselves as connected to the wider community, human history, and the universe itself. Guiding the process of achieving an "ego-Self axis," a grounding of the ego in this broader psychic center, is the archetype of Self. The Self is in fact the very

---

13. James A. Hall, *Jungian Dream Interpretation: A Handbook of Theory and Practice* (Toronto: Inner City Books, 1983), 10.

14. Ibid., 11.

"archetype of archetypes" in the collective unconscious, the most central and comprehensive ordering pattern.

The concept of the Self takes psychology to its very limits. We cannot truly say what the Self is, for we know ourselves as egos, while the Self remains indescribable. Mysterious source of our own self-realization, it is therefore "indistinguishable from a God-image." Thus human self-realization "amounts to God's incarnation."[15] To become a fully functioning person, in other words, is to integrate the God-image into one's own being. The psychological value of the Christian myth of the incarnation therefore lies in its expression of the human potential for self-realization. Jung's indebtedness to John at this point should be obvious.

In Jung's terms, there is a psychological equivalence between incarnation and individuation. For to be incarnate is to take on "fleshy" existence, i.e., the conditions of human life, and individuation is precisely the process that defines our humanity. This realization also puts us in touch with the significance of another aspect of the Christ-symbol: "Because individuation is an heroic and often tragic task, the most difficult of all, it involves suffering, a passion of the ego."[16] The lure of self-realization, in other words, is a frightening lure; it is not easy to abandon our narrow and neatly defined patterns of behavior in quest of that elusive, larger Self. We are afraid of losing ourselves altogether. "Through the Christ-symbol," however, we can "get to know the real meaning" of our suffering: it is the gateway toward the realization of our wholeness.

For Jung, then, Christ constitutes an archetype of the Self, which explains the enormous appeal the Christian message had as it expanded into the ancient world. The psychological significance of the Christ-drama is that it symbolizes the transformation of the individual human life by a "higher destiny."[17]

5. The Johannine Logos and Ecological Theology

The reader who comes to the New Testament looking for direct support for environmentalism is likely to be disappointed. It can hardly be said that the early Christian writings exhibit a developed ecological consciousness. And later Christian theology in the Western world, both Catholic and Protestant,

---

15. C. G. Jung, *Collected Works*, vol. 11, trans. R. F. C. Hull, 2d ed. (Princeton, N.J.: Princeton Univ. Press, 1969), 157.

16. Ibid.

17. Ibid.

has put such great emphasis upon the theme of God's action in human history that it has tended to neglect the question of God's relation to nature.

The Eastern Orthodox churches, however, have nurtured a mystical theology, based largely upon the notion of the Logos in John 1, that refuses to make such a sharp distinction between nature and history. It is not surprising, then, to find a contemporary Orthodox thinker, Paulos Mar Gregorios, making use of the Johannine notion of the Logos as the basis of an ecological theology:

> Neither art nor literature, neither mountain nor river, neither flower nor field came into existence without Christ and the Holy Spirit. They exist now because they are sustained by God. The creative energy of God is the true being of all that is; matter is that spirit or energy in physical form. Therefore, we should regard our human environment as the energy of God in a form that is accessible to our senses.[18]

Gregorios's proposal, made from a very traditional point of view, entails nothing less than the respiritualization of nature. Process theology obtains a similar result from a nonsupernaturalist perspective. Stressing the interrelatedness of all parts of reality and understanding the universe itself as the "body" of God, it too has a strong ecological emphasis that can be related to John 1 and similar passages we will note later (see below, p. 430). So although direct support for environmentalism may be lacking in the New Testament, some interpreters would claim indirect support that might be significant in its own way.

STUDY QUESTIONS

1. What specifically does the narrator tell the reader about Jesus' identity in chapters 1–3?

2. How do Jesus' "signs" contribute to the reader's understanding?

3. List specific ways in which the narrator "educates" the reader in how to read this Gospel.

4. What are the most prominent examples of symbolic language in chapters 5–12?

5. Describe Jesus' interactions with the Jewish people in chapters 5–12. How is Jesus' relationship to God understood in these chapters?

---

18. Paulos Mar Gregorios, "New Testament Foundations for Understanding the Creation," in *Liberating Life: Contemporary Approaches to Ecological Theology*, ed. Charles Birch, William Eakin, and Jay B. McDaniel (Maryknoll, N.Y.: Orbis Books, 1990), 40.

6. What theological points does the raising of Lazarus make, and how does this story contribute to the plot?

7. Give examples of the use of irony in chapters 1–12.

8. What is the significance of Jesus' symbolic action in 13:1-30?

9. What is the primary content of Jesus' farewell discourses and prayer for the church?

10. What can you tell from the Gospel about the identity of the "beloved disciple"? What does his significance seem to be?

11. What is the significance of Mary Magdalene's postresurrection encounter with Jesus? What is the significance of Thomas's encounter with Jesus?

12. What specific themes are developed in the epilogue (chap. 21)?

13. Explain why some scholars doubt that we have John in its original form.

14. Contrast the views of Bultmann and R. E. Brown regarding the identity of the "beloved disciple."

15. Contrast the views of Brown and Bultmann on the background of this Gospel.

16. Explain how Bultmann employs this Gospel in his demythologizing project, and give your own evaluation of his use of specific passages.

17. How specifically does the Gospel of John contribute to Jung's interpretation of the Christ-symbol?

18. Explain how some theologians find John 1 useful in reflecting on ecological themes.

FOR FURTHER READING

Barrett, C. K. *The Gospel according to St. John*. 2d ed., rev. Philadelphia: Westminster, 1978. A detailed, technical treatment, requiring a knowledge of Greek.

Bultmann, Rudolf. *The Gospel of John: A Commentary*. Trans. G. R. Beasley-Murray, et al. Philadelphia: Westminster, 1971. Detailed, making extensive use of the Greek text; otherwise readable and extremely rewarding. A classic.

Dodd, C. H. *The Interpretation of the Fourth Gospel*. Cambridge: Cambridge Univ. Press, 1953. A detailed commentary, making extensive use of Greek and Hebrew. Extensive treatment of the background of the Gospel. An important work; a classic.

Brown, Raymond E. *The Gospel according to John*. 2 vols. Garden City, N.Y.: Doubleday, 1966 and 1970. Exhaustive in scope, with an extensive introduction on critical issues. Already a classic.

————. *The Community of the Beloved Disciple: The Life, Loves, and Hates of an Individual Church in New Testament Times*. New York: Paulist, 1979. A well-argued presentation of the author's reconstruction of the history of the Johannine community. Complex but fascinating reading.

Culpepper, R. Alan. *Anatomy of the Fourth Gospel: A Study in Literary Design.* Philadelphia: Fortress Press, 1983. Detailed. A groundbreaking application of literary methods to John.

Howard, Wilbert Francis. *The Fourth Gospel in Recent Criticism and Interpretation.* 4th ed. Revised by C. K. Barrett. London: Epworth, 1955. A detailed summation of Johannine research in the first half of the century.

Kysar, Robert. *John, the Maverick Gospel.* Atlanta: John Knox, 1976. Brief, readable introduction to the thought and symbolism of John in light of the general human religious quest.

—————. *John's Story of Jesus.* Philadelphia: Fortress Press, 1984. A brief and readable treatment from a literary perspective.

Moloney, Francis J. *Belief in the Word: Reading John 1–4.* Minneapolis: Fortress Press, 1993. A reader-response analysis, with attention to the Johannine community. Detailed, readable, helpful.

Schnackenburg, Rudolf. *The Gospel according to St. John.* 3 vols. Trans. K. Smyth et al. New York: Crossroad, 1982. A major technical work.

Segovia, Fernando F. *The Farewell of the Word: The Johannine Call to Abide.* Minneapolis: Fortress Press, 1991. An extended study of the farewell discourse, employing a combination of approaches with an emphasis on the literary rhetorical method.

Smith, D. Moody. *Johannine Christianity: Essays on its Setting, Sources, and Theology.* Columbia: Univ. of South Carolina Press, 1984. The introduction surveys the main lines of recent research, and the subsequent essays express the author's views on key issues.

Epilogue to Part Two

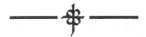

1. Diversity within the Canon: Four Stories of Jesus

No one who studies the Gospels closely can fail to notice that the four stories are in many ways quite different. Most prominent are the variations in content, wording, and sequence of events. John stands out in this regard, with a distinctive set of characters and episodes, but the differences among the Synoptics are by no means minor. And the contrast between Mark's ending and those of the other three is dramatic. While Matthew, Luke, and John stress in varying ways Jesus' presence with the postresurrection community, Mark's final scene leaves the reader in paradox and ambiguity—though not without hope.

Subtler, but no less significant, are the differences in theological perspective. John alone clearly presents Jesus as the incarnation of a preexistent being, while only Matthew and Luke include the virgin birth in their understanding of his divine origin. Luke is distinctive by virtue of its prophet-Christology that seemingly precludes the saving significance of Jesus' death, and John contains an emphasis on realized eschatology unmatched in the Synoptics.

While some interpreters might prefer to speak of variations on a single story, then, there is a sense in which we really have four different stories. Admittedly, all share some overall themes as well as characters and plot elements, and the Synoptics have in common a good bit of sequence and wording. More importantly, all in some way present Jesus as savior, and all in some way see the Christian story as a continuation of the Jewish story. Nevertheless, the differences raise an important question for the interpreter.

As long as we treat the stories separately, there is no real problem. The difficulty arises when we ask about the *New Testament* understanding of

311

Jesus, when we ask whether there is some unity in what the New Testament teaches about the meaning of his life. This question is most serious for the Christian believer, but it has some significance for the secular reader who comes to the New Testament seeking help in defining what Christianity most essentially *is*.

The problem is not confined to the Gospels; the other materials contain their own understandings of Jesus, as well as varying views on quite a few other matters. But attention to the literary character of the Gospels is particularly useful in calling into question the practice of approaching the New Testament as a repository of Christian doctrine, as if one could make a simplistic, one-to-one correlation between New Testament passages and definitive Christian belief. Not only is story something quite different from doctrine, but insofar as our stories do present theological ideas they also conflict with one another. It may be, then, that we will have to understand the relationship between New Testament writings and Christian doctrine as a much more open-ended, dynamic, and imaginative process than many believers have envisioned. That relationship, in other words, may involve a rather complex hermeneutic.

The desire for unity and simplicity is strong, however, and many Christians through the centuries have had difficulty with the diversity of the Gospels. We know from the testimony of early writers that a man named Tatian in the late second century produced a conflation of all four Gospels into a single narrative, entitled *The Diatessaron*. It is in some ways remarkable that the church chose to canonize the diverse documents rather than an attempt at harmonization such as Tatian's.

2. Beyond the Canon: The Limits of Diversity

The toleration of diversity was not limitless. We know of many early Christian writings, which have been termed the "New Testament apocrypha," that the church did not accept as canonical. Quite a few of these are generally designated Gospels, although many of them do not really fit the format of a narrative account of Jesus' life. Some have been completely lost but are mentioned by early Christian writers; most others have been preserved only in fragments and/or brief quotations in other works.

A number of these writings are clearly dependent either upon the canonical Gospels themselves or upon the same strands of tradition found in them. In some cases they take the form of lengthy expansions of specific episodes in the canonical accounts. There are, for example, several infancy narratives that provide extended accounts of Jesus' birth and childhood. And some of the apocryphal Gospels are gnostic in orientation. These often take the form of sayings of the risen Jesus, as does the Coptic Gospel of Thomas, discussed in chapter 3.

Although much theological reflection is evident in some of these materials, particularly those of gnostic character, many are also in large measure the product of the folk imagination. And the very fact of their rejection by the early church has made them a gold mine for additional flights of fancy throughout the centuries. Both these ancient documents and contemporary equivalents have been used to convince gullible readers that a secret tradition, historically accurate and theologically sound, has been maliciously suppressed by a conniving church hierarchy.

It is true enough that the church suppressed some of these materials, but that does not mean one can simply pronounce them to be the authentic Jesus tradition and the canonical tradition false. My point here is not to defend the canonical tradition but to argue that we can answer the question of historical accuracy only through historical research. And no one familiar with the work done in the last century on the development of the Jesus traditions should be susceptible to the extravagant claims of some of the popular writers on the apocryphal materials. Although some of the apocryphal works claim an apostle as author, no serious scholar would take such claims at face value. What one finds meaningful and helpful on a spiritual level is of course another matter altogether.

Although the vast majority of scholars are convinced that these materials have very little to contribute to our knowledge of the historical person Jesus, some do find them useful at a few specific points. Many scholars think that on occasion the Coptic Gospel of Thomas may have preserved a saying of Jesus in an earlier form than did the Synoptic tradition. And John Dominic Crossan has made some limited use of the Gospel of Peter in his treatment of the resurrection tradition.[1] These scholars, however, make their cases on carefully thought out historical criteria, and their claims are debated in an atmosphere of scholarly reflection.

Wholly apart from the problem of the historical Jesus, these writings contribute much to our understanding of the diversity of Christian thought and the life of Christian communities in the early period. The church suppressed them only because they were in fact read and did in fact have influence.

---

1. John Dominic Crossan, *The Historical Jesus: The Life of a Mediterranean Jewish Peasant* (San Francisco: HarperSanFrancisco, 1991), 385–91, and *The Cross That Spoke: The Origins of the Passion Narrative* (San Francisco: Harper & Row, 1988).

3. Some Motifs in the Apocryphal Gospels

a. The Folk Imagination

In some cases the sheer delight of the folk imagination in storytelling is evident in the apocryphal materials, and it sometimes takes rather bizarre and unfortunate (if perhaps entertaining) forms. The classic example is an infancy Gospel written under the name of Thomas (but different from the Coptic Gospel of Thomas). Expanding upon the brief references to Jesus' childhood in Luke, it depicts a divine child with more miraculous power than human concern. Along with stories such as his bringing clay sparrows to life with a clap of his hands and stretching a beam of wood to help Joseph in the carpenter's shop, we also find several, such as the following, that take a less innocent turn:

> After this again he went through the village, and a lad ran and knocked against his shoulder. Jesus was exasperated and said to him: "You shall not go further on your way," and the child immediately fell down and died. But some, who saw what took place, said: "From where does this child spring, since his every word is an accomplished deed?" (4.1)[2]

b. Devotional and Theological Interests

At other points the storytelling reflects more pious and theological interests. In particular, a book written under the name of James, often called the Protevangelium of James, contains a number of motifs that became a part of accepted tradition and have played a major role in Christian devotion and art through the centuries. It is here that we read that Jesus' maternal grandmother was named Anna and that Mary was sixteen years old at the time of her pregnancy.

We also find in this writing several elements apparently intended to deal with problems raised by the canonical Gospels. The notation that Mary was a descendant of David emphasizes the Davidic lineage of Jesus in the face of the objection that Joseph was not his biological father. And the tradition that Joseph was considerably older than Mary and had children by an earlier marriage is a way of reconciling the canonical references to Jesus' siblings with the tradition (not mentioned in the canon) of the perpetual virginity of Mary. This explanation was in fact accepted for some time, but it later gave

---

2. Wilhelm Schneemelcher, ed., *New Testament Apocrypha*, vol. 1: *Gospels and Related Writings*, rev. ed., trans. R. McLachlan Wilson (Cambridge: James Clark; Louisville: Westminster/John Knox, 1991), 444.

way to the view that that those called Jesus' brothers and sisters in the Gospels were really cousins.

This book exalted Mary and by implication held up celibacy as an ideal. In doing so it both reflected and contributed to movements that would become increasingly popular within the church as time moved on. Such was not the case, however, with the emphases found in some other apocryphal Gospels, which are clearly Jewish-Christian in orientation.

c. Jewish-Christian Motifs

Although Jesus and his first followers were Jews, within a generation the church had become largely gentile in orientation, dispensing with much of its distinctively Jewish heritage. But not all Christians of Jewish origin followed the majority in moving in this direction; some groups preserved various aspects of the Jewish heritage, although doing so cut them off from what eventually became the mainstream movement. There is some indication that some Jewish Christian communities continued to require circumcision and that some rejected the virgin birth of Jesus.

We know very few specifics about these forms of Jewish Christianity, which eventually died out. In some ways they may have preserved the views of Jesus' first followers, but there is also some indication that their doctrines underwent change as time went on. There is, for example, evidence of gnostic influence along the way.

One of the Jewish-Christian works, which scholars have called the Ebionite Gospel, seems to have been closely related to the canonical Matthew. But it dispensed with the genealogy and birth stories, perhaps in order to avoid the virgin birth motif. Another such work, known as the Gospel of the Hebrews, embraced a motif that was probably characteristic of Jewish Christianity in general: the exaltation of James, the brother of Jesus, who led the church in Jerusalem for many years. The following account not only makes him the recipient of what is apparently the first appearance of the resurrected Jesus to a follower, but also implies (in the reference his having drunk "the cup of the Lord") that James was present at the last supper:

> And when the Lord had given the linen cloth to the servant of the priest, he went to James and appeared to him. For James had sworn that he would not eat bread from that hour in which he had drunk of the cup of the Lord until he should see him risen from among them that sleep. And ... the Lord said: Bring a table and bread! And ... he took the bread, blessed it and brake it and gave it to James the Just and said to him: My

brother, eat thy bread, for the Son of man is risen from among them that sleep.[3]

The Jewish Christian groups remained outside the majority church by choice. The matter was fundamentally different, however, with the gnostic Christians, whose writings provide particularly vivid and interesting glimpses into the diversity of the early Christian movement.

d. The Gnostic Gospels and Church Authority

Scholars have generally argued that the eventual concentration of power in the office of the bishop was in large measure a response to rampant diversity in doctrine among various Christian groups. Elaine Pagels, however, suggests that the reverse process might have been at work in the case of Christian Gnostics. The leaders of what became the majority church, in other words, might have rejected gnostic writings precisely because they constituted a challenge to the official authority structure.[4]

The issue of authority is particularly clear in a work called the Gospel of Mary, in which a woman, who is presumably Mary Magdalene, is presented as having more accurate teachings than Peter and the other apostles. After Mary reports her conversation with the risen Jesus, Andrew and Peter dispute her testimony:

> But Andrew ... said to the brethren, "Say what you (wish to) say about what she has said. I ... do not believe that the Savior said this. For certainly these teachings are strange ideas." Peter ... spoke concerning these same things. He questioned them about the Savior: "Did he really speak privately with a woman ... ? Are we to turn about and all listen to her? Did he prefer her to us?"[5]

Mary receives the support of Levi, however, whose words serve to legitimate secret gnostic teachings.

> Levi ... said to Peter, "Peter, you have always been hot-tempered. Now I see you contending against the woman like the adversaries. But if the Savior made her worthy, who are you indeed to reject her? Surely the Savior knows her very well. That is why he loved her more than us.

---

3. Schneemelcher, *New Testament Apocrypha*, 2:178.

4. Elaine Pagels, *The Gnostic Gospels* (New York: Random House, 1979), chaps. 1 and 2; see, however, Pheme Perkins, *The Gnostic Dialogue: The Early Church and the Crisis of Gnosticism* (New York: Paulist, 1980), esp. 191–217, for an opposing view.

5. James M. Robinson, gen. ed., *The Nag Hammadi Library in English*, 3d ed. (San Francisco: Harper & Row, 1988), 525–27.

Fig. 57. The Gospel of Thomas, title page

Rather let us be ashamed ... and preach the gospel, not laying down any other rule ... beyond what the Savior said."

Whether official authority in the church developed to combat gnostic teachings or the Gnostics were rejected because they denied official authority, the end result was the same. The increasingly hierarchical majority church rejected the gnostic groups, who indulged in rather free-floating speculation in their teachings. And their teachings did differ significantly from what eventually emerged as the "orthodox" view. The disputed conversation between Mary and Jesus in the Gospel of Mary provides a case in point:

"I saw the Lord in a vision and I said to him, 'Lord, I saw you today in a vision.' He ... said to me, 'Blessed are you, that you did not waver at the sight of me. For where the mind is, there is the treasure.' I said to him, 'Lord, now does he who sees the vision see it <through> the soul <or> through the spirit?' The Savior ... said, 'He does not see through the soul nor through the spirit, but the mind which [is] between the two....'"

This teaching obviously stands in stark opposition to the view, eventually endorsed by the majority church, that Jesus' resurrection involved a physical body. For it interprets Jesus' original appearance to Mary as a matter of "the mind." Pagels raises an important question point, however, when she comments that the New Testament itself is not consistent in stressing the literal, physical nature of the resurrection. And if it is important to understand just how radically some forms of gnostic Christianity differed from the majority church, it is equally important to understand the Gnostics' intentions. Their point regarding the resurrection, Pagels comments, was that it "was not a unique event in the past: instead, it symbolized how Christ's presence could be experienced in the present."[6]

4. The Canon as Theological Problem

Behind the popular fascination with the apocryphal materials there lurks a question of real substance. To the pure historian, all sources are fair game; there is no reason to deny the legitimacy of looking to the apocryphal materials, along with any other documents we can get our hands on, for reconstructing the history of early Christianity. For the theologian and the Christian believer, however, the phenomenon of rejected tradition presents something

---

6. Pagels, *The Gnostic Gospels*, 11.

of a problem. For it invites reflection on the limits of acceptable belief. It raises, in other words, the question—which is essentially hermeneutical in nature—of just how rigidly one should understand the boundary between the canonical and the noncanonical to be.

According to one school of thought, the canon defines absolutely and for all times what is acceptable and unacceptable Christian doctrine. According to another, the boundaries of the canon are only relative; for they were drawn by human beings who were subject to all the limitations of historical existence. From this latter perspective, not all material within the canon is of equal value, and not all outside it is to be rejected absolutely. And as the church finds itself in new and different circumstances, it discovers new needs, new interests, and new perspectives. According to this way of thinking, the church should continually mine the marginalized and rejected traditions for new insights, and it should take the boundaries of the canon as an important indicator of authentic Christian belief but not as an absolute limit.

This debate is a theological and hermeneutical one, and it cannot be settled by historical research. But attention to the apocryphal Gospels makes it necessary to give equal emphasis to three points. First, the noncanonical Gospels are diverse among themselves, with widely varying interests and points of view. Second, they tend to differ markedly from the canonical materials. Third, however, what the authors of some of these materials did was not in principle different from what the authors of the canonical Gospels did. They reflected on the meaning of Jesus' life and/or teachings from some particular perspective, reshaping traditional materials on the basis of their own interests and intentions. However one might evaluate them theologically, then, for the historian they remain a part of the broad stream of Christian tradition.

5. Ethics and Hermeneutics

If Christians have often read the canonical Gospels in order to mine them for their theological content, they have also looked to them for specific ethical norms. In doing so they have encountered the hermeneutical problem in some very concrete ways.

One particularly difficult issue has been that of divorce and remarriage. The problem at one level is that the various Gospel sayings on the issue (Matt. 5:31-32; Matt. 19:7-9; Mark 10:11-12; Luke 16:18) are not entirely consistent with one another. Mark and Luke, for example, seem to prohibit divorce altogether, whereas Matthew seems to allow it in cases involving a wife's unfaithfulness. So it is difficult to speak of the New Testament's position on this matter.

The problem at another level has to do with how the Christian community should apply the New Testament teachings in contexts far removed from the ancient world. From one point of view, the biblical passages are normative in a direct and literal way and no further considerations are relevant. But from a different perspective some other questions need to be asked. Can we determine which if any of the various forms of the teaching actually come from Jesus himself? And can we say anything about the possible motives behind these particular sayings? Some scholars, for example, think that Jesus did in fact issue a strict prohibition against divorce, but did so precisely as a way of protecting women's rights in a society in which those rights were severely limited.

At the second level, the question is how the Bible should function as ethical norm in the Christian community. Are Christians bound to the literal commands of Jesus and/or the Gospels, or should they make an attempt to formulate ethical teachings that are in the "spirit" of the New Testament and/or the early Christian witness, even if they depart from the specific positions taken in those materials? And how much weight, if any, should be given to one's own specific culture and set of circumstances in formulating such teachings? These are not easy questions, and Christian groups have given various answers throughout the centuries.

Another specific ethical question that has given rise to debate throughout Christian history is that of violence. The strong condemnation of violence in the Sermon on the Mount (Matt. 5–7) has led many Christians from earliest times to adopt various forms of pacifism. Many others, however, have endorsed the right to self-defense and the defense of others and have maintained the appropriateness of participation in wars and revolutions fought for just causes. Here again, the question of the nature of biblical authority comes into play. And here again the interpreter of the New Testament faces the hermeneutical issue in a particularly difficult and agonizing way.

As complex as the process of deriving ethical norms from the New Testament might be, however, Christians through the centuries have generally been able to agree upon one central principle as indispensable: the command to love God and one's neighbor. There have been widely varying ways of applying this standard concretely, and historians have no trouble in identifying many points in Christian history when it has been stretched far beyond the breaking point. But all who seriously attempt to engage in ethical reflection based upon the New Testament know that they must in some way give a prominent place to the love command.

STUDY QUESTIONS

1. In what sense do the four Gospels tell different stories? In what sense do they tell the same story?

2. Do you think the church was right or wrong in accepting four Gospels with their diverse perspectives rather than a harmonization such as Tatian's *Diatessaron?* Defend your answer.

3. What would you say to someone who claims that the true Christian tradition is found in "apocryphal" materials rather than the canonical writings? What knowledge have you gained from reading this text that is helpful in answering this question?

4. Give a brief overview of the different kinds of traditions found in the apocryphal Gospels.

5. In what sense is the canon a theological *problem* for Christians? Give your own views on how a canon should function for a religious community.

6. Imagine that you, as a New Testament scholar (of international reputation!), have been appointed to a council commissioned to produce a position paper on the relevance of the New Testament for either of these problems: (*a*) divorce and remarriage; (*b*) the use of violence for just causes. Of which portions of the Gospels would you make use, and what kind of hermeneutic would you employ in applying those portions to the question?

FOR FURTHER READING

Pagels, Elaine. *The Gnostic Gospels.* New York: Random House, 1979. A fascinating and highly readable account by a competent scholar; raises important questions.

Perkins, Pheme. *The Gnostic Dialogue: The Early Church and the Crisis of Gnosticism.* New York: Paulist, 1980. An important study of the gnostic revelation dialogues, with reflection on contemporary issues such as Jung's use of gnostic thought. Critical of Pagels on some points.

———. *Gnosticism and the New Testament.* Minneapolis: Fortress Press, 1993. An accessible account of the origins of Gnosticism and its interaction with early Christianity.

Robinson, James M., gen. ed. *The Nag Hammadi Library in English.* 3d ed. San Francisco: Harper & Row, 1988. Translations of gnostic writings that are important for understanding the environment of New Testament Christianity.

Schneemelcher, Wilhelm, ed. *New Testament Apocrypha.* Vol. 1: *Gospels and Related Writings.* Rev. ed. Trans. R. McLachlan Wilson. Cambridge: James Clark; Louisville: Westminster/John Knox, 1991. Translations of noncanonical writings important for understanding the environment of New Testament Christianity.

Part Three

The Pauline Corpus

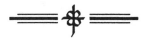

Prologue to Part Three

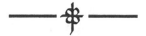

The figure of Paul looms large in the New Testament. Thirteen of its writings are letters in which the author is self-identified as Paul. Another work, the book of Hebrews, made its way into the canon because some early Christians attributed it to Paul. And the lengthy book of Acts is devoted largely to an account of his work as missionary and apostle.

As one New Testament writer (2 Pet. 3:15-16) acknowledges, Paul's letters are not always easy to understand. It is thus imperative, in approaching these works, to know something about who Paul was and about the background against which he wrote.

1. The Letters, the Book of Acts, and the "Historical" Paul

Since Acts is our only source for Paul's life outside his own writings, it might seem that a knowledge of this work would be the best introduction to his letters. Such knowledge, however, might actually be a hindrance. For a comparison of Acts with the letters on some important points reveals that the author of Acts has pressed Paul's life into a mold designed to make specific theological points. Whereas he appears in Acts as in full accord with Peter and the leaders of the Jerusalem church, in Galatians Paul reveals a deep-seated conflict between himself and these other leaders. Not only does he differ from them on an important matter of policy, but he clearly understands his own commission as apostle as completely independent of the authority of Peter or Jerusalem. It is not too much to say that Acts has come near to reversing the roles of Peter and Paul as Paul himself understood them. For Galatians 2:7 discloses that Peter brought the gospel to Jews and Paul brought it to Gentiles, whereas in Acts it is Peter who initiates the gentile mission while Paul spends some of his time preaching to Jews.

Scholars generally agree that when Paul's letters conflict with Acts, the letters are to be preferred. There is less consensus on the extent to which we can rely upon Acts in relation to matters that Paul does not mention at all. I will begin by noting some details we can learn from the letters alone.

As to his background, Paul says he was born into a family of practicing Jews and was himself a Pharisee totally committed to the Jewish law (Phil. 3:5-6; 2 Cor. 11:22; Rom. 11:1). His extensive use of the Jewish Scriptures, moreover, attests his thorough familiarity with them. That he seems to use the Septuagint and demonstrates familiarity with Greek literary conventions shows that he was, more specifically, a Hellenized Jew.

Paul also mentions that at one point in his life he persecuted the church, seeking to destroy it (Gal. 1:13-14). Although he does not disclose his motivation, we may speculate that he "saw the developing freedom with regard to the law, especially among Hellenistic Jewish Christians, as a threat to Judaism and as an affront to God."[1]

In response to a dramatic experience, Paul became a follower of Jesus. He never describes the details of this experience, but he does interpret it as an appearance of Jesus to him (1 Cor. 15:8; 9:1). He also interprets it as a specific commission to become an apostle to the Gentiles (Gal. 1:15; 2:7-9).

Paul provides some specific chronological information in Galatians 1–2. Following his "call," he went to "Arabia" (by which he meant the region just south of Damascus, Syria) and then, three years later, visited Peter in Jerusalem. After that he spent more than a decade preaching in Syria and in Cilicia of Asia Minor before journeying again to Jerusalem for a meeting with the other leaders to hammer out some questions raised by his inclusion of Gentiles into the Christian fellowship. Paul reports an agreement at this meeting, but it apparently did not settle all questions. For he later had a serious confrontation with Peter and others (Gal. 2:11-14) over whether Jewish Christians should eat with gentile Christians who had not undergone circumcision and did not observe the law.

We also know from Paul's correspondence that he carried his missionary activity beyond Asia Minor to Macedonia and Greece. And we know that he founded churches in the gentile world and played an ongoing role in their supervision. It is also clear that he generally supported himself through the practice of a trade, which he never names explicitly.

Paul claimed apostolic status on the basis of his revelatory experience and

---

1. Leander E. Keck, *Paul and His Letters,* 2d ed. (Philadelphia: Fortress Press, 1989), 27.

Fig. 58. "Paul's Dispute at Damascus" (Palermo mosaic)

exercised authority over the churches he founded, although this authority was sometimes disputed (Gal. 2:11-14). When he could not actually visit a congregation, he communicated by way of letters. In some cases it is clear that the letters are responses to crisis situations. As we will see, he exercised his authority through them. He was not, by the way, the only person outside the Twelve who functioned as apostle, for he applies this term to several others who also had not been in this inner circle.[2]

As a sign of his solidarity with the Jerusalem leadership, Paul agreed to take up a collection among his gentile churches for "the poor" in the Jerusalem church (Gal. 2:10). Successful in this endeavor, he wrote the church at Rome about his intention to deliver the collection to Jerusalem and then to visit Rome on his way to Spain to continue his missionary work (Rom. 15:22-29).

The letters give us no information beyond this point. Early church tradition has it, however, that Paul made his way to Rome, but not to Spain: imprisoned

---

2. James the brother of Jesus (Gal. 1:19; 1 Cor. 15:7), Barnabas (1 Cor. 9:6), and Andronicus and Junia (Rom. 16:7).

during a time of persecution, he was put to death by the Roman government. It is a tradition that most scholars have accepted.

We can be virtually certain of these details about Paul's life; the question is whether we should accept some other details recounted only in Acts. Was he really born in the city of Tarsus in Asia Minor, and was he really a Roman citizen? Did he actually study with the Jewish teacher Gamaliel in Jerusalem, and was his trade in fact tentmaking? A good rule of thumb is that points that most obviously serve the theological interests of Acts must remain the most suspect. Thus, for example, the connection between Paul and Gamaliel is uncertain because it fits well with the tendency in Acts to show the early Christians as pious Jews. The tradition regarding Tarsus is far less suspect, on the other hand, since it is more difficult to imagine a motivation for connecting Paul to that particular city.

Most scholars grant some credibility to the Acts accounts of Paul's missionary travels, but there is little consensus on how much weight to give them. The reconstruction of Pauline chronology remains a complex matter.[3]

2. Studying Paul's Letters

If interpreters through the centuries have tended to treat the New Testament writings as repositories of doctrine, they have done so particularly in the case of Paul's letters. But just as contemporary scholarship has rediscovered the Gospels as stories, it has also rediscovered Paul's writings precisely as letters. It has thus become commonplace to say that they should be studied not as theological treatises but as communications between two parties on specific occasions for specific reasons. Paul wrote not in order to work out the details of Christian teaching in an abstract way but to deal with concrete questions and problems. For that reason, it is important to try to reconstruct the specific situations that occasioned the letters. And in some cases the tools of sociological research can provide important insights into "what was going on" in such situations.

This does not mean that the letters were merely private communications. Paul wrote specifically in his capacity as apostle, and he constantly addressed his readers in the second-person plural. It is clear also that he expected the letters to be read to the entire congregations (1 Thess. 5:27; Phlm. v. 2). We must therefore imagine that he composed them very carefully, taking pains to think his points through. While not formal doctrinal statements, they are the

---

3. See Appendix 2.

products of considerable reflection on complex issues. It is legitimate to read them with a view to understanding Paul's theological thinking, as long as one keeps in mind the specific situations he is addressing.

It is nevertheless important to remember that they are letters and to note that letter writing in the Greco-Roman world was bounded by stereotyped conventions regarding both formal structure and phraseology. A comparison of Paul's letters to others written in that environment shows that he followed the conventional format but modified it to suit his purposes.

William G. Doty gives the following outline of the typical Greek letter:

Introduction (prescript or salutation)
> including: sender, addressee, greetings, and often additional greetings or wish for good health

Text or Body, introduced with characteristic introductory formulae

Conclusion
> including: greetings, wishes, especially for persons other than the addressee; final greeting or prayer sentence; and sometimes dating.[4]

Paul modifies the Hellenistic introduction with his phrase, "Grace to you and peace," which reflects his Jewish background, and he makes the conclusion into a benediction. He also generally replaces a typical sentence of thanks to the gods for the writer's rescue from danger with a sometimes elaborate thanksgiving for the faith of the congregation to which he writes.[5] And, following the main body of the letter, he typically adds specific exhortations regarding behavior, the scholarly term for which is "parenesis" (or paraenesis).

The result is a format that generally characterizes Paul's letters:

Opening (sender, addressee, greeting)

Thanksgiving or Blessing (often with intercession and/or eschatological climax)

Body (introductory formulae; and often having an eschatological conclusion and/or an indication of future plans)

Paraenesis

---

4. William G. Doty, *Letters in Primitive Christianity,* Guides to Biblical Scholarship (Philadelphia: Fortress Press, 1973), 14.

5. Ibid., 22, citing John L. White, "The Structural Analysis of Philemon: A Point of Departure in the Formal Analysis of the Pauline Letter" (photocopy for the Society of Biblical Literature on the Form and Function of the Pauline Letters, 1971).

Closing (formulaic benedictions and greetings; sometimes mention of the writing process).[6]

Paul also made use of specific modes of argumentation drawn from both Greek and Jewish learning. Rhetoric, the art of persuasion through speaking and/or writing, was a major component of Greek and Hellenistic education and the subject of much reflection and analysis. And Jewish teachers, who in this period sometimes studied Greek rhetoric, had their own distinctive modes of argumentation. Rhetorical criticism is increasingly making its way into New Testament studies and has been of particular interest to Pauline scholars. It will be helpful, at several points in our discussion, to pay attention to the rhetorical features of Paul's letters.

3. Critical Questions about the Letters

Thirteen letters bear Paul's name, but many scholars are convinced that some of these were written by other Christians in his name. Whereas the modern person is apt to think of writing in someone else's name as dishonest, it was not considered so in the ancient world. Those who wrote in Paul's name did so to lend authority to their attempt to say what they genuinely believed Paul would have said in a particular situation.

In chapters 9–11 I will treat the seven letters that are almost universally accepted as authentically Pauline: Romans, 1 Corinthians, 2 Corinthians, Galatians, Philippians, 1 Thessalonians, and Philemon. The remaining six will come under discussion in chapter 13.

The question of authenticity is not the only critical question the student of Paul faces. Some of the letters read very unevenly, raising suspicions that we do not have them in their original forms. There is general agreement that 2 Corinthians is a composite of more than one letter, and many scholars have made a similar judgment regarding Philippians. At some points, however, the presence of material that seems out of place is best attributed to an editor's interpolation. And in still other cases scholars suspect that readers made comments in the margins of manuscripts and later scribes copied them into the text. It will be important to take note of such possibilities as we seek to read and interpret the letters of Paul.

---

6. Doty, *Letters in Primitive Christianity*, 27.

4. Paul in Context

Generally dated in the 50s C.E., Paul's letters are the earliest of all New Testament writings. Although we will approach these letters primarily in order to understand Paul and only secondarily as sources for the history of the early church, they do provide us with some important insights into early Christianity. In chapter 3 we drew upon Paul in reconstructing the resurrection tradition. At this point we may note that Paul is also an important source for the early tradition regarding Jesus' words at the last supper (1 Cor. 11:23-26). There are also numerous points at which scholars identify traditional materials of other types—such as, for example, the Christ-hymn of Philippians 2:6-11—which Paul has quoted.

The recognition of these traditional materials is important not only for its value in reconstructing the history of the early tradition; it also gives us insight into Paul's relationship to the wider Christian community. Despite his insistence upon his independence from the authority of the Jerusalem leadership, he worked, spoke, and wrote from within an ongoing tradition.

It is important to note also that this tradition had made inroads into both the Jewish Diaspora and the gentile world itself prior to Paul's own missionary activity. The story of Stephen and the "Hellenists" in Acts 6 reflects the presence of Hellenized Jews within the early Christian community in Jerusalem, and later passages in Acts (8:1; 11:19-26) report that the departure of Christians from Jerusalem following Stephen's martyrdom led to a mission to Diaspora Jews and to Gentiles. The historical likelihood is that it was only *Hellenized* Jewish Christians who were forced to flee Jerusalem and that it was they who extended the Christian mission into the synagogues of the Diaspora.[7] They apparently had some success in this endeavor, and not only among Jews. It was commonplace that Gentiles who were attracted to Jewish monotheism and ethics, but perhaps unwilling to undergo circumcision or observe dietary regulations, attached themselves to synagogues without formally converting. From their point of view, Christianity would have appeared as a "universalized" form of Judaism, which in a real sense it was. It was undoubtedly among such people that Christianity first moved outside the Jewish community.

It should thus be clear that the picture of Paul as the "second founder" of Christianity, who single-handedly transformed the simple message of Jesus into a complex Hellenistic cult, is an extremely distorted view. The gentile mission was in progress before Paul became a part of it. It is nevertheless

---

7. See Marcel Simon, *St. Stephen and the Hellenists in the Primitive Church* (London and New York: Longmans, Green, 1958).

apparent that Paul was a major figure in that mission; and, in any case, the letters he wrote were eventually deemed so important that they were recognized as Scripture.

5. A Note on Method

The primary method with which I will approach the Pauline letters will be reader-response criticism. Because this method is normally used in relation to narratives rather than letters, however, it will be necessary to make certain modifications in the version employed in studying the Gospels in Part Two.

The Prologue to Part Two calls attention to two technical terms used by reader-response critics in the treatment of narratives: "the *narrator*" and "the *reader.*" "The narrator" is not the actual author of the work but the "voice" that tells the story. Although sometimes a character in the story, the narrator is more often anonymous. "The reader," similarly, is not some actual person but a mental construct of the critic, devised as an aid to understanding the story. "The reader" posited by the critic is a hypothetical person who follows the narrator's clues and responds through various mental actions such as anticipating future events, filling in gaps in the story, and forming opinions about the characters.

The concept of narrator serves us well in reading a story; but a letter is not a story. Since Paul identifies himself as the writer of the letters we will be studying, I will refer not to a narrator, but simply to Paul himself, when dealing with the letters of undisputed authenticity.[8]

I will preserve the term "the reader," but the student should be aware of a subtle shift in meaning. Historical knowledge plays some role in the construction of the readers in the analyses of the Gospels in Part Two. It is necessary, for example, to posit readers who are familiar with the Septuagint. Nevertheless, the emphasis there is not upon what we can learn about the *original* readers of these works but upon how the writings themselves implicitly define their own readers. When we approach the authentic letters of Paul, however, the situation is a little different. Each letter is addressed to a *specific*

---

8. The difference between letters and stories in not absolute in this regard, however. In writing a letter, an author assumes a particular stance (or "persona") that might differ in some respects from her or his everyday way of thinking and speaking. So we cannot make a simple equation between the total person Paul and the Paul who writes Romans. Paul-writing-Romans is thus somewhat akin to the narrator of a story, but is closer to what literary critics call the "implied author," that is, the "image" or "projection" of the author that is expressed in a text. By the same token, the author of a letter also construes the recipients in a particular way. Thus the Galatians as addressed by Paul might be rather different from the Galatians as observed by someone else or, indeed, as addressed by Paul on another occasion.

audience, such as the Christian churches Galatia, a man named Philemon, or the Christian community in the Corinth. Although we will look primarily to the letters themselves for help in constructing "the readers," then, the readers we construct will represent actual, historical situations. And at some points it will be important to supplement this construction with information drawn from other sources.

The disputed letters present a special case, since Paul may not be the actual author and we cannot be certain of the original audience. I will discuss the modifications necessary in their case at the beginning of chapter 13.

Having stressed the differences between letters and stories, it is necessary now to point out that a letter nevertheless presupposes a story of sorts, the story of how the person who wrote the letter came to do so. People write letters for specific reasons, which sometimes involve earlier interactions with their intended audiences. Prior to a reader-response analysis of each of Paul's letters, then, I will seek to reconstruct the story behind it. It is particularly important to do this, since reading a letter is, as Leander Keck has remarked, "somewhat like overhearing a telephone conversation: one must always infer what is being said on the other end of the line, as well as the context of the conversation."[9] We need all the help we can get in making both types of inference.

STUDY QUESTIONS

1. Assess the historical value of the various sources for the life and work of Paul.

2. What are the most important things we can know about Paul's life from his letters alone?

3. Discuss whether it is legitimate to study Paul's letters as theological treatises.

4. Why is it not appropriate to speak of Paul as the "second founder" of Christianity?

FOR FURTHER READING

Doty, William G. *Letters in Primitive Christianity.* Guides to Biblical Scholarship. Philadelphia: Fortress Press, 1973. A brief and helpful introduction.
Stowers, Stanley K. *Letter Writing in Greco-Roman Antiquity.* Philadelphia: Westminster, 1986. A study of the phenomenon in terms of its relevance for understanding early Christian letters; includes translations of various types of letters.

---

9. Keck, *Paul and His Letters,* 1.

Chapter 9

Philemon, 1 Thessalonians, Philippians, and Galatians

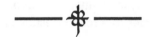

1. Philemon

a. The Story behind the Letter

Alone among the undisputed letters of Paul, the Letter to Philemon is addressed to an individual. Philemon is a Christian, apparently converted by Paul's preaching. He is also in some sense the leader of a local Christian congregation, since it meets in his house. In writing the letter, Paul presupposes some earlier events linking himself and Philemon.

It seems that Philemon has a slave named Onesimus, who escapes—possibly having helped himself to some of his master's possessions as he departed, or perhaps simply in debt to him. Somewhere (the letter does not tell us where), Onesimus encounters Paul during a period of the latter's imprisonment. And, like Philemon, he becomes a Christian through Paul's influence. Paul, for his part, becomes deeply attached to Onesimus, who is of great assistance to him during the imprisonment. Now, however, Paul sends Onesimus back to Philemon with a letter, addressed primarily to Philemon but also to the church that meets in his house and other specific members.

b. Reading the Letter to Philemon

The opening salutation (vv. 1-3) does more than identify the writer and the recipient. It places the entire communication in the context of Christian faith, and it reinforces this point with the secondary address: although in one sense for Philemon, the letter is in another sense for the whole house church. That Paul writes also on behalf of Timothy, an associate in his Christian work, is another sign of the "semiofficial" nature of the communication. The salutation also underscores Paul's imprisonment, which he interprets as "for Jesus Christ."[1] Philemon must therefore read the letter as a fellow Christian, as fellow-worker of someone imprisoned because of his faith, and as a member of a Christian community. Paul's prayer of thanksgiving for Philemon's faith, love, and work in the church (vv. 4-7) underscores the point in another way. Having read this much, Philemon must now read on in light of his own past deeds; he must read on as someone who has up to this point proved a faithful Christian servant.

Addressed initially as a "co-worker," Philemon is confronted in v. 8 with Paul's apostolic authority: Paul asserts that he could simply command what he is about to ask. The emphasis upon authority, however, gives way to a different approach. Without yet stating what he is getting at, Paul indicates that he prefers, out of love, to issue an appeal rather than an order, for Philemon to do his "duty" in relation to Onesimus. His appeal nevertheless uses some strong persuasion. While not confrontational in tone, it buries Philemon in the ethos of the Christian fellowship: Paul is "father," Onesimus his "child"—indeed, Paul says, his "very heart." Making a pun on the runaway's name, which means "useful," Paul says that Onesimus will now be useful both to Philemon and to himself, and then proceeds to note how much he would in fact like to have Onesimus stay with him during his imprisonment!

Only in vv. 15 16 does Paul finally state what he wants: that Philemon should receive Onesimus back, "no longer as a slave but more than a slave, a beloved brother." And only at that point does he refer to the sensitive matter of Onesimus's debt (theft?), which he quickly defuses with an offer to make restitution himself.

Having thus made his appeal to Philemon's love and free will, Paul picks up the pen at v. 19 (apparently having dictated to someone else up to this point) and finishes the letter in his own hand. But now his tactics shift again. Philemon is reminded of his own debt to Paul, presumably his conversion, and then reads in v. 20 what comes very close to a command. Paul then asserts his confidence that Philemon will render *obedience* and "will do even more than" he asks. To top all this off, Paul mentions his coming visit before adding the final greetings.

---

1. RSV. The NRSV obscures the point with the translation "*of* Jesus Christ."

Where does the letter leave Philemon? At the very least, he will perceive it as his Christian duty to receive Onesimus back without reproach and treat him as a brother in Christ. He will also know that, should he not do so, other church members who read the letter will be available to call him to account and that Paul himself hopes to visit after his release from prison. The implication is that to fail to do what Paul asks is to deny the very ties that Christians know in Christ.

This is the very least that Philemon can hear in the letter; but he can hardly miss some additional undertones. What is the "even more" that Paul suggests? Should Philemon send Onesimus back to continue to aid Paul? More fundamentally, what are the implications of receiving Onesimus back as a brother? Does a person hold a brother or a sister as slave? Does not the master-slave relationship clearly violate the meaning of Christian fellowship?

c. A Socioliterary Analysis

Employing a complex methodology combining literary and sociological approaches, Norman Petersen has gained some interesting insights about the Letter to Philemon.[2] What interests Petersen is not Paul's theology, but the sociology implicit in what he calls Paul's "narrative world."

To understand the term "narrative world," it should be helpful to reflect on the fact that the "story behind the letter" recounted above was reconstructed from the letter itself; we have no independent knowledge of the events. While one can legitimately approach this reconstruction as "what actually happened" (and there is little reason to doubt that it is in fact a reasonably accurate reconstruction), it is just possible that Paul completely distorts the actual events. Whether he does or does not, however, makes no difference in terms of Petersen's interest. The point is that Paul does imply a story, a story that contains characters who relate in particular ways within a particular story-world. And because the story implies a world, it also embodies a "sociology," i.e., a system of social relations among the characters.

The interesting point that Petersen discovers is that in Paul's story the Christian fellowship constitutes a kind of anti-structure over against the sociological structure of the world at large. In the "outside" world, masters own slaves and relate to them in terms of a superior/inferior hierarchy. In the church, however, there can be no master-slave relationship. In Christ, all have

---

2. Norman R. Petersen, *Rediscovering Paul: Philemon and the Sociology of Paul's Narrative World* (Philadelphia: Fortress Press, 1985).

equal status as siblings in one family; Onesimus and Philemon are therefore brothers!

The matter is complicated by the fact that Paul can assert his hierarchically based authority precisely in order to enforce the anti-hierarchical nature of the church. But this contradiction is partially mitigated by the fact that Paul refers to Philemon as "co-worker" and "brother" (v. 7). In the world outside, by contrast, there is nothing to mitigate the vast chasm between master and slave, debtor and debtee, and the like. Although not utterly devoid of hierarchical relations, the church nevertheless stands for anti-structures that "*invade* the world's social structures in the story of Philemon."[3]

In Petersen's scheme, the relationships among human beings constitute only one level of Paul's narrative world. Those relationships are undergirded by a "symbolic universe,"—a set of symbols expressing one's most basic assumptions about reality, in which God and Christ appear as characters. According to this analysis, Philemon's decision regarding Onesimus really constitutes a choice between symbolic universes. To refuse to accept the slave as brother would be to opt for the understanding of reality embraced by the world at large. Simply said, it would be a denial of Christ.

The Onesimus incident has thus precipitated a crisis in Philemon's life. Before Onesimus ran away, Philemon apparently lived rather comfortably in two worlds: the world at large, in which he was master over a slave, and the world of brothers and sisters in the church. "Now," however,

> he finds that "being in Christ" makes a totalistic claim upon him from which there are no exceptions. *If he is to remain in the service of Christ the Lord, he cannot be "in Christ" only when he is "in church."*[4]

d. Concluding Comments

While Petersen confines himself largely to Paul's "narrative world," it is relevant to ask now about the actual church in the actual world. Can the Letter to Philemon teach us anything about the early Christians' stance regarding slavery? Although we cannot learn a great deal from one small document, two brief observations seem justified. First, the fact that Philemon continued to hold slaves after his conversion and during the time that a church was meeting in his house suggests that Christians did not automatically abandon the practice of slavery within the fellowship. Second, however, it seems clear

---

3. Ibid., 169.
4. Ibid., 269; italics original.

Fig. 59. The City Walls of Thessalonica. Although parts of these walls may be traced to the Hellenistic and Roman periods, the substantial circuit preserved today dates from the 4th to the 9th cent. C.E. Constructed of stones and mortar and alternating with brick, they range in height from 8 to 10 m. and originally stretched for about 7 km.
(Photo: Koester/Hendrix)

that Paul was able to call upon a set of assumptions shared in the church—Petersen's "symbolic universe"—that contained the seeds of a challenge to that practice.

We might also ask what we have learned about Paul from this letter. For one thing, we have seen concretely how he made use of the medium of a letter to carry out his apostolic function. We have also had a glimpse of his understanding of the authority he believed attended his apostolic status. And, most importantly, we have learned something about what was important to Paul and about the basis from which his thinking proceeded. One's being in Christ is not, in Paul' view, one aspect of life parallel to other aspects. It is the very center and substance of one's existence. It is the norm by which one orders one's whole life and makes all decisions. It is everything.

2. 1 Thessalonians

a. The Story behind the Letter

Acts 17:1-15 gives an account of Paul's sojourn in Thessalonica, and most scholars make use of this account in fitting his work there into a chronological scheme. But there is reason to be skeptical of Acts on some points. For example, Acts typically has Paul preach in the synagogue and make Jewish converts. The Letter to the Thessalonians, by contrast, makes no mention of this practice and rather clearly presupposes a congregation that is at least predominantly gentile (1:9).

Here, then, is the "story" we can derive from the letter itself. Paul and his companions come to Thessalonica, teeming capital of the Roman province of Macedonia, and are successful in gaining converts and founding a Christian community. When Paul moves on, however, he becomes concerned about the new Christians and sends Timothy to inquire about them. Timothy returns to Paul with a generally positive report, but with some questions also. In response, Paul writes the letter known as 1 Thessalonians.

b. Reading 1 Thessalonians

(1) 1:1—3:13. Following the greeting, Paul launches a lengthy thanksgiving to God for the faith, love, and hope of the Thessalonians. The readers will be encouraged by his report that the story of their response to the mission has become well known in other areas, and they will feel drawn into an ongoing process. As was the practice among Hellenistic teachers, Paul had presented himself as an example, i.e., he sought to embody his own teaching. Thus the Thessalonians, by imitating him, have now become an example to others. Paul also encourages the readers to remember the paradoxical joy they experienced in accepting the Gospel under adverse circumstances (1:6) and reminds them of the content of their faith: they have turned from idols to await the return of Jesus, whom God raised from the dead (1:10).

In reading Paul's account of the behavior of his group in their presence (2:1-12), the Thessalonians will be led to compare this group favorably to the wandering philosophers, so prevalent in the Greco-Roman world, many of whom were regarded as charlatans. Remembering how Paul and his associates supported themselves rather than burden the congregation, how they nurtured the new Christians and gave of themselves, the readers will be encouraged to follow Paul's earlier exhortations regarding the conduct of their lives (2:11-12).

Fig. 60. Pilaster depicting Cabirus. Cabirus was a dying/rising god worshiped at Thessalonica. This marble pilaster is dated to the 3rd cent. C.E. *(Photo: Koester/Hendrix)*

Turning back to the theme of imitation in 2:13, Paul now links the adversities the Thessalonians experienced in receiving the gospel to that of Judean Christians. The readers will understand that both groups suffered rejection—the Judean Christians by other Jews, the Thessalonians by their fellow Gentiles. Picking up on the point, Paul then moves into a bitter invective against the Jews. (The end of this passage—"But God's wrath has come upon them"—may reflect the fall of Jerusalem in 70 C.E., in which case we must regard it as a later interpolation. Some scholars, in fact, believe the whole passage is secondary.)

In 2:17—3:10 Paul recounts the events leading up to the letter and, in the tenderest terms, expresses joy in the Thessalonians' faith and his desire to visit them. Along the way, he reminds the readers of his own adversities and of the role their steadfastness plays in his comfort. The thanksgiving concludes (3:11-13) with a benedictory prayer combining Paul's desire for a visit with a pronouncement of God's blessings.

Having read thus far, the Thessalonians should feel encouraged by Paul's appraisal of them and strengthened by their bonds to others in the faith. Re-

Fig. 61. Imperial coin,
depicting Cabirus*

Fig. 62. Imperial coin,
depicting Tyche (Fate or Fortune)*

minded of their original joy and of the content of their faith and hope, they should be renewed in their commitment.

(2) 4:1—5:28. With a transitional phrase—"finally," in English—Paul turns from thanksgiving to exhortation, referring to prior "instructions." The readers will hear his injunctions regarding sexual ethics (4:3-8) in light of God's desire for their "sanctification," their being "set apart" for a holy purpose. Then, addressing the life of the community (4:9-12), Paul enjoins mutual love and a quietistic life-style defined by manual labor and noninterference in the lives of others. The readers will feel a responsibility not only to live ethically responsible lives but to gain the respect of outsiders through irreproachable behavior.

In 4:13 Paul addresses a question the Thessalonians have asked through Timothy. Apparently, some members of the community have died since Paul left, and their fellow-Christians are wondering about their ultimate fate: will they share in the salvation that comes with Christ's return? Paul's answer is that when the end comes the "dead in Christ" will be raised, and then all, dead and living together, will be caught up "in the clouds to meet the Lord in the air" (4:17).

Paul thus not only declares that those who have already died have a share in the world to come, but he gives his readers a powerful image of ultimate victory. He invites them to look forward to a triumphal procession in which they will accompany Christ either into heaven or back to a renewed earth (it is

---

*The obverse and reverse sides respectively of a bronze coin minted in Thessalonica in the Roman Imperial period. *(Photos: Koester/Hendrix)*

not clear which). And he assures them of eternal fellowship with one another and with Christ.

Perhaps the Thessalonians had also asked about when Christ's return would be. In any case, in 5:1 Paul proceeds to discourage all speculation on this point. Echoing in 5:2 an image from the Jesus tradition (Matt. 24:43; Luke 12:39), he says that the end will come "like a thief in the night." As he then enjoins the readers to sobriety, watchfulness, and mutual encouragement, they will understand his words as both warning and promise: God has granted them salvation through Christ, but they must be on guard as the end draws near.

In 5:12 Paul turns again to the life of the fellowship, counselling respect for the leaders, admonition of idlers, and encouragement of the weak and fainthearted. The tone is positive: the Thessalonians should rejoice and give thanks in all circumstances. They will understand the admonitions (5:19-20) not to "quench the Spirit" or "despise prophesying" as a call to allow God's gracious gifts to work among them. And they will hear in 5:23-24 not only an eschatological warning but a promise. In the injunction regarding the "holy kiss" in 5:26 they will recognize a common practice signifying the bond of love that united all in Christ.

Encouraged in the faith, instructed on matters of concern, and admonished in various ways, the readers will receive the benediction with which the letter concludes as the blessing of a nurturing pastor. Surely they will in fact read the letter aloud in their meetings—and be renewed!

c. Critical Problems

First Thessalonians is a simple pastoral letter, devoted largely to the task of encouraging new Christians to continue in the faith. And Paul's theology seems straightforward and uncomplicated: as far as we can tell from this letter, Christian faith consists mainly in accepting Jesus, whom God raised from the dead, as the agent of salvation (5:9) and in faithfully awaiting his return.

There are some questions, however, which are not so easily answered. Was the encouragement offered in the thanksgiving Paul's main reason for writing, or were the Thessalonians' questions about eschatology his primary concern? Or, perhaps, are there other problems regarding which the letter gives us only hints? Does the fact that Paul goes to such lengths to defend the behavior of his group when they were in Thessalonica mean that someone there has been critical of him? What precisely are the "afflictions" (RSV: 3:3) the Thessalonians have suffered? And what was the root of their eschatological misunderstanding?

According to one reading (reflected in the NRSV translation of 3:3), the Thessalonians have recently undergone persecution, which is the reason for their eschatological anxiety. And if one accepts the Acts account, this persecution was at the hands of the Jews. Abraham Malherbe, however, thinks that Paul refers to the new Christians' psychological distress brought on by the alienation from friends, associates, and family that accompanied the abandonment of their former lives. It is clear, he argues, that in 2:14 Paul refers to rejection not by Jews but by fellow Gentiles.[5]

Malherbe also claims that Paul's self-defense in 2:1-8 follows a pattern common among Hellenistic philosophers distinguishing themselves from those among their number of bad reputation.[6] While many scholars have sought to identify specific opponents of Paul at Thessalonica, Malherbe finds their attempts unnecessary. In his reading, 1 Thessalonians is a letter born solely of pastoral concern.

Some scholars, however, remain convinced that a conflict lies in the background. Robert Jewett argues that when Paul stresses that his mission was not "in vain" (2:1), we must imagine that some group in Thessalonica has claimed that it was.[7] But on what grounds would such a group make such an attack? Jewett seeks to answer this question by reconstructing the social situation in which the Thessalonian congregation might have existed.

Drawing upon sociological studies of the Pauline churches, Jewett characterizes the group as made up largely of handworkers, people who, while not destitute, suffered relative deprivation. Many such people, Jewett notes, would at one time have been attracted to the cult of Cabirus, which once flourished in Thessalonica and which centered around a dying/rising god who conferred great blessings. This religion was highly ecstatic in nature and offered the "divinization" of the initiates. By the time of Paul, however, it had been absorbed into the imperial cult that flourished at Thessalonica. The result, one may imagine, was that the followers of Cabirus among the common people became alienated from the cult, feeling it had been co-opted by the rich and powerful.

Perhaps, then, the new converts to Christianity brought expectations that led to disappointment with Paul. They might have expected dramatic demonstrations of charismatic power. And they might have interpreted Paul's message as an extreme form of "millenarianism" that placed so much em-

---

5. Abraham J. Malherbe, *Paul and the Thessalonians: The Philosophic Tradition of Pastoral Care* (Philadelphia: Fortress Press, 1987), 46–47.

6. Ibid., 2–3.

7. Robert Jewett, *The Thessalonian Correspondence: Pauline Rhetoric and Millenarian Piety* (Philadelphia: Fortress Press, 1986), 102.

phasis upon the nearness of the new age that it seemed appropriate to shirk all worldly responsibilities. That would explain why Paul found it necessary to say a word about "idlers" in 5:14. It might also explain the Thessalonians' extreme distress at the death of community members: how could that happen to participants in the new age? In such a reading Paul's instructions regarding sexual morality (4:3-8) might also indicate that some at Thessalonica were arguing that the new age freed them from ordinary constraints.

Paul's instructions, however, can be interpreted as part of the stock advice of those who nurtured Hellenistic philosophical and religious groups. And Malherbe notes that some philosophical schools were severely criticized for their lack of social responsibility.[8] It is thus possible that Paul's concern was simply to distinguish the Christians from those groups that tended to opt out of society altogether. The precise situation at Thessalonica remains a matter of speculation.

3. Philippians

a. The Story and Some Critical Problems

We know from 1 Thessalonians that Paul and his companions experienced extreme opposition in their mission at Philippi, prior to coming to Thessalonica. According to Acts 16, the Roman authorities imprisoned them for creating a disturbance. The Letter to the Philippians shows, however, that Paul was successful in founding a Christian community there, a community with which he developed a very special relationship. We can also determine from the letter that Paul is writing from prison and that at some point he has received financial assistance from the Philippian Christians, delivered by Epaphroditus. Having fallen ill and subsequently recovered, Epaphroditus is now returning to Philippi with the letter.

Further reconstruction of the story behind the letter is complicated by a critical problem. In 3:1, Paul seems to be bringing the letter to a close, but in 3:2 he suddenly launches a biting attack upon some unnamed proponents of circumcision and then goes on to criticize those whose "god is the belly" (3:19). Again in 4:2-9, the letter seems to be moving toward a conclusion. Now, however, Paul proceeds (4:10-20) to thank the Philippians for their gift.

Many scholars take these breaks in thought sequence and in the standard letter format as evidence of the composite nature of the present letter. One among several reconstructions is that suggested by F. W. Beare: 3:2—4:1 and

---

8. Malherbe, *Paul and the Thessalonians*, 97.

4:10-20 are fragments of other letters which an editor has woven into the "main" letter.

Other scholars remain unconvinced by this evidence and interpret the material following 3:1 as a series of postscripts. In the treatment that follows, I will proceed through the letter as it stands but will address the disputed passages in a way that does not presuppose an original connection to the present context.

b. Reading Philippians

(1) 1:1—3:1. Following the salutation, Paul offers a heartfelt thanksgiving that encourages the Philippians to persevere in their faith, assured of God's work among them in preparation for the "day of Christ," and that expresses Paul's affection for them. The thanksgiving also serves to comfort the readers in the face of Paul's imprisonment by including them as "partakers" in this experience and in the grace that somehow issues from it. One aspect of that grace is the fact, expounded in 1:12-14, that Paul's misfortune has actually emboldened others to preach the gospel. The readers are thus encouraged to take heart, just as Paul himself can rejoice—even if some of this preaching issues from unworthy motives (1:15-18). In speaking of the possibility of his death with equanimity (1:19-23), Paul adds a different dimension to the comfort he offers; but then he quickly assures his readers of his intention to preserve his life, precisely for their sake, and of his hope to see them again.

Having offered his own resounding note of joy in the midst of afflictions, Paul now exhorts the Philippians to remain committed and unified in the face of their own adversities (1:27-30). Then, in a poetic appeal for unity, humility, and mutual concern (2:1-11), he apparently quotes an existing hymn in order to present Christ as an example of selflessness. Following an additional appeal that reiterates earlier points (2:12-14), he informs his readers of an eventual visit by Timothy, adds words of praise for Epaphroditus, who will presumably bear the letter, and once again (3:1) counsels the Philippians to rejoice.

The readers will feel included in a community grounded in Christ and dedicated to selfless concern for others, and they will be motivated to give attention to the quality of their life together. They will sense a particularly warm relationship to Paul himself and will be inspired by his courage in the face of adversity. And they will reflect upon the deep joy mediated by their Christian faith.

(2) 3:2—4:1 (a fragment of a later letter?) Warning the readers against the "evil-workers" who propose circumcision, Paul bolsters his argument with a biographical point. Having found righteousness before God through faith in

Christ, Paul himself counts his former blamelessness under the law utterly of no worth. The readers are thus encouraged to conclude that physical circumcision is unnecessary for Christians, who in Christ participate in the "true circumcision."

Paul's reference to faith in Christ leads him to a statement on the hope for resurrection (3:10), which in turn leads into a lyrical confession of the goal of the Christian life (3:12-16). Presenting himself as a model for imitation, Paul then warns against those "whose god is their belly" (3:19) and makes an appeal (4:1) for steadfastness. The readers will be motivated to give attention to their personal behavior in light of their ultimate destiny.

(3) 4:2-9. Addressing a dispute by two women in leadership positions in the Philippian community, Paul asks his readers to help them reach a reconciliation. Then, returning to the theme of rejoicing, he counsels his readers to engage in prayer and thanksgiving, to focus upon the positive aspects of community life, and to imitate him.

(4) 4:10-20 (a fragment of an earlier letter?). Rejoicing in the Philippians' concern for him, Paul first asserts that he has learned to be content in any set circumstances. Then, acknowledging the gifts the Philippians have sent through Epaphroditus, as well as earlier contributions, he takes pains to interpret them as a contribution to his work and an act of worship. The readers will be moved by Paul's strong images of a faith that survives extreme difficulties.

(5) 4:21-22. With a traditional greeting and benediction, Paul concludes the letter.

c. Philippians 2:6-11 and the Development of Christology

Scholars universally maintain that in 2:6-11 Paul quotes an early Christian hymn to Christ. There is less consensus on whether it was composed by Paul himself at an earlier time, by a member of one of Paul's communities, or by an earlier Christian in the pre-Pauline church, although this third possibility is the most frequently assumed.

There is also a dispute about the interpretation of the hymn, which has some bearing on one's understanding of the development of early Christology. It seems almost self-evidently to contain a reference to the preexistence of Christ (vv. 6-7), and most scholars interpret it in that way. If they are correct, this means that Christians developed the view of Christ as a preexistent being at a very early date. And some see it as evidence for a pre-Christian redeemer myth of gnostic orientation.

If, however, ones takes "form of God" in v. 6 as the equivalent of the "image of God" in which Adam was created, it need not imply preexistence. On the basis of such a reading, some scholars find here an Adam-Christology in which Christ reverses Adam's fateful choice in the face of the temptation to seek "equality with God." Translating the Greek verb in v. 7 not as "born," but, literally, as "becoming," they understand this verse to mean simply that Christ, *during his lifetime,* took on the slave-status that Adam brought upon all humanity by his sin.[9] Scholars who accept this interpretation frequently argue that the notion of preexistence did not come to full expression until the Gospel of John.

To the majority of scholars, however, the preceding interpretation seems quite strained. Not only does another Christ-hymn, quoted in Colossians 1:15-20, seem to contain a notion of preexistence, but in several passages Paul himself seems to embrace such a Christology: 1 Corinthians 1:24, 8:6, and 10:1-5. The first two of these passages in 1 Corinthians are of particular interest because they can be interpreted as applications of the motif of personified Wisdom to Christ. This would mean that the notion of preexistence was an early development, not a late one; but it might also mean that this notion was adopted directly from Jewish wisdom speculation and does not presuppose a developed Gnosticism in the first century.

d. Other Critical Problems

The traditional assumption has been that Paul wrote Philippians while imprisoned in Rome. The letter, however, does not specify the place of composition, and some scholars have challenged this view. Philippians 2:19-24 seems to presuppose relative ease in visitation, but Rome is a great distance from Philippi; and the problem is increased if one accepts the theory of multiple letters. Paul in fact mentions numerous imprisonments (2 Cor. 6:5, 11:23), so that any number of places are possible. Because of a negative reference to Ephesus in 1 Corinthians 15:32, many scholars have seen this city as the most likely candidate.

A final question is whether Paul is combatting specific opponents within the Christian community at Philippi. We know that he contended with proponents of circumcision in Galatia, and some scholars have found similar groups

---

9. James D. G. Dunn, *Christology in the Making: A New Testament Inquiry into the Origins of the Doctrine of the Incarnation* (Philadelphia: Westminster, 1980), 114–21.

at both Thessalonica and Philippi. According to one theory, Christians who sought to bring Christianity into full conformity with Judaism dogged Paul in his missionary travels. Another view is that Paul was opposed, in these cities and in Corinth as well, by Jewish-Christian Gnostics who urged circumcision but also embraced a libertine life-style.

Evaluation of these views will have to await treatment of Galatians and the Corinthian correspondence. Suffice it to say now that we have seen other possibilities for understanding the situation in Thessalonica, and the evidence for organized opposition within the church is slim with respect to Philippi. Paul could as easily be speaking in Philippians 3 of non-Christian Jews seeking to bring the gentile converts into their own fold as he could of a group of Christians urging circumcision.

4. Galatians

a. The Story behind the Letter

The Letter to the Galatians presupposes that sometime during his ministry Paul established churches in the region of Galatia in Asia Minor. It is less clear whether this designation applies to the old Galatian territory in the central region of the peninsula or to the larger Roman province of Galatia, although the former view is the more generally accepted. In any case, Paul's initially positive view of the Galatian churches is shattered when he receives news that some missionaries have appeared in Galatia and have apparently convinced some of the people to accept a version of the gospel different from Paul's own. According to their teaching, it is necessary for male gentile converts to undergo circumcision, which would mean that all Christians are subject to the Jewish law. In response to this development, Paul writes to the churches in Galatia to win them back to the gospel he originally preached to them—the gospel without law.

b. Reading Galatians

(1) 1:1—2:21. Paul confronts his readers almost immediately with argumentation. The very prescript contains an unusual emphasis upon the divine origin of his apostolic authority, and he follows the greeting with an accusation that the Galatians have deserted the gospel. The expression of astonishment in 1:6, moreover, puts the readers on the defensive from the outset, suggesting that their position is absurd. And then Paul proceeds to pronounce a curse upon

anyone preaching a gospel different from his own. That he includes himself—and even a hypothetical angel from heaven!—among the potential recipients of the condemnation defines the issue in the sharpest possible terms. There can be no compromise: what is at stake is the very substance of the gospel itself, that is, "the grace of Christ." Paul thus places before his readers a clear-cut yes/no decision.

In denying in 1:10 that he seeks to please human beings, Paul sets himself apart from Hellenistic rhetoricians of bad reputation. His goal is not to impress the readers with his persuasive abilities but to serve God. This point leads to a reiteration of the divine origin of his commission (1:11), which he then supports with a long narration of supportive facts (1:12—2:14).

There are two key points Paul stresses in this narration. First, he received his gospel in a direct revelation from God, not from any human teachers. The readers should therefore conclude that anyone claiming the authority of the apostles in Jerusalem to dispute Paul's teaching is barking up the wrong tree. Second, however, in a conference in Jerusalem these apostles agreed with Paul that he was entrusted with the gospel to the Gentiles, just as Peter was sent to Jews. That they "contributed nothing" to Paul, but asked only that he "remember the poor" (in the form of a collection for the Jerusalem church), indicates that they accepted a gospel *without the law* for Gentiles.

Having made these points, Paul turns to a later incident that has immediate bearing upon the situation in Galatia: a conflict between himself and Peter at Antioch. What the Galatians should grasp is that Peter's behavior was inconsistent; having first adopted the practice of eating with Gentiles—and thus acknowledging the uncircumcised as full members of the Christian fellowship—he later caved in under pressure from a "circumcision faction" reputedly sent from James (the brother of Jesus, in Jerusalem).

At this point, the reader is already boxed in. All arguments for circumcision have been demolished, and the unanswerable question Paul once asked of Peter (2:14) now implicitly challenges the Galatians. But Paul pushes on in 2:15 to a larger point, which he makes by way of self-reference. As a Christian, Paul is "dead" to the law, and Christ lives in him. And the life he now lives is defined precisely by his faith in Christ, who died for him. The issue comes to a head in 2:21. The question is how human beings can stand justified, i.e., be accounted in good standing, before God. And Paul's answer is unequivocal: "If justification were through the law, then Christ died to no purpose." One cannot, in other words, have it both ways. The central point the readers must understand is that if human beings are justified by faith in Christ, they have no need of the law; if they look to the law for justification, they deny the efficacy of Christ's death.

(2) 3:1—4:31. In 3:1 Paul resumes the intimidating tone of 1:6. Terming the Galatians "foolish" and "bewitched," he confronts them, in a series of rhetorical questions, with the irrefutable testimony of their own experience. They have in fact received the Spirit through Paul's earlier preaching, and they have continued to witness "miracles" in their midst. But all this happened through their faith in Christ, before anyone ever mentioned circumcision or the law! The readers are therefore forced to a conclusion of their own: to supplement faith in Christ with adherence to the law would be a denial of what they themselves have experienced.

The argument now turns (3:6) from experience to Scripture. Assuming a knowledge of the story of Abraham—who accepted God's promise to make him ancestor of a great people, even though his wife was infertile!—Paul quotes Genesis 15:6, according to which God counted Abraham's faith as righteousness. The Galatians should thus understand that Abraham stood "righteous" or "justified" (these both translate the same Greek word) before God not because of his good deeds or his obedience to the law but precisely because of his *faith*. It is thus persons of faith—those who rely upon God's gracious act in Christ, not upon their own obedience to the law—who are in fact justified before God.

Citing additional scriptural evidence, Paul then underscores the point with intricate interpretation. The unstated assumption in 3:10-14 is that perfect obedience to the law is impossible. That is why the law brings a curse upon those who rely on it for justification. In 3:15-18 Paul compares God's promise to Abraham to a will, arguing that this promise, fulfilled in Christ, was not nullified by the law, which came after Abraham. The readers must remember that the whole argument pits faith against law: the point, again, is that faith has always been the means by which God justifies human beings.

If that is so, however, the readers may well ask why the law was needed at all. Paul's answer is that it was given as an interim measure, a kind of disciplinarian until Christ came (3:21-24). But this answer opens into a resounding proclamation that may reflect a baptismal formula familiar to the readers: when the Galatians were baptized, they were all incorporated into Christ in a way that transcends all human distinctions—Jew/Greek, male/female, slave/ free—and thus received the promise to Abraham. The conclusion that the readers must again supply is that if the Jew/Greek distinction is obliterated in Christ, the law is unnecessary.

Picking up on the metaphor of disciplinarian, Paul then (4:1-11) contrasts humanity's slave-like status apart from Christ to Christians' status as heirs who have received the Spirit and can call God "Abba" (Daddy,

Dear Father). And, with the readers where he wants them, he can now ask the devastating rhetorical question: why would an heir become a slave again?

After reminding the readers once more of their joy in the gospel they originally heard (4:12-21) from him, Paul adds another argument from Scripture regarding the two sons of Abraham. The slave Hagar and her son Ishmael stand as a prototype of present Jews under the law. But the free woman Sarah and her son Isaac stand for Christians, free from the law. Children of freedom, the readers must conclude, have no part in "slavery."

(3) 5:1—6:18. The preceding verses have prepared the readers for the exhortation that now follows. Having been freed in Christ, the Galatians must not submit again to the "slavery" of circumcision. Contending that to do so is to sever oneself from Christ, Paul completes his line of logic with a bit of brutal humor (5:12): those demanding circumcision should go all the way and castrate themselves!

In light of such a resounding endorsement of freedom, the readers might well conclude that life in Christ is pure permissiveness. Paul thus shifts his emphasis in 5:13. Freedom in Christ is in fact an opportunity to fulfill the whole law through obedience to one simple command: "You shall love your neighbor as yourself." Paul can even list, in typical Hellenistic fashion, those behaviors that should be avoided and those that should be embraced. And he is strong in his condemnation of "the works of the flesh" (5:19). But the Christian is led to love, joy, peace, patience, kindness, etc., not through the law but through the Spirit. "Live by the Spirit" (5:16)—that is the essence of Paul's exhortation.

After further injunctions on intracommunity relations and behavior (6:1-10), Paul concludes with a summary note and postscript in his own hand. In 6:15 a single sentence reminds the readers of the entire argument: circumcision is irrelevant for Christians—precisely because life in Christ is a *new creation!*" The final verses that follow reinforce the point and leave the reader fully aware of the paradoxical character of the letter. Paul has admonished the readers severely in order to lift up the message of overwhelming grace.

c. Critical Problems

(1) Rhetorical Criticism of Galatians.
In his 1979 commentary, Hans Dieter Betz sought to analyze the Letter to the Galatians in terms of the categories of

Greek rhetoric.[10] He found it to be an "apologetic" (or "defense") letter and thus an example of judicial rhetoric, that is, an argument calling for a judgment about the past. In Galatians, according to Betz, Paul defends himself, as if arguing before a jury.

While contributing to the renewal of interest in rhetorical criticism, Betz's treatment has also provoked criticism. More recent analysts suggest that Galatians is not judicial but deliberative, an attempt to persuade an audience to take action in the future. Classics scholar George Kennedy, for example, argues:

> The letter looks to the immediate future, not to a judgment of the past, and the question to be decided by the Galatians was not whether Paul had been right in what he had said or done, but what they themselves were going to believe and to do.[11]

Read as deliberative rhetoric, Galatians is intended primarily to encourage the readers to reject circumcision, on the one hand, and "to love one another and practice the Christian life" on the other.[12] In such a reading, Paul's self-defense appears not as the primary thrust of the letter but as a secondary way of supporting the gospel without law, while the exhortation in the concluding chapters takes on greater importance.

Brevard Childs raises a rather different point. "It is one thing," he notes, "to suggest that recognition of Paul's cultural background aids in interpreting his letter, but quite another to argue that he has been deeply influenced by traditional Greek rhetoric."[13] From his perspective, both Betz and his critics are at risk of distorting Paul's intentions by trying to fit his letters too neatly into preconceived molds. Granted that Paul constructed his letter with some care, the question is whether he consciously followed the models provided by rhetorical handbooks.

(2) The Problem of the "Stoicheia."

Twice in Galatians Paul uses the Greek term *stoicheia*. The basic meaning of the word is "elements" or "fundamental principles," but precisely what it means and how it should be translated at the various points at which it occurs in the New Testament is the subject of much debate.

---

10. Hans Dieter Betz, *Galatians: A Commentary on Paul's Letter to the Churches in Galatia* (Philadelphia: Fortress Press, 1979); see also Betz, "The Literary Composition and Function of Paul's Letter to the Galatians," *New Testament Studies* 21 (1975): 353–79.

11. George A. Kennedy, *New Testament Interpretation through Rhetorical Criticism* (Chapel Hill: Univ. of North Carolina Press, 1984); see also Joop Smit, "The Letter of Paul to the Galatians: A Deliberative Speech, *New Testament Studies* 35 (1989): 1–26.

12. Ibid.

13. Brevard Childs, *The New Testament as Canon: An Introduction* (Philadelphia: Fortress Press, 1984), 301.

Paul speaks in 4:3 of the *"stoicheia* of the world" and in 4:9 of "weak and beggarly *stoicheia."* When the NRSV renders the term "elemental *spirits,"* it accepts the prevailing scholarly view that Paul refers to "demonic forces which constitute and control 'this evil aeon.' "[14] Certainly people in the Hellenistic world, including Jews, believed in the existence of such demonic forces. And certainly Paul believed that this present world order is in some sense held in bondage (Rom. 8:18-25; 1 Cor. 15:24-28). It is not so clear, however, that Paul refers to demonic forces with this particular phrase, which he applies not only to the former religion of the gentile converts (4:9) but to his own former beliefs as a Jew (4:3)! Walter Wink has argued, convincingly to my mind, that in Galatians *stoicheia* refers "to those basic practices, beliefs, rituals, and celebrations which are fundamental to the religious existence of all peoples, Jew and Gentile alike."[15]

(3) The Problem of Paul's Opponents. There is no question but that in Galatians Paul was combatting an organized opposition. There are divergent views, however, of the precise nature of this opposition.

The most widely accepted opinion is that those who came into Galatia preaching circumcision were conservative Jewish Christians seeking to keep the Christian movement within the Jewish fold. Some scholars, however, argue that Paul's injunctions against licentiousness in 5:13-25 do not fit such opponents, who would more likely support rigorous adherence to the moral aspects of the Jewish law. It has thus been suggested that Paul was arguing on two fronts: not only against advocates of the law but against libertines.

Walter Schmithals accounts for Paul's moral injunctions in another way.[16] He argues that Paul's opponents were members of a gnostic group embracing many Jewish elements but also advocating libertine behavior, a group that Schmithals believes also opposed Paul in Corinth, Philippi, and Thessalonica. Schmithals's characterization of this hypothetical sect is consistent with what we know of the various forms of later Gnosticism, but the moral injunctions in Galatians provide inadequate basis for such a conclusion. The characterization of Paul's opposition in Galatia as conservative Jewish Christian remains the most widely accepted hypothesis. The majority of scholars, moreover, see no need to posit a libertine group in Galatia. Paul's moral injunctions are a standard part of his message and are readily understandable in this case as a hedge against overinterpretation of his emphasis upon freedom.

---

14. Betz, *Galatians,* 204; see also 213-16.
15. Walter Wink, *Naming the Powers: The Language of Power in the New Testament* (Philadelphia: Fortress Press, 1984), 72.
16. Walter Schmithals, *Paul and the Gnostics,* trans. J. E. Steely (Nashville: Abingdon, 1972).

d. Concluding Comments

In Philemon, Philippians, and 1 Thessalonians we have observed Paul primarily as apostle and pastor. Galatians, too, is a pastoral letter, but it also exhibits Paul at work as theologian. His notions regarding righteousness/justification, law, and faith—stated only in the briefest form in Philippians 3:8-10—reach programmatic status in Galatians. Paul also develops with some clarity the point that life in Christ is (as a "new creation") a radically new mode of existence, a life pervaded by the Spirit and standing in stark opposition to a life based upon "the flesh." Just what he means by "flesh" and "Spirit," however, will need some elaboration. And the same must be said of his use of "participation" language regarding Christians' relationship to Christ: "As many of you as were baptized into Christ have clothed yourselves with Christ" (3:27).

STUDY QUESTIONS

1. Reconstruct the "story" behind Philemon.

2. Explain the "socioliterary method" Petersen employs in studying Philemon. What does Petersen learn about the letter through this method?

3. Are Paul's ideas on slavery adequate for our own time in history? Say why or why not.

4. Reconstruct the "story" behind 1 Thessalonians. What are the main theological themes Paul stresses in this letter?

5. Contrast the views of Malherbe and Jewett on the reason for Paul's writing 1 Thessalonians.

6. Reconstruct the "story" behind Philippians.

7. Why do some scholars think Philippians might be a composite of fragments?

8. Characterize Paul's relationship to the church at Philippi.

9. What are the two interpretations of the Christology of Philippians 2:6-11?

10. Reconstruct the "story" behind Galatians.

11. Characterize the understanding of Paul's relationship to the leadership of the Jerusalem church expressed in Galatians. From what source does Paul claim to have received the message he preached?

12. What issue was at stake in Paul's confrontation with Peter at Antioch?

13. Explain Paul's understanding of the Jewish law in Galatians.

14. What role does the Spirit play in Christian life, according to Galatians?

15. What are the competing views of the meaning of the term *stoicheia?*

16. What are the competing views of the identity of Paul's opponents in Galatia?

FOR FURTHER READING

Bassler, Jouette M., ed. *Pauline Theology.* Vol. 1: *Thessalonians, Philippians, Galatians, Philemon.* Minneapolis: Fortress Press, 1991. Essays by members of the Pauline Theology Consultation of the Society of Biblical Literature, approaching Paul's theology on the basis of individual letters rather than as a totality. An important contribution.

Beare, Frank W. *A Commentary on the Epistle to the Philippians.* New York: Harper & Row, 1959. A solid, competent treatment.

Best, Ernest. *The First and Second Epistles to the Thessalonians.* New York: Harper & Row, 1972. A thorough, detailed treatment; defends Pauline authorship of 2 Thessalonians.

Betz, Hans Dieter. *Galatians: A Commentary on Paul's Letter to the Churches in Galatia.* Hermeneia. Philadelphia: Fortress Press, 1979. An important resource that makes use of the categories of Greek rhetoric.

Cousar, Charles B. *Galatians.* Atlanta: John Knox, 1982. A competent, readable contribution.

Craddock, Fred. *Philippians.* Atlanta: John Knox, 1985. A readable and helpful contribution.

Jewett, Robert. *The Thessalonian Correspondence: Pauline Rhetoric and Millenarian Piety.* Philadelphia: Fortress Press, 1986. Interprets the letters as a response to eschatological fervor; considers 2 Thessalonians authentically Pauline.

Knox, John. *Philemon among the Letters of Paul: A New View of Its Place and Importance.* London: Collins, 1960. Derives interesting insights regarding Paul from the letter.

Lohse, Eduard. *Colossians and Philemon.* Hermeneia. Trans. William R. Poehlmann and Robert J. Karris. Philadelphia: Fortress Press, 1971. Detailed, technical treatment.

Malherbe, Abraham J. *Paul and the Thessalonians: The Philosophic Tradition of Pastoral Care.* Philadelphia: Fortress Press, 1987. Argues that Paul distinguishes the gospel from current philosophical schools but is not combatting opponents in the church.

Martin, Ralph P. *Philippians.* London: Oliphants, 1976. A strong, competent treatment.

Petersen, Norman R. *Rediscovering Paul: Philemon and the Sociology of Paul's Narrative World.* Philadelphia: Fortress Press, 1985. A fascinating treatment combining sociological and literary methods.

Schmithals, Walter. *Paul and the Gnostics.* Trans. J. E. Steely. Nashville: Abingdon, 1972. Argues that Paul was opposed by Gnostics throughout his ministry.

Chapter 10

1 and 2 Corinthians

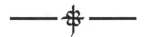

1. The City of Corinth

Refounded in 44 B.C.E. as a Roman colony after an earlier destruction, Corinth was apparently the capital of the Roman province of Achaia, home of the old Greek city-states. Located on the narrow isthmus from which the Peloponnesian peninsula dangles, and thus with access to both the Aegean and the Adriatic seas, it was a flourishing center of trade as well as industry. In terms of religion, it was a typical Hellenistic city, with the usual array of sanctuaries and cults.

2. 1 Corinthians

a. The Story behind the Letter

As is clear from 1 Corinthians 2–3, Paul founded the Christian community in Corinth. According to Acts 18, he went there after leaving Athens and stayed with a couple who had come from Rome, with whom he worked as a tentmaker. In 1 Corinthians 16:19 Paul sends greetings from this couple, Prisca and Aquila, who are now with him in Ephesus. Romans 16:3 reveals that they were associates in his missionary activity. Paul also mentions three others who preached in Corinth: Silvanus (Silas in Acts) and Timothy, both of whom worked concurrently with him (2 Cor. 1:19), and Apollos, who came to Corinth after he had left (1 Cor. 1:10-17). Acts 18:24-28 characterizes Apollos as an eloquent missionary and recounts how Priscilla (Prisca) and Aquila

Fig. 63. Ancient Corinth and Gulf from the Demeter Sanctuary *(Photo: Koester/Hendrix)*

converted him from "the baptism of John" to Christianity when they were in Ephesus.

We know from 1 Corinthians 5:9-11 that after leaving Corinth Paul wrote the Corinthians a letter, which is now lost, containing advice regarding association with immoral people. Later he received two communications from Corinth: a letter raising a number of serious questions, and a verbal report from "Chloe's people" that painted a disturbing picture of the state of affairs in the church. Now in Ephesus in Asia Minor, Paul writes back to answer the Corinthians' questions and to speak to the problems revealed in the report.

b. Reading 1 Corinthians

(1) 1:1—4:21. In the opening and thanksgiving, Paul places the letter in the context of his apostolic authority and reminds the readers of the spiritual gifts they have received as they await Christ's return. Having written to Paul earlier, the Corinthians will anticipate answers to their questions. What they hear first, however, is a response to the negative report from "Chloe's people." Paul begins the body of the letter (1:10) with an appeal to unity in the face of their factionalism, apparently based upon loyalty to various leaders—himself, Apollos, Peter. He attacks this divisiveness with devastating rhetorical questions and (1:13) portrays it as antithetical to the message of the cross. The irony in his contrasts between the divine and human perspectives will jolt his readers. As he links God with foolishness, lowliness, and weakness and human beings with wisdom, nobility, and strength, they will hear a bitter denouncement of the claim of some members—those who "boast" (1:31)—to a superior wisdom.

Hellenistic audiences expected philosophers to teach on two levels: basic doctrines for average hearers and an advanced wisdom for the spiritual elite. They also expected rhetorical excellence. Some of the Corinthians must have complained about Paul on these matters, for in 2:1 he applies his ironical argument to his own case: foreswearing lofty words, he instead preached the message of the crucified Christ, which brought the gift of the Spirit. He does in fact have a secret wisdom (2:6-14), but as the gift of the Spirit it remains unintelligible to the "rulers of this age." When Paul then pronounces the Corinthians not ready for the higher wisdom (3:1), the readers must draw the unflattering conclusion: they remain too closely tied to the present corrupt world—as their factionalism shows (3:3-4)!

Returning to the issue of divisiveness, Paul stresses that he and Apollos are complementary servants of Christ, not leaders of factions. Christ alone is the foundation of the church, and it is what one builds upon this foundation, what one *does* on the basis of faith in Christ, that counts in the final judgment (3:12-15). The readers are thus prepared to hear that because their "wisdom" misses this point, it is utterly futile (3:18-20). But they can also understand that this is so precisely because "all things" are already theirs, simply because they are in Christ!

Presenting himself and his associates as "stewards of God's mysteries," Paul defends his performance in that capacity (4:1-5)—implying that some in Corinth have criticized him. But then in 4:6 he turns the tables by attacking those who act in a "puffed up" way against their fellow Christians. With powerful irony, he contrasts the weakness, foolishness, and vulnerability of the apostles to the attitudes of those who think they already know the fullness of the new age: "Already you have all you want!" The readers must conclude that the fullness of God's Rule has not in fact come and must draw a contrast between the "triumphalist" theology of those who are "puffed up" and Paul's paradoxical theology of the cross, which recognizes that Christians must continue to live in a world in which suffering is real.

The readers will detect a more conciliatory tone as Paul distinguishes his admonitions from an attempt to shame them and refers to himself as their "father" (4:14-17). They will feel chastised but still accepted and included in the Christian fellowship. When Paul then resorts to bitter sarcasm as he speaks of his impending visit (4:18-21), however, they will realize that the nature of that visit depends upon their response to his admonitions.

(2) 5:1—6:20. Shifting to other aspects of the report he has heard, Paul turns first to the case of a man having relations with his stepmother, something prohibited by both Jewish and Roman law. The readers will presumably understand the punishment Paul pronounces in 5:5 as excommunication, expulsion from the community. Familiar with his terminology, they will interpret "the destruction of the flesh" as a reference not to the killing of the physical body but to release from an alien power holding human beings in bondage. With Paul, they will hope that this man's severance from the fellowship will lead to his repentance and eventual salvation. From 5:6-8 the readers can identify Paul's primary concern as the effect of the incident upon their community. And they will get two messages through the metaphor of "yeast": a warning about the "contagious" effects of immorality and a charge that "puffed up" Christians live on the basis of the old age, not the new.

Following the clarification of a point in his earlier letter (5:9-13) and an attack upon Christians who sue other Christians (6:1-8), Paul launches a general condemnation of unrighteousness (6:9-11) that leads to a confrontation with his opponents' views. Quoting their slogans ("All things are lawful," etc.) with apparent approval, he attacks their use of these fundamental premises. The readers must conclude that neither freedom from the law nor the destructibility of the body constitutes permission for immorality. Affirming the sacredness of the body, Paul also asserts the reality of the relationships a person enters through it: that is why "members of Christ" cannot be joined to the "members of a prostitute." The readers will understand by "body" not a material entity in the simplistic sense but the entire human being, something that a person "is" rather than "has."[1] When Paul concludes his line of argument with a use of the "ransom" metaphor ("you were bought with a price"), the readers will understand that the whole person is redeemed through Christ.

(3) 7:1-39. Mindful of Paul's displeasure in the report he has received, and clear that this displeasure is grounded in his understanding of the "word of the cross" that precludes activities disruptive of solidarity in Christ, the readers now read that Paul will answer their questions. First on the list is a set of is-

---

1. Rudolf Bultmann, *Theology of the New Testament*, vol. 1, trans. Kendrick Grobel (New York: Scribner's, 1951), 194–95.

sues regarding marriage, divorce, and sex. Initially expressing his preference
for celibacy, Paul nevertheless affirms marriage. Some of the Corinthians
have apparently thought that sexual relations are incompatible with Christianity, and Paul clearly states otherwise. He counsels against the attempt to
practice celibacy within marriage, affirming the conjugal rights of both the
husband and the wife.

As the argument progresses, it becomes clear to the readers that Paul's
reservations about marriage stem not from any disparagement of the physical but solely from his belief in the nearness of Christ's return. Because "the
appointed time has grown short" (7:29), Christians should live in an attitude
of "as if not" in relation to all matters—whether marriage or finances or whatever. The readers will understand that they should be as free as possible from
anxieties in order to devote full attention to matters related to faith (7:32-
35). While discouraging marriage for those who have the "gift" of celibacy,
Paul prefers that people marry rather than risk giving in to desires outside
marriage.

The nearness of the end also provides the context for Paul's counsel that it
is best to remain in whatever state one was in when one became a Christian (7:17-24). The readers are expected to understand that this advice is
grounded in Paul's strong sense of God's grace. The assumption behind his
indifference toward circumcision in 7:19 is that changes in status—whether
of marriage, condition of servitude, or circumcision—do not affect one's justification before God. The readers will conclude that any attempt to insure
one's status before God through circumcision, celibacy, or anything else is a
denial of grace.

Paul's readers will also hear his views on divorce and remarriage (7:10-16)
in light of his counsel to remain as one is. And they will accept his argument
that an unbeliever is made holy through a believing spouse, as well as his
general preference for reconciliation, as a sign of the sacredness and power
of the marriage bond.

(4) 8:1—11:34. The readers will have an immediate interest in the issue Paul
addresses next: whether Christians should eat meat consecrated to deities
other than the Jewish/Christian god. For much of the meat found in the
markets had undergone such consecration. The "wise" in Corinth had apparently argued that the practice was harmless, since these deities did not
really exist anyway. Paul accepts the premise of this argument (8:4-6), but
not before he undercuts the Corinthians' use of it with a critique of their
supposedly superior "knowledge" (8:1-3). And he qualifies his acceptance by
noting that although there is only one true god, there are many "so-called

gods"—apparently accepting the reality of demonic beings. Then, admitting that those who take offense at the practice are "weak," he lays down a principle by which to judge such matters, namely, concern for one's Christian fellows. To eat consecrated meat is harmless in itself but dangerous if it confuses a "weak believer," who might not be able to separate the practice from "pagan" worship.

The point the readers must grasp is that the life of the community, the fellowship of those for whom Christ died (8:11), takes precedence over individual enjoyment. They will accept the characterization of some members as weak but will also remember the ironical contrasts in chapter 1, in which Paul declared God's preference for what is weak, lowly, and despised. Once again, they are forced to associate God with what appears foolish by human standards.

In the course of his argument (8:10), Paul mentions the specific possibility of eating a meal in a pagan temple, where guilds and social clubs frequently held banquets. Without directly prohibiting such practice, he points out the possible consequences if a "weak believer" should see one partaking of such a meal. Once again, the reader must recognize concern for fellow Christians as a central criterion of behavior.

In 9:1 Paul turns to a defense of his apostolic authority. Someone in Corinth has apparently challenged him on the matter, arguing that because he has not exercised the apostolic right to financial support from the community and to a wife, he must not be a real apostle. Paul inverts the argument: after piling up several analogies and scriptural quotations to make the case for his rights, he says that for the sake of the gospel he has chosen not to exercise them. Then he presents this choice as part of his general strategy of entering into the specific situations of those to whom he preaches (9:19-22). Confronted with Paul's own willingness to sacrifice everything for the gospel, the readers are assured of his authority and encouraged to make a similar dedication of their own lives (9:24).

Paul's story of God's displeasure with the disobedient Israelites in the wilderness (10:1-5; Num. 14:29-30), together with his general attack upon idolatry (10:6-15), sets the stage for his condemnation of actual participation in "pagan" cult meals. Reminded that although idols have no real existence they are somehow connected to demonic beings, the readers must recognize that those who participate in the Lord's Supper cannot also share "the table of demons" (10:21). The presupposition shared by Paul and his readers is that sacred meals carry a genuine power with them.

The quotation of the Corinthian slogans in 10:23 signals the readers that Paul's argument has come full circle. In the verses that follow he expands upon earlier points and adds injunctions to do everything to God's glory and to imitate his own behavior (10:31—11:1). Then the compliment in 11:2 prepares the readers to look for another train of thought.

The new subject concerns women: Paul issues an injunction (11:3-6) regarding women who pray or prophesy during worship.[2] He does not, however, prohibit them from performing these roles, and in 11:11-12 he pauses to underscore the *interdependency* of female and male. The readers will know that Paul's regulation is specifically for women, but they will understand his view of the relationship between the sexes less in terms of hierarchy and subordination than in terms of a simple distinction in roles. And in any case "the presupposition of the whole discussion is that women can and do share fully in the leadership of worship."[3]

Contrasting Paul's refusal to commend the Corinthians in 11:17 with his compliments in 11:2, the readers will feel the severity of his criticism of their behavior at the Lord's Supper. In an allusion back to the problem of factionalism (11:19), Paul notes that some people are eating their meals and getting drunk before others arrive. And he cites a tradition regarding Jesus' institution of the last supper (11:23-26) as he accuses the Corinthians of desecrating the rite. The readers must acknowledge that their behavior in this matter, as in others, is an utter violation of their unity in Christ.

(5) 12:1—14:39. "Now concerning spiritual gifts...." Paul thus introduces the discussion of another topic, religious ecstasy, about which the Corinthians must have inquired. And he immediately (12:2-3) puts those among the readers who have apparently boasted of such gifts on the defensive. When the Corinthians were pagans, he notes, they were "led astray." The readers must conclude that spiritual ecstasy can lead in more than one direction, "that ecstasy alone is no criterion for the working of the Spirit, but itself requires such a criterion."[4] What Paul proposes is the confession of Jesus as lord in Christian worship: only spiritual gifts that lead to that confession are to be sought and valued.

With that point made, Paul turns directly to those gifts (12:4-31). Speaking of the Christian community as Christ's body, he argues that all gifts of the one Spirit are necessary to the body's functioning. The Corinthians will know that he is criticizing those among them who claim superiority on the basis of

---

2. See chap. 12, p. 406, n. 27.

3. Victor Paul Furnish, *The Moral Teaching of Paul: Selected Issues,* rev. ed. (Nashville: Abingdon, 1985), 101.

4. Hans Conzelmann, 1 *Corinthians: A Commentary on the First Epistle to the Corinthians,* trans. James W. Leitch (Philadelphia: Fortress Press, 1975), 206.

their special gifts. And they will understand that no one in the community has the right to lord it over others on such a basis.

Paul nevertheless indicates that some gifts are "greater" than others—a point that leads him into the famous "love chapter" (chap. 13). Without disparaging the various spiritual gifts, he subordinates them all to love. Writing in the manner of Jewish wisdom, he presents love as a universal value, recognizable by anyone.[5] But the readers will be clear that he speaks specifically of the self-giving love associated with Christ.

Although Paul subordinates prophecy to love, in chapter 13 he pointedly elevates prophecy over "speaking in tongues"—ecstatic, unintelligible utterance under the influence of the Spirit. Here is the rub for the Corinthian "boasters": they undoubtedly excel in speaking in tongues and take this gift as a sign of their spiritual superiority. Without denying the validity of this practice—he himself engages in it (14:18)—Paul once again points to the communal context of all decision making. Speaking in tongues should not be prohibited but should be regulated: only two or three persons should be permitted utterances in a given service of worship, and only then if an interpreter is present. The overall principle the readers should grasp is that all components of a service, including both tongues and prophecy, should function as edification of the community, not as individual exercises in spirituality (14:26).

(Critical note: Many scholars consider 14:33b-36 a later addition to the text by a hand other than Paul's. They argue that these verses not only interrupt the flow of thought but also express a point—that women should keep silent in church—that seems to contradict Paul's presuppositions in 11:5.)

(6) 15:1-58. In 15:1 Paul signals another turn in his thought by reminding his readers of the fundamentals of the gospel, hinting (15:2) that they have departed from the teaching that grounds their salvation. Relating a traditional proclamation of Jesus' resurrection, he comes to the point in 15:12: some of them are denying the resurrection of the dead. Arguing that such denial undercuts Christ's own resurrection, and hence their own deliverance from sin, he bursts forth with a resounding declaration that ends in an account of the eschatological events: Christ's resurrection; his return; the raising of "those who belong to Christ"; the destruction of all competing authorities, including death; and, finally, Christ's own subjection to God. In 15:29-34 Paul rounds out his argument, appealing both to the Corinthians' own practice of receiving baptism in behalf of the dead and to his own empowerment to face difficulties. The readers should conclude that denial of the resurrection is simply absurd.

5. Ibid., 221.

Employing elements of a rhetorical form known as diatribe, Paul now raises a series of questions, only to declare how foolish they are (15:35-36). Then he tries actually to answer the question of the manner of the resurrection. Drawing upon analogies from nature and the scriptural image of Adam, he describes resurrection as transformation of the person into a "spiritual body," rather than the resuscitation of "flesh and blood." The readers learn that the final resurrection will come before all now alive have died and that the living will be instantly transformed.

Quoting a triumphant passage from Isaiah, Paul closes his argument with a ringing declaration of victory over death and a final exhortation to faithfulness. He has encircled the readers with logic, Scripture, and reference to experience. They should conclude that they cannot deny the resurrection without denying the heart and soul of their Christian faith.

(7) 16:1-24. His arguments completed, Paul turns to instructions regarding the collection for Jerusalem and to his travel plans. After brief notes and instructions, he adds greetings and brings the letter to a close with an expression of his love, but not before a final warning (16:22). The readers are left with the dual feelings of severe chastisement on the one hand and inclusion within the community on the other—and with sharp ironies to ponder.

c. Knowledge, Wisdom, Status, and Gender: Paul's Opponents in 1 Corinthians

(1) The Identity and Theology of the Opposition Group. Scholars have made many attempts to identify the specific group or groups Paul attacks in 1 Corinthians. Some have taken his reference to the slogans, "I belong to Paul," "I belong to Apollos," etc., in 1:10-17 as a sign that the church was split into several different factions. But Paul also lists among the slogans, "I belong to Christ," and it is difficult to imagine what kind of group would have been behind it. So the majority opinion is that he is fighting on only one front. But who, then, are his opponents? Schmithals's view is that they are Jewish-Christian Gnostics. They claim a superior wisdom (1:18-2:14) and experience of the new age in its fullness (4:8-13), and they exercise radical freedom from the law (6:12-20; 8:1-13; 10:14-11:1). Schmithals also claims that the phrase "Let Jesus be cursed" in 12:3 is among their slogans, a rejection of the physical person Jesus in favor of the spiritual Christ.[6]

---

6. Walter Schmithals, *Gnosticism in Corinth: An Investigation of the Letters to Corinth*, trans. John E. Steely (Nashville: Abingdon Press, 1971), 127.

The letter, however, gives no hint of the complex mythological systems of developed Gnosticism. And the phrase "Let Jesus be cursed" can be understood as a rhetorical device providing a contrast to the confession "Jesus is Lord."[7] Many scholars therefore characterize Paul's opponents simply as Hellenistic "enthusiasts," persons so enamored of their sense of possession by the Spirit that they think of themselves as transcending the present age. This type of religious consciousness, of course, does provide part of the background out of which the developed Gnostic systems of the second century c.e. grew.

Whoever the opponents were, they differed from Paul on some crucial issues. Their eschatology has been particularly interesting to scholars: many have argued that Paul was mistaken in assuming that their denial of resurrection (15:12) was a denial of eternal life. One view is that they rejected the Jewish notion of resurrection because they embraced the Greek idea of the immortality of the soul. Another is that they pushed "realized eschatology" to the point of believing that the resurrection had already taken place.

(2) The Social Status of the Opposition Group. Without denying the theological dimension of Paul's conflict with his opponents, Gerd Theissen has argued that class conflict is in the background.[8] It is clear from 1:26-31 that the Corinthian church was made up primarily of persons from the lower classes. Paying close attention to Paul's statements about specific persons in Corinth and to material in Acts, however, Theissen determines that most of these were persons of considerable means. The phrase "Chloe's people," for example, suggests that this woman was mistress of a large household including slaves and/or servants; in other cases the mention of houses or households is explicit. The community in Corinth apparently embraced a cross-section of society.[9]

Theissen argues that the groups Paul identifies as "the weak" and (by implication) "the strong" fall out along class lines. "The strong" advocate freedom to eat meat offered to idols: only the affluent were frequently invited to banquets, and only they could have afforded meat as a regular part of their diet. "The weak" are scandalized by eating consecrated meat: the poor would have received meat most often through public distributions on ceremonial occasions and, associating it with religious celebration, would have had trouble disconnecting it from pagan worship. The affluent, moreover, would have been better educated and more interested in the speculative wisdom that

---

7. Conzelmann, 1 *Corinthians,* 204.

8. Gerd Theissen, *The Social Setting of Pauline Christianity: Essays on Corinth,* trans. John H. Schütz (Philadelphia: Fortress Press, 1982).

9. Ibid., 69–110.

Fig. 64. The Archaic Temple and Acrocorinth. Originally built around 700 B.C.E. of buff-colored poros limestone with a heavy tile roof (estimated to weigh more than sixteen tons), this temple was destroyed by fire ca. 570 B.C.E. *(Photo: Koester/Hendrix)*

characterized the Corinthian "enthusiasm." Possession of a higher knowledge would also have fit in with their sense of superiority.

On an intellectual level, Paul sides with "the strong." But his understanding of the Christian message leads him to advocate what Theissen calls a "love-patriarchalism." He does not challenge the social system, but he asks "that the higher classes accommodate their behavior to the lower classes."[10]

Theissen also finds class conflict in the controversy over the Lord's Supper.[11] Of those who arrive early for the meal, Paul asks rhetorically (11:22), "Do you not have houses to eat and drink in?"—suggesting their affluence. It is difficult to know exactly what was going on: wealthy hosts might have provided better meals for their peers (a typical custom), or perhaps *only* the bread and wine for the poor. In any case, Paul brings a theological perspective to the social conflict. He understands the disruptions as part of the eschatological testing of the congregation (11:19), and he views the meal itself in an eschatological context: unworthy participation leads to condemnation at the

10. Ibid., 139.
11. Ibid., 145–68.

judgment. The Corinthians' behavior is unworthy because it denies the unity the meal establishes (10:16-17).

Another aspect of the letter that may reflect conflict between rich and poor is Paul's criticism of some church members for taking others to court (6:1-11). As Alan C. Mitchell shows, the probable situation is that it is rich members who are suing the poorer ones.[12] This interpretation is suggested by Paul's ironical use of the term "wise" in v. 5, which would be most effective against an elite who thought of themselves as possessing wisdom. And it is reinforced by the consideration that ancient standards of honor and shame mitigated against taking one's peers to court, since to do so would imply an inability to deal with one's equals. The likelihood is thus that the rich, with far greater access to the legal system, are resorting to court procedures to settle debts with those beneath them on the social scale.

(3) Status and Gender. Antoinette Clark Wire has painted a rather different picture of Paul's opponents in her attempt to reconstruct their point of view through a study of the rhetoric of 1 Corinthians.[13] She believes that women prophets were among those Paul attacked in this letter. And, drawing upon anthropological studies, she argues that the conflict was rooted in the different ways in which inclusion into the church affected the social standing of Paul on the one hand and these women on the other.

For Paul, an educated male, the decision to enter the Christian fellowship entailed a voluntary loss of status. For the uneducated segment in Corinth, however, that decision brought a gain in status. And that was particularly true for the women. They would have experienced greater freedom within the church than outside it and would have gained a new sense of empowerment.[14]

This difference in experience resulted in different perspectives. Paul stressed humility and emphasized that God inverts the values of the world. Having made his own decision to give up status, Paul also expected those of low status to remain in that condition, precisely because God has chosen to work with the foolish and weak. But to the Corinthian women prophets the new life in Christ meant a destruction of the old boundaries within which they had lived. It brought them wisdom, power, and honor. Thus if Paul thought of them as arrogant persons seeking social advantage, they must have thought of him as denying the social transformation God had brought about. And if Paul

---

12. "Alan C. Mitchell, Rich and Poor in the Courts of Corinth: Litigiousness and Status in 1 Corinthians 6.1-11," *New Testament Studies* 39, no. 4 (1993).

13. Antoinette Clark Wire, *The Corinthian Women Prophets: A Reconstruction through Paul's Rhetoric* (Minneapolis: Fortress Press, 1990).

14. Ibid., 58–71.

thought their claims to wisdom ignored the difference between this life and the next, they must have thought that he was denying the power of the Spirit to work dramatic changes in human beings in the here and now.

Wire rejects the view of many scholars that 14:33b-36, which forbids women to speak in church, is a non-Pauline addition. And she argues that the conflict between Paul and the women is a central aspect of the letter. Comparing 1 Corinthians 12:13 to Galatians 3:27-28, she notes that although in the latter context Paul can proclaim that in Christ "there is no longer Jew or Greek...slave or free...male and female," in the present letter he omits the reference to male and female from the formula. Although in other contexts he can take the more inclusive view, the conflict at Corinth leads him to reinforce a traditional social boundary.[15]

It is not Wire's intention to take sides in the conflict, to endorse either Paul or his opponents. What she does intend, however, is to hear the side of the conversation that did not find its way into the New Testament canon.

3. 2 Corinthians

a. The Story and a Critical Problem

Any attempt to speak of the story behind 2 Corinthians runs into a critical problem: there is widespread agreement that the canonical book is a composite of two or more letters of Paul.[16] Chapters 1–9 presuppose that the Corinthian church has passed through a crisis of some sort. Paul extends forgiveness (2:10), expresses his confidence in the Corinthian Christians (7:16), and looks forward to their contribution to his fund for the Jerusalem church (8:1—9:15). While he addresses some problems, the tone is basically positive. In 10:1, however, the tone changes abruptly. From here on, Paul is highly argumentative, speaking frequently and threateningly of a coming visit, something that is never mentioned in the earlier part.

In addition, 6:14—7:1 seems intrusive in its present context, and its severe attitude toward unbelievers is at least in tension with 1 Corinthians 5:9-10 and 7:12-16. Many scholars believe it is a non-Pauline interpolation.

While scholars have proposed numerous ways of accounting for the apparent breaks in the thought flow, the following reconstruction of the story behind 2 Corinthians assumes that the canonical book combines two letters

---

15. Ibid., 123–28.
16. For extended discussion of this issue, see Victor Paul Furnish, *II Corinthians* (Garden City, N.Y.: Doubleday, 1984), 30–41, whose solution I have followed.

Fig. 65. Head of Serapis, Corinth.*

of Paul and a (probably non-Pauline) fragment.[17] After writing 1 Corinthians, Paul pays a "painful" visit to Corinth (2 Cor. 2:1) to deal with the problems discussed in that letter. Then, with the problems still unresolved, he sends another letter, now lost (which he characterizes in 2 Corinthians 2:4 as severe and written out of anguish). Later, he dispatches Titus to Corinth, and Titus returns with basically good news. The letter has apparently accomplished its purpose, but there are problems that need attention. Some in Corinth are probably hurt and puzzled by Paul's harshness and by his reneging on a promised visit (2 Cor. 1:15—2:11). More seriously, a group claiming apostolic status has arrived in Corinth and is causing concerns about Paul's own authority. From somewhere in Macedonia (2 Cor. 9:1-4), Paul writes back (2 Cor. 1–9) to express his joy over the healing that had taken place but also to lay the problems to rest.

---

*Serapis was the Hellenistic version of Osiris, consort of Isis. The cult of Isis and Serapis was one of the most popular of the mystery cults in Hellenistic times. In time, however, Isis outstripped Serapis in importance and took on characteristics of a universal deity. *(Photo: Koester/Hendrix)*

17. Because there are actually numerous breaks in thought in both 1 and 2 Corinthians, some scholars have proposed complex theories of partition involving both canonical letters. Sometimes 2 Corinthians is split up into four Pauline fragments, in addition to the non-Pauline interpolation. The more complex a theory becomes, however, the more difficult it is to verify. And a majority of scholars remain convinced that 1 Corinthians is a unity.

Later, Paul somehow learns that the rival apostles have been successful in gaining adherents and pose a serious threat to his relationship to the Corinthian church. It is impossible to say whether this is a new development or Paul had been naively optimistic about the earlier situation. In any case, he writes again (2 Cor. 10–13) to defend his authority and discredit his opponents.[18]

Long after the incidents in Corinth, an editor combines Paul's two letters. And, either at this point or a later time, the short passage in 6:14—7:1 is added and becomes a part of the composite writing that is eventually accepted into the canon.

b. Reading 2 Corinthians 1–9

(1) 1:1—5:19. Following the address, Paul offers (instead of his usual thanksgiving) a blessing, in the Jewish liturgical style, of God as comforter. This leads into an interpretation of his recent afflictions as participation in Christ's sufferings. Then, disclosing an apparent brush with death in Asia (Minor), he creates a feeling of solidarity by drawing the Corinthians, in turn, into his own experience: his suffering is for their "consolation and salvation," and by participating in it they also share the comfort God provides. The readers will assume that Paul has suffered precisely for the gospel and will be motivated to pray for God's continuing protection of him and his associates.

Paul begins the body of the letter (1:12) with a reminder of his own conduct among the Corinthians, illustrative of his concern for them, and an explanation of his failure to visit and of his severe letter. Having spared them the pain of a disciplinary visit, he nevertheless wrote harshly because of his love for them. Referring to a specific situation the readers will recognize (2:5)—apparently an offense against Paul by a member of the Corinthian church—he stresses the pain of the community itself rather than his own. As he adds his own forgiveness to that extended by the community, the readers will feel deep satisfaction regarding the reconciling spirit within the community.

In 2:14, Paul turns to the theme of apostleship, stressing the good effects of his missionary work. Disavowing personal credit, he nevertheless contrasts

---

18. It is not absolutely certain that 10–13 were written after, rather than before, 1–9. Since Paul mentions a harsh and "tearful" letter in 2:4 and 7:8, some scholars have identified it with the concluding chapters of 2 Corinthians. This would mean that 10–13 was written prior to 1–9. The problem, however, is that the "tearful" letter concerned a Corinthian Christian who in some way wronged Paul, but this matter is not mentioned in 10–13; and 10–13, on the other hand, is concerned with "false apostles," while there is no indication that this issue came into play in the "tearful" letter. There is evidence, moreover, that 10–13 was written after 1–9. In 8:16-24 Paul says he is sending Titus and two other "brothers" to Corinth, presumably with the letter (1–9). When in 12:18 Paul speaks of a *past* visit by Titus and mentions the "brother" sent with him, it is natural to assume that the same visit is in view. See Furnish, *II Corinthians*, 37–38.

his role to that of others who "peddle" God's word, thus encouraging the readers to question the integrity of those claiming apostleship in Corinth. Through the metaphor of letters of recommendation, common among travelers in the Greco-Roman world, he denies the charge that he has been commending himself: the success of his message among the Corinthians themselves is sufficient attestation of his commission.

Disavowal of personal credit leads to another point: Paul's confidence in his apostolic ministry issues from God and is based upon the new covenant. Using a rabbinic mode of argumentation—reasoning from the lesser to the greater—he shows that the splendor of this new covenant, rooted in the Spirit, must exceed that of the old covenant based merely upon the written law. The reader must supply part of the logic from prior knowledge of Paul's gospel: the written code is associated with death because it does not lead to righteousness (Gal. 2:16; 3:13, 21-24; Rom. 7:7-24; 8:2-4). The new covenant, by contrast, is rooted in the Spirit, which gives freedom, life, and direct access to God (3:18). The contrast leads into a discourse on the story in Exodus 34 of how Moses wore a veil, after coming down from the mountain, to hide the splendor of his face. Paul uses the veil as a metaphor to serve his contrast between the old and new covenants, claiming that it obscured the temporary nature of the old and still causes Jews to misinterpret Scripture. To make the argument work, the reader must assume that the Jewish Scriptures point to Christ.

It is the superior splendor of the new covenant, Paul argues, that gives Paul and his associates boldness (3:12). Turning back explicitly to this point in 4:1, he contrasts his straightforward proclamation of the truth to others' underhanded ways. The Corinthians will know he refers to his opponents.

In 4:7 Paul launches a poetic discourse on the sufferings of himself and his associates. The paradox they must grasp is that Paul's vulnerability, which his opponents may have ridiculed, is an instrument through which God works for the Corinthians' good. If "death" is at work in him, it is only because he shares in Christ's sufferings and only so that "life" might be at work in the readers (4:12). In the end, he can view his afflictions as "momentary," aware that the whole present existence is temporary and that the world rushes on toward the final judgment (5:10). Understanding that Paul has suffered for them, the readers will now view the arrogant claims of his opponents in a more negative light; and they will be reminded of the life-through-death paradox that lies at the heart of the gospel message.

In 5:11-19, Paul brings his discussion of his apostolic ministry full circle. Far from indulging in self-commendation, he says, he has laid bare the nature of his work so that the readers can refute those who boast of externals. The readers will probably think of the ecstatic gifts Paul discussed in 1 Corinthians. They will contrast his ministry with that of his opponents and will feel "enlisted" in his cause against them. As they read on, they will find the entire argument rounded out in the assertion of the radical effect of Christ's death in vv. 16-19. Paul's readers will thus feel reestablished in the central tenets of the Christian message: those who participate in Christ become part of God's new creation; through Christ, God has reconciled the world to God's own self and created the ministry of reconciliation.

(2) 5:20—6:11; 7:2—9:15 (deleting 6:14—7:1). The reader will understand by this point that Paul's ministry needs no external validation; the word of reconciliation, grounded in the cross, is attested by Paul's willingness to suffer on their behalf and by its effects among the Corinthians themselves. In 5:20 Paul begins to appeal to the Corinthians to act upon this knowledge. Extending the theme of reconciliation, he now calls upon the Corinthians to be reconciled to God so that their original acceptance of grace might not be in vain. Buttressing his appeal with a renewed statement of his own sufferings on their behalf, Paul then pleads for acceptance of his own ministry (6:11-12; 7:2-3). The readers must conclude that a turn away from Paul's ministry would be a turn away from God's grace and that reconciliation to God is entwined with recognition of Paul's apostolic mission.

Paul's expression of pride and confidence in the Corinthians (7:4), followed by his conciliatory rehearsal of the events surrounding his earlier harsh letter (7:5-16) will encourage the readers to accept the reconciliation he offers. Commended for their repentance and reminded of Titus's good report of them, they will feel fully accepted by Paul and motivated to complete the restoration of good relations. At this point (8:1—9:15), Paul makes an extended appeal to the Corinthians to complete the offering for the Jerusalem church, closing it with an exclamation of thanks to God.

(Critical note: The original letter probably contained a closing that was deleted when it was joined with chaps. 10–13. It is possible, of course, that the closing was already lost, which would have provided motivation for combining it with other material.)

c. Reading 2 Corinthians 10–13

(Critical note: The editor who dispensed with the ending of 1–9 presumably deleted the opening of 10–13 also. In 10:1 we find ourselves in the body of the letter.)

Paul begins with an appeal to the Corinthians not to force him to make his

Fig. 66. Mosiac in the Demeter Sanctuary at Corinth. According to the cult legend, Demeter, the "Mother of Grain," searched the underworld for her daughter Kore (Persephone), who had been abducted by Hades (Pluto). Because in Demeter's absence the grain was unable to grow, Zeus decreed that Kore should spend one-third of the year in the underworld and the rest with her mother. *(Photo: Koester/Hendrix)*

upcoming visit unpleasant. They will understand his sarcasm in the opening verse: as he will shortly make explicit (10:10), his opponents have accused him of ineffectiveness when he is present and boldness only when he is writing letters. Paul assures the readers that he is capable of severe disciplinary action in dealing with disobedience on crucial matters. Then, in 10:7, he turns directly on his opponents with an argument touched with irony: apologizing for his own boasting, he exposes the opponents as the true boasters (13-17); and declining to compare himself to those who commend themselves (10:12), he exposes the absurdity of self-commendation (10:18).

The irony continues as, in 11:1, Paul asks his readers to indulge him in some "foolishness," which turns out to be extended boasting and self-commendation—such as he has just criticized in his opponents. Comparing his care for the congregation to the care for a betrothed daughter by her father (who is responsible for her virginity), Paul worries that they will be led astray. The readers will know, of course, that it is Paul's opponents who correspond to the serpent who deceived Eve. Having thus characterized the rivals as deceivers, he can now compare himself to them. Even if he cannot match their rhetorical skill, he is not inferior to them in knowledge (11:6). And even if he did not demand his right to free keep—as the opponents apparently did (11:20)!—this does not mean he did not have that right as an apostle. Apologizing for his foolishness all the while, he draws a sharp contrast between himself and the opponents, whom he now openly terms "false apostles" and agents of Satan (11:12-14). While he acted out of love for the Corinthians, these others have degraded and exploited them.

Heightening his "boasting" in 11:21, Paul runs through a checklist of credentials, matching the opponents point by point and then turning to the one category on which they presumably could not compete at all—his sufferings for Christ. Then in 12:1-4 the boasting reaches its crescendo as Paul speaks of a revelatory experience in which he was "caught up into Paradise."

Having indulged in self-commendation, Paul has put himself in a precarious position. By explicitly labeling his speech as "foolish," however, he distinguishes his blatant "boasting" from actual self-glorification. He speaks foolishly only because there is no avenue left open to him (12:11). How, after all, does one answer the challenges of the arrogant? Paul's apparent answer is "with an ironical counterarrogance!" Paul the recipient of numerous revelations is nonetheless subject to an unnamed physical infirmity (12:7-10); and Paul who performed signs and mighty works in Corinth, by no means inferior to the "super-apostles," is in himself "nothing"!

In 12:14 Paul returns to the theme of his coming visit. Assuring the readers of his concern, he also reiterates some of his earlier points regarding his own behavior. But he moves quickly back to the visit in 12:20, expressing concern over what he will find upon his arrival. Then in 13:1 he turns to explicit warnings and exhortations. After a final appeal to the Corinthians to mend their ways (13:11), Paul closes the letter with brief greetings and a benediction.

What will the readers make of Paul's arguments? Ultimately, the truth or falsity of Paul's claims hinges upon the effects of his mission upon the Corinthians' lives. But how does one call upon this evidence without self-glorification? Paul's strategy has been to dismantle his opponents' seeming advantage by giving the readers a complex task. Vacillating between straightforward speech on the one hand and irony, paradox, and sarcasm on the other, he constantly pushes the readers to look beneath the surface and beyond appearances. What the readers must do as they follow the argument is to see past mere claims and rhetoric, and even beyond such flashy credentials as ecstatic experience, to their own human experience and to the character of the one who originally brought them into Christ.

d. The Problem of 6:14—7:1[19]

While all commentators admit that 6:14—7:1 interrupts the thought flow between 6:13 and 7:2, many treat it as a simple digression: in the midst of a conciliatory appeal to the Corinthians to open their hearts, Paul pauses to add a cautionary note about relations with unbelievers. An alternative view is that the passage is a fragment of another letter of Paul, perhaps the one mentioned in 1 Corinthians 5:9-11. Since the vocabulary is somewhat uncharacteristic of Paul, however, some scholars contend that Paul is quoting material he did not write. And, for others, the severe attitude toward unbelievers seems so incompatible with Paul's views in 1 Corinthians that they think it was added by someone other than Paul himself.

The passage is in any case Christian (v. 15), although it has some striking affinities with the Qumran literature. It seems to counsel a rather rigid separation from non-Christians on the grounds that the unbelieving world is inherently unclean.

e. Paul's Opponents in 2 Corinthians

Many scholars have assumed that in 2 Corinthians Paul is combatting the same opponents he disputed in 1 Corinthians. The issues seem quite different in 2 Corinthians, however, and recent commentators have tended to see them as a group that arrived on the scene after 1 Corinthians was written. Although they were Jewish Christians of some sort (2 Cor. 11:22-23), they do not appear to have advocated circumcision as did the group in Galatia. Nor is there any direct evidence of a gnostic orientation. One influential theory is that they were Hellenistic Jewish Christians, deeply influenced by the "divine man" tradition, who claimed that their ecstatic experiences and wonder-working abilities attested their possession of the same divine power that worked through Moses and Jesus.[20] Any specific solution, however, is speculative; but it is clear that they claimed charismatic gifts and apostolic status.

STUDY QUESTIONS

1. Reconstruct the "story" behind 1 Corinthians.

2. What issues are at stake between Paul and his opponents in 1 Corinthians?

---

19. For a full discussion, see Furnish, *II Corinthians,* 371–83.
20. Deiter Georgi, *The Opponents of Paul in Second Corinthians* (Philadelphia: Fortress Press, 1986).

3. Summarize Paul's views, as expressed in 1 Corinthians, on sex, marriage and divorce, eating meat offered to idols, and participation in "pagan" worship.

4. Characterize Paul's understanding of the nature of Christian community as expressed in 1 Corinthians 12.

5. What is Paul's understanding of spiritual "gifts" in 1 Corinthians 13-14?

6. What does 1 Corinthians 15 reveal about Paul's eschatological views?

7. In his sociological analysis of 1 Corinthians, what use does Theissen make of the categories of "the strong" and "the weak"?

8. According to Wire, how did the discrepancy in status between Paul and the women prophets in Corinth result in different perspectives regarding claims to wisdom?

9. Why do many scholars think 2 Corinthians is composed of two or more separate letters?

10. What is problematic about 2 Corinthians 6:14—7:1, and what are the different views about its origin?

11. Reconstruct the "story" behind 2 Corinthians.

12. What part does the story of the veil of Moses play in Paul's argument in 2 Corinthians?

13. How does Paul meet the challenge regarding letters of recommendation in 2 Corinthians?

14. According to Paul, what is the meaning of the sufferings he endures?

15. What strategy does Paul adopt in making his argument in 2 Corinthians 10-13? Give your own evaluation of the advantages and disadvantages of such a strategy.

16. Why do many scholars think Paul is arguing against a different set of opponents in 2 Corinthians than he is in 1 Corinthians?

FOR FURTHER READING

Barrett, C. K. *A Commentary on the First Epistle to the Corinthians*. New York: Harper & Row, 1968. Competent and readable.

———. *A Commentary on the Second Epistle to the Corinthians*. New York: Harper & Row, 1973. Competent and readable.

Conzelmann, Hans. *1 Corinthians: A Commentary on the First Epistle of Paul to the Corinthians*. Hermeneia. Trans. James W. Leitch. Philadelphia: Fortress Press, 1975. Thorough, technical treatment.

Furnish, Victor Paul, *II Corinthians*. Garden City, N.Y.: Doubleday, 1984. Detailed and technical, but readable, with helpful summary sections; an important contribution.

Georgi, Dieter. *The Opponents of Paul in Second Corinthians.* Philadelphia: Fortress Press, 1986. Identifies opponents as Hellenistic Jewish Christians influenced by the "divine man" tradition.

Wire, Antoinette Clark. *The Corinthian Women Prophets: A Reconstruction through Paul's Rhetoric.* Minneapolis: Fortress Press, 1990. A reconstruction of the theology of some of Paul's opponents. A demanding and complex treatment of an important issue.

Chapter 11

Romans

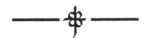

1. The Story and Some Problems

The basic story behind the Letter to the Romans is easy enough to reconstruct from Romans 15:14-29. Convinced that he has completed his mission on the eastern end of the Mediterranean, Paul decides to extend his work to the west after delivering the collection for the Jerusalem church. He writes to the Christians in Rome to inform them that he will stop for a visit on his way from Jerusalem to Spain.

It is more difficult to say why Paul wrote the particular letter he did. Some interpreters think the content has little to do with the specific situation in the Roman church; Paul wrote this letter as a kind of summary of his message, perhaps in order to introduce himself to this important congregation that he did not found. One scholar calls it his "last will and testament," and another suggests that it was actually a "round letter," sent to more than one church. Others, however, maintain that Paul's attention to the themes of the law, circumcision, and God's relation to Israel show that he was addressing a church in which relations between Jewish and Gentile Christians were problematic.[1]

Opinions on the motivation behind Romans remain divided, but the general character of the letter seems clear enough. However much Paul may have been responding to a specific situation, he did in fact bring together a number of themes that had been central to his thinking as he carried out his missionary and pastoral work. Romans is, nevertheless, a letter and not a theological

---

1. See Karl P. Donfried, ed., *The Romans Debate*, rev. and expanded ed. (Peabody, Mass.: Hendrickson, 1991) for articles outlining the various positions; also Brevard Childs, *The New Testament as Canon: An Introduction* (Philadelphia: Fortress Press, 1984), 247–49.

treatise. Although it responds to questions Paul had faced throughout his ministry, it is not a summary of Christian doctrine; and 15:15 shows that Paul expected some of his statements to provoke controversy.

The question of the purpose of the letter overlaps with the problem of chapter 16, which many scholars have argued was not part of the original. Their case rests in part upon the fact that 15:33 sounds very much like a conclusion. But the content of chapter 16 also raises some questions; for here Paul greets numerous persons, and one may wonder how he would have known so many people in a church he had not yet visited. There is also some ambiguous manuscript evidence that has been cited in support of this view.[2]

Not surprisingly, a number of theories have developed regarding chapter 16. One view is that this material once constituted a completely separate letter of recommendation on behalf of Paul's co-worker Phoebe (16:1). Another theory is that Paul wrote Romans as a "round letter," intended for more than one church, and that 16 was included in a version sent to the church at Ephesus, with which many of the persons mentioned in this chapter were in fact associated. If this hypothesis is accepted, it lends force to the interpretation of Romans as more of a programmatic statement than a response to a situation in a specific church.

There is no real consensus on the problem, but the trend among recent interpreters seems to be toward acceptance of chapter 16 as part of the original letter sent to Rome. Although the arguments for an original fifteen-chapter letter are impressive, they are far from conclusive. The manuscript evidence is in fact ambiguous, and many scholars maintain that chapter 16 makes sense as an ending to Romans if the persons mentioned there are Jewish Christians who left Rome during a period when Jews were persecuted but subsequently returned.[3]

It is very likely, however, that the doxology in 16:25-27 is a later non-Pauline addition. Not only does it occur at various points in different early manuscripts (after 14:23, as well as 15:33 and 16:23); it is also unlike any of Paul's other closings.

---

2. The twentieth-century discovery of a manuscript of Romans, older than any formerly known, places the doxology, normally found at the end of chapter 16, between the end of chapter 15 and the beginning of 16. Scholars have sometimes asked, therefore, whether this manuscript might "possibly bear witness to a text tradition in which Romans consisted only of 1:1—15:33, followed by a doxology, to which the rest of chap. 16 was extrinsically added" (Joseph A. Fitzmyer, *Romans: A New Translation with Introduction and Commentary* [New York: Doubleday, 1993], 50).

3. See Donfried, "A Short Note on Romans 16" and "False Presuppositions in the Study of Romans" in Donfried, ed., *The Romans Debate,* for a defense of chapter 16 as original to the letter. See Willi Marxsen, *Introduction to the New Testament: A Concise and Up-to-date Guide to the New Testament Literature and Its Historical Setting,* trans. G. Buswell (Philadelphia: Fortress Press, 1968), 95–104, for the theory that Jewish Christians have recently returned to Rome.

Fig. 67. The Arch of Titus at Rome, erected to honor Titus's victory over the Judeans at Jerusalem in 70 C.E. *(Photo by Thomas Hoffman)*

Fig. 68. Detail from the arch depicting the triumphal march of Titus in which Judean captives can be seen carrying the seven-branched candlestick from the Temple, along with other trophies. *(Photo by Thomas Hoffman)*

2. Reading Romans

a. 1:1—3:20

Through an elaborate address and greeting, Paul introduces the readers to his understanding of the content of the gospel and of his ministry. As apostle to the Gentiles, he preaches the resurrection of God's son in order to bring about "the obedience of faith." In the thanksgiving (1:8-15), Paul defines his coming visit in terms of mutual encouragement in the faith but goes on to state his intention of "preaching the gospel" in the congregation. The Roman Christians are thus encouraged to make balanced judgments: Paul is someone with special authority who will carry on a ministry among them, but he will not try to "lord it over" them; his gospel is the Christian message pure and simple, yet he does have something distinctive to say.

The capsule definition of the gospel in 1:16-17 signals the readers that Paul will now give an extended exposition of it. That it brings salvation for Jews first and then Greeks means it is based upon God's promises to Israel but is ultimately for all humankind. In hearing that it concerns God's righteousness, the readers familiar with the Jewish Scriptures will understand that it somehow demonstrates God's faithfulness to the covenant promises and activity as a just judge. Hearing also that this righteousness of God is intimately related to faith, they will read on for further explanation.

Paul's first point, by way of explanation, is that God's wrath is revealed from heaven against all forms of ungodliness (1:18). Associating wrath with eschatological judgment on the basis of the Jewish Scriptures, the readers will understand that God is presently exercising such judgment. Hearing Paul's argument that human beings are responsible for the wickedness they do, since certain aspects of God's being are evident in creation itself, the readers will also realize that Paul is speaking of Gentiles, who do not have the advantage of God's law. This point becomes clearer as Paul illustrates human corruption through the examples of idolatry and homosexual acts. The readers will know that the Torah condemns both, and they will associate the latter with the exploitative relations between men and boys that were common in the Hellenistic world (see below, pp. 407–10).

Having thus documented both the sin and the responsibility of the Gentiles, Paul interprets the corrupt human condition itself as God's judgment. God manifests wrath precisely in abandoning people to their own perverse ways. Their punishment for failing to acknowledge their Creator is that they must live without God.

Pointedly, in 2:1 Paul shifts his argument. To any who feel comfortable in condemning the Gentiles for their idolatry, he poses a series of rhetorical questions implying such persons' own guilt. Declaring these also subject to God's wrath, Paul then states that as those sinning apart from the law perish, so those sinning under the law are judged by it (2:12). It thus becomes clear to the reader that he is now speaking of Jews: the implication is that even though they received God's law they did not obey it and are thus found guilty. At this point Paul's logic leads him back to the Gentiles, and he makes explicit what he had earlier implied: although they do not have the Torah, they do have a law "written on their hearts" (2:15) and are therefore accountable for their sin. Quickly (2:17), however, Paul turns back to his main point, this time addressing the Jews directly. Following another series of rhetorical questions, he contrasts physical circumcision to an inward disposition (2:25-29).

Having disparaged circumcision and charged Jews with unfaithfulness to the law, Paul now raises a question with himself. What about his earlier endorsement of the priority of Jews in God's plan of salvation? Resoundingly, he insists that this priority is real (3:2) and argues that human failure in no way nullifies God's faithfulness. What the readers should understand is that God, having made promises to Israel, cannot go back on them; on the other hand, if Israel itself rejects God, then God must exercise justice. Paradoxically, then, Israel's unfaithfulness becomes the occasion for the manifestation of God's wrath. To say this, however, raises another question: can God rightly hold Jews responsible for their sin, if that sin results in God's own glory? Paul answers by insisting that God's condemnation is just—deserved by those who receive it (3:8).

When in 3:9 Paul asks, "Are we any better off?" (i.e., are Jews any better off than Gentiles), he brings his readers back to the question of Jewish "advantage" (3:1). When he answers in the negative, they must conclude that although the advantage is in one sense real, it does not affect salvation. For, as Paul demonstrates through Scripture, all human beings, Jew and Gentile alike, are actually held under "the power of sin" (3:10-20).

The long argument of chapters 1–3 thus concludes with an unequivocal declaration of the universality of sin. The readers should understand that all humanity stands condemned and that not even God's law is capable of justifying human beings.

b. 3:21—8:39

With the phrase "but now," Paul signals a turning point in his argument. Having demonstrated the impossibility of a righteousness based upon the law, he now announces the righteousness of God, based upon faith, which is manifest in God's putting forth Jesus Christ "as a sacrifice of atonement" (3:21-26). To understand how this action demonstrates God's righteousness, the reader must make two assumptions: first, that a just God cannot simply overlook sin; second, that God in the past has not passed judgment against sin but has shown "forbearance" toward it. Paul's point is that now, through the death of Jesus Christ, God has acted justly by providing a way of judging the sinner, a way, however, that leads not to condemnation but to justification. That is to say, God's own righteous action in Christ results in the restoration of a right relationship between human beings and God.

The readers should now understand more clearly the point made in 1:17, namely, that human righteousness before God comes through faith. And, as in 1:17, they will connect the righteousness of God to divine faithfulness to the covenant with Israel. In declaring that human beings stand justified before God through faith in Christ, Paul implicitly declares those promises fulfilled, but in a way that includes all humankind. His notion of the "righteousness of God" will thus have many nuances for the reader. It is God's just judgment and faithfulness to the covenant (and all creation). It is also the human righteousness, appropriated by faith, that God brings about through Christ. And, since Paul can speak of the gospel as "the power of God for salvation" (1:16), the righteousness of God revealed in that gospel is in some sense also the *power* through which God brings human righteousness about.[4]

Paul's next point (3:27-31) is that if human beings are justified by faith, no one has grounds for boasting. Anticipating the reader's conclusion that the law is thus overturned, he insists that his teaching actually upholds the law. For evidence he turns to the Torah, arguing that Abraham himself was justified not by works of the law but by faith (4:1-25). God accounted him righteous, because of his trust, even before his circumcision. Abraham therefore became the ancestor not of Israel alone (the circumcised) but of all humankind, since all would eventually be justified by faith. For, Paul argues, from the beginning God intended the promise to Abraham to reach beyond Israel. That is why justification/righteousness could not be based upon the law. The readers will thus understand that they are included in Paul's declaration in 4:22-25 that those who believe in the one who raised Jesus from the dead will also be justified.

"Therefore, since we are justified by faith"—Paul thus signals the reader in 5:1 that he has made his point and can build upon it. Noting that justification creates peace between humanity and God, he goes on to pile up terms ex-

---

4. See the Appendix by Manfred T. Brauch, "Perspectives on 'God's Righteousness' in Recent German Discussion," in E. P. Sanders, *Paul and Palestinian Judaism* (Philadelphia: Fortress Press, 1977), for a summary of some of the views on this difficult but rich concept.

pressing the consequences of God's act in Christ: it provides access to *grace* and a basis for *hope* (5:2-5); and it demonstrates God's love, effecting *reconciliation* of humanity with God and signalling eventual *salvation* (5:6-11). Then, presenting Christ as the antitype of Adam, Paul contrasts the condemnation resulting from Adam's sin to the *grace, righteousness*, and *eternal life* issuing from Christ's obedience (5:12-19).

Declaring that when the law came in to increase sin, grace abounded all the more (5:20-21), Paul then pulls up short and raises the logical question: Should one then revel in sin to increase grace (6:1)? He answers by interpreting Christian baptism as an act of dying and rising with Christ, an incorporation into Christ that frees the believer from sin and opens up a new mode of existence. The "death" one dies in the rite is precisely a death to sin. The readers' task at this point is less one of logic than of penetration into the meaning of baptism. Those "in" Christ know what newness of life is all about: nothing more is needed to support the exhortation, "do not let sin exercise dominion in your mortal bodies." (6:12). The problem of misunderstanding is serious enough, however, that Paul restates his point with another set of metaphors (slavery to sin, slavery to God) and another term expressive of the new life: "sanctification," being "set apart" by God for a holy purpose (6:15-23).

In 7:1 Paul's rhetorical question brings the readers back to the law. Employing the metaphor of a woman's release from marriage through her husband's death and reiterating the point in terms of dying and rising with Christ, he declares the Christian's freedom.

Because his argument links the law with sin and death, however, Paul must now anticipate the readers' questions: is the law itself sinful, and does it bring death? Answering negatively in both cases, he gives a complex explanation. Sin uses the law to deceive human beings into thinking they can find salvation by obeying it. Because humanity itself is enslaved by the power of sin (7:14), the attempt to do good results in evil (7:21-23). The reader must thus conclude that obedience to the law is an absolute dead end. The law does, however, expose sin for what it is (7:13), and it thereby opens the way for an alternative solution to humanity's despair. Paul thus brings his readers to a crucial point in 7:21-25, implicitly inviting them to share both his cry of despair and his exclamation of praise.

The readers can already conclude that Christ provides what the law could not: deliverance from sin and death. But Paul states the point explicitly in 8:1 and then elaborates on it in a lilting, passionate declaration of the nature of Christian existence. Life in Christ is lived "according to the Spirit," not "according to the flesh"; as such it *is* "life and peace" (8:6)—that is, *authentic* human existence, the life of those who have become the children of God.

The readers will understand that people must be "adopted" as God's children because the world apart from Christ is in bondage to sin. And they will understand that for that reason the process of adoption remains incomplete in the present. But they will also hear Paul proclaiming a hope of deliverance that far outweighs the suffering they must endure (8:18, 31-39). They will hear him declaring that, although the Christian "victory" over the world is a paradoxical one, since suffering remains, it is the most profound victory imaginable. For Christians experience the one reality that makes real life possible: "the love of God in Christ Jesus our Lord" (8:39).

c. 9:1—11:36

When Paul expresses his anguish for his fellow Jews in 9:1-5, the readers will understand that he is wrestling with the implications of the Jewish rejection of Jesus. From 9:6-7 they can detect that he is also concerned about whether this rejection has nullified God's promise to Israel. To demonstrate that it has not, Paul uses biblical stories to distinguish between physical descent from Abraham and reception of the promise God gave Abraham. What the readers should conclude is that the rejection of Jesus by some Jews does not nullify the promise, since other Jews, along with Gentiles, receive that promise through faith in Christ.

Because Paul believes that justification issues from God's mercy and is not a reward for human action (9:16-17), he can stress that those who receive the promise do so by God's *election* (9:11). To say this, however, is to raise the question of justice: if God elects those who will respond and those who will not, then how can God pass judgment (9:14, 19)? On one level, Paul's answer is a simple assertion of the sovereignty of God; it is God's prerogative to choose the recipients of mercy and of wrath. If the readers focus on the negative side of election, this answer may appear grossly inadequate. Paul's emphasis, however, is on the positive side. God's seemingly negative acts— the rejection of Esau and the hardening of Pharaoh's heart—are not ends in themselves but serve to show forth God's mercy. Hearing in 9:30 that Gentiles have found righteousness through faith, the readers should conclude that all God's actions somehow play into the purpose of offering salvation as a free gift to everyone.

The readers' attention, however, is directed not to Gentiles who found righteousness but to Jews who did not. Although expressing a desire for their salvation (10:1), Paul charges them with treating the law as a matter of works rather than faith (9:32) and contrasts their approach with the righteousness of God, based on confession of Jesus, that embraces both Jews and Gentiles

(10:3-13). Arguing then that the confession of Jesus depends upon the Christian mission, Paul quotes a series of biblical passages that the reader must apply to the case at hand (10:18-21): as God's word goes out to all the world, disobedient Israel becomes jealous.

With the question posed in 11:1—Has God rejected Israel?—the readers will sense that Paul is bringing the discussion of the Jewish people to a head. And in the ensuing verses they will hear an emphatic rejection of this suggestion. To begin with, Paul argues, there is already a "remnant" (11:5), a small number of Jews who believe. But that is not all. Reasoning in rabbinic fashion from the lesser to the greater, he states that if Israel's trespass brings salvation to the Gentiles, the eventual *inclusion* of the whole Jewish people will have to mean something even greater! For the first time, the readers pick up a hint that Israel as a whole might in fact turn to Christ.

In 11:13 Paul speaks specifically to Gentiles, undercutting any basis for gloating or pride with his metaphor of a wild shoot grafted onto a tree. Not only have Gentiles been incorporated into someone else's community, but they are subject to being "broken off" as were some Jews. The argument reaches a climax in the explicit declaration that "all Israel will be saved" (11:26), and Paul summarizes the whole discussion in the statement that God has "imprisoned all in disobedience" only in order to "be merciful to all." The readers, sensing the depth of Paul's feeling, will grasp the appropriateness of the thanksgiving and doxology that conclude the argument (11:33-36). God has not only kept the promises to Israel but has shown mercy to all humanity!

d. 12:1—15:33

The phraseology of 12:1 ("I appeal to you therefore") combines with the "Amen" in 11:36 to mark the transition from the body of the letter to exhortations. It also coaches the readers to understand these exhortations as intimately related to what has gone before. The worship they should render is based upon the "mercies of God" Paul has just recounted. And the call for a renewal of their minds in contrast to conformity to the world is based upon the notion that through Christ God has set the world free from sin and death: the ethic Paul urges is that of the new age. In humility, all are to fulfill their functions within the body of Christ, as they are assigned by the Spirit; and their decisions should be grounded in a self-giving love that ministers to the enemy, seeks harmony within the community, and fully accepts the lowly.

Paul's injunctions on being subject to governing authorities (13:1-7) encourage the readers to accept the secular government as instituted by God. The readers will conclude that a "quietistic," nonconfrontational relationship to the political order is appropriate, and they will understand that this is so in part because of the nearness of the end (13:11-14). Coming on the wake of the broader exhortation not to conform to worldly standards, however, the assertion of rulers' authority presupposes the exercise of conscience (13:5), discernment of the good (13:3), and recognition of *God's* authority behind that of the ruler. And Paul's statement in 13:8-10 puts all the preceding injunctions in context: the one absolute requirement for Christians is the unqualified demand to love one's neighbor as oneself.

That Paul presents the love command as the fulfillment of the law (13:8, 10) will remind the readers that the gospel is rooted in God's promises to Israel. Although the law in the formal sense does not remain for Christians and must never be understood as the instrument of salvation, it does express God's will. The readers will thus understand that Christians owe God obedience, but they will link this obedience to *faith and love*. Far from an attempt at self-salvation, love is an act that fulfills one's trust that, through Christ, God has made salvation available as a free, unmerited gift.

Coming to chapter 14 with these thoughts in mind, the readers will be prepared to grasp several points. Observance of the Sabbath or of dietary constraints cannot bring about salvation and cannot be made mandatory for Christians; to that extent Paul sides against those he calls "the weak." Those who are by implication "strong," however, must remember that love is the ultimate rule of the Christian life. They should make sacrifices to avoid causing others to stumble and should recognize that the practices of "the weak" are done out of devotion. But since the attitudes of "the strong" are rooted in similar devotion, the weak should honor their decisions also. As a broad rule, then, Paul proposes the exercise of individual conscience (14:5). The net result of the discussion is that Christians who make differing decisions on these matters are encouraged to live harmoniously with one another. And Paul concludes his argument by making just that point in 15:5-13.

The benedictory statement in 15:13 suggests to the readers that Paul has concluded his exhortations and is turning to other matters. That impression is borne out in 15:14 as he as expresses his general satisfaction with the Roman church and then explains his remarks in terms of his apostolic ministry (15:15-21). If the readers retain suspicion regarding his teachings, they are implicitly asked to consider them in light of Paul's special calling.

Paul's delineation of his mission leads into an announcement of his ensuing visit, which he places in the context of his projected journeys to Jerusalem and Rome. His final appeal (15:30-33), therefore, serves to draw the readers into his ongoing ministry. The one who will visit them is one in whose ministry they share; they can therefore look forward to his visit as a time of mutual refreshment and joy.

e. 16:1-23

By commending Phoebe to the readers (16:1-2), Paul encourages them to accept her as a co-worker in their mission. The greetings and commendations in 16:3-15 reaffirm his ties to the individuals mentioned and should strengthen the readers' resolve to continue in their work. These verses will also create a sense of solidarity, both between the congregation and Paul and within the Christian fellowship generally, which will make the exhortations in 16:17-20 seem appropriate. With final greetings, including a note from the scribe, Paul concludes the letter (16:21-23).

f. 16:25-27 (a doxology, probably added by another hand)

In its setting at the end of chapter 16, the doxology provides a conclusion to the whole letter as it now stands.

STUDY QUESTIONS

1. Reconstruct the "story" behind Romans. On what points do scholars disagree in the reconstruction of this story?

2. Why do many scholars think that chapter 16, although written by Paul, might not have been part of his original letter to Rome? What are the arguments in defense of chapter 16 as part of the original?

3. According to Romans 1–8, how are human beings enabled to stand justified before God? What are the steps in his argument on this matter? What specific role is played by his statement in 2:15 that the demands of the law are written on Gentiles' hearts?

4. What does Paul seem to mean by the phrase "righteousness of God"?

5. What does Christian baptism mean for Paul, and what specific role does his discussion of it in chapter 6 play in his argument?

6. How does Paul answer, in Romans 7, the hypothetical charge that because the law increases sin it is itself sinful?

7. According to Romans 1–8, what are the specific characteristics of the Christian life?

8. According to Romans 9–11, what role does Israel play in God's plan for salvation? Explain why you do or do not find Paul's argument logical and/or meaningful at this point.

9. What is the specific meaning of Paul's metaphor of the body in Romans 12?

10. What advice does Paul give Christians in terms of their relationship to the Roman Empire?

FOR FURTHER READING

Barrett, C. K. *A Commentary on the Epistle to the Romans.* New York: Harper & Row, 1957. A strong, helpful work; scholarly, but readable and reasonably brief.

Cranfield, C. E. B. *Romans: A Shorter Commentary.* Grand Rapids: Eerdmans, 1985. A condensation of a major technical commentary; very helpful.

Donfried, Karl P., ed. *The Romans Debate.* Rev. and expanded ed. Peabody, Mass.: Hendrickson, 1991. A collection of articles taking different positions on the nature and purpose of Romans.

Dunn, James D. G. *Romans 1–8* and *Romans 9–16.* Dallas: Word Books, 1988. An exhaustive work, including both technical and more accessible portions; an important contribution.

Fitzmyer, Joseph A. *Romans: A New Translation with Introduction and Commentary.* New York: Doubleday, 1993. A detailed, highly competent treatment; an important contribution.

Heil, John Paul. *Paul's Letter to the Romans: A Reader-Response Commentary.* Mahwah, N.J.: Paulist, 1992. Stresses Paul's use of rhetoric to persuade his audience.

Käsemann, Ernst. *Commentary on Romans.* Trans. Geoffrey W. Bromiley. Grand Rapids: Eerdmans, 1980. Complex and technical, requiring Greek; a major work; already a classic.

Chapter 12

Perspectives on Paul

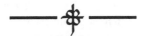

With the seven undisputed letters of Paul now in view, it is meaningful to ask some questions about his thought as a whole. In this chapter I will first (section 1) make some observations about key elements in Paul's theology and then (sections 2-4) examine his views from the perspectives of three distinctively modern or postmodern methodologies. Section 5 will review some recent attempts to relate Paul's writings to moral issues in our own contemporary world.

1. Cornerstones of Paul's Theology

Scholars in recent years have become increasingly skeptical about approaches to Paul's writings that try to find in them a comprehensive, self-consistent system of thought. Because the letters are writings produced for specific occasions with limited purposes in mind, interpreters should not treat them as chapters in a systematic theology. Paul was, nevertheless, a theological thinker, and there are concepts and lines of logic that appear frequently in his letters. It thus seems both legitimate and important, after examining each letter in its specificity, to try to identify the central components of the broad understanding of the Christian faith that seems to have emerged through the course of his ministry.

a. Searching for a Center

(1) The "Juridical" Perspective. Ever since Martin Luther, whose reading of Paul's letters was a major factor in the Protestant Reformation, Protestant scholars have generally identified "justification by faith" as the center of Paul's theological thought. From this perspective, the primary question in Paul's mind was how human beings could stand "justified" before God. And his answer was that justification came not through works of the law but through God's grace, which is appropriated by faith. Roman Catholic interpreters, however, have generally opposed the notion that justification is Paul's central concept, understanding it as "one of the many metaphors describing the new Christian existence." They have also insisted that Paul's understanding of God's grace does not rule out human cooperation with that grace in the process of salvation.[1]

Part of the difficulty in interpreting Paul is that the Greek term *dikaiosynē* can be translated either as "righteousness" or as "justification." It is thus unclear whether, when Paul speaks of "*dikaiosynē* by faith," he means that the believer somehow actually *becomes* "righteous" in the moral sense or simply that the believer is acquitted, given a new standing before God. Catholic interpreters have tended toward the former view, and Protestants toward the latter, which is often termed the "juridical" interpretation.[2] According to the juridical reading, *dikaiosynē* is not a moral category at all, but simply signifies a legal status: to be justified is to be acquitted before God, solely on the basis of God's act in Christ, rather than one's own merit.

(2) The "Participationist" Perspective. In recent decades, Catholics and Protestants have come much closer in their readings of Paul.[3] A major challenge to the dominant Protestant interpretation came early in this century from Albert Schweitzer, himself a Protestant, in a book entitled *The Mysticism of Paul the Apostle.*[4] Focusing on passages expressing the believers' existence "in Christ" or in the "body of Christ" and the indwelling of Christ or the Spirit in believers, Schweitzer argued that these "mystical" passages, rather than Paul's statements regarding justification, constitute the true center of his thought. The theme of justification comes into play only when Paul is addressing the controversy regarding the Jewish law, whereas the "mystical" theme appears in connection with other central Pauline motifs such as the Spirit, resurrection, and ethics.

---

1. Joseph Plevnik, *What Are They Saying about Paul?* (New York: Paulist, 1986), 57.

2. Ibid., 55–57.

3. See, e.g., Joseph A. Fitzmyer, "The Biblical Basis of Justification by Faith: Comments on the Essay of Professor Reumann," in John Reumann, *Righteousness in the New Testament: With Responses by Joseph A. Fitzmyer and Jerome D. Quinn* (Philadelphia: Fortress Press, 1982), 208.

4. Albert Schweitzer, *The Mysticism of Paul the Apostle,* trans. William Montgomery (New York: Macmillan Company, 1956). Originally published in 1931.

Pauline interpretation has always had a problem with the relationship between justification and ethics, or between faith and works. Many commentators have pointed out that for Paul the "indicative" precedes and grounds the "imperative." That is to say, the proclamation that sinners are justified through Christ's sacrifice (the indicative), provides the basis for the ethical imperative: *because* sinners are already accepted by God, they can now be addressed with an ethical demand.

One may still ask, though, just how the ethical demand follows from the fact of justification. According to Schweitzer, there is actually no connection between the two. For Paul derives ethics not from justification but from incorporation into Christ; it is a fruit of the spirit, a natural result of one's new state of being. In other words, while mere acquittal carries with it no drive toward or empowerment for good works, the experience of a renewed life as a member of Christ's body does.

Catholic interpreters have had less trouble finding a connection between indicative and imperative. They have rejected the view that by *dikaiosynē* Paul means the mere fact of acquittal, devoid of moral content. From their perspective, the term refers to "the whole new being in Christ, the new relationship, the new creation, in which ethical uprightness is made possible and required."[5]

Many scholars have objected to Schweitzer's use of the term "mysticism," but some recent interpreters have defended modified versions of his thesis, generally preferring to speak of Paul's "participationist" language rather than his "mysticism."[6] Although the precise relationship between Paul's notions of justification on the one hand and incorporation into Christ on the other remains a matter of debate, it seems clear that one cannot rightly understand Paul without taking both into account. For Paul, it is by faith that the believer becomes a member of the body of Christ and remains within it. Faith thus brings a new status before God, but it also places one in a new *relationship to* God. Those who are "in Christ" have entered a new sphere of influence, in which they are both called and empowered to do the good. They are "raised" to a new life in the Spirit and have become, in short, a "new creation."

b. Community in Christ

However one resolves the question of juridical and participationist language, it is clear that for Paul those who are "in" Christ are also in community with

---

5. Plevnik, *What Are They Saying about Paul?* 69.
6. See particularly E. P. Sanders, *Paul and Palestinian Judaism* (Philadelphia: Fortress Press, 1977), chap. 5.

one another. "We have no evidence," J. Paul Sampley writes, "that Paul ever conceived of a solitary, isolated believer." Christians are "brought together by their shared death with Christ," not by virtue of common backgrounds or social standing.[7] Belonging to Christ, they have a responsibility to build up the community itself, to be productive members of the corporate whole. Each individual counts and is a recipient of special gifts from God, but the new life is inherently a life lived in communion with others who have received God's grace in Christ.

c. Freedom in Christ

The new life in Christ is also a life in freedom. Negatively, this means there can be no basis for salvation other than God's grace, the free gift of salvation through Christ's death and resurrection. Thus any attempt to earn what God has already given is a denial of faith, a failure to trust solely in God. The positive meaning is that those in Christ are free from the power of sin. Of course they still live in the world and remain subject to all the limitations of existence. They still face temptation, death, and suffering. But they are no longer bound by the iron necessity of sin; by the power of the Spirit, they *can* do the good.

d. Flesh and Spirit

In their freedom, believers confront two possible modes of existence. They can live "according to the Spirit" or "according to the flesh." To live "according to the Spirit" is to make proper use of the power one has newly received; it is to follow the Spirit's promptings. Concretely, this means moral action, most especially love. To live "according to the flesh," on the other hand, is to turn away from the Spirit and live in another sphere of influence. In playing flesh and Spirit off against one another, however, Paul is not endorsing a dualism in which material reality appears as evil. Material reality is not in and of itself evil for him, as it is for Gnosticism, but it is subject to domination by evil. To live "according to the flesh" is to live as if the material world were a self-sufficient reality, as if there were no Spirit; it is to live under an alien power in competition with that of Christ.[8]

---

7. J. Paul Sampley, *Walking between the Times: Paul's Moral Reasoning* (Philadelphia: Fortress Press, 1991), 37–38.

8. See Rudolf Bultmann, *Theology of the New Testament*, vol. 1, trans. Kendrick Grobel (New York: Charles Scribner's Sons, 1951), 192–210, 232–39, for a discussion of the terms "body," "flesh," and "spirit."

Fig. 69. St. Paul
(Vincenzo Foppa; Italian,
1425/30–1515/16)

e. This Age and the Age to Come

The alien power is that of Satan, who has since the sin of Adam held the world in bondage. It is a power, however, that belongs to an age that is passing away. Through Christ's death and resurrection, God has already inaugurated the eschatological age, a fact manifested in the Spirit's presence and in "spiritual gifts" such as prophecy and tongues. In living "according to the Spirit," believers participate already in the age to come.

Although underway, the new age is not fully present. That is why believers are still subject to temptation, suffering, and death; and that is why they cannot claim full knowledge. They live in an "in-between time," in which the competing powers are still in conflict, although the eventual outcome is apparent to them. As followers of a Messiah who died a shameful and humiliating death, Christians are not magically freed from the conditions of earthly existence. The cross of Christ must in some sense be their own, as it is indeed Paul's.

f. The Body

If for Paul "spirit" is a totally positive term and "flesh" usually negative, "body" is neutral. The body is the person as a whole, which is mortal but capable of redemption. Whereas "flesh and blood cannot inherit the kingdom of God" (1 Cor. 15:50), life in the resurrection will be a life in a transformed body. Paul's use of the term "body" shows that he does not view matter itself as evil.

g. Human Hope and the Redemption of the Cosmos

It is not human beings alone that will be transformed in the age to come. The "present evil age" is in Paul's view the result of a cosmic disruption brought about by sin. To say that Satan rules this age is to say that the universe itself, what we would call the natural world, is corrupted and exists under a curse. The fullness of the new age will bring not only human redemption but a total cosmic renewal. The life of the believer is therefore not only a life lived in faith, one that heeds the message of God's redemption of the world through Christ, but also a life lived in hope. To believe in Christ is to hope for final salvation and the restoration of the universe to its intended glory.

h. Faith Active in Love

Above all, however, the life of the believer is a life of love. For faith fulfills itself only as it becomes active in love, only as it treats the neighbor as a child of God. But Christians do not immediately and automatically become perfect, loving human beings. In the "in-between" time in which Christians live they are continually in a process of growth. Paul is clear that believers are "at various stages in their faith journey toward maturity" and "that his life too is marked by a pressing on toward maturity or perfection."[9] Such progress in the Christian life is a gift of God, the work of the indwelling Spirit.

2. Existentialist Interpretations of Paul

a. Bultmann: Contradictions in Paul

It should be clear that Paul's theology reflects the thought patterns of the ancient world, patterns that Bultmann identified as "mythological." In Paul

---

9. Sampley, *Walking between the Times*, 47–48.

as well as the Gospel of John, however, Bultmann found evidence that the New Testament itself actually begins the process of "demythologizing," or existentialist interpretation.

According to Bultmann, the entire New Testament is pervaded by a contradiction. On the one hand, human beings appear as pawns in the hands of cosmic powers, with no control over their own destinies. On the other hand, the New Testament constantly addresses its readers and calls them to decision, thus clearly presupposing human freedom.

An example of this contradiction is found in Paul's conception of the Spirit. Sometimes Paul refers to the Spirit as if it were a natural force: it is the source of wondrous deeds and psychic phenomena, and possession of it guarantees resurrection (Rom. 8:11). He can even "speak of the 'Spirit' as a kind of supernatural matter (1 Cor. 15:44ff.)." The implication is that it is a power working deterministically upon human beings, wholly apart from their own decisions. Clearly, however, it is not Paul's deepest intention to present such a view. For he often appeals to the reader's decision to *obey* the Spirit's promptings: "If we live by the Spirit, let us also be guided by the Spirit" (Gal 5:25).

"So it is," Bultmann argues, "that the concept of the 'Spirit' is demythologized." In other words, Paul's insistence upon human responsibility cuts through the mythological view of the Spirit as a supernatural force working independently of human decision and presents it as "the possibility in fact of the new life that is disclosed in faith."[10] The option to "be guided by the Spirit" is thus an existential possibility, a possibility belonging to human existence as such, and not something supernaturally imposed upon the human condition.

Something similar can be observed in Romans 6. In v. 5, Bultmann notes, Paul repeats an early Christian understanding of baptism as a guarantee of eventual resurrection to eternal life: "If we have been united with [Christ] in a death like his, we shall certainly be united with him in a resurrection like his." In v. 4, however, he breaks the parallel between dying with Christ (in baptism) and eternal life: "so that, just as Christ was raised from the dead ... *so we too might walk in newness of life.*" In effect, Paul has reinterpreted the believer's resurrection as "an already present resurrection which realizes itself in ethical conduct."[11]

Because Bultmann finds that the New Testament writings themselves have begun the process of demythologizing, he argues for a contemporary mode

---

10. Bultmann, *New Testament and Mythology*, 20.
11. Bultmann, *Theology of the New Testament*, 1:140–41.

of belief that rejects the supernaturalist or mythological worldview reflected in those writings. Salvation through the cross of Christ, for example, appears in the New Testament as a mythical event through which Christ atones for human sin through his blood and frees humanity by taking upon himself the consequences of sin. Existentialist interpretation reveals, however, that such views do not represent the deepest intention of the New Testament itself.

> Thus, to believe in the cross of Christ does not mean to look to some mythical process that has taken place outside of us and our world or at an objectively visible event that God has somehow reckoned to our credit; rather, to believe in the cross of Christ means to accept the cross as one's own and to allow oneself to be crucified with Christ.[12]

In other words, when Paul says, "I have been crucified with Christ" (Gal. 2:19), he shows that Christian faith does not at its base mean believing that Jesus' death somehow created an objective change in God's relationship to the world. It does not mean that this death somehow actually accomplished the redemption of humanity, as if God could not accept human beings apart from it. What it does mean is that when human beings hear the proclamation of this event as redemptive and accept it as such, it in fact *becomes* so for them. The redemption takes place in human experience, not on a cosmic level.

b. Beyond Bultmann: Christology as Re-Presentation

Now Bultmann always insisted that the New Testament maintains a consistent connection between faith on the one hand and the Christ-event on the other. In other words, it is only in relation to the Christian proclamation that authentic faith is really possible. Other interpreters, however, have found some indications to the contrary in Paul's letters. In Romans 4, for example, Paul presents Abraham as an example of the person of faith. But Abraham's faith is not in Christ; it is trust *directly in God* to give him a child. Paul thus speaks of faith in a general way: what Abraham illustrates is a trusting attitude, which is also exemplified in the Christian's faith in Christ.[13]

Such an interpretation provides some basis for arguing that existentialist interpretation should go beyond Bultmann and understand the Christ-event not as the unique event through which God has brought redemption about

---

12. Bultmann, *New Testament and Mythology*, 34.

13. Hendrikus Boers, *Theology out of the Ghetto: A New Testament Exegetical Study concerning Religious Exclusiveness* (Leiden: E. J. Brill, 1971), 74–104; Russell Pregeant, *Christology beyond Dogma: Matthew's Christ in Process Hermeneutic* (Philadelphia: Fortress Press; Missoula, Mont.: Scholars Press, 1978), 148–50.

but as a paradigm for the way in which God provides for human salvation in all times and places.[14] The New Testament, in this view, does not at its most basic level witness to a new human possibility that comes about through Christ; it rather re-presents the possibility that God is always making available to human beings, i.e., "the original possibility of authentic existence."[15] What finally matters is not faith in Christ per se, but faith in God—as *definitively disclosed* in the proclamation of Jesus as the Christ.

It should be clear that such a reading of the New Testament does an end run around traditional Christian exclusivism. For it finds the key to salvation not in a necessary relationship to Jesus or the church, but in a specific human attitude, trust in God, which is in some sense made possible for people anywhere at any time, although definitively re-presented in Jesus. It should be equally clear that one cannot obtain this view by a simplistic reading of the New Testament. The dominant way of presenting the Christ-event in the New Testament is as the exclusive, supernatural event through which God literally redeems the world. It is only if one chooses to look "beneath" the supernaturalism of the text to an "existential" level that either Bultmann's understanding or that of his more radical followers makes sense.

3. A Structuralist Interpretation of Paul

Existentialist interpretation is one way of attempting to state what the New Testament "means" as opposed to what it merely "says." It is concerned primarily with New Testament theology, and its intent is to show that the messages of the various authors are not bound to the ancient worldview but can speak to human beings across the ages.

Some more recent interpreters, also interested in getting at what New Testament texts "mean," have focused not on the theological perspectives of the writers, but on their faith. The distinction is crucial: a person's faith is constituted by what she or he presupposes, whereas one's theology consists in rational explanation of what is presupposed. The analysis of a text from the point of view of such a distinction constitutes a form of structuralism. By identifying the presuppositions at work in a text the interpreter gets hold of the "system of convictions" upon which it is built, i.e., the underlying "struc-

---

14. Schubert M. Ogden, *Christ without Myth: A Study Based on the Theology of Rudolf Bultmann*, 2d ed. (Dallas: Southern Methodist University, 1979); Boers, *Theology Out of the Ghetto*; Pregeant, *Christology beyond Dogma*.

15. Ogden, *Christ without Myth*.

ture" that is more basic than any specific point the writer seeks explicitly to make.

In a book entitled *Paul's Faith and the Power of the Gospel,* Daniel Patte has applied such a structuralist analysis to Paul's letters. Noting that a system of convictions cannot always be stated in the form of a logical argument, Patte contends that in order to identify it one has to look precisely for "what is odd in the argument, what does not contribute to the unfolding of the argument or even hinders it." More explicitly, one must look for apparent contradictions, strange reasonings, repetitions that seem to lead nowhere, and metaphorical language.[16] The point is that one's system of convictions is something one is not prepared to give up; and one will resort to strange forms of argument to defend it. So when we find Paul's logic odd, when we find him straining to make a point, we can bet that his system of convictions, the faith he presupposes, is at stake.

Patte's attempt to locate Paul's convictions leads him to conclude that Christ plays a different role in his basic faith than in his theological reasoning. On the theological level, Paul understands Christ's death as an event in the past through which God brought about human salvation. One might thus think that Christian faith is faith in the saving power of that event, and passages such as Galatians 1:3-4 support such a view. When one identifies Paul's system of convictions, however, it becomes evident that the significance of the cross is that it constitutes a pattern that is repeated in the believers' own personal experiences. And it is in those experiences themselves that faith is actually anchored.

How Patte reaches these conclusions is a complex matter. Beginning with Galatians, he finds a set of convictions related to the opposition of freedom and bondage to be central to Paul's faith. Understanding the gospel as freedom, Paul plays it off against other systems of convictions, for example, those of the Pharisees and of his opponents in Galatia, which he interprets as forms of bondage. Thus it is precisely when he is defending the gospel as freedom from the law that he resorts to "odd" argumentation. A case in point is that in 3:19-20 Paul compromises the divine origin of the law even though it is clear from Galatians as a whole that this is not his intention.

According to Patte, Paul's system of convictions differs from some other systems by virtue of the fact that it is open-ended, rather than closed. One sign of this open-endedness is the fact that Paul's faith includes elements in common with Judaism (God, Scripture) on the one hand and Hellenism

---

16. Daniel Patte, *Paul's Faith and the Power of the Gospel: A Structural Introduction to the Pauline Letters* (Philadelphia: Fortress Press, 1983), 39–46.

(virtues) on the other; it does not entail total rejection of those other systems. Another such sign appears in Paul's criticism of his opponents in Galatia. These opponents require circumcision because they take Torah as absolute, as containing in itself the pathway to righteousness before God. From Paul's point of view, however, "Torah is Scripture precisely because it points beyond itself (and away from concern about one's right relationship with God), that is, because it is 'promise' pointing to Christ and to the Gentiles' experience of the Spirit."[17]

Now it would be possible to limit this open-endedness by presenting the revelation in Christ as absolutely final, just as Paul's opponents thought Torah was final. Patte argues, however, that Paul believed that new revelations continue after Christ. As evidence, he cites 1 Thess. 1:3-10, where Paul speaks of God's "choosing" the Thessalonians. This notion is obviously parallel to the Jewish concept of God's election of Israel, but Paul does not justify his declaration of the Thessalonians' chosenness by referring to an event in the past. Instead, he points to their own immediate experience, their reception of the gospel message "in power and in the Holy Spirit and with full conviction" (1:5). The point is that by understanding election as something that *"happens in the believers'* experience,"[18] Paul implies that the process of revelation did not end with Christ but continues in the present.

Patte also finds it significant that Paul speaks of the Thessalonians as imitators both of himself and of Jesus who are themselves "types" for yet others to imitate. In all these cases "imitation" means something more than simply following a prior example: the Thessalonians are imitators of those who have gone before because "the same things *happened* to them."[19] In 2:14-16 the point is particularly clear: just as Jesus and the churches in Judea suffered persecution by their own people, so did Paul and his associates; and so now the Thessalonians have suffered persecution by *their* own people. And it is precisely such experience that qualifies the Thessalonians themselves to becomes "types" for others to imitate (1:6-7).

According to Patte's reading, Paul believes that it is in the Thessalonians' own experiences that God is present to them. And this means that their faith is actually centered on these experiences rather than on the cross of Christ as an event in the past. If we ask, then, about the specific role of Christ in Paul's system of convictions, the rather startling answer is that "Jesus Christ is a type, a promise (and not a complete and final revelation)."[20] That is to

---

17. Ibid., 83.
18. Ibid., 133; italics original.
19. Ibid.; italics original.
20. Ibid.

say, Christ constitutes a pattern that is repeated in the believers themselves, not the once-for-all event that somehow wins salvation.

Now Patte acknowledges that at many points Paul's letters reflect "the view that Jesus' death (in the past) is salvific."[21] Yet he is equally certain that not only 1 Thessalonians, but also Philemon and Philippians, get along quite well without any such presentation of Jesus' death. It thus appears that

> Paul simultaneously held both views of Jesus' death. On the one hand, he viewed the cross as a salvific event in the past (Jesus died for our sins) which is the necessary precondition for the believers' faith. On the other hand, he viewed the cross merely as a prefiguration (a type) of Christ-like events in the believers' experience which are the center of the believers' faith.[22]

How are we to make sense of this apparent contradiction? Patte's solution, as already noted, is that Paul's two views belong to two different levels of thought. Paul's *system of convictions* involves the view that God is at work in the lives of those to whom he has preached the gospel, just as God has also been at work in his own life and in the life of Jesus. His *theological explanation* of his convictions, however, takes the form of the declaration that it is specifically through Jesus' death that God has somehow brought about human salvation, i.e., that this death is an expiation for sin, or that through it God justifies humankind.

By centering on Paul's convictions rather than on his theology, Patte opens the way for an evaluation of what is most significant in Paul that is parallel to Bultmann's existentialist interpretation. For one may now ask whether Paul is best interpreted when readers repeat the apostle's own theological explanations of those convictions or when they work out their own explanations, taking their own contemporary situations into account. If one accepts the view that Paul held even his convictions in an open-ended way, then the latter view would seem unavoidable. No less than an existentialist interpretation, however, Patte's structuralist reading constitutes a challenge to much traditional theology.

4. A Freudian Interpretation of Paul

In a book entitled *Paul for a New Day,* Robin Scroggs has drawn upon Freudian theory to illuminate Paul's notion of justification. Scroggs notes that

---

21. Ibid., 191.
22. Ibid.

according to Freud the superego develops as a way of resolving a developmental crisis in childhood. Although Freud differentiated male and female development, in both cases the child at the oedipal stage represses desire, internalizes the image of the feared parent, and directs aggression inward. The result is the emergence of the superego, the conscious part of which is the conscience. Accepting Freud's characterization of one's image of God as a projection of the father-image (which has nothing to do with the question of the actual *existence* of God), Scroggs finds a parallel between the child who is obedient in order to avoid punishment and Paul's understanding of humanity under the law.

> To be obedient to the Torah in an attempt to justify oneself by works covertly expresses that primal hostility and aggression against God the Father. Aggression is the reaction against the authoritative, awesome Father, who says "Thou shalt not...," thus putting an end to freedom.[23]

Through his proclamation of justification by faith, Paul undermines this threatening image of God with the assertion that through Christ God has brought about a reconciliation: the hostility is resolved. Reception of the new relationship, however, demands that human beings abandon their false (and unconsciously hostile) ways of seeking God's favor:

> All that we grasped to ourselves must be willingly thrown away. No longer do we *have* to look over our shoulders to see what others think of us; we are liberated from that anxiety—but no longer *can* we use our place in the community to satisfy our self-assurance. Thrown away must be all the support gained from our carefully constructed life-facade— business skills, intellectual accomplishments, community esteem, and especially our ethical performance, the most insidious and demonic crutch of all.[24]

5. Paul as Ethicist

Paul is as controversial a figure today as he was in the first century. This is particularly the case when his ethical views are under discussion. Social activists often find Paul less than adequate when it comes to the issues of slavery and civil disobedience, yet some liberation theologians have enlisted

---

23. Robin Scroggs, *Paul for a New Day* (Philadelphia: Fortress Press, 1977), 13.
24. Ibid., 16.

him in their cause. Many conservative Christians cite Paul's letters in support of "traditionalist" views on homosexuality and the status and role of women, and for that reason he is often condemned by feminists and advocates of lesbian/gay rights. On the other hand, some interpreters have found in him the inspiration for a distinctively modern "new morality" that revolutionizes traditional attitudes toward sex. It is thus important not only to pay close attention to what Paul actually says on matters such as these but also to notice the presuppositions of those who have sought to evaluate his views.

It is also important to understand that Paul does not simply rattle off random pronouncements on ethical and unethical behavior. He engages in a complex process of moral reasoning that is influenced by various cultural factors but is firmly grounded in his faith and theological understanding. And just as he himself engages in moral reasoning, he expects those to whom he writes to do the same. Although he can at a few points provide sayings of Jesus and lists of virtues and vices that serve as the boundaries of ethical reflection, he invites Christians (Rom. 12:2) to "discern" the will of God, that is, to puzzle out for themselves what is right and what is wrong. This does not mean that they should simply do whatever feels comfortable to them, however, for Paul links the ability to carry out such reasoning to the renewed mind that one has in Christ. And he also lays down specific criteria for discernment:

> Projected deeds have to be evaluated in two ways: how they bear on the one who might do them and how they bear on others in the community of faith. It is not enough to ask whether some action might be appropriate to oneself, one must also ask whether the deed would help build up others in the body of Christ.[25]

Paul's ethics is influenced by his conviction that in Christ human beings participate in the new age, even though they must continue to live in the old one. Because their minds have been renewed by dying and rising with Christ, they are capable of reasoning out proper action. But they must always remind themselves that they do not yet live in the fullness of God's Rule and that the presence of the neighbor is a check upon their own desires. And that is why the final criterion for ethical action must be service to the community as a whole, the body of Christ, why it must, in other words, be love. It is important to remember all this as we approach Paul's views on specific ethical questions.

---

25. Sampley, *Walking between the Times*, 60.

a. The Status and Role of Women

What roles should women play in the church? Should they be ordained as ministers? What is the role of a wife in relation to her husband? Conservative theologians cite the Pauline writings, more than any other part of the New Testament, in defense of the "traditional" answers to these questions: women should be subservient to their husbands, and their roles in the church should be different from those of men; most importantly, ordination should be reserved for males.

While support for all of these answers can be found in letters attributed to Paul, it is important first of all to note that the passages that make the sharpest distinction between female and male roles are found in those letters that many scholars are convinced Paul did not actually write. This fact alone does not of course answer the question as to whether and in what sense such passages should be accepted as authoritative by the present-day church. At a later point it will be important to make some observations relevant to that question. But since our present concern is with Paul's own views, I will confine this discussion to the undisputed letters.

The clearest example of a distinction in roles is 1 Corinthians 14:33-36, which prohibits women from speaking in church and charges them to ask all questions of their husbands at home. As we noted in chapter 9, however, many scholars think that this passage is a non-Pauline interpolation.

But even if Paul did try to silence women in Corinth, there is also overwhelming evidence that he generally accepted women in prominent leadership roles.[26] He mentions Euodia and Syntyche (Phil. 4:3), as well as Prisca and her husband (Rom. 16:3-5), as fellow workers in spreading the gospel. Prisca's leadership role is underscored by the additional facts that she and Aquila hosted a church in their home and that Paul, against the custom, mentions her before her husband. And the reference to Chloe in 1 Corinthians 1:11 suggests that this woman also exercised some type of authority in the church.

Paul's references to two other women illustrate how cultural bias can enter into interpreters' decisions about the meaning of a text. In Romans 16:1-2 he mentions Phoebe, to whom he applies the Greek term *diakonos*. The literal meaning of this word is "servant" or "helper," but it eventually came to designate a person ordained to a formal, ministerial office in the church. When used in this latter, technical sense, it is usually translated "deacon." Paul generally employs the term in its nontechnical sense, but the phrase "of

---

26. Victor Paul Furnish, *The Moral Teaching of Paul: Selected Issues,* rev. ed. (Nashville: Abingdon, 1985), 101–12.

Fig. 70. "Christa"
(Bronze sculpture
by Edwina Sandys
© 1975)

the church" in this passage suggests that he has an actual office in mind, although we do not know precisely what duties the title might have carried at this early date. Translators, however, assuming that a woman could not have held such a position, have traditionally avoided the term "deacon" at this point. Only a little short of two thousand years late, the NRSV has granted Phoebe the title of "deacon"—and even suggested "minister" as an alternative rendering.

The second case is even more dramatic. In Romans 16:7, Paul sends greetings to two persons whom he apparently recognizes both as his predecessors in Christianity and as apostles. As grammatical objects in the sentence, the names appear in the accusative case, i.e., with a final *n*: Andronik*on* and Junia*n*. The first of these is the accusative form of the male name Andronicus, and the latter of the female name Juni*a*. Assuming that a woman could not have been an apostle, however, translators have posited a male equivalent,

Juni*as*. But we have no evidence of such a male form. It would thus appear that Juni*a* is original, which would tend to indicate that Paul did in fact recognize a woman as an apostle. We cannot be entirely certain on this matter, since the meaning of the sentence is somewhat ambiguous, and some manuscripts read "Ju*l*ian" instead of "Ju*n*ian." But this latter point may simply illustrate that bias was at work even among early manuscript copyists.

To say that Paul recognized women in leadership roles in the church does not mean that he made no distinctions whatsoever between men and women. For in 1 Corinthians 11:2-16 he insists upon a restriction upon women during worship that does not apply to men.[27] And he also says that "the husband is the head of his wife," just as a man's head is Christ and Christ's head is God (11:3). We thus come upon a passage in which Paul seems not only to draw a distinction between male and female roles but to place women at the bottom of a hierarchical power-relationship: God, Christ, man, woman.

Nevertheless, in the course of his argument Paul makes a remarkable point that does not serve his immediate interest at all: in 11:11-12 he injects a comment reasserting an equalitarian relationship between man and woman. Although Paul can resort to traditional thinking regarding woman's status at some points, at others he can assert that "in Christ" all traditional distinctions among people are in some sense dissolved.

This latter point is made explicit at Galatians 3:28: "There is no longer Jew or Greek, there is no longer slave or free, there is no longer male and female; for all of you are one in Christ Jesus." Scholars are generally agreed that here Paul quotes a baptismal formula current in the churches[28]; so we may assume that his equalitarian views are not innovative but reflect the radicalism of the earlier community. In fact, as Schüssler Fiorenza shows, Paul modified this radicalism in a more traditional direction.[29] It is nevertheless clear that, although from our modern perspective he was not always true to the principle at work in Galatians 3:28, it was an important influence on both his thought and his action. And his counsel to some women to remain unmarried (1 Cor. 7:8)

---

27. The Greek of verses 4-6 is somewhat ambiguous. Most interpreters have assumed that Paul wants Christian women to cover their heads with veils, according to Jewish custom, and this assumption has affected the English translations. Some recent interpreters, however, argue that he is insisting that the women keep their hair bound up rather than letting it down, since free-flowing hair was "quite common in the ecstatic worship of oriental divinities" (Elisabeth Schüssler Fiorenza, *In Memory of Her: A Feminist Theological Reconstruction of Christian Origins* [New York: Crossroad, 1983], 223). In this reading, Paul's real concern is to distinguish Christianity from ecstatic cults that would be suspect among some segment of the Greco-Roman populace, not to enforce a rigid distinction in male-female roles. Not all interpreters accept this interpretation of the passage, however.

28. Schüssler Fiorenza, *In Memory of Her,* 229-30, 205-18.

29. Ibid., 219-36.

in and of itself constitutes a radical challenge to the traditional, patriarchal family structure.[30]

In conclusion, we may say that from a feminist perspective Paul's legacy is ambiguous. On the one hand, both his message and his practice involved a gospel in which traditional sex roles were transcended. On the other, he occasionally resorted to traditional distinctions and unwittingly laid the groundwork for the eventual resurgence of patriarchal structure in the church, a resurgence we will observe in chapter 13.

b. Homosexuality

Is a homosexual life-style an acceptable one for Christians? Should Christian churches accept practicing homosexuals into the ordained ministry? While Paul's writings figure prominently in the contemporary debate over the status and role of women, they stand at the very center of the controversy regarding homosexuality. For in two passages in the undisputed letters, 1 Corinthians 6:9-10 and Romans 1:24-27, Paul seems to condemn the homosexual life-style. It is important, however, not only to note precisely what Paul does and does not say on this subject, but to ask the more difficult question of why he says what he does.

Before examining these two passages, two observations are in order. First, although texts from the Hellenistic world referred to specific homosexual *practices,* neither Greek nor Hebrew in the ancient world had words "equivalent in meaning to our English words 'homosexual' and 'homosexuality.' "[31] This suggests that Paul's world knew nothing of what modern persons mean by "sexual orientation." And this conclusion is borne out by an examination of the writers of this period who criticize homosexual activity: they universally assume that it is a matter of conscious choice and show no awareness that some people might experience themselves simply to "be" homosexual.[32]

The second observation is that the specific form of homosexual practice most widely known and discussed in Paul's time was pederasty—the love of a man for a boy. In ancient Greece the close relationship between mentor and student had been an important aspect of the educational process, and when Plato praised such love "his thought was not of a physical relationship but of a 'higher' form of love uniting two persons."[33] The physical dimension was probably present in many instances, however. In any case, by

---

30. Ibid., 224–26.
31. Furnish, *Moral Teaching,* 53.
32. Ibid., 65.
33. Ibid., 59.

Paul's time pederasty had come more and more to be associated not only with a physical relationship but with utter, self-indulgent lust. In particular, the boys were often "call-boys"—male prostitutes—or slaves, who were sometimes castrated.[34] Not surprisingly, then, when writers of the period criticized homosexual practice they generally directed their attention to the issue of exploitation of one person by another: they tended to see it as a degenerate activity of the idle rich.[35]

This second observation is of immediate relevance for understanding 1 Corinthians 6:9-10. Here Paul lists several types of persons who will not inherit God's Rule; on the list are two terms difficult to translate, *malakos* and *arsenokoitēs*, which apparently have something to do with homosexual activity. What specifically does Paul mean by these words, and why does he use them both?

The root meaning of *malakos* is "soft," and it eventually took on the connotation of "effeminate." Scroggs argues that in a context suggesting pederasty it would bring to mind "images of the effeminate call-boy."[36] The second term, *arsenokoitēs*, is problematic in that its earliest known occurrence is 1 Corinthians 6:9. But it is a compound of two words: *arsēn*, meaning "male," and *koitē*, meaning "bed," and then, by extension, "sexual intercourse." Thus Scroggs argues that the compound term refers to person who has sex with males. And he also makes a good case that it was a term that arose in Hellenistic Judaism as a translation of a Hebrew phrase denoting the stereotypically active partner in a homosexual relationship.[37]

Scroggs's investigations thus point to a reason why both terms, *malakos* and *arsenokoitēs*, appear in 1 Corinthians 6:9. In this passage Paul is thinking specifically of pederasty; and his condemnation is of "call-boys" and the adult males who use them.[38]

The Romans passage is quite different. Here Paul can cannot be thinking exclusively of pederasty, since he mentions female homosexual practices as well as male. It is also clear that he condemns such practices as "unnatural." For some contemporary Christians considering the issue of homosexuality, this observation settles the issue; for others, however, some additional considerations carry weight.

For one thing, if we ask about the function of this passage in Romans we

---

34. Robin Scroggs, *The New Testament and Homosexuality: Contextual Background for Contemporary Debate* (Philadelphia: Fortress Press, 1983), 39.
35. Furnish, *Moral Teaching*, 59–63.
36. Scroggs, *The New Testament and Homosexuality*, 65.
37. Ibid., 108.
38. Ibid., 62–65, 101–9.

can see that it is incidental to Paul's main point. In Romans 1:1-3:20, he is arguing that all human beings are sinners before God, as a prelude to his declaration of universal grace in 3:21-26. The passage, in essence, serves as a metaphor for humanity's general "perversion" of God's creation by worshiping creatures rather than the creator. Interestingly, he does not even list homosexual practice in his catalogue of vices with which he concludes the illustration. It is thus evident that Paul did not write Romans 1 in order to teach that homosexuality is a perversion; but because he assumed it to be such, he used it as an illustration of humanity's overall corruption.

If we now ask why Paul made such an assumption, we may easily identify two sources of his attitude. One is the association of homosexual practice with pederasty, especially in its most exploitative forms. Even though female homosexual relationships were obviously known, they are seldom mentioned in texts of the period. So it is probable that his view of all same-sex relationships was in fact shaped by his knowledge of pederasty.

The other source of Paul's attitude was Judaism: both the Jewish Scriptures and later Jewish texts condemned homosexual practice, although the passages in which it is discussed are extremely sparse. If we ask about the reason for this condemnation, we can only speculate. The Scriptures give no reason, but it is interesting that only male homosexual practice is mentioned. This may indicate that a primary concern was that it diverted men from the task of procreation, a value that lay close to the heart of the ancient Jew. It is also worthy of note that Jews associated homosexuality with Gentiles and idolatry. The legal prohibition of homosexual activity (Lev. 18:22; 20:13), which prescribes the death penalty, occurs in a law code (Lev. 17–26) that is explicitly defined as distinguishing the Hebrew people from their neighbors who have "defiled" themselves through practicing various "abominations" (18:24-30; 20:23).[39]

A rather different explanation is possible on the basis of insights from anthropology regarding the notions of ritual purity and pollution. As noted in chapter 2 (see above, pp. 51–55), ancient people had a deep-seated concern for what they perceived to be the proper order of things; disorder brought confusion, danger, and, ultimately, destruction. Leviticus 19:19—with its prohibitions against cross-breeding cattle, planting two kinds of seed in the same field, and wearing garments made of more than one kind of cloth—expresses this thoroughgoing concern for order. Such forms of mixing presumably suggested the confusion of disparate elements and were thus rejected. Fernando Belo argues that the ancient Hebrew view of homosexuality is to be understood in a similar light: "even compatible elements can be joined only if they

---

39. See Norman H. Snaith, *Leviticus and Numbers* (London: Thomas Nelson and Sons, 1967), 126.

are different." The logic would thus be that union of the *same* sex creates a confusion, a disruption of order, similar to that created by mixing *different* kinds of cloth, seeds, or cattle.[40]

So what relevance, then, do Paul's writings have to the contemporary Christian debate about homosexuality? It should be evident that the answer will depend upon how one understands the Bible as authoritative. According to some models of biblical authority, Christians are obligated to accept Paul's views in a direct and literal way, even if they are expressed only in passing. According to other models, however, the issue cannot be settled so easily. Some Christians might contend, for example, that since Paul knew nothing of sexual orientation in the modern sense, his statements cannot be applied without qualification to the contemporary question. Such interpreters might value his rejection of exploitative sex, pointing out that it is no less reprehensible in heterosexual than in homosexual relationships, while finding the assumptions expressed in Romans 1 to be irrelevant to the contemporary debate. From their point of view, the issue would be one on which the Bible gives no direct guidance, so that it would be best discussed in conversation with modern sociology, anthropology, psychology, and biology. This would not mean, of course, that the Bible could not in some more general way define a Christian context for such discussion.

c. Paul and Social Activism

Paul often gets low marks from social activists on two crucial counts. Not only does he seem far too accepting of the institution of slavery, but by counselling his readers in Romans 13:1-7 to be subject to the governing authorities he seems to undercut any basis for civil disobedience on behalf of just causes.

With respect to slavery, it is argued, Paul shows no inclination to challenge the social order on this or any other question. And although he counsels his readers not to sell themselves into slavery (1 Cor. 7:23), he also tells slaves not to worry about their status (7:21).[41] Must we say, then, that Paul teaches nonresistance to social injustice?

The first point that needs to be made is that the passages that lean most clearly in that direction come not from the undisputed letters but from Colossians (3:22), Ephesians (6:5), Timothy (6:1-2), and Titus (2:9): in each of

---

40. Fernando Belo, *A Materialist Reading of the Gospel of Mark,* trans. Matthew J. O'Connell (Maryknoll, N.Y.: Orbis Books, 1981), 38; see also Mary Douglas, *Purity and Danger: Analysis of Concepts of Pollution and Taboo* (New York: Frederick A. Praeger, 1966), 48–53.

41. The meaning of the second half of 7:21 is disputed; some interpreters think it means slaves should gain their freedom if they can, but others take it to mean that slaves should make the best of their present circumstances.

these passages the writer enjoins slaves to be obedient to their masters. The second point is that by envisioning a church community in which all are brothers and sisters and by proclaiming that all Christians are slaves *of Christ,* Paul makes an implicit challenge to social structures. It is true, of course, that he does not make this challenge explicit through an endorsement of social activism; nor does he explicitly endorse civil disobedience. But in evaluating these facts one should keep in mind the eschatological context of Paul's teaching: along with other early Christians he looked for the imminent close of the age, when God's Rule itself would restructure the social order.

With respect to Romans 13:1-7, it is important to note that Paul does not command his readers to "obey" the authorities but to "be subject" to them. The difference is real: to be subject to a government is to recognize its legitimate right to exist, whereas to obey it means to comply with some specific law.[42] One may note, for example, that Martin Luther King Jr. disobeyed specific laws he found unjust or unjustly applied while nevertheless recognizing governmental authority by accepting legal consequences of his actions. Because Paul shared the ancient Jewish and Hellenistic belief that governments were appointed by God, he could in good conscience counsel loyalty to the state. But it is clear throughout Romans and Paul's letters in general that the Christian's ultimate sovereign is Christ. That he would have expected Christians to resist the Roman Empire when faith itself was at stake is unquestionable, as his own prison record makes amply clear.

d. Paul's Ethics Today: Competing Approaches

Anyone who wants to apply Paul's ethics to life in the modern world cannot do so without facing the question of *how* such an application is to be made. Some interpreters make such an application in a one-to-one fashion: to be faithful to Paul is to repeat in our situation the views he held in his. Others, however, contend that such an approach is particularly problematic when dealing with Paul. For them, a rule-morality, an ethical system consisting in specific rights and wrongs, runs into conflict with a key element in Paul's own thinking. If human beings are justified not by the law but by faith, they argue, then Christian morality cannot consist in adherence to specific rules. While Paul certainly refers to such rules, the real heart of his morality is found in the broad principle of faith working through love (Gal. 5:6). Such interpreters do not find Paul's specific judgments irrelevant. But they do argue that such judgments should be subordinated to an attempt to apply

---

42. Furnish, *Moral Teaching,* 126.

Paul's love ethic to the contemporary situation, taking into account the radical differences between Paul's world and our own.

These two approaches to Paul, based upon two different models of biblical authority, place Paul in a rather odd position in modern Christian thought. Quoted by the most conservative thinkers on specific issues, he is also hailed by the most liberal as setting the precedent for an open-ended mode of theological reflection. As Paul's letters themselves show, of course, this diversity in the interpretation of Paul goes all the way back to his own day. And, as chapter 13 and the Epilogue to Part Three will make clear, it was equally evident in the decades immediately following his ministry.

STUDY QUESTIONS

1. Describe the roles played in Paul's thought by each of the following: Spirit, Spirit/ flesh, body, faith, grace, *dikaiosynē,* freedom, love, present age/age to come, hope, resurrection, salvation, the death of Christ/the cross. Then discuss the relationship between Paul's "juridical" language and his "participationist" language.

2. Assess the potential of each of the following approaches to Paul for showing the relevance of his thought in the modern/postmodern world: existentialist interpretations, Patte's structuralist interpretation, Scroggs's Freudian interpretation.

3. Give and defend your own views as to whether and how Paul's views on the status and role of women, homosexual practice, and social activism have relevance for the contemporary discussion of these issues.

FOR FURTHER READING

Beker, J. Christiaan. *Paul the Apostle: The Triumph of God in Life and Thought.* Philadelphia: Fortress Press, 1980. Finds the center of Paul's thought in an apocalyptic perspective more fundamental than the juridical or the participationist language. Detailed and complex; a major contribution.

————. *The Triumph of God: The Essence of Paul's Thought.* Minneapolis: Fortress Press, 1990. An accessible summation of the author's view.

Bornkamm, Günther. *Paul.* Trans. D. M. G. Stalker. New York: Harper & Row, 1971; Minneapolis: Fortress Press, 1995. A lengthy but readable treatment of both Paul's life and work and his theology; for many years the definitive account.

Furnish, Victor P. *The Moral Teaching of Paul: Selected Issues.* 2d ed. Nashville: Abingdon, 1985. A brief, readable, helpful investigation of Paul's views on specific issues.

————. *Theology and Ethics in Paul.* Nashville: Abingdon, 1968. A detailed study of how Paul's ethical perspective is grounded in his theology. An important contribution.

Hock, Ronald. *The Social Context of Paul's Ministry: Tentmaking and Apostleship.* Philadelphia: Fortress Press, 1980. A brief, readable study that makes an important contribution.

Käsemann, Ernst. *Perspectives on Paul.* Trans. Margaret Kohl. Philadelphia: Fortress Press, 1971. Technical essays by an influential student of Bultmann, who is critical of his teacher on some points.

Keck, Leander E. *Paul and His Letters.* Proclamation Commentaries. 2d ed. Philadelphia: Fortress Press, 1989. A brief and highly readable introduction to Pauline studies. Contains a valuable appendix on the history of modern interpretations of Paul's theology. An excellent starting point.

Marrow, S. B. *Paul: His Letters and His Theology: An Introduction to Paul's Epistles.* New York and Mahwah, N.J.: Paulist, 1986. A basic, readable introduction; a good starting point.

Neyrey, Jerome H. *Paul, in Other Words: A Cultural Reading of His Letters.* Louisville: Westminster/John Knox, 1990. A helpful approach to Paul through anthropological categories.

Patte, Daniel. *Paul's Faith and the Power of the Gospel: A Structural Introduction to the Pauline Letters.* Philadelphia: Fortress Press, 1983. Lengthy and complex, but a remarkably readable application of structuralism.

Sampley, J. Paul. *Walking between the Times: Paul's Moral Reasoning.* Minneapolis: Fortress Press, 1991. A clear and concise treatment in light of the thought world that informed Paul's views.

Sanders, E. P. *Paul and Palestinian Judaism: A Comparison of Patterns of Religion.* Philadelphia: Fortress Press, 1977. A major contribution, critical of traditional Protestant readings of Paul and Christian interpretations of Judaism of the New Testament period.

————. *Paul, the Law, and the Jewish People.* Philadelphia: Fortress Press, 1983. Elaborates aspects of the former volume and introduces discussion of Paul's view of the Jewish people.

Sandmel, Samuel. *The Genius of Paul.* Philadelphia: Fortress Press, 1979. A sympathetic treatment by a Jewish scholar.

Schoeps, H. J. *Paul: The Theology of the Apostle in the Light of Jewish Religious History.* Trans. Harold Knight. Philadelphia: Westminster, 1959. An important study by a Jewish scholar.

Stendahl, Krister. *Paul among Jews and Gentiles.* Philadelphia: Fortress Press, 1976. A Lutheran scholar's criticism of traditional Protestant readings of Paul. Brief, readable, and important.

Theissen, Gerd. *The Social Setting of Pauline Christianity.* Ed. and trans. John H. Schütz. Philadelphia: Fortress Press, 1982. A fruitful application of sociological method.

Whiteley, D. E. H. *The Theology of St. Paul.* Oxford: Oxford Univ. Press, 1972. Among the more highly regarded attempts to summarize Paul's theology systematically.

Chapter 13

The Disputed Letters:
2 Thessalonians, Colossians,
Ephesians, 1 and 2 Timothy,
Titus

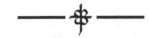

The six letters now to be considered are those whose authenticity as writings of Paul has been disputed. It will thus be important in each case to preface the reader-response analysis with comments on the question of authorship. The arguments against authenticity are more widely accepted in some cases than in others. The letters to Timothy and Titus, often called the "pastoral letters" because of their focus on ministerial functions, are almost universally assigned to a period later than Paul. Scholarly opinion on the three remaining letters is divided, however.

Because the Pauline authorship of all these letters is in doubt, I will not try to place them in actual situations in Paul's life but will seek only to describe in broad fashion the circumstances to which they speak. The readers I posit in the reader-response analyses are therefore defined in a very general way. And I will refer not to the actual, historical person Paul but only to "the author." When I do use the term "Paul" (in quotation marks), I indicate the role that the author has assumed in writing the letter.

1. 2 Thessalonians

a. The Question of Authenticity and the Author's Purpose

One argument against the authenticity of 2 Thessalonians has to do with its relationship to 1 Thessalonians. The theme development, terminology, and wording of the two letters is so close as to suggest that the author of one had the other in hand while writing. Yet there are apparent discrepancies on specific points. In 1 Thessalonians 5:1-2, for example, Paul cautions readers that the day of the Lord will come without warning. In 2 Thessalonians 2:1-12, however, the writer lays out an apocalyptic scheme that seemingly undercuts the element of surprise and suggests to some interpreters that the author no longer expects the imminent end of history. Another key point is the strange ending of 2 Thessalonians, in which the author makes such a point of claiming to be Paul as to recall Shakespeare's line about protesting too much.

Many scholars remain unconvinced on these points, however, and have made various attempts to explain why Paul would have written this letter as a follow-up to the earlier one. Robert Jewett believes that eschatological fervor in Thessalonica led some members of the community to misunderstand 1 Thessalonians and claim that the "day of the Lord" had already arrived. So Paul wrote again to state his point more carefully.[1]

It is notable, though, that in none of the undisputed letters does Paul resort to an apocalyptic timetable, such as is found in 2 Thessalonians, to meet the challenge of eschatological enthusiasm.[2] And many scholars believe that the reference to a pseudo-Pauline letter (2:2), used by the author's opponents, reflects a time after that of Paul. Their presupposition is that such a letter could hardly have been accepted during Paul's lifetime.

In any case, the recent trend is toward regarding the letter as the pseudonymous work of someone in the generation after Paul, who used 1 Thessalonians as a base and enlisted the apostle's authority to combat an "erroneous" eschatological teaching. There is disagreement, however, on the nature of the "error." Some think those the author opposed taught a realized eschatology of the gnosticizing sort that denied apocalypticism altogether in the belief that the resurrection of the dead had already occurred. Others argue that they

---

1. Robert Jewett, *The Thessalonian Correspondence: Pauline Rhetoric and Millenarian Piety* (Philadelphia: Fortress Press, 1986), 191-92, 177-78.

2. Gerhard Krodel, "The 2 Letter to the Thessalonians," in J. Paul Sampley, et al., *Ephesians, Colossians, 2 Thessalonians, the Pastoral Epistles* (Philadelphia: Fortress Press, 1978), 75.

simply believed that the final events in the apocalyptic drama had already begun.[3]

Whoever wrote 2 Thessalonians, and whatever the precise nature of the "false" teaching, the letter is directed to readers who had suffered persecution (1:4-5) and whose minds were unsettled by the eschatological claims of some among them. The author's purpose is apparently "to demonstrate that the Day of the Lord is not present and simultaneously to give consolation and hope by pointing to Christ's inevitable, ultimate victory over all satanic forces."[4]

b. Reading 2 Thessalonians

(1) 1:1-12. Following the salutation, which establishes the authorship of the letter, "Paul" launches a lengthy thanksgiving (1:3-10) that addresses the readers' sufferings by placing these tribulations in the context of their own continuing faith and God's eschatological victory. Punishment of their persecutors underscores the ultimate vindication of the faithful. The prayer that closes the thanksgiving furthers the sense of encouragement by reminding the readers of the power of God at work among them in the present.

(2) 2:1—3:5. In 2:1-2 the readers can identify the topic for discussion as the return of Christ and the immediate problem as a letter purporting to be from Paul. They are told that this prior letter's proclamation of the day of the Lord as already present is false, since that "day" is to be preceded by specific events that have not yet taken place: the "rebellion" and the revelation of "the lawless one" who will work wonders by Satan's powers. The readers are expected to recognize these events as matters about which they have already been taught (2:5), and they are also reminded that they are already aware of some force or person that temporarily restrains the "lawless one" in the present (2:6-7).[5]

Noting that "the mystery of lawlessness" is already at work in the present (2:7), "Paul" invites the readers to identify its manifestations in the world they know. Against the background of this identification, the readers are assured of Christ's eventual victory (2:8) and reminded that God will be at work even in the midst of the delusion worked by evil forces (2:9-12).

---

3. See Krodel, "The 2 Letter to the Thessalonians," 86–88, for arguments against the "gnosticizing" interpretation.

4. Ibid., 89.

5. The term for the restraining agent appears in the neuter in vs. 6 (*to katechon:* "what is restraining") and in the masculine in vs. 7 (*ho katechōn:* "the one who restrains").

Through words of thanksgiving, admonition, benediction, and encouragement (2:13—3:5), "Paul" bids the readers to "stand fast," keeping the traditions he has taught them. The request for the readers' prayers (3:1) includes them in the apostle's own role in "speeding on" the final triumph, and statements regarding God's faithfulness and the readers' own obedience create a feeling of confidence about their ultimate destiny.

(3) 3:6-18. "Paul" now turns to a series of admonitions regarding the "idle," whom the readers will presumably recognize as those who have abandoned work because they believe the end is already upon them. Then, with general admonitions, benedictory sentences, and indications of Pauline authority, the letter comes to a close.

c. Problems of Interpretation

A number of points in 2 Thessalonians remain obscure. The "rebellion" (2:3) can hardly refer to the disobedience of humanity as a whole, since the Greek word (*apostasia*) indicates the falling away of someone who was formerly faithful. The writer could envision the eventual apostasy of some Christians or, perhaps more likely, refer to continued Jewish rejection of the gospel.

There have been numerous attempts to identify "the lawless one" (2:3-9), but none has gained wide acceptance. Satan is among the suggestions, but 2:9 seems to present this figure as a subordinate in the hierarchy of evil. Other suggestions are the Roman Empire or emperor and a supernatural being of some sort. The lawless one, in any case, is clearly related to a notion that apparently became widespread toward the end of the first century: prior to Christ's return, an evil force of some sort would arise, in opposition to the gospel, as an antitype of Christ.[6] The Johannine letters, for example, mention the expectation of an "antichrist" (1 John 2:18, 22; 4:3; 2 John 7).

The precise nature of the agent that restrains the "lawless one" in the present (2:6-7) is even more difficult to pin down. Among the suggestions are Paul himself as a preacher of the gospel, Satan, and God. According to Gerhard Krodel, the restrainer "represents the present power of oppression in the world," oppression wrought by those who do not know God.[7]

---

6. Ernest Best, *The First and Second Epistles to the Thessalonians* (New York: Harper & Row, 1972), 283–86.

7. Krodel, "The 2 Letter to the Thessalonians," 94.

2. Colossians

a. The Question of Authenticity

Anyone who reads the Letter to the Colossians in Greek after the undisputed letters is in for something of a shock. The sentences are longer and more cumbersome, and the text abounds with unfamiliar words.

Many interpreters also find subtle theological divergences. For one thing, the Christology of Colossians has a "cosmic" thrust not found in so developed a form in the uncontested letters. In Christ, "all the fullness of God was pleased to dwell" (1:19; see also 2:9), and through him "all things have been created" and "all things hold together" (1:16-17). He is the one who "disarmed the "rulers and authorities" (2:15) and through whom "all things" were reconciled to God (1:20). While some of these phrases occur in a hymn the author quotes (1:15-20), others do not; so it is clear that the "cosmic" emphasis is the author's own.

Another difference is that Colossians consistently presents salvation as already having taken place, not as something to be awaited in the future. In 2:12, for example, the writer declares that "you *were* also raised with him through faith." And although the theme of Christ's return appears in 3:4, there is no mention of the imminence of this event. Colossians also presents Christ as exercising sovereignty already in the present. In an undisputed letter (1 Cor. 15:28) Paul says that all things have not yet been subjected to Christ and that in the end even Christ will be subjected to God; but in Colossians 3:11 we find that "Christ is all, and in all."

While all commentators grant the differences between Colossians and the undisputed letters, many defend its authenticity as a letter of Paul. Some explain the differences by pointing to the specific nature of the "false teaching" that the letter opposes. Faced with what seemed to be a head-on challenge to the ultimacy of Christ, their argument goes, Paul had to struggle to make his point. Hence the new vocabulary and complex sentences; hence also the "cosmic" Christology, which after all can be seen as a legitimate extension of that found in the other letters; and hence the emphasis upon salvation and Christ's sovereignty as already present.

As with 2 Thessalonians, however, the recent trend is to view Colossians as pseudonymous. For some scholars, the deciding factor is that it seems to reflect more formalized views on the church, tradition, and Paul's apostleship than are found in the undisputed letters. The term "faith" seems now to refer to a well-defined body of teaching, and Paul's apostolic office seems to function as its insurer (1:5-8, 23, 25, 28; 2:6-7; 3:16). And while in the undisputed letters Paul speaks of Christians collectively as Christ's body, in Colossians the terminology changes: Christ is the "head" of the body, which is specifically designated by the term "church" (1:18; 2:19).

It is also significant that Colossians contains a clear statement of woman's subjection to man (3:18) and an injunction to slaves to obey their masters (3:22), neither of which find unqualified parallels in the undisputed letters. Thus by some accounts Colossians involves not only an extension of Paul's theology but the absorption of that theology into a less radical stance in relationship to the dominant culture. It is true that these statements occur within a "household code" (a traditional compilation of social regulations) that the author has incorporated. But the very use of such material may speak against Pauline authorship, since no such codes occur in the undisputed letters.

A substantial number of scholars thus reject the authenticity of Colossians. There is no consensus among these scholars, however, on where to place the letter historically. Some argue for the generation after Paul, while others think a follower of Paul might have written it while Paul was still alive. The issue to some extent hangs upon how far one thinks Colossians has moved from Paul in developing more formalized notions of church, tradition, and ministry. As we will see, it is not as far as Ephesians and nowhere near as far as the pastoral letters.

b. Reading Colossians

(1) 1:1—2:23. Following the prescript that identifies himself as the sender and the Colossian Christians as recipients, "Paul" offers a thanksgiving that reminds the readers of the gospel they have already heard through Epaphras, his emissary. The intercessory prayer that follows (1:9-11) encourages the readers themselves to give thanks to God.

The declaration in 1:13-14 directs the readers' reverent attention to Christ and leads into what they will presumably recognize as a familiar hymn (1:15-20). Eliciting a feeling of adoration, it also states Christ's sovereignty over all things. Perhaps the readers will recognize some phrases as the author's additions: "the church" in 1:18 and "through the blood of his cross" in 1:20.[8] In any case, they will understand from the interpretive comments in 1:22-23 that the reconciliation they have experienced was won through Christ's death and that they have appropriated it precisely through the church and Paul's own apostleship.

---

8. See, e.g., Eduard Lohse, *A Commentary on the Epistle to the Colossians and Philemon*, trans. William R. Poehlmann and Robert J. Karris (Philadelphia: Fortress Press, 1971), 42–43.

As "Paul" continues to stress his apostolic office (1:24—2:5), the readers also hear that through him they have received the "mystery," God's plan from the beginning, which is identified as Christ's presence among them. Presenting this mystery as containing the true wisdom and knowledge, "Paul" also warns them against being deceived. The conclusion will stare them in the face: the teaching they have recently been entertaining is not the *true* wisdom and knowledge.

With that conclusion implied, "Paul" leads the readers in a new direction in 2:6-7: they must live on the basis of the (true, complete) faith through which they received salvation. And the first thing they hear is an explicit condemnation of the "philosophy" of merely human origin that is spreading among them, a condemnation interspersed with another declaration of Christ's sovereignty over the elements of the universe and all "rulers and authorities" (2:8-15). Again the readers are directed back to their original experience: it was in Christ that they were raised from the dead, through baptism.

Now "Paul" attacks the specifics of the "false" teaching (2:16-23). Condemning the festivals, dietary regulations, etc., he presents these as a mere shadows of the true reality. Since in Christ the readers have already "died" to such things, he can pose the devastating rhetorical question: "Why do you submit to regulations?" And he can declare that these regulations do not in fact accomplish what they promise, that is, to stop "self-indulgence."

(2) 3:1—4:18. The implication of the preceding point is that Christ can accomplish what the "philosophy" cannot. Reasserting that the readers have been raised with Christ, then, "Paul" can now issue specific instructions that presuppose their power to struggle meaningfully against the flesh. Having received a new nature in Christ—a nature in the image of God, which transcends all human distinctions among people—they are exhorted to bring that nature to realization through avoiding vices and embracing virtues. The readers will find the lists of good and bad behaviors typical of other moral teachings with which they are familiar, but they will also understand that Paul calls them to perform their deeds specifically in the name of Christ.

The lists of virtues and vices are followed by a table of instructions, designated as service to Christ (3:23), that pertain to various relationships. In the midst of more general exhortations, "Paul" refers again to his own apostleship and now mentions his imprisonment.

The personal greetings in 4:7-17 strengthen the sense of a relationship between "Paul" and the readers. The mention of the Christians in two other communities (Laodicea and Hierapolis), however, subtly places the letter in a wider context, suggesting that its argument might be relevant to other churches as well. A closing reference to "Paul's" imprisonment is a final reminder of his apostolic role in the progress of the gospel.

c. The Nature of the Colossian "Heresy"

Can we be more specific about the "false teaching" Colossians was written to counteract? Suggestions have ranged from a conservative Jewish Christianity such as Paul opposed in Galatia to an early Gnosticism. The emphasis on Sabbath observance and dietary regulations does suggest Jewish influence, but there is no indication that circumcision was an issue. One can find an asceticism, characteristic of some gnostic sects, behind the slogans "Do not handle, Do not taste" (2:21) and in the claim to wisdom (2:23). And since the term "fullness" plays an important role in Gnosticism, one can argue that the use of this word in 1:19 and 2:9 is intended specifically to undercut gnostic claims. On the other hand, there is neither any reference to the mythological systems so characteristic of gnostic thought nor any indication of "the radical dualism that marks the Gnostic spirit."[9]

The truth is that we cannot be very specific in describing the teaching the letter opposes. Perhaps the most we can say is that it was a syncretistic teaching combining some Jewish elements with ideas that, at least later, became characteristic of Gnosticism. Two matters relating to this teaching are, however, worthy of comment.

First, the phrase "worship of angels" in 2:18 has occasioned some debate. Commentators have generally assumed that means that the people were worshiping angels. Another possibility accepted by a number of scholars is that they understood themselves to be participating in the worship that *angels perform*.[10]

Second, the term *stoicheia* ("elements," "fundamental principles"), which we discussed earlier in relation to Galatians, occurs twice in Colossians, in 2:8 and 2:20. Most commentators continue to treat the term as referring to cosmic beings. According to Wink's interpretation, however, in 2:8 it means "the first elements or founding principles of the physical universe," because what the author attacks in this specific context is "philosophy" and "human tradition." In 2:20, on the other hand, the usage is parallel to that in Galatians: it means "the elements common to religion, pagan and Jewish alike."[11]

---

9. Joseph Burgess, "The Letter to the Colossians" in Sampley, et al., *Ephesians, Colossians, 2 Thessalonians, the Pastoral Epistles,* 45.

10. Fred O. Francis, "Humility and Angelic Worship in Col. 2:18," *Studia Theologica* 16 (1962): 109–34.

11. Walter Wink, *Naming the Powers: The Language of Power in the New Testament* (Philadelphia: Fortress Press, 1984), 74–76.

3. Ephesians

a. The Question of Authenticity

Much like Colossians, Ephesians is characterized by lengthy, complex sentences and an unusual number of words not found in the undisputed letters. It is particularly striking that many of the unfamiliar words occur frequently in the later writings of the New Testament and in Christian literature shortly after the New Testament period. And familiar Pauline terms are often displaced by alternatives: instead of "heaven," for example, one finds "heavenly places."

Ephesians also stands apart theologically. It tends to present salvation as already having taken place and makes no mention of the imminence of Christ's return. It also speaks, as does Colossians, of Christ as the "head" of the body, which is the church. And whereas in the undisputed letters the word "church" frequently designates a local congregation, in Ephesians it is used only of the "worldwide" church.

Even more significant is the view of the apostolic office in Ephesians. In 2:20 the author speaks of the church as "built upon the *foundation* of the apostles and prophets, Christ Jesus himself being the cornerstone." And in 3:5 we read of the "*holy* apostles and prophets." Paul frequently defended his apostolic office, but in none of the uncontested letters does he speak of apostles and prophets as the church's foundation. And the specialized usage of "holy" seems at odds with his application of this term to the Christian community at large.

Another consideration is the literary relationship of Ephesians to Colossians. There is so much overlap between the two that many scholars conclude either that one author copied from the other or that both used a common source. The most popular view is that the author of Ephesians used Colossians and expanded upon it. Interestingly, there is a shift in meaning in one of the most important instances of dependence: whereas in Colossians the "mystery" of God's plan, revealed to Christians, is Christ's presence among them, in Ephesians the mystery is the unity of Jews and Gentiles in the church.

In Ephesians we again find a "household code" with injunctions regarding women's subordination to their husbands and slaves' obedience to their masters. And a final point is that many scholars regard Ephesians not as a "real" letter but as a treatise presented in letter form. The best manuscripts do not contain a reference to Ephesus in the salutation, and the work is almost devoid of personal references. Nor does it address any specific problem as do the other letters.

Many scholars defend the authenticity of Ephesians. For the reasons given, however, many others credit it to a second-generation follower imitating a revered master in an attempt to set forth a particular theological statement.

b. Reading Ephesians

(1) 1:1—3:21. Following the salutation, which establishes the "letter" as a writing of the apostle Paul, the author launches a lengthy doxology that places a number of key ideas before the readers. Christians are blessed "in the heavenly places," chosen "before the foundation of the world," and called to be "holy and blameless" before God. The readers will get a strong sense of their vocation as Christians and their place in an overarching mystery: God's plan to unite all things in Christ. The phrase "all things" invites them to think in the widest possible terms: God's plan is the reconciliation of all components of the universe. Assuring the readers in 1:11-14 of their eventual redemption, "Paul" then encourages them to think confidently of the present in light of the eschatological future.

The intercessory prayer that follows (1:15-22) conveys a sense of the rich possibilities of Christian life in the present—wisdom, enlightenment, hope, power—that issue from Christ's exaltation. Imagining Christ as reigning over "all things" as "head" of his body/the church, they should feel enormously empowered.

In 2:1 "Paul" focuses on the readers' own experience of salvation. Declaring that Christ has made Christians "alive" (2:5), he contrasts the new, resurrected state to the old life of sin. And, presenting their salvation as issuing from God's grace (2:8), he places the present writing in the context of "his" other letters. Through the metaphor of a "walk" (obscured in the NRSV), he also issues a call for good works: although once walking in the ways of "this world," Christians are now enabled to live differently (2:1, 10).

Reminded in 2:11 that (as Gentiles) they once had no share in God's promises, the readers also hear that God has abolished the Jew/Gentile distinction. They should thus feel a strong sense of undeserved inclusion. And the image of the new humanity resulting from the union of Jew and Gentile, together with the metaphor of "household of God" for the church, brings the cosmic unity of 1:10 into narrower focus: God's reconciliation of "all things" through Christ is manifest in the church's own inclusiveness.

The characterization of the church in 2:19-22 reminds the readers of Christians' calling to be "holy and blameless" in 1:4. Now, however, "Paul" introduces the metaphor of a temple: with Christ as cornerstone and apos-

Fig. 71. "St. Paul at Ephesus" (Acts 19:19) (Engraving by Gustave Doré, 1865)
Paul's new converts at Ephesus renounce their former practice of magic
and burn the books they had used in this practice.

tles and prophets as foundation, it is a unified structure in which God's Spirit dwells.

The references to Paul's imprisonment in 3:1 and 3:13 serve to place the intervening discourse on the "mystery" in the context of Paul's own place in God's plan. The readers should understand that the "mystery of Christ" has been revealed to the "apostles and prophets"—and more specifically to Paul himself, who has received the insight that Gentiles are included in Christ's body. But Paul's role also points beyond itself. His commission to preach the gospel to Gentiles is also a commission to declare the role of the church in God's purpose: it too is called to declare God's wisdom (by which the readers will again understand God's mystery/plan) "to the rulers and authorities in the heavenly places." The reference to Paul's sufferings in 3:13 thus becomes a word of encouragement to Christians who are themselves in mission.

This encouragement is strengthened through a lengthy doxology, in 3:14-21, that closes with a pronouncement of "glory in the church." The readers will finish this section with a strong feeling of empowerment as members of the church, graciously included by God's own mercy and called to a mission of cosmic dimensions that is attested by the apostles and prophets and Paul himself.

(2) 4:1—6:23. The words "I therefore" signal the readers that "Paul" is now about to draw out the implications of what has gone before. Beginning with general ethical exhortations, he quickly places them in the context of an understanding of the church as united by Christ, a single faith, and baptism. Statements on Christ's ascension then ground a discourse on the various gifts given to church members. The readers are encouraged to understand that these gifts serve to "build up" the church and to provide a defense against false doctrine (4:14). And the notion of Christ's body, now removed from its cosmic context and made concrete, asks them to image the church as an organic unity. All individuals should thus think of their roles as essential to the whole and should also feel responsibility to maintain both doctrinal purity and loving relationships with others.

In 4:17-24 "Paul" places general exhortations in the context of Christology. What the readers have learned in Christ contrasts with the way the "Gentiles" (which here means non-Christians) live. And by asking the readers to put away their old way of life, he implicitly presents their new ethical possibilities as the result of God's action in Christ.

"Paul" now turns to specifics, offering some initial instructions on behavior (4:25-32) that he sums up in the injunction to "be imitators of God" and "live [walk] in love" (5:1-2). Then comes a more detailed list of admonitions that closes with a call to constant thanksgiving (5:18). It is followed by a lengthy "household code" that includes instructions for wives, husbands, children, fathers, slaves, and masters (5:21—6:9). The readers will recognize typical Hellenistic morality in the code, but they will also receive it as a statement of their Christian duty. "Paul" presents both the subordination of the wife to the husband and the obligation of the husband to love the wife as analogous to Christ's relationship to the church. The readers will thus understand marriage as holy but will also conceive it within the context of a hierarchical arrangement of power. And they will notice that Paul links slaves' duty to obey their masters to their duty to obey Christ.

Duly admonished, the readers are once again encouraged, now with combat metaphors, to stand strong in the struggle against insidious powers (6:10-17). They will think back to the cosmic dimensions of Christ's body and of their mission as the church. And they will understand both ethical action and doctrinal fidelity as prime components in that mission. "Paul's" self-reference in 6:19-20, together with the closing comments and benediction, serves once again to place all that has been said in the context of his apostolic authority.

c. Ephesians 3:10 and the "Language of Power": A "Postmodern Rereading"

In 3:10, the author of Ephesians declares that the church should make God's wisdom known "to the rulers and authorities" [RSV: "principalities and powers"] in the heavenly places." What are these "rulers and authorities," and how can the church be expected to preach in "heavenly" places? These questions play a crucial role in Wink's study of "the language of power" in the New Testament. As a way of understanding such language in our own context, Wink offers a "postmodern" interpretation that draws upon Bultmann's existential interpretation, Jungian psychological interpretation, and insights from both liberation theology and process thought—one of the schools of "postmodern" thinking discussed earlier (see above pp. 21, 32–33, 49–51, and below pp. 533–35).

(1) The *Stoicheia,* "the Powers," and Idolatry. Before discussing the Ephesians passage, it is important to take a broader look at Wink's project. We noted earlier his view that the term *stoicheia* in Galatians and in Colossians 2:20 refers not to supernatural beings, as many scholars have believed, but to the "elements" constitutive of any religion, that is, beliefs, rituals, etc. The important point now is to understand the sense in which such "elements" appear

as powers to which human beings are enslaved. Wink identifies the problem as idolatry:

> What is most basic to existence begins to be worshiped, either overtly or, as more often happens, unconsciously, as people abandon themselves to religious practices or philosophical ideals or ideological principles. When that happens, the stoicheia become functional gods, and their devotees are alienated from the One in and through and for whom even these most basic things in existence were created.[12]

The *stoicheia,* then, while not evil in themselves, actually become "demonic," as human beings falsely invest ultimacy in them. They enslave those who give final allegiance to them.

The term *stoicheia* is only one among many words and concepts found in the New Testament indicating powers that can enslave human beings. Among the others are authorities, powers, rulers, thrones, evil spirits, angels, fallen angels, and angels of the nations, i.e., "guardian" angels of specific peoples. While it might seem puzzling that apparently good powers, such as angels, are included in the list, Wink argues that "the powers" are both good and bad. They have their proper place in creation, but can become evil through their ignorance of God's plan. And, as in the case of the *stoicheia,* human beings can give them the absolute allegiance that belongs only to God: thus "even the good, made absolute, becomes evil."[13]

(2) Witnessing in the "Heavenly Places." A problem that has consistently bothered interpreters is whether such terms as "rulers" and "authorities" refer to earthly institutions/persons or to supernatural beings. This issue comes to a head in Ephesians 3:10, where the church is commissioned to witness to these powers "in the heavenly places." This phrase clearly refers to the supernatural realm. In Ephesians 1:3, however, the author says that Christ has blessed *the church* in the heavenly places. Since the church is on earth, Wink concludes, "the heavenly places" must mean "that sphere where Christians, with one foot in each of two worlds, already experience the risen life in Christ."[14] "The heavenly places," in other words, refers not to a place spatially removed from earthly existence but to a transcendent dimension where "earth" and "heaven" intersect.

What, then, would it mean for the church to makes its witness "in the heavenly places"? In answering this question, Wink also proposes a solution to the

---

12. Ibid., 77.
13. Ibid., 49.
14. Ibid., 89.

problem of the "rulers and authorities." Acknowledging the difficulty that the mythological notion of heavenly powers poses for many people in our day, he suggests that we can best understand the "rulers and authorities" as "the inner and outer manifestations of any given manifestation of power."[15] This statement will need elaboration.

(3) The Projection from Lived Experience. As Wink's analysis shows, the New Testament writers seem to refer to the powers in a way that embraces both the "earthly" and the "supernatural" senses, both human institutions/ persons *and* supernatural beings. If we ask why, the obvious answer is that they are projecting from their lived experience. Encountering an earthly government as oppressive, for example, they would come to understand it as the manifestation of an evil supernatural force.

While other interpreters have made similar points, Wink's contribution is to treat such projection as more than a fiction. Far from something "made up," it is a reflection of the actual impact of human institutions upon the unconscious. Every such institution manifests some type of "inwardness" or "spirituality," whether positive or negative. It is pervaded with a sense of human dignity and worth, or it stifles creativity in an atmosphere of fear; it fosters cooperation and mutual respect, or it sets one group against another; it looks lovingly on the world at large, or it stands belligerently against anything outside itself. Whatever the particular "spirit" of a given institution, the point is that it is *experienced* by human beings; and it is this very real experience that is projected in the creation of myth, an observation Wink credits to Jung.[16]

In their "inward" manifestations, then, the powers are "the inner essence of outer organizations of power." In their "outward" manifestations, "they are political systems, appointed officials, the 'chair' of an organization, laws—in short, all the tangible manifestations which power takes."[17] And what does it mean for the church to witness to them in "the heavenly places"? It means to seek to "convert" actual human institutions, to turn them away from their perversions to an understanding of their proper role in creation. More than changing mere structures, however, it means changing their very "souls."

(4) The Sources of Wink's Postmodernism. In highlighting the demand for change in human institutions, Wink is heavily influenced by liberation theology. He is also indebted to Alfred North Whitehead's school of process

---

15. Ibid., 5.
16. Ibid., 134.
17. Ibid., 5.

thought on several points. This way of thinking, too, emphasizes change, since it understands reality as dynamic, always in flux. It also envisions all components of reality as parts of one spiritual whole, which is God.

The notion of God as the transcendent whole of reality is reflected in Wink's treatment of the proper and improper behavior of the powers. Properly understood as parts of the whole, they ignorantly and foolishly aspire to ultimacy: "The parts do not or cannot know the effect of their acts on the whole, and some, less innocently, by their worship of their own selfish short-term interests, have become detrimental to the good of the whole."[18]

Process thought also stresses that if all things are parts of one spiritual whole, then the Western dualism of matter and mind (or spirit) simply will not hold. Reality is of one kind only, which is a physical/spiritual unity. Wink's emphasis upon the unity of "the inner" and "the outer" is a direct reflection of this rejection of dualism.

Wink also looks to Whitehead for insight into the phrase, "heavenly places." Finding inadequate the popular conception of heaven as an "otherworldly sphere qualitatively distinct from human life, to which the dead go if they have been good," Wink proposes to understand it as the "home of possibility." According to Whitehead, God feeds possibilities into the world, ever luring it toward the greater good. One way to get hold of the meaning of "heavenly places," then, is to understand this dimension of reality as the source of the lures to overcome the influences that lead human beings to oppress one another, accept such oppression, and remain victims of "inertia, fear, and neuroses." When human beings respond to such positive lures, Wink comments, they "quite rightly speak of the experience of ecstasy that accompanies that realization as 'heavenly.' "[19]

(5) The Reason for "Rereading." As is especially evident from these latter statements, Wink is engaged in a self-conscious "rereading" of the New Testament language of power. He does not imagine that the New Testament writers thought precisely in such terms. He claims for this "rereading," however, solid grounding in the biblical passages he examines; and he presents his "postmodern" interpretation as a way that persons in our day can get hold of what those passages actually say and mean. Certainly the New Testament writers knew nothing of Bultmann, Jung, liberation theology, or process thought; but that is not the question. The question is whether when we think in

---

18. Ibid., 115.
19. Ibid., 119.

these terms we are better able to grasp what they meant when they proclaimed Christ as sovereign over "the powers."

d. Restoration Eschatology, Cosmic Christology, and Ecological Theology

According to Ephesians 1:10, God will at the end time "gather up all things" in Christ." This reference to a final "gathering up" of all things, paralleled by a similar phrase in Acts 3:21,[20] seems to reflect the notion that the entire cosmos—not just individuals and not just human beings!—will be the object of God's ultimate redemption. It therefore stands alongside John 1 and Colossians 1:15-17 in exhibiting a decidedly cosmic dimension. Like these other passages, it has a strong appeal to theologians interested in ecological themes (see above, p. 308).

4. The Pastoral Letters: 1 and 2 Timothy and Titus

Designated the "pastoral letters" since the early eighteenth century, the three remaining writings attributed to Paul have much in common. All are concerned with ministerial functions but also speak to wider community concerns. They presuppose similar conditions in the church, speak to similar problems, and share distinctive characteristics of vocabulary and theological perspective. We have every reason to treat them as the work of a single author.

a. The Question of Authenticity

What the pastorals have in common with one another also sets them apart from the undisputed letters. The difference in word usage is striking. To begin with, a number of shorter words appearing frequently in the other letters— such as the Greek terms for "now," "therefore," "so that"—do not occur in the pastorals. In addition, a number of key words in the pastorals are found rarely or not at all in the other letters. Thus, for example, *eusebeia*—translated as "godliness," "piety," or "religion"—occurs ten times in the pastorals but never in the uncontested letters. It is also significant that the terminology in these writings closely parallels that of Christian writings from the second century, long after the time of Paul.

---

20. Acts 3:21 refers to the fulfillment of what God spoke through the prophets and probably includes the promises to Israel. But the term "universal restoration" seems to have a broader, cosmic dimension.

In some cases, differences in usage suggest theological differences. In the undisputed letters, the word "faith" refers to a dynamic reality, the act of the total human being in appropriating God's grace. In the pastorals, however, it generally designates a body of doctrine, a set of specific beliefs. The author of the pastorals, moreover, never uses the term "son" for Christ, never employs the formula "in Christ" in its "mystical" sense, and never mentions the cross at all![21]

The pastorals also presuppose a situation quite different from that depicted in the undisputed letters. While the latter make references to various functions within the Christian community, authority seems to be primarily charismatic in nature. The term *episkopos,* translated as either "overseer" or "bishop," occurs once in the undisputed letters (Phil. 1:1), but does not seem to be intended in the later, more formalized sense and may even be an insertion. The bishops mentioned in the pastorals probably did not possess the "monarchical" authority later associated with this term, but the lengthy discussions of the office of *episkopos,* along with that of deacon and elder, reveal a greater degree of formalization in church order than is evident in the undisputed letters.

There is, moreover, at least one apparent reference to an early form of ordination in the pastorals (1 Tim. 4:14). Although we cannot find here any sign of the hierarchical arrangement of power that eventually developed, scholars generally agree that in the pastoral letters we have clear evidence of "early Catholicism," the beginnings of an institutionalized church. The emphasis upon an ordained ministry dovetails with that upon formalized doctrine: a function of the officers of the community is to insure sound doctrine.

Scholars also find difficulty in fitting the pastorals into the chronology of Paul's life. To meet this difficulty, some have argued that he was released from his Roman imprisonment, visited Spain according to the plan laid out in Romans 15:28, and was later imprisoned again in Rome and put to death. In this view, Paul wrote the pastorals in the period after his release. The pastorals themselves, however, provide no real evidence for this theory.

Several scholars defend Pauline authorship on the grounds that the personal details in the letters are not the sort of thing a pseudonymous writer would invent. But others argue that such details might have been available through legend or projected from material in Acts and the other letters. And in some cases the personal details actually speak against authenticity. Although 2 Timothy 1:5 presents Timothy's faith as the product of Christian training in the

---

21. A. T. Hanson, *The Pastoral Epistles: Based on the Revised Standard Version* (Grand Rapids: Eerdmans, 1982), 3.

home, Paul's reference to him as his own "child in the Lord" in 1 Corinthians 4:17 suggests he was actually a convert.

Some scholars propose a compromise solution, arguing that the author expanded upon fragments of authentic letters. But such a view is difficult to substantiate and accomplishes little; one must still reckon with letters that are on the whole pseudonymous.

It should be noted, finally, that the pastorals draw extensively from Hellenistic sources, not only household codes, with their hierarchical views on women and slaves, but maxims from popular philosophy. Such borrowing, uncharacteristic of Paul, is one more item in a long list of arguments against authenticity. It would appear almost certain that 1 and 2 Timothy and Titus are the work of a pseudonymous author writing sometime between the last decade of the first century and the middle of the second.[22]

b. Approaching the Pastoral Letters

It was possible to offer reader-response analyses of 2 Thessalonians, Colossians, and Ephesians on a neutral basis, without making hard and fast judgments regarding authenticity. But such a strategy is less satisfying in the present case, since the pastorals are addressed to individuals rather than churches. We cannot trace the effects upon the readers without deciding whether we have in mind the actual persons Timothy and Titus or Christians of a later generation. In the following treatment, I will assume that the letters are pseudonymous. The readers whose responses will concern us are the people in the churches of the author's own generation.

There is no way to determine the sequence in which these three letters were written; the canonical arrangement is based upon length. But because 1 Timothy and Titus share an emphasis upon church regulations, it will be helpful to treat them in direct sequence. And because 2 Timothy focuses most clearly upon Paul himself, and thus can be understood as providing a personal background for these regulations, it makes a good starting point.[23]

c. Reading 2 Timothy

(1) 1:1—3:9. With the salutation (1:1-2), the author establishes the letter as a communication from Paul to Timothy. The designation of the latter as the

---

22. On dating the pastorals, see, e.g., Fred D. Gealy, "The First and Second Epistles to Timothy and the Epistle to Titus: Introduction and Exegesis," *The Interpreter's Bible*, vol. 11 (New York: Abingdon, 1955), 368–70.

23. Martin Dibelius and Hans Conzelmann, *The Pastoral Epistles*, trans. Philip Buttolph and Adela Yarbro (Philadelphia: Fortress Press, 1972), 71.

apostle's "beloved child" encourages the readers to revere Timothy as well as Paul and to pay close attention to the words "Timothy" is about to receive.

"Paul" then offers a "grateful remembrance" of the tradition in which both he and Timothy stand (1:3-14).[24] References to Timothy's mother and grandmother subtly encourage the readers to value Christian training. And the notation on cowardice vs. power (1:7) combines with the reference to Paul's suffering (1:12) to prepare the reader to hear exhortations to courageous action. Exhortations to Timothy, in fact, follow immediately, although they concern adherence to the "sound teaching." When in verses 15-18 "Paul" returns to the theme of his suffering by contrasting those who abandoned him in his distress with one who stood by him, the readers will make a connection: imitation of Paul in their day, faithfulness to his example, means guarding the Christian tradition; and to depart from it is equivalent to a refusal to share his lot.

With the above point made, "Paul" can now (2:1) issue explicit exhortations to "Timothy." Beginning with an injunction to "be strong," he quickly follows with two commands: to entrust Paul's teaching to the next generation and to accept his share in suffering. The readers, depending upon their roles in the community, will identify either with those Timothy will appoint or with the larger body of Christians. In any case, they will understand that all Christians must share in the apostle's suffering—that is made clear in 2:10-14—and that the injunctions in verses 14-26 apply to them. The readers will also note the condemnation of the teaching that the general resurrection has already taken place (2:18).

When in 3:1 "Paul" mentions the stress associated with the "last days," the readers will hear his statement as a prophecy pointing to their own time. And they will associate the vices listed in 3:2-5 with the "false" teaching regarding the resurrection, which they will also connect with a phenomenon in their contemporary situation. The reference to Jannes and Jambres (names given in Jewish tradition to Pharaoh's magicians who contended with Moses in Exodus 7) serves as a warning: those who oppose God come to a bad end (3:8-9).

(2) 3:10—4:22. "Paul's" injunction to "Timothy" in 3:10-11—to look back over the apostle's entire career—encourages the readers to focus on the image of Paul. They will hear in the statement on Paul's sufferings and deliverance a message made partially explicit in verses 12-13: those who pursue godliness

---

24. Willi Marxsen, *Introduction to the New Testament: An Approach to Its Problems*, trans. G. Buswell (Philadelphia: Fortress Press, 1968), 205.

can expected persecution, but the God who rescued Paul will be with them also; the ungodly, however, will presumably reap destruction.

In 3:14—4:8 "Paul" admonishes "Timothy" to continue in Paul's teaching, study the (Jewish) Scriptures, and pass on sound doctrine. Readers who are entrusted with the tasks of preaching and teaching will hear these instructions as directed toward them. Others will understand themselves as the recipients of such teaching and will be encouraged to distinguish between what has come from the apostle and what has not. They will know that the "coming" time (4:3) has arrived in their own day. The reference to "myths" in 4:4 will identify more specifically what is to be avoided.

In 4:6 "Paul" focuses on his own situation in prison. The reference to his "departure" will remind the readers of what they already know from tradition, that Paul in fact died for his faith, and will once again inspire them to take heart from his example and stand fast. Envisioning the great apostle as abandoned by everyone but Luke, having been attacked by Alexander the coppersmith, and so poor he must send for a cloak, they will be moved to consider their own lives as Christians. Will they be like those who fall away in times of trouble, or like the faithful Timothy? And the notation in 4:15 will remind them of the specific form faithfulness must take in their day: the crime of the evil coppersmith was opposition to Paul's message.

The readers are face to face with Paul's death and will receive the letter as a kind of last will and testament; the author has insured that with 4:6. It thus becomes important to know his final words. God stood by Paul in his distress and delivered him from destruction; the readers should believe that God is with them also. He must die now, but he stands to inherit God's heavenly rule. The readers can expect the same if they remain faithful.

The final greetings and benediction bring the letter to a close, leaving the readers with the final impression that they have read a letter of Paul, one that speaks directly to their own situation.

d. Reading 1 Timothy

(1) 1:1-20. Informed by the prescript that this is a letter from Paul to Timothy, the readers will conclude from 1:3-7 that its purpose is to deal with the matter of "false" teachings that involve "myths," "genealogies," and the Jewish law. They will recognize a complex of ideas, current in their midst, that combines aspects of Judaism with gnostic speculation on the origin of the universe. Whether officers or rank-and-file members of the Christian community, they will thus hear "Paul's" words to "Timothy" as applicable to their own sit-

uation: they must reject such deviant teachings. The letter thus presents itself as instruction in maintaining a proper Christian "household."

Having said that the "false" teachers refer to the law but misunderstand it (1:7), "Paul" hastens to comment on its proper function: to instruct ungodly people (1:8-11). Following a thanksgiving and personal testimony, he then charges "Timothy" to "fight the good fight" (1:18-20). The readers will receive "Timothy's" commission as their own, understanding it as an injunction to maintain "sound teaching" (1:10) and keep a good conscience (1:5, 19).

(2) 2:1—6:21. The phrase "first of all" in 2:1 signals the readers to expect a series of instructions. What they immediately receive is a command regarding prayer for all persons, including government officials, supported by an appeal to Paul's own commission and a statement on the universality of God. They will conclude from 2:2 that Christians are expected to live peaceably in the world, worthy of the respect of all persons.

In 2:8-15 they hear instructions regarding the internal life of the community. Statements on the subordination of women are grounded in an interpretation of the story of Adam and Eve. If the readers assume that the serpent's "deception" of Eve involved sexual seduction, they may understand woman's salvation through "childbearing" as a reversal: one is saved through a means corresponding to the way one becomes lost.[25] Along with the theme of woman's subordination, they may also hear a polemic against the gnostic teachers: the emphasis upon childbearing is also in some sense an affirmation of sexuality, the family, and the present world order.

In the statement of qualifications for the offices of bishop and deacon (3:1-13), the readers will hear typical Hellenistic moral instruction. Here again, the readers are encouraged to image the church as an orderly household and to view it as living inoffensively in its social context: the bishop should be well thought of by non-Christians (3:7).

When in 4:1 "Paul" turns to the "false" teaching of "later times," the readers will think of their own situation. What was earlier implied now becomes explicit: the heretics' prohibition of marriage and certain foods constitutes a denial of the goodness of God's creation. The exhortation given to "Timothy" (4:11), together with the reference to his "ordination" by the elders (4:14), reminds the readers of their own duties. If they are church officials, they have a special responsibility to guard the community from unsound teaching. As Christians, in any case, they are expected to reject false teaching and pursue training in godliness. Their salvation depends upon it (4:16).

---

25. Dibelius and Conzelmann, *The Pastoral Epistles*, 48–49.

In 5:1 "Paul" comments on the treatment of persons of varying statuses and then in 5:3-16 gives explicit instructions regarding "widows," who apparently constituted a somewhat formalized group. Readers will presumably recognize the problems "Paul" associates with some women claiming this status. And the negative characterization of younger widows in 5:13 warns the readers against what these women say. Both the emphasis upon marriage and the reference to the community's relationship to outsiders reinforce the image of the church as at peace with the world, although the reference to non-Christians as "the enemy" shows that those who follow Christ should not embrace the world uncritically.

In 5:17-20 the readers find instruction to elders, followed by personal exhortations to "Timothy." The injunction to moderate wine-drinking in 5:23 challenges the asceticism of the false teachers and affirms the goodness of creation. The injunction to slaves in 6:1-2 enhances the general image of the church as an orderly household, moral by the standards of society at large. Behind the command that slaves must not be disrespectful of Christian masters lies the assumption that they have no right to expect liberation.

The general exhortation at the end of 6:2 signals the readers that the main points have been made and encourages them to think back over all the instructions they have read. The warnings against false teaching in 6:3-10 reinforce the point, as do the positive exhortations to "Timothy" in 6:11-16.

After an exhortation to the rich (17-19) and a warning to "Timothy" regarding "what is falsely called knowledge" (*gnōsis*), "Paul" brings the letter to a close with the briefest of benedictions. The readers, by now, know what is necessary to maintain a Christian "household": they must reject the false teaching, hold fast to sound doctrine, demand proper demeanor in their leaders, and live as good Christian citizens in the world.

e. Reading Titus

(1) 1:1-16. The prescript in 1:1-4 not only establishes Paul as the writer and Titus, whom Paul has left in Crete, as the recipient; it also identifies the purpose of the letter as to strengthen "God's elect" (or chosen) in their faith and knowledge. The readers will identify with the "elect" and understand the letter as applicable to their situation.

In 1:5 "Paul's" reference to his commission to "Titus" to appoint elders reveals that the letter will explain how congregations should be organized. The immediate transition (1:6) to a discussion of the office of bishop reveals either that the terms "elder" and "bishop" are interchangeable or that a bishop is someone chosen from among the body of elders—the readers will presumably know which. In any case, "Paul" underscores the importance of the bishop by referring to the problem with which this person must deal, that is, teachers who recommend circumcision and seek personal gain. The negative impression of these teachers is reinforced by the quotation of a line, attributed to the Cretan poet Epimenides, that makes an ethnic slur against Cretans.[26] Perhaps the readers will know that many in the Hellenistic world thought of Cretans as liars because of their claim that the tomb of Zeus was in their land.[27] In any case, the quotation and its elaboration exploit their presumed prejudices in order to enhance a negative view of those who teach "falsely."

(2) 2:1-15. With false teaching thus denounced, "Paul" exhorts "Titus" in 2:1 to the teaching of sound doctrine and then includes a household code that encourages women and slaves to be submissive. In 2:11-15 the readers find a summary statement on the ideal behavior of the community. The eschatological hope is present, but the readers will have no sense of an imminent end to history: as Christians await Christ's return, they should live as good citizens in the world.

(3) 3:1-15. In 3:1-2 the reader finds a list of admonitions, such as to submit to authorities and act courteously toward all people, which are given a Christian interpretation in verses 3-7. Again the readers will interpret the Christian life in terms of good relations with the world at large. There follow a few more injunctions, including some more specific references to the "false" teachings (3:9), and a specific word on dealing with factious people (3:10). Then "Paul" adds some personal notes and a final admonition (3:14) and closes with a greeting and benediction. The personal elements leave the readers with the image of Paul, a faithful missionary busy at his work and concerned about others in the fellowship, fresh in mind.

STUDY QUESTIONS

1. Why do many scholars think 2 Thessalonians, Colossians, and Ephesians were not actually written by Paul?

2. What specific point does 2 Thessalonians make regarding eschatology?

3. What seems to be the specific nature of the Colossian "heresy," and how does the author argue against it?

---

26. Walter Lock, *A Critical and Exegetical Commentary on the Pastoral Epistles* (New York: Charles Scribner's Sons, 1924), 134.
27. Dibelius and Conzelmann, *The Pastoral Epistles,* 137.

4. According to Ephesians, what is the role of the church in God's plan? How, specifically, are the readers expected to express their loyalty to the church?

5. Explain how Wink intends his "postmodern" interpretation to enable contemporary readers to get hold of the "language of power." In what specific ways does his interpretation make use of "liberation" and "process" theologies?

6. Summarize the arguments for rejecting the pastoral letters as authentic letters of Paul.

7. How does the author of the pastorals make use of the figure of Paul himself in 2 Timothy as a way of engaging the reader?

8. Characterize the "false teaching" combatted in 1 Timothy.

9. In what ways does the author of the pastorals present the church as an "orderly household"?

10. What attitude toward the world outside the church is expressed in the pastorals? How do the "household codes" express this attitude?

FOR FURTHER READING

Barth, Markus. *Ephesians: Introduction, Translation, and Commentary.* 2 vols. Garden City, N.Y.: Doubleday, 1974. A major work treating the letter as authentic.

Best, Ernest. *The First and Second Epistles to the Thessalonians.* New York: Harper & Row, 1972. See chapter 9.

Dibelius, Martin, and Hans Conzelmann. *The Pastoral Epistles.* Hermeneia. Trans. Philip Buttolph and Adela Yarbro. Philadelphia: Fortress Press, 1972. Detailed and technical; a valuable resource.

Gealy, Fred D. "The First and Second Epistles to Timothy and the Epistle to Titus: Introduction and Exegesis." *The Interpreter's Bible.* Vol. 11. New York: Abingdon, 1955). Pp. 343–51. Strong commentary with an excellent introduction.

Goodspeed, Edgar J. *The Meaning of Ephesians.* Chicago: Univ. of Chicago Press, 1933. Argues that the person who compiled the Pauline letters composed Ephesians as an introduction to the collection, an influential but disputed theory.

Hanson, A. T. *The Pastoral Epistles: Based on the Revised Standard Version.* Grand Rapids: Eerdmans, 1982. Strong, readable, with a good introduction.

Jewett, Robert. *The Thessalonian Correspondence: Pauline Rhetoric and Millenarian Piety.* Philadelphia: Fortress Press, 1986. See chapter 9.

Krodel, Gerhard, ed. *The Deutero-Pauline Letters: Ephesians, Colossians, 2 Thessalonians, 1–2 Timothy, Titus.* Proclamation Commentaries. Rev. ed. Minneapolis: Fortress Press, 1993. Brief, readable competent treatments.

Lohse, Eduard. *Colossians and Philemon.* Hermeneia. Trans. William R. Poehlmann and Robert J. Karris. Philadelphia: Fortress Press, 1971. See chapter 9.

Martin, Clarice J. "The *Haustafeln* (Household Codes) in African American Biblical Interpretation." *Stony the Road We Trod: African American Biblical Interpretation,* ed. Cain Hope Felder. Minneapolis: Fortress Press, 1991. Examines the codes in light of Philemon and reflects on the biblical materials in relation to American slavery.

Mitton, C. L. *Ephesians.* Grand Rapids: Eerdmans, 1976. A sold commentary treating the letter as inauthentic.

Schweizer, Eduard. *The Letter to the Colossians: A Commentary.* Trans. Andrew Chester. Minneapolis: Augsburg, 1982. Detailed but readable; argues that Timothy composed the letter on behalf of the imprisoned Paul.

Epilogue to Part Three

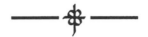

Thinkers have no control over the later use of their ideas, and Paul is no exception to this rule. Historians who study the writings of Paul's spiritual heirs in the late first century and the second century encounter radically divergent understandings of what "the apostle," as he came to be designated, was all about. In fact, we can see from 2 Peter 3:15-16 that the interpretation of Paul's letters had become problematic even before the New Testament period had ended. There should thus be little wonder that we find him claimed as an ally by persons with sharply opposing views today.

The passage in 2 Peter presupposes the existence of a collection of a Paul's letters before the middle of the second century. We do not know which letters were in the earliest grouping, but by the late second century the thirteen letters treated in Part Three were generally accepted. Hebrews, which eventually made its way into the canon as a letter of Paul, was by this time accepted by many churches but did not as yet have a secure status.

1. Marcion's Interpretation of Paul

One of Paul's most ardent heirs in the second century was a man named Marcion. Excommunicated in 144 c.e., Marcion subsequently founded his own church. He also constructed a canon of Scriptures that included only a shortened version of the Gospel of Luke and a collection of ten letters of Paul from which the pastorals were absent.

For Marcion, who was influenced by gnostic thought, Paul's contrast between law and grace necessitated a rejection of the Jewish heritage altogether. He not only denied the authority of the Jewish Scriptures but taught that the God of Jesus Christ was not the Jewish God at all. The latter, in his view,

440

was an inferior, harsh, and tyrannical deity who created the world out of evil matter. The Christian god, who appeared for the first time in Christ, was characterized by love and grace. Christ, who appeared on earth without being born and without a material body, came to rescue souls from this inherently corrupt world. Those who received him were required to abstain from all sexual intercourse and eating of meat.[1]

Marcion edited the Pauline letters he used, excluding all positive references to the Jewish heritage. That is one way to deal with perceived contradictions, but it is not the only way. An alternative is to read some passages as symbolic rather than literal. This is the route taken by the teachers of the second-century Christian gnostic groups.

2. Gnostic Interpretation of Paul

A particularly prominent Christian gnostic school was that founded by Valentinus, who was born in Egypt and later taught in Rome. Although our knowledge of Valentinus himself is limited, anti-gnostic Christian writers of the period have left us detailed accounts of the teachings of his followers, each of whom offered different versions of a complex system of thought. And there are some Valentinian materials among the gnostic documents of the ancient library discovered at Nag Hammadi in Egypt.[2]

Gnostic mythologies are populated not with goddesses and gods but with "aeons," personified abstract notions that represent both spatial realms and "divine, semi-divine, or demonic beings."[3] These aeons make up the spiritual light-world known as the Fullness. In the Valentinian system, the incomprehensible, perfect aeon named "Fore-Beginning, Forefather, and Abyss" plants a seed in the womb of his female counterpart named Thought, Grace, and Silence.[4] The result is a lengthy chain of emanations of aeons in male-female pairs.

The last of the female aeons, Sophia, precipitates a crisis. Separated from her male counterpart, she desires what is impossible—knowledge of the Father—and risks being lost in the Father's depth or Abyss. Although she is eventually convinced of her error and reclaims her place in the Fullness, her

---

1. Williston Walker et al., *A History of the Christian Church*, 4th ed. (New York: Charles Scribner's Sons, 1985), 67–68.

2. See James M. Robinson, gen. ed., *The Nag Hammadi Library in English*, 3d ed. (San Francisco: Harper & Row, 1988).

3. Hans Jonas, *The Gnostic Religion: The Message of the Alien God and the Beginnings of Christianity*, 2d ed., rev. (Boston: Beacon, 1963), 53–54

4. Ibid., 180.

Intention takes on a life of its own and produces Passion, which is a "detached complex of mental states," a formless "abortion."[5] Thus Christos and Holy Spirit are emanated to restore harmony to the Fullness, a harmony that produces yet another aeon, Jesus.

All is still not well. Sophia's Intention lives on outside the Fullness, producing a lower counterpart to Sophia named Achamoth (from a Hebrew word for wisdom), whose passions cause her great suffering. Jesus comes to save her and in the process transforms her emotions into the substances from which the Demiurge, who is produced by her longing to return to the light, creates the material world. Ignorant of all the worlds above him, this Demiurge thinks he is the true and only god.

From the beginning, the lower world contains a spiritual element, the result of Achamoth's longing for the light. But it must be awakened through knowledge (*gnōsis*). Thus Jesus, united with the Christos, eventually sojourns in the world to impart this knowledge and bring salvation to human beings. This salvation is not, however, available to all. Some persons are simply "fleshly" and cannot be helped at all, while others are "spiritual" and predestined to return to the light. A third group, who are "psychic," can be saved only through the "spirituals."

With this outline of the Valentinians' teaching in view, we can turn to their interpretation of Paul. Our guide will be a major treatise on this subject, written by Elaine Pagels.[6]

In their reading of Paul, the Valentinians made much of their distinction between the true god (the Forefather) and the inferior deity (the Demiurge) who created the material world. They argued, for example, that when Paul calls Abraham "our ancestor according to the flesh" in Romans 4:1, Abraham symbolizes the Demiurge. And they interpreted Romans 1:25 in a similar way, understanding those who "served the creature rather than the Creator" as persons who worshiped the lesser god rather than the Forefather.[7]

The distinction between the spirituals and the psychics was also important. Paul's words on Jews and Gentiles, law and grace in Romans provided a gold mine on this theme. According to the Valentinians, Paul taught that the spirituals are free from the law and exempt from the notions of sin and judgment. Lacking only the glory of the Father, they are justified by grace, which they receive through faith in the spiritual *Christos*. The psychics, however, who are under sin and subject to the law, are saved through faith in the psychi-

---

5. Ibid., 183.
6. Elaine Pagels, *The Gnostic Paul: Gnostic Exegesis of the Pauline Letters* (Philadelphia: Fortress Press, 1975).
7. Ibid., 16, 24, 27–28.

cal *Jesus*. It is they, so the Valentinians maintained, whom Paul has in mind when he says that "all have sinned" (Rom. 3:23) and declares that the law is upheld (Rom. 3:31).[8]

The psychic/spiritual distinction is again in view in the Valentinians' reading of 1 Corinthians 11:11-15, which speaks of the interdependence of man and woman. Male and female are symbolic, respectively, of spirituals and psychics, and the passage means that "only in conjunction with one another can either gain access" to the Fullness.[9] When Paul speaks of the limited character of knowledge, prophecy, etc. in 1 Corinthians 13, he has the gifts of the *psychics* in mind. It is only the spirituals who have true knowledge and love.[10]

The Gnostics' negative view of material reality also played its part in Valentinian interpretation. One interpreter took Paul's phrase in Romans 8:3—"in the *likeness* of sinful flesh"—to mean that the Son had only the appearance of a physical body. And, assuming that Paul could not have referred to a bodily resurrection in Romans 6, they argued that he was speaking symbolically of the process of receiving *gnōsis*. To be dead was to be ignorant of (the true) God, and to be resurrected meant to receive the knowledge they taught.[11]

Christian interpreters from earliest times have generally assumed that the Gnostics simply read their own systems of thought into Paul. Pagels, however, cautions against such a simplistic judgment, concluding that at many points the Valentinians' theology was a genuine outgrowth of their reading of Paul, not a preconceived set of ideas they imposed upon him. In this sense the Valentinian teachers qualify as genuine interpreters.[12] Indeed, as another writer states, "their distinction between 'spiritual,' 'psychic,' and "fleshly' . . . owes much to Pauline language."[13] It should be said also that their "realized eschatology," while clearly one-sided, did in fact get hold of an important aspect of Paul's own teaching.

We may consequently speak of both Marcion and the Christian Gnostics as representing schools of Pauline interpretation that were rooted in serious attempts to understand Paul's views. Some works of early Catholicism, of course—the pastorals—made it into the New Testament canon, whereas the Gnostic interpretations of Paul did not. This is hardly to say, however, that the

---

8. Ibid., 22.
9. Ibid., 76.
10. Ibid., 76–79.
11. Ibid., 28–33.
12. Ibid., 9.
13. Walker, *A History of the Christian Church*, 66.

author of the pastorals interpreted Paul correctly but Marcion and the Gnostics did not. It was, in fact, clearly the latter two, whatever one must conclude about the "accuracy" of their readings, who made the more serious attempts to expound Paul's *theology*.

3. The Paul of Legend

The author of the pastorals perpetuated Paul's legacy by enlisting his apostolic authority in the service of "sound teaching" and a church structure designed to maintain it. Marcion and the Gnostics did so by interpreting Paul theologically. But there was yet another way Paul's memory was kept alive: early Christians told stories about him, some of which are collected in an apocryphal book called "the Acts of Paul."

Dennis MacDonald has recently sought to determine the relationship between the pastoral letters and some of the stories in the Acts of Paul. In one of these, Paul plays the hero in a variant of the ancient tale on which George Bernard Shaw based his play "Androcles and the Lion." According to the original version, an escaped slave hiding in a cave befriends a lion by removing a splinter from its paw. The slave is eventually captured, condemned to death, and stands helpless in an arena as a lion is released upon him. When the lion, who turns out to be the slave's old friend, gently licks his feet, the spectators are moved to spare the man's life. The Pauline variation is wonderfully appropriate. Paul too is spared by a lion. But instead of removing a splinter in the earlier scene, he preaches to the lion—who immediately repents and is baptized![14]

Even more interesting is the story of Thecla, a young and beautiful woman who is converted by Paul's preaching on the eve of her wedding to the wealthy Thamyris and dedicates herself to a life of chastity. MacDonald summarizes:

> When Thamyris fails to woo her back from Paul, he and Thecla's mother, Theocleia, take her to the governor, who orders her brought to the theater naked to be burned at the stake. A hailstorm extinguishes the fire, and Thecla is saved. She finds Paul, tells him she will cut her hair short—i.e., like a man's—and follow him if he will baptize her. But Paul is not yet sure of her commitment. Together they go to Antioch of Pisidia, where another frustrated would-be lover condemns Thecla before

---

14. Dennis Ronald MacDonald, *The Legend of the Apostle: The Battle for Paul in Story and Canon* (Philadelphia: Westminster, 1983), 21–23.

the governor. In spite of the protests of the women of the city, including a Queen Tryphaena, she is thrown naked to the beasts, baptizes herself in a pool of seals, is saved by a series of miracles, sews her mantle so that she will look like a man, and flees to Paul, who ordains her to teach.[15]

MacDonald gives good evidence that these stories were originally passed on in oral form by female storytellers. The dominant and sympathetic characters in every story are women, and men often appear in hostile roles. In the lion story, for example, Paul converts two women in prison to the consternation of their husbands. The stories thus reflect a dissenting voice against the mores of a patriarchal society. The image of Thecla, a woman outside the traditional household and a teacher, served to legitimate women's independence and right to serve in leadership roles. It is significant that the stories seem to come from Asia Minor, where women were particularly prominent in church leadership.[16]

MacDonald thus argues that a primary motivation of the author of the pastorals was to silence female storytellers who told such tales as later appeared in the Acts of Paul. In 2 Timothy 3:6-7, for example, "Paul" warns against "those who make their way into households and captivate silly women . . . who are always being instructed and can never arrive at a knowledge of the truth." And 1 Timothy 4:7 speaks explicitly against "old wives' tales"!

The reason for silencing women was to protect the institution of the patriarchal household. It is thus understandable that the pastorals not only object to stories that empower women but also reject the practice of celibacy (1 Tim. 5:11-14), which encourages their independence. If this motive is in fact at work, the statement that women are saved through childbearing (1 Tim. 2:11-15) becomes all the more intelligible: the point is quite literally that women should be kept in their place at home.[17]

To maintain a stable patriarchal household, one must maintain the authority of a patriarch. That, according to MacDonald's reading, is why the pastorals give so much attention to the offices of the church, which must be filled with males. And that is why the requirements for these offices are so consistent with typical Hellenistic morality. Their role, in fact, is to maintain the church as a stable household as defined by Hellenistic society.

The Paul of legend, however, stands in marked contrast to the church officials who pass on the Pauline heritage in the pastorals. "Nothing in the legends," MacDonald writes, "suggests that Paul or any other Christian could

---

15. Ibid., 18–19.
16. Ibid., 26–53.
17. Ibid.

be characterized as moderate or dignified; rather, they are proudly presented as socially deviant, impudent, and incorrigible."[18]

4. Perspectives on the Issues

It is always a temptation to caricature one's opponents. During the late first and early second centuries, the Pauline legacy developed in several radically different directions. While the options that appeared during that time cannot be equated with the ways in which twentieth-century interpreters sort out the issues, one can meaningfully point out parallels. Modern opponents of women's ordination are in some sense heirs of the pastoral letters, and feminist theologians stand in some sense in the line of those ancient Christian women who told the story of Paul and Thecla. While it is important to recognize these connections, however, it is also important not to reduce the ancient issues to the modern ones but to see them in their original complexity.

It is easy enough for interpreters who consider themselves "orthodox" to reject the Marcionite and gnostic readings of Paul out of hand. There can be little doubt that such readings distort Paul's thought. We may legitimately ask, however, whether such "distortions" were any greater than those found in the pastoral letters. Do the pastorals rightly represent Paul's views on women? Does their emphasis upon "sound doctrine" do justice to Paul's understanding of faith?

It is all too easy, on the other hand, simply to condemn the pastorals as representing a degeneration of an early, charismatic movement into a staid institution. It is important to remember that in opposing Gnosticism the Pastorals were preserving Christianity's Judaic heritage, with its emphasis upon the goodness of God's creation. And when the church accepted a canon including the pastorals and four Gospels it reaffirmed that point. One should also recognize that what the pastorals sought to preserve was unity within the Christian community, a profoundly Pauline theme.[19]

It is nevertheless true that the price the early church paid for shoring up the boundaries of the community and preserving an affirmation of the material world was the adoption of a patriarchal structure. Whether that particular price was necessary is a matter of conjecture, and whether it was justified is a matter of opinion. It should be clear enough from the preceding investiga-

---

18. Ibid., 72.

19. See, e.g., the comments of Jerome D. Quinn, *The Letter to Titus: A New Translation with Notes and Commentary and an Introduction to Titus, I and II Timothy, the Pastoral Epistles* (New York: Doubleday, 1988), 21.

tion that theological speculation was indeed running wild and that loss of any meaningful connections to the earliest level of the Jesus tradition and to the Judaic heritage was a real possibility. But that is not to say that the patriarchal structure was the only way to preserve those links. And, above all, it is not to deny the consequences of the choice the early church made.

How one evaluates the perspective of the pastorals and the decision of the church depends to some extent upon one's perception of the nature of the "danger" the communities faced. Interpreters of the pastorals have often concluded that the author recommends silencing women because women have been particularly active in propagating gnostic teaching. MacDonald points out, however, that there are no discernible gnostic elements in the stories in the Acts of Paul.[20] Although we find gnostic teaching and women's stories lumped together in the pastorals, this does not mean that such lumping was accurate. Alongside the anti-gnostic thrust of the pastorals we have also seen a general interest in settling down in the world. The author's attitude toward women seems motivated in part by a desire to accommodate to the dominant culture. Certainly, the church would acquire a "bad" reputation if its women became known as disrupters of households!

Because early Catholicism—ancestor of later Orthodox, Catholic, and Protestant Christianity—adopted the patriarchal structure, many contemporary feminists have been inclined to look upon Gnosticism as more favorable to women's interests. Certainly, Gnosticism included feminine aspects in the deity, and there is evidence that women played active roles in gnostic circles. According to Elisabeth Schüssler Fiorenza, however, this does not mean that Gnosticism was pro-feminist:

> Gnosticism... employed the categories of "male" and "female," not to designate real women and men, but to name cosmic-religious principles or archetypes.... In Gnosticism, the pneumatics [spirituals], men and women, represent the female principle, while the male principle stands for the heavenly realms, Christ, God, and the Spirit. The female principle is secondary, since it stands for the part of the divine that became involved in the created world and history. *Gnostic dualism shares in the patriarchal paradigm of Western culture. It makes the first principle male, and defines femaleness relative to maleness.*[21]

That both the early church and Gnosticism adopted aspects of the patriarchal ideology is hardly surprising; it was central to the dominant culture. The

---

20. MacDonald, *The Legend of the Apostle*, 63.

21. Elisabeth Schüssler Fiorenza, *In Memory of Her: A Feminist Theological Reconstruction of Christian Origins* (New York: Crossroad, 1983), 274; italics added.

victory of patriarchy, however, was not absolute. The church eventually made a place for celibate women and thus provided an escape from the household, although this status fell short of full equality. And, in preserving the undisputed letters of Paul, along with the Gospels, it also passed along fragments of an alternative vision of social structure.

5. The Interpretation of Paul as a Hermeneutical Problem

The wide variation in the early readings of Paul provides a vivid illustration of hermeneutics in process, that is, the attempt of interpreters not simply to understand Paul in a merely technical, descriptive way but to make ultimate sense of his point of view, to find meaning in his writings that is of genuine significance to one's life. The discrepancies also illustrate, to be sure, the problematic character of hermeneutics: how does one decide between competing interpretations? But they can also be viewed as evidence that hermeneutical endeavor is a necessary corollary of the attempt to understand, that the interpreters always bring some value-laden agenda to their work.

It should come as no surprise, then, that the hermeneutical issue arises in more recent attempts to understand Paul. To be sure, some of the variations in the characterizations of Paul's theology are rooted in technical questions such as the meaning of certain terms and concepts, the motivation for a particular writing, and the nature of a conflict within which Paul was involved. At other points, however, it is evident that interpreters understand Paul differently because they read him in different ways, that is to say, from varying hermeneutical perspectives.

STUDY QUESTIONS

1. Compare and contrast the "Paul of legend" to the Gnostic Paul, the Paul of the pastoral letters, and the Paul who wrote the seven undisputed letters. State which aspects of these various "Pauls" you personally find acceptable or unacceptable, interesting or uninteresting, and explain why.

2. Give your own arguments as to whether the "main" body of the church was justified in rejecting gnostic teachings such as found in Valentinianism.

3. It has been argued that many Gnostic teachings actually survived within the "main" body of Christianity. Give your own opinions regarding this claim.

FOR FURTHER READING

MacDonald, Dennis R. *The Legend and the Apostle: The Battle for Paul in Story and Canon.* Philadelphia: Westminster, 1983. Brief, readable, and interesting; traces "feminist" origins of extra-canonical stories about Paul.

McGinn, Sheila E. "The Acts of Thecla." In Elisabeth Schüssler Fiorenza, ed. *Searching the Scriptures,* vol. 2: *A Feminist Commentary.* New York: Crossroad, 1994. Distinguishes "The Acts of Thecla" from "The Acts of Paul," in which it was included, and challenges traditional explanations of its exclusion from the canon. Important reading.

Pagels, Elaine. *The Gnostic Paul: Gnostic Exegesis of the Pauline Letters.* Philadelphia: Fortress Press, 1975. A competent and interesting study; raises important questions.

Part Four

Hebrews, the General Letters, and Revelation

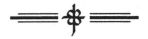

Prologue to Part Four

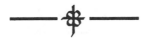

1. On the Margins: Inside

The nine writings to be examined in Part Four form a somewhat diverse body of materials. One factor that does bind them together, however, is that, with the exception of 1 John and 1 Peter, they were all subjected to some degree of dispute in their process toward final acceptance into the canon. In that sense, seven of them stand "on the margins" of the New Testament. Christians have valued some of these very highly through the centuries, however, as they have 1 John and 1 Peter.

Tradition has assigned each of these nine works to an apostolic author, but in every instance modern scholars have raised serious doubts. As is the case with other New Testament writings, the titles are undoubtedly secondary, supplied not by the authors but by later Christians who preserved them.

Although the influence of these books on Christian thought and practice does not equal that of the Gospels or the letters of Paul, they contain much that is of interest to the student of the New Testament. We find here not only material that is useful for the reconstruction of the history of the early church, but some of the most distinctive theological perspectives in the New Testament. And some of the works have played important roles in theological thinking in our own time.

The complexity of the problem of organizing the New Testament materials for study becomes particularly apparent when we come to these materials. In chapter 14 we will study the Letter to the Hebrews, an anonymous work traditionally attributed to Paul. The ambiguity of the early church's judgment about its authorship is reflected by its place in the canon. In the New Testament, the letters of Paul are arranged in the order of decreasing length; yet Hebrews, much longer than several of the other letters attributed to Paul,

453

stands at the very end of the collection. Although a strict canonical approach would have warranted including it in Part Three as an addendum to the Pauline letters, its theological distinctiveness was the deciding factor in my decision to treat it separately.

Hebrews is followed by seven writings that from early times have been called the "general" or "catholic" (i.e., "universal") letters. This designation presumes (wrongly in at least some cases) that they were intended not for a specific church in a specific locale but for the church at large. Three of these form a subgroup of "Johannine" letters, traditionally attributed to John the son of Zebedee, the supposed author of the Gospel of John. As we will see, these writings must have come from the same Christian community that produced that Gospel. Were it not for the decision to follow the broad canonical divisions and treat the four Gospels and Acts together, the Johannine letters could have been studied in conjunction with the fourth Gospel. Two of the other four general letters reflect historical situations closely paralleling those of the pastoral letters and could have been treated in connection with that group. In the present arrangement, the seven writings are placed in two groupings. Chapter 15 is devoted to James, 1 and 2 Peter, and Jude; the Johannine Letters receive separate treatment in chapter 16.

The subject of chapter 17 is a writing entitled the Revelation to John, the final book in the New Testament. Since tradition also assigned this work to John the son of Zebedee, it too might have been studied in another connection. But few critical scholars accept that tradition. And, in any case, separate treatment seems justified not only by its distinctive content but by the apparent reason for its placement in the canonical order. As the work most heavily influenced by apocalyptic themes, most clearly focused on the question of the "last things," it stands rather appropriately as the conclusion of the New Testament canon.

2. On the Margins: Outside

If there are writings that stand in some sense marginally within the canon, there are others that stand marginally outside it in the sense that they fulfill one or more of the following criteria: they appeared on one or more of the canonical lists in the early centuries; they were treated as authoritative by some church leaders; they were included in collections of New Testament texts. Unlike works such as the gnostic Gospels that were specifically branded heretical by the emerging majority church, these writings were often considered valuable resources for use in Christian worship. The five I have chosen to discuss here are 1 Clement, the Didache, the Shepherd of Hermas, the Letter of Barnabas, and the Apocalypse of Peter.

a. 1 Clement

The letter that came to be known as 1 Clement was sent from the church in Rome to the church in Corinth, and is generally dated late in the final decade of the first century. An early and apparently reliable tradition attributes the actual composition to one Clement of Rome. A later tradition identifies this Clement as bishop of the Roman church, but many scholars discount it because the letter's own terminology seems to indicate that the practice of investing exclusive authority in a single bishop in each church had not yet developed.[1]

The letter is a response to an incident in the Corinthian church: a dissident group has deposed the established leadership. The author (on behalf of the Roman church) defends the established leadership by referring to a chain of authority. As Christ is from God, so the apostles are from Christ. And it is the apostles who appointed the bishops and deacons. Many scholars see here the notion of apostolic succession, the belief that Jesus gave, through Peter and the other apostles, a formal authority to bishops. Helmut Koester argues, however, that the author does not connect specific apostles with specific churches and therefore "is not interested in the doctrine of apostolic succession, but wants to speak generally about the continuance and stability of offices in the Christian churches."[2] It would seem, nevertheless, that we have here a clear step in the direction of such a doctrine, which in any case begins to take shape shortly after 1 Clement and is found in explicit form by the end of the second century.

The author speaks to the situation not only by condemning the removal of the leaders, but by engaging in a long parenetic discourse, drawing upon such sources as the Jewish Scriptures, sayings of Jesus, the letters of Paul, Christian traditions regarding Peter and Paul, and "pagan" materials as well. The bulk of the letter consists of extended exhortation to maintain authentic Christian piety and ethical behavior. Prominent, for example, are the condemnation of envy and rivalry and the recommendation of humility and repentance.

Some scholars think there was a theological dispute behind the controversy between the rival leadership groups, and it is possible those who deposed the

---

1. Cyril Richardson et al., trans. and ed. *Early Christian Fathers* (Philadelphia: Westminster, 1953), 36.
2. Helmut Koester, *Introduction to the New Testament*, vol. 2: *History and Literature of Early Christianity* (Philadelphia: Fortress Press, 1982), 290.

leadership were the spiritual heirs of Paul's opponents in 1 Corinthians. There is, however, no definite indication of this in the letter.

The writing is notable for its mention of the deaths of Peter and Paul and its use of the legend of the phoenix. According to this legend, when the bird dies a worm is formed from its decaying flesh. Feeding off the carcass, it eventually grows into a new bird which then repeats the cycle. The author uses the story as an analogy to the Christian belief in the resurrection of the dead.

b. The Didache

The Teaching of the Twelve Apostles—or the Didache (Greek for "teaching"), as it is popularly known—is composed of two prior documents that an editor has brought together relatively intact. The first of these is a tractate on the "two ways," a kind of moral catechism that exists in slightly different forms as an independent document and as a part of the Letter of Barnabas. The second is basically a manual of church order.

Many scholars think that the first part is a slightly reworked Jewish document, but others dispute this. In its present form, in any case, it contains many points of contact with the Gospels. The two ways are the way of life and the way of death. The former is characterized by such virtuous activities as loving God, loving one's enemies, giving to those in need, and honoring church leaders; and the latter by murder, adultery, fornication, magic, astrology, sorcery, greed, and jealousy.

The church manual contains instructions for sacred practices such as baptizing, fasting, and the celebration of the sacred meal. The last is called the "eucharist" (Greek for thanksgiving), but some scholars doubt that this term is used here in the technical sense applied to the Lord's Supper and think it refers only to the love feast, or common meal, at a time after the Lord's Supper had been split off from it. It is possible, however, that the separation has not yet taken place. In any case, the instructions indicate an actual meal, not just bread and wine, and explicitly exclude from it anyone who has not undergone Christian baptism.

The manual also offers guidance on the treatment of apostles, teachers, and prophets and urges the election of worthy bishops and deacons. In addition, it informs churches how to distinguish between true and false leaders among those who arrive as visitors, and it closes with an admonition about false prophets who will appear in the last days.

The Didache claims to represent the teaching that Jesus gave to the "twelve apostles," but its final form clearly dates from the end of the first century or a little later. It has points of contact with several New Testament writings, most notably the Gospel of Matthew, which the final editor may have used.

c. The Letter of Barnabas

The Letter of Barnabas is really an anonymous treatise rather than a letter, and there is no reason to accept the early attribution of it to Barnabas the companion of Paul. The greater part of the work is devoted to Christian allegorical interpretations of the Jewish Scriptures, and in this respect it has a similarity to the canonical book of Hebrews. Unlike Hebrews, however, it is disparaging of the Jewish people, whom the author believes proved unworthy of the revelation given to them.

Addressing a wide range of topics in the Scriptures, the author understands the dietary regulations as allegorical statements of moral commands. The prohibition against eating pork, for example, is really an injunction for human beings not to act like swine. And the reference to the six days of creation in Genesis means that Christ's return will come six thousand years after the world was made. What "Barnabas" considers the most important piece of wisdom in the treatise, however, concerns the account in Genesis 14:14, 17:23 that Abraham circumcised 318 of the males in his household.

> Now the (number) 18 (is represented by two letters), J=10 and E=8—thus you have "JE" (the abbreviation for) "Jesus." And because the cross, represented by the letter T (=300), was destined to convey special significance, it also says 300....No one has learned from me a more trustworthy lesson! But I know you are worthy of it. (Barnabas 9:8-9)[3]

Allegorical interpretation appears bizarre to modern readers influenced by historical criticism. But it is in many ways typical of ancient Jewish interpretation in general and has clear points of contact within the New Testament, not only in Hebrews but, for example, in Paul's use of the story of Sarah and Hagar in Galatians 4:21-31.

d. The Shepherd of Hermas

The Shepherd is a long apocalyptic work that recounts three sets of visions of the author, Hermas. Highly moralistic in tone, it extends a final call to repentance before a coming persecution and/or the end of the age. The presupposition is that those who refuse this opportunity to repent will be lost, as

3. Robert M. Grant, *The Apostolic Fathers: A New Translation and Commentary*, vol. 3: *Barnabas and the Didache* (New York and Toronto: Thomas Nelson and Sons, 1965), 109.

will any who do repent but later fall into sin. In offering a new opportunity for repentance, however, it gives a different answer to the question of whether those who sin after baptism can subsequently be forgiven than does Hebrews. The latter takes a harder line (Heb. 6:4), proclaiming that there is in fact no forgiveness for those who fall from grace.

Hermas identifies himself as a freed slave, and the first set of visions comes to him through an appearance of the figure of his former owner, Rhoda. Eventually turning out to be a symbol of the church, she convicts Hermas of his sin and demands that he repent, which he does. The remaining visions, which constitute the greater part of the work, come through the figure of the shepherd, who is identified as the angel of repentance. And Hermas's explicit commission is to announce the time of repentance to his readers.

In the second set of visions, the shepherd delivers a series of mandates, or extended commandments. The first is the injunction to believe in the one god. The others range from prohibitions of illicit sexual thoughts, anger, and greed to commendation of cheerfulness, purity, and endurance in suffering. Both men and women are commanded to divorce unfaithful spouses and remain single afterward but to take them back if they repent.

The final visions take the form of lengthy allegories, which the author calls parables. They are devoted largely to symbolic representation of the various categories of people in the church, such as those who have remained pure, those who are generally pure but have sinned in minor ways, and those who have placed themselves beyond repentance by committing blasphemy.

The Shepherd of Hermas contains very little explicit theology, but it is notable in several respects. An adoptionist Christology, the notion that Jesus became the Son of God during his life, is evident at some points, although at others the preexistence of the Son is clear. And the writing seems to contain an early form of the notion of works of supererogation, good deeds above and beyond the commandments, which receive special merit from God.

Also, there is frequent reflection upon the question of poverty and riches within the church. In an attempt to trace the social history of the Shepherd's community, however, Carolyn Osiek concludes that there were probably few truly upper class persons to be found there.[4] The "rich," in her account, were, like Hermas himself, former slaves who had become relatively successful in business and were increasingly abandoning their responsibilities to the church in favor of quests for luxury and status in the wider society. Hermas's criti-

---

4. Carolyn Osiek, *Rich and Poor in the Shepherd of Hermas: An Exegetical-Social Investigation* (Washington, D.C.: Catholic Biblical Association of America, 1983).

cisms of wealth are thus an attempt to get such persons to exercise their duties to the rest of the community.

The Shepherd of Hermas was apparently written in Rome. But it is hard to date, because it is probably composed of several earlier documents. Most scholars think, however, that it achieved its final form by the middle of the second century.

e. The Apocalypse of Peter

The Apocalypse of Peter, which should not be confused with a gnostic work of the same name, purports to be the apostle Peter's account of revelations given to him by Jesus on the Mount of Olives. Although some early church leaders considered it authentic, that judgment did not prevail; and it is universally considered pseudonymous today.

Despite its eventual rejection, the work did have some lasting influence on Christianity. It is the first example we have of a Christian writing that gives detailed descriptions of the rewards and punishments in heaven and hell, the kind of material later appearing in Dante's *Inferno*. Among those singled out for special punishment are blasphemers, people guilty of sexual sins, murderers, and slaves who do not obey their masters. The flavor is amply evident in the following excerpts:

> Then will men and women come to the place prepared for them. By their tongues with which they have blasphemed the way of righteousness will they be hung up. There is spread out for them unquenchable fire.... And the murderers and those who have made common cause with them are cast into the fire, in a place full of venomous beasts, and they are tormented without rest, as they feel their pains.[5]

The obvious point of comparison among the canonical writings is the book of Revelation. But, as we will see, in Revelation the detailed descriptions of divine punishment are confined to the earthly sphere and serve a somewhat different function. And the Apocalypse of Peter is entirely lacking in the theme of vindication of the oppressed that is so strong in Revelation—whose author would never have listed disobedient slaves among the candidates for eternal torture.

---

5. Wilhelm Schneemelcher, ed., *New Testament Apocrypha*, vol. 2: *Writings Relating to the Apostles: Apocalypses and Related Subjects*, rev. ed., trans. R. McLachlan Wilson (Cambridge: James Clark; Louisville: Westminster/John Knox, 1992), 628–29.

STUDY QUESTIONS

1. Based upon the brief treatments of the noncanonical works in this prologue, try to formulate arguments both for their inclusion and for their exclusion. What aspects of each do you think you would value? Why? What aspects might you not value? Why?

2. State why you agree or disagree with the author's statement that the approach to the Jewish Scriptures found in the Letter of Barnabas is not very different from the approach employed in canonical New Testament writings.

3. Did the early Christians do the right thing in settling upon a definite canon? Give arguments on both sides of the question.

FOR FURTHER READING

Grant, Robert M. *The Apostolic Fathers: A New Translation and Commentary.* 6 vols. New York and Toronto: Thomas Nelson and Sons, 1964–69. Contains all the works treated in section 2 above except the Apocalypse of Peter. Vol. 1 is a valuable introduction; vol. 2 includes 1 Clement, vol. 3 Barnabas and the Didache, and Vol. 6 Hermas.

Chapter 14

The Letter to the Hebrews

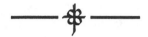

1. Searching for the Story

Despite many attempts to reconstruct the story behind the writing that bears the title "To the Hebrews," there is no consensus on the matter. An old tradition in Alexandria assigned the work to Paul, although his name does not appear in it. On the basis of that tradition, the churches in the East had generally accepted it as canonical by the third century. Modern critical scholarship is virtually unanimous in rejecting Pauline authorship, however. Although Hebrews exhibits some similarities to Paul's letters, the author's style, vocabulary, and theology are quite different from Paul's.

Some scholars have sought to find the author among the New Testament characters linked in one way or another with Paul: Barnabas, Apollos, Luke, Priscilla, Epaphras. None of these suggestions, however, has gained wide acceptance.

The original audience of the work is nearly as difficult to identify as the author. The title reflects the early view that it was written to Jewish Christians on the verge of abandoning their Christian faith and reembracing Judaism. Some scholars accept this judgment because of the extensive use of quotations from the Jewish Scriptures and the detailed knowledge of Jewish institutions the author presupposes. But gentile as well as Jewish Christians accepted the authority of the Jewish Scriptures. And the author's dialogue is not with the living Judaism of the original readers' world but with the ancient sacrificial system described in Leviticus. On the other hand, attempts to prove that the audience was specifically gentile do not fare much better.

Another problem in reconstructing the story behind Hebrews is its unusual

461

form. Since it lacks the usual prescript or salutation as well as the writer's self-identification, many scholars classify it as a sermon or theological treatise. But it does exhibit some characteristics of a letter. In chapter 13, the author offers specific exhortations and asks for the readers' prayers, and the conclusion in 13:22-25, which contains a reference to Timothy, is typical. Some scholars think that both v. 19 and this conclusion are later additions designed to present the work as a letter of Paul. But one may wonder why Paul's name was not added also. Many scholars thus accept the work as a real, although anonymous, letter. As to the date of composition, we can say only that it was probably written before the end of the first century, since it is apparently quoted in 1 Clement. The place of composition remains even more indefinite. Because the conclusion contains greetings from "those from Italy," some interpreters argue that the author wrote from Rome to Jewish Christians in Jerusalem. Others think the author, writing *to* Rome, is referring to Christians originally from Italy but residing in the place where the letter was composed. The truth is that we know neither where the author wrote, nor specifically to whom, nor who that author was.

Although we cannot be very specific in our reconstruction of a story behind the writing of Hebrews, it is clear that the author regards the addressees as Christians in danger of falling away from their faith. At some point in their common history they had probably experienced persecution and had conducted themselves admirably in the midst of it. Now, however, some are neglecting communal worship and losing heart. The writer's broad intention is to rekindle the faith of the community and encourage perseverance. We thus find much of the work devoted to exhortation. Undergirding this exhortation, however, is a complex theological statement somewhat different from anything else in the New Testament.

2. Reading Hebrews

a. *1:1-4*[1]

The first four verses contain a refined theological statement identifying the subject of the discourse. Although God has spoken to the Christians' "ancestors" or predecessors "in many and various ways," God has now, in the "last days," spoken through the Son. The reader will draw a contrast between an

---

1. Text divisions are based upon Harold W. Attridge, *The Epistle to the Hebrews: A Commentary on the Epistle to the Hebrews* (Philadelphia: Fortress Press, 1989), 19.

Fig. 72. The Western Wall in Jerusalem. The only part of the temple that remained after its destruction by the Romans in 70 c.e. It is also known as the "wailing wall" because of its continuing significance for Jews as a site of mourning the destruction and the loss of their homeland in the first century. *(Photo by Marshall Johnson)*

earlier and partial revelation, or divine self-disclosure, and a later and complete one. The subsequent elaboration of the Son's status and function will reinforce this contrast and encourage the reader to think of the Son in the loftiest possible terms: as the agent through whom God created the world, as the one who made purification for human sins, and as the one who was granted a station higher than that of angels.

b. 1:5—2:18

Shifting from what God has said to humanity *through* the Son, the author turns to what God says *to and about* the Son, quoting a series of passages from the Jewish Scriptures. The reader will view these passages as confirming the unique status of God's son. Then, in the verses following the "therefore" in 2:1, the logic of the discourse becomes clear. Presupposed is a tradition according to which God gave the Torah through angels. The reader must conclude that if defection from God's earlier, incomplete revelation through angels merits punishment, how much more so defection from the full revelation now provided.

In further support of the point, the author adds that this revelation, this salvation, was first "declared" by Jesus himself ("the Lord") and then attested by God. The description of Christian salvation as conveyed through a "declaration" complements the opening statement regarding God's "speaking" and suggests a continuity between the spoken word as a bearer of religious testimony and miraculous events as forms of God's communication with human beings. The reader is thus encouraged to see such divine communication in all the events making up the Christian story, from Jesus' own ministry to the workings of the Holy Spirit in the church.

Turning again to the subject of angels in 2:5, the author states that God "did not subject the coming world...to angels" and quotes Psalm 8 to the effect that God has actually subordinated "all things" to humankind itself. Noting then that human beings do not yet exercise the authority thus implied, the author explains that Jesus does; it is he who was "for a little while" made lower than the angels. The reader will conclude that Jesus' work won an exalted status for all humanity and will learn from vv. 10-18 that God subjected Jesus to suffering in order to bring him to perfection. Because Jesus shared the fragile human condition, he could function as the "pioneer" of salvation for other human beings and, through his own death, destroy the Satanic power of death and atone for human sins.

c. 3:1—5:10

Elaborating on Jesus' status, the author now designates him as God's appointed apostle and introduces the theme of his faithfulness. The metaphor of a house then provides a vehicle for asserting Jesus' superiority over Moses. From 3:6 the reader learns that Christians are themselves God's house— which is to say, the people of God—to the extent that they stand fast in hope. And the "if" in this verse takes on force as the reader proceeds through the quotation from Psalm 95 in 3:7-11 and the exhortations in 3:12-19. The rebellion of the Jewish people against God following the exodus is a reminder that only the faithful receive what God has promised: the rebellious followers of Moses were denied entrance into God's "rest."

On one level, the readers will interpret this "rest" as the land of Canaan. But in 4:1-10, in a scriptural argument demonstrating that the promise of that rest is still open, a broader reference becomes evident: God's own Sabbath rest, instituted at the creation of the world. Equating that rest with the salvation mentioned in 2:10, the readers are prepared to hear the author's call to faithfulness in 4:11-13.

Verses 14-16 summarize much of the preceding argument: because Christians have as their heavenly high priest Jesus, who is at once Son of God and a person who can sympathize with human weakness, they should hold fast to their confession, their faith. Explaining then that high priests in general sympathize with human weakness and assume their offices only at God's call, the author declares that Jesus is high priest by God's appointment and goes on to connect his priestly office to that of Melchizedek (5:1-10). The reader will know that in Genesis Melchizedek appears as king and priest in Salem, pre-Hebrew Jerusalem, but will wonder what the author means by placing Jesus in his priestly order.

d. 5:11—10:25

Acknowledging that the reference to Melchizedek requires further explanation, the author focuses instead on the readers' lack of understanding as a sign of spiritual immaturity. The readers will be shamed by the accusation that, although they ought themselves to be teachers who grasp the deeper aspects of faith, they remain in need of basic instruction. They can take comfort from the call to progress in the faith in 6:1 but will again be brought up short by the warning that those who fall away from the faith cannot be restored. The reassurances that follow, however, encourage the readers to receive such warnings as directed toward their own good. In 6:1-20, words of warning and encouragement lead into a ringing declaration of God's promise to Abraham, guaranteed by a divine oath.

The reference to Melchizedek in 6:20 reminds the reader that the author has promised to elaborate on this theme. There follows in 7:1-3 an account of Abraham's homage to Melchizedek in Genesis 14, from which the author derives two points. The first, based upon Melchizedek's name and title, is that this mysterious figure symbolizes the peace and righteousness associated with the rest/salvation God has promised. The second point is derived from the fact that the Genesis story mentions nothing about Melchizedek's parentage. From this omission the author concludes that, like the son of God, he has no beginning or end but "remains a priest forever." The readers must draw an analogy between Melchizedek and Jesus: remembering the term "forever" in 6:20, they will conclude that Jesus' own priesthood is without end. But in 7:4-10 the author proceeds to elaborate on Melchizedek, demonstrating that his status was greater than that of either Abraham or Levi, ancestor of the priestly tribe of Levi.

The argument in 7:11-19 presupposes two points: the connection of the levitical priesthood with Levi (and Moses' brother Aaron), and the fact that Jesus himself constitutes a new priesthood in the order of Melchizedek. The claim is that the institution of Jesus' priesthood implies the inadequacy of the old one. The reader must also make a connection between priesthood and the law: since the law institutes the levitical priesthood, when the latter is transcended the former undergoes change as well. In 7:20-25 the author further contrasts the two priesthoods, reiterating the point about God's oath and emphasizing that the levitical priests were subject to death. This latter point is elaborated in a dramatic description of Jesus' high priestly office (7:26-28) underscoring the once-for-all character of Jesus' sacrifice.

In 8:1 the reader is alerted to a restatement of the main point of the preceding argument. Proclaiming that Jesus is indeed such a high priest as has been described, the author elaborates on his differences from earthly priests, now with an added twist: the sanctuary in which the earthly priests served is itself but a "shadow" of the heavenly one. The reader, familiar with the Hellenistic distinction (going back to Plato) between the ultimately real spiritual world and the present world of only derivative reality, will have no trouble understanding how service in the heavenly sanctuary renders Jesus' ministry "more excellent" and the basis of a "better covenant." Citing scriptural support for the notion of a new covenant, the author interprets the passage as declaring the old covenant obsolete (8:13).

In 9:1-10 the author describes the earthly sanctuary in terms that relate to the moveable tabernacle used by the followers of Moses in the wilderness (not the later temple in Jerusalem). The key point is the distinction between the outer portion of the sanctuary and the inner holy of holies. The reader should conclude from the fact that only the high priest enters the most sacred area, "and he but once a year," that true access to God is not in fact achieved under the old covenant. Then in 9:11-14 Christ's priesthood is presented in contrasting terms: based upon his own blood sacrifice, it effects a true and lasting purification.

In 9:15-23 the author explains that all covenants require purification by blood sacrifice and that heavenly matters require a better kind of sacrifice than do earthly ones. Verses 24-26 then describe that better sacrifice, building upon distinctions made earlier: heavenly sanctuary vs. earthly copy, and repeated sacrifice vs. once-for-all offering. Locating the time of Christ's sacrifice for sin "at the end of the age," the author goes on in 9:28-30 to point ahead to his eschatological return that will bring salvation.

The contrast between shadow and reality is elaborated in 10:1-10, where the author, quoting a psalm as a saying of Christ, focuses upon the speaker's intention to do God's will. The reader should conclude that although the blood of animals cannot atone for sin, Jesus' blood can, precisely because he was obedient to God. Following a reiteration of the final and lasting quality of Christ's sacrifice in 10:11-18, the reader is alerted by the "therefore" in v. 19 that the major implication of the preceding argument is now to be stated. What follows is an exhortation based upon a declaration. Because the blood of Jesus offers unprecedented access to God, Christians should approach God confidently and hold fast to their faith; they should be faithful in attending the community's gatherings and should encourage one another. The readers will note in v. 25 the author's indictment of those who neglect communal worship as well as the eschatological reference that supports the exhortation.

e. 10:26—12:13

In 10:26-31 the author reiterates an earlier warning, stating more clearly that it is those who "willfully persist in sin" for whom no sacrifice can atone. The reader will understand that—after having once received forgiveness—one cannot turn intentionally back to the old life, counting on Christ's sacrifice as a kind of magical or mechanical operation. Reminded (10:32-34) of their exemplary lives shortly after their original enlightenment, the readers are then urged not to lose heart. They will get the point: if they turn back now, they will lose the precious salvation they have awaited.

Picking up on the term "faith" in the quotation in 10:37-38, the author offers in 11:1-3 both a definition and a brief statement on its effects. Then, in a dramatic rehearsal of key moments in the history of the Hebrew people, the reader finds concrete examples of faithful action. In 11:13-16 the author pauses to note that the exemplary folk of old kept the faith even in the face of unfulfillment, since they died before God's promises were realized. They thus lived as "strangers and foreigners on the earth," people "seeking a homeland." The author identifies the latter as a "heavenly" country and indicates that God has in fact prepared it for them.

The rehearsal continues, concluding in verses 32-40 with emphasis upon the difficulties endured by the people of God. Acknowledging that the faith of these servants of God was commendable, the author emphasizes they did not in fact receive what God had promised, for "God had provided something better so that they would not, apart from us, be made perfect." The reader will have to think back through the entire argument to understand the point. The old covenant provided a promise, but not fulfillment; that has come only in Jesus, the heavenly high priest who has made a once-for-all purification for sins. Christians thus experience that which the heroic figures of old awaited in faith.

Speaking as a fellow believer, the author issues a powerful exhortation in 12:1-2. The readers will understand that, given the witnesses of those who earlier awaited the promise in faithfulness, they should persevere in their faith, looking to Jesus who himself persevered and was exalted to God's side. The contrasts between Jesus' endurance and their own fainthearted-ness, in 12:3-4, together with the interpretation of their tribulations as God's way of disciplining them (12:5-11), lead to further a summary exhortation in 12:12-13. Assorted warnings in 12:14-17 precede a reminder of the su-periority of the new covenant (12:18-24), and the admonitions in 12:25-29 emphasize the seriousness of rejecting the complete and final revelation given in Christ.

The readers find assorted injunctions regarding attitudes and behavior in 13:1-6 and in v. 7 a call to imitate those who brought the Christian message to them. The statement on Christ's eternal, unchanging nature in v. 8 com-bines with the admonitions against strange teachings and dietary regulations to ground another contrast between the old sacrificial system and Christ's sac-rifice in 13:9-12. Having noted that Jesus suffered outside the city gate, the author then issues a call (v. 13) to "go to him outside the camp and bear the abuse he endured." When the readers then hear in v. 14 that Christians have "no lasting city" but are "looking for the city that is to come," they will understand the significance of the site of the crucifixion. They will equate the holy city of Jerusalem with "the realm of security and traditional ho-liness"[2] and conclude that as his followers they also must remain aliens in the present world. That is why they must bear abuse if they are to remain in solidarity with him. They will also understand that although Christians are privy to the "perfected" revelation in Christ, they are still in some sense, like the heroic figures of the Hebrews Scriptures, the "wandering people of God."[3]

In vv. 15-19 the author gives additional injunctions: praise of God, sharing within the community, obedience of leaders, prayer for the writer. Reference to the possibility of a visit in v. 19 gives the writing the tone of a letter, as do the benediction and farewell comments in 20-25.

---

2. Ibid., 399.
3. Ernst Käsemann, *The Wandering People of God: An Investigation of the Letter to the Hebrews*, trans. Roy A. Harrisville and Irving L. Sandberg (Minneapolis: Augsburg, 1984).

3. A Critical Problem: Background of the Author's Thought

Much attention has been given to the question of the background of the author's thought. There is a strong reliance upon the Jewish Scriptures, but the author seems to depend upon the Septuagint and also to reflect many components of Hellenistic thought. Attempts to be more specific about influences have resulted in a variety of theories.

Ernst Käsemann, influenced by Bultmann's theory of a well-developed pre-Christian Gnosticism, argued that several themes in Hebrews betray a gnostic background: the earthly/heavenly contrast, the notion of a heavenly redeemer, and the movement toward a heavenly homeland. Recent scholars have tended to reject this aspect of Käsemann's work. A major failing of the gnostic thesis is that it tends to downplay the author's eschatological emphasis, which, while infrequent, should probably not be dismissed as unimportant. One may also note that the author's emphasis upon the world as God's creation (1:1-2) runs counter to gnostic thought.

Other scholars have argued for the influence of the writings of Philo of Alexandria, and it is easy to cite numerous parallels. Yet there are important differences, most notably the absence in Hebrews of the allegorical interpretation so prominent in Philo. For many scholars, it is enough simply to note the general Hellenistic component in the theology of Hebrews, with a possible acknowledgment of its affinities with Alexandrian thought, of which Philo may have been only one of many representatives.

Attempts have also been made to find direct links between Hebrews and the Dead Sea Scrolls. Here again, however, the more judicious judgment appears to be that the author was familiar with broadly based Jewish notions also shared by the residents of Qumran.

With respect to the Christian background of Hebrews, scholars have pointed out similarities to both Paul and the Gospel of John. Most notable in the latter case are the author's use of the concept of "word" and the clear statement of Christ's preexistence. But it is not really possible to demonstrate direct dependence; what seems more likely is that the author drew from a fund of ideas spread widely within the early Christian community. As to Paul, some important theological differences should also be noted. The crucial term "faith," while prominent, is used in a rather different sense than it is in Paul; in Hebrews it suggests a kind of steadfast endurance rather than "trust." Hebrews, moreover, lacks the central Pauline contrasts of faith/works, flesh/spirit, Jew/Gentile; nor does it employ the notion of being "in Christ." Paul, on the other hand, knows nothing of the notion of Jesus as high priest or of the impossibility of returning to the faith after willful defection.

In the end, we can say that the author drew upon a wide range of ideas from early Christianity, the Jewish Scriptures, and Hellenistic thought. Even the speculation about Melchizedek, which seems so strange to modern readers and so distinctive in its New Testament context, is not without parallels. This mysterious figure played a role not only among Jewish apocalyptic writers but also in Philo, the Dead Sea Scrolls, and the Nag Hammadi writings. We must not imagine that Hebrews was written in a vacuum. Yet, on the other hand, there can be little doubt of the author's creativity. When all is said and done, Hebrews remains a distinctive writing of great complexity and depth.

4. The Old and the New in Hebrews

Graham Hughes, in his study of the interpretive method of the author of Hebrews, divides scholars into two broad groups.[4] Those who think Hebrews was written to Jewish Christians beginning to turn back to Judaism generally read it as a sharp polemic against Judaism. From this perspective, the author wrote to encourage allegiance to the Christian confession and was largely concerned to state correct doctrinal positions. Those who think it was written to gentile Christians see it as a more general call "for a more spiritualised conception of faith." From their point of view, "the Jewish motifs are employed simply as examples or symbols of an unworthily materialistic form of faith," and the author was far less concerned to state doctrine than to exhort the readers to faithfulness.

Hughes argues that neither of these views does justice to the author's main concern, which he identifies as the question of how to understand "the Word of God . . . as being subject to historical processes and yet remaining, recognisably, God's Word." In other words, the argument in Hebrews focuses on the problem of the old and the new, how Christianity is related to the Hebrew faith that preceded it.

According to Hughes, the author solves the problem by reading the Jewish Scriptures from a Christian perspective, according to which incomplete and fragmentary revelations can be seen as part of a continuous process leading up to the final revelation in Jesus. When, however, the author asks how the question of the Jewish Scriptures apply concretely to the life of a Christian congregation, the matter becomes more complex. Since in Christianity Jesus is God's complete self-disclosure, Jewish institutions are understood as

---

4. Graham Hughes, *Hebrews and Hermeneutics: The Epistle to the Hebrews as a New Testament Example of Biblical Interpretation* (Cambridge: Cambridge Univ. Press, 1979), 2–3.

outmoded. One therefore finds a strain of realized eschatology in this work. The eschatological perspective changes, however, when the author addresses the community's awareness of its existence within the historical process with all its contingencies, i.e., its acknowledgment that the "city" it seeks is not yet present. At these points one finds a futuristic eschatology and a sense of close continuity between the Christian community and the people of the Jewish Scriptures.

One must therefore reckon with both continuity and discontinuity in describing the relationship between old and new in Hebrews. Recognizing a kind of finality in the Christian revelation, it nevertheless presents the new community as continuing the pilgrimage of the people of old, as responding to the word of the same God who has spoken in various ways throughout human history, although definitively in Jesus.

STUDY QUESTIONS

1. What is it possible to say about the authorship and original audience of Hebrews?

2. What problem does the author of Hebrews seem to be addressing?

3. What is distinctive about the way Jesus is presented in Hebrews?

4. What is the role of the list of heroic figures in Hebrews 11?

5. Explain the role of each of the following in the argument of Hebrews: Melchizedek, shadow (or copy) versus reality, Jesus' faithfulness to God.

FOR FURTHER READING

Attridge, Harold W. *The Epistle to the Hebrews: A Commentary on the Epistle to the Hebrews*. Hermeneia. Philadelphia: Fortress Press, 1989. Detailed and technical, but readable; a major contribution. Extensive bibliography.

Hagner, Donald A. *Hebrews*. San Francisco: Harper, 1983. Solid, competent, and readable.

Hughes, Graham. *Hebrews and Hermeneutics: The Epistle to the Hebrews as a New Testament Example of Biblical Interpretation*. Cambridge: Cambridge Univ. Press, 1979. Technical but highly interesting.

Jewett, Robert. *Letter to Pilgrims: A Commentary on the Epistle to the Hebrews*. New York: Pilgrim, 1981. A solid interpretation with an interesting attempt to relate the writing to contemporary experience in postindustrial society.

Johnson, William G. *Hebrews*. Atlanta: John Knox, 1980. Brief and readable.

Chapter 15

The General Letters A:
James, 1 and 2 Peter, Jude

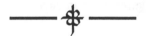

1. The Letter of James

a. Searching for the Story

The writing included in the New Testament as "the Letter of James" begins with a typical salutation, but there are few other marks of a genuine letter. Consisting entirely of exhortations, the work lacks the references to specific people that characterize, for example, the letters of Paul. The author is self-identified as a teacher, and the document may be described as a parenetic treatise.

The author is also self-identified as James, and the work came into the canon on the supposition that it was written by James "the brother of the Lord"—also known in tradition as "James the Just"—the longtime leader of the Jerusalem church. Those who believe that the author was in fact the brother of Jesus presume that the intended audience, described as "the twelve tribes in the Dispersion" (1:1), was the group of Christians who fled Jerusalem during the persecution mentioned in Acts 8:1.

Most critical scholars, however, reject the traditional view of authorship. The work is written in rather polished Greek and employs Hellenistic rhetorical devices. One may also note that the author, who is definitely steeped in the Jewish Scriptures, seems to have known them in their Greek form. And it is significant that this writing achieved acceptance only gradually and rather late; its place in the Western canon was not fully secure until the end of the fourth century. In fact, we have no sure evidence of its existence before the third century.[1]

Scholars who argue for authenticity point out that the work seems to have drawn upon sayings of Jesus in their pre-Synoptic form. They also claim that only James the Just had such widely acknowledged authority as to be able to put out a treatise under this name without further explanation. The problem of the sophisticated Greek is sometimes answered with the claim that James was aided by a secretary or that a later editor revised the original work.

There is evidence, in any case, that the work reflects more than one historical situation, which suggests that the present text is the result of the revision of earlier material. But this does not mean that the earliest stratum actually came from James the brother of Jesus. In the following analysis, I will assume that in its present form this writing comes from a time around the end of the first century. It is the readers of the finished product in this later situation whose reactions I will seek to trace in the reader-response analysis.

If we cannot say a great deal about the author of James, we can say even less about the place of composition. There is practically nothing to go on in the work itself, so that there is little to say by way of reconstructing the story behind it. Attention to the author's interests, however, provides a basis for sociological observations. Pedrito U. Maynard-Reid argues that James must be read against the background of extreme social stratification and that it was written for a community of the poor.[2] While Maynard-Reid accepts the traditional view of authorship and relates the work to an early period in Palestine, many of his observations hold good even with other presuppositions. If, as seems likely, the passages on wealth and poverty are ultimately rooted in the experience of the early Palestinian church, it is also evident that they continued to have relevance for the situation in which the work received its final form.

If we ask whether it is possible to identify a specific purpose on the (final) author's part, we again find opinion divided. Many scholars have found no real unity in the work, interpreting it as a string of largely unrelated exhortations. Peter H. Davids, however, has offered an outline presupposing a unified structure, which I have followed here.[3]

---

1. Some scholars find allusions to James in late first-century materials, but these are vague parallels that might simply be drawn from a common tradition.

2. Pedrito U. Maynard-Reid, *Poverty and Wealth in James* (Maryknoll, N.Y.: Orbis Books, 1987).

3. Peter H. Davids, *The Epistle of James: A Commentary on the Greek Text* (Grand Rapids: Eerdmans, 1982), 27–28.

b. Reading James

(1) 1:1-27. Addressed as "the twelve tribes," the readers will understand that they as Christians consider themselves the "true Israel." The qualifying phrase "in the Dispersion" will probably suggest that they are living outside Palestine, the site of God's original dealings with the people of Israel.[4] In any case, they are being addressed, in the name of James the brother of Jesus, on matters regarding their identity as the people of God.

In vv. 2-11 the readers hear advice and comments on assorted topics. They should accept the trials of life as testing that produces maturity, and they should pray earnestly for wisdom if they lack it. In hearing next that the lowly should "boast in being raised up" and that (ironically) "the rich will disappear like a flower in the field," they will discern the theme of reversal. They will accept the matter of wealth and poverty as loaded with religious significance and conclude that God in some sense favors the poor.

The advice in vv. 12-18 includes reflections on God's ways with the world. Encouragement to endure temptation leads to the insistence that temptation comes from within the individual, not from God; but all good and generous things do in fact come from God, who is unaffected by any degree or kind of change. The implication is that the readers, God's "first fruits," should actualize generosity in their lives. Counsel against anger and related dangers in 19-21 is followed by an injunction on hearing and doing; and a statement in 26-27 defines genuine religion in terms of actual behavior, most especially deeds of mercy.

(2) 2:1-26. The rhetorical question in 2:1, with its accusation regarding "favoritism," prepares the readers for the description of an instance of discrimination against the poor and deference toward the rich, which builds upon the earlier statement on wealth and poverty. The similar questions in vv. 5-7, punctuated by another accusation, assume that the readers are themselves primarily poor, a point that lends irony to the indictment: they turn against their own in favor of the rich who oppress them! The argument hinges, however, not upon an appeal to crude self-interest but upon the notion that God has "chosen the poor in the world to be rich in faith." The readers must thus be prepared to reverse the standards of the world, rejecting the common tendency to cater to the wealthy.

---

4. Some commentators think this phrase reflects a "pilgrim" theology such as that in Hebrews and indicates that Christians in this world are away from their true home in heaven. There is little in the writing to suggest such an interpretation. See John H. Elliott, *A Home for the Homeless: A Sociological Exegesis of 1 Peter, Its Situation and Strategy* (Philadelphia: Fortress Press, 1981), 38, 45.

When in vv. 8-13 "James" contrasts discrimination against the poor to the "royal law" of love, the readers will recognize a dual appeal, to the Hebrew Scriptures and to Jesus' summation of the law. That general point is immediately applied to the case at hand—treatment of the rich and poor—and is supported by an assertion of the "wholeness" of the law. The readers will conclude that they will be judged on the basis of the whole law, which includes the demand for mercy. When in v. 14 the author declares the uselessness of faith without works, the readers will know that it is specifically deeds of mercy that are meant.

The logical conclusion in v. 17, that faith without works is dead, becomes the occasion for a broader treatment of the theme. First demonstrating that mere belief in the existence of God is religiously neutral, the author then illustrates the necessity of works with biblical examples. The repetition of the general statement on faith and works in v. 26 signals the reader that the argument has been completed.

(3) 3:1—4:12. Beginning with a statement on the special responsibility of teachers in 3:1, "James" now comments on the judicious use of speech. In 3:13 the point is broadened to an injunction to acquire wisdom, which is supported by a contrast between true wisdom and its "earthly, unspiritual, devilish" imitation. The reader will notice that the author presents true wisdom as the source of the works of mercy enjoined earlier and that the term "partiality" reappears in conjunction with hypocrisy.

After the rhetorical questions in 4:1 encouraging the readers to identify their "cravings" as the source of their conflicts, the author makes specific indictments in vv. 2-3. Then in v. 4 the metaphorical accusation "Adulterers!" leads into a discourse setting God's way in stark opposition to the way of the world. Laced with imperatives, this discourse concludes with injunctions to the readers against slandering or judging one another. Already reminded of the love command, the readers will now understand that speaking evil of one another impugns the law that issues that command.

(4) 4:13—5:6. The readers will realize that it is now the rich, those who can afford lengthy business travel, who are being addressed with the dramatic "Come, now." If there are a few such persons in the community, they will recognize themselves and hear in the ensuing verses a direct confrontation. The poor, however, will hear it as a rhetorical way of pointing up the sins of the rich in general and of the upper stratum of the merchant class more specifically.

The repetition of "Come, now" in 5:1 signals the readers that the new material will parallel the preceding verses. But now God's judgment against the rich is laid out in vivid detail as the social aspect of their sin—their unfair treatment of laborers and murder of the righteous—is made explicit. Here they will recognize the prophetic mode of speech and the echoes of a familiar prophetic theme: the condemnation of the oppression of the righteous poor.[5]

(5) 5:7-20. Beginning with a discourse commending eschatological patience alluding to a final judgment (vv. 7-11), "James" now issues a series of injunctions. Included are a condemnation of oaths, a recommendation of prayers for the sick and confession of sin, and a final admonition (vv. 19-20) to seek the restoration of those who fall away from the faith.

c. Theological Issues

Belated acceptance into the canon is not the only indignity suffered by the Letter of James. It has often been disparaged as theologically weak. Martin Luther, avid proponent of a doctrine of justification by faith based upon Paul's writings, called it an "epistle of straw" because of its view of faith and works. Thus Protestants have often accused it of a "legalistic" approach that links salvation to human achievement rather than God's grace.

Consequently, the relationship between this writing and Paul's thought has been the subject of much debate through the centuries. Some interpreters have tried to press Paul and James into the same mold. But while Paul insisted that it is faith *and not works* that brings justification, the author of this writing believed that faith without works is ineffective. Thus other scholars have argued that James was written in explicit opposition to Paul.

Although Paul's teachings are in the background, it is not at all clear that the author is responding directly to Paul. The way in which the faith/works issue is cast suggests a familiarity only with the generalized notion that faith need not be supplemented with works of the law, and not with the subtleties of Paul's views. For this author seems to understand faith as simply the acceptance of monotheism—belief in the existence of one God (2:19)—whereas for Paul it is an act of trust involving the whole of one's being. Given a reduction of faith to intellectual assent, one will naturally argue that it is insufficient without deeds in which it becomes actualized. But for Paul, as we have seen, real faith at least contains within itself the drive toward this actualization; it does not exist in some privatized internal dimension of the self. There is therefore a certain truth in the claim that although Paul and James by no

---

5. Isaiah 3:10; Proverbs 1:11; Wisdom of Solomon 2:10, 12, 19.

means say the same thing about faith and works, they do not really disagree either; for they are to some extent talking about different matters.

It is not only the statement on faith and works that has perpetuated the view that James is theologically weak. Many scholars have noted that there is in fact little theology at all in the work. So little in James is distinctively Christian, in fact, that some scholars view it as a Jewish treatise only slightly reworked by a Christian redactor. The more recent judgment, however, is that it is dependent upon the Jesus tradition, most particularly the kind of material underlying the Sermon on the Mount. And the charge of theological weakness is a matter of perspective. Liberation theologians criticize the neglect of this writing and find its attention to problems relating to social class and its emphasis upon deeds of mercy an important corrective to the tendency to understand faith as a purely internal attitude. Thus Cain Hope Felder, in a study carried out from a perspective defined by the interests of the black church, disputes the notion that James represents a legalistic point of view:

> There is a profound difference between "legalism" (rigid adherence to religious regulations of the cultus to gain merit and guarantees) and moral obligations by which persons of faith are held accountable to God's law and purposes for humanity.... Christian faith, no less than God's moral law, for James, necessarily involves criteria for Christian social behavior.[6]

2. 1 Peter

a. Searching for the Story

Although the prescript of 1 Peter presents this work as a letter from Peter the apostle to Christians in Asia Minor, there are good reasons to regard it as pseudonymous. To begin with, the excellent Greek and consistent use of the Septuagint seem unlikely for a Galilean fisher. Defenders of the traditional view point out that the author acknowledges use of a secretary (5:12), but there are other considerations that speak against Petrine authorship. Some scholars think that 1 Peter shows the influence of Pauline thought, and it seems clearly directed to churches that are predominantly gentile, whereas Peter's mission seems to have been primarily to Jews (Gal. 2:7).

Many scholars also find reasons to date the work after Peter's death, which is usually dated ca. 65–67. On the supposition that it reflects a situation in

---

6. Cain Hope Felder, *Troubling Biblical Waters: Race, Class, and Family* (Maryknoll, N.Y.: Orbis Books, 1989), 130–31.

which the church is undergoing persecution, some have placed it in the reign of the emperor Trajan (98–117), under whom some Christians were put to death in Pontus and Bithynia, two of the provinces named in the salutation. Others opt for the reign of Domitian (81–96), although it is not clear that the same policies were in effect regarding Christians at that time. Not all scholars agree that 1 Peter reflects a background of persecution, but there are other reasons for accepting a late date. Arguing that most of the letter's intended recipients were in rural areas, John H. Elliott concludes that Christianity would not have had time to spread there before the last quarter of the first century.[7]

Scholars who think 1 Peter was written during a persecution naturally interpret it as a response to that crisis. For them, the characterization of the readers as "the exiles of the Dispersion" means that Christians remain pilgrims on the earth with their true home in heaven. Elliott disputes this reading, however, arguing that the terminology of "homelessness" and "alienation" is used not metaphorically but sociologically. That is to say, the author addresses persons who are literally noncitizens and who have probably experienced economic deprivation as well. Their alienation is not from heaven but from society.[8]

If the original readers of 1 Peter were in fact social outsiders, they would have embraced the new movement with hope of finding a sense of belonging. Although they must have experienced this initially, Elliott surmises, they soon discovered that membership in the Christian community made them even more unacceptable to their neighbors. According to this view, what they were suffering through was not the official persecution of the Roman Empire but social ostracism from their neighbors; and the author's purpose was to counteract the disintegrating effects of this problem on the community.

Whereas many commentators understand 1 Peter's use of "household codes" as a sign of accommodation to the "bourgeois ethic" of the larger society, in this reading they contribute to the internal solidarity of the "household of God." The "socioreligious strategy" of the letter was to remind the readers of their identity as Christians and to stress the importance of internal discipline and cohesion as well as separation from the world outside.

Elliott's view remains a minority opinion, but it provides a caution against too easy an acceptance of the presence of a sharp dichotomy in this work between "this world" and "the other world." Although a "pilgrim theology" emphasizing Christians' homelessness in this world is present in Hebrews, Elliott gives some reason to doubt that it should be applied to 1 Peter. As Brevard Childs points out, however, 1:4, which mentions an imperishable in-

---

7. Elliott, *Home for the Homeless*, 87.
8. Ibid., chap. 1.

Fig. 73. The Crucifixion of St. Peter (c. 1450). It is probable that both Peter and Paul suffered martyrs' deaths. Tradition has it that Peter, feeling himself unworthy of the same death as Christ, requested to be crucified upside down.

heritance "kept in heaven for you," is difficult to accommodate to Elliott's position.[9] Thus some interpreters think Elliott may have gone too far in denying metaphorical force to the terminology of homelessness.

That the author in any case wrote to strengthen Christians facing difficulties in their social situation is evident and accounts for the largely parenetic character of the writing. We may also presume that it was written from Rome, since that is the probable metaphorical meaning of the reference to "Babylon" in the conclusion (5:13). The references to Silvanus and Mark at this point are also interesting, since the reader will undoubtedly think of the companions of Paul, which raises a question as to why the author chose the name of Peter. As Helmut Koester points out, however, by the time the letter was probably written both Peter and Paul were honored as martyrs, so that it mattered little which name was chosen. While Paul's letters were the only ones available for imitation, Peter's association with Rome must have been the determining factor in the choice of a pseudonym.[10]

Some scholars detect two different attitudes toward persecution in the work—one assuming that the persecution has not yet begun, the other assuming that it has—and have speculated about stages of composition. And it is often noted that apart from the prescript and conclusion there are few marks of a genuine letter. It is enough for our purposes to note that the author may have drawn upon existing materials to create a writing that encourages Christians in the face of some kind of hostility.

b. Reading 1 Peter[11]

(1) 1:1-2. Through the salutation the readers will understand the writing as coming from Peter the apostle and will receive it as authoritative. Addressed as "visiting strangers of the Dispersion" (Elliott's translation) and as God's chosen ones, they will think of themselves as heirs of God's promises to Israel and also of Israel's sufferings. As the church, they are God's chosen people who remain alienated from the society around them. The conclusion of the greeting with words of grace signal that what follows will bring comfort.

(2) 1:3—2:10. The optimistic note continues as "Peter" praises God for Christians' new birth through the resurrection of Jesus that brings the hope

---

9. Brevard Childs, *The New Testament as Canon: An Introduction* (Philadelphia: Fortress Press, 1984), 458.

10. Helmut Koester, *Introduction to the New Testament*, vol. 2: *History and Literature of Early Christianity* (Philadelphia: Fortress Press, 1982), 293.

11. Divisions based upon Elliott, *A Home for the Homeless.*

of salvation. The readers should understand that this hope can comfort them in the face of current tribulation. Not only that, but they should receive their present suffering as a test that prepares them for Christ's eventual return. Reminded of their actual faith and love (1:8-9), and told (10-12) that the prophets of old only anticipated what they have now received, they will look to their own experience in the Christian community as confirmation of the author's words.

The author's "therefore" in v. 13 signals the readers to look for the implications of the preceding declarations. What they find are concrete injunctions regarding the proper behavior of a "holy" people, interspersed with further reminders of their distinctive status. They should maintain self-discipline, putting aside the desires that plagued their old lives; they should nurture love and avoid negative attitudes and deeds; and they should continue to feed upon the "spiritual milk" of Christian teaching.

The appeal in 2:4—"Come to him"—now directs the readers' attention to Christ and to their status as the "spiritual house" of which he is the cornerstone. The readers will understand the quotation in v. 6 as a reference to Christ and his rejection by the world; and they will interpret the quotation in v. 7 as drawing a sharp distinction between themselves as Christ's church and those "outside." The metaphor of the stone thus takes on a dual quality: the precious cornerstone of God's household is for the outside world only an obstruction on which they stumble.

Understanding that their community is grounded in Christ, the readers are ready to hear the poetic declaration of who they are in vv. 9-10. Although once they had no identity, no sense of ultimate belonging, by God's action they have become a chosen people. They have taken on the role of a priesthood commissioned to tell the world of those wonderful acts by which they themselves have received a new identity. Reminded of their distinctive status and of the mercy they have received, the readers will feel joy, empowerment, and a sense of mission.

(3) 2:11—4:11. In 2:11-12 the theme of separateness from the world is reinforced. The readers are addressed as "beloved" and "aliens," while the people in the world outside (i.e., non-*Christians,* not non-*Jews!*) are termed "Gentiles." And the injunction to abstain from "the desires of the flesh" builds upon the distinctive identity of the community.

Distinctiveness need not mean direct confrontation, however. Although acknowledging the hostility of outsiders, "Peter" counsels the readers to conduct themselves honorably—precisely so that "the Gentiles" will learn to glorify God! The readers will understand that their godly conduct is one way of fulfilling their "priestly" mission declared in 2:9. Although separate from the world, they are to be in creative interaction with it.

A similar line of thought underlies the ensuing injunctions. Told in 2:13 to obey the secular authorities and "honor everyone," the readers are also counselled to "love the family of believers" and "fear God" (2:17). Implying that the Christians owe their ultimate allegiance to God, the author nevertheless assumes the possibility of living in relative harmony with the Roman Empire. The readers then hear commands, supported by biblical examples, that slaves should obey their masters (2:18-25) and wives should obey their husbands and live simple and reverent lives (3:1-6). Husbands are then enjoined to honor "the weaker sex [literally: "vessel"]" (3:7), and the entire community is encouraged to reject vengeance and to pursue unity, humility, and love (3:8-12).

In 3:13 the author turns to the topic of suffering. Beginning with the suggestion that outsiders are unlikely to harm them if their behavior is good, "Peter" argues that it is in any case better to suffer for doing good than for doing wrong. The point is then supported by an appeal to Christ's example that mentions his preaching, apparently between his death and resurrection, to "the souls in prison," those who were disobedient in the time of Noah. In 4:1-6 admonitions against falling into the wanton behavior of the "Gentiles" are supported by a reference to the coming judgment. And the eschatological note leads into a series of injunctions regarding community life in 4:7-11. The readers will hear in these verses a call to mutual love and service directed toward the glory of God.

(4) 4:12-19. In 4:12-19 the author turns explicitly to the "ordeal" the readers face. Told that suffering specifically as Christians is a sign that God's Spirit rests upon them, the readers will understand that their present plight is a mark of their distinctive role in the world. They must therefore rejoice in their present situation. Reference to the eschatological judgment supports the injunction to rejoice even as it constitutes a warning.

(5) 5:1-11. Applying the title "elder" to himself, "Peter" turns to the relationship between the elders of the communities and "the flock of God." The readers will understand the notation that the author has witnessed "the sufferings of Christ" as an indication that he has lived through ordeals similar to their own. As elders are counselled to exercise oversight and to avoid seeking personal gain, the people are encouraged to obey the elders. Humility before God is then urged upon all, as is discipline and resistance of the devil.

A promise of eschatological deliverance (5:10) is then followed by a brief doxology (v. 11).

(6) 5:12-13. With a conclusion containing greetings from a "sister church" and "Mark," as well as an additional word of encouragement, the author brings the letter to an end.

c. The "Spirits in Prison" and the Preaching to the Dead: 1 Peter 3:18-20 and 4:6

Few passages in the New Testament have received attention so disproportionate to their length as have 1 Peter 3:19 and 4:6. Sadly, however, both remain obscure.

Many scholars regard 3:18-20 as the application to Christianity of a motif of a descent into the underworld that was widespread in pre-Christian Eastern religions and appeared also in Greek myths (Orpheus and Eurydice, Persephone). As to the specific meaning of the verse in 1 Peter, one interpretation is that the "spirits in prison" are the people—symbolized by the generation swept away in the flood in Noah's time—who died in a state of sin before the time of Christ. According to this reading, it indicates that between his death and resurrection Jesus descended into hell to provide a chance for these otherwise lost souls to accept the salvation offered through the gospel. Ephesians 4:8-10 is sometimes interpreted along similar lines, and in any case the notion of such a descent did have a place in early Christianity. A similar motif appears in the apocryphal Gospel of Peter (10:39-42), and the Apostles' Creed contains the affirmation that "[Christ] descended into hell," a phrase omitted by many Protestant churches. An alternative understanding of the descent motif, however, one that does not seem to fit 1 Peter 3:18-20, is that those imprisoned in hell were not the sinners but the *righteous* who lived before Christ.

Another view of 3:18-20 is that the spirits in prison are those heavenly beings of Genesis 6:1-4 who corrupt the women of the earth. These beings appear in the noncanonical book of 1 Enoch as fallen angels who are eventually destroyed in the flood (1 En. 6-10). This interpretation tends to support the view held by a number of recent interpreters—that Christ descended not to save the prisoners but to proclaim his victory over the powers of evil.

It is possible to interpret 4:6, the notation that the gospel was preached to the dead, in conjunction with the "second chance" motif. An alternative interpretation, however, is that it refers to Christians who are now dead but who responded to the gospel when they were alive. Another is that the dead are the righteous ones mentioned in the Jewish Scriptures, understood as having believed the gospel ahead of time.

d. Church and World in 1 Peter

Elliott's sociological reading of 1 Peter calls into question the tendency to dismiss this work as a simple accommodation to the "bourgeois ethic" of the surrounding society that ultimately compromises the distinctive character of the Christian worldview. From his perspective, 1 Peter fosters a sense of internal solidarity that sets the church radically apart from the "outside" world. Whatever the author's intention, however, it is difficult to deny that the advice given women and slaves does in fact reflect the ethical standards of the larger Hellenistic society. And to that extent it is similar to the Pastoral Letters, Colossians, and Ephesians.

3. 2 Peter

a. Searching for the Story

The story behind 2 Peter is entwined with that behind the Letter of Jude. For parts of the two are so close in subject matter and wording as to make it virtually certain that one of the authors was dependent upon the other. In fact, almost all of Jude is in some way paralleled in 2 Peter.

The vast majority of contemporary scholars are convinced that it is 2 Peter that is dependent. A key argument is that the absence in this work of Jude's use of Jewish works (such as 1 Enoch) that were eventually excluded from the canon of Jewish Scriptures is best explained as the result of the intentional deletion of "suspect" material. And the fact that some passages in 2 Peter are obscure until read in light of their parallels in Jude suggests the author of 2 Peter, in reworking old material for a new context, unthinkingly deleted material the new readers would need to get the full meaning.

If 2 Peter is dependent upon Jude, it seems highly unlikely that it was actually written by the apostle Peter. And there is much evidence to confirm this negative judgment. Not only do the language and rhetorical style of the work show heavy influence of the Hellenistic environment, but there is strong indication that it comes from a time long removed from the apostolic age. For one thing, it presupposes not only that the letters of Paul have been collected, but that they have already attained the status of Scripture (3:15-16); for another, it is mentioned by no Christian writer before the third century. And, finally, although the writing purports to be a "testament" of Peter before his death, in which he predicts the appearance of false teachers in the later church, the author shifts from the future tense to the present when actually denouncing these teachers.

It is therefore safe to say that 2 Peter was not written before the last decade or so of the first century, and many scholars, regarding it as the latest writing in the New Testament, place it as late as 140 C.E. It was almost certainly written after 1 Peter, since there is a rather clear allusion to the latter in 3:1-2. But scholars generally conclude that the two letters were written by different authors.

It is clear that 2 Peter was written to combat certain teachings, regarded by the author as heretical, that were becoming popular in the churches in the Hellenistic environment. Many scholars have identified the "heretical" teachers as Gnostics. A more recent judgment is that the author opposed Christians who were accommodating their faith to popular Hellenistic ideas, such as those found in Epicureanism, by deleting such traditional notions as apocalyptic eschatology and the divine inspiration of the Jewish Scriptures.

The author's strategy is to construct a "testament" left by the apostle Peter, warning the church of such teachings as those the readers are now encountering. As apostle, "Peter" reminds these readers of the fundamentals of the faith and warns them regarding the fate of those who fall away from the truth. In a rhetorical analysis of 2 Peter, Duane Frederick Watson classifies it as primarily deliberative rhetoric because it seems designed to dissuade the audience from a particular set of views and give advice regarding future action. He also finds elements of judicial and epideictic rhetoric, however. The former appears in 1:16—2:20, which calls for judgments about the past, and the latter in 2:10b-22, which denounces the opponents and seeks to persuade the audience to take a negative view of them in the present.[12] The following treatment follows Watson's outline.

b. Reading 2 Peter

(1) **1:1-2.** Finding themselves addressed by "Simeon Peter, a servant and apostle of Jesus Christ," the readers will receive the writing as having great authority; and the reference to their own faith and the blessing serve to remind them that they are professing Christians. They will therefore begin to read the

---

12. Duane Frederick Watson, *Invention, Arrangement, and Style: Rhetorical Criticism of Jude and 2 Peter* (Atlanta: Scholars Press, 1988), 85–86.

Fig. 74. St. Peter, traditional founder of the Church at Rome. Peter is represented as giving the scarf, the symbol of holy office, to Pope Leo III, and the standard, the symbol of royal power, to Charlemagne. From a ninth-century mosaic (restored).

body of the letter in a positive light, looking for help in their attempts to live out their faith.

(2) 1:3-15. Initially placing himself alongside his readers through the use of the first-person plural ("us"), "Peter" reminds them of the benefits and promises Christians have received through their faith. Quickly, however, he shifts to the second person (v. 5) to drive home some implications for the readers: they must support their faith with specific virtues to secure their place in Christ's eternal Rule. As the readers then learn of the author's intention to continue to offer such reminders (v. 12), they will prepare to hear more. And "Peter's" reference to his imminent death and the time following it (vv. 13-15) will contribute to their feeling that what he has to say has particular importance for them. They will read on in the hope that the words of the great apostle of the past will in fact help them hold onto the knowledge and faith that is theirs as Christians.

(3) 1:16—3:13. In 1:16-19, "Peter" draws a contrast between the message regarding Jesus' "power and coming" on the one hand and "cleverly devised myths" on the other. To support the point, he states that he was an eyewitness to the "glory" of Jesus Christ and describes an event reminiscent of the transfiguration scene in the Gospels (Mark 9:2-13). Since they have been taught that Peter actually saw the event and heard the heavenly voice proclaim Jesus as God's Son, the readers should listen well to what the author says and be wary of those who cast aspersions on the traditional teaching of the church: it is not "myth," as they claim. For this majestic revelation has reconfirmed "the prophetic message," i.e., presumably, the messianic prophecies of the Jewish Scriptures (1:19). More specifically, the readers will understand the transfiguration scene as a preview of the majesty that will surround Jesus at his eschatological return. A general defense of prophecy (1:20-21) then rounds out the author's point: interpretation of biblical prophecy is not a matter of individual interpretation, since the Holy Spirit speaks through it.

Understanding now that the traditional teaching of the church is rooted in prophecy and is not human invention, the readers are prepared for the next stage of the argument in 2:1-3: even though prophecy is inspired, human beings can distort and misuse it. The reference to false prophets of the past thus provides a context for understanding the false teachers of the readers' own time: they too are persons who corrupt tradition and bring themselves to destruction. In 2:4-10 the latter claim is supported with examples of God's punishment of the unrighteous. Concluding these examples with a statement on the final judgment, the author uses the remainder of chapter 2 to issue a fiery denunciation of those who defect from the faith.

The allusion to an earlier letter in 3:1-2, together with the references to the words of the prophets and "the commandments of the Lord and Savior spoken through your apostles," reminds the readers that the message they have received as Christians stands within a long history of God's communication with the world. This brings them back to the author's main point and prepares them for a resumption of the argument.

In 3:3 the readers hear a prediction of the appearance of scoffers in "the last days." The characterization of the teaching of these scoffers will sound like a description of those among their own number who have challenged traditional eschatology. Since the "prediction" has thus apparently come true, they will listen attentively to the refutation of the false teachers in vv. 5-7. What the readers should conclude is that God has acted in past history and will therefore do so again at the end of the age.

As further refutation of the false teachers, "Peter" explains the delay in Christ's return by noting the difference between divine and human perspectives on time and then interprets this delay as God's way of granting further opportunity of repentance (3:8-9). Affirmations of Christ's return (3:10, 13), together with the rhetorical question they bracket (3:11-12), then encourage the readers to renew their eschatological hope and order their lives in accordance with it.

(4) 3:14-18. Encouragement becomes explicit exhortation in 3:14-16, which summarizes the arguments made in vv. 8-13. The reference to Paul reinforces the entire argument with an appeal to a second apostle's authority. And it further undermines the views of the "false teachers" by presenting Paul's letters as Scriptures and reiterating the point that human beings can twist revealed truth. The readers should conclude that instead of accepting the opinions of any teacher who comes along, they should hold to the apostolic tradition—passed on in the letters of Paul, but also by Peter in the letter at hand. The basis is thus laid for a final warning in v. 17 against being "carried away." The implication that the readers are basically stable in their faith combines with the final blessing and doxology to conclude the letter on an optimistic note. The readers will be encouraged to persist in the faith they originally adopted and to reject the teachings of those who scoff at certain aspects of it.

4. Jude

a. Searching for the Story

The Letter of Jude purports to be written by "Jude, a servant of Jesus Christ and brother of James." Early tradition identified this Jude with a brother of Jesus and James mentioned in Matthew 13:55 and Mark 6:3. Scholars generally agree that this indeed is the Jude that is meant, but the majority treat the work as pseudonymous. Not only is it written in sophisticated Greek, but the reference to "the predictions of the apostles" in v. 17 seems to presuppose a situation in the postapostolic age. And the phrase "the faith that was once for all entrusted to the saints" (1:3) reflects the notion of a fixed body of beliefs—a concept, characteristic of the Pastoral Letters, that probably did not develop until late in the first century.

We have no way of identifying the original recipients of the letter. The characterization of the "heretics" the author attacks would seem to indicate a gentile context, however, and the author was likely a Hellenistic Jewish Christian.

Many scholars think that the references to the licentiousness of the "heretics" indicate that they were Gnostics. Others find the evidence too scant to make such a judgment. We may be sure, in any case, that the work was written to combat persons the author considered heretical. Indications are that they were itinerants who worked their way into the community to which the letter is sent (v. 4). And we have a good idea of how the author viewed them: not only are they immoral, but they deny Christ (v. 4), reject authority, revile angels (8), and seek personal gain (11).

Watson classifies the work as deliberative rhetoric; it is "intended to advise and dissuade the audience," and its "time referent" is primarily future, although occasionally present.[13] The author's strategy is simple: to remind the readers of the apostolic faith and to denounce the "heretics" by exposing their unworthiness.

b. Reading Jude

(1) **Verses 1-2.** The prescript not only establishes the author's authority by establishing a link with James and by implication with Jesus, but also defines the context in which this impressive figure addresses them. His designation of the recipients as the "called" and the "beloved," who are "kept safe for

---

13. Ibid., 32; the following analysis make use of Watson's outline.

Jesus Christ," combines with the blessing in v. 2 to encourage them to read the letter as an attempt to secure their salvation.

(2) Verses 3-4. In v. 3, "Jude" announces his purpose in writing. By claiming to have foregone an earlier intention to write on another subject, he underscores the urgency of his present appeal for the readers to hold to the traditional faith. Verse 4 both explains why it is necessary to do so and gives a preliminary denunciation of those "ungodly" persons who created the unfortunate situation.

(3) Verses 5-16. Stating in v. 5 his intention to remind the readers of God's acts of judgment, "Jude" provides vivid examples in vv. 6-7. The comparison in v. 8 is designed to shock the readers: the actions of the "ungodly" persons in their midst parallel those of the ancient evildoers, even down to the matter of reviling angels! And vv. 9-10 place such actions in an even worse light with a contrast: the archangel Michael would not even revile Satan, yet the ungodly ones "slander whatever they do not understand." Pronouncing a woe upon these persons in v. 11, "Jude" gives further examples of their degenerate nature in 12-13. The readers should conclude that these people are indeed worthy of God's condemnation and will in fact receive it. And the contention in vv. 14-16 that the (noncanonical) book of Enoch predicted the coming of these "ungodly sinners" should further confirm that judgment.

(4) Verses 17-23. Verses 17-19 serve as a summation of "Jude's" argument, and the contention that the apostles predicted the advent of the "scoffers" places the entire issue in the context of apostolic authority. Then in vv. 20-23 the author appeals to the readers to take action: they should nurture their own faith and seek to rescue those who are falling away.

(5) Verses 24-25. The doxology with which "Jude" concludes adds a deeply emotional touch to the argument. It reminds the readers of the author's intention to keep them "safe" in the faith and encourages them to believe that it is through their Christian faith that they can finally appear, in contrast to the "ungodly" ones, "without blemish" before God.

5. Theology, Doctrine, and the Hermeneutical Question

There is a certain irony in the fact that although Jude and 2 Peter are deeply concerned about doctrinal purity, they contain virtually no theology at all. To this extent, they are similar to the pastoral letters. In none of these writings do the authors really struggle to refute their opponents with argumentation; they simply condemn them. Jude and 2 Peter go much farther in this direction and take on a harsher polemical tone. But in the pastorals no less than in Jude and 2 Peter we can hear the echoes of a time in which the dynamic, open-ended kind of theological reflection characteristic of Paul is giving way to the process of sheer doctrinal pronouncement.

Many scholars and theologians have for this reason portrayed all these writings as a degeneration from the creative early years of Christian thought. Others, however, have seen the movement toward doctrinal stability as necessary and inevitable in light of tendencies toward fragmentation. I will not try to settle the debate here but will only point out that it involves a question that is at base hermeneutical. To what extent is theological endeavor an ongoing, never-end process of formulation and reformulation, and to what extent must it involve the strict definition of boundaries?

STUDY QUESTIONS

1. What is it possible to say about the authorship and original audience of James?

2. Martin Luther, an admirer of Paul, thought James was theologically weak; but contemporary liberation theologians think highly of it. Can you explain why, in each case?

3. What is it possible to say about the authorship and original audience of 1 Peter?

4. How does the author of 1 Peter expect Christians to relate to the outside world?

5. Give your own opinion of Elliott's sociological interpretation of 1 Peter.

6. Why do scholars think 2 Peter is dependent upon Jude? What is it possible to say about the authorship of these two works?

7. To what specific problems are 2 Peter and Jude directed, and what are the authors' strategies for dealing with them?

8. Give your own arguments on the question as to why each of the works studied in this chapter should or should not have been accepted into the canon.

FOR FURTHER READING

Davids, Peter H. *The Epistle of James: A Commentary on the Greek Text*. Grand Rapids: Eerdmans, 1982. A detailed technical study, particularly helpful in discerning the organization of the work; argues that Silvanus, the secretary, wrote the letter at Peter's direction, whether before or after the latter's death.

Dibelius, Martin. *James: A Commentary of the Epistle on James.* Hermeneia. Rev. by Heinrich Greeven. Trans. Michael A. Williams. Philadelphia: Fortress Press, 1976. Detailed, technical; contains an important discourse on the comparison between the Letter of James and Paul; finds no unity in James.

Elliott, John H. *A Home for the Homeless: A Sociological Exegesis of 1 Peter, Its Situation and Strategy.* Philadelphia: Fortress Press, 1981. Somewhat technical, advancing an important thesis.

Laws, Sophie. *A Commentary on the Epistle of James.* San Francisco: Harper & Row, 1980. A solid, readable work, widely quoted.

Maynard-Reid, Pedrito U. *Poverty and Wealth in James.* Maryknoll, N.Y.: Orbis Books, 1987. A readable study stressing the social radicalism of the work; accepts apostolic authorship.

Tamez, Elsa. *The Scandalous Message of James: Faith without Works Is Dead.* New York: Crossroad, 1990. Brief, readable, insightful; stresses the social radicalism of the work and its emphasis upon oppression, hope, and action.

Watson, Duane Frederick. *Invention, Arrangement, and Style: Rhetorical Criticism of Jude and 2 Peter.* Atlanta: Scholars Press, 1988. A helpful technical study making use of the categories of Greek rhetoric.

Chapter 16

The General Letters B:
The Johannine Letters

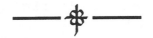

1. Searching for the Stories

a. The Problem of Authorship

None of the three writings that appear in the New Testament as the letters of John actually claim to have been written by a person of that name. The first of these, which bears hardly any traits of a letter, does not name an author at all. The two shorter writings, which follow the form of a Hellenistic letter rather closely, indicate simply that they are sent by "the elder." The close similarity in language and theology between the Gospel of John and these three books, however, convinced the early church that all were written by the same person.

That person was generally presumed to be John the Son of Zebedee, one of "the Twelve," who was also identified with "beloved disciple" of the Gospel. Although many modern scholars reject all aspects of this traditional view of the authorship of the Gospel, we may still ask whether the letters were written by the person who wrote the Gospel and whether the three letters themselves had a common authorship.

Opinion is divided on both questions, but there is reason to answer the first negatively. Despite similarities in thought between the Gospel and the letters, there are significant differences in emphasis. While the Gospel stresses Jesus' divine nature, both 1 and 2 John are more concerned to make the point that the Son of God came "in the flesh"; and 1 John contains a much stronger emphasis upon futuristic eschatology than does the Gospel. Also, the phrase "the beginning," which seems at first glance to bind 1 John (1:1) so closely

493

to the Gospel, might actually count in the other direction. In the Gospel it refers to the creation of the world, but in 1 John it indicates the initial stage of the Christian tradition. Many scholars also claim that 1 John reveals a later historical situation, since the opponents it attacks are not those outside the community but false teachers within it.

Not all critics are convinced by such evidence, since it could be replied that the author changed tactics to meet a new situation. And the question is complicated by the possibility that the Gospel has gone through one or more stages of revision. Some scholars believe that the person who wrote 1 John, while not the author of the original version of the Gospel, was responsible for its final state. The question of whether the author of 1 John also wrote 2 and 3 John is even more difficult, because the latter two works are so brief as to yield little evidence. But there is no real reason to doubt that 2 and 3 John were written by one person, i.e., "the elder."

Given the difficulty of all these questions, any attempt to tell the story behind the letters of John will be speculative. But there is one point upon which virtually all scholars agree. Whether written by one, two, or more authors, the four Johannine writings came from the same Christian community, which was marked by a distinctive theological outlook.

b. The Conflict with the "Secessionists"

In chapter 7 we noted Raymond E. Brown's view that the Johannine community was made up originally of Jewish Christians who developed a very high Christology involving a belief in the preexistence of the son of God, were expelled from the synagogue, and began to receive gentile converts. Far from the Christianization of an already-developed Gnosticism, Johannine theology was in Brown's view a step, initially taken within Jewish Christianity, that fed into later Gnosticism.

According to Brown, the letters of John date from a stage in the community's life somewhat later than that in which the author of the Gospel wrote.[1] After this community was fully separated from other Jewish Christians who would not accept its high Christology, it went through a period of internal conflict. Some members began to emphasize Jesus' divine nature to the point of compromising his full humanity. Brown refers to this group as the secessionists, because they apparently separated from the rest of the community.

---

1. Raymond E. Brown, *The Community of the Beloved Disciple: The Life, Loves, and Hates of an Individual Church in New Testament Times* (New York: Paulist, 1979), and *The Epistles of John* (Garden City, N.Y.: Doubleday, 1982).

In the opinion of many scholars, the letters of John oppose a fully gnostic point of view characterized by "docetism" (from the Greek verb *dokeō*, to "think," or "seem"), the view that Jesus only "seemed" to be human and had no real human body at all. But Brown thinks that the secessionists had not moved that far, since they too were Johannine Christians, and it would be difficult to justify a truly docetic Christology on the basis of the Gospel of John. What they denied, according to Brown, was not that Jesus was human, but only that the human Jesus had significance for salvation. They understood salvation as the result of the knowledge of God Jesus brought, not of any action that took place in the world, such as his death on a cross.

Any Christology will have implications for other aspects of belief and practice, and the letters of John associate the secessionists with a number of specific views. We may assume from 1 John 1:8, 10 that they claimed to have reached a state of sinlessness. This view is consistent with their strong sense of union with God and their rejection of futurist eschatology. The emphasis upon commandments in 1 John is also evidence that the author's opponents thought that ethical behavior was unnecessary for salvation.

On some other matters, we must be more careful about accepting the author's characterization of the opponents. Many scholars take the charge that the secessionists lack love (1 John 2:9) at face value, assuming that those who de-emphasized the humanity of Jesus and the importance of commandments would feel no sense of obligation to the human neighbor. Brown thinks it more likely, however, that each camp was characterized by internal solidarity on the one hand and animosity toward the opposition on the other. The author of 1 John may well have appeared as unloving to those called "antichrists" and "liars" (2:18, 22) as they did to that author! And they undoubtedly understood the author's group, not theirs, as the one that had fallen away from the truth.

c. The Purposes of the Letters

In Brown's view, 1 John was written for the author's immediate community, the home base of Johannine Christianity, in order to combat the teachings of the splinter group. Because the potential readers were close at hand, there was no reason to use the format of a letter. In 2 John, however, "the elder" writes to a Johannine house-church some distance away to warn about the secessionists and to urge rejection of any missionaries whose views do not conform to "the teaching of Christ"—as, of course, the author defines it.

The specific story behind the third letter is the most difficult to reconstruct. In it "the elder" writes to one Gaius, praising him for "faithfulness to the

Fig. 75. "Jesus at the Limbo" (Duccio; Italian, 14th cent.). Based upon a traditional interpretation of 1 Peter 3:18-20, 4:6, according to which Jesus descended into hell following the crucifixion to offer the gospel to those who died before his coming. See above, p. 483.

truth" and criticizing someone named Diotrephes. The author charges the latter with usurping authority and refusing to welcome some group, presumably emissaries from the home base community. We do not, however, know the specifics of the controversy. Why, for example, did Diotrephes turn the travelers away? The author does not speak directly about the secessionists of 1 and 2 John. But was Diotrephes perhaps a secessionist? Or did he think the emissaries were? We do not even know whether Diotrephes and Gaius were in the same local community, or what specific office (if any) each held.

Brown thinks Diotrephes was an early example of a local leader invested with great authority, such as the bishops of the pastoral letters. He agreed with "the elder" in rejecting the secessionists, but disagreed about authority in the church. Whereas "the elder" retained a community-based version of authority, characteristic of the earlier stages of Johannine Christianity, Diotrephes thought that controversies were best dealt with through concentrated power. He therefore assumed the authority to expel members from the community (v. 10) and probably dealt with the problem of false teaching by rejecting all missionaries. When he refused to accept the emissaries from the home community, "the elder" wrote to Gaius, who may have received the missionaries after their rejection by Diotrephes (vv. 3, 5-8), to shore up support for a confrontation on this issue.

We do not know who won the immediate dispute. But, if Brown's view is correct, we do know which point of view ultimately prevailed: the church finally invested authority in the office of bishop. So it is likely that the letters of "the elder" represent a model of community-based authority within Johannine Christianity that finally disappeared as the Johannine churches were absorbed into the church at large. The apparent acceptance of Peter's authority in the Gospel of John 21 is a sign that it was only a modified version of Johannine Christianity that was ultimately acceptable to the wider body. For it was a revised, "ecclesiastical" version of the Gospel of John that achieved canonical status. (This view of Peter also makes it unlikely that the author of the letters is responsible for chapter 21 of the Gospel.)

d. The History of the Johannine Community

From Brown's perspective, the Johannine writings give a glimpse of several stages in the history of a distinctive form of early Christianity. The precanonical version of the Gospel reflects a middle period of the community, when it is still in dispute with Jewish Christians with a lower Christology. In the letters we see a later situation in which one segment of the community rejects another, which in its eyes has taken the Johannine high Christology to an extreme. This latter faction, which increasingly de-emphasizes Jesus' humanity, is eventually cut off from the larger church altogether and finally feeds into a developing Gnosticism. And the secessionists take with them a range of community traditions, including the Gospel of John, that gain great popularity in gnostic circles. The wider body of the Christian church does not accept the perspective of "the elder," with its communitarian authority base. But it does receive from the Johannine tradition a high Christology, a version of its central writing (the Gospel of John), and the three letters as well.

2. Reading 1 John

a. 1:1-4

In vv. 1-4 the author, using the first-person plural, discloses an intention to declare "what was from the beginning." Three terms in the introduction will remind the readers of the prologue to the Gospel of John—"the beginning," "life," and "word" (logos). But the emphasis is not upon the preexistent Logos, as in the Gospel; it is upon the extension of that word through the tradition of the community. The readers will thus hear themselves addressed by the Johannine community itself, by the tradition they associate with the beloved disciple. They will recognize the terms "eternal life" and "joy," as well as the notions of revelation and fellowship, as central to that tradition; and they will understand that the author is claiming authority precisely by speaking on behalf of the tradition that has brought life, in the qualitative sense, to believers. As Johannine Christians, the readers will identify with the author's "we," but will also be aware that they are addressed as "you." They will thus be prepared to have the author in some way extend or correct their understanding of the tradition.

The readers will also sense an intense concreteness in the author's description of the community's experience of the word: witnesses, Johannine Christians, have "seen" it with their eyes, "touched" it with their hands. The eternal word, having become manifest in an actual human being, continues to be present in a very tangible way in the life of the community. Thus when the author indicates a purpose in writing in 1:4, the readers, as members of that living community, will want to know what the author has to say that will make joy "complete."

b. 1:5—3:10

In 1:5 the author specifies the content of the tradition, the "message" that has brought life, fellowship with God, and joy: God is pure light, containing no darkness at all. The readers will recognize the qualified dualism that pervades the Gospel of John. To say that God is light is to say that God is the source of the illumination that engenders authentic human existence. To mention darkness at all, however, is to recognize an antithetical force in the world, a power that stands in stark opposition to all that is good. Against the background of this dualism, the author implies in 1:6 that some who claim fellowship with God actually walk in darkness and goes on to assert that it is those who walk in the light who alone have such fellowship. The readers are thus prepared to distinguish between true and false claims.

As the author turns to the theme of sin (1:7), the readers will presumably understand the reference to those who claim sinlessness as a condemnation of the secessionists. Hearing that those who are in the light are cleansed and forgiven through "the blood of Jesus," they will conclude that all human beings stand in need of such forgiveness, which means that those who deny their own sinfulness are liars. The reference to atonement in 2:1-2 combines with the appeal to the readers as "little children" to clarify the author's view of sin: those in the light should not sin; but if they do, they are forgiven through Christ's sacrifice. The readers will conclude that the secessionists, in claiming sinlessness, miss the significance of his death as atonement.

The readers will hear the statements regarding the knowledge of God in 2:3-6 against the background of the author's earlier statements on fellowship. They will now understand that keeping the commandments, which is the path to "perfection," is a sign that one does in fact walk in the light. And they will also note reminiscences of the Gospel of John, both in the theme of the knowledge of God (prologue to the Gospel) and in the reference in 1 John 2:8 to the new commandment.

The author thus encircles the readers with the Johannine tradition and hones in on the content of the commandment: love of one's fellow believers. The readers must thus see that hatred of other community members places one on the side of darkness. In stating that "the darkness is passing away," the author interprets the Johannine dualism in the light of a futuristic eschatology, subtly indicating that the time of absolute fulfillment lies in the future. Although passing away, the darkness is still present in the world, which is one reason no one can claim sinlessness. But to say that "the light is already shining" is to acknowledge the Johannine tradition of fulfillment in the present.

In 2:12-14, the author offers assurances to the readers: their sins are forgiven; they do have knowledge of God. Then an admonition, once again reflective of Johannine dualism, follows in vv. 15-17: the readers must not love the world, which stands in opposition to the Father and is passing away.

The proclamation in 2:18 that "it is the last hour" makes explicit the eschatological point subtly indicated earlier. And the references to the "antichrists" identify the object of the author's scorn: the readers will presumably know from their tradition that some sort of demonic figure was expected to arise, in opposition to Christ, just before the end of the age. Now there can be no doubt about the identify of the group the author opposes: it is those who "went out from us"—the secessionists. Their very presence is itself a sign of the nearness of the end, and in identifying them with the expected antichrist the author expects the readers to reject them outright.

In 2:22-25 the author plays off those who deny that "Jesus is the Christ" against those who confess the Son and thereby know the Father also. Although the specific point of contention is not mentioned, the readers will presumably recognize in the conjunction of "Jesus" with "Christ" something that the secessionists deny, rendering their Christology inadequate. And the reference to what the readers "heard from the beginning" will remind them that this confession of Jesus stands at the center of their tradition. That tradition once again appears as the source of authority, and vv. 26-27 invite the readers to contrast it to the teachings of the secessionists, whom the author now presents as deceivers. In proclaiming that the community members have no need of teachers, since they are anointed, presumably by the Spirit, the author binds the Spirit and the tradition together. This move undercuts the secessionists' position, since they too undoubtedly appealed to the Spirit as justification for their views: did not the Gospel of John (16:13) promise that the Spirit would guide the community "into all the truth"? On the basis of 2:26-27, the reader will understand tradition as dynamic, yet not simply free-floating, since what was heard in the beginning remains the point of departure.

In the immediately following injunction (2:28) to "abide in him," the readers will hear a reference to Christ, since the author goes on to refer to "his coming." Abiding in Christ and remaining true to the tradition thus appear as equivalents, and the eschatological significance of faithfulness to the tradition implied in 2:18 is made explicit. The author also promises (v. 29) confidence to those who so "abide" and presents right action as the sign of one's relation to Christ. This thought leads into a brief discourse on what it means to be "children" of God in 3:1-3, where use of "the world" in its negative sense and additional eschatological references emphasize the distinction between the readers and the secessionists.

When the author refers to those who commit sin in 3:4, the readers will presume that the secessionists are in view. Hearing then that those who abide in Christ do not sin, they will understand that the author is pointing up two incompatible modes of existence and will be prepared for the contrast that follows, that between the children of the devil and "those who have been born of God." If the statement that those in Christ do not sin sounds very much like the secessionists' view, the readers will nevertheless remember that the author has condemned the claim to sinlessness, has written of atonement and confession of sin, and in the present context continues to press the obligation to "do what is right" and love one's fellow Christians.

c. 3:11—5:12

In 3:11 the author both builds upon the immediate context and signals a new beginning. The reference to "the message you have heard from the beginning" takes the reader back to 1:1, 5 and indicates a new expansion upon that message. But it is in fact love, mentioned in 3:10, that constitutes the new summation of the message. In vv. 12-17 the story from Genesis 4 of Cain's murder of his brother sets the two ways of existing in the world over against one another in the sharpest terms. Those who hate their fellows are murderers like Cain, abiding "in death." The readers, included in the author's "we," must accept a different way of life. Abiding in life rather than death, they will be hated by "the world" and are called to imitate Christ in laying down their lives for others. The rhetorical question in v. 17 then brings the point home in terms of economics: the readers will understand that the "haves" cannot claim to manifest God's love if they ignore the needs of the "have nots."

After an injunction to actual deeds (as opposed to mere words) of love in 3:18, the author offers assurance in vv. 19-24. If the readers worry about whether they are "from the truth," they need only ask themselves whether they do in fact obey the commandments, specifically the commandment to love, which the author links to the confession of Jesus Christ as God's Son.

Verse 24 also states that the readers may be certain of Christ's presence in them by the testimony of the Spirit. But this raises a question, since the readers will experience many spirits in the world. The author acknowledges the problem in 4:1, noting the presence of false prophets, and thus provides a way to test the spirits manifest in the various teachings: any true spirit will confess "that Jesus Christ has come in the flesh." The readers will conclude that the motivating force behind the teaching of the secessionists is "antichrist," since that teaching does not adequately acknowledge the full humanity of Jesus. Then in 4:4-6 the author again assures the readers that they are from God, contrasting true believers with "the world."

In 4:7 the author breaks out into a poetic sequence, bracketing an exposition on the relationship between God and love with injunctions to realize love in the community. Love is the necessary sign of the knowledge of God and is descriptive of the essence of God's own being; and God's love is revealed in the sending of the Son as a sacrifice for sin. Although human beings cannot see God, those who love one another in Christ can experience God's presence (4:12).

Reemphasizing several points in 4:13-21, the author also presents love as the basis for confidence in the day of judgment and contrasts it with fear. Told that fear of punishment is a sign of imperfect love, the readers will understand that the way to achieve eschatological assurance is to love their fellow believers; for when love reaches perfection, its full potential, it drives out fear. Verse 20 uses a logical argument to reveal the absurdity of the separation of love of God from love of neighbor. The readers will conclude that the secessionists' disruption of the community negates their professed love of God. And the strong term "liar" underscores the point.

In 5:1-4 the author extends the love theme through an analogy: as love of a parent entails love of the child, so love of God entails love of God's children. Since God's children are identified as those who confess Jesus (the human being) as the Christ, the readers will understand that it is the author's own faction within the community that is meant. The secessionists are thus excluded as unloving, whereas the readers can prove themselves to be God's children by loving one another. The author's words thus constitute both a demand and a promise. The readers should love one another; and in doing so they are able to "conquer the world," to overcome the darkness.

In 5:5 the author reiterates the theme of conquering and leads into a discourse on the Son of God in vv. 6-12. The readers will undoubtedly grasp the significance of the statement on "water and the blood" in a way that modern critics cannot. They will presumably identify in the view that relates Jesus' coming to "water only" some aspect of the secessionists' teaching, which probably had something to do with the statement of John the Baptist in the Gospel (John 1:26): "I baptize with water"; and they will connect the more inclusive formula, "the water and the blood," to the death scene in the Gospel of John 19:34, where blood and water pour out of Jesus' wounded side. It would be consistent with the author's earlier statements to see here an insistence that Jesus' atoning death on the cross is an essential aspect of Christian faith.

The readers will also understand that in Jewish tradition witnesses were demanded in court cases (Deut. 19:15) and will therefore receive the author's statement regarding the three witnesses—water, blood, and Spirit—as confirming the identify of Jesus as the Son of God. Believers may thus look to various sources for confirmation of their confession of faith: the water and blood from Jesus' side, John the Baptist's testimony at Jesus' baptism, and the testimony of the Spirit at various points—at Jesus' baptism and death and in the continuing life of the community. And what that testimony confirms, apparently, is the saving significance of Jesus' death.

In 5:9 the author contrasts God's own testimony to merely human testimony, which the readers will identify with the secessionists' views, very likely their appeal to John the Baptist. When the readers read in v. 11 that this testimony is God's gift of eternal life in the Son, they will understand that it is their own possession of eternal life that constitutes God's testimony. Since eternal life is the sign that one is truly related to God through the Son, the author can then in 5:12 assure the readers that a true confession of Jesus brings life, whereas a defective confession leads to death.

d. 5:13-21

Restating in 5:13 the purpose in writing, the author reminds the readers of the earlier statement of purpose (1:4) and so brackets all the intervening material as the main body of the writing. Told earlier that the purpose is to make joy complete, they now hear that the author wants to secure their knowledge that they do have eternal life. After presenting that knowledge as the ground of confidence in prayer, the author turns in vv. 16-17 to the issue of praying for those who sin. The readers must distinguish between sins that lead to eternal death and those that do not; they should pray for those who commit the latter, but not those who commit the former. The implication is probably that since the secessionists' position makes them guilty of mortal sin, the readers should not pray for them.

With the emphatic threefold use of the phrase "we know," the author now offers a final set of assurances regarding the readers' knowledge of God. Having earlier denied the secessionists' claims to sinlessness, the author can now (5:18) address the readers with the more positive, empowering statement that "those who are born of God do not sin." The readers will understand that although sin remains a possibility for them, it is ultimately incompatible with knowledge of God; and that God in fact protects them from sin. Including in the assurances the affirmation that the god known in Christ is the true god, the author closes with a warning against idolatry. The readers will understand that the secessionists' false Christology leads to a false understanding of God.

3. Reading 2 John

With the self-designation "the elder" (v. 1), the author indicates his link with tradition, which, together with the references to "the truth," establishes both the context and the authority of his writing. The readers are addressed as Christians, who have been taught "the truth." The elder also creates a bond with the recipients by expressing his love and terming the recipient church "the elect lady and her children," a bond that is strengthened through the assurances given in v. 3.

The bond with the readers is strengthened again through the expression of joy in v. 4, although this verse also hints that the author also has some concern about the church to which he writes: only *some* of the "children" walk in the truth. After enjoining the love commandment as central to the Johannine tradition—it is "from the beginning"—the author then alerts the recipients to the problem of the deceivers (vv. 7-11). Identifying the false teaching as denial "that Jesus Christ has come in the flesh," he warns the readers against receiving into their community any who "go beyond" traditional teaching.

With the essential point made, the elder indicates in closing (v. 12) that he will have more to say when he visits in person. The phrase regarding the completion of joy, apparently stock Johannine phraseology, again solidifies the author's bond with the readers. The final greeting from the elder's own church community brings the letter to a close on a note of confessional solidarity.

4. Reading 3 John

The salutation in v. 1 not only identifies the sender and recipient but also binds them together as Christians through the terms "elder," "love," and "truth." Gaius will know that he is addressed by a fellow Christian who speaks on behalf of the tradition. The health wish in v. 2 increases the bond between sender and recipient. And the expression of joy in vv. 3-4 not only contributes to this bond but also prepares Gaius to hear discourse regarding "the truth." Complemented so warmly for walking in the truth, he will anticipate that the elder will write of others who do not so walk.

In vv. 5-8 the elder requests that Gaius continue the practice of welcoming emissaries. Although he does not identify the persons, it is assumed that the recipient will know who is meant. References to Gaius's prior practice on the matter and to his love for the church combine with v. 8, with its gentle "we ought" and its reference to "the truth," to present reception of the emissaries as his Christian duty.

Against this background, the author can in vv. 9-10 place the issue in a wider context. Disclosing now that Diotrephes has refused the emissaries, rejected the authority the elder represents, and spread false charges, the elder implicitly asks Gaius to side with him against Diotrephes. The mention of a possible visit increases the urgency of taking sides, and reference to Diotrephes's practice of expelling opponents from the church further discredits the latter's position.

The injunction to do good in v. 11 is couched in theological language and implies that to follow the elder's advice on the matter at hand is to do God's will. The author's testimony on behalf of Demetrius, possibly one of the emissaries, will commend the latter to Gaius. The closing reference to a visit suggests that the elder has much more to say on the matter at hand; and the final greeting is worded so as to play up the close relationship between the elder and the members of Gaius's community. Gaius will finish the letter with a strong sense that to refuse the emissaries is an outright denial of the tradition through which he has learned "the truth."

5. Note on "Antichrist"

Students of literature know that a hero needs an opponent. The creator deities of ancient Middle Eastern mythology battled primordial monsters representing chaos and Judaism itself made a place for an archfiend when it embraced apocalypticism. So it is hardly surprising that as messianic thought of various types developed in Judaism, various kinds of "anti-messiahs" were introduced to play a role in apocalyptic dramas. Nor is it surprising that the New Testament, heir to Jewish apocalypticism, would pick up on this broad theme also.

It is important to understand that just as there were no unified, self-consistent concepts of either a Messiah or an anti-Messiah in pre-Christian Judaism, but a diverse range of ideas on these themes, so in the New Testament there is no unified concept of an "antichrist." In the New Testament, in fact, the term appears only in the Johannine letters. There are, however, several different images of an eschatological opponent of Christ. The Synoptic Gospels, for example, mention "false messiahs" (e.g., Matt. 24:24) who will arise to lead people astray. We have already seen that 2 Thessalonians 2:9 mentions "the lawless one," who clearly appears as an eschatological antitype of Christ, and in chapter 17 we will see that the broad notion appears in more than one form in the Revelation to John.

Post–New Testament Christian writings, not surprisingly, continued the tradition. And later interpreters tended to put together all the diverse images, including those in the Jewish Scriptures, to create self-consistent *concepts* of an antichrist that, century after century, they identified with one after another historical figure.

What is interesting about the use of the term "antichrist" in the Johannine letters is that they apply it quite literally to the secessionist movement. And this identification shows that the eschatology of the letters is related to that of the Gospel on the one hand and the church at large on the other in a complex way. At one stage, the Gospel of John reshaped the traditional, futurist eschatology of the wider church, giving it a strong realized component. The letters, which for the most part move back toward futurist thought, nevertheless introduced a new kind of realized eschatology. For their claim that the antichrist has already appeared means that the present moment, the time in which the letters are written, is in their view the "last hour," the actual beginning of the eschatological drama.

STUDY QUESTIONS

1. What is it possible to say about the authorship of the Johannine letters?

2. According to Raymond Brown's theory, at what stage of the Johannine community's development was each of these letters written?

3. In Brown's view, what was the teaching of the "secessionists"?

4. What is central in Christian teaching according to 1 and 2 John?

FOR FURTHER READING

Brown, Raymond E. *The Community of the Beloved Disciple: The Life, Loves, and Hates of an Individual Church in New Testament Times.* New York: Paulist, 1979. A well-argued presentation of the author's reconstruction of the history of the Johannine community. Complex, but fascinating reading.

———. *The Epistles of John.* Garden City, N.Y.: Doubleday, 1982. An important contribution by a leading Johannine scholar.

Bultmann, Rudolf. *The Johannine Epistles.* Hermeneia. Trans. R. Philip O'Hara with Lane C. McGaughy and Robert W. Funk. Philadelphia: Fortress Press, 1973. Technical and detailed, but important.

Dodd, C. H. *The Johannine Epistles.* New York: Harper, 1946. Still an important resource; strong on Greek background.

Kysar, Robert. *I, II, III John.* Augsburg Commentary on the New Testament. Minneapolis: Augsburg, 1986. Brief, competent, readable.

Perkins, Pheme. *The Johannine Epistles.* Wilmington, Del.: Michael Glazier, 1979. Brief, competent, readable; stresses relationship of the style of writing to oral culture.

Smith, D. Moody. *First, Second, and Third John.* Louisville: Westminster/John Knox, 1990. Readable and highly instructive.

Schnackenburg, Rudolf. *Johannine Epistles: Introduction and Commentary.* Trans. Reginald and Ilfe Fuller. New York: Crossroad, 1992. A major scholarly contribution.

Chapter 17

The Revelation to John

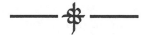

1. Searching for the Story

The Revelation to John gives rise to a certain paradox. Many people who know nothing else of the Bible are at least vaguely aware of popular claims that Revelation contains prophecies regarding the "end of the world" that are supposedly being fulfilled in the late twentieth century. On the other hand, many who have some familiarity with the Bible will name Revelation as the most puzzling of all the biblical books, and quite a few find it either frightening or morally repugnant. It is therefore important to pay careful attention to questions regarding the story behind this writing.

a. Who Was the Author?

The author identifies himself as John. By the middle of the second century, many Christians assumed this John to be one of the Twelve, namely, the son of Zebedee, who had supposedly written the Gospel and letters of John also. And by the end of that century the churches of the West had accepted the work as apostolic and canonical. In the East, however, many leaders denied apostolic authorship, and the canonical status of Revelation was not secure until the end of the fourth century.

In the third century, a bishop in Alexandria noted the distinct linguistic differences between Revelation and the Gospel and letters of John. And many modern scholars are convinced that the same person cannot have authored all these works. Not the least of the problems is the fact that Revelation is per-

507

meated with futuristic eschatology, whereas the Gospel has a strong emphasis upon realized eschatology.

Some scholars do find enough similarity between Revelation and the other works to think that its author was associated with the Johannine community. In Revelation 19:13, for example, Jesus is called "the Word [Logos] of God." This is the only passage in the New Testament outside John 1:1 where the term "Logos" is used in this way. Other scholars, however, find the similarities superficial. Elisabeth Schüssler Fiorenza points out that Revelation has no great affinity with the Johannine writings in vocabulary—less, indeed, than with the letters of Paul.[1]

The author's knowledge of Jewish apocalyptic literature is evident. In fact, the entire genre gets its name from this writing, which came to be known as "the Revelation [*apokalypsis*] to John" on the basis of the author's designation in 1:1: "The revelation of Jesus Christ...." It is also clear that the author speaks as a Christian prophet, since he refers to the work as "the words of the prophecy" (1:3). And we may be fairly certain that he lived in Asia Minor. For he has constructed the writing as an extended letter to seven churches in that region and locates the scene of his vision on the isle of Patmos, just off its western coast.

b. In What Sense Is Revelation "Prophecy"?

There is a range of scholarly views on the questions treated so far. But the big difference of opinion is that between critical scholars and popular interpreters regarding the author's purpose and the nature of the work. All agree that John understood his work as "prophecy." But there are different understandings of what prophecy is.

In popular thinking, prophecy is virtually synonymous with prediction, and prophets are people who, under divine inspiration, predict the (usually distant) future. Those who understand Revelation on the basis of this model of prophecy believe that John predicted events centuries removed from his own time. According to one version of this approach, Revelation gives a preview of human history from the first century to the "end of the world." Another version, which appeared in the nineteenth century, is represented in recent popular works and is often endorsed by media evangelists. In this view, John's predictions concern only the end of history, not its entire sweep.

---

1. Elisabeth Schüssler Fiorenza, *The Book of Revelation: Justice and Judgment* (Philadelphia: Fortress Press, 1985), 93–95.

Proponents of this interpretation believe that Revelation foresees incidents in twentieth-century international politics.

Critical scholars understand Revelation differently, in part because they understand prophecy differently. When one reads the prophetic books of the Jewish Scriptures—such as Amos, Hosea, Isaiah, and Jeremiah—in light of the circumstances in which they were written, it becomes clear that the prophets interpreted their own times in light of what they understood as God's will and God's intentions.

The prophets saw God at work in the sociopolitical events in which Judah, Israel, and the neighboring countries and empires were involved. They often declared God's displeasure with the actions of the people and their monarchs and thus spoke of a coming judgment. But they expected this judgment in the immediate, not distant, future. On other occasions, they spoke of the promise of God's eventual restoration of Israel and/or Judah. In some instances they envisioned this restoration very soon, and in others they spoke more vaguely, in the vein of "someday." But they did not give an outline of specific events stretching out into centuries to come. They sometimes declared what was to happen in the future, getting it right in some instances and wrong in others. But "prediction" is an inadequate understanding of their primary intentions.

Detailed "predictions" of historical events are, to be sure, found in apocalyptic works such as Daniel. But these works were written pseudonymously, in the name of heroes of earlier ages. By writing in the name of persons in the distant past, the apocalyptic authors could make their reviews of events that were actually in the past look like predictions of the future. Typically, when an apocalyptic writer deals with the actual future, the "predictions" become extremely vague.

For critical scholars, John was a prophet who used the apocalyptic medium to speak to readers in his own time about the events of that time. Revelation is not a book about the distant future, which would have remained meaningless to persons in the first century. It does speak of the eschatological future, of the end of the age; but John made it perfectly clear that he believed the eschatological events to be very near (1:3; 2:16; 3:11; 6:11; 10:6; 12:12; 22:6, 7, 12, 20).

Why did John believe this, and why did he write this apocalyptic work? The clues are in the book itself. John believed that his readers were about to face persecution (2:10; 7:14) and that some of them had already suffered (2:3, 9, 19). His statement in 1:9 may well indicate that because of his Christian faith he himself was banished to Patmos by Roman authorities, who often used the island as a place of exile.

Christians in general believed that Jesus' resurrection from the dead had

Fig. 76. The Roman Province of Asia, showing the churches of Revelation 2:1—3:22.
(Map by C. Kim Pickering)

inaugurated the eschatological age. Given that belief and given an apocalyptic tradition that frequently included a period of "woes" just preceding the end of the age, it was natural for John to conclude that the end was near. Apparently, then, he wrote to the churches of Asia Minor as a way of bringing hope in the midst of tribulation, interpreting their present distress as a prelude to God's final victory.

c. Whom Did the Author Oppose? And When Did the Author Write?

If John wrote primarily to offer hope to his readers, he also wanted to admonish them to avoid certain teachings and practices. In 2:6, 15 he rails out against a group he calls the Nicolaitans, and in 2:20-25 he disparages a prophet by dubbing her "Jezebel"—an infamous idolater in the Jewish Scriptures. He also condemns both "Jezebel" and another group to which he applies names from the Jewish Scriptures (2:14) for approving the practice of eating meat offered to idols. But we saw in Part Three that Paul had no objection to that practice as long as it did not unsettle other Christians. So what was it about these groups that offended John? To answer that question, we must be more specific about the situation in which he wrote.

According to a Christian writer in the late second century, Revelation was written near the end of the reign of the Roman emperor Domitian, which lasted from 81 to 96 C.E., and the majority of modern scholars think this is the most likely time of composition. Although evidence for a persecution of Christians under Domitian is ambiguous, we know that a few years later, during the reign of Trajan (98–117), when persons were accused of being Christians the authorities would execute them if they refused to sacrifice before the emperor's image and/or curse Christ. Thus scholars who date Revelation during Domitian's reign think that a similar situation must have existed at that time. Christians were not being put to death in great numbers, but the precarious situation of the community created a feeling of alienation from the wider society and a sense of imminent danger.

It is possible, however, that the situation was somewhat more critical than this description would indicate. J. Christian Wilson has made a strong case for dating Revelation in an earlier period (the 60s), either late in the reign of Nero, for which time we have ample evidence of the persecution of Christians, or under the rule of his immediate successor, Galba.[2] This would mean that John wrote either during or shortly after a time of a bloody and system-

---

2. J. Christian Wilson, "The Problem of the Domitianic Date of Revelation," *New Testament Studies* 39, no. 4 (1993): 587–605.

atic attempt to exterminate the church. Thus his audience was either in the midst of a genuine crisis or feared another outbreak of the terror they had just been through. The usual objection to this dating, though, is that the author employs a metaphorical identification of the Roman Empire with Babylon, and we can document this usage among Jews only after the destruction of the temple in 70 C.E.

Whether Revelation was written under Nero, Galba, or Domitian, the broad issue at stake would have been the same. In a situation in which faithful Christians faced the possibility of death for refusing to perform a sacrifice to the emperor, the eating of meat offered to idols took on a different meaning than it did for Paul. In John's eyes it was outright idolatry. It seems likely, in fact, that all the groups he opposed advocated, in one way or another, an accommodation to the ways of the Roman Empire, that is, full participation in business and social activities. But for John the empire was an agent of Satan; to accommodate to it was to deny the faith. So when he wrote to encourage Christians to "keep the faith," he meant that his readers should not compromise with the demands of the empire just to keep themselves alive. They should be prepared, if necessary, to go to their deaths.

d. Who Were the Readers?

If John seems uncompromising and quick to condemn, it is important to note another aspect of the story behind Revelation. The fact that Christians were singled out for persecution reveals their marginalized status in the empire. "They were," Eugene Boring writes,

> considered to be adherents of a sect that primarily appealed to the lower classes, a sect that had no long history or glorious institutions.... Even Christians who were of a social status that permitted them to participate in the social and political life of the Roman Empire were hesitant to do so, because of the association of such participation with the Roman gods. Christians were thus considered to be unpatriotic and irreligious, sometimes being called "atheists" because they had no "gods." Thus, they were likely candidates to become scapegoats for disasters, such as the fire which destroyed much of Rome in 64. Nero could accuse Christians of arson and arrest and kill many of them... only because the public already considered them to be outsiders within the social structure and because the Christians thus tended to look upon themselves as outsiders.[3]

---

3. M. Eugene Boring, *Revelation* (Louisville: Westminster/John Knox, 1989), 11.

From the perspective of a marginalized community, anyone who advocates accommodation to the larger society threatens the identity of the smaller community. To do so in a time of overt persecution is to compound the injury.

e. Christians and Jews in Revelation

It is important to remember both the background of persecution and the sense of alienation and vulnerability that John and other Christians felt when one comes upon a passage such as 2:9: "I know the slander on the part of those who say that they are Jews and are not, but are a synagogue of Satan." By the time of Christianity, Judaism was a well-established religion in the Roman Empire. And although Jews were considered strange by the general populace and often harassed in various ways, the empire had learned to tolerate them and accord them a measure of respect. They were exempt from military service and any obligation to participate in the emperor cult.

When Christianity became a separate religion, it lost the special status accorded Jews. And, given the precarious position of any group that could not participate fully in the emperor cult, it was almost inevitable that the bitterness between Christians and Jews would increase during a time of persecution. Because Christians threatened the very structure of Judaism by including uncircumcised Gentiles in a faith that claimed Jewish roots, Jews would be inclined to distance themselves from Christians, even to the point of denouncing them to the authorities. From the Christians' perspective, of course, Jesus was the Messiah whose coming had broken down the barrier between Jew and Gentile. They considered themselves the true heirs of Abraham, which can only have infuriated members of the synagogue.

Against such a background, John made harsh statements against non-Christian Jews. In so doing, he reflected a tragic instance of the frequent situation in which rival marginalized groups, powerless in the face of the dominant power structure, turn their anger on one another.

f. The Author's Use of Language

The Revelation to John is a book that gives vent to anger. While this anger is sometimes directed at Jews and rival prophetic groups within the church, it is more often directed against the Roman Empire. John brands this enemy with a name that Jews had already given it following the destruction of the temple in 70 C.E., the name of the capital of that earlier empire that had destroyed the temple long before: Babylon. In announcing the end of the age, John also announces the end of Rome, the end of a human power structure responsible for untold injustice and human misery.

John's anger is apparent, but there is another dimension of his message that is often missed. To declare an end to oppression is to declare the beginning of freedom; to proclaim an end to human injustice is to proclaim the justice of the Rule of God. The story behind the Revelation to John is the story of a prophet writing to instill hope in people who felt themselves marginalized and oppressed, hope for a time in which "mourning and crying and pain will be no more" (21:4). It is the story of a visionary who looked forward to the ultimate "healing of the nations" (22:2). The reverse side of the language of judgment is that of hope, joy, and reconciliation.

Another aspect of the author's language is its symbolic nature. Almost all interpreters recognize that John did not intend for images such as the great beast rising out of the sea (13:1) and the locusts with tails like scorpions who torture human beings (9:1-11) to be interpreted literally. But there are different ways in which symbolic language can function.

Some interpreters of Revelation have assumed that every symbol in the book has an exact meaning, corresponding in a one-to-one fashion to something outside the text. A symbol that functions in this way is called a steno-symbol. For these interpreters, just as Rome stands for Babylon, every one of the "woes" visited upon the earth by angels in chapters 8–9 points to some definite set of events the author expected to take place. Interpreters at the other extreme deny that any of the symbols have exact meaning or point to specific realities in the actual world. Even Babylon, from this perspective, does not stand in simplistic fashion for the Roman Empire but functions more generally as a symbol of oppressive, God-denying power in any time or place.[4]

Scholarship remains divided on how to interpret the symbolic language of Revelation, but there is increasing recognition that John's use of such language falls somewhere between the two extremes. Some of the symbols seem to have a definite reference, most notably Babylon. But to try to interpret Revelation as a whole by simply "decoding" it—by assigning to each symbol a referent in the actual world, whether that of the first century or a later time—is to miss an important aspect of the author's intention. It would be absurd, for example, to try to identify the "event" John envisions in 20:14, the casting of Death and Hades into the lake of fire. As Schüssler Fiorenza notes,

---

4. Paul S. Minear, *I Saw a New Earth: An Introduction to the Visions of the Apocalypse* (Washington, D.C.: Corpus Books, 1968), esp. chaps. 4–5.

The strength of Revelation's language and images lies not in theological argumentation or historical information but in their evocative power inviting imaginative participation. The symbolization and narrative movement of Revelation elicits emotions, feelings, and convictions that cannot, and should not, be fully conceptualized. The phrasing of the images and metaphors in propositional, logical, factual language robs them of their power of persuasion. The mythopoetic language of Revelation is akin to poetry and drama. Therefore, any adequate exploration and comprehension of revelation has to experience the evocative power and "musicality" of the book's language since it was written to be read aloud as a liturgical poem and to be heard in the worship gatherings of the Asian communities.[5]

In the following treatment, I will interpret Revelation against its first-century background, and this means in terms of the sociopolitical, economic, and religious situations in which the author lived. But I will also keep in mind that the book's symbolic language is not for the most part the simplistic language of the steno-symbol. It is the powerful, emotionally charged language of the open-ended symbol, which grows out of the impact of deeply lived experience upon human persons and communities. And since John probably wrote the work to be read aloud in Christian worship, I will try to recapture something of the impact this work would have had in that context. It will therefore be more appropriate to speak of "hearers" than of "readers."

2. Hearing the Revelation to John

a. 1:1-8[6]

The opening words of John's writing will command the hearers' attention. The reading they are about to hear will recount a revelation from Jesus Christ and God, delivered by an angel. The blessing in v. 3 combines with the promise that "the time is near" to create an initial sense of consolation and positive expectations.

The greeting that begins in v. 4 will increase this sense of well-being. The reference to God's throne and the seven spirits that surround it remind the hearers that God's power is ultimate. The allusion to Jesus' resurrection points both to the salvation it has effected and to the general resurrection to

---

5. Elisabeth Schüssler Fiorenza, *Invitation to the Book of Revelation: A Commentary on the Apocalypse with Complete Text from the Jerusalem Bible* (Garden City, N.Y.: Doubleday, 1981), 18–19.
6. Text divisions are based upon Elisabeth Schüssler Fiorenza, *Invitation to the Book of Revelation.*

come. And the proclamation of Christ as "the ruler of the kings of the earth" is an invitation to look beyond the oppressive powers of this world to the power of God. The thought that it is God who rules will create an ecstatic mood that is heightened by the doxology in v. 6 and the scriptural allusion in v. 7 and brought to a climax in John's representation of God's words in v. 8. Caught up in the proclamation that God is "Alpha and Omega" (the first and last letters of the Greek alphabet) and "the Almighty," the hearers come to the end of the introductory section in a mood of exultation.

b. 1:9—3:22

Hearing John refer to himself in v. 9 as a brother who has shared in the persecution, the audience will feel a sense of solidarity with him. That he claims to share with them "patient endurance" and God's Rule creates a feeling that in some sense the peace of the coming age is possible even in the present adversity. The account of the command of the loud voice and subsequent description of "one like the Son of Man" (1:10-16) then re-create a sense of awe and remind the hearers of Christ's divine status and cosmic power.

John's response to the vision—he falls at the feet of the awesome figure—confronts the audience with the inadequacy of all human beings before the divine; yet the figure's compassionate response reminds them that the effect of Christ's resurrection is their own deliverance from the power of death. The explanation of the meaning of the seven stars and lampstands then focuses the hearers' attention on the message that they, as the seven churches of the region, are about to receive. And the formula that introduces each of the seven "letters," or prophetic messages—"to the angel ... write"—will encourage a receptive and reflective mood.

The hearers will understand the "angels of the seven churches" (1:20) as "guardian angels," analogous to those that in Jewish thought represented each of the nations of the world. By addressing the messages to these angels, John adds to the authority of his words: each congregation will feel that the message is reinforced by its local heavenly representative.

Members of each of the seven congregations will undoubtedly listen with particular interest to the message directed to their particular church, but they will also understand the seven as representative of all the churches of the region. Every hearer is addressed in the formula that closes each message: "Let anyone who has an ear listen to what the Spirit is saying to the churches."

The prophetic proclamation to the churches, stretching from 2:1 to 3:22 and presented as the words of Christ, alternates between complements and encouragement on the one hand and sharp criticism on the other. When appropriate, John praises congregations for their endurance, faith, service, and love; when necessary, he chides them for their failings. At some points he expresses the latter in general terms, as when he calls Sardis "dead"; but at other points the charges are specific, as when he condemns those who tolerate the Nicolaitans or one of the other groups he opposes.

The mention of Satan at several points places the issues in the context of an either/or decision. Heard against the background of the awesome vision of Christ in 1:12-20, the messages to the churches concern ultimate matters. To fail at endurance, faith, or love is to take one's stand on Satan's side, whereas to side with Christ is to accept God's power as the true power. Heard against the background of persecution, the messages constitute a call to keep the faith in the face of the temptation to make one's peace with the surrounding social order. The repeated injunction to "conquer" encourages the hearers to persevere, despite the difficulties they face; and the various references to Christ's eventual return bolster the appeal with the promise of eventual vindication.

The reference to Satan's throne in the message to Pergamum (2:12) creates a contrast with the reference to God's throne in 1:4 and gives the either/or choice an unmistakably political content. Aware that Pergamum was a major center of the emperor cult, the hearers will understand that to side with the empire is in fact to side with Satan.

At some points John's words will challenge and even reverse the hearers' self-appraisals. To the afflicted at poverty-stricken Smyrna, he can proclaim that "you are rich." But to Laodicea, which considers itself rich, he applies a devastating description: "wretched, pitiable, poor, blind, and naked." These words are all the more powerful since he has charged this congregation not with the blatant infidelity found in some other groups but only with being "lukewarm." And since the message to Laodicea is the last of the seven, the effect on the audience is particularly powerful: at the conclusion of the messages they do not hear words that soften John's harsh judgments but find that any "middle ground" is swept away. One is either on Christ's side or Satan's; neutrality and compromise are in fact the worst forms of unfaithfulness.

The promise in 3:21, combined with an allusion to Christ's exaltation, picks up on the earlier compliments to the faithful and encourages the hearers to maintain a sense of hope. The presentation of Christ as one who himself "conquered" presents the reader with a positive model, and reference to his throne reminds them of the ultimacy of the power he represents. In hearing the formulary injunction for the seventh time in 3:22, then, the readers are not only warned but are given positive encouragement.

c. 4:1—9:21

The image in 4:1 of the open door in heaven, combined with the command of the heavenly voice that spoke in 1:10-11, rekindles the hearers' anticipation and awe and signals a major turn. The anticipation is fulfilled as John describes the heavenly court in majestic language. Notions of God's sovereignty are stretched to the limit of human imagination as the audience hears of twenty-four elders, seated upon thrones, casting their crowns before the central throne, and of lightning, thunder, and awesome creatures. The vivid descriptions combine with the hymns of the creatures (4:8, 11) to catch the hearers up in the ecstasy of worship and a sense of wonder and adoration. And the wonder and mystery of the divine are underscored by the fact that John never actually describes God, the "one who is seated on the throne."

The promise of the voice to disclose "what must take place after this" (4:1) alerts the hearers to listen for a word about the future, and the image of the scroll with seven seals in 5:1 signals that the disclosure is about to take place. The search for one worthy to open the seals then creates a moment of suspense that heightens the hearers' exultation when the conquering Lion of Judah is deemed worthy of the task.

Easily recognizing Jesus as this Lion, as the Messiah from the line of David, the hearers immediately experience (5:6) a clash of images. What John actually sees before God's throne is not a lion at all, but a lamb, "standing as if it had been slaughtered." Falling before this figure, the elders sing a hymn of praise to the one whose death has ransomed the saints from every tribe in the world and enabled them to "reign on earth." And the paradox is completed as angels, the rest of the heavenly court, and finally all creatures in the universe join in the worship of this bloodied little creature. Caught up in this ecstatic scene, the hearers will feel reassured that, despite the vulnerability they experience, followers of the crucified Jesus have access to the ultimate power in the universe.

In 6:1 the lamb starts to open the seals. The first four of these release horses and riders that bring conquest, war, famine, and death upon the world. And the fifth is followed by a vision of the souls of those slaughtered for God's word, crying out and asking how long they must wait for justice and vindication.

The promise that these martyrs need wait only "a little longer" (6:11) will remind the hearers that the end of the age is very near. And they will understand the horrible events released by the four riders and by the opening of the sixth seal in 6:12-17 as the eschatological woes that must precede God's ultimate victory. Because the image of the first rider will have called up asso-

Fig. 77. "The Four Horsemen of the Apocalypse" (Revelation 6:1-8)
(Engraving by Raymond Hawthorn)

ciations with the Parthians   whose troops rode white horses and carried bows
and were a constant threat to Roman power—the hearers will link the end of
the age to the dissolution of the empire. They will view the death, destruction,
and cosmic disruption not as something God wills in a simplistic sense but as
the necessary culmination of human corruption and injustice, the very forces
that resulted in the martyrdom of the righteous. By pitting evil forces against
one another and allowing them to run their course, God indirectly brings the
old world order to an end—precisely to initiate the new.

To the hearers, then, the wrath of the Lamb and of God mentioned in 6:16-
17 will appear not as sheer vengeance but as justice. Nevertheless, the initial
effect of the images of God's wrath is fear, so that the question posed here
will seem pertinent: "who is able to stand?"

The hearers will not really expect an answer to that question at this point, since the seventh seal remains to be opened. But the unexpected happens: the vision of five angels in chapter 7 provides a dramatic answer. Carrying the "seal of the living God," the fifth angel marks God's servants, twelve thousand from each of the tribes of Israel. The hearers will interpret the tribes of Israel as the Christian community and will understand that those marked with God's seal will emerge victorious from the eschatological woes. They will also think of the total number of those marked, 144,000, not as a literal count but as symbolizing the "completed" church, consisting of an enormous multitude.

The sense of ultimate victory will increase as John describes the triumphal march of a great throng from every nation of the world, ending in another majestic scene of heavenly worship. In the vision John himself identifies the throng as those who have come through "the great ordeal" and brings the scene to a close with a poetic description of the heavenly peace in which all the sufferings and injustices of life are overcome (7:15-17). Right in the midst of a description of the eschatological woes, then, the hearers get a foretaste of ultimate bliss and are reminded that their present sufferings will soon give way to the glorious age to come. And through the image of white robes washed in the blood of the Lamb (7:14) they are reminded that it is the death of the lamb that has made their ultimate victory possible.

The opening of the seventh seal in 8:1 brings the preceding interlude to a close and reminds the hearers of the eschatological woes. Instead of immediately resuming an account of these woes, however, John notes that "there was silence in heaven for about half an hour." The effect will be an increase in the hearers' sense of awe and reverence in the presence of the holy and their awareness that the woes, horrible as they are, issue from God and serve God's purposes.

The vision of the angels in 8:2-5 not only perpetuates the feeling of reverence but invites the hearers to strengthen their sense of connection between the peace of heaven and the life of the church in the world. The image of the prayers of the saints presented to God with the heavenly incense is a reminder that human prayers are not in vain. As Christians on earth live through the terrible events accompanying the break-up of the present world order, they can be confident that God is aware of and responds to their plight.

Dramatically, however, v. 5 directs attention back to the woes as an angel throws fire on the earth; and quickly the hearers are confronted with seven angels sounding trumpets that release a new sevenfold pattern of events. The first six trumpets bring cataclysmic disruptions in the natural world, described in terms that abound with allusions to the Jewish Scriptures. The hailstorm (8:7), the turning of the sea to blood (8:9), the darkness (8:12), and the locusts

(9:3) are reminiscent of the plagues visited upon the Egyptians in the story of the exodus (Exod. 7–10); and the reference to the bitter drug wormwood recalls Jeremiah 9:15 and 23:15, where it is a sign of divine chastisement. The audience will thus think in terms of God's judgment, and the voice of the eagle in 8:13 heightens the anticipation of even further woes. But since the plagues of Exodus were a prelude to the escape of the Hebrew people, the readers will also understand the woes in Revelation as leading ultimately to liberation.

Familiar with the widespread Jewish identification of the stars with angels and also knowledgeable of the story of Satan's fall from heaven in writings outside the Jewish canon (2 Enoch 29:4-5; Wisdom of Solomon 2:24; Life of Adam and Eve, 12–16), the audience will probably think of the fallen star in 9:1 as Satan. They will thus be reminded of the supernatural character of all the events described. Yet they will also connect the destructive forces under Satan's direction with the Roman Empire. They will remember, too, that these destructive forces are unleashed by God, and they will be comforted by John's notation (9:4) that it is only those who do not bear God's seal who are vulnerable to the locusts' attack.

In 9:12 the audience hears that what has just taken place is the first in a series of three woes, so they will prepare to hear of further disasters. The sixth trumpet then announces the release of four angels at the Euphrates River, which makes way for the destructive march of a ghastly army of horses and riders that will remind them of the white horse and rider of 6:2. Since the Euphrates separated the Roman Empire from the Parthians, the audience will once again envision the forces of evil pitted against one another in a cosmic battle signaling the empire's eventual fall. But 9:20-21 also encourages the hearers to identify the ultimate goal of God's unleashing these destructive forces: far from sheer punishment, the woes are a dramatic call to repentance—which, unfortunately, goes unheeded.

d. 10:1—15:4

The audience will expect a seventh trumpet in 10:1; but, as in the earlier series, they are met with an interlude instead. John's description of the enormous angel creates intense interest in what that figure says in a voice accompanied by the seven thunders. And that interest is intensified by the mysterious heavenly command to "seal up what the seven thunders have said." The thought that not everything regarding the end is revealed to John increases the audience's sense of awe in the presence of the divine; and it combines with the promise of no more delay (10:6) to remind the hearers that God is ultimately in control and will in fact bring deliverance.

The eating of the angel's scroll in 10:9-10 will call to mind the similar scene in Ezekiel 3:1-3, where the scroll symbolizes prophecy. The hearers will interpret the paradoxical account of its taste in terms of the dual character of the prophetic word: bitter because it brings God's judgment, sweet because it is ultimately redemptive. They will also be reminded of John's original description of his writing as prophecy (1:3), as well as the prophetic commission he received from the angel in the initial vision (1:19), and will be prepared to reflect upon the phenomenon of prophecy itself.

John's measuring of the temple in 11:1-2 will recall Zechariah 2:1-5, where a similar action signifies God's protection in the face of coming destruction. The audience will know that once again John speaks of the church—those who have received God's "mark." The death of the two prophetic witnesses, however, shows that God's protection does not mean exemption from suffering. Identifying the city to which John gives the symbolic names of Egypt and Sodom as Rome (11:8), the hearers will understand that those who bear the word of prophecy are vulnerable to the empire's oppressive power. The resurrection of the witnesses (11:11) is nevertheless a reminder of the ultimate vindication of the faithful. And the scene in which the survivors of the earthquake praise God contrasts with the people's refusal to repent (9:20-22), reinforcing the notion that repentance stands together with vindication of the righteous as a goal of God's acts of judgment.

In 11:14 John notes the end of the second woe and speaks of the third to come. Then, at the sound of the seventh trumpet, the audience is caught up once again in a description of heavenly worship that begins with a proclamation of Christ's rule (11:15) and ends with an awe-inspiring vision of the ark of the covenant within the temple. This vision, following the proclamation that God destroys "those who destroy the earth" (11:18), is yet another powerful assertion of the superiority of God's power to that of oppressive forces that seem to rule the world.

The announcements in 12:1, 3 of two great portents in heaven alert the hearers to expect something particularly dramatic, and they are not disappointed. An initial vision of a cosmically adorned, goddess-like woman leads into an ominous dragon's pursuit of her and the male child to whom she gives birth. And an account of a war in heaven between the forces of the dragon and those of Michael the archangel, resulting in a resounding proclamation of victory in heaven, leads to a sequence on earth in which the dragon pursues the woman's other children.

John makes certain (12:9) that the audience will identify the dragon as Satan, and they will easily see Christ in the image of the child. The woman will probably call up numerous associations, including Mary the mother of Jesus, but will stand in a more general way for the people of God throughout history. In her other children, of course, the Christians will see themselves, pursued by the Satanic power of Rome precisely because they "keep the commandments of God and hold the testimony of Jesus" (12:17). And the either/or choice between the church and the empire is heightened by the regal appearance of the woman in 12:1, which casts her as an antitype of Roma, the goddess of Rome.

The drama continues as a horrible beast rises from the sea (13:1) and, in league with the dragon, commands worship in the world. In 13:9-10 John's narration (based on Jer. 15:2; 43:11) intrudes to make two explicit points. First, although permitted to exercise authority for a time, the beast will eventually receive punishment; and second, the hearers should interpret the account of this vision as "a call for the endurance and faith of the saints." Following the intrusion, John speaks briefly of a second beast that will encourage worship of the first, and then brings the sequence to a close with an invitation to puzzle out the identity of the original beast on the basis of a numerical symbol.

The audience will in a general way associate the beast with the empire, understanding its "mark" as participation in Roman society. And they will in all probability respond to John's invitation (13:18) and decode the number, 666, as a reference to the emperor Nero.[7] If Revelation was written after Nero's suicide, they will be reminded of the current belief that he was not really dead, but only in hiding and planning to resume control of the empire. And they may interpret the mortal wound, now healed, to one of the beast's heads (13:3), as a reference either to Nero's suicide or to the assassination of an earlier emperor.[8] In any case, the mortal wound and the mark will also serve to present the beast as an antitype of Christ, who died and was resurrected and gave a mark to his followers. And the audience will certainly see themselves as those who would be killed for failure to worship the beast (13:15). They will thus come to the end of chapter 13 painfully aware that the forces that oppress them in this world issue from a demonic source. And they

---

7. The letters of the Greek and Hebrew alphabets were assigned numerical values. The sum of the values of the name NERON KAISER in Hebrew is 666. Although many other suggestions have been made for decoding the number, this interpretation remains by far the most likely and is widely accepted by critical scholars. It is strengthened, moreover, by the existence of a textual variant in which the number appears as 616, the numerical value of the same name in Greek.

8. This latter possibility, that the reference is to the assassination of Julius Caesar, is reported by Christian Wilson, "The Problem of the Domitianic Date of Revelation," 559–600, as a suggestion made by David Barr.

will have only one possible answer to the question in 13:4 as to who can fight against the beast: no ordinary human being!

Just at the point at which the image of the beast brings the audience's awareness of the vulnerability of the church to its highest level, John breaks in (14:1) with a dramatic image of hope: the Lamb, standing now on Mount Zion, surrounded by the 144,000 of chapter 7. Invited to imagine the glorious music of the heavenly court, the audience also hears John's characterization of the 144,000. They will understand the references to the throng's "undefiled," "virginal" status and their innocence of lying as metaphors for their refusal to corrupt themselves through emperor worship. Bearing God's name on their foreheads, they are followers of the Lamb—and hence the redeemed. The hearers will thus be reminded that it is only God whose power is greater than that of the beast.

On the wake of this insight, the audience is asked (14:6-11) to envision a series of three angels announcing that God's judgment has now come, that Babylon (by which they will understand Rome) is fallen, and that the worshipers of the beast will be punished. After intruding to interpret the preceding vision as another call to endurance (14:12), John records a voice from heaven and a vision of the Son of man. The audience will be comforted by the dramatic pronouncement of rest for those who "die in the Lord" (14:13). And they will gain a sense of ultimate vindication through the harvest-images (14:14-20), which signify the final judgment.

Announcing yet a third portent in heaven in 15:1, John conjures up the image of seven angels ready to bring seven plagues upon the earth—which, he assures the audience, will be the last. Before the plagues commence, however, he portrays another joyous scene in heaven where those who have endured sing songs of praise to God. References to the sea and to the song of Moses (15:2-3) call up associations with the exodus story and encourage the audience to think of ultimate liberation.

e. 15:5—19:10

The seven angels of 15:1 now receive golden bowls full of God's wrath and proceed to pour them out on the earth in scenes that once again recall the plagues in Exodus. As at earlier points, the audience is reminded of the purpose of the woes by the comments on the people's refusal to repent (16:9, 11). The actions of the fifth and sixth angels bring mounting drama as the throne of the beast itself is submerged in darkness and the Euphrates dries up to make way for "the kings of the East," a phrase that will once again call to mind the Parthian troops. Then the seventh bowl, poured into the air itself, brings the sequence to a climax as a voice announces the completion of the drama of judgment, and Babylon—together with the cities, islands, and mountains of the world—disintegrates. The hailstorm in 16:21, which causes the people to curse God, adds a touch of finality and leaves the audience with a sense of awe in the presence of God's wrath.

When one of the angels announces the judgment of "the great whore who is seated on many waters" (17:1), the audience will understand that John will now view the destruction of Rome from a different angle. The identity of the whore is made plain by her identification with Babylon (17:5), the allusion to the blood of Christian martyrs she has drunk (17:6), the seven mountains (= seven hills of Rome) on which she sits (17:9), and the description of her as "the great city" (17:18). The audience will presumably puzzle out an allusion to a specific Roman emperor in the reference to the beast in 17:11. More importantly, they will understand that the beast forms an alliance with ten kings and turns against the whore. Once again, the hearers must conclude that God uses the forces of evil against one another in the final conflict.

The mood shifts abruptly at the beginning of chapter 18. John now depicts the earth as brightened with the splendor of an angel, who pronounces a dirge over the fallen Babylon that will give the audience a feeling of relief and vindication. These feelings are only momentary, however. When another voice from heaven (18:4) enjoins the hearers to "come out" of Babylon, proceeding to list her many sins, they will hear a warning to resist the allure of Roman civilization and power.

If the audience has expected gloating over the whore's destruction, what they find instead is a description of great mourning by all the kings and merchants of the world who once had traffic with her. They will note painful ironies in her destruction. Once seemingly indestructible, she has come to her downfall "in one hour" (18:19); once wallowing in luxury, she has seen her wealth "laid waste" (18:17). Overwhelmed by John's description of her dazzling riches, the hearers will be astonished by her fate. And they will be shocked by John's exposé of the true character of her wealth. Associating that wealth with "fornication" (18:9), he concludes the long list of her cargo items with "slaves—and human lives" (18:13). The audience will understand the metaphor of "whore" as symbolizing Rome's willingness to sell its very soul, by its oppressive and unjust policies, for the price of great material wealth.

The irony is heightened as those who had once traded with the whore turn from mourning to a joyous proclamation of God's justice in 18:20. But John does not allow the audience to heed the call to rejoicing immediately. In 18:21 an angel casts a millstone into the sea and pronounces a heart-rending descrip-

Fig. 78. "Babylon Fallen" (Revelation 18:9-10)
(Engraving by Gustave Doré, 1865)

tion of the activities that no longer animate the great city. Far from gloating, the hearers will feel a sense of tragic loss, mixed with their awe at the fearfulness of God's judgment. Irony returns, however, when the angel concludes this litany (18:24) with words that gather up all that been said about the evil at the heart of the magnificent empire. As dazzling as she was, she was a murderer.

Now the audience can in fact rejoice. In 19:1 John once again invites them to listen to the sound of triumphant heavenly song and liturgy, in which God is praised as just judge and cosmic regent. The hearers will understand the announcement of the marriage feast of the Lamb (19:7-9) as a proclamation of the joyous moment of eschatological consummation, the realization of God's Rule. And they will know that those invited to the supper are precisely the righteous, those who have endured in the faith. When in 19:10 the angel forbids John to worship him, they will hear a reminder that worship belongs to God alone—not angels, and certainly not earthly kings and empires. And when the angel speaks of those "who hold the testimony of Jesus" and says that "the testimony of Jesus is the spirit of prophecy," they will hear a call to maintain the prophetic spirit in their midst. They will hear a call to witness to Jesus, even in the face of the threat of death.

f. 19:11—22:9

In 19:11 the author assumes once again an earthly perspective and describes the opening of heaven. The vision of the rider on the white horse will at first remind the audience of the similar figure in 6:2. It becomes immediately apparent, however, that this time the rider is Christ. The hearers will therefore contrast his messianic rule with the conquest in which the earlier figure engaged. Whereas Christ's awesome appearance signifies ultimate power, the blood on his robe reminds the audience that he has conquered precisely by submitting to death. Because his sword, the symbol of judgment, is in his mouth, and because he himself is designated the Word of God, they will understand that it is the prophetic word itself by which he rules. They will therefore interpret his "rod of iron" as a metaphor for justice, not oppressive power. And his title, "King of kings," will once again set God's power and authority over against the false powers that have seemed to rule the world. Although the audience will have seen graphic illustrations of God's power manifested in wrath, they will know it is a power rooted in justice and love.

The gruesome scene in 19:17-18 symbolizes in the starkest terms the downfall of the unrighteous, and the gathering of the beast and the kings against the rider suggests a showdown between the forces of good and evil. The immediate capture of the beast illustrates Christ's superior power and invites the hearers to imagine the destruction of the false power of the empire, while the binding of Satan in 20:1-3 signifies a more fundamental victory over the very source of evil. The audience will know that the victory is not final, however, from the notation that Satan will be loosed for a short time after a thousand years.

The significance of the thousand years becomes apparent as John speaks of the resurrection of the martyrs who remained faithful during the great persecution: reigning with Christ during this period, they will be immune to the power of the "second death." The hearers will listen well for further explanation.

Describing yet another showdown between Christ and Satan (20:7-10), John now calls up the figures of Gog and Magog from the book of Ezekiel, which had become the subject of much elaboration in later apocalyptic literature. Symbols of the powers of evil, they are immediately defeated and cast into hell with Satan. The phrase "forever and ever" allows the hearers now to imagine the final defeat of these powers. And the sense of finality is strengthened as they hear a description of the appearance of the dead from the sea, the last judgment, and the casting of Death and Hades into the eternal fire. They will understand that John is symbolizing the "death of death," the breaking of the stronghold death has had upon humanity. They will interpret the books that are opened in 20:12 as the record of human deeds and the book of life as the list of the righteous. Told that the lake of fire is the "second death" mentioned earlier, they will understand it as the eternal fate of those whose names do not appear in the "book of life."

Dramatically, John now recounts his vision of the new heaven and earth and the new Jerusalem (21:1-2). The characterization of the latter as Christ's bride will remind the audience of the invitation in 19:9 to the wedding supper and will encourage a feeling of joyous celebration. And the fact that it descends from heaven suggests that the new world does not simply negate everything belonging to the old, but takes up within itself all positive human accomplishments. This point is underscored by the notation that God will now dwell among human beings (21:3) and the words of the voice from the throne: "See, I am making all things new." The eschatological order is not totally new, created out of nothing, but a renewal of what already is.

The audience will nevertheless be impressed with the contrast between old and new, since the latter is characterized precisely by the absence of all the defects that have plagued human existence. Death, suffering, and pain will not be present (21:4).

The further words from the throne in 21:6 increase the hearers' sense of finality and remind them that God is both the origin and destiny of their lives and all creation. And the ensuing statement serves as a summary exhortation: it is only those who "conquer" who will enter this blessed realm.

That point made, John now (21:9) invites the audience to share an angel's tour of the new Jerusalem, the eschatological reality itself. What they behold is a vision that creates a sense of wonder, glory, and peace. The abundance of worldly splendor is so great as to suggest the unworldly, and the absence of a temple (21:22) sets the heavenly city apart from anything in the present order. Described as a perfect cube, it recalls the "holy of holies," the most sacred part of the earthly temple. The audience will understand that the eschatological world abolishes all distinction between the sacred and the profane in time and space. All reality and every moment have become holy, and God's presence is all-pervasive. So inclusive is the vision that the hearers are told that kings and nations will bring their earthly glory into this new world (21:24-26). They will understand again that the new reality is purified, but not absolutely new.

As the audience is brought to the center of the city in 22:1 they will recognize similarities with the Garden of Eden and will feel a strong sense of peace. They will think of the eschatological reality as in some sense restoring the original creation, before the human rebellion against God, but will also understand that aspects of human history and culture are valued positively; for the leaves of the tree of life are "for the healing of the nations."

The assuring words in 22:6-7, which include Christ's promise of his imminent return, leave the audience with a sense of expectation of the truth and seriousness of John's prophetic account. And the scene in 22:8-9 reminds them yet again that worship belongs to God alone.

g. 22:10-21

The emphasis upon the nearness of the end of history continues as John receives a command not to seal up the prophecy and as Christ announces that he will come soon and exercise judgment. That announcement becomes the occasion for exhortation in 22:14-16, but the poetic invitation in 22:17 stresses grace by presenting the water of life as a gift.

In 22:18 John directs the hearers' attention to the writing itself, reasserting its prophetic character and warning them against altering its words. The audience will be reminded of the claim that the content of this writing was given in a revelatory experience, and they will be comforted by the promise and

Fig. 79. "New Jerusalem" (Revelation 21)
(Woodcut by Lucas Cranach for Martin Luther's Bible of 1522)

blessing in verses 20-21. Assured of ultimate vindication and justice in the near future, reminded that the god they worship is indeed the ultimate power in the universe, and inspired by the visions of eschatological peace they have just entertained, they will resolve to remain faithful in the face of whatever terrors the immediate future brings.

3. Reflections on the Sources and Structure of Revelation

No careful reader of Revelation will miss the complexity of the progression of eschatological "events" throughout the several visions. While interpreters have tried to plot a continuous chronology of these events, it is a sign of the difficulty of this task that the distinguished scholar R. H. Charles could do so only by rearranging many of the passages with the assumption that the final editor was incompetent.[9] Recent scholars therefore tend toward the view that the several visions do not present a continuous chain of events but describe roughly the same events over again from alternative angles. Evidence for this view is found in the fact that partial visions of eschatological glory occur throughout the book.

The complex structure of Revelation, then, is to some extent explained by the author's purpose, which was not to outline a chronology of coming events but to inspire hope and confidence in his readers. By using multiple symbols, he immersed the audience in imaginative portrayals of God's judgment on the one hand and the blessedness of God's eschatological rule on the other. His appeal was not to the intellectual urge to calculate but to the deep-seated emotional needs of his readers.

There is, however, another reason for the complexity of the work. It is apparent to anyone familiar with the environment within which John wrote that his visions, for the most part, are literary creations, not scenes that he actually saw in a dream or trance. For they are replete with allusions not only to the canonical Jewish Scriptures but to other apocalyptic texts. To some extent, that is to say, John's account was shaped by the extensive literary sources he employed. The notions of a thousand-year messianic reign and of the eschatological woes are only two of the many items he drew from the standard apocalyptic repertoire.

---

9. R. H. Charles, *The Revelation of St. John.* 2 vols. (Edinburgh: T. & T. Clark, 1920).

4. A Social-Psychological Interpretation

Adela Yarbro Collins has argued that the Revelation to John functions as a means of reducing the cognitive dissonance experienced by the audience.[10] "Cognitive dissonance" is a sociological term for the state of mind that arises in the face of great discrepancy between "what is" and "what ought to be," between expectations and social reality.

Revelation accomplishes this task in two ways. First, it induces a kind of "catharsis," or cleansing of emotions, akin to that which Aristotle attributed to Greek tragedies. In Aristotle's view, a tragic drama brings threatening emotions to the surface, enabling the audience to deal with them. According to Yarbro Collins, Revelation serves in a similar way to enable John's audience to identify, express, and ultimately to manage their fear of Roman power and resentment of Roman wealth.

The second way in which Revelation deals with cognitive dissonance is to convince the audience "that what ought to be *is*."[11] By imaging a heavenly reality in which the crucified Jesus is already enthroned and by announcing an already determined future in which the forces of oppression are overcome, John enabled the audience to participate imaginatively in the eschatological peace in the here and now. "From a social-psychological viewpoint," Yarbro Collins writes, "the vision of a heavenly reality and of a radically new future functions as compensation for the relatively disadvantaged situation of the hearers or as an imaginative way of resolving the tension between expectations and social reality."[12]

Resentment easily leads to feelings of aggression, and Yarbro Collins believes that Revelation offers two strategies for "containing aggressive feelings."[13] The first is transference. John never depicts the Christian believers as engaged in combat with Rome or Satan, but he does present Christ and God as defeating and judging these forces. In psychological terms, he transfers his aggressive feelings to other subjects and to the eschatological future.

The second strategy is internalization. John enjoins his readers to accept martyrdom and to embrace rigorous life-styles in relation to wealth, sexuality, and participation in the general culture. It may be argued from a psychological perspective that such an ascetic set of demands manifests an aggressiveness turned inward on one's self.

---

10. Adela Yarbro Collins, *Crisis and Catharsis: The Power of the Apocalypse* (Philadelphia: Westminster, 1984).

11. Ibid., 154.

12. Ibid.

13. Ibid., 156.

5. A "Process" Interpretation

a. The Process Understanding of the Power of God

We have, on several occasions, taken note of the process philosophy/theology associated with Alfred North Whitehead (see above, pp. 21, 49–51, 426–30). It will be recalled that according to this worldview, the universe is both dynamic and relational. Not only is everything in constant flux, but things are what they are only by virtue of the relationships in which they exist.

Even God, according to this perspective, is relational. Just as the world is inherently related to God, so God is inherently related to the world. This means that God is actually changed by what happens in the world and therefore does not have absolute control over the course of events. Process thinkers thus understand God's power as persuasive rather than coercive; in their view God can exert strong influence on the world but cannot absolutely control what happens in it.

b. Affinities with Process Thought

At first glance, nothing seems farther from the process understanding of divine power than the Revelation to John. For is it not clear that according to John God controls the course of history and ultimately exercises coercive power over the forces of evil in bringing them to final judgment? Whitehead, in fact, held up Revelation as a prime example of the "barbaric elements" in Christianity, such as the image of God as despot, that have worked against what is deepest and best in that faith.[14] Ron Farmer, however, has recently noted some surprising similarities between the views of God's power in Revelation and in process thought.[15]

Farmer focuses on the vision in Revelation 4–5, in which the Lamb receives a scroll. The first point he notes is that the angel asks in 5:2, "Who is worthy to open the scroll and break its seals?" Since the scroll apparently contains God's redemptive plan, the implication is that God's intention to redeem the world depends upon human action. A human agent must, through some sort of test, become worthy to open the scroll and thereby enact the plan. Already one can see an affinity with process thought, since the implication is that God cannot simply impose the plan upon the world. But this is only the first step in Farmer's argument.

---

14. Alfred North Whitehead, *Adventures of Ideas* (New York: The Free Press, 1967; originally published in 1933), 170.

15. Ron Farmer, "Divine Power in the Apocalypse to John," in Eugene H. Lovering, ed., "Society of Biblical Literature: 1993 Seminar Papers" (Atlanta: Scholars Press, 1993), 70–102.

The statement in 5:3 that no one was found worthy dramatizes the announcement in v. 5 that "the Lion of the tribe of Judah, the root of David, has conquered, so that he can open the scroll and its seven seals." The messianic image here clearly suggests militaristic, coercive power; David was known as a warrior, and lions are associated with raw aggressiveness. This image, however, is immediately balanced by that of the "Lamb standing as if it had been slaughtered" in 5:6. Not only are lambs associated with gentleness, but the fact that this one bears the marks of a violent death calls to mind the notion of Jesus as the innocent lamb whose death is a sacrifice for sin.

The presence of contradictory images, Farmer argues, forces the audience to interpret each in light of the other. The image of Jesus as conquering lion interprets his death: it is victory, not defeat. And that of Jesus as lamb interprets his role as conqueror: God, through Jesus, conquers precisely through "suffering, redemptive love."[16] As in process thought, then, the lamb imagery suggests that God achieves the divine purposes not through coercion but through the persuasive power of what appears as weakness. The power that Christ wields, Farmer notes, is the power of a sword that comes from his mouth (1:16; 2:12, 16; 19:15). This means that his power is that of words that pierce the souls of human beings—words that *persuade.*

c. A Process Hermeneutic

Farmer is aware that the imagery of persuasive power in Revelation is an "undercurrent" within a dominant emphasis upon coercion. He therefore turns to another aspect of process thought, its understanding of language, to approach the interpretation of this work on another level. His project thus moves beyond exegesis into an exercise in "process *hermeneutic.*"

According to process thought, language is never absolutely precise. Rather than expressing perfectly clear and distinct notions, it always contains an element of imprecision that invites the hearer to interpret it in an imaginative way. Of course some types of language (for example, poetry) have a stronger imaginative component than others (for example, a simple statement such as "Maria is reading the Gospel of Mark"). But all language, in however small a degree, invites the hearer to engage in creative thought. No interpretation of a text is ever final and complete, since every new situation demands a different creative response.

Creative thought becomes particularly necessary when the reader of a text finds a discrepancy between points of view within the text itself. One response

---

16. Ibid., 94.

to such a discovery is to decide that the text is confused. Another, however, is to find a new perspective from which the competing points of view can be brought together into a synthesis. Known as a "contrast" in the technical vocabulary of process thought, such a synthesis achieves a kind of harmony without destroying any of the conflicting elements.

On the literal level, the strain of imagery in Revelation that presents God's power as persuasive is clearly incompatible with the deterministic strain that presents divine power as coercive. Farmer argues, however, that it is possible to hold the two perspectives together if one interprets the deterministic strain nonliterally, i.e., as an imaginative, exaggerated expression of the view that "creative-responsive love . . . is the most powerful force in the universe."[17] Farmer thus suggests a synthesis in which the hearer moves beyond the literal meaning of Revelation's deterministic imagery and, bringing it into conversation with the competing undercurrent of thought, entertains a more complex set of propositions. Reading Revelation as Farmer does, then, one might well be led to consider the possibility that God does not control the events in history absolutely, but works precisely through contingencies and seeming weakness to effect the divine purpose.

6. Evaluating the Revelation to John

Whitehead is not alone in his criticism of Revelation; it has had many detractors through the centuries. Martin Luther found it theologically inadequate, and quite a few scholars and theologians have read it as a sub-Christian desire for revenge. The writer D. H. Lawrence, who called it the "Judas" in the New Testament, thought it reflected an envy of the strong and a hatred of civilization.[18] To many modern readers Revelation has the ring of anti-worldly escapism, and if Yarbro Collins is correct in finding in it an aggressiveness turned inward on the self, one must ask what distinguishes that attitude from masochism.

Many interpreters, however, have found great value in the work. Elisabeth Schüssler Fiorenza echoes the views of many liberation theologians when she writes that

Revelation's theology is not so much interested in describing the "reversal of fate," because of an unchristian resentment of civilization or of the city, as it is in spelling out hope and encouragement for those

---

17. Ibid., 98.
18. D. H. Lawrence, *Apocalypse* (New York: Viking Press, 1932), 14–15.

who struggle for economic survival and freedom from persecution and murder.[19]

We may also recall that John's image of eschatological glory is one of peace and ultimate reconciliation, symbolized by the fruit of the tree of life that accomplishes "the healing of the nations" (22:2).

One's evaluation of Revelation will depend to some extent upon one's judgment as to whether the extreme rhetoric of either/or is appropriate and healthy. Revelation clearly sets up the audience's choice in terms of absolute good and absolute evil. For John, there is no legitimate compromise; the hearers must either stand by their faith and risk rejection and death or deny their faith and side with Rome. To some people, such a dichotomy is a sign of fanaticism. Real life, they argue, is complex; and choices are seldom so clearcut. From another perspective, however, this dichotomy is the expression of the moral nature of the universe. According to this view, even if compromises are necessary at some points, one must begin with the notions of absolute good and evil to provide a basis for any talk of justice and faithfulness at all.

Evaluating Revelation is not an easy task. Yarbro Collins finds on the one hand that "Revelation works against the values of humanization and love insofar as the achievement of personal dignity involves the degradation of others. The imagery of Revelation suggests a reversal of roles."[20] This same scholar recognizes, however, that "for persons and groups living at subhuman levels, anger and violence may be constructive and life-giving, a step toward becoming more fully human." And she can even grant that "Revelation serves the value of humanization insofar as it insists that the marginal, the relatively poor and powerless, must assert themselves to achieve their full humanity and dignity."

So although Yarbro Collins views Revelation in a much more negative light than does Schüssler Fiorenza, who de-emphasizes the theme of the reversal of the roles of oppressor and oppressed, she does not simply reject the work. She speaks rather of its accomplishment as ambiguous and advocates a "critical reading" that takes place in full awareness of its "flaws." Such a process, she contends, can lead to a "personal reinvolvement with the text," a way of reading Revelation "in which a partial, imperfect vision can still speak to our broken human condition."

Talk of a "critical reading" and of "personal involvement" raises once again the question of the nature of interpretation that we met in the preceding section. The problem of evaluating Revelation is but a fragment of the

19. Schüssler Fiorenza, *Invitation to the Book of Revelation*, 173.
20. Yarbro Collins, *Crisis and Catharsis*, 171–72.

larger problem of evaluating the various New Testament materials and finally the New Testament as a whole. There is internal tension within many individual writings and even greater tension among the various elements of the canon. The question of critical reading thus forces itself upon anyone who either seeks to make personal use of the works we have read or who simply wants to be able to understand and evaluate that body of religious writings known as the "New Testament."

STUDY QUESTIONS

1. What is it possible to say about the authorship of Revelation?

2. Describe the specific situation of the original audience, and explain why the author uses such dramatic language to address this situation.

3. What are the competing views regarding the relationship of the "events" mentioned in Revelation and actual human history? How do the interpretations of critical scholars differ from those of many popular interpreters?

4. What is the function of the letters to the seven churches in Revelation 1-3?

5. What specific emotions might chapters 4–9 elicit from those who hear them read? What is the function of the "eschatological woes" described in these chapters?

6. With what or whom would a first-century reader have identified the symbols of the beast, Babylon, and the whore?

7. What effect might it have had on a first-century congregation to hear chapters 17–22 read aloud during worship?

8. Evaluate the claim that Revelation predicts events in the late twentieth century.

9. Does the book of Revelation have any relevance, *when not interpreted literally,* for people living in our place and time? Compare and contrast the views of Yarbro Collins and Schüssler Fiorenza on this issue, and then give reasons for your own judgment.

10. Explain the roles of (*a*) the distinction between coercive and persuasive power and (*b*) the process understanding of language in Farmer's interpretation. Then give your own evaluation of his reading of Revelation.

11. In what specific ways does Revelation raise the question of a "critical reading" of the New Testament?

FOR FURTHER READING

Boring, M. Eugene, *Revelation*. Louisville: Westminster/John Knox, 1989. A readable, scholarly, and insightful commentary, with an excellent introduction. An important contribution.

Caird, G. B. *A Commentary on the Revelation to St. John the Divine*. New York/ Evanston: Harper, 1966. An important contribution.

Charles, R. H. *The Revelation of St. John*. 2 vols. Edinburgh: T. & T. Clark, 1920. For many years the definitive work on Revelation, but marred by the author's hypothetical rearrangement of the text.

Minear, Paul. *I Saw a New Heaven and a New Earth: An Introduction to the Vision of the Apocalypse*. Washington/Cleveland: Corpus Books, 1968. An interesting and instructive account, following a nonhistorical interpretation of the author's symbolic language.

Pilch, John J. *What Are They Saying about the Book of Revelation?* New York: Paulist, 1978. A brief, readable, and competent survey of key issues of interpretation.

Schüssler Fiorenza, Elisabeth. *Invitation to the Book of Revelation: A Commentary on the Apocalypse with a Complete Text from the Jerusalem Bible*. Garden City, N.Y.: Doubleday, 1981. A relatively brief but excellent commentary.

———. *The Book of Revelation: Justice and Judgment*. Philadelphia: Fortress Press, 1985. Essays on the structure, theology, composition, language, setting, etc. of Revelation by a leading specialist in the field. An important work.

———. *Revelation: Vision of a Just World*. Proclamation Commentaries. Minneapolis: Fortress Press, 1991. An extensively revised version of *Invitation to the Book of Revelation,* emphasizing rhetorical analysis.

Yarbro Collins, Adela. *Crisis and Catharsis: The Power of the Apocalypse*. Philadelphia: Westminster, 1984. A highly interesting and readable contribution, employing historical, literary, and psychological methods.

Epilogue

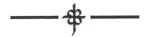

1. After the New Testament

The New Testament leaves the historian in mid-stream. For there is much that is characteristic of the church of a few centuries later that we do not find here: the explicitly stated doctrines, the hierarchical church structure, the institutionalized ministry.

We do, of course, find the foundations of later doctrine. The major writings share a general understanding of Jesus as Messiah and Son of God as well as other beliefs such as a final judgment and the resurrection of the dead. And some of the later books manifest an explicit concern for the purity of a body of beliefs. The pastoral letters in particular reflect a movement toward institutionalized authority. And, finally, the New Testament in general gives us clear evidence of the practice of baptism and the observance of the Lord's Supper.

With all of this, however, we are still a long way from the highly institutionalized church, with a formally stated body of doctrine, that enters the Middle Ages. But the transition was not long in coming. By the end of the second century the writings of Irenaeus, the bishop of Lyons, reflect a situation in which each church is under the authority of a single bishop and this authority is understood in terms of apostolic succession. That is to say, the belief is securely in place that Jesus appointed specific apostles over specific churches and that they in turn appointed bishops who passed on the apostolic authority in unbroken chain. Irenaeus can therefore speak of a worldwide church sharing one apostolic faith. In time, a formalized understanding of the ordained ministry is worked into the notion of apostolic succession.

Irenaeus specifically associated the church in Rome with Peter and Paul and provided a list of bishops supposedly going back to their original appointee. And gradually, because of the unique status of Rome in the empire,

539

the bishop of that city began to assert authority over other churches. Eventually, the bishop of Rome was accorded formal authority over the church in general: he was the pope (or "papa") of the church universal, standing in a line of succession beginning with Peter.

The church that thus emerged from the New Testament period understood itself as catholic, or universal, and apostolic, the authentic continuation of the faith delivered by Jesus to the apostles. But in naming itself universal, it was in fact distinguishing itself from other bodies that claimed a common heritage. For from the beginning there were individuals and communities that dissented from what became the majority view. We have seen that some scholars believe there were early groups that followed Jesus but did not attach saving significance to his death. And, in any case, there were conservative Jewish Christians who never accepted the way in which others dispensed with the Jewish law; continuing for a time as small sects, they eventually died out. And then in the second century the Gnostics and Marcionites were excluded. So also was a group known as the Montanists, who stressed the renewal of prophecy and eschatological fervor and demanded a more rigorous Christian life-style than they observed in the late second-century churches.

Further splits came in the ensuing centuries as a result of the effort to settle the issues surrounding the doctrine of the two natures of Christ. The eventual formulations excluded three major groups along the way: the Arians, who denied that the Son was co-eternal with the Father; the Nestorians, who argued that the two natures of Christ remained separate; and the Monophysites, who said that the two natures merged completely into one and whose doctrine survives in the Coptic church in Egypt today.

The church that defined itself early on as catholic and apostolic is the ancestor of most of the Christians of the world. But it has not remained whole. A split between its eastern and western regions resulted in a distinction between the Roman Catholic Church on the one hand and a group of national churches under the umbrella of Eastern Orthodoxy on the other. The western church was rent asunder yet again in the English and Protestant reformations, and these divisions were followed by innumerable divisions down to the present time.

Recent years have brought a strong movement toward reunification, however, and all bodies that issue from the "apostolic and universal" church that emerged in the early centuries can look to a common heritage. But one must never forget, in reflecting on the nature of Christianity and the meaning of its canonical writings, that there have been and are other groups who have shared at least part of that heritage.

2. Evaluating the New Testament: The Necessity of Hermeneutics

At a corner of Central Park, a man in a black suit waves a tattered Bible and cites John 3:7, urging his hearers to be born again. Meanwhile, a woman in Nicaragua speaks of Jesus—who challenged the power structure through his action in the temple—as liberator of the oppressed. Students who have worked through the present text have come a long way since the little panorama in chapter 1 that posed the problem of multiple interpretations of the New Testament. And no serious reader can have failed to sense the reality of that problem as we approached the materials from numerous perspectives.

The problem of varying interpretations, however, is only one dimension of a much broader and deeper question. We have also encountered differing viewpoints among the various New Testament writings. If the formula Paul quotes in Galatians 3:28 proclaims that in Christ female and male are no longer divided, the pastoral letters are equally clear in asserting male authority. And we have even observed tensions within the individual writings themselves. The unavoidable question is whether and how readers can understand and evaluate the New Testament in its totality.

If we broaden our concern beyond the canonical writings to the early Christianity that produced them, yet another aspect of the problem appears. For the books of the New Testament are selections from a wider range of materials that the early communities produced. When one surveys all the types of early Christianity that died out after a time, and then imagines all the ways in which the movement might have developed but did not, some rather crucial questions begin to arise. To what extent is the kind of Christianity that survived as the "mainstream" movement the inevitable result of Jesus' words and deeds, and to what extent is it the result of contingent factors and of decisions that might have been made differently? Does the New Testament as a finished product ultimately express, or does it perhaps in some ways betray, the deepest insights of the Jesus movement? It is, one must admit, a long trek from Jesus' open-ended parables to the tight doctrinalism of Jude, 2 Peter, and the pastorals. And one can easily question whether the route is a straight one.

Although it might seem otherwise, my intention here is not to drive the reader into despair. It is, rather, to raise for a final time the all-important question of hermeneutics. Hermeneutics, as noted in chapter 1, has two dimensions. On the theoretical level, it explores the question of how understanding takes place. But on the more concrete level, a given hermeneutical perspective will entail a specific strategy for finding meaning in a text. My point is that now, after having given close attention to the writings in the New

Testament and having approached them from a number of different angles, the reader of this text should be prepared to reflect more deeply and systematically on the question of how to read these writings, the question of a strategy for understanding and evaluating them in a more than superficial way.

For many interpreters, the tasks of understanding and evaluating the New Testament are relatively simple matters. One takes the writings at face value, perhaps making use of historical criticism to determine their original meanings. And then one decides for or against them, decides whether to accept or reject their various claims to truth, assertions of value, and moral injunctions.

For those who take this approach—whether they are Christian believers, adherents of other faiths, or secular interpreters—the encounter with the ancient text is essentially a one-way conversation. That is to say, the meaning of the text is fixed, unchanging. It makes a clear and definite claim, and the interpreter's first task is to understand that claim in an objective way, a way untarnished by her or his own prejudices, preconceptions, and desires. The second task, which is often understood as entirely separate, is to evaluate the witness of the text, to make positive or negative judgments about it. These two tasks, taken together, constitute one rather widespread hermeneutical strategy.

There are, however, more complex hermeneutical approaches that are more like dialogues than one-way conversations. From these perspectives, the tasks of understanding and evaluation, while generally regarded as relatively distinct, cannot be separated in such an absolute way. Interpreters who employ such approaches therefore allow their own world-pictures, interests, and concerns a much greater role in the discovery, and perhaps creation, of meaning. And because they recognize something problematic about understanding the biblical writings, they adopt strategies that seek to look beneath the face value, or surface meaning, of the texts.

In some cases, the hermeneutical strategy makes the problematic character of understanding explicit. Bultmann's existentialist interpretation is a way of finding a meaning in the New Testament that is, for many readers, obscured by the mythological or supernaturalistic language in which it is couched. In a similar way, Ron Farmer's use of a process hermeneutic to uncover and mediate tensions within the book of Revelation is a way of rendering intelligible a text that might otherwise appear incoherent at some points. And Adela Yarbro Collins's call for a "critical reading" of that same work is a conscious attempt to discover its value despite some objectionable aspects.

In other cases, the problematic character of understanding remains implicit. Neither psychological interpretation nor Patte's structuralist method explicitly identifies anything problematic about the New Testament as it stands. But the psychological approach does make possible a different way of appreciating certain themes and stories that can engage some readers who might otherwise remain uninterested. And Patte, by focusing on Paul's faith, cuts beneath doctrinal formulations that might be difficult for contemporary readers to appropriate.

The reader-response criticism that has played the dominant role in this book also has the potential to overcome difficulties in understanding. Precisely by focusing upon the Gospels as stories, it encourages the student to delay certain questions that grow out of training in Christian doctrine or a concern for historical factuality. In doing so, it enables a fresh reading that can lead to a new level of interest and personal involvement. And similar results can issue from reading the letters and other materials in light of their possible effects upon the reader.

The problem that has interested many hermeneutical theorists is that of the conflict in world-pictures held by the ancient writers on the one hand and modern or postmodern readers on the other. But quite a few recent thinkers are drawn to the question of sociopolitical ideology. More specifically, many feminist and politically minded interpreters find the New Testament to be quite bound up with the hierarchical and patriarchal models of society and the universe that were characteristic of the ancient world.

One way scholars have met this problem is through historical reconstruction, often aided by sociological and anthropological methods. The contributions of Elisabeth Schüssler Fiorenza and Richard Horsley are cases in point. To discover a historical Jesus or an early Christian community that stands in some degree at odds with the canonical writings has the potential of allowing some readers to find a point of contact in a collection of texts that might otherwise appear alienating and oppressive.

In part for that reason, the hermeneutical importance of the historical method must not be overlooked. Although the early proponents of this approach tended to ignore the subtle prejudices in their own presuppositions and judgments, the method itself, I would argue, remains indispensable. When subjected to continuing critique, particularly by those with a perspective different from that of the dominant elements in society, it becomes an important check upon the interpreter's subjectivity.

The two broad divisions of hermeneutical methods mentioned here will of course have different ways of dealing with the specific problem of diversity within the New Testament. One version of the first school will simply deny that the diversity exists. But as we move toward the more complex, dialogical strategies, we find increasing emphasis upon other ways of meeting the problem. Some interpreters try to identify a common core of agreement beyond all the disagreements in the New Testament. Others select some portion of the canon, or some level of tradition behind the canon, as a normative center by which the whole can be measured. An alternative approach is to interpret the various strains within the New Testament in light of traditions (such as those of women) that have been suppressed or even rejected and can be identified only through historical reconstruction.

This latter way of meeting the problem is sometimes combined with an emphasis upon the role of the experiences of the interpreters themselves and/or the communities in which they live in determining the value of the writings and traditions. Schüssler Fiorenza, for example, denies that it is possible to find a central, normative core of teaching in the Bible itself. From her perspective, the contemporary community of women must look to its own experience for help in sorting out the various biblical materials, which are to be valued less for the specific positions they take than for the process of reflection they initiate.

The two general types of hermeneutical approach also lead to different ways of dealing with the problem of multiple interpretations. The first tends to treat texts as containing fixed meanings, while the more complex approaches tend to view meaning as inexhaustible and to grant the reader an active role in its creation. I would hope that by now the reader of this text can understand why many interpreters have moved in this latter direction. I would also hope, however, that the reader will be aware of the difference between saying that we contribute to the meaning of a text and saying that we can make the Bible say anything we want it to, that any interpretation is as good as any other. Let me say, in any case, that this is a distinction that I as an interpreter of the New Testament find not only possible but necessary to make. Psychological interpretation reveals a different kind of meaning than does historical criticism, but it does not sanction just anything anyone wants to read into the text. Nor do structuralism, existentialist interpretation, readings informed by the various liberation theologies or process thought, or moderate reader-response approaches.

One may read the Gospel of Mark in many ways, but one cannot legitimately understand it as a call to save one's neck in a time of crisis. One may read Paul's Letter to the Romans in many ways, but those who bypass the theme of grace on the one hand or that of God's promise to Israel on the other have missed something essential. And one may read the Letter of James in many ways, but not in a way that justifies the oppression of the poor by the rich. Nor is it possible, short of utter distortion, to find in the deeds and words of Jesus an endorsement of the maxim that one must "go along to get along."

Although I suppose it is evident to the reader that my own hermeneutical stance fits within the second broad category, I would also hope that my emphasis upon the various methods of "critical reading" has not prejudiced the case against those who approach the New Testament in a more "straightforward" way. My intention has not been to force a particular interpretive strategy upon the readers but simply to confront them with the hermeneutical problem. For it is a problem, I maintain, that is ultimately unavoidable. However we choose to read the New Testament, our way of reading is in fact a choice; and that is no less true of the first broad hermeneutical division than of the second. Those who desire an informed and thoughtful evaluation of the New Testament writings must give attention to the question of reading strategy.

I do not mean, however, to insulate hermeneutics from criticism. A number of theorists have charged that it is simply a sophisticated way of saving the text at all costs, that is to say, a way of making a text that is unacceptable appear acceptable. I would grant that hermeneutics can in fact degenerate into such a practice. And it is up to the reader to decide in any given instance whether a hermeneutical move is just such an act of desperation. My conviction, however, is that at its best hermeneutics does not deny the interpreter the right to reject a text. What it does is to help insure, by exposing a broad potential for meaning in a text, that the decision to accept or reject is not made on a superficial basis. And, in the end, it should be said that even the decision to reject a text involves some sort of hermeneutical decision as to how it is to be read.

So here, finally, are the two points for which I do want to argue and which I hope this introductory text has helped to demonstrate. If we wish to read the New Testament with genuine understanding, we must pay close attention to what it actually says. We must, in other words, nurture an appropriate objectivity. But if our reading and understanding are to be more than superficial, we will also have to nurture an appropriate subjectivity, precisely by allowing what it has to say to engage us on the deepest level. And if we are to do that, then we simply cannot escape the question raised in the second half of Jesus' query in Luke 10:26: "What do the Scriptures say? *How do you interpret them?*" (Today's English Version).

Appendix 1

"Son of Man"

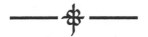

No problem in New Testament studies is more difficult than that regarding the term "Son of man," or, as the *Inclusive Language Lectionary* translates it, "the Human One."[1] The phrase occurs numerous times in the Gospels, always in passages involving Jesus' own speech, whether in direct or indirect discourse. Whatever the ultimate origin and original meaning of these passages, in their present contexts in the Gospels they present Jesus himself as the Son of man. The aspect of the problem that most concerns us here is how Jesus came to be known as Son of man and what the phrase might have meant in its earliest application to him. Many scholars believe that Jesus actually did use the term, although there has been much disagreement as to what he meant by it. Others think that it was the early postresurrection community that placed it on his lips.

It is important to note, in beginning, that the phrase "son of..." in Semitic languages (such as Hebrew and Aramaic) is often a way of designating membership in a general category. Thus "son of a prophet" can refer to a member of a prophetic community, and "son of man" can mean simply "human being."

The term appears in Jewish writings both within and outside the canon. There are numerous instances, such as Psalm 8:4 and Isaiah 51:12, in which it is clearly the equivalent of "human being." In Ezekiel it refers to the prophet Ezekiel himself and seems simply to be a way of emphasizing his status as a human being, in contrast to God. In the book of Daniel it occurs in an apocalyptic context, in the midst of a vision of things to come: "I saw one like a human being [a son of man] coming with the clouds of heaven. And he

---

1. *An Inclusive Language Lectionary* (Atlanta: John Knox, 1983–88).

came to the Ancient One and was presented before him. To him was given dominion ... " (Dan. 7:13-14).

The reference in Daniel is apparently to a figure that looks like a human being, to whom God (the Ancient One) gives power. Some scholars think that the author drew at this point upon imagery from ancient Canaanite mythology, according to which a younger god takes power from an older one. Whatever the background of the term, there is some dispute regarding its precise meaning in Daniel. Many interpreters think it designates a supernatural individual of some sort. But others, on the basis of Daniel 7:27, take it as a collective symbol of he people of Israel, who receive "kingship and dominion" from God at the climax of history.

Outside the canon, we find the term in the book of Enoch, in a section that is apparently of separate origin from the rest of the book and the dating of which remains uncertain. In chapter 46, for example, we find the following: "This is the Son of Man to whom belongs righteousness ... for the Lord of the Spirits has chosen him. . . . This Son of Man whom you have seen is the one who would remove the kings and the mighty ones from their comfortable seats ... and crush the teeth of the sinners."[2] Also, in 2 Esdras, a Jewish apocalyptic work probably written near the end of the first century c.e., we find a reference to "something like the figure of a man" (13:3) who arises out of the sea. And in both Enoch and 2 Esdras the figure in question is also identified as "Messiah."

In the Gospels, the term is used in three different ways. Some of the passages are apocalyptic, highly reminiscent of Daniel 7 and Enoch; in them Jesus is identified with the son of man who will appear at the end of history. At other points the term appears in the context of Jesus' prediction of his coming death and resurrection. And in still other passages it is Jesus' self-designation with respect to his earthly ministry. Among the questions scholars have debated is which, if any, of these three usages actually stems from Jesus himself.

For a long time it was a standard assumption among New Testament scholars that prior to the time of Jesus there was a widespread expectation among Jews of a supernatural redeemer designated by the term "Son of man" as a formal title. They presumed that the concept of such a supernatural being was reflected in Enoch and 2 Esdras and that it grew out of the mythology on which the Daniel passage had drawn. Scholars who took this position be-

---

2. James H. Charlesworth, ed., *Old Testament Pseudepigrapha* (Garden City, N.Y.: Doubleday, 1983), 1:34.

lieved either that Jesus thought of himself as that heavenly Son of man or that he spoke of a coming heavenly redeemer distinct from himself.

Many recent scholars, however, doubt that there was any such widespread expectation of an apocalyptic Son of man prior to the time of Jesus. Some deny that the term is actually intended as a formal title in the Enoch passage or any other Jewish literature of the time. Others argue that Enoch and the Gospels represent two independent attempts to interpret the passage in Daniel 7 but do not draw upon a preexisting concept. In other words, at some time of crisis a Jewish individual or small community of people read Daniel 7 and, out of a longing for supernatural help, took the term "son of man" not as a symbol but as a literal reference to a heavenly being. In a somewhat similar way, early Christians, looking back on the life and death of Jesus, took the same passage in Daniel to be a reference to Jesus' eventual return at the end of history. But neither the Jewish nor the Christian interpreters were, in this view, drawing upon an already formalized notion of a heavenly redeemer.

On the other hand, not all scholars are convinced that the passages in Enoch and 4 Ezra are simply the products of the interpretation of Daniel. John J. Collins notes that these two apparently independent texts share a number of assumptions, including the interpretation of the "son of man" as an individual. Noting that the question of a formalized Son of man concept is "evidently a matter of definition," he argues that "anyone in the late first century who spoke of one in human form riding on the clouds, or appearing with an Ancient of Days, or in any terms reminiscent of Daniel 7, would evoke a figure with distinct traits which go beyond what was explicit in the text of Daniel's vision."[3]

Was the term "son of man" used in pre-Christian Jewish apocalyptic literature as a title for a supernatural figure? This question remains a matter of debate. But in any case, many recent scholars—whatever their position on the presence of such a concept in first-century Judaism—deny that it was Jesus himself who introduced the notion of an apocalyptic Son of man into the thinking of his followers. It was rather those followers themselves, as they awaited his return, whether they did so on the basis of a prior Jewish hope for a supernatural redeemer or as their own creative act of interpretation of the Jewish Scriptures in light of their allegiance to Jesus.

Another possibility is that Jesus did use the term apocalyptically but, perhaps following Daniel, in a symbolic rather than a literal way. He might, for

---

3. John J. Collins, "The Son of Man in First-Century Judaism," *New Testament Studies* 38 (July 1992): 466.

example, have spoken of "the days of the Son of Man" (Luke 17:26) and meant that phrase as a reference to the dawn of the Rule of God that would bring with it the restoration of Israel. Then, after his death, his followers interpreted the term in a literal way as Jesus' self-designation.

What all these theories have in common is the notion that the apocalyptic Son of man passages represent the earliest usage of the term by Jesus or his followers. According to this view, it would tend to follow that the nonapocalyptic passages represent a later stage of the tradition. First applied to Jesus in an apocalyptic context, the term was then read back into the actual lifetime of Jesus.

Some scholars, however, think it is the nonapocalyptic passages that come from the earliest layer of Christian tradition. Since "son of man" is the equivalent of "human being," they argue, Jesus probably used the term in a nonapocalyptic way as a self-designation. It was an indirect, somewhat mysterious, and perhaps humble way of saying simply "I" or "this man." This argument tends to hinge, however, on the assumption that "son of man" was in fact used in this way in Aramaic, that is, as a circumlocution for "I." But the evidence for such usage is highly ambiguous and not universally accepted.

A related possibility is that Jesus used the term in a nonapocalyptic way, but with a generic meaning rather than as an exclusive self-designation. That is to say, he could have employed it as a reference to human beings in general (including himself), in which case it would have been the equivalent of the impersonal "one." In this view, it would have been only in the postresurrection community that it became either a title or an exclusive self-designation.

It cannot be said that anything near a consensus has been reached by New Testament scholars on the problem of the term "son of man." Just about every theory has competent defenders. My own guess is that if Jesus used the term in any way other than as an equivalent of the impersonal "one," it was as a bit of apocalyptic language intended metaphorically, and that later tradition made it into a self-designation, both in the apocalyptic and the nonapocalyptic contexts.

It should be noted, in any case, that the issues discussed here have little direct effect upon one's reading of the Gospels as literary wholes. The term appears in each of them as Jesus' self-designation, but one must determine from each work what precise nuances it takes on in that context.

FOR FURTHER READING

Collins, John J. "The Son of Man in First-Century Judaism." *New Testament Studies* 38 (July 1992): 448–66.

Crossan, John Dominic. *The Historical Jesus: The Life of Mediterranean Jewish Peasant.* San Francisco: HarperSanFrancisco, 1991, pp. 238–59.

Fuller, Reginald H. *The Foundations of New Testament Christology.* New York: Charles Scribner's Sons, 1965.

Johnson, S. E. "Son of Man." In *The Interpreter's Dictionary of the Bible: An Illustrated Encyclopedia,* Vol. 4. New York: Abingdon, 1962.

Perrin, Norman. "Son of Man." In *The Interpreter's Dictionary of the Bible: An Illustrated Encyclopedia, Supplementary Volume.* New York: Abingdon, 1962.

Tödt, H. E. *The Son of Man in the Synoptic Tradition.* Trans. Dorothea M. Barton. London: SCM, 1965.

Chronologies of Paul
by John A. Darr

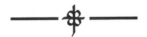

Our resources for calculating the sequence, time, and date of events in Paul's ministry are essentially restricted to the Pauline letters and to the Acts of the Apostles. Neither of these sources is directly concerned with Pauline chronology, although Acts may provide a rough schema of Paul's later ministry. Since Paul's letters dealt primarily with religious issues and were geared to current circumstances in his churches, there was little opportunity for him to recount his personal history in his writings (with one important exception). The modern historian is therefore forced to reconstruct the chronology of Paul's life from meager and diverse sources which must be constantly evaluated and interpreted. This results in a wide range of scholarly opinions as to the dating of Paul's various activities. Nevertheless, two basic approaches to Pauline chronology may be delineated:

1. *Chronologies based on the sequential outline found in Acts.* In this category, the general procedure has been to fit the various phenomena mentioned or presupposed by the Pauline letters into the narrative framework provided by Acts (the three missionary journeys, Paul's trip to Rome, etc.). This procedure implies a highly positive evaluation of the basic historical trustworthiness of Acts. Dates are supplied by those references which can (to the scholar's satisfaction) be supported by extrabiblical historical evidence, such as ancient inscriptions mentioning Roman officers with whom Paul dealt.

2. *Chronologies based on the Pauline letters.* A number of scholars have been skeptical of the historical narrative found in Acts and have preferred

---

This appendix is taken from D. Patte, *Paul's Faith and the Power of the Gospel* (Fortress).

to base their chronologies almost exclusively on evidence gleaned from the Pauline letters, scanty though it may be. The reasoning behind this approach is that Paul's own letters constitute primary evidence, while the Acts account can be considered only secondary evidence at best. Acts is not to be trusted, except at those points where it is supported by a specific statement in Paul's letters. Thus, use of the Acts material must be restricted and is advisable only after the essential structure of Pauline chronology has already been developed on the basis of the letters alone. Dating is achieved by reference to certain extrabiblical evidence.

The primary question in a study of Pauline chronology is the placement of the so-called Jerusalem conference in which Paul took part. This incident is crucial in that Paul himself, in one of his few backward glances, recounts all of his previous visits to Jerusalem up to and including the conference visit (Galatians 1 and 2). Acts also knows of Paul's important visit to Jerusalem, but mentions at least one "extra" visit not accounted for by Paul in Galatians. How are we to place the various visits of Paul to Jerusalem? The answer to this question is the basic distinguishing characteristic of all modern reconstructions of Pauline chronology. Historians highly dependent on Acts have identified the conference visit either with the event in Acts 15 or in Acts 11:30. The chronologies based on Paul's writings reject both these options and point instead to Acts 18:22 as an oblique reference to the real conference visit of Paul. For apologetic reasons, the author of Acts inserted two fabricated Jerusalem visits early in Paul's career. The real conference visit took place late in Paul's career and was marked by the instigation of Paul's "collection for the poor in Jerusalem." The progress of this collection process can be traced through almost all of Paul's letters and thus provides a point of reference for Pauline chronology.

The two most significant extrabiblical pieces of evidence used in Pauline chronologies are the following. First, the so-called Gallio Inscription, uncovered at Delphi, from which it has been deduced that Gallio held office at Corinth from the year 51 to 52. Gallio is mentioned in Acts 18:12 in connection with Paul's activities in Corinth. The second piece of evidence is Claudius's edict expelling the Jews from Rome, which is generally assumed to have been issued in the year 49 (based on Orosius) and to have been the reason for Aquila and Priscilla arriving in Corinth from Rome (Acts 18:2). The near coincidence of these dates is taken by many to be a sure sign that Acts' picture of Paul's *first* ministry at Corinth is essentially accurate. Other incidents in Paul's European ministry are then ordered around this time period. Those who are less accepting of Acts' historical accuracy point out that the Claudius edict may well be dated at 41 rather than 49, and thus a chronology based on Acts 18:2, 12 will begin to unravel. These latter scholars see two widely separated Pauline missions to Corinth, one near the beginning or middle of Paul's career (thus the reference to Aquila and Priscilla) and one at the end (thus the Gallio reference in Acts). The author of Acts simply mixed these two traditions in one narrative about Paul at Corinth.

The evolution of Paul's thinking within his letters has often been used as an *internal* source of evidence for Pauline chronology. Determining the sequence and spacing of Paul's letters through careful comparison of their content could provide a valuable criterion for the chronologist. Toward this end, at least three areas of Pauline thought have been examined:

1. *Ecclesiology* (the doctrine of the church). Can we perceive in Paul's letters a growing awareness of the ongoing institutionalization of the early church (the establishment of specific church offices, a centralization of authority, developed sacramentalism, and so on)? Scholars who feel that Paul wrote the pastoral letters find this criterion especially significant and helpful; others do not.

2. *Christology* (the doctrine of Christ). How is it that in some letters (1 Thessalonians, Philippians) Paul does not speak of Christ's death as an atonement, while in other letters (Romans, 1 Corinthians) Christ's atoning death is a prominent theme? Could this disparity be another indication of long-term development in Paul's thinking?

3. *Eschatology* (the doctrine of the end). In 1 Thessalonians, Paul apparently feels that Christ's Second Coming is imminent and that virtually all Christians will still be alive when Christ returns (cf. 4:13ff.). In 1 Corinthians, however, Paul takes for granted that many Christians will die (indeed, *have* died) before the Second Coming (cf. 6:14; 11:30; 15:6, 18, 51). In the latter case he speaks of a bodily transformation of Christians which will take place at the eschaton (end); yet bodily transformation is not even alluded to in 1 Thessalonians, where one would expect it to be a major motif. Does this indicate a progression in Paul's thought, and if so, how much time would have passed between the writing of 1 Thessalonians and 1 Corinthians? Since answers to these and other such questions are subjective, few concrete results have been obtained, and no consensus of opinion has been established concerning the sequence or spacing of the letters. There is, however, widespread agreement among scholars that 1 Thessalonians is our earliest authentic letter written by Paul, and that Romans is our latest. Conjectures concerning the sequence of the letters are often used as warranting or supporting arguments for chronological schemas, but rarely form the foundation of such reconstructions.

Some of the basic types of Pauline chronology are schematized below. It should be emphasized that these charts are not comprehensive summaries of the full-scale chronological reconstructions by the scholars in the footnotes. Rather, they are intended to provide elementary conceptualizations of these varying chronologies, The sequence and spacing of events in the charts are much more important than the absolute dates (which, for the most part, are highly conjectural). Note once again the different placements of the "Jerusalem conference" and the varying degrees of reliability accorded the account in Acts.

Fig. 80.

I. CHRONOLOGIES DEPENDENT ON THE OUTLINE OF ACTS

A. *The Jerusalem Conference Visit of Paul (Galatians 2) = Acts 11:30*[1]

33	Paul's conversion	
35	Paul's first Jerusalem visit	Acts 9:26
35–46	Paul in Syria and Cilicia	
46	Paul's conference visit to Jerusalem (Galatians 2)	Acts 11:27-30; described as a famine visit
47–48	Paul and Barnabas in Cyprus and Galatia (first missionary journey)	
?48	*Letter to the Galatians*	
49	Council at Jerusalem. Paul's third Jerusalem visit	Acts 15
49–50	Paul and Silas travel from Syrian Antioch through Asia Minor to Macedonia and back (second missionary journey)	
50	*Letters to the Thessalonians*	Claudius's edict (49) = Acts 18:2
50–52	Paul in Corinth	Gallio Inscription (51-52) = Acts 18:12
52	Paul's fourth Jerusalem visit	Acts 18:22
52–55	Paul in Ephesus	
55–56	*Letters to the Corinthians*	
55–57	Paul in Macedonia, Illyricum, Achaia	
57	*Letter to the Romans*	
57	Last visit to Jerusalem	Acts 21:17
57–59	Imprisonment at Caesarea	
60	Paul's arrival at Rome	
60–62	Paul under arrest in Rome ?Writes the *Captivity Letters*	
?65	Paul visits Spain	
?65	Paul dies	

---

1. Based on F. F. Bruce, *Paul: Apostle of the Heart Set Free* (Grand Rapids, Mich.: Wm. B. Eerdmans, 1978), p. 475.

B. The Jerusalem Conference Visit of Paul (Galatians 2) = Acts 15[2]

35	Paul's conversion	Acts 9
38	Paul's first Jerusalem visit	Acts 9:26
38–47	Paul in Syria and Cilicia	
46	Famine relief visit to Jerusalem	Acts 11:30; ?12:25
47–48	First missionary journey (Cyprus and Galatia)	Acts 13, 14
48	Council at Jerusalem (conference visit)	Gal. 2:1-10=Acts 15
49–52	Second missionary journey (Asia Minor, Macedonia, Caesarea)	Acts 15:36—18:22
49	Jews expelled from Rome	Claudius's edict (49); Acts 18:2
50	Paul reaches Corinth	
50	*Letters to the Thessalonians*	
51	Gallio becomes proconsul of Corinth	Gallio Inscription 51–52
52	*Letter to the Galatians*	
52–56	Third missionary journey (Macedonia and Achaia)	Acts 18:23—21:15
52–55	Three years spent at Ephesus	
55	*Letters to the Corinthians*	
56	*Epistle to the Romans*	
56	Arrival at Jerusalem	
56–58	Imprisonment at Caesarea	Acts 24:27
59	Paul reaches Rome	Acts 28:16
59–61	Paul at Rome *Philippians, Philemon, Colossians, Ephesians*	
61(64)	Paul's martyrdom	Neronian persecution (64)

2. Based on B. W. Robinson, The Life of Paul, 2d ed. (Chicago: University of Chicago Press, 1928), pp. 240–41.

C. The Jerusalem Conference Visit of Paul (Galatians 2:1-10) = Acts 15 = Acts 11:30[3]

30–32	Paul's conversion	
32–34	Paul's first Jerusalem visit	
44/45	Paul's conference visit to Jerusalem	Gal. 2:1-10/Acts 15/11:30
46	Mission to Cyprus and Asia Minor	
46/47	Quarrel with Barnabas (equated with the disagreement in Gal. 2:13)	
47–51	Mission to Macedonia and Achaia; *1 Thessalonians*	
52–58	Mission in Galatia, Phrygia, and Asia; collection journey; *Galatians, 1 and 2 Corinthians, Romans*	
58	Arrest in Jerusalem and Caesarean imprisonment; *Philemon*	
60	Journey to Rome	
60—	Roman imprisonment; *Philippians* (?)	

---

3. A. J. M. Wedderburn, "Keeping up with Recent Studies, VIII, Some Recent Pauline Chronologies," *ET*, January 1981, p. 107. Notice that the second and third missionary journeys of Acts are inverted and also that the first journey is placed after the conference rather than before it. While maintaining that Acts is basically trustworthy, adherents of this approach feel that the account of the famine visit (Acts 11:30) resulted from a simple historical misinterpretation by the author of Acts and not from any conscious attempt to distort the facts. A famine did take place, and the Antioch church did send aid to Jerusalem. However, it may be that Paul himself never did accompany Barnabas on a trip solely for the purpose of bringing relief to Jerusalem; and/or that Paul took a donation to Jerusalem at the same time he went for the conference visit (Acts 15/Gal. 2:1-10). In either case, the author of Acts (or his sources of information) was not clear in making these historical distinctions. Thus we have two accounts rather than one. Conjectures of this sort are intended to solve (somewhat at the expense of Acts' trustworthiness) the problem of an "extra" Jerusalem visit by Paul in Acts while at the same time preserving the basic integrity of the greater part of Acts.

Fig. 81.

II. CHRONOLOGY DERIVED FROM PAUL'S LETTERS

A. *The Jerusalem Conference Visit of Paul (Galatians 2) = Acts 18:22 (J. Knox and G. Lüdemann)*[4]

33/34	Paul's conversion	Gal. 1:15, 16; 2 Cor. 12:2
36/37	Paul's first Jerusalem visit	Gal. 1:18
36/37–38/39	Mission activity in Syria, Cilicia, and Galatia	Gal. 1:21
38/39–50/51	Independent Pauline mission activity in Macedonia, Achaia, and perhaps elsewhere	
41	Paul in Corinth; *1 Thessalonians* Aquila and Priscilla come to Corinth from Rome	Claudius's edict, (41)= Acts 18:2
50/51	Paul's conference visit to Jerusalem (a dramatic and skewed rendering of this is [mis]placed at Acts 15)	Gal. 2:1=Acts 18:22
50/51–54/55	Collection for the Jerusalem church and other mission activity in Asia Minor and Greece	
51	Paul in Galatia	
51–53	Paul based in Ephesus	
52	*1 Corinthians*	
52	Quick trip to Corinth and back to Ephesus	Gallio Inscription (51– 52); Acts 18:12
53	Paul travels to Troas and Macedonia; *2 Corinthians and Galatians*	
54	Paul arrives in Corinth; *Romans*	
54/55	Final journey to Jerusalem to deliver the collection	
	We have no hard evidence on Paul after this)	

---

4. This table is constructed from two slightly varying chronologies which employ the same basic presuppositions and methodology; the spacing and sequence of events is similar despite the difference in the absolute dates (indicated by the diagonals). This display does not represent the entire range of dates proposed by these scholars, but it does accurately represent the sequential aspects of their chronologies of Paul: J. Knox, *Chapters in a Life of Paul* (Nashville: Abingdon Press, 1950), pp. 83–88; G. Lüdemann, *Paulus, der Heidenapostel*, vol. 1, *Studien zur Chronologie* (Göttingen: Vandenhoeck & Ruprecht, 1980), pp. 272–73.

B. The Jerusalem Conference Visit of Paul (Galatians 2:1-10) = Acts 18:22 (R. Jewett)[5]

34	Paul's conversion	
35–37	Activities in Arabia; return to Damascus	
37	Escape from Aretas IV; first Jerusalem visit	2 Cor. 11:32-33
		Acts 9:23-26
37–46	Activities in Syria and Cilicia	
43–45	First missionary journey: Antioch, Cyprus, Pamphylia, and South Galatia	
46–51	Second missionary journey: Antioch, North Galatia, Troas, Philippi, Thessalonica, Berea Athens, Corinth; *1 and 2 Thessalonians*	Claudius's edict (49)
51	Hearing before Gallio at Corinth	Gallio Inscription
51	Second Jerusalem visit: apostolic conference	Acts 18:22/Gal.
		2:1-10
52	Conflict with Peter	Gal. 2:14-17
52–57	Third missionary journey	
	North Galatia	
52–54	Ephesus; *Galatians*	
54/55	Ephesian imprisonment; *Philippians*	
55	Visit to Corinth; return to Macedonia and Asia; *1 and 2 Corinthians*	
56/57	Back to Corinth; *Romans*	
57	Philippi to Jerusalem; arrest	
57–59	Imprisonment in Caesarea	
61	Imprisonment in Rome	
62	Execution in Rome	

---

5. R. Jewett, *A Chronology of Paul's Life* (Philadelphia: Fortress Press, 1979), foldout. This simplified chart can present only a fraction of the information Jewett includes in his complex chronology. Note that although Jewett places the conference visit at Acts 18:22 and opts for only three Jerusalem visits (as per the letters), he is much more dependent on Acts for his chronological framework than Knox (see previous table).

Glossary

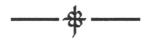

Agrippa II. (28 C.E.–ca. 100 C.E.) Son of Agrippa I (Herod Agrippa), great-grandson of Herod the Great, and the last reigning member of the Herodian dynasty; ruled a mostly gentile kingdom, under Roman appointment, that eventually included Galilee and parts of Judea. In Acts 25–26, Paul, under arrest, defends himself before Agrippa II just prior to his departure to Rome to pursue his appeal to Caesar.

Allegory. A type of story whose various elements point symbolically to realities, with which the readers/hearers would be familiar, outside the story-world. Many of the stories called parables in the New Testament are actually allegories; in some cases the parables of Jesus have been made into allegories either by the Gospel writers or earlier handlers of tradition.

Apocalyptic literature. A type of writing in exilic and postexilic Judaism involving a revelation given to a human subject by a heavenly messenger. The revelation can consist of secrets of the heavenly realm and/or a divinely ordained plan for history. Apocalypses of the historical type generally focus on a dramatic end to history followed by the resurrection of the righteous to eternal life.

Apocrypha. A term, used largely in Protestantism, to refer to a collection of ancient Jewish writings, most of which were included in the Septuagint but did not become a part of the final canon of the Jewish Scriptures. They are considered "deuterocanonical" (belonging to a second level of canonicity) by the Roman Catholic Church; and there are several books that appear in the Greek and Slavonic Bibles but not in the Catholic, or in appendices to one or more of these canons. The literal meaning of the term is "hidden," and it has sometimes been used to designate materials considered heretical;

561

in the present context, however, it indicates only a secondary status. In Catholicism, the term "apocrypha" is used for the writings Protestants call the pseudepigrapha. See Pseudepigrapha.

Apocrypha, New Testament. A term applied to wide range of early Christian writings not included in the canon; these vary widely in theological perspective, from what came to be known as orthodox to what was considered severely heretical. Many of them are the products of sectarian groups of Christians that eventually died out. The term is somewhat misleading, since the books considered New Testament Apocrypha are not really parallel to the Apocrypha (see Apocrypha above) of the Jewish Scriptures. The latter have a kind of secondary canonical status among Christians (although not among Jews), whereas the former have no official standing at all in relation to the canon.

Apostle. Literally, "one who is sent"—an emissary, agent, or ambassador. The Christian usage seems related to a Hebrew term with similar meaning. In the early church an apostle was understood as someone belonging to the first generation of Christians with a special divine commission for mission and leadership. The circle of apostles included, but was not limited to, "the Twelve"—those believed to have been called into leadership by Jesus himself. Paul considered himself an apostle and was apparently widely accepted as such; and he recognized a few others, beyond the Twelve, as having this status also.

Archetype. Literally, an original pattern, from which all copies derive. In Jungian psychology, the archetypes are specific patterns of thinking that all human beings share by virtue of their common evolutionary history; and the notion of "the self" is the controlling archetype, which guides human beings toward their ultimate fulfillment.

Babylonian Empire. More technically designated Neo-Babylonian, it flourished 625–529 B.C.E. Centered in the city of Babylon in Mesopotamia, it extended eastward and included Palestine. In 587, following an attempt of Judah to gain independence, the Babylonians sent the ruling class into exile in Babylon. The period from that point until 538, when the conquering Persian king decreed that the Judahites could return home, is known as the Babylonian exile.

B.C.E./C.E. Abbreviation for Before the Common Era and Common Era—nonreligious alternatives, respectively, to B.C. and A.D.

Canon. A Greek word designating a reed and, by extension, anything straight (as reeds are straight). It also took on the metaphorical meaning of rule, measure, or standard; hence in the early church it was applied to religious law and doctrine and to a list of writings understood to provide an authoritative standard of faith. The various books of the Bible thus constitute a canon, and those included are termed "canonical."

C.E. See B.C.E./C.E.

Cosmic empathy. A term used by the author of this book to describe the perception, common in prehistorical society, that all components of reality are organically related and that all aspects of the universe, including those that moderns consider inanimate, are pervaded with vitality and feeling.

Covenant. In Hebrew thought, a compact between God (Yahweh) and the people of Israel, including two components: God's promise to be with the people (evidenced by God's prior actions on their behalf) and the people's obligation to serve and obey God.

Decapolis. A region in Palestine, east of the Jordan, that was home to a federation of Greek cities. There were originally ten in the federation, but ancient sources are not entirely consistent with respect to which cities were included.

Demystification. The process of explaining some phenomenon, which previously appeared to be mysterious and/or supernatural, in such a way as to render it intelligible in nonmysterious terms. Whereas ancient people tended to view nature as mysterious, modern science has tended to demystify it, often explaining it in mechanistic fashion.

Demythologizing. See Existentialist interpretation.

Deuterocanonical. See Apocrypha.

Devil, The. A Greek term (*diabolos*) meaning "slanderer," used in the Septuagint to translate "Satan." In the New Testament, the Devil and Satan are basically interchangeable designations for the archfiend, author of evil and cosmic opponent of God.

Diaspora. A Greek word meaning "dispersion." Refers to the Jewish people living outside the homeland, beginning in the period of the Babylonian exile.

Diatribe. A type of argumentation, probably used in philosophical schools, in which the speaker (or writer) uses vivid images and rhetorical questions to take up and refute the arguments of imaginary opponents.

Dispersion. See Diaspora.

Docetism. From a Greek word meaning "to think" or "to seem"; the doctrine, considered heretical by what emerged as "mainstream" Christianity, that Jesus, as a divine being, only seemed to have a physical body. Many forms of Gnosticism embraced a docetic Christology.

Dualism. In philosophy, the view that there are two different types of reality—one mental/spiritual, the other material—neither of which is reducible to the other.

Eschatology. Teaching regarding the "last things," the end of history or of the present age.

Essenes. A Jewish subgroup of the Hellenistic period, characterized by sectarian teachings and strict community discipline. They do not appear in the New Testament but are mentioned in other ancient sources. The majority of scholars identify the community at Qumran, who produced the Dead Sea Scrolls, as Essenes.

Exegesis. From a Greek term, with the literal meaning "leading out," that signifies the process of interpretation. In biblical studies exegesis is systematic interpretation of the meaning of a text. See also Hermeneutics.

Exile, Babylonian. See Babylonian Empire.

Existentialist interpretation. An approach to biblical interpretation first proposed by the German scholar/theologian Rudolf Bultmann. Bultmann's method involved looking for an "existential" meaning—a meaning not dependent upon supernatural categories, but referring to human existence as all persons experience it—beneath the mythological language of biblical texts.

Exodus, The. The event recounted in the Jewish Scriptures (Exod. 14) wherein God, acting through Moses, led the Hebrews out of slavery in Egypt, parting the waters of the sea for them as they went.

Feminist criticism. An approach to the interpretation of texts from the explicit standpoint of a commitment to full equality for women. Feminist critics engage in such operations as critiquing the patriarchal nature of texts, recovering the lost history of women by reconstructing history through the critical use of texts, and challenging traditional interpretations of texts on the basis of explicit attention to questions of particular interest to women.

Galilee. A region in northern Palestine, where Jesus grew up (in the town of Nazareth) and carried out most of his ministry.

Gentiles. Derived from a Latin term used to translate Greek and Hebrew words that literally mean "the nations." It is employed only when those words are taken to have the specific connotation of non-Jews as opposed to Jews. "Gentile" thus means "non-Jew."

Gnosticism. A modern term, based upon the Greek word for knowledge, that refers to a wide range of religious teachings dating from the second century C.E. (and perhaps earlier). Gnostics typically claimed to possess a secret knowledge that ensured their immortality; and they tended to see the physical universe as completely under the sway of evil, so that the goal of religious enlightenment was the eventual escape of a divine spark within the individual from this world into the realm of light. Many Gnostics considered themselves Christians, although the church eventually so defined its beliefs as to exclude them. See also Docetism.

Gospel(s). From an Anglo-Saxon (and Middle English) term meaning "good news," it translates the Greek *euangelion,* with the same meaning. In New Testament Christianity, the gospel is first of all the message, or proclamation, about Jesus Christ; then, by extension, it is applied to the four narratives of Jesus's life in the New Testament—the Gospels.

Greco-Roman. The term means influenced by both Greece and Roman; the Greco-Roman world was the sphere of the Roman Empire, which retained much of Greek culture.

Griesbach Hypothesis. See Two-Gospel Hypothesis.

Hasidim. A Hebrew term with the literal meaning of "those who practice *ḥōsedh*"; *ḥesedh* connotes a rich range of meaning including such notions as loyalty, mercy, and lovingkindness. In the broad sense, then, persons who are particularly faithful and loyal to God are termed "hasidim." And in the period of the Maccabean Revolt, those who refused to comply with orders from the Seleucid king to violate the Jewish law became known as the Hasidim.

Hasmonean Dynasty. The Jewish dynasty that ruled following the Maccabean Revolt, 142–63 B.C.E.

Hellenism. A term referring to Greek culture. It is most frequently applied to that of the Hellenistic Age (see Hellenistic Age).

Hellenistic Age. Most narrowly, the period from the death of Alexander the Great (323 B.C.E.) to the ascendancy of Octavian (later to become Caesar Augustus) in 31 C.E. But Hellenistic culture permeated the Roman imperial period also.

Hermeneutics. A technical term relating to the process of interpretation. Once used simply to indicate the rules of interpretation, it has taken on two broader connotations. One is philosophical reflection upon the conditions under which the understanding of a text takes place. The other is methodology for extracting meaning from texts, most especially methodology designed to overcome a specific problem, such as a discrepancy between the worldview of the text and that of the interpreter.

Herod. A native of Idumea, he was appointed "king of the Jews" by the Roman emperor and came to be called "Herod the Great." He reigned as a vassal of the Romans from 37 to 4 B.C.E. He appears in the Gospel of Matthew as a jealous king seeking the life of the child Jesus.

Herod Antipas. A son of Herod the Great, he ruled Galilee and Perea after his father's death. He appears in the New Testament as the Herod who questions Jesus in Jerusalem prior to his trial.

Hierarchical. From a Greek term referring to someone who is a steward or keeper of sacred things. A hierarchical power structure is a system of authority in which persons are arranged according to rank.

Historical-critical method. An approach to the study of materials from the past that attempts to place them in their original historical contexts. Interpreters employing this method seek objectivity by trying to take up a disinterested attitude toward the results of investigation, distancing themselves from their own beliefs and commitments. And they try to bridge the gap between their own worldview and that of the materials in view by immersing themselves in the historical world of the latter.

Holy Spirit. In the Jewish Scriptures, the power and/or presence of God, operative in such divine activities as empowering heroes, inspiring rulers and prophets, creating the world, and sustaining life. The Spirit was also associated with the eschatological expectation, and in the New Testament it is understood as descending upon Jesus and as empowering both individual Christians and the church collectively. In post–New Testament times, Christian theology defined the Holy Spirit as the third person of the Trinity, alongside the Father and the Son.

Humanism. In philosophy, its predominant usage is for the view that human beings are the center and source of value. Although theists will sometimes identify themselves as humanists, the term generally indicates a rejection of any notion of God or the supernatural.

Idealism. In philosophy, the view that there is only one type of reality, which is mental or spiritual.

Irony. A mode of expression in which the speaker or writer intends a meaning that is the exact opposite of that which the words would normally carry; also, a situation in which the result of events is the opposite of what one would normally expect. Sarcasm is a form of irony.

Isis. An Egyptian goddess, originally envisioned as the consort of the god Osiris. In Hellenistic times, Isis worship underwent extensive syncretism in which various other deities were identified with her. Among some worshipers she came to be understood as the one universal deity.

Israel. The term can be used in several ways. It may indicate the Hebrew/Jewish people, their homeland as a totality, or the northern monarchy that split off from the south (Judah) following the death of King Solomon.

Jamnia. See Yabneh.

Jewish Palestine. See Palestine.

Josephus, Flavius. A Jewish historian living in the first century C.E. A commander of Jewish forces during the war against Rome in 66–70, he gained favor with the Romans following his surrender. Residing in Rome and living on an imperial pension, he spent his remaining years writing. Although they must be used critically, his works are an important source for the period.

Jubilee, Year of. Leviticus 25:11 provides that the "fiftieth year shall be a jubilee...." Although some scholars interpret the passage to refer to a one-time occurrence, it has generally been taken to mean that every fiftieth year should be such, as the culmination of a cycle of seven sabbatical years. In any case, the Jubilee Year entailed the emancipation of any Israelite who had become enslaved to another Israelite and also the return of all property that had been sold during the period to the original owner or family. Scholars debate whether it was ever put into practice.

Judea. See Judah.

Judah. The name of one of the twelve tribes of Israel; also of one of the twelve sons of Jacob whom tradition named as the ancestors of these tribes. Upon the division of ancient Israel into northern and southern monarchies after the death of Solomon, the southern region took the old tribal name Judah as its designation. In the period after the Babylonian exile, this region became known as Judea.

Kingdom of God. See Rule of God.

Koinē. A Greek word meaning "common." The language of the Hellenistic world, a simplified form of Greek, is called the *koinē.*

Liberation theology. A type of theological thinking stressing God's identification with and action on behalf of the poor and oppressed; it also values engagement with the world rather than abstract speculation. The term in its narrowest sense refers to a particular strain of Latin American thought originating in the 1960s, but it is increasingly used in a broad sense that includes other perspectives with related interests, such as certain types of black, feminist, and Asian theological thought.

Logos. A Greek term with a wide range of meanings, including word, speech, subject, reckoning, reason. The Stoics used it to indicate both the divine principle in which all reality coheres and a spark of the divine within each human being. The Gospel of John uses it to indicate God's eternal Word that became incarnate in Jesus.

LXX. Abbreviation for the Septuagint.

Maccabean War. The insurgency of the Jewish people, led by one Judas, nicknamed Maccabeus ("the Hammer"), against the Seleucids (one of the Hellenistic monarchies) in 168–167 B.C.E. It eventually resulted in victory and the founding of the Hasmonean Dynasty.

Manuscript(s), biblical. Copies of the biblical writings dating back to the ancient world. None that we possess, however, are the original or autograph copies; thus textual critics must seek to reconstruct the originals from the various manuscripts.

Materialism. In philosophy, the view that there is one type of reality, which is matter; there is no spiritual dimension, and what is popularly called "mind" is simply a function of matter.

Mechanism. In philosophy, the view that reality can be explained totally in terms of mechanical operations, without reference to any overarching purpose or design. It is the opposite of teleology, the belief that there is some purpose at work in the very nature of things.

Mediterranean world. The area surrounding the Mediterranean sea, including Italy, Greece, Asia Minor, Syria, Israel/Palestine, the northern coast of Africa, etc. Anthropologists identify certain cultural traits that bound this broad area together in ancient times.

Messiah. Literally, "anointed"; in Judaism the kingly figure expected to serve as God's agent in bringing in the age of peace and justice at the end of history. Rooted in the ideology surrounding the reign of David, the concept developed over a great expanse of time and probably did not take its final form until after the time of Jesus.

Midrash. A type of Jewish commentary on the Scriptures intended to explain their meaning and apply them to the situations in which the interpreters lived.

Mishnah. In the broad sense, Jewish laws passed on orally rather than in written form; eventually applied to a written compilation of such materials, arranged topically, in the second century C.E.

Monotheism. The belief that there is only one god.

Mysteries. A term applied to a broad range of religious phenomena in the Hellenistic world, characterized by initiation through secret rites, that generally promised a renewed life in the present and immortality after death.

Myth. From a Greek term meaning "story" or "legend." In the field of religion, a traditional story passed on in a community in order to provide a sense of the nature of reality and the people's place in it. In Bultmann's usage, however, it carries further implications. See Mythological.

Mythological. Having the character of myth. In Bultmann's demythologizing project, it refers to a view of reality involving belief in the supernatural in which ultimate or other-worldly reality is presented in terms that properly apply only to this world. Thus, for example, God is envisioned as "above" the earth. See Myth.

Narrator (in literary criticism). In a narrative, the voice—whether anonymous or that of a character—that tells the story. Not to be confused with the author, an actual person.

New Testament Apocrypha. See Apocrypha, New Testament.

Orthodox. From Greek roots for "straight" and "thinking," the term indicates correct, as opposed to wrong or heretical, religious doctrine. It is also used in relation to one branch of Judaism and in the formal names of one family of Christian churches—Greek Orthodox, Russians Orthodox, etc.—that is parallel to Roman Catholicism and Protestantism.

Palestine. As used in relation to the ancient world, the preferred term to refer to the total area on which the ancient Israelites, the twelve tribes, had their homeland. "Israel" is ambiguous, since it can also designate the Hebrew people or only the northern monarchy in the period following the death of King Solomon. The term "Palestine" is derived from the name of one of the tribes of the "sea people," the Philistines, who entered the land in the early twelfth century B.C.E. and struggled with the Israelites for domination. Some recent scholars use the term "Jewish Palestine," indicating that in the period in question it was home to Jewish society and religion.

Pantheism. The belief that the universe as an entirety is divine, that nature is the only god there is.

Pantheon. A Roman temple, dedicated to all the gods; more broadly, the whole array of deities worshiped by a polytheistic people.

Parable. A story suggesting metaphorical meaning but demanding creative interpretation on the part of the audience. Authentic parables must be distinguished from allegories. See also Allegory.

Parenesis (or Paraenesis). From a Greek root meaning exhortation or admonition to order one's life in accordance with specific moral/religious teachings.

Patriarch. From Greek roots meaning "father" and "rule." The patriarchs in the Jewish Scriptures—of which Abraham, Isaac, and Jacob are primary—were the forefathers of Israel.

Patriarchal. Pertaining to a patriarch or father. A patriarchal system is one in which power is invested in the father; the term is used in a negative way by feminists to refer to a male-dominated, hierarchical social arrangement.

Pericope. A small, self-contained literary unit, taken out of a larger whole.

Pharisees. A Jewish subgroup of the Hellenistic period, apparently drawn from the retainer class. Rivals of the Sadducees, they advocated strict obedience to the details of the law and held certain beliefs, such as the resurrection of the dead, not contained in the Torah. They appear in the Gospels, where they receive extremely negative characterizations, as opponents of Jesus.

Pilate, Pontius. The Roman procurator of Judea, 26–36 C.E., who presided at the trial of Jesus in the Gospels.

Postmodernism. An intellectual movement in the late twentieth century that moves away from the confidence, characteristic of the modern Western world, that human reason is able to comprehend the nature of reality. Postmodernists stress that all such attempts are carried out from some perspective limited by culture, bias, experience, etc. One variety of postmodernism tends to be agnostic on the question of God and extremely skeptical of human claims to knowledge; another, known as constructive postmodernism, which is rooted in process thought, thinks that provisional understandings of reality are possible and that it is meaningful to construct new models of God in light of recent scientific theory.

Process thought (also process theology, process philosophy). A twentieth-century philosophy stressing the dynamic quality of reality and viewing the most basic realities as events rather than things. It understands an electron, for example, not as a single, self-consistent entity that moves through time and space, but as a series of energy events. Also, it envisions God not as a being separate from the universe but as the mind of the universe. Emphasizing freedom, it understands God's power as relational or persuasive rather than absolute or coercive.

Prophet. In Israelite religion, a person commissioned by God to bring a message to the people in a particular set of circumstances. Because prophets announced God's intentions, they were also understood in a secondary way as predicting the future, but only through God's power. In early Christianity, prophets spoke to Christian communities in the name of the risen Jesus.

Pseudepigrapha. A largely Protestant designation for a group of ancient Jewish writings, outside both the Jewish canon and the apocryphal/deuterocanonical books, which Catholics generally designate Apocrypha. The term, which indicates pseudonymous authorship, derives from the fact that some of these works claim authorship by biblical characters, e.g., the Psalms of Solomon and 2 Enoch.

Q. A hypothetical document purported to have been used by the authors of Matthew and Luke, defined by the material these two have in common with each other but not appearing in Mark.

Qumran. An ancient settlement near the Dead Sea, uncovered in twentieth-century excavations; the site of the discovery of the Dead Sea Scrolls. The majority of scholars believe that Qumran was inhabited by the Essenes.

Rabbi. At first, a title accorded to revered teachers. In the period following the establishment of the academy at Yabneh (see Yabneh), there was a succession of such rabbis, and the type of Judaism they helped fashion became known as Rabbinic Judaism. In time, the rabbinate became a formalized status marked by ordination.

Rabbinic Judaism. See Rabbi.

Retainer class. According to modern sociological analysis, a class of persons in agrarian societies who were directly responsible to the governing class. Among them were government officials, educators, soldiers, etc.

Rhetorical criticism. A study of texts in light of the standardized forms of expression (rhetoric) employed in the ancient world.

Rule of God. Most basically, God's action in the manner of a monarch, reigning over human society, and also the sphere of such action. The notion underwent many changes over the course of time. In the prophetic and apocalyptic traditions, it came to refer to a time in the future, but in the wisdom tradition it meant something always present. There is much scholarly debate as to its precise meaning in the teaching of Jesus. Traditionally translated "kingdom of God."

Sadducees. A Jewish subgroup of the Hellenistic period, apparently drawn from the ruling class. Rivals of the Pharisees, they were concerned primarily with the temple cult and rejected all beliefs (such as resurrection of the dead) not found in the Torah. They appear in the Gospels as opponents of Jesus.

Samaria. The region in Palestine to the north of Judah and the south of Galilee named for the capital city of the northern monarchy (Israel). In the postexilic period, the Samaritans were bitter enemies of the Jews; the two peoples shared roots in the ancient Hebrew faith, but the Samaritans were at this point a separate society with their own version of the Torah, which constituted their sole canon, and for a time they had their own temple.

Satan. In the New Testament, Satan appears as the supernatural archfiend who opposes God on a cosmic level. This usage, however, develops late in Jewish history, appearing in the Apocryphal/Deuterocanonical writings and the Pseudepigrapha but not the Jewish Scriptures. Derived from a root with the meaning "obstruct," it appears in the latter not as a proper name for the archfiend but as the designation for a prosecutor or accuser in the heavenly court or a spirit. Alongside Satan, other names were applied to the archfiend, such as Belial.

Scribes. Scholars have had some disagreements as to precisely what the term "scribes" in Jewish society of the New Testament meant, but there is no real reason to see them as a unified group. They were employed in positions demanding skills in reading and writing. Many of them were thus engaged in such tasks as keeping records, copying documents, and collecting taxes. The temple employed scribes, and it was undoubtedly scribes who were primarily responsible for preserving religious writings. In the New Testament, "the scribes" are usually portrayed in a negative light and associated with the Pharisees.

Septuagint. The ancient Greek translation of the Jewish Scriptures. Abbreviated LXX.

Social-scientific criticism. In biblical studies, a broad term indicating any approach to a text that employs methods drawn from the social sciences, such as sociology and anthropology.

Syncretism. The process of combining formerly distinct traditions. The Hellenistic Age was characterized by extreme religious syncretism.

Synoptic Gospels. The Gospels of Matthew, Mark, and Luke; designated the "Synoptics" (meaning "seeing together") because, as opposed to John, they share a great deal of wording and sequence.

Synoptic problem. The difficult question of the literary relationships among the Synoptic Gospels, i.e., which was written first and which drew upon the others.

Torah. The Hebrew term for the first five books of the Jewish Scriptures, understood to be the most important part and attributed to Moses. Its root meaning has to do with pointing the way, and it is sometimes translated as "instruction." The Torah contains both law and narrative, but it was translated in the Septuagint as *nomos*, the Greek word for law.

Two-Document Hypothesis. The predominant solution to the Synoptic problem; the view that Mark was the first of the Synoptic Gospels written and that the authors of Matthew and Luke drew upon both Mark and another document, which scholars term Q. See Q, Synoptic problem.

Two-Gospel Hypothesis. One proposed solution to the Synoptic problem. The view that Matthew was the first of the Synoptic Gospels written, that the author of Luke used Matthew, and that Mark combined Matthew and Luke in abridged form. Also known as the Griesbach hypothesis, after its first proponent.

Wisdom. A type of literature found in the Jewish Scriptures that involves reflection on life as ordinarily experienced, apart from specific reference to distinctively Hebraic notions such as covenant. In a philosophical strain of this tradition, there eventually emerged the personified figure of Wisdom—

imaged as a female, because of the feminine gender of the noun—who was present with God and creation and whose presence permeates the universe. There is evidence that the notion of personified Wisdom played a part in the development of Christology.

Yabneh. Or Jamnia, or Jabneel. A town near the coast of the Mediterranean in northern Judah. At the time of the Jewish revolt against the Romans in 66–70, the Pharisee Yohanan ben Zakkai secured Roman permission to establish a Jewish academy there. It became an important center for the preservation of Jewish tradition, and its establishment signaled the beginning of what became known as Rabbinic Judaism. See Rabbi.

Yahweh. The distinctive Hebrew/Jewish name for God; the sacred name that according to ancient and Orthodox Jews should not be pronounced (although the high priest spoke the name once a year in the Holy of Holies, the innermost sanctuary of the temple).

Zealots. A coalition of freedom fighters probably formed in a late phase of the Jewish rebellion against Rome in 66–70 C.E. At one time scholars believed that the Zealots were a longstanding revolutionary party that would have been active during the time of Jesus, but the recent trend is away from this view.

Index

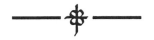